# A-Z LEICESTER and RUTLAND

C000246667

## CONTENTS

| | |
|---|---|
| Key to Map Pages | 2-3 |
| Large Scale City Centre | 4-5 |
| Map Pages | 6-157 |

Road Map Pages

Index to Streets, Stations and selected Places of Interest

Index to Hospitals & Hospices                     224

## REFERENCE

| | | | |
|---|---|---|---|
| Motorway | M1 ═══ | Airport | ✈ |
| Primary Route | A6 | Car Park (Selected) | P |
| Under Construction | | Church or Chapel | † |
| A Road | A594 | Cycleway (Selected) | ◉◉◉ |
| Proposed | | Fire Station | ■ |
| B Road | B6416 | Hospital | H |
| Dual Carriageway | | House Numbers (Selected Roads) | 13    8 |
| One-way Street | → | Information Centre | i |
| Traffic flow on A Roads is also indicated by a heavy line on the driver's left. | → | National Grid Reference | 420 |
| Restricted Access | | Park & Ride | Meynells Gorse P+ |
| Pedestrianized Road | | Police Station | ▲ |
| Track / Footpath | | Post Office | ★ |
| Residential Walkway | | Toilet | ▽ |
| | | with facilities for the Disabled | ▽ |
| Railway | Heritage Sta. / Level Crossing / Station / Tunnel | Viewpoint | ⋇ ☀ |
| Local Authority Boundary | | Educational Establishment | ◰ |
| Posttown Boundary | | Hospital or Hospice | ◰ |
| Postcode Boundary (within Posttown) | | Industrial Building | ◰ |
| Built-up Area | MLL ST. | Leisure or Recreational Facility | ◰ |
| | | Place of Interest | ◰ |
| | | Public Building | ◰ |
| Map Continuation | 58 | Shopping Centre or Market | ◰ |
| Large Scale City Centre | 4 | Other Selected Buildings | ◰ |
| Road Map Pages | 160 | | |

## Scale

Map Pages 6-157
1:16,896   3¾ inches (9.52 cm) to 1 mile   5.9cm to 1km

0   ¼   ½ Mile
0   250   500   750   1 km

Large Scale City Centre Page 4-5
1:8,448   7½ inches (19.04 cm) to 1 mile   11.8cm to 1km

0   ⅛   ¼ Mile
0   125   250   375   500m

## Copyright of Geographers' A-Z Map Company Ltd.

Fairfield Road, Borough Green, Sevenoaks, Kent TN15 8PP
Telephone: 01732 781000 (Enquiries & Trade Sales)
01732 783422 (Retail Sales)

www.a-zmaps.co.uk

Copyright © Geographers' A-Z Map Co. Ltd.

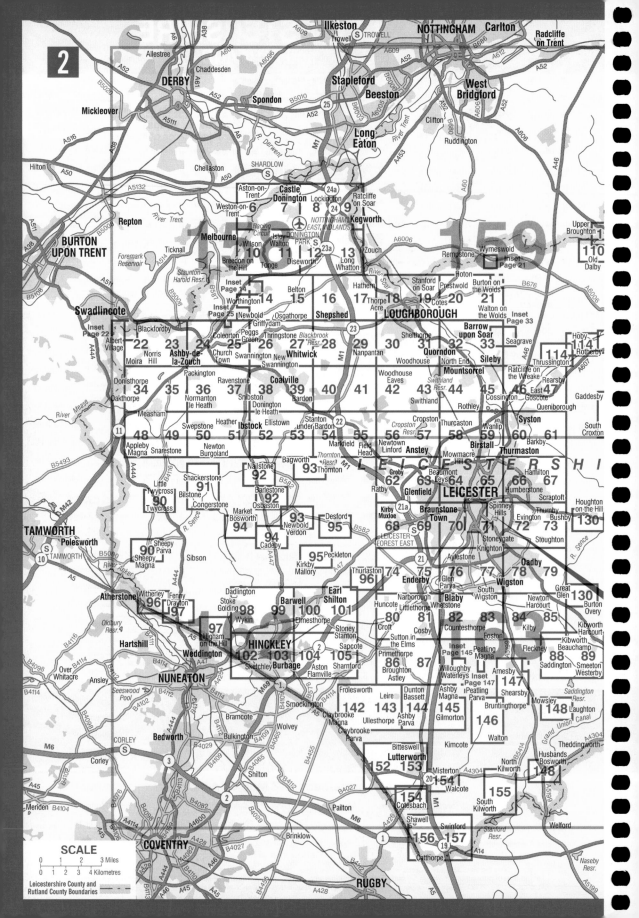

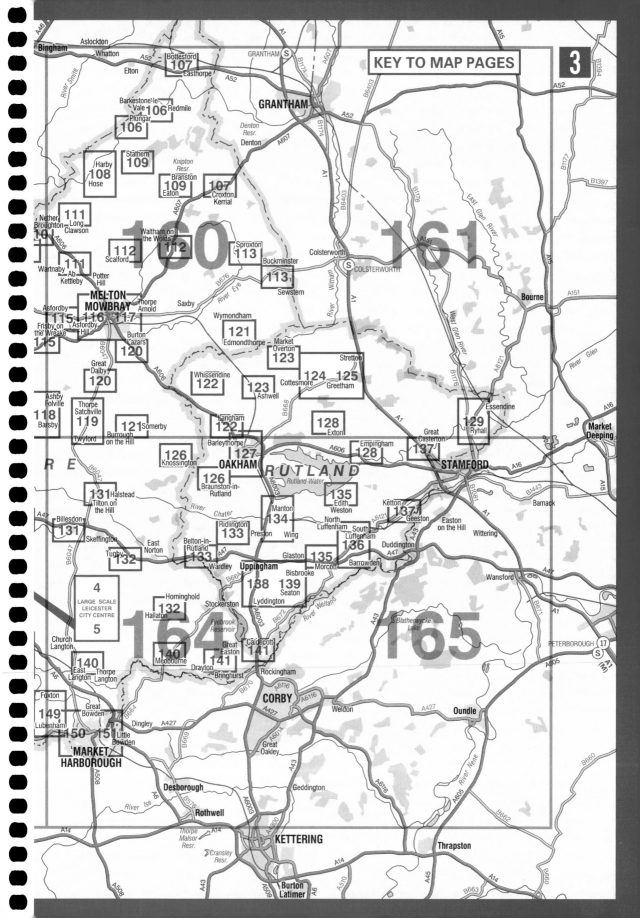

KEY TO MAP PAGES

**3**

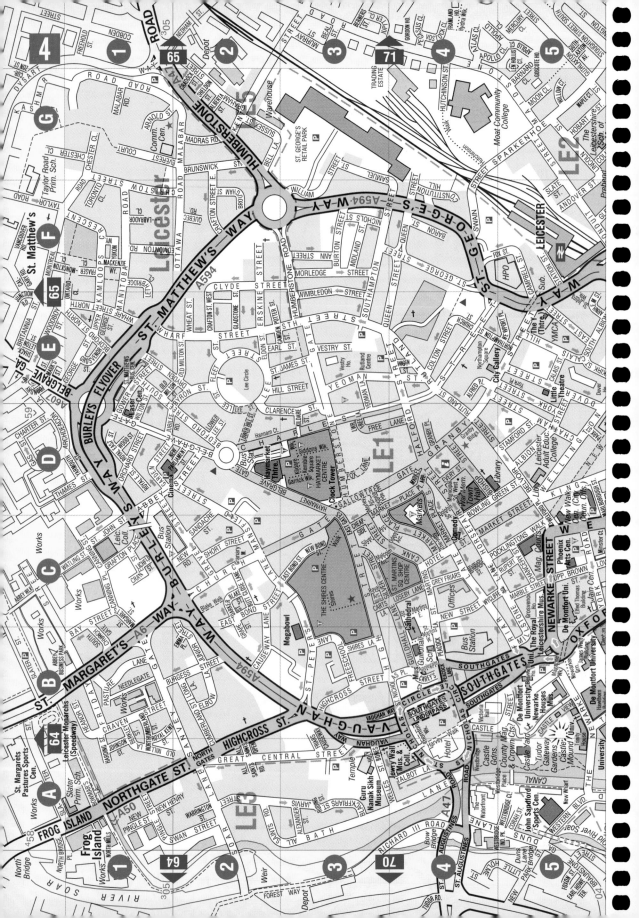

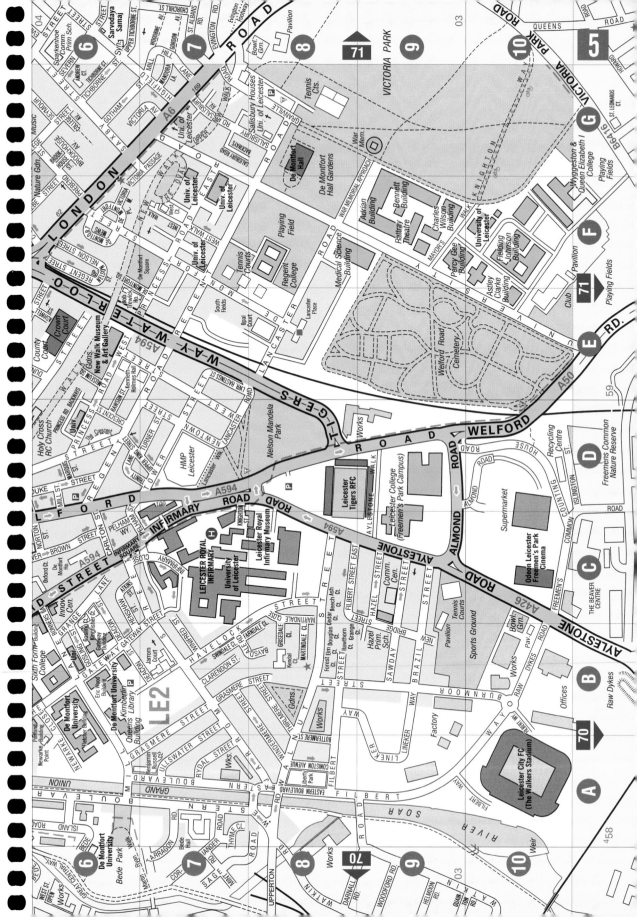

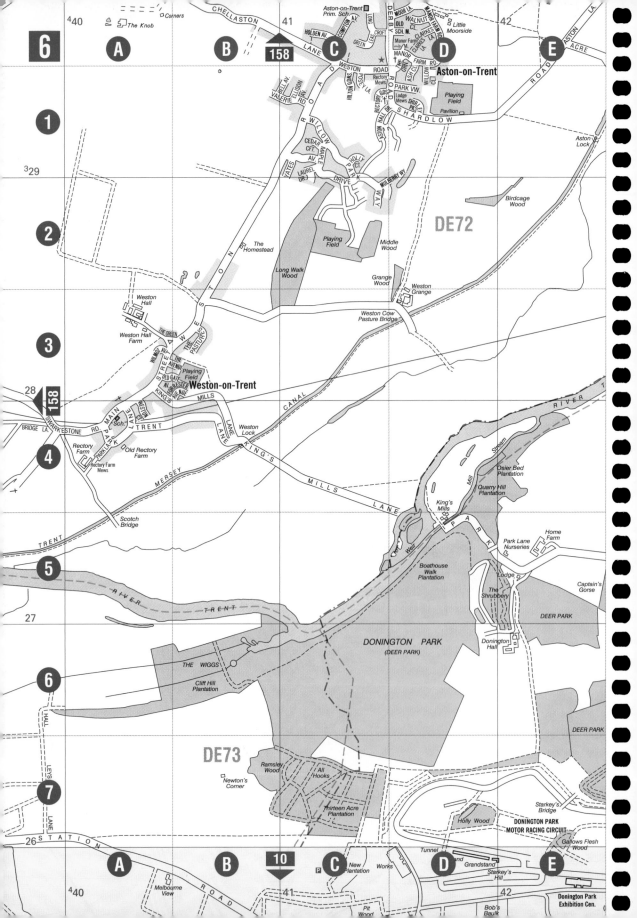

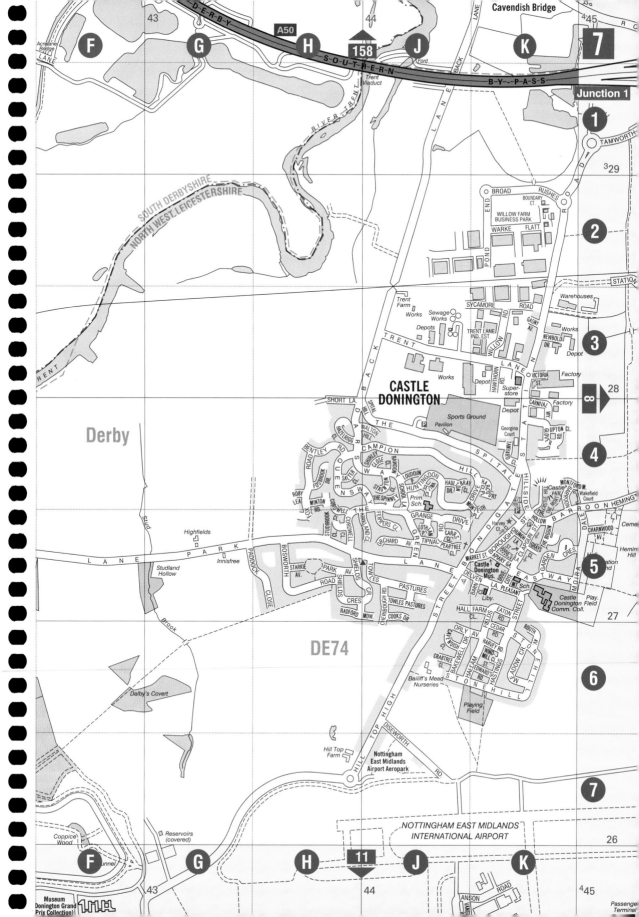

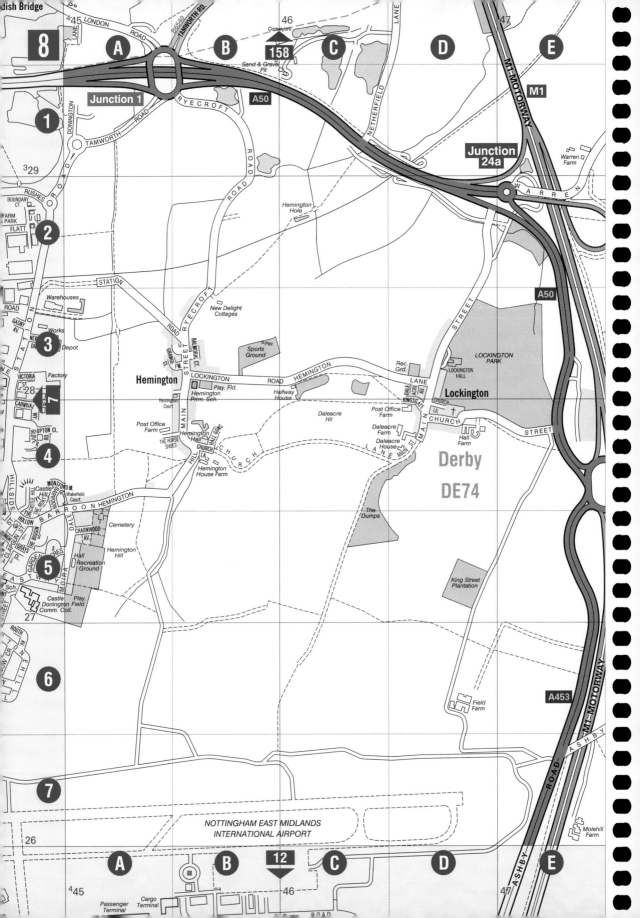

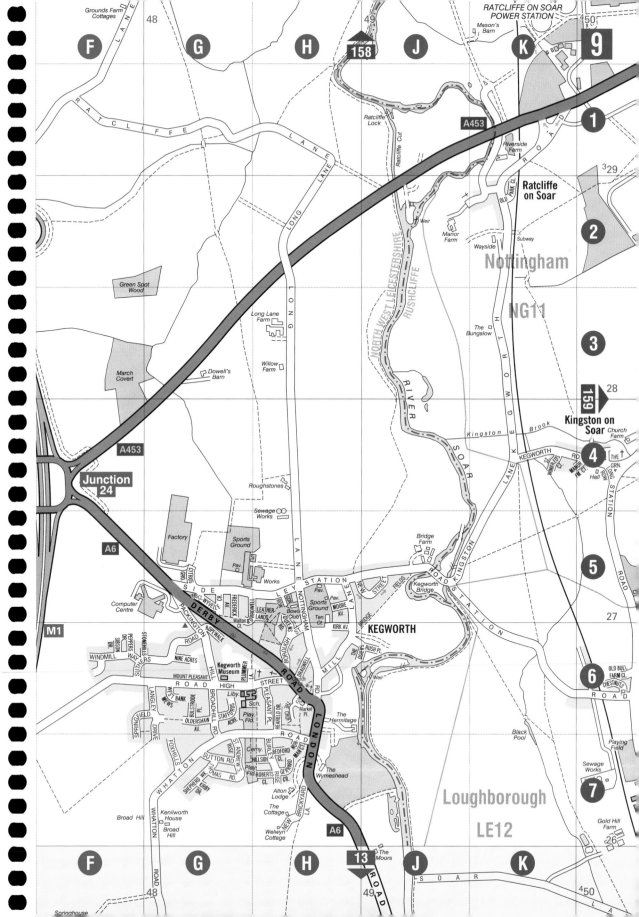

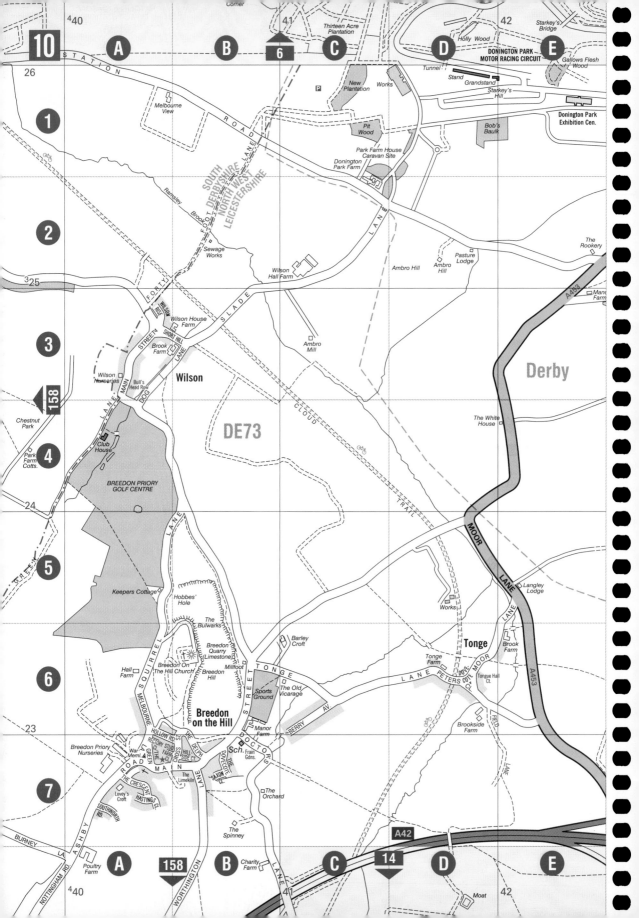

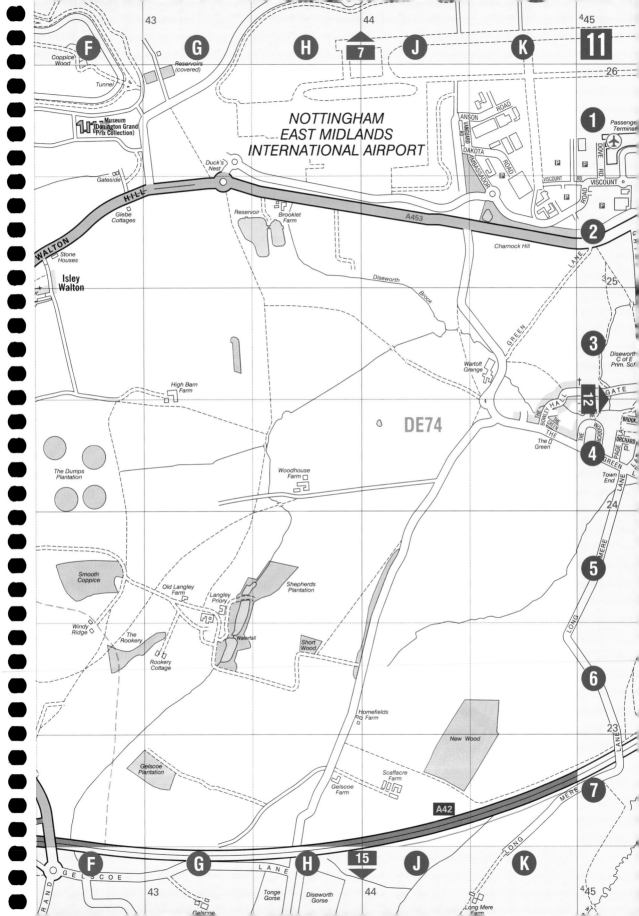

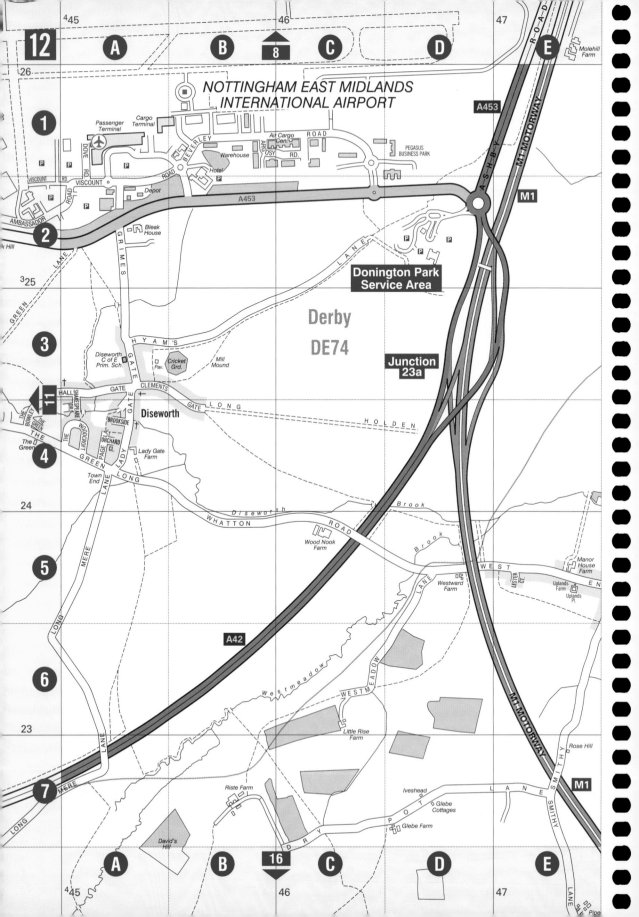

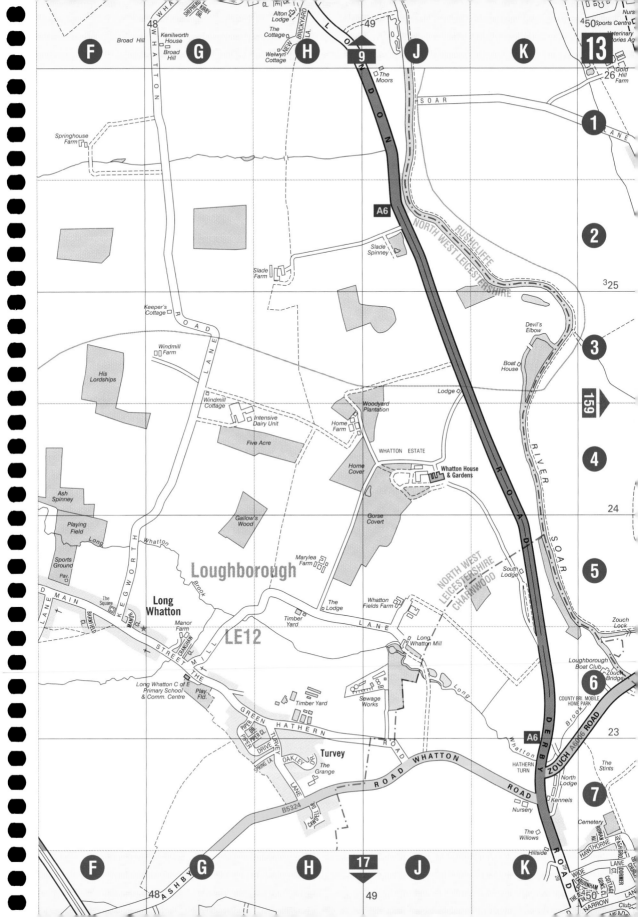

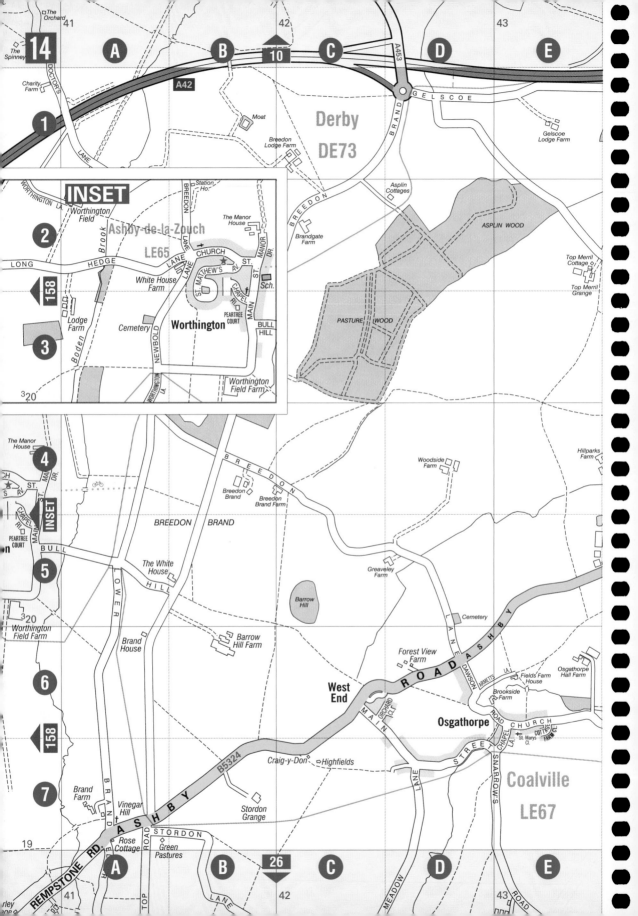

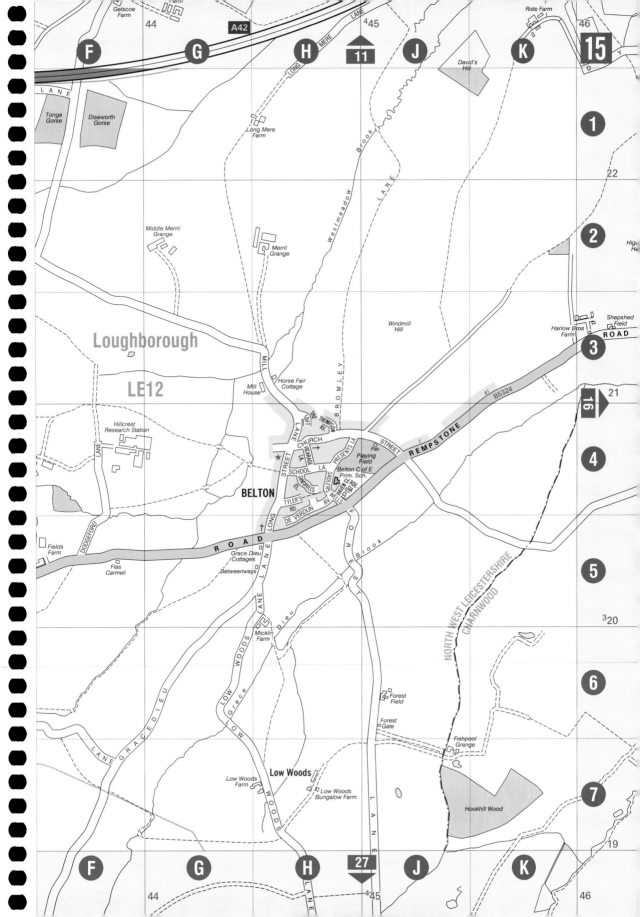

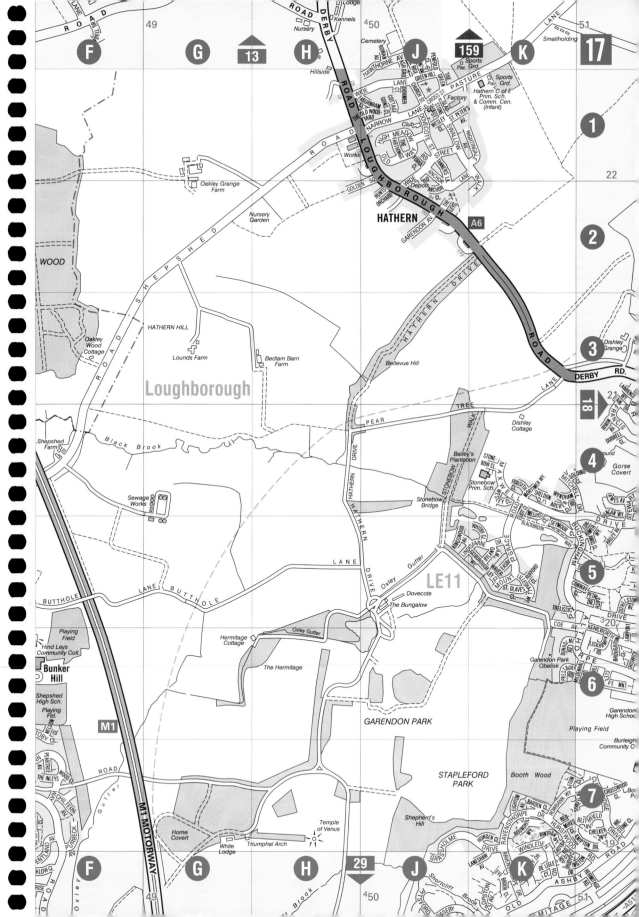

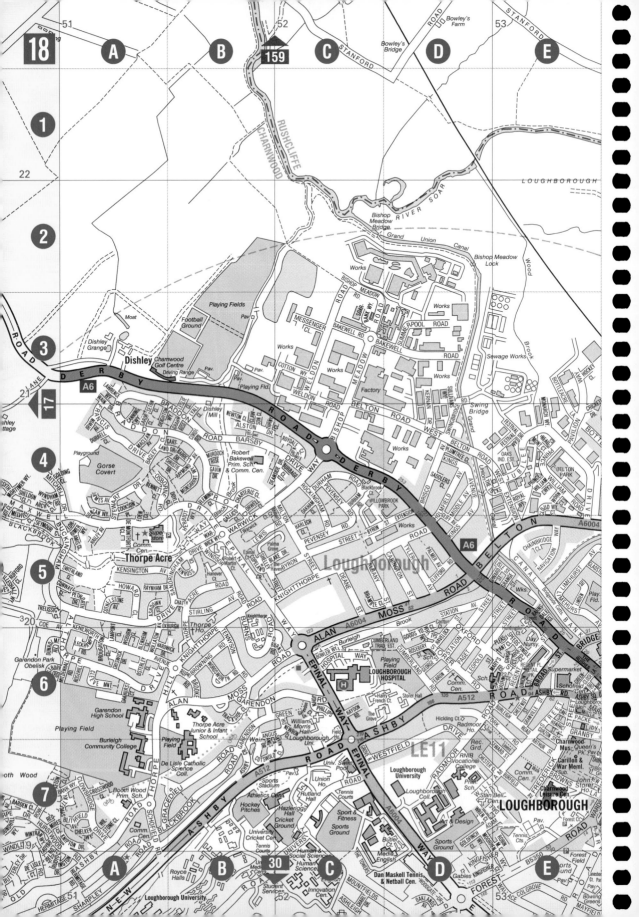

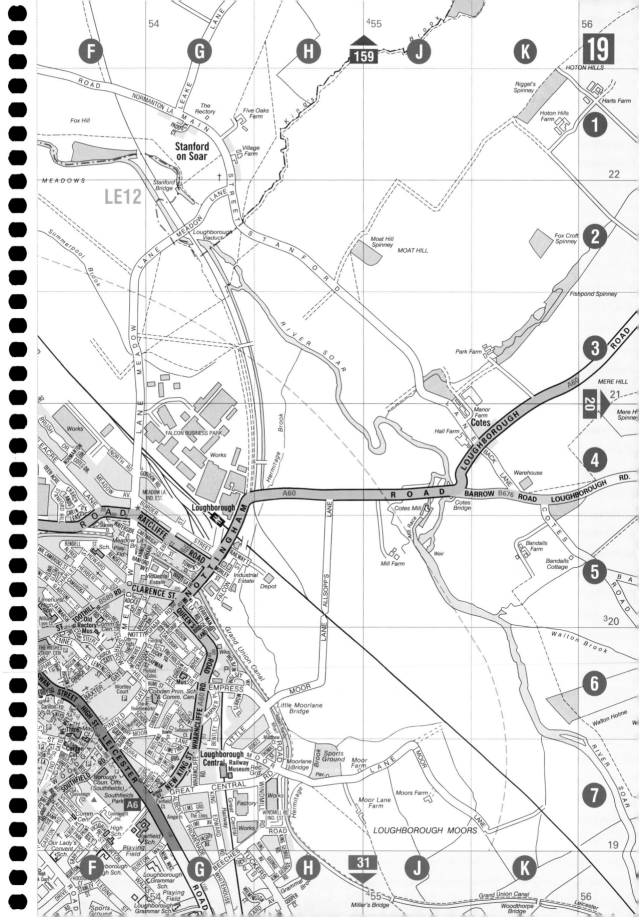

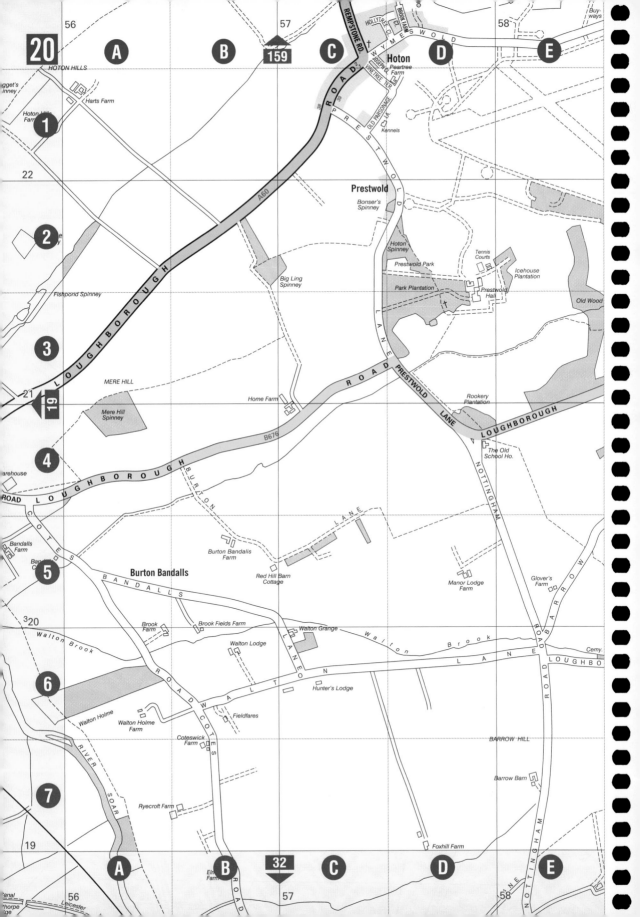

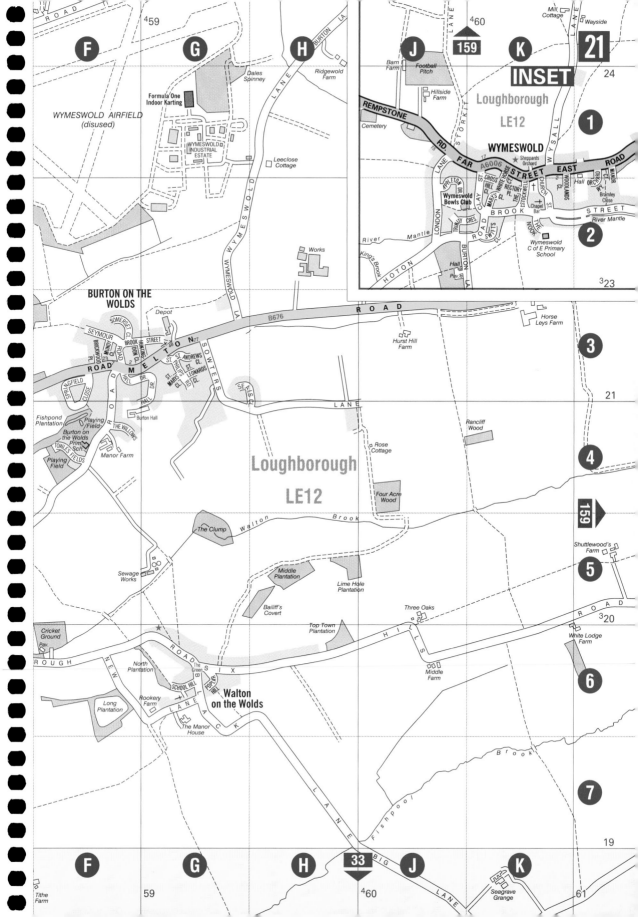

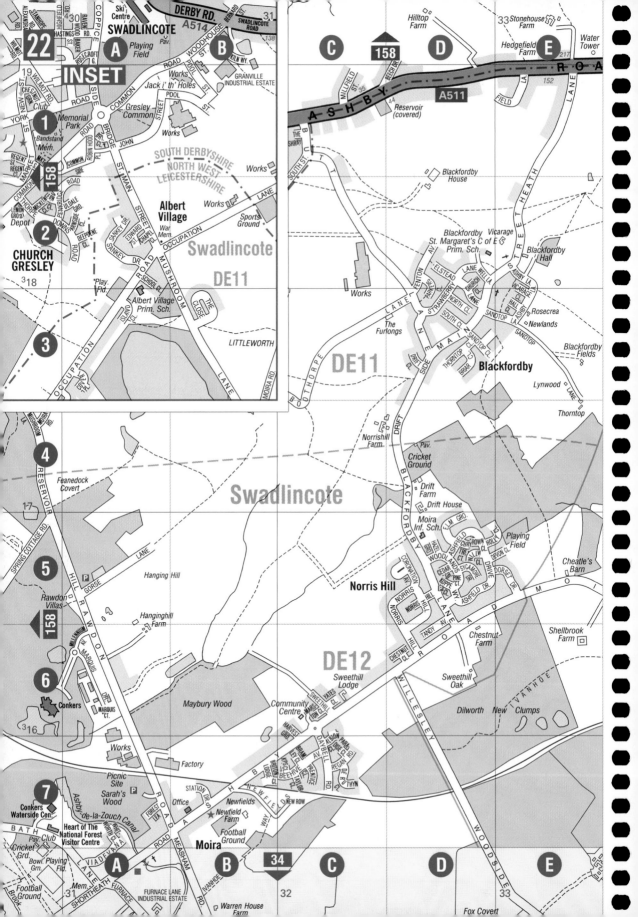

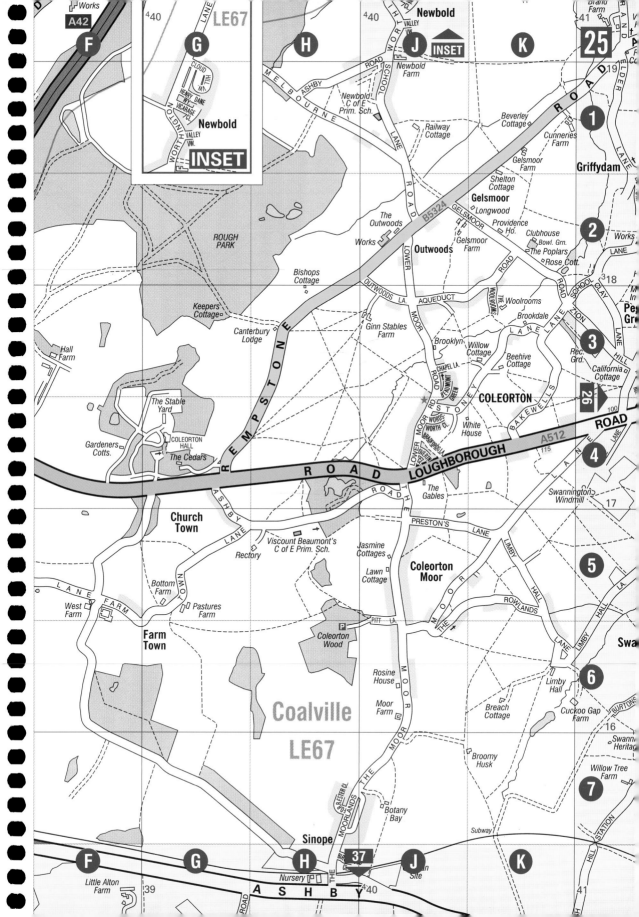

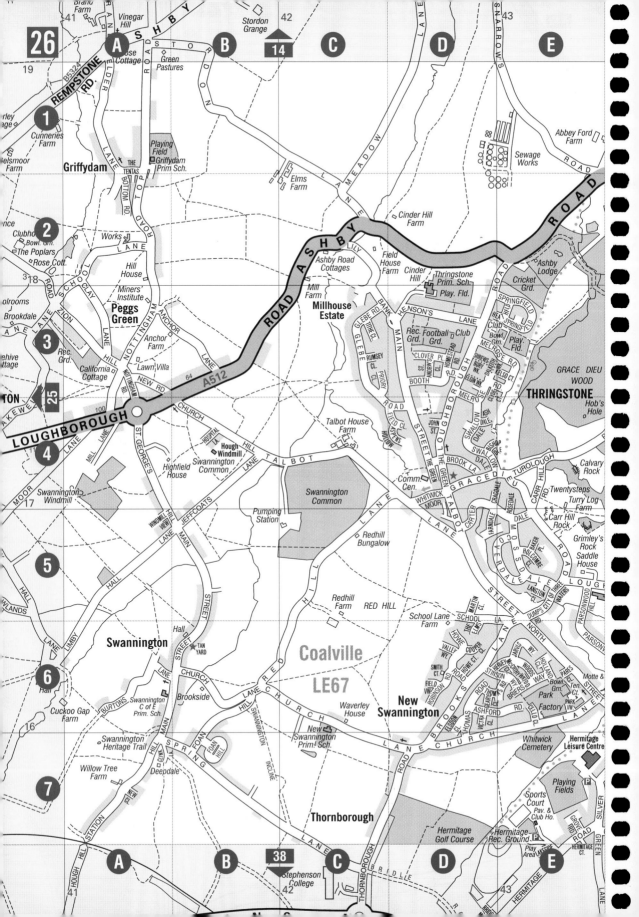

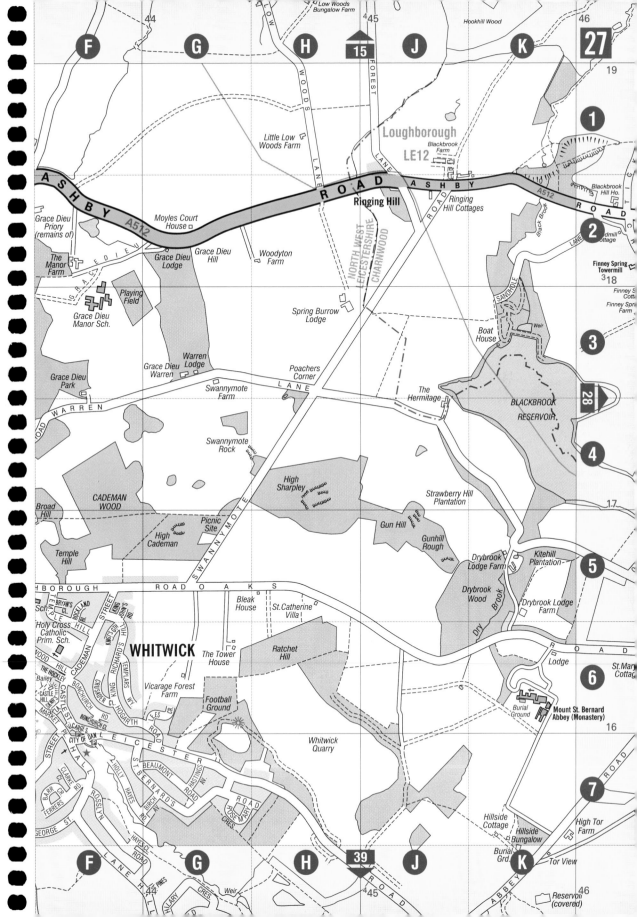

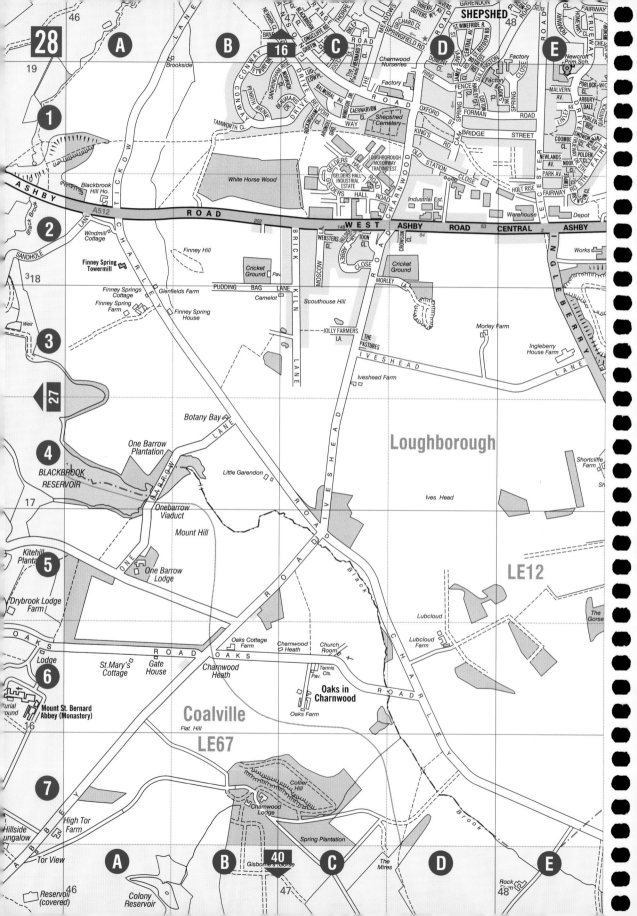

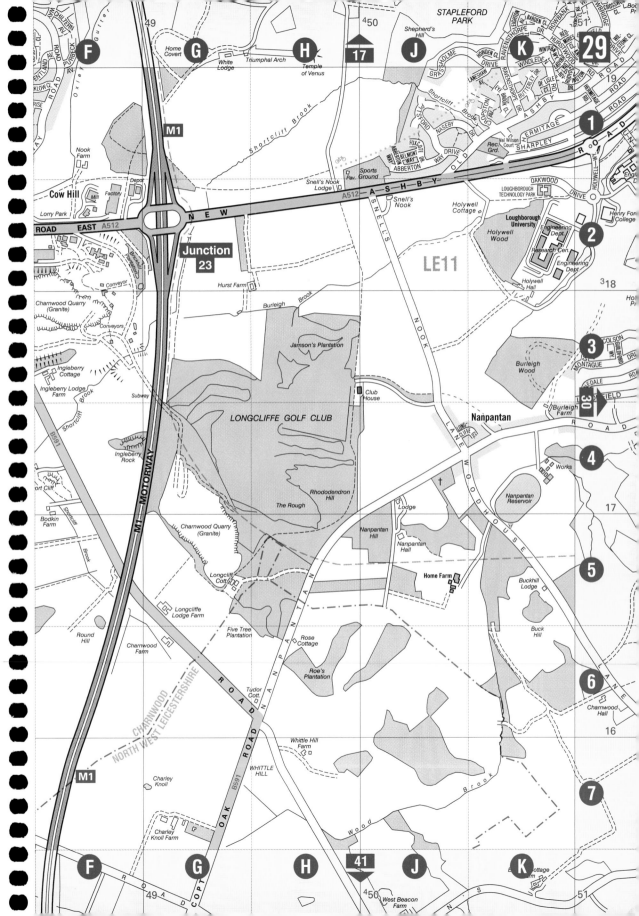

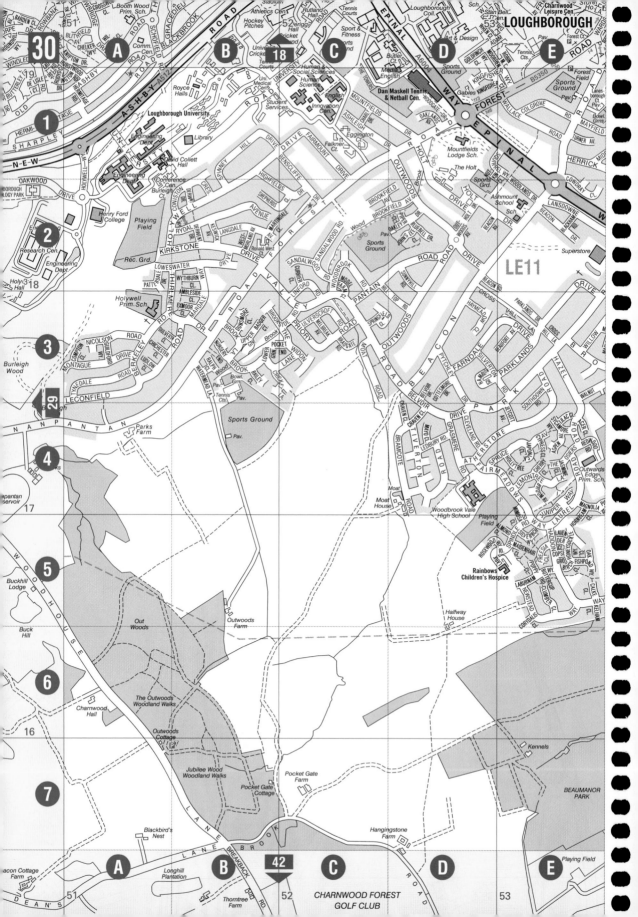

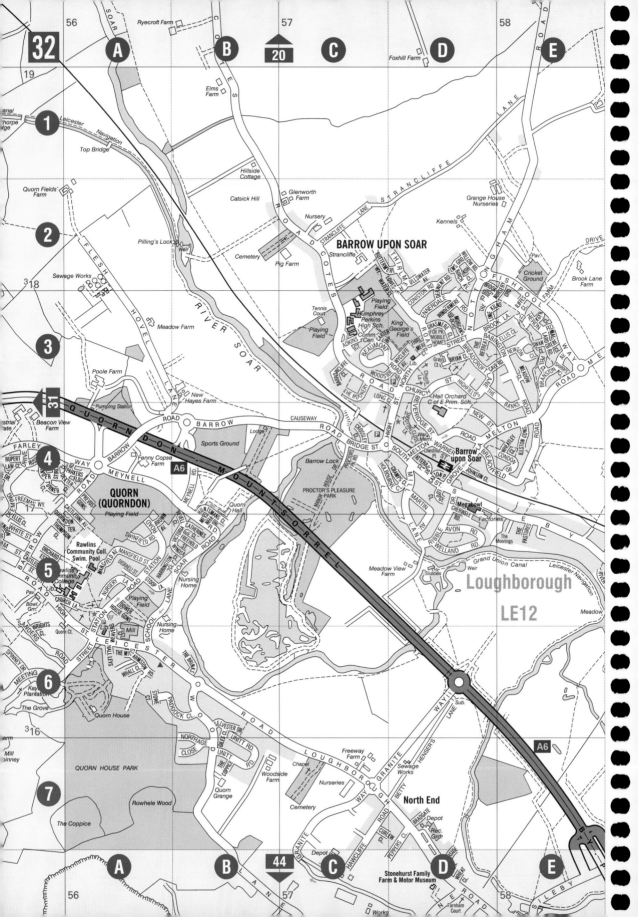

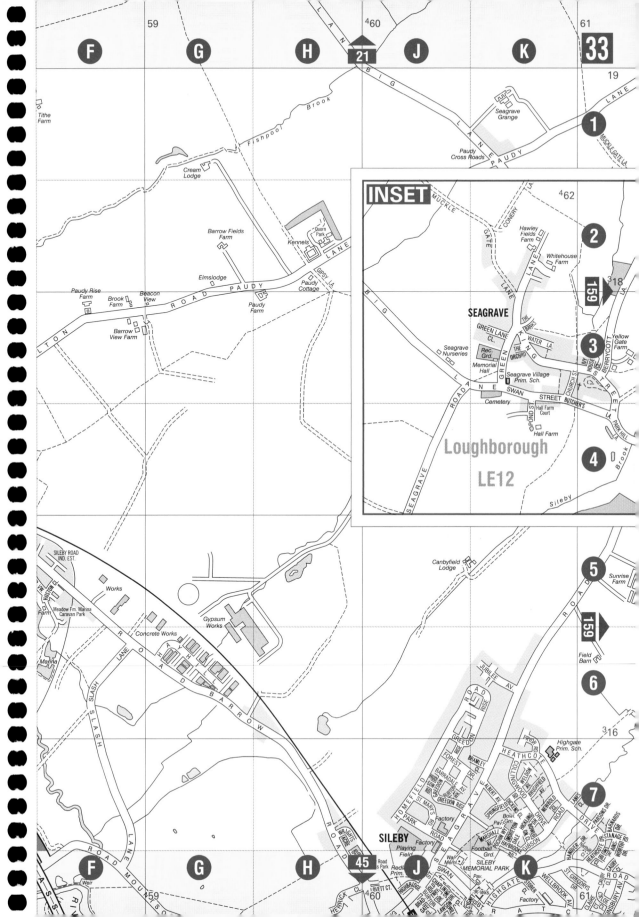

F   G   H   **21**   J   K

Tithe Farm

Brook

Fishpool

Seagrave Grange

Paudy Cross Roads

**1**

MUCKLE GATE LA.

Cream Lodge

**INSET**

MUCKLE GATE LANE

CONERY LANE

462

Hawley Fields Farm

Whitehouse Farm

**2**

**159**   318   LA.

Barrow Fields Farm

Quorn Park

Kennels

Elmslodge

GIPSY LA.

Paudy Cottage

ROAD   PAUDY   LANE

Paudy Rise Farm

Brook Farm

Beacon View

Paudy Farm

Barrow View Farm

Seagrave Nurseries

THE BANKS

**SEAGRAVE**

GREEN LANE CL.

GREEN LANE

WATER LA.

THE ORCH'RD

THE HOUSE

IVY HOUSE ST.

CHURCH ST.

BERRYCOT LA.

Yellow Gate Farm

**3**

Rec. Grd.

Memorial Hall

Seagrave Village Prim. Sch.

SWAN   STREET   BUTCHER'S LA.

PARK HILL

Cemetery

Hall Farm Court

Hall Farm

POND ST.

**Loughborough**

**LE12**

Brook

**4**

Sileby

SEAGRAVE ROAD

BIG LANE

LANE

BOLTON

SILEBY ROAD IND. EST.

Works

HUSTON CL.

Meadow Fm. Marina Caravan Park

Concrete Works

Gypsum Works

Canbyfield Lodge

Sunrise Farm

**5**

ROAD

**159**

Field Barn

**6**

316

Marina

SLASH LANE

HAY ROAD

BARROW ROAD

JUBILEE AV.

ROAD RISE

Highgate Prim. Sch.

**7**

GREEDON

FOREST

BRAMLEY

HEATHCOTE

PRYOR RD

WILSON

COLLINGWOOD RD

BRISSHEID

ALBERT AV.

NEWBOLD AV.

ROAD

PARSONS DR.

HOMEFIELD

BARRADALE

GREEDON RISE

SPRINGFIELD

ST. MARY'S RD

Factory

MARSHALL

GIBSON

Bowl. Pav'n.

DRIVE

BARNARD'S

HANOVER DR.

STANAGE RD

WORTHEY

**SILEBY**

Factory

SEAGRAVE ROAD

Playing Field

Football Grd.

SILEBY MEMORIAL PARK

HEATHCOTE DR.

SWAN

ROAD MOUNTSO

Weir

RIVER

SLASH

F   G   H   **45**   J   K

Road s Park

Redla Prim.

HERRICK CL.

LOVETT CT.

HIGHBRIDGE

SWAN

CHAPLIN LA.

BROAD ST.

WAR Mem'l.

Pav.

WELLBROOK DR.

HIGHGATE

ST. GREGORY'S DR.

CAULEY

ASHBURY AV.

Factory

59   460   61

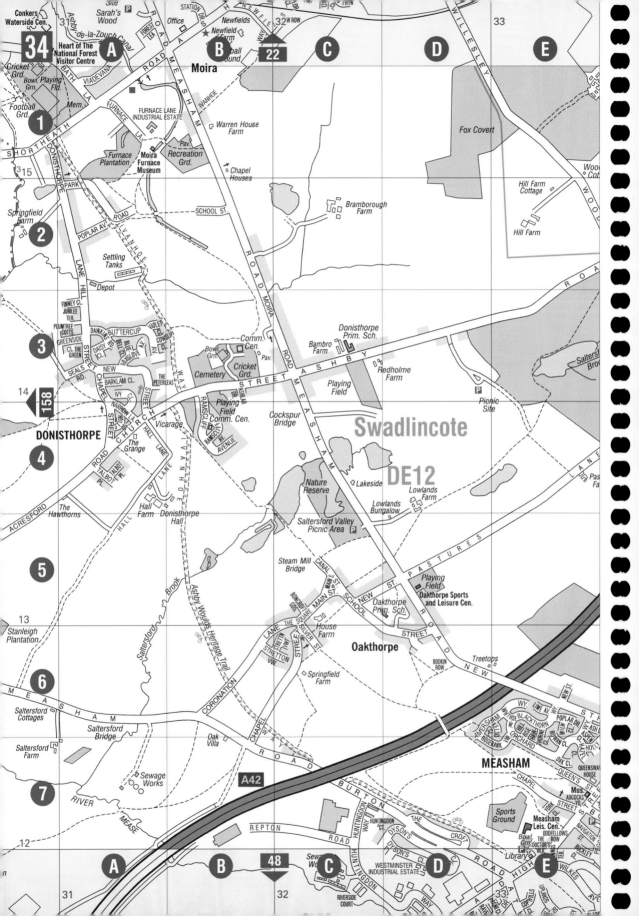

# 34

**A** **B** **C** **D** **E**

Conkers
Waterside Cen.
Ashby-de-la-Zouch Canal
Sarah's
Wood
P
STATION DRIVE
Forest Lea
Office
Newfields
Newfield Farm
32 W ROW
33
Heart of The
National Forest
Visitor Centre
Football Ground
22

**1** Cricket Grd. Bowl. Grn. Playing Fld.
Football Grd.
Mem.
VIADEVANA
BATH LA.
ROAD
MEASHAM
FURNACE LA.
IVANHOE
**Moira**

315
Warren House Farm
Furnace Lane
INDUSTRIAL ESTATE
Fox Covert
Wood
Cot.

SHORTHEATH
DONISTHORPE
PARK
Furnace Plantation
Pav.
Moira Furnace Museum
Recreation Grd.
Chapel Houses
Hill Farm Cottage
Hill Farm
WOOD ROAD

**2** Springfield Farm
POPLAR AV.
IVANHOE
ROAD
SCHOOL ST.
Bramborough Farm
MOIRA ROAD

LANE HILL
Settling Tanks
Depot
Donisthorpe Prim. Sch.

**3** FINNEY CL. JUBILEE TER.
PLUMTREE COTTS.
GREENSIDE CL.
THE GREEN
BUTTERCUP
DAISY CL.
DAWKINS
BLUEBELL CL.
FOXGLOVE AV.
CONSLIP
VIOLET CL.
Comm. Cen.
Pav.
Bowl Grn.
Cemetery
Cricket Grd.
Bambro Farm
Redholme Farm
Playing Field
Saltersford Brook

SEALS RD.
NEW CHAPEL STREET
STREET
BARKLAM CL.
IVY
THE PETERLEAS
WAY
ASHBY STREET
ASHM. ST.
MEASHAM

14
158
NARROW
HO.
CL.
RAMSCLIFF AV.
Playing Field Comm. Cen.
Cockspur Bridge
Picnic Site
P

**4** **DONISTHORPE**
Vicarage
CHURCH
HALL LANE
IVANHOE WAY
AVENUE
**Swadlincote**
**DE12**

ROAD
TALBOT PL.
The Grange
Nature Reserve
Lakeside
Lowlands Farm
PASTURES LANE

ACRESFORD
The Hawthorns
HALL LANE
Hall Farm
Donisthorpe Hall
Saltersford Valley Picnic Area
P
Lowlands Bungalow

**5**
Saltersford Brook
Ashby Woulds Heritage Trail
Steam Mill Bridge
CANAL
SCHOOL ST.
Playing Field
Oakthorpe Sports and Leisure Cen.
Oakthorpe Prim. Sch.

13
Stanleigh Plantation
MAIN ST.
THE SQUARE
BONCROFT GDNS.
House Farm
NEW STREET

**6**
MEASHAM
CORONATION WAY
STRETTON
SILVER ST.
STRETTON VW.
Springfield Farm
**Oakthorpe**
BODKIN ROW
Treetops
NEW

Saltersford Cottages
Saltersford Bridge
CHAPEL WAY
ROAD
Oak Villa
**MEASHAM**
AMBASTON
WHITWYSE BLACKTHORN
W. ORCHARD
ROSEBANK
ROWAN CL.
POPLAR DR.
LIME AV.
NEW ST.
OAK CL.
QUEEN'S
QUEENSWAY HOUSE

Saltersford Farm
Sewage Works

**7**
RIVER
MEASE
A42
REPTON ROAD
BURTON ROAD
HUNTINGDON WAY
HUNTINGDON CT.
THE CROFT
DYSON'S CL.
Sports Ground
Measham Leis. Cen.
Bowl Grn.
Library
CHAPEL STREET
Mus.
ADCOCKS YD.
THE DOCTOR'S
ODDFELLOWS ROW
NAVIGATION ST.
BUCKLEY CL.
YORK STREET
HIGH STREET

12
**A** **B** 48 **C** **D** **E**
Sewage Works
WESTMINSTER INDUSTRIAL ESTATE
RIVERSIDE COURT
HUNTINGDON WAY
WILKES
UPLANDS AVE.

31
32
33

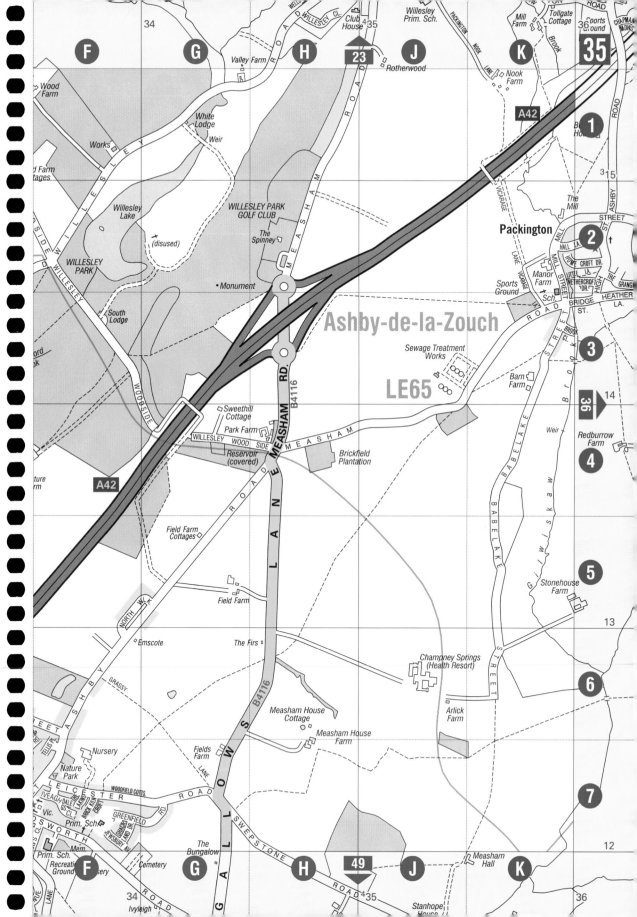

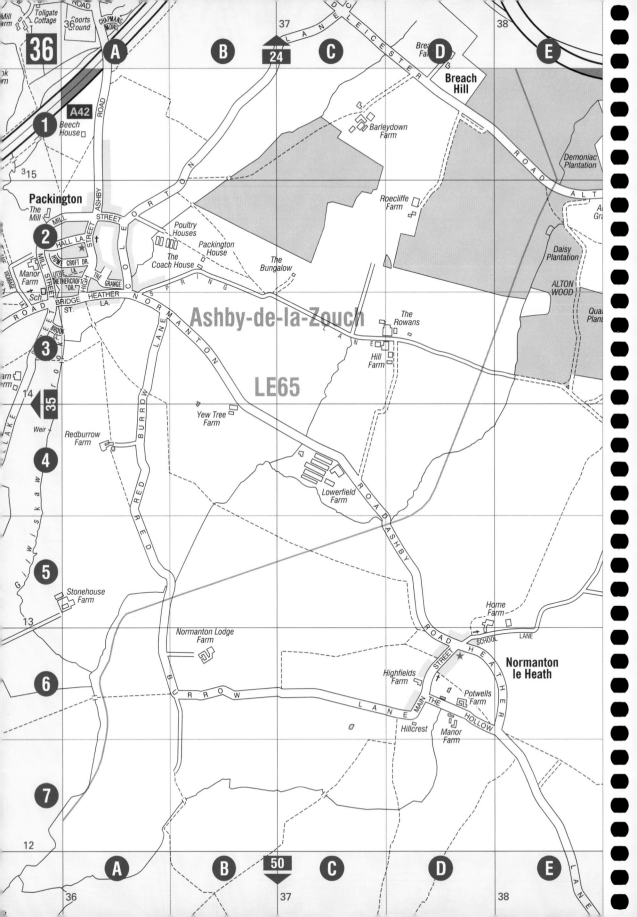

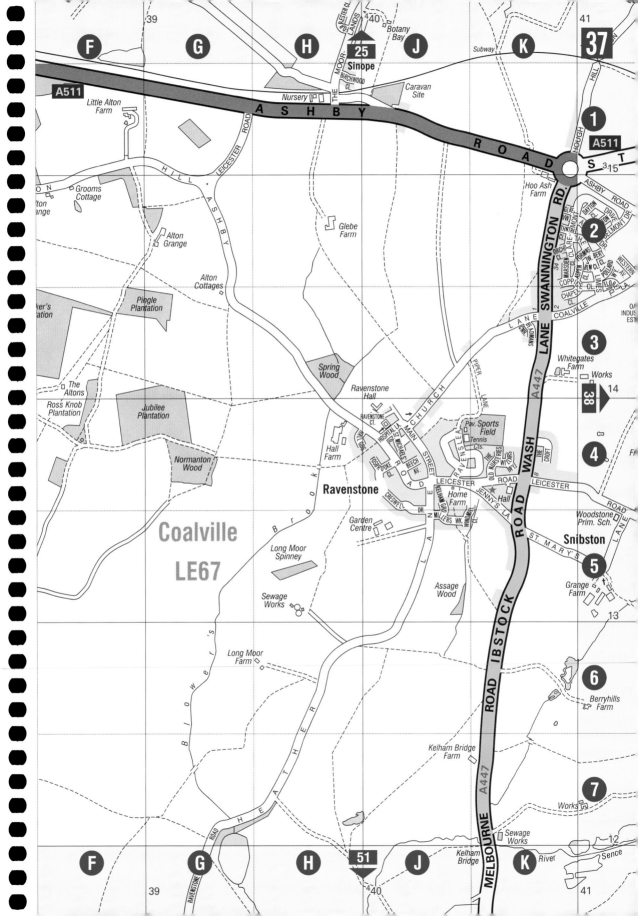

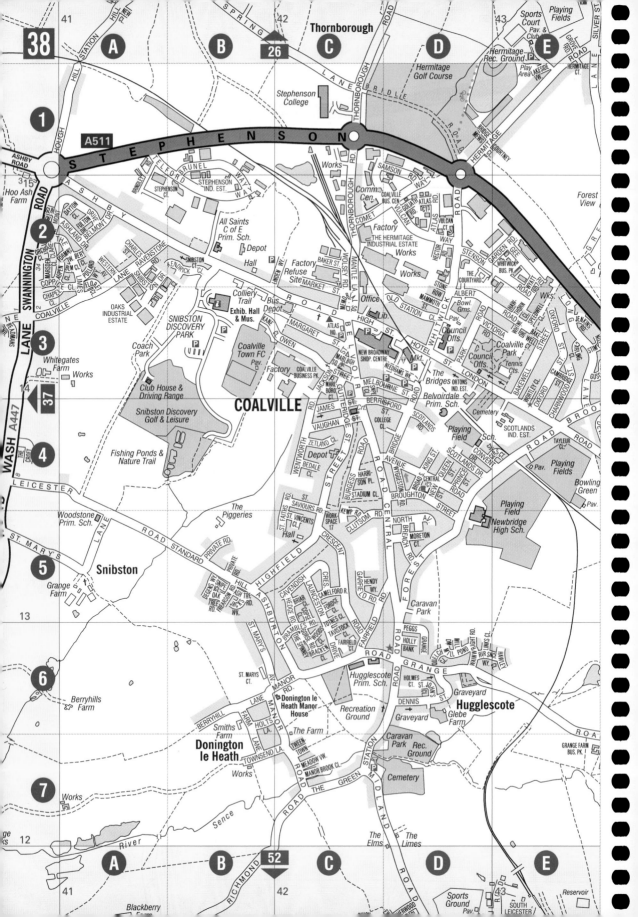

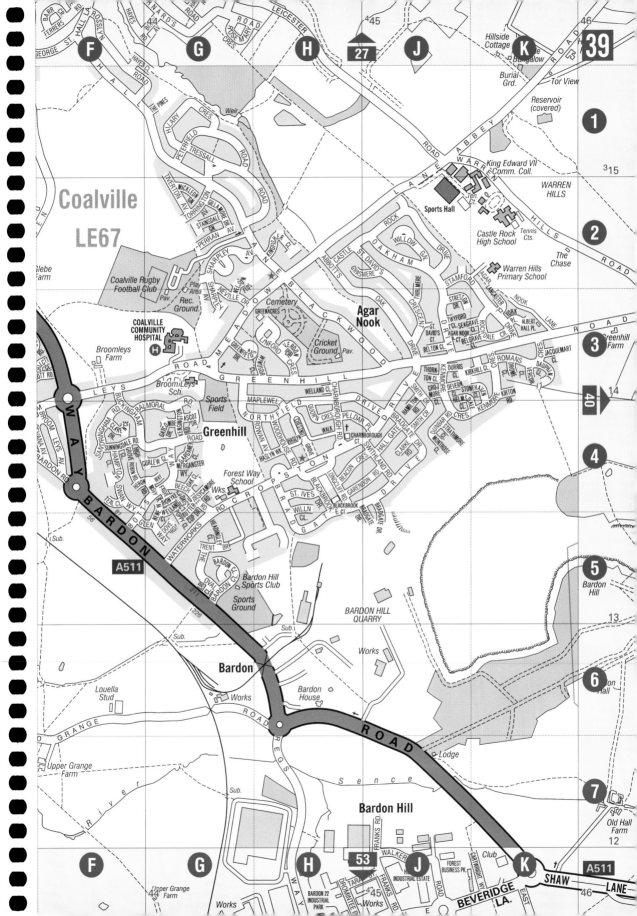

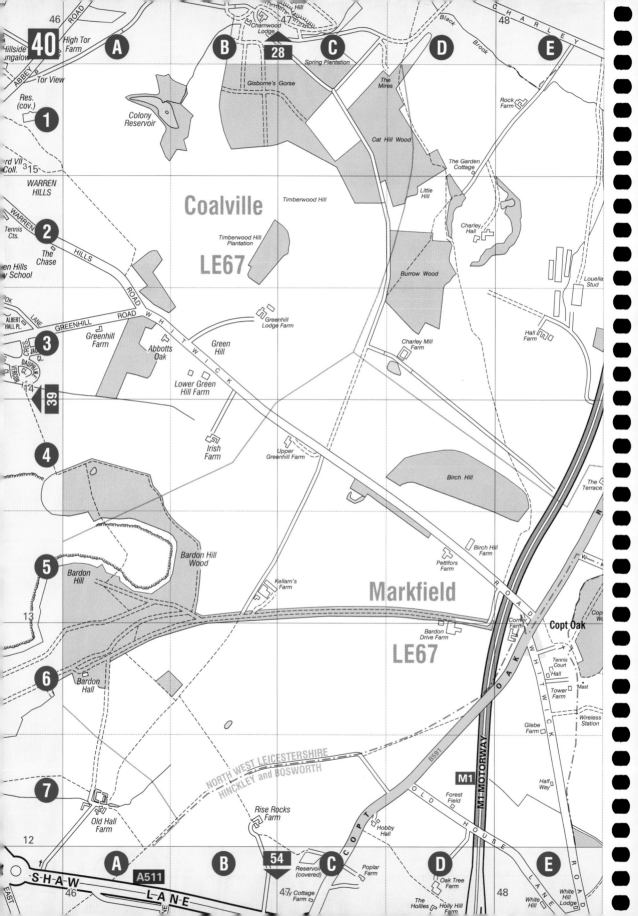

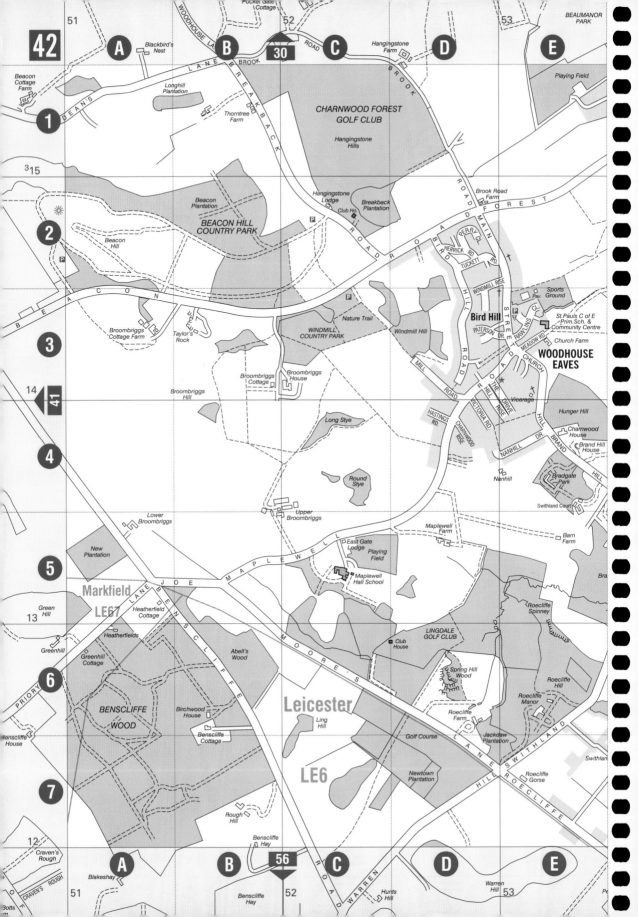

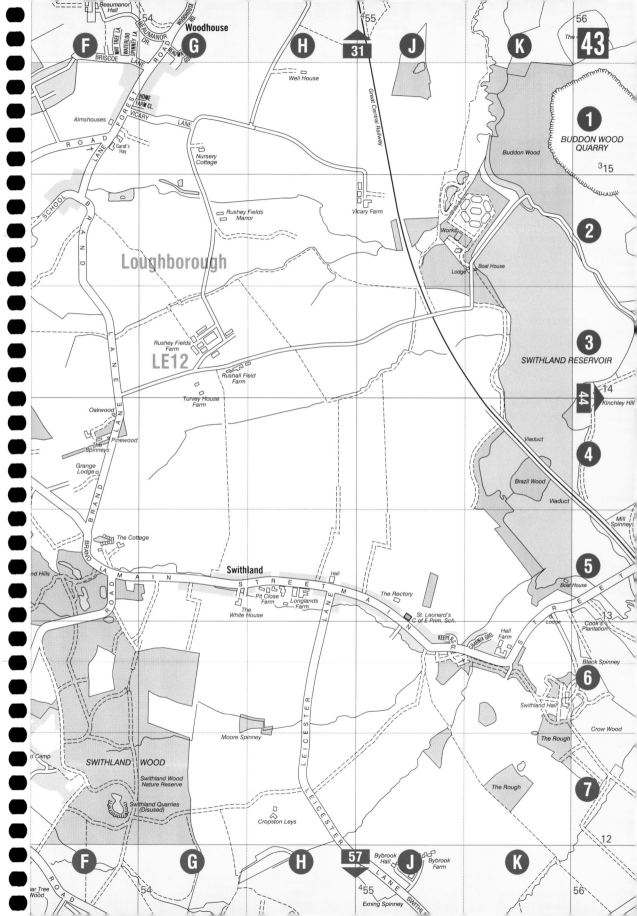

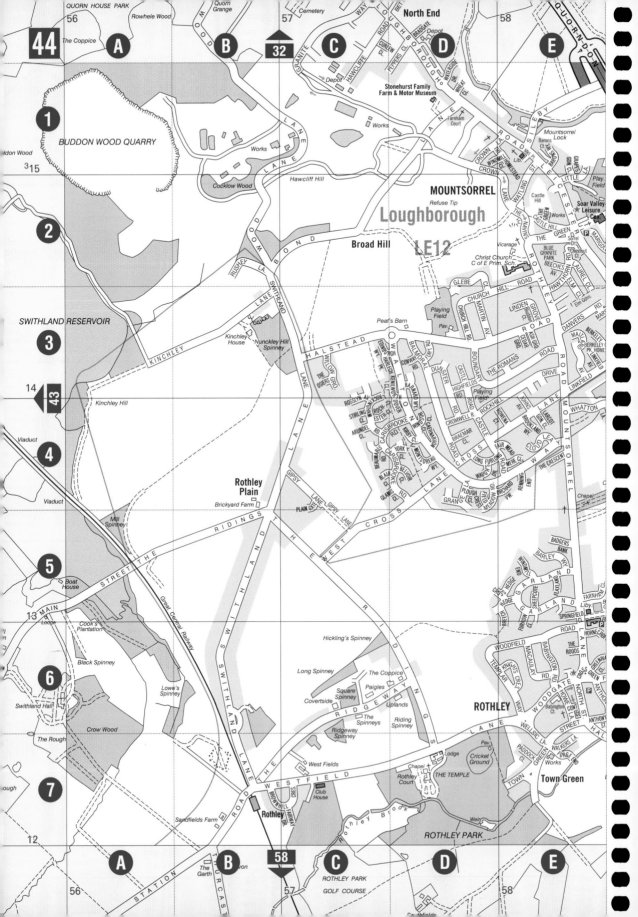

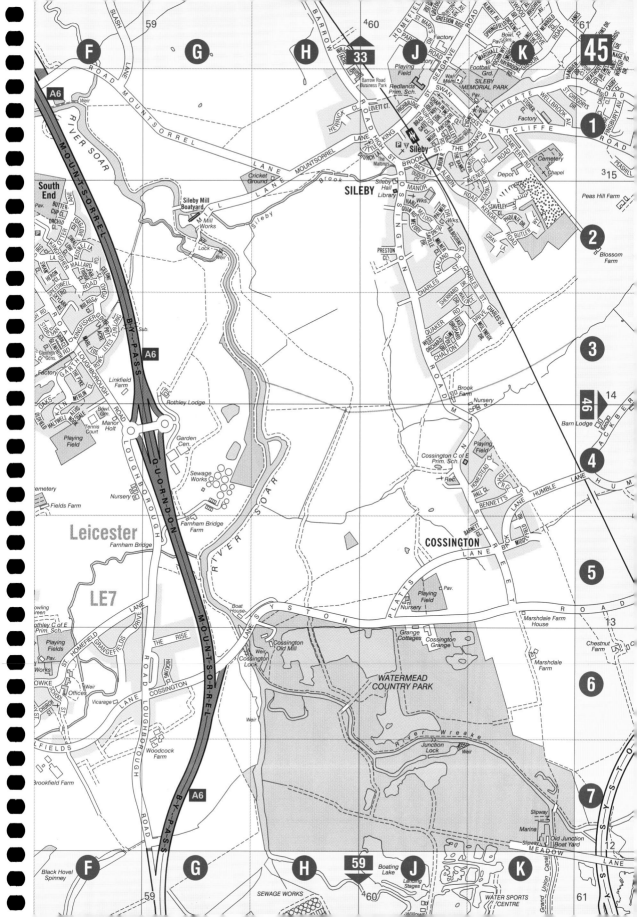

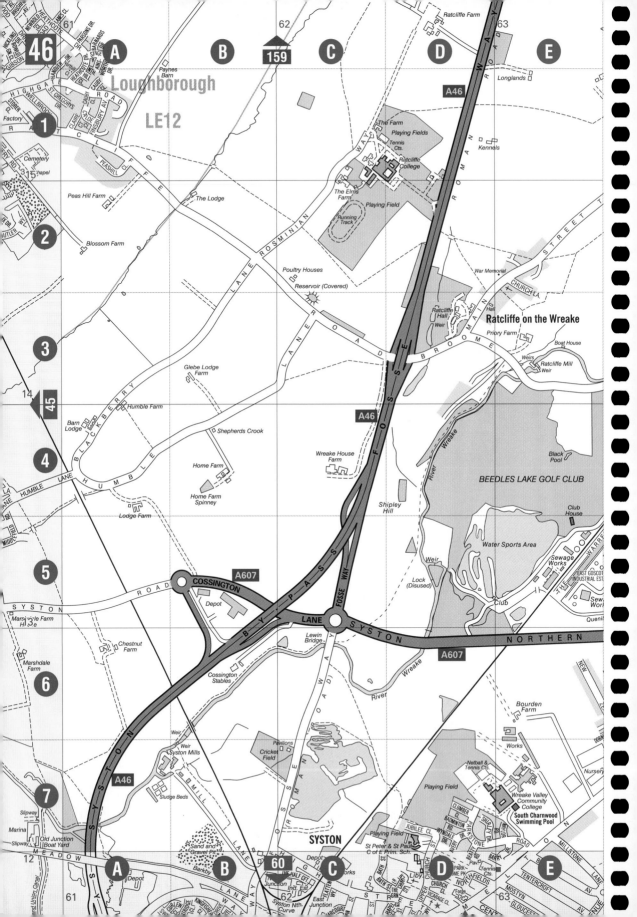

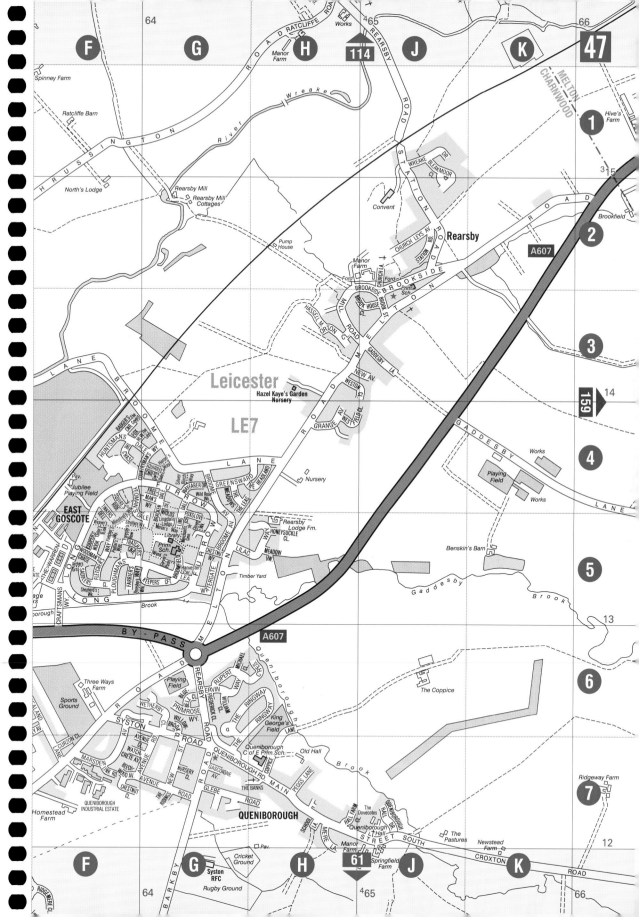

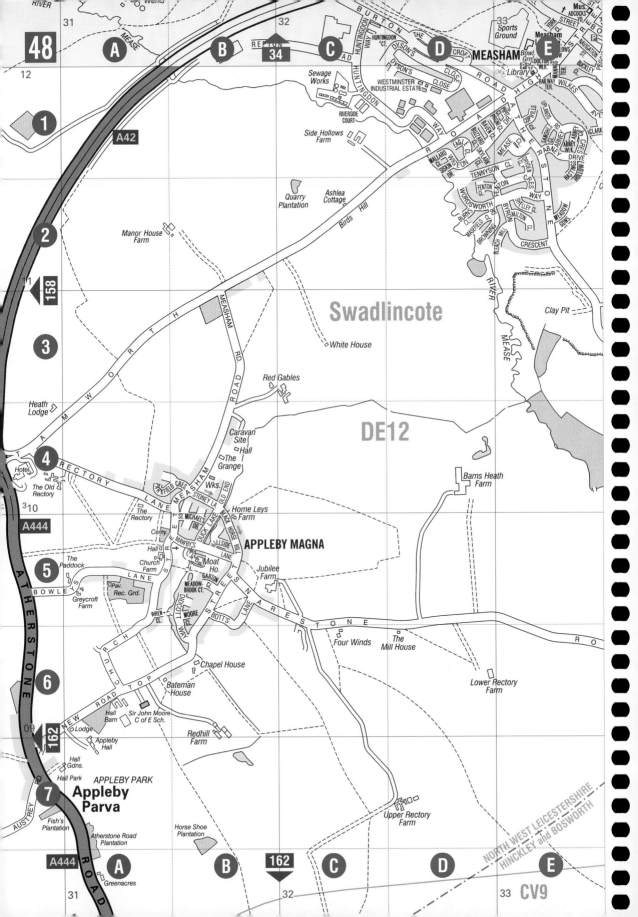

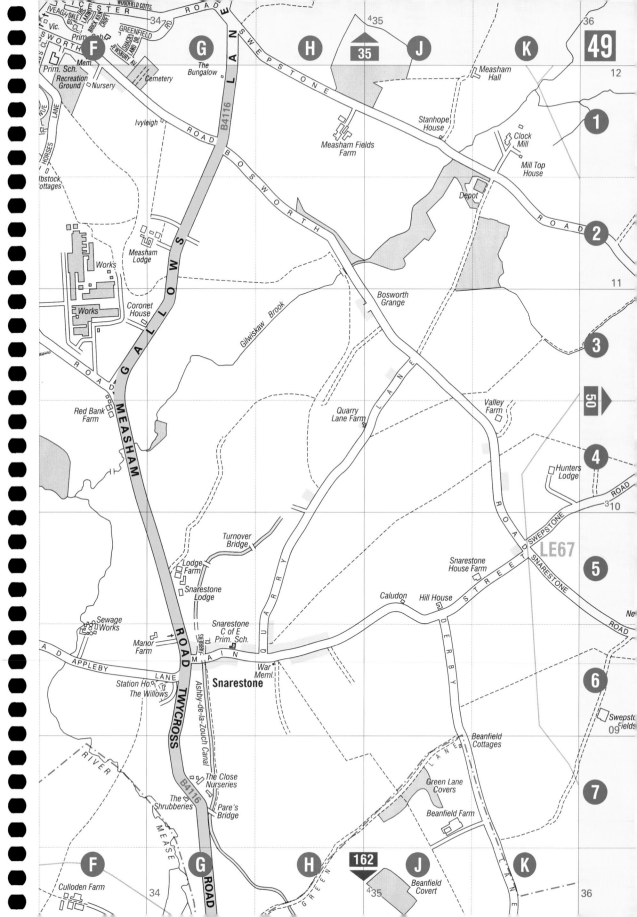

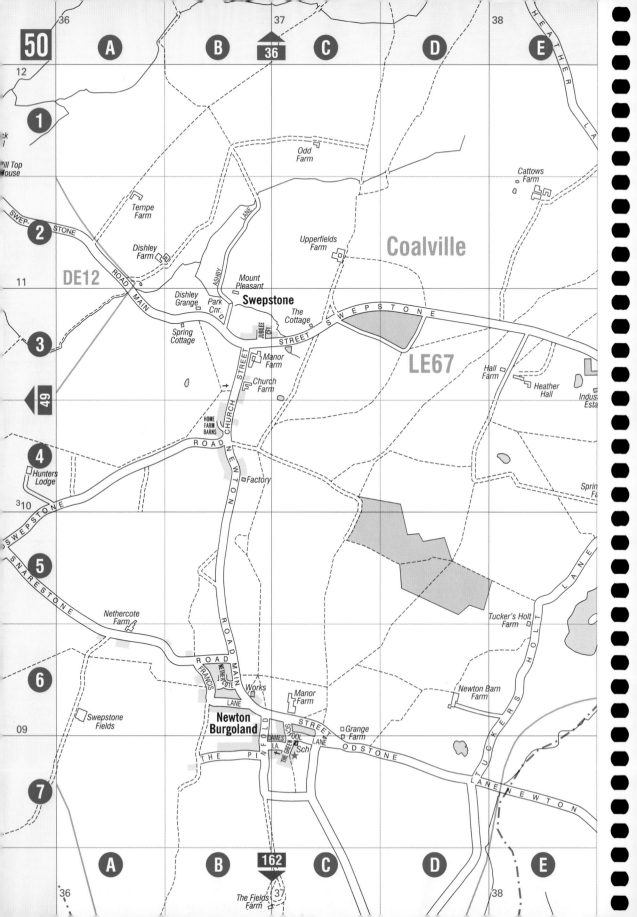

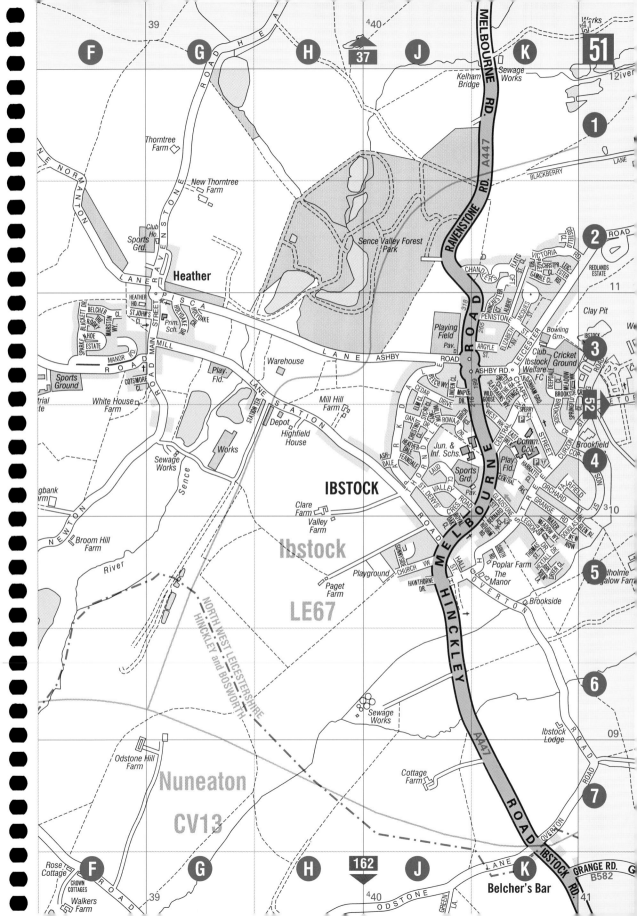

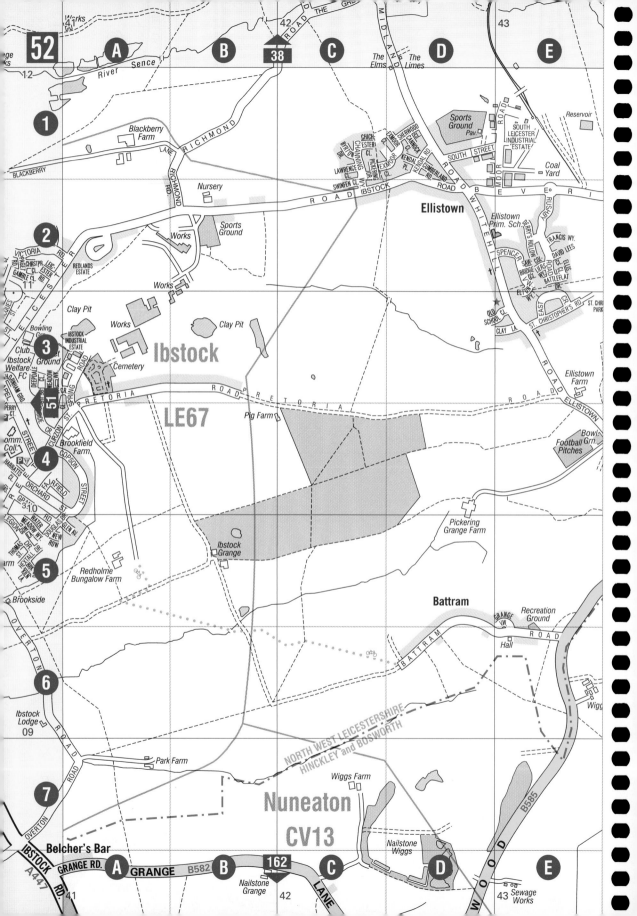

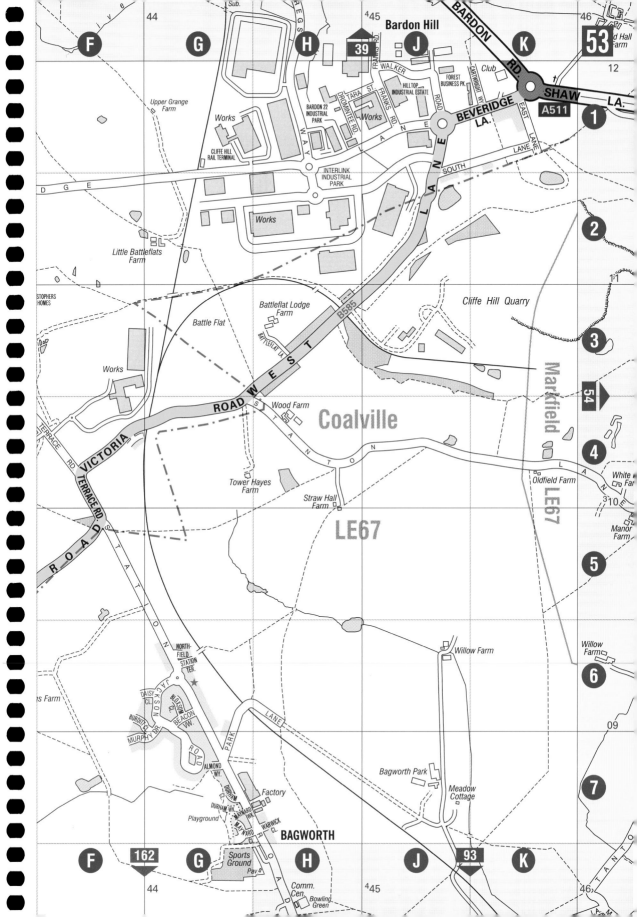

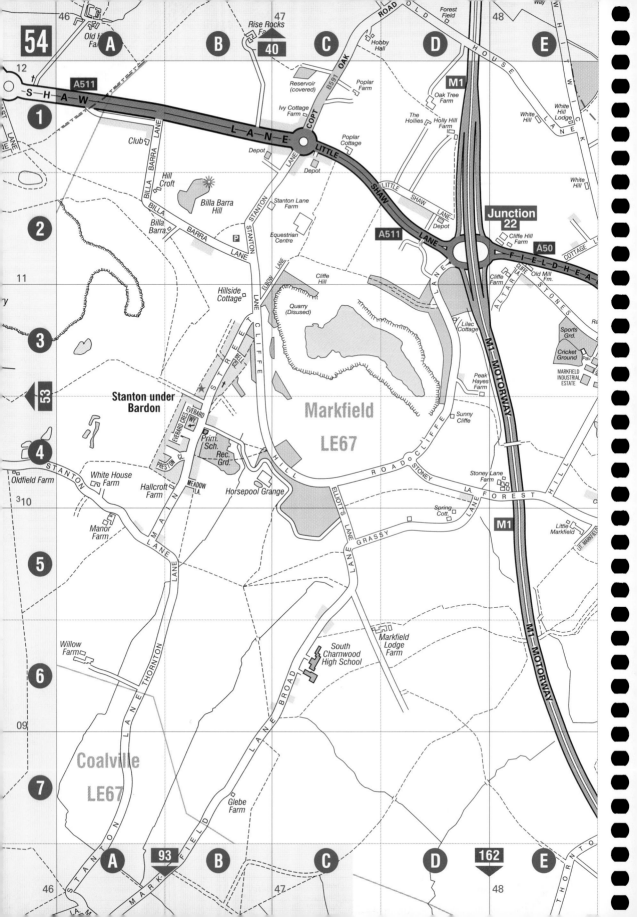

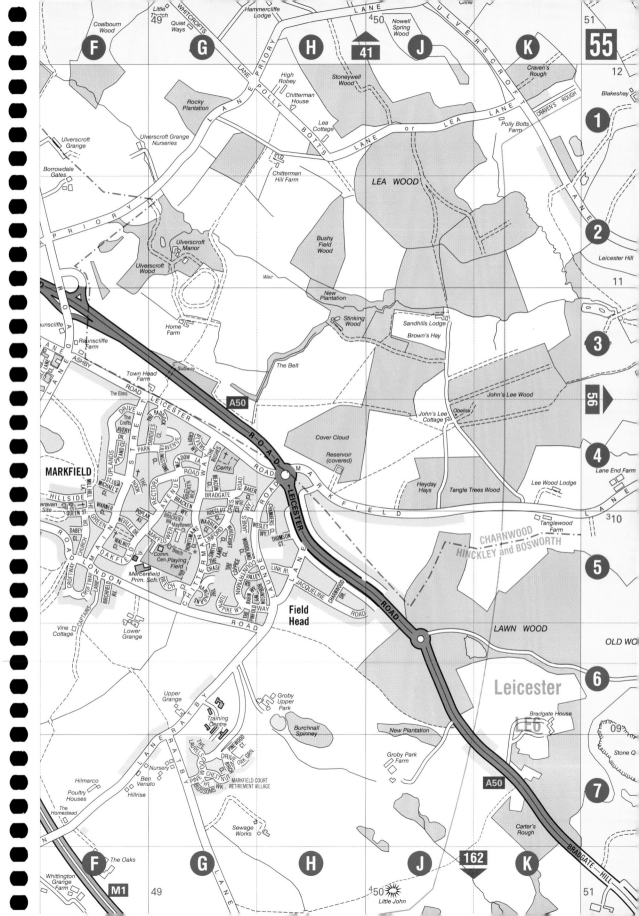

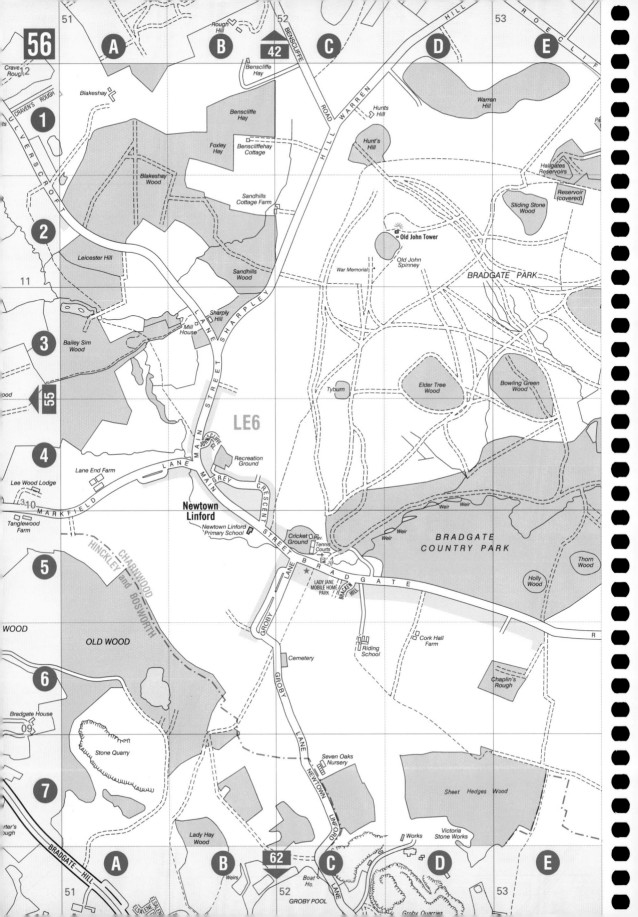

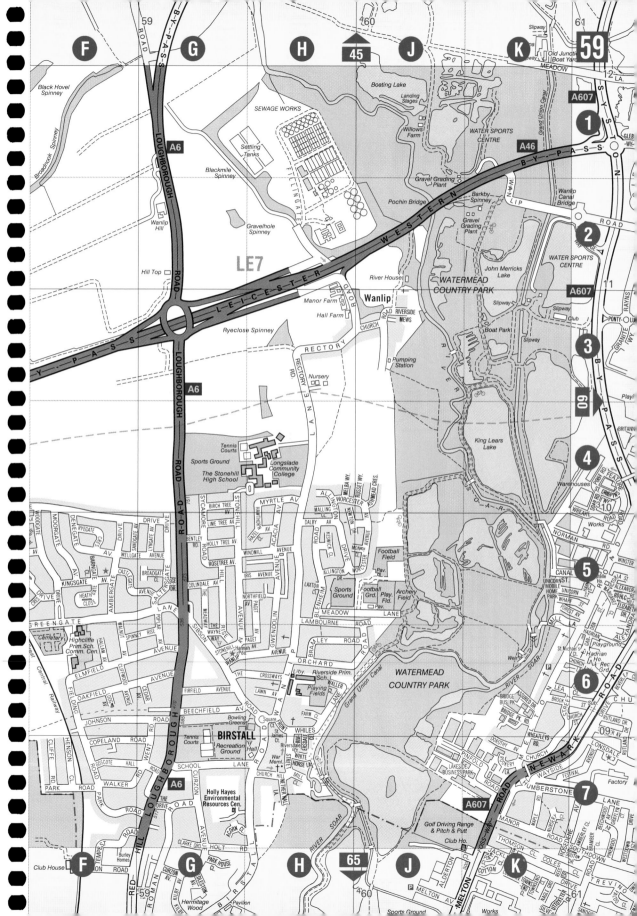

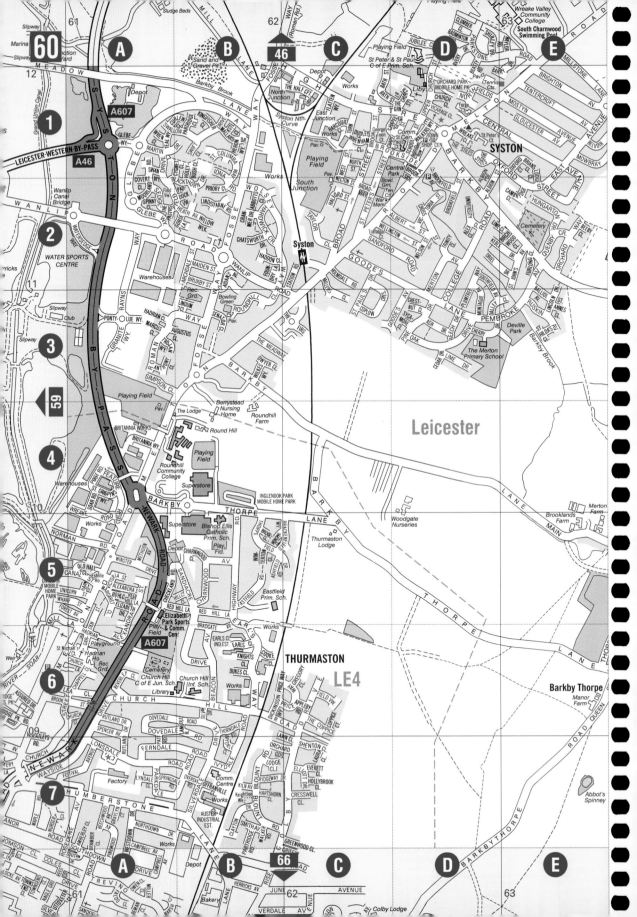

QUENIBOROUGH

Homestead Farm
QUENIBOROUGH INDUSTRIAL ESTATE
64
THE BANKS
GLEBE ROAD
THE RIDINGS
CHESTNUT CL
AVENUE
ROAD
66
12

**F** **G** **H** **47** **J** **K**

Queniborough Hall
MAIN STREET
MERE LA.
QUENIBOROUGH STREET
QUENIBOROUGH HALL DR.
Dovecotes
Manor Farm
Springfield Farm
Pav.
SOUTH CROXTON ROAD
The Pastures
Newstead Farm

**1**

Cricket Ground
Syston RFC
Rugby Ground
Hillcrest

**2**

RIDGEMERE
BARKBY ROAD
The Ridgemere Centre
Nursery
Redlands Farm
ROAD
Syston Grange
LANE
**159** 11
11

**3**

New York Farm

**4**

$^3$10

QUENIBOROUGH ROAD
Cemetery
The Hall
Barkby
Dairy
VICARAGE LA.
BROOKSIDE
HOLT LANE

**LE7**

**5**

**163**

STREET
Cricket Grd.
Pav.
The Pochin Sch.
BARKBY
CHURCH LA.
BROOKSIDE
BARKBY
Barkby Brook
Grange Farm
Beeby Paddocks

**6**

THORPE
Thorpe Farm
KING ST.
Hill Top Farm
ROAD
09
Chestnut Farm

**7**

Works

**F** **G** **H** **67** **J** **K**

Spring Grange
BARKBY ROAD
Brooke House Farm
Beeby

64
Barkby Thorpe Spinney
$^4$65
66

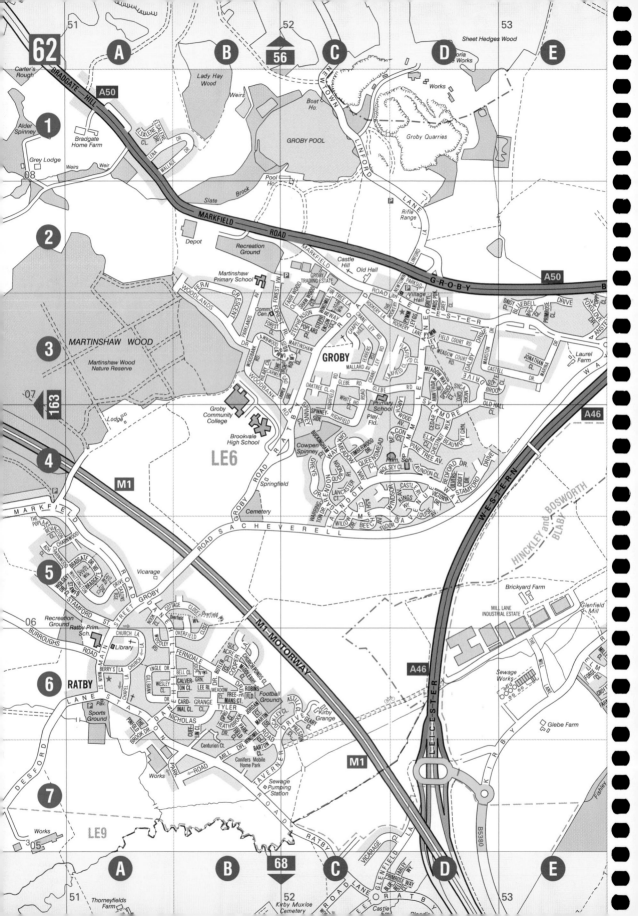

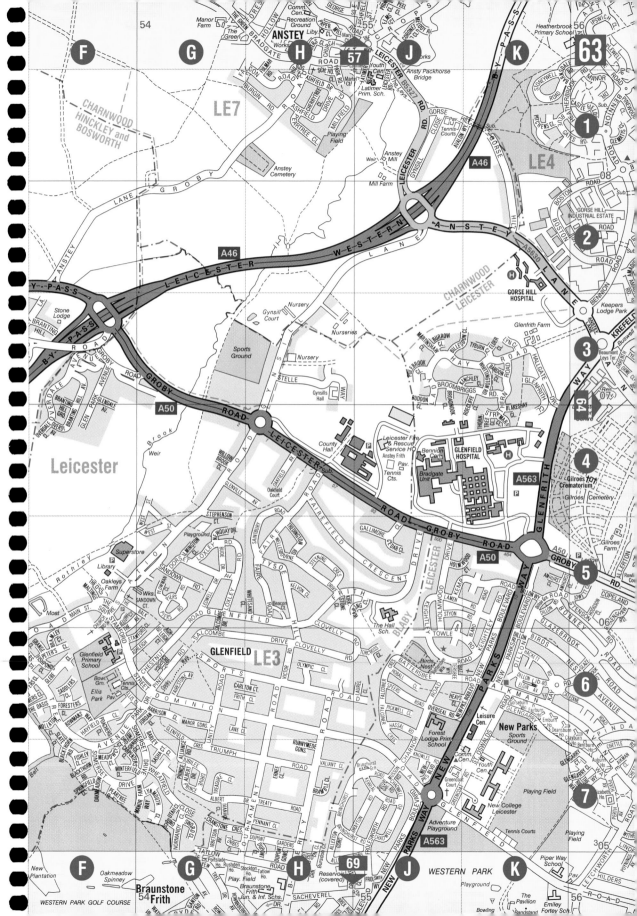

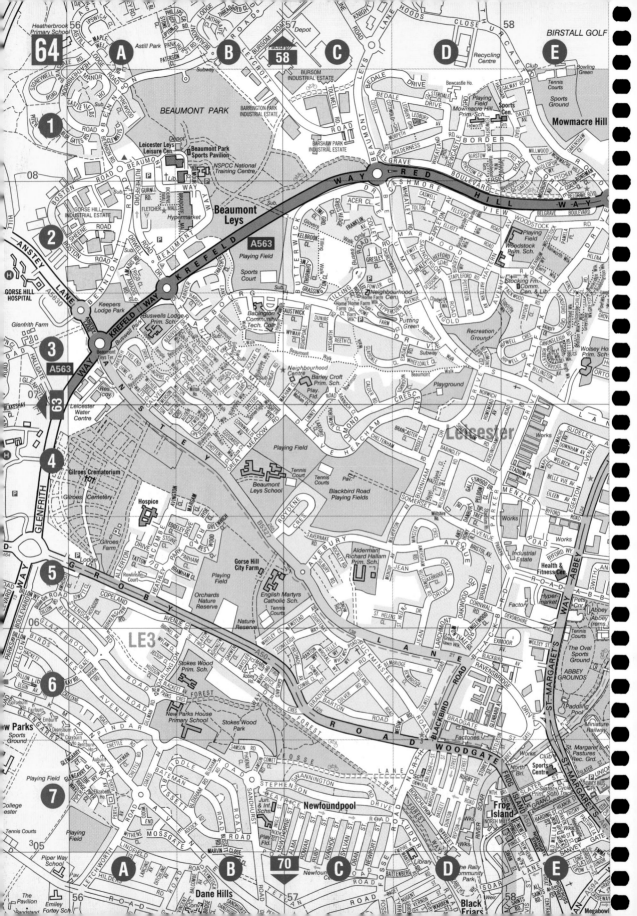

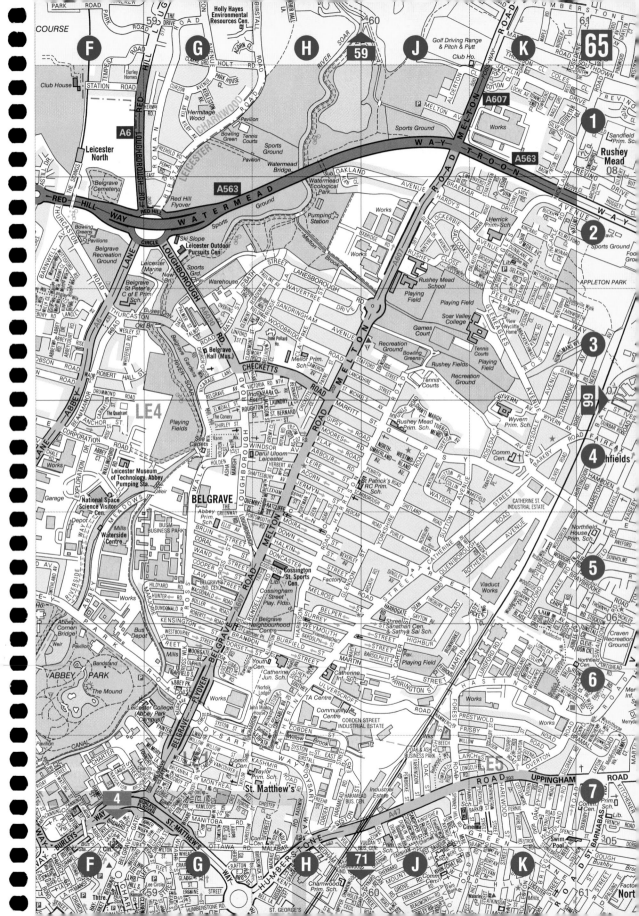

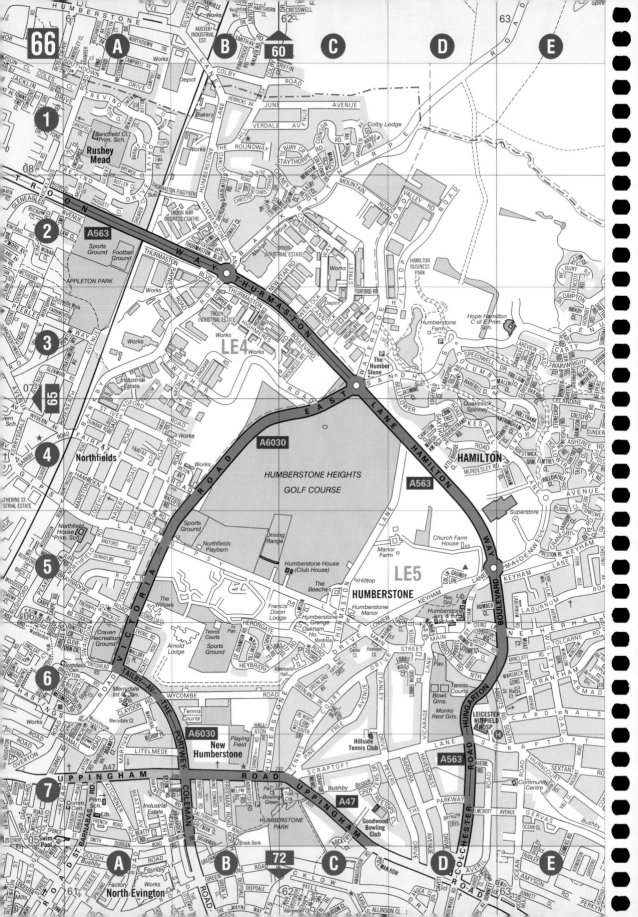

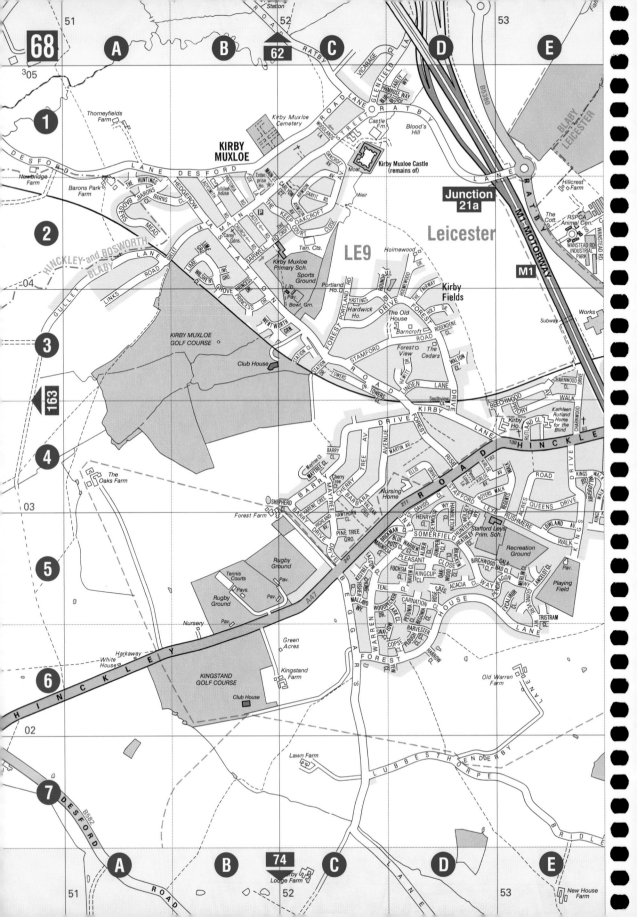

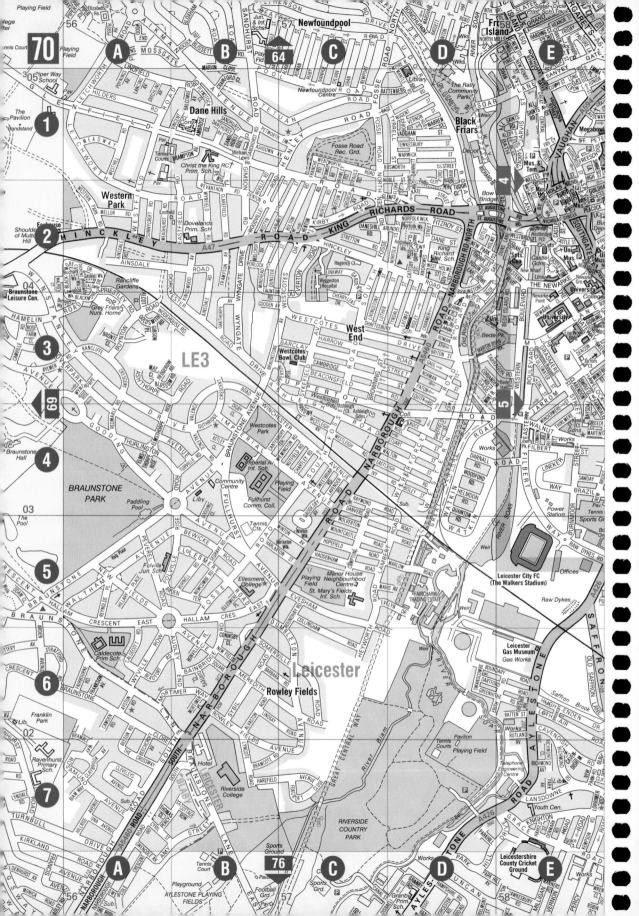

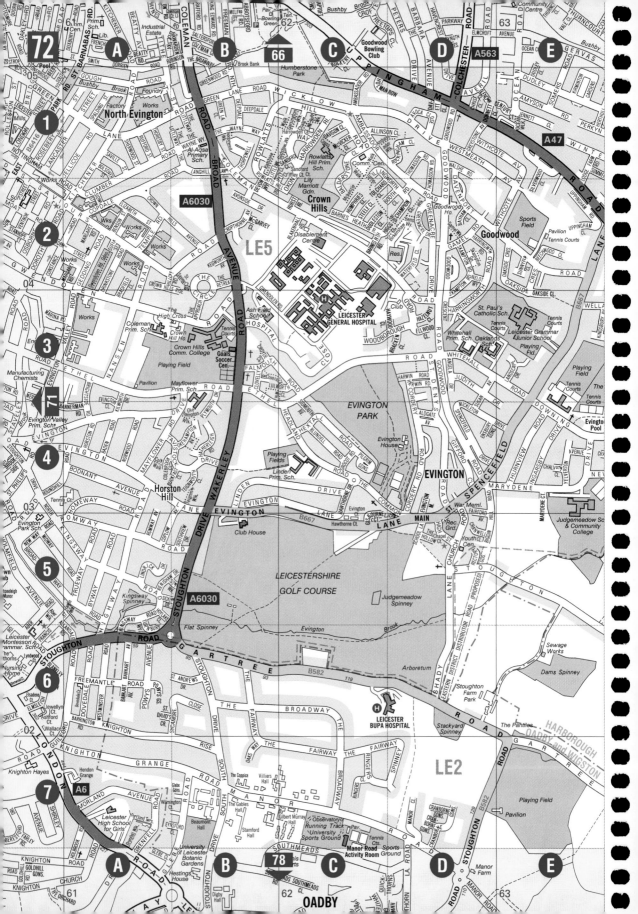

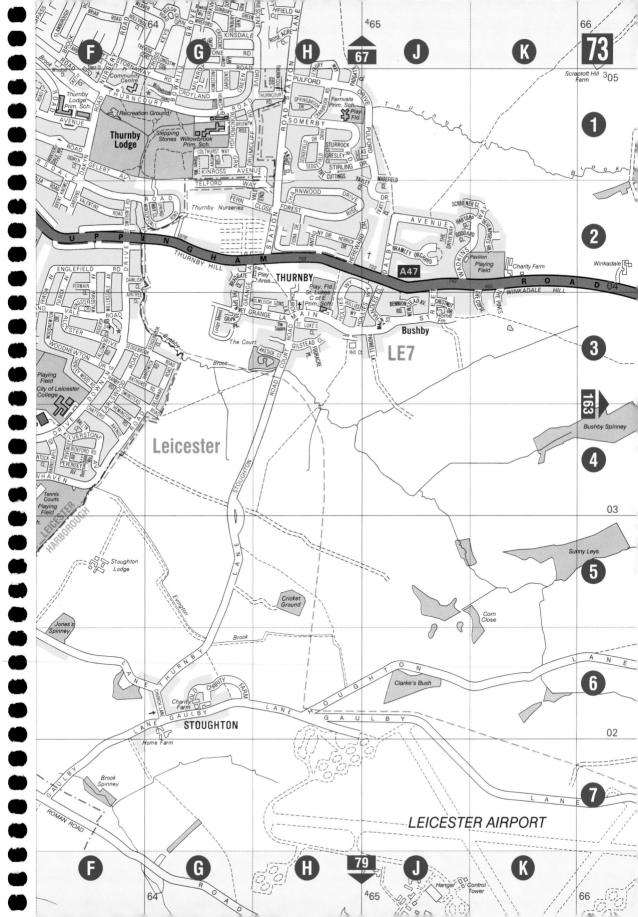

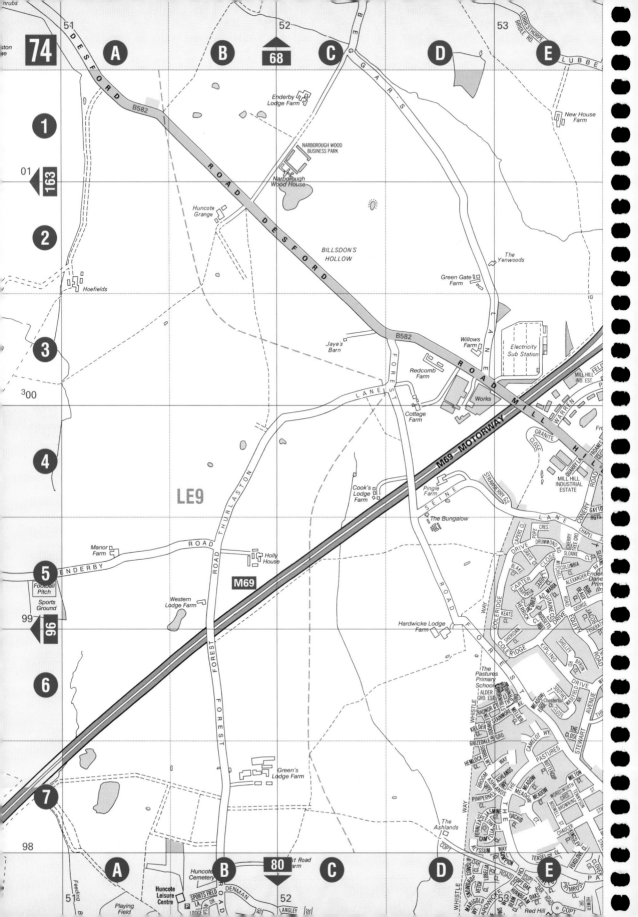

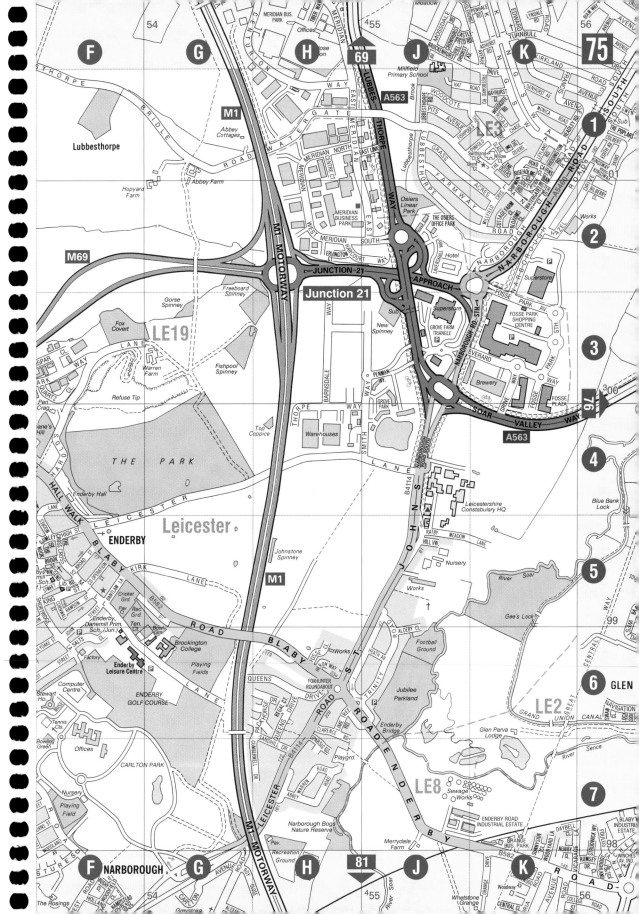

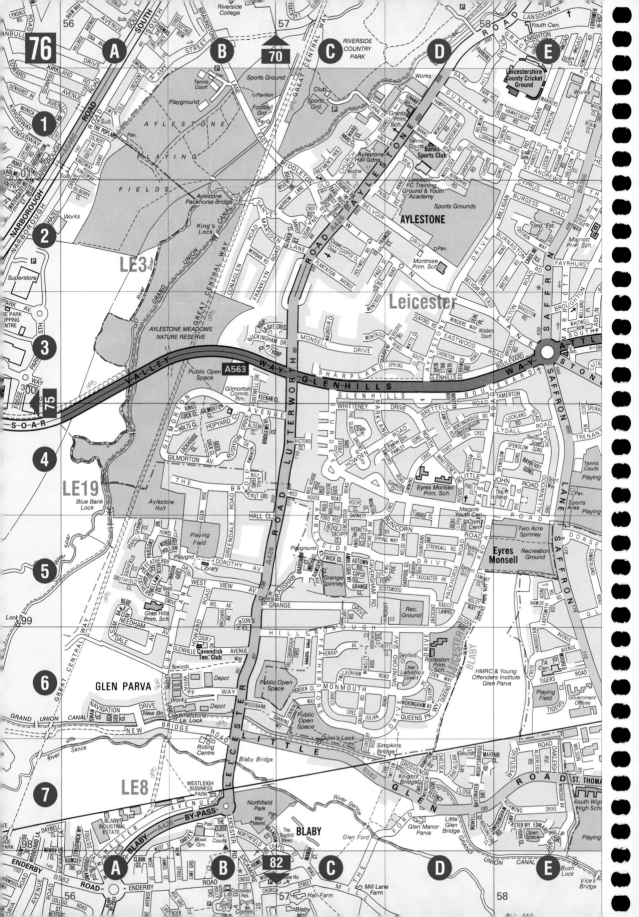

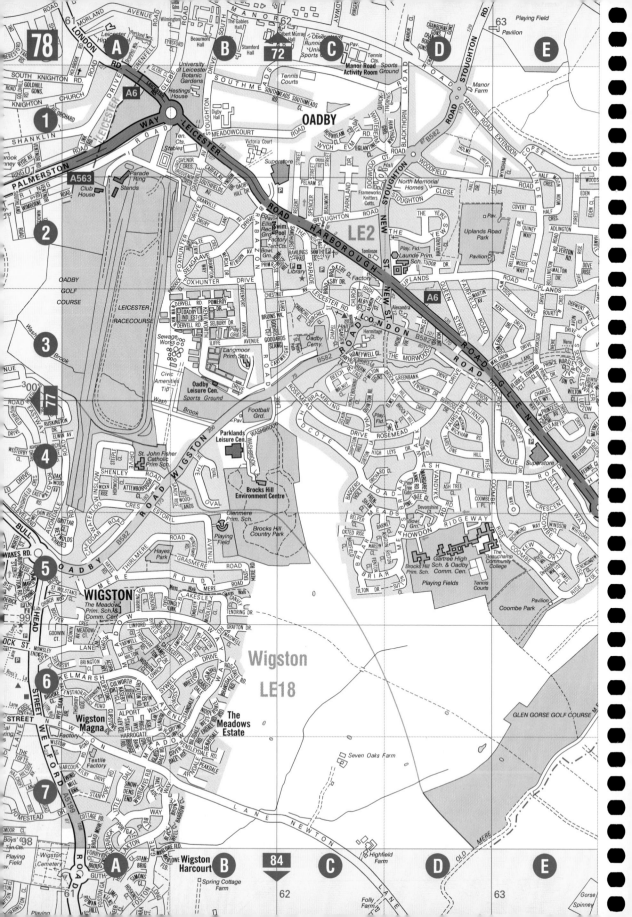

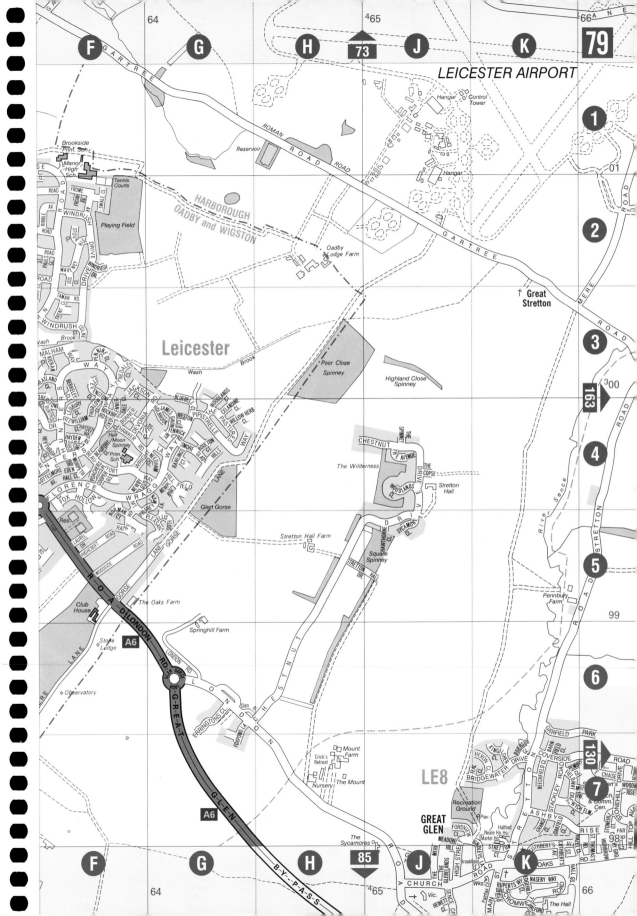

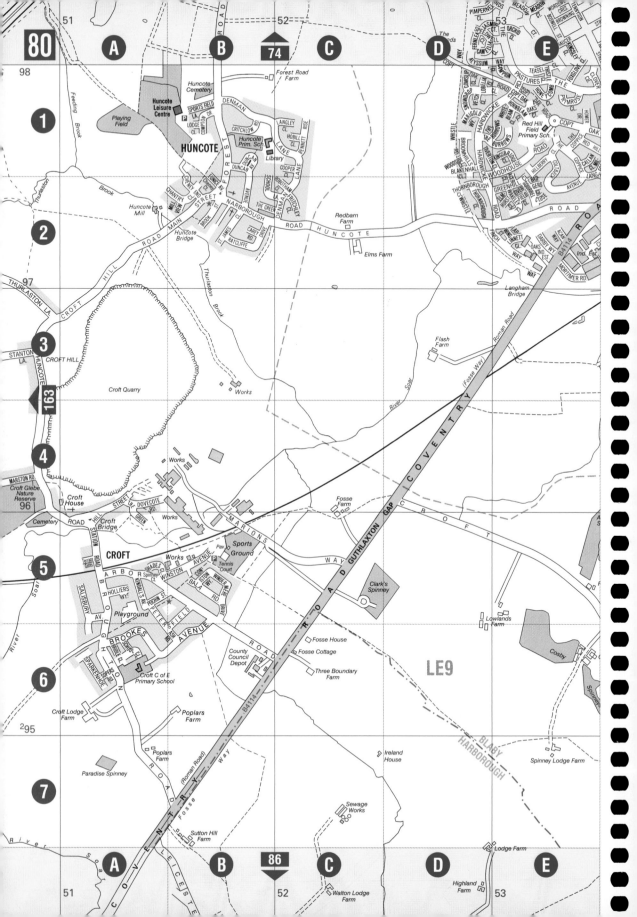

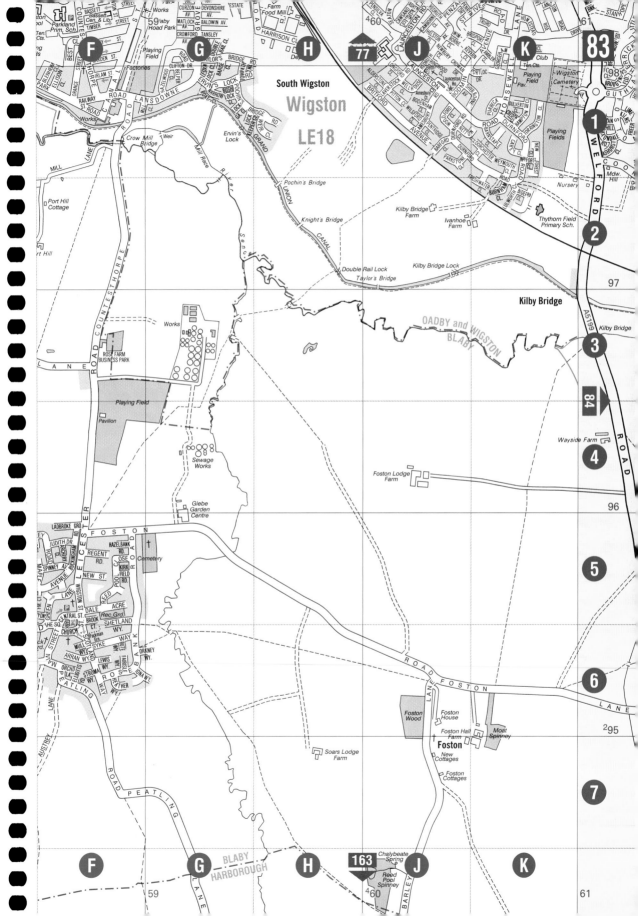

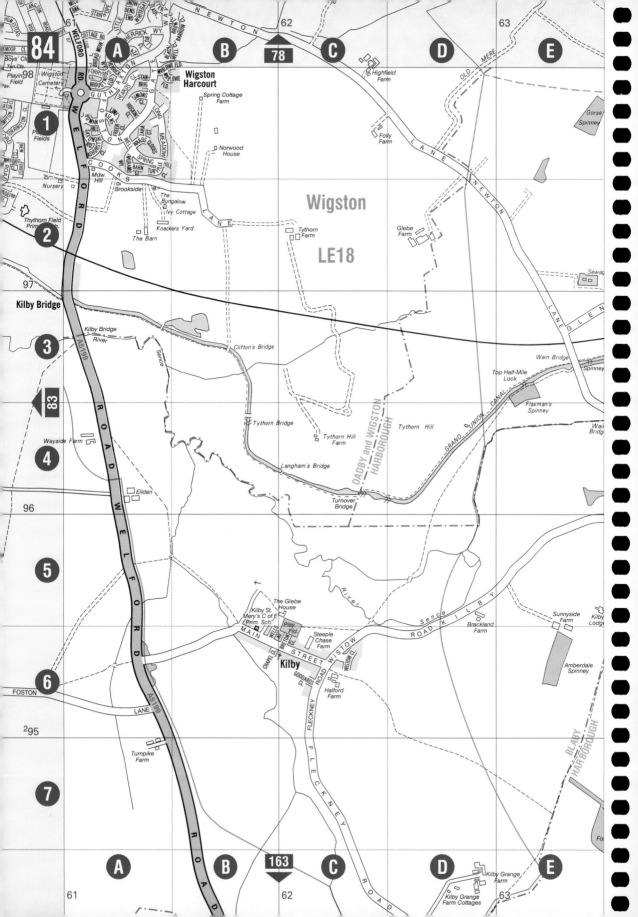

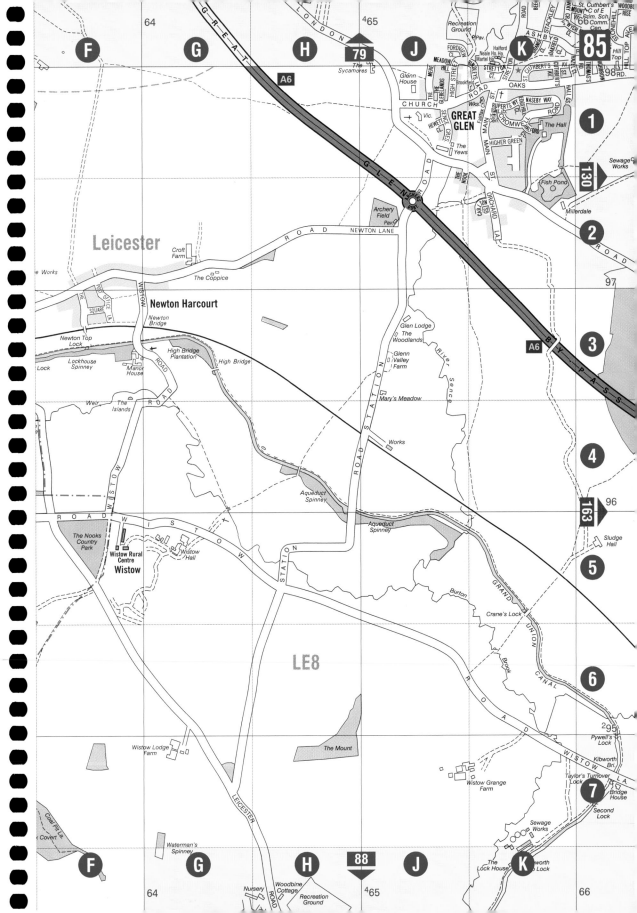

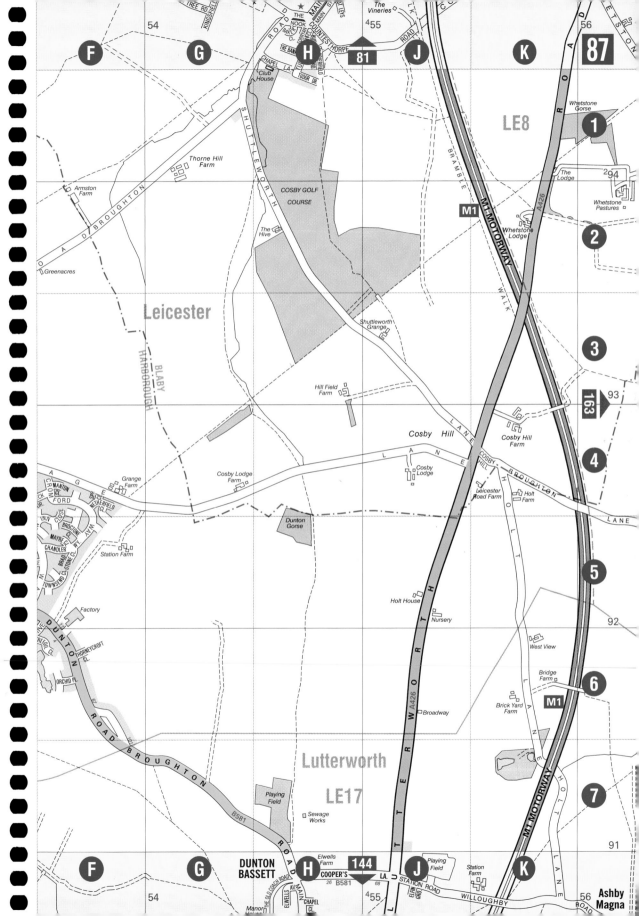

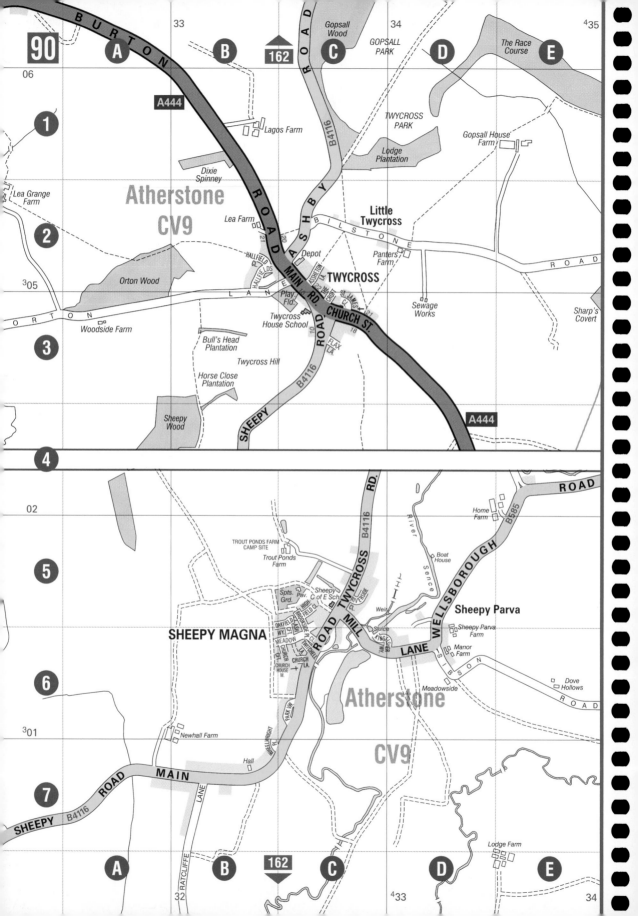

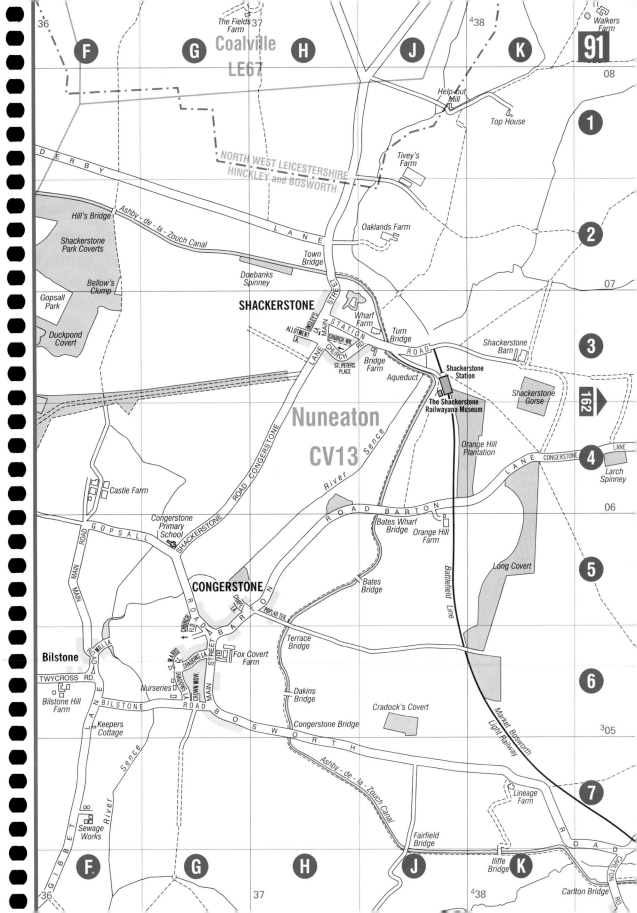

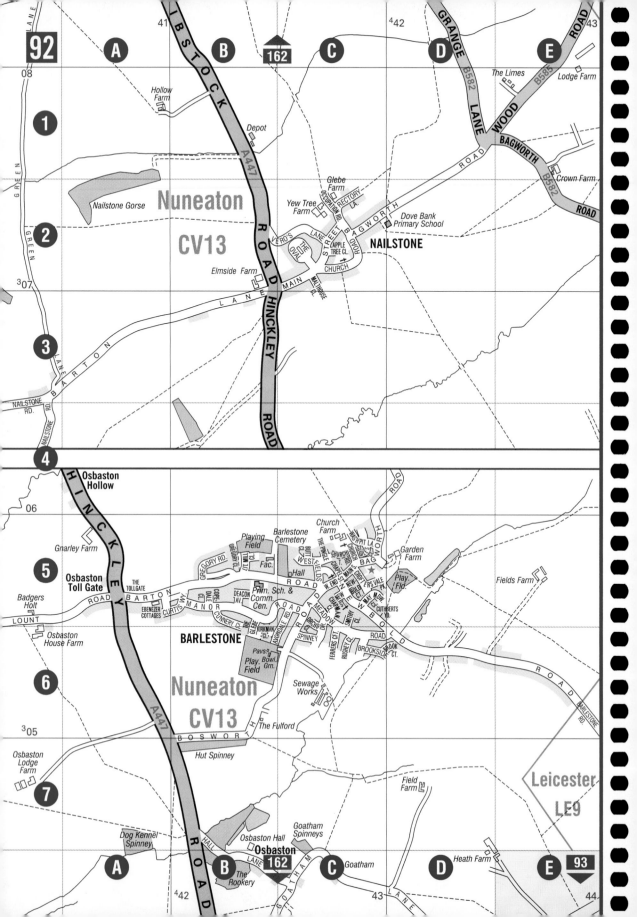

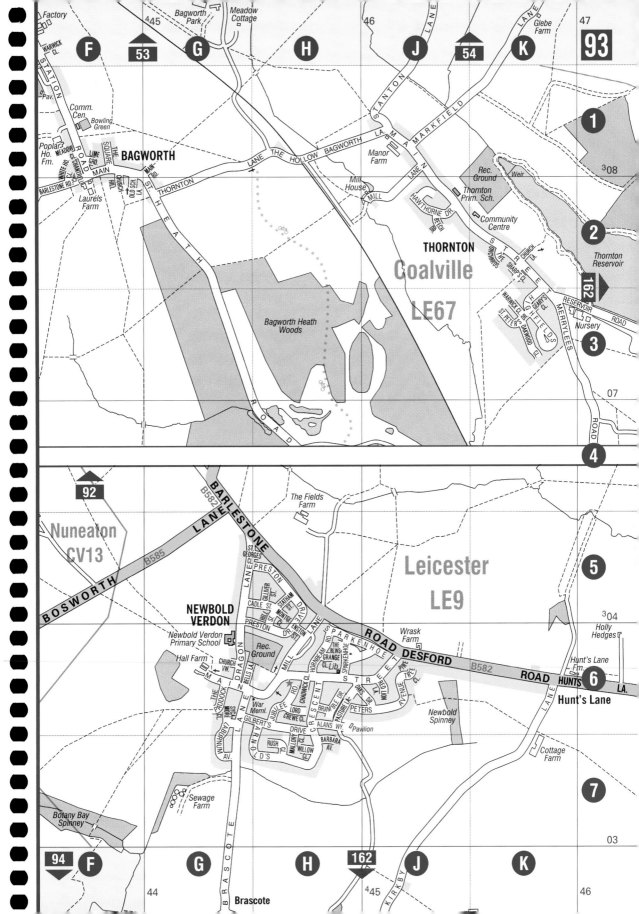

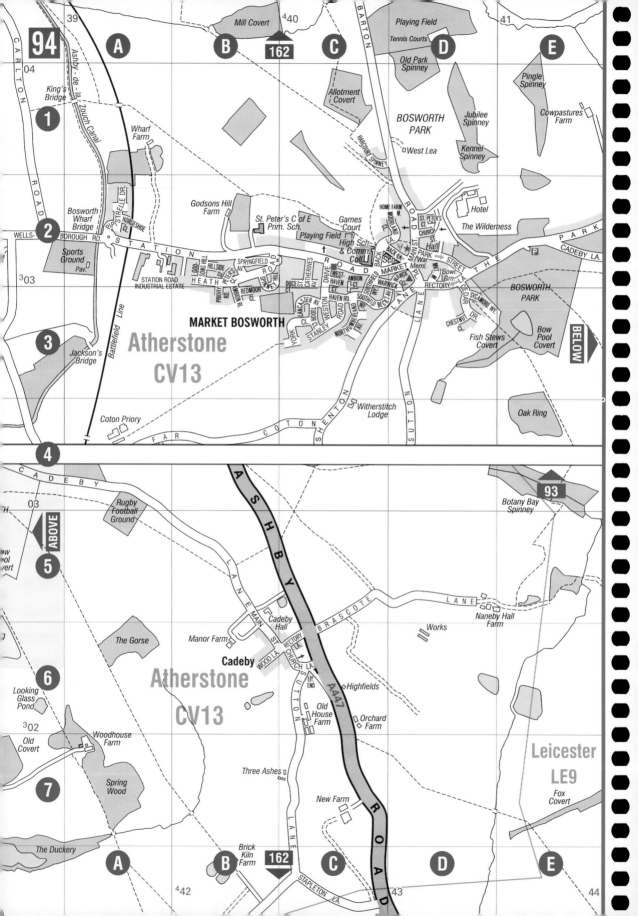

**Top map (grid 94):**

39 | 40 | 41
A | B | C | D | E

04

King's Bridge
1

Mill Covert
162

Playing Field
Tennis Courts
Old Park Spinney

Pingle Spinney

Cowpastures Farm

Allotment Covert

BOSWORTH PARK

Jubilee Spinney

West Lea

Kennel Spinney

CARLTON ROAD

Ashby-de-la-Zouch Canal

Wharf Farm

Bosworth Wharf Bridge
2
WELLS- | BOROUGH RD.

STRELLE DR.
HORSESHOE CL.

Sports Ground
Pav.

STATION ROAD INDUSTRIAL ESTATE

³03

Godsons Hill Farm

HEATH

STATION ROAD

GODSONS HILL
HILLSIDE
PRIORY RD.
PETER'S AV.
MANOR RD.
REDMOOR CL.
SPRINGFIELD
SONS HILL
SPRING HILL

St. Peter's C of E Prim. Sch.

Playing Field

Games Court

High Sch. & Comm. Coll.

HARBOUR SPINNEY

HOME FARM M.
MOORLAND
BACK LA.
BACK LA.
MAIN ST.

ST. PETER'S CT.
ST. PETER'S CHURCH

Hotel

The Wilderness

PARK

CADEBY LA.

P

DUCEY CT.
CATHERINES AV.
LANCASTER AV.
WOOL CL.
STANLEY
YORK
WESTON RD.
NORTHUMBERLAND
WEST HAVEN CT.
HAVEN RD.
SOUTHFIELD
BECT. IN.
SOUTHED RD.
AMBION CT.
WARWICK CT.
WARWICK SQ.
MARKET
RECTORY
WAR MEML.
PARK
WAR. WY.
CEDAR LA.
BOWL. GRN.
CHESTNUT CL.
SYCAMORE WY.
CHURCH ST.
ST. HALL

**MARKET BOSWORTH**

*Atherstone CV13*

BOSWORTH PARK

BELOW

3

Jackson's Bridge

Battlefield Line

Fish Stews Covert

Bow Pool Covert

Witherstitch Lodge

SHENTON LA.

COTON RD.

FAR

SUTTON LA.

Oak Ring

Coton Priory

4

**Bottom map (grid 93):**

03

CADEBY

Rugby Football Ground

ABOVE

5

H

ow ol vert

ASHBY LANE

Cadeby Hall

Manor Farm

MAIN ST.
WOOD LA.
RECTORY LA.
CHURCH LA.

**Cadeby**

*Atherstone CV13*

BRASCOTE

LANE

Works

Naneby Hall Farm

Botany Bay Spinney

93

6

Looking Glass Pond

³02

Old Covert

Woodhouse Farm

SUTTON LANE

A447

Highfields

Old House Farm

Orchard Farm

LIT. END

**Leicester LE9**

7

Spring Wood

Three Ashes

New Farm

ROAD

Fox Covert

The Duckery

A

Brick Kiln Farm
162
B

STAPLETON LA.
C

D

E

⁴42 | 43 | 44

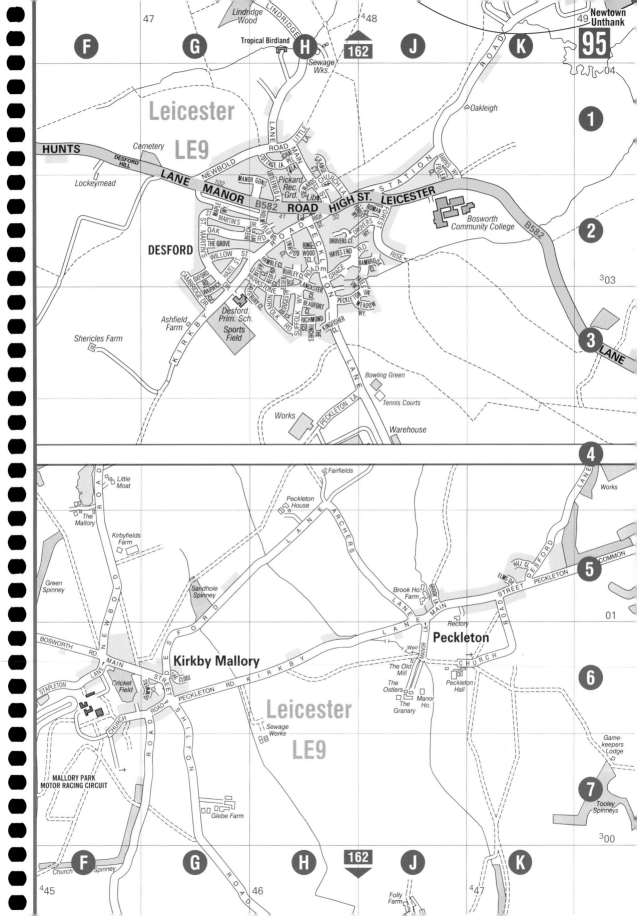

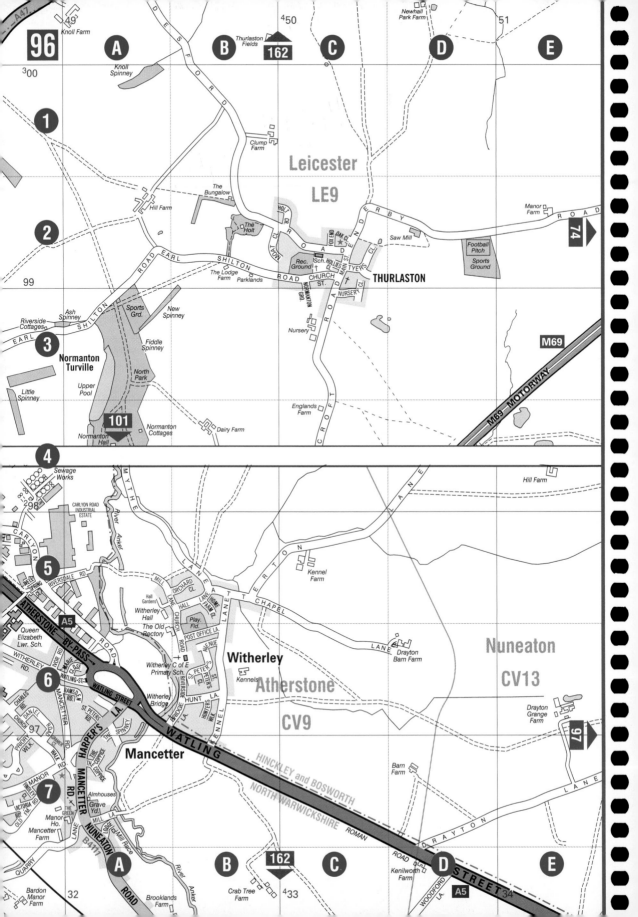

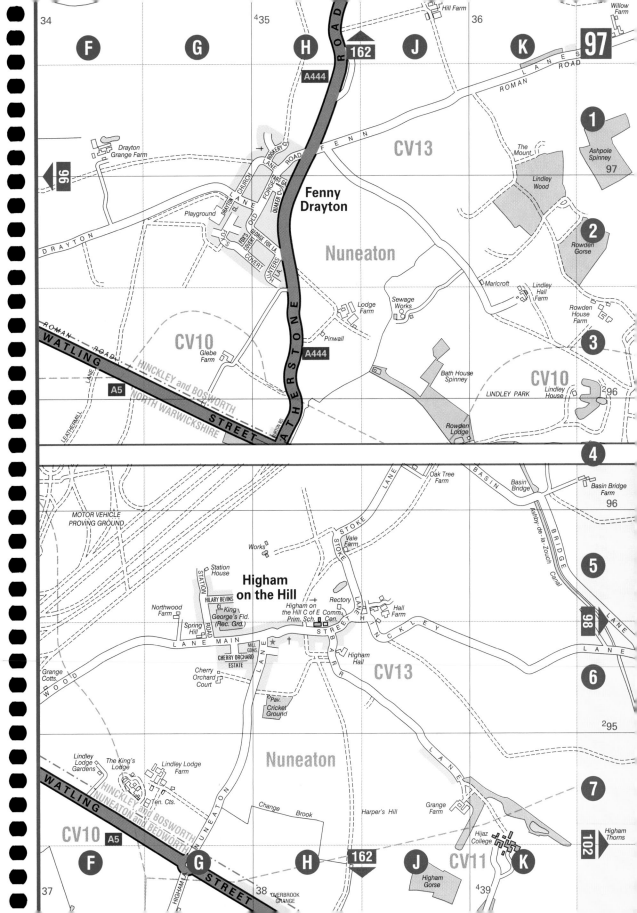

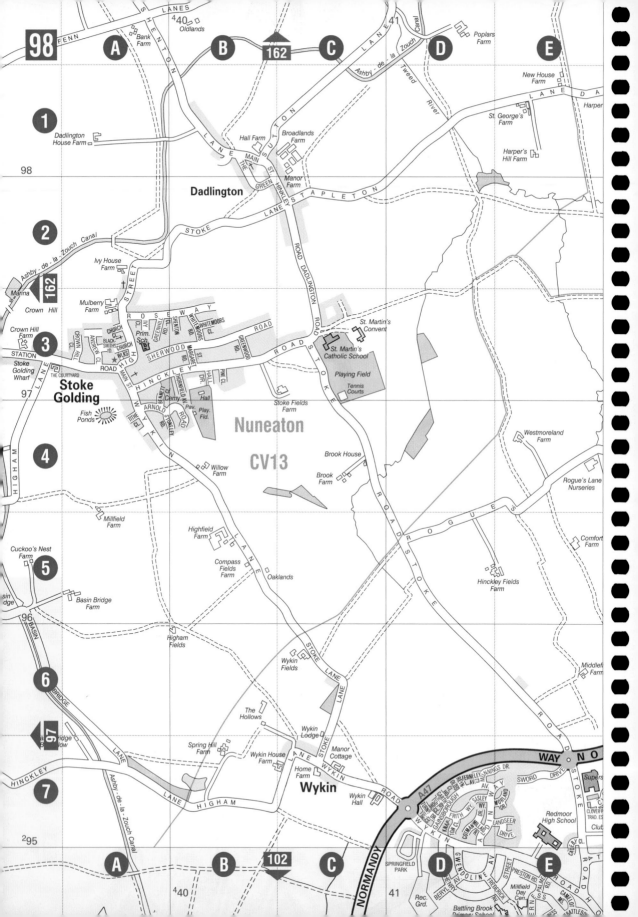

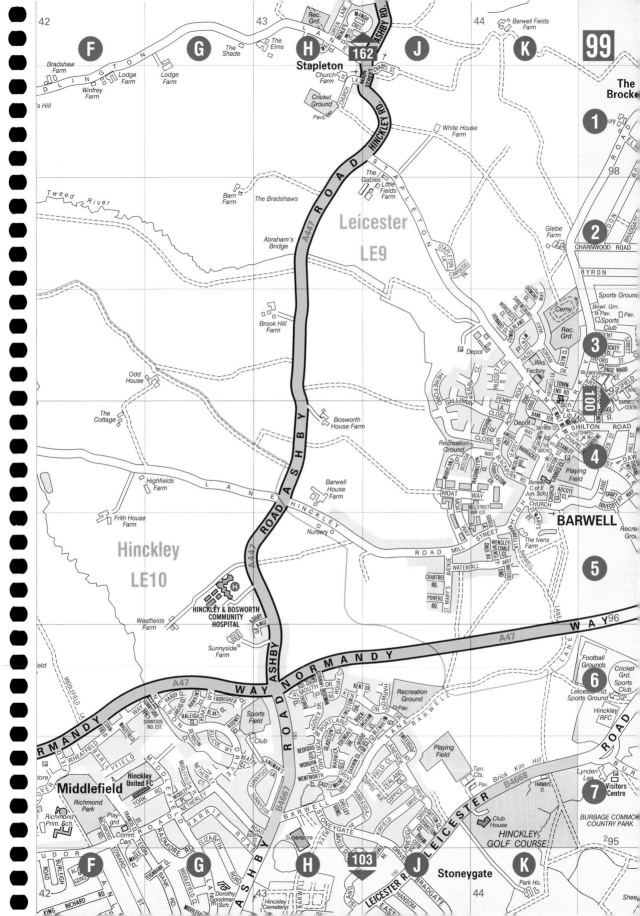

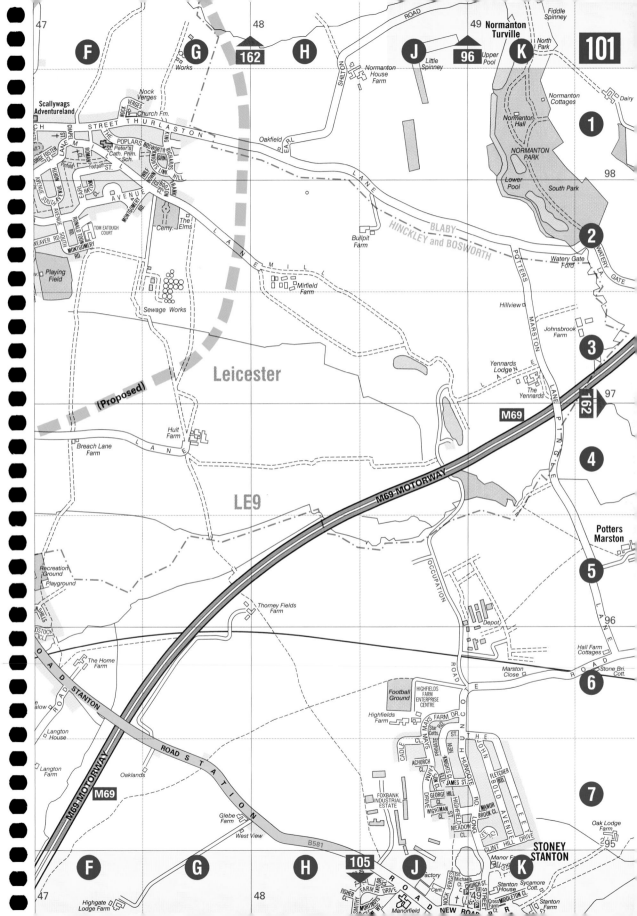

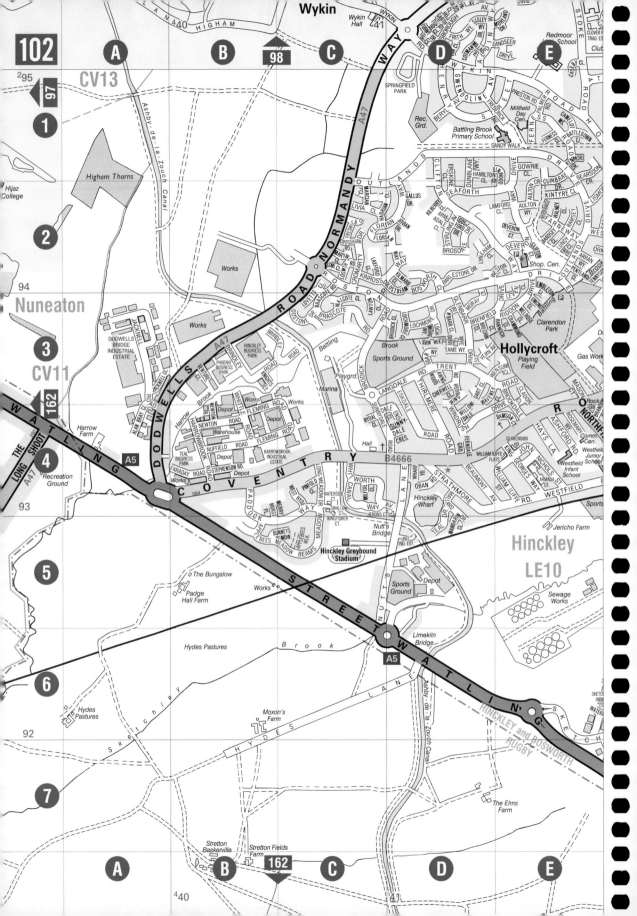

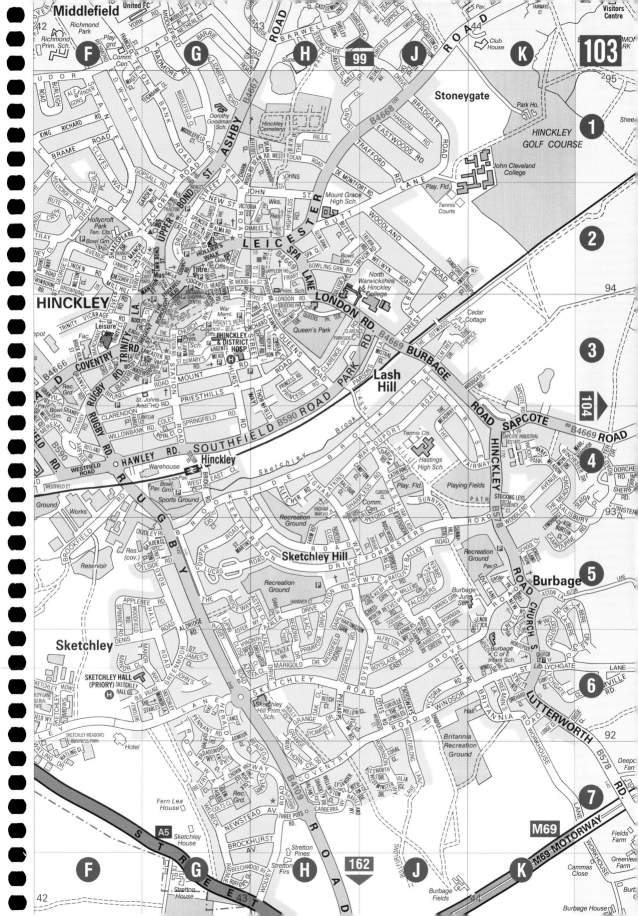

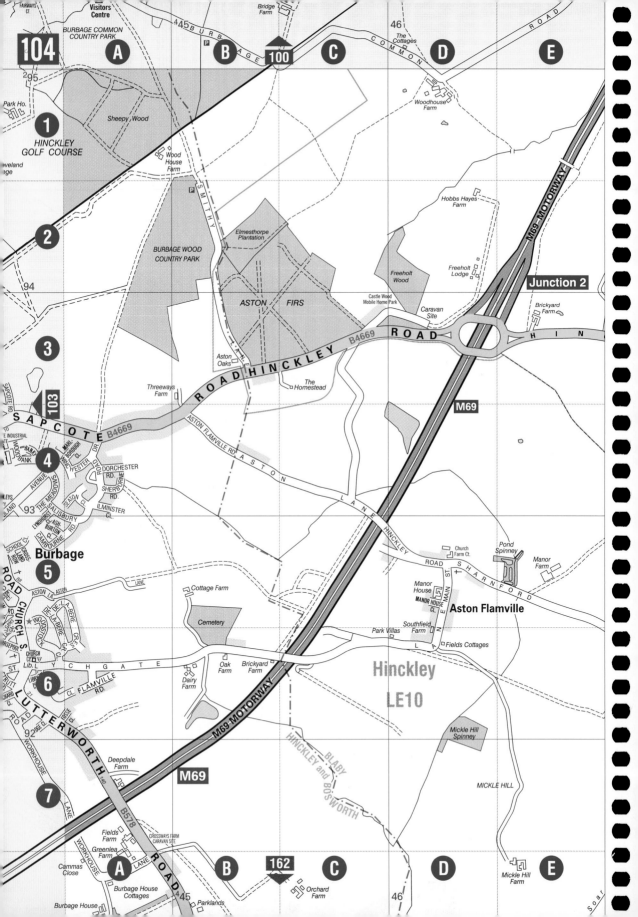

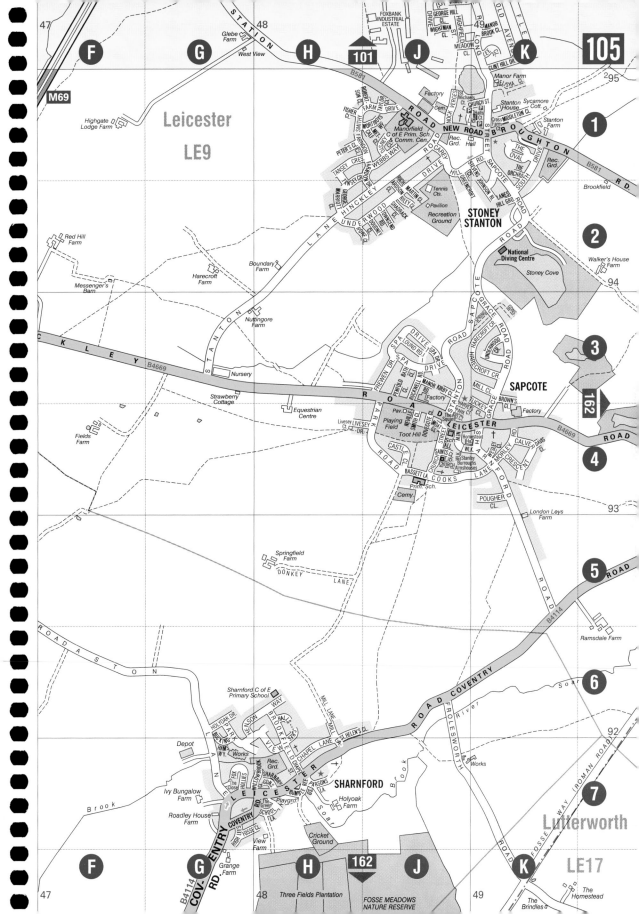

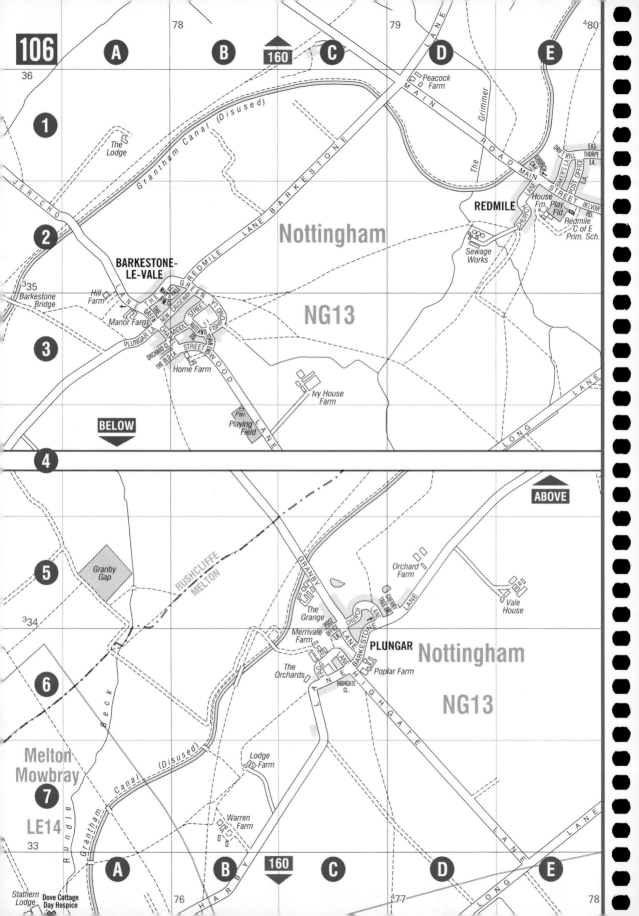

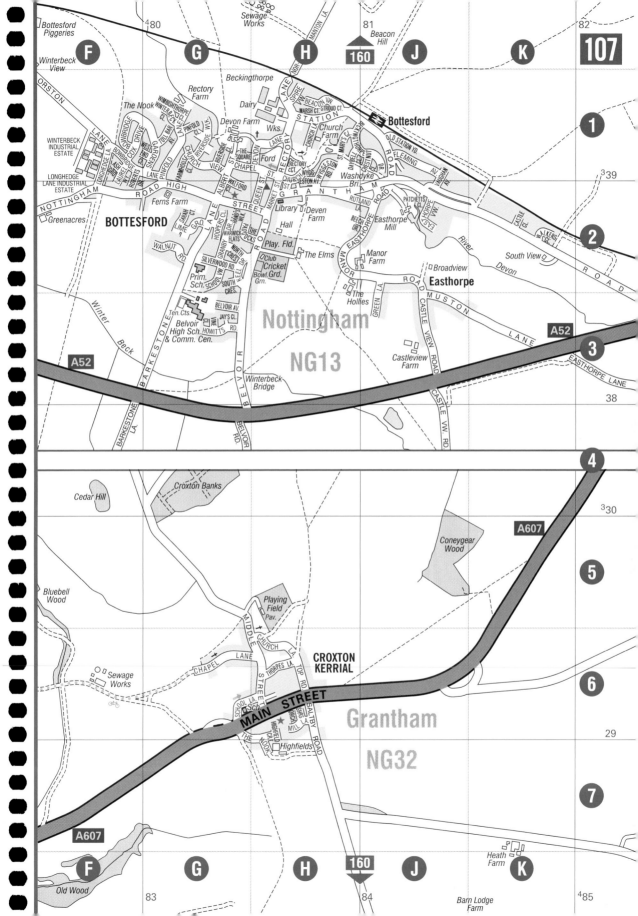

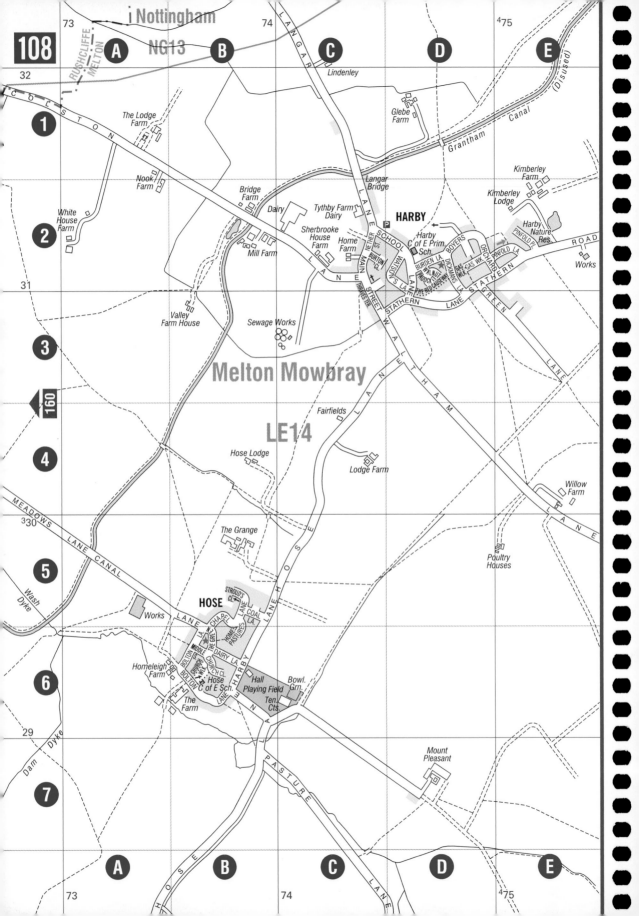

i Nottingham

NG13

RUSHCLIFFE
MELTON

**A** **B** **C** **D** **E**

73 74 475

32

Langar

Lindenley

1

COLSTON

The Lodge
Farm

Glebe
Farm

Grantham Canal (Disused)

Nook
Farm

Kimberley
Farm

2

White
House
Farm

Bridge
Farm

Dairy

Tythby Farm
Dairy

Langar
Bridge

HARBY

Kimberley
Lodge

Harby
Nature
Res.

ROAD

Sherbrooke
House
Farm

Home
Farm

Harby
C of E Prim.
Sch.

BOYERS

Works

Mill Farm

SCHOOL LANE

MAIN STREET

MASON'S LANE

BURDEN LA.

WALNUT

PYE RD

GAS WK.

DICKMANS LA.

GAS WK.

PINFOLD LA.

ORCHARD WK.

STATHERN

GREEN LANE

PINFOLD PL.

31

Valley
Farm House

Sewage Works

STATHERN LANE

WALTHAM LANE

Melton Mowbray

3

160

Fairfields

LE14

Hose Lodge

Lodge Farm

4

HOSE LANE

Willow
Farm

MEADOWS LANE CANAL

330

The Grange

Poultry
Houses

5

Wash
Dyke

Works

STROUD'S CL.

HOSE

CHAPEL LANE

COAL LA.

PASTURES LANE

6

Homeleigh
Farm

THE GREEN

BOLTON LANE

MIDDLE CL.

DAIRY LA.

CHURCH CL.

Hose
C of E Sch.

Hall
Playing Field

Bowl.
Grn.

HARBY LANE

Ten.
Cts.

The
Farm

29

Dam Dyke

PASTURE LANE

Mount
Pleasant

7

**A** **B** **C** **D** **E**

73 74 475

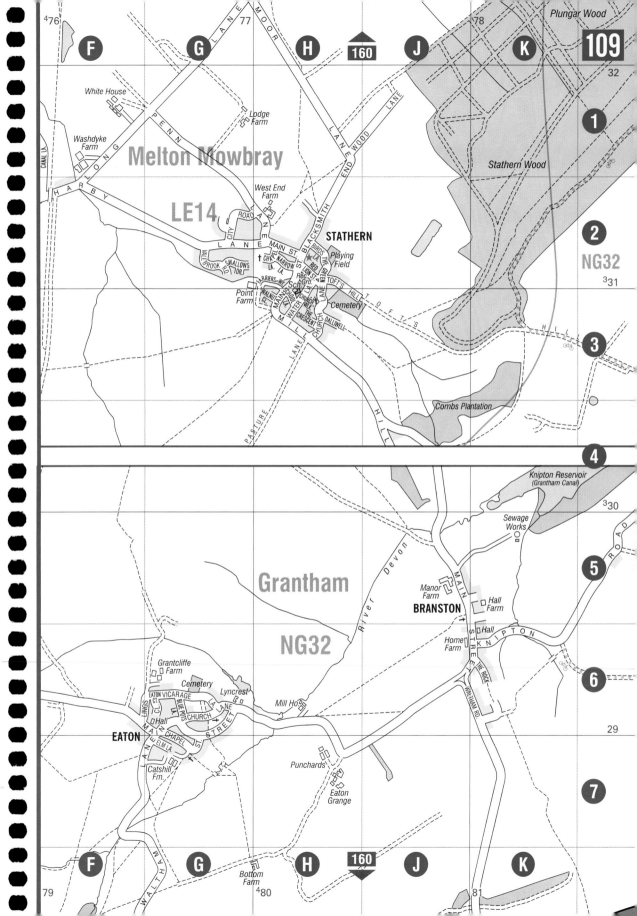

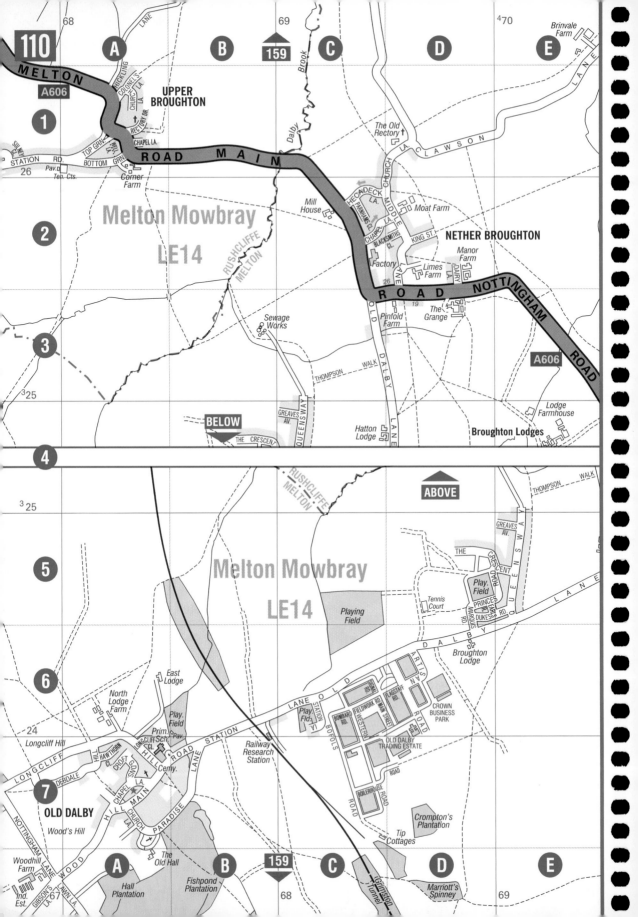

**68**     **A**     **B**     **69**    159    **C**     **D**     ⁴**70**    **E**

MELTON

A606

UPPER BROUGHTON

Brinvale Farm

1

The Old Rectory †

STATION RD.
Pav. Cts.
Ten. Cts.
26
TOP GRN.
WELL LA.
BOTTOM GRN.
CHAPEL LA.
ROAD MAIN
Dalby
CLAWSON LA.
HUCKLING LA.
COLONELS LA.
CHURCH LA.
RECTORY DR.

Corner Farm

Melton Mowbray

LE14

RUSHCLIFFE MELTON

2

Mill House

CHEADECK LA.
PARKING CL.
CHAPEL LA.
BLACKSMITHS CL.
MIDDLE LA.
KING ST.
Moat Farm

NETHER BROUGHTON

Manor Farm

Factory
Limes Farm
DAIRY

3

³25

Sewage Works

THOMPSON WALK

OLD DALBY LANE

Pinfold Farm
The Grange

ROAD NOTTINGHAM ROAD
26
19
A606

Lodge Farmhouse

BELOW
GREAVES AV.
QUEENSWAY
THE CRESCENT
Hatton Lodge

Broughton Lodges

---

**4**

**³25**

RUSHCLIFFE MELTON

ABOVE

THOMPSON WALK

5

Melton Mowbray

LE14

Playing Field

Tennis Court

Play. Field

THE
CRESCENT RD.
QUEENSWAY LANE
PRINCES RD.
MARQUIS RD.
DUKES RD.
GREAVES AV.

6

East Lodge

North Lodge Farm

Play. Field

Broughton Lodge

DALBY LANE

LANE OLD
STATION RD.
BOTOLS
BOMBARD RD.
FENWICK RD.
FLAGSTAFF RD.
MAIN STREET
WESTERN
ARTISAN RD.
Play Fld

CROWN BUSINESS PARK

24

Longcliff Hill

LONGCLIFF
THE HAWTHORN
CROFT CL.
DEBDALE
Longcliff CL.
Prim. Sch.
Pav.
HILL RD.
CHAPEL LA.
MAIN
HILL
Cemy.
PARADISE
CHURCH LA.
STATION LANE
Railway Research Station

OLD DALBY TRADING ESTATE
BOLENHOUSE ROAD
ROAD

Crompton's Plantation

7

OLD DALBY

Wood's Hill

Woodhill Farm
Ind. Est.
GIBSON'S LA.
NOTTINGHAM LANE
WOOD LA.
TWIN LA.
HILL

The Old Hall

Hall Plantation

**A**

Fishpond Plantation

**B**

159

**68**

**C**

Tip Cottages

Marriott's Spinney

**D**

**69**

**E**

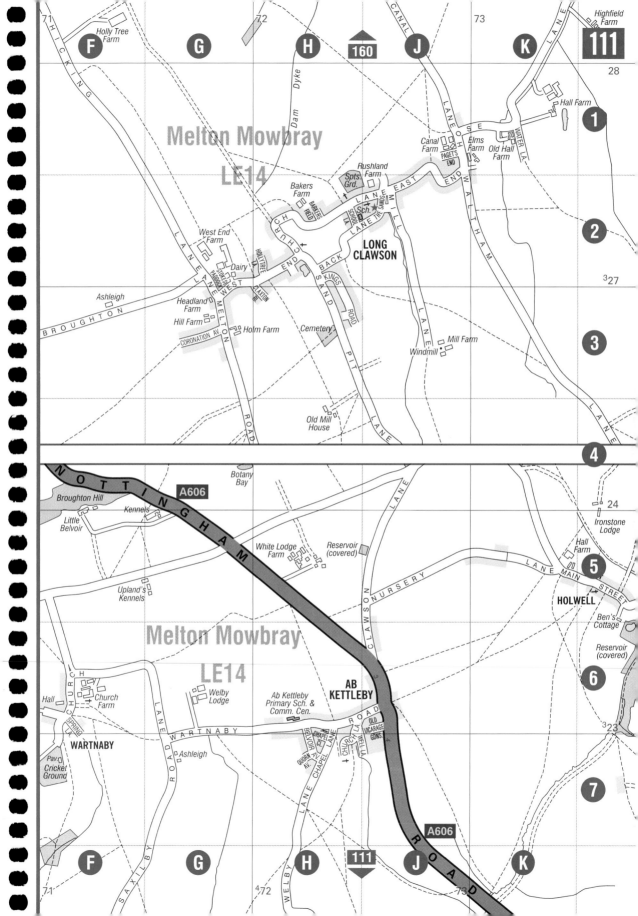

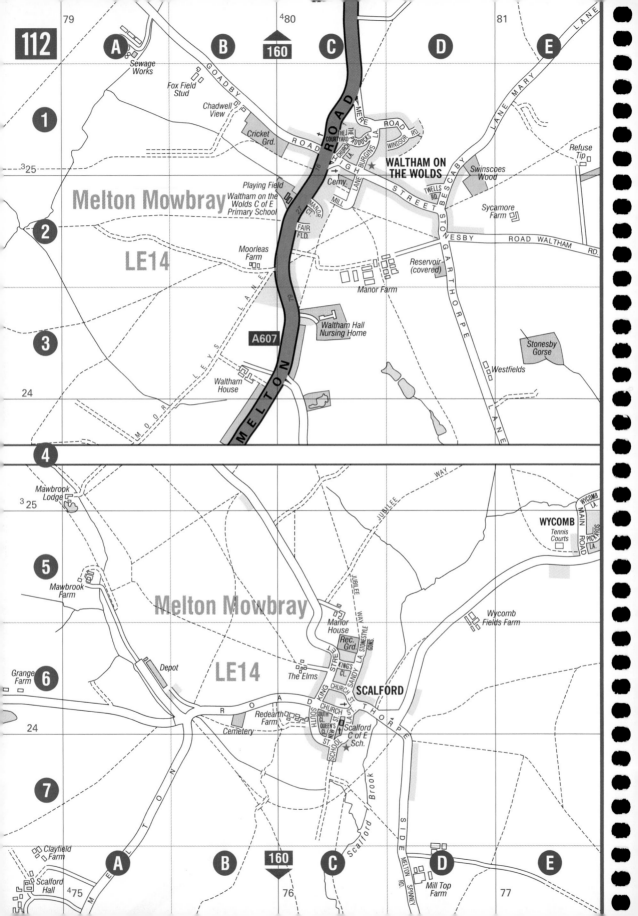

**112**

79    <sup>4</sup>80    81

A    B    **160**    C    D    E

1

Sewage Works
Fox Field Stud
Chadwell View
Cricket Grd.

GOADBY ROAD

<sup>3</sup>25

ROAD

HIGH

MERE

CHURCH LA.

THE PADDOCKS
THE COURTYARD

WINDSOR RD.

ROAD

MARY LANE

LANE

Refuse Tip

**Melton Mowbray**

Waltham on the Wolds C of E Primary School

Playing Field

CEMY.

**WALTHAM ON THE WOLDS**

Swinscoes Wood

2

**LE14**

Moorleas Farm

MANOR CT.

MILL LANE

BURGINS LA.

STREET

TWELLS RD.

BESCABY

STONESBY

Sycamore Farm

ROAD WALTHAM RD.

FAIR FLD.

Reservoir (covered)

Manor Farm

GARTHORPE

LANE

3

A607

MELTON

Waltham Hall Nursing Home

Stonesby Gorse

Westfields

24

LEYS LANE

Waltham House

M O O R    R.

4

Mawbrook Lodge

<sup>3</sup>25

WAY

JUBILEE

WYCOMB LA.

**WYCOMB**

Tennis Courts

MAIN ROAD

PICKRS LA.

5

Mawbrook Farm

**Melton Mowbray**

Manor House

Rec. Grd.

JUBILEE WAY

STREET

STONESTYLE GDNS.

SANDY LA.

Wycomb Fields Farm

Grange Farm

6

Depot

**LE14**

The Elms

KING'S CL.

KING STREET

CHURCH CL.

SOUTH CL.

CHURCH ST.

LAST

THORPE

**SCALFORD**

ROAD

Redearth Farm

QUEEN'S CL.

NEW ST.

SCHOOL

Scalford C of E Sch.

Scalford Brook

SIDE

MELTON RD.

SPINNEY

Cemetery

24

MELTON

7

Clayfield Farm

Scalford Hall

<sup>4</sup>75

A    B    **160**    C

Mill Top Farm

D    77    E

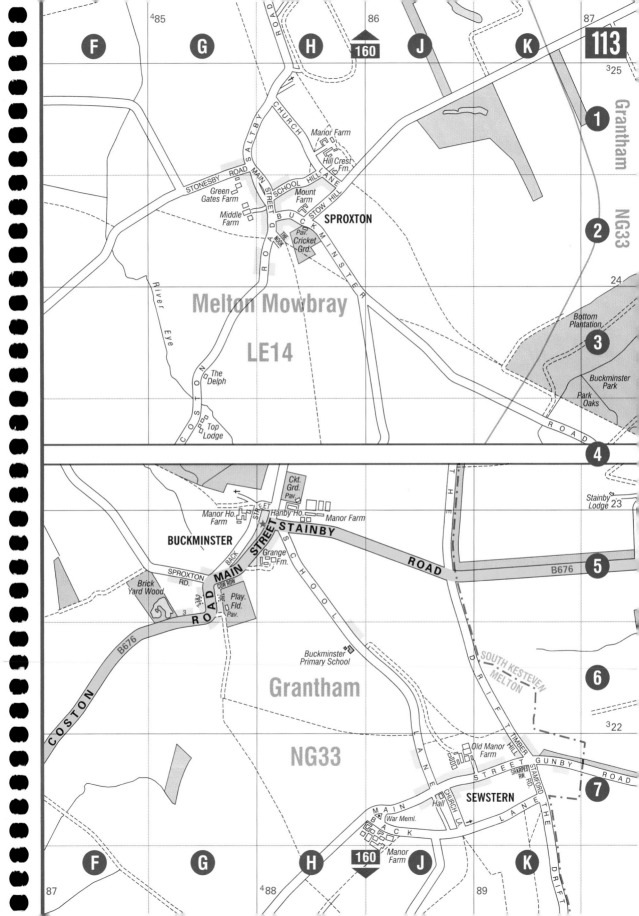

F G H J K

160

1

**Grantham**

**NG33**

³25

2

24

3

CHURCH HILL LANE

SALTBY ROAD

MAIN STREET

SCHOOL HILL

STOW HILL

STONESBY ROAD

Green Gates Farm

Middle Farm

Mount Farm

THE NOOK

BUCKMINSTER

Marior Farm

Hill Crest Fm.

**SPROXTON**

Pav. Cricket Grd.

**Melton Mowbray**

**LE14**

River Eye

COSTON ROAD

The Delph

Top Lodge

Bottom Plantation

Buckminster Park

Park Oaks

ROAD

4

F G H 160 J K

Ckt. Grd. Pav.

STREET

Manor Ho. Farm

Hanby Ho.

Manor Farm

Stainby Lodge 23

**BUCKMINSTER**

**STAINBY**

MAIN STREET

BACK

SPROXTON RD.

Grange Fm.

**ROAD**

THE DRIFT

B676

5

Brick Yard Wood

COW ROW

Play. Fld.

Pav.

SCHOOL LANE

B676

COSTON ROAD

Buckminster Primary School

**Grantham**

**NG33**

SOUTH KESTEVEN MELTON

6

³22

TIMBER HILL

Old Manor Farm

STREET

STAMFORD RD.

SHARPES RW.

GUNBY ROAD

THE DRIFT

7

MAIN

LANE

CHURCH LA.

**SEWSTERN**

Hall

BACK

War Meml.

160

Manor Farm

87 ⁴88 89

F G H J K

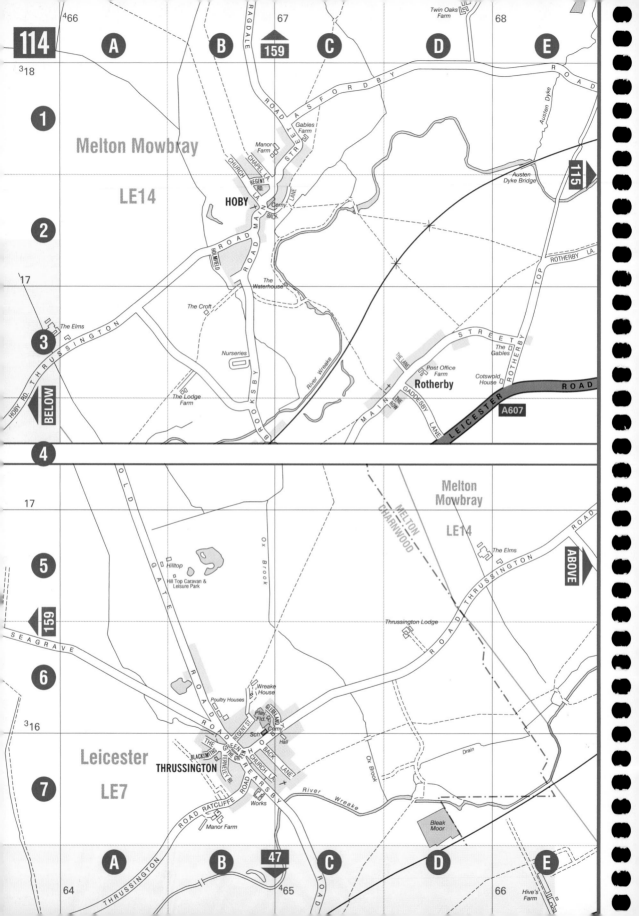

**114**

³18

⁴66

67

68

A  B  ▲ 159  C  D  E

**115** ▶

1

**Melton Mowbray**

RAGDALE

EAS FORDBY ROAD

Twin Oaks Farm

Austen Dyke

**LE14**

Gables Farm

Manor Farm

Austen Dyke Bridge

2

CHAPEL LA.

CHURCH

REGENT RD.

STREET

HOLMFIELD

ROAD MAIN

ROAD MAIN

LANE

LANE

BACK

**HOBY**

Cemy.

ROTHERBY LA.

ROTHERBY

TOP

17

3

THE ELMS

The Elms

The Waterhouse

The Croft

Nurseries

BROOKSBY

River Wreake

STREET

The Gables

ROTHERBY

Post Office Farm

**Rotherby**

Cotswold House

ROAD

THRUSSINGTON

HOBY RD.

◀ **BELOW**

The Lodge Farm

THE LANE

MAIN

GADDESBY LANE

THE FRITH

LEICESTER

**A607**

4

17

OLD GATE

**Melton Mowbray**

MELTON CHARNWOOD

**LE14**

ROAD

The Elms

THRUSSINGTON

ROAD

5

Hilltop

Hill Top Caravan & Leisure Park

Ox Brook

Thrussington Lodge

**ABOVE** ▶

◀ **159**

SEAGRAVE

6

GREEN ROAD

REARSBY

RATCLIFFE ROAD

Poultry Houses

Wreake House

REGENT ST.

Play Fld.

Sch.

GLEBELAND

Hall

BACK LANE

Cemy.

Ox Brook

Drain

³16

**Leicester**

**LE7**

THE GREEN

FERNLEY Rd.

BLACKSMITHS

CHURCH LA.

**THRUSSINGTON**

River Wreake

7

Works

Bleak Moor

Manor Farm

A  B  ▼ 47  C  D  E

64

THRUSSINGTON ROAD

⁴65

66

Hive's Farm

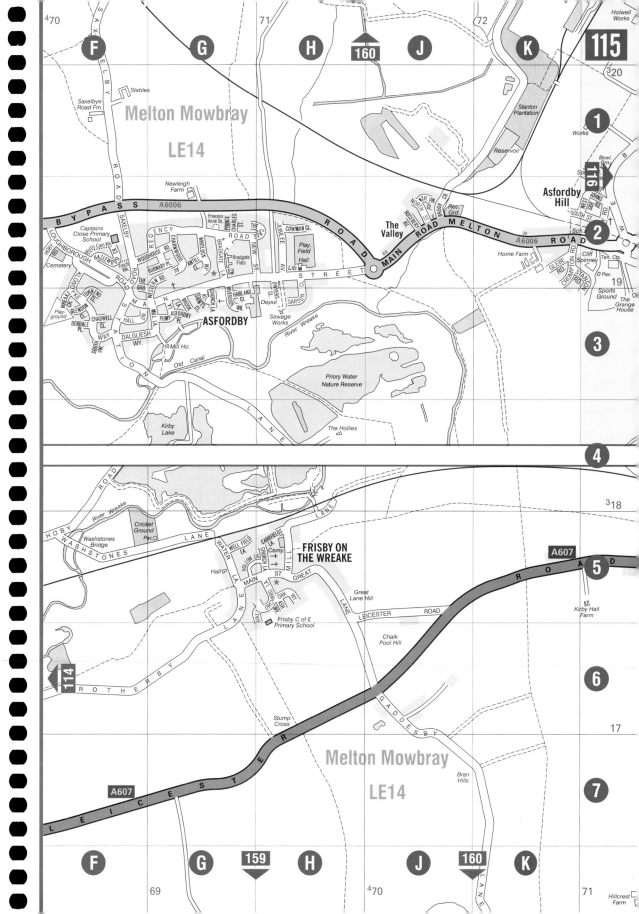

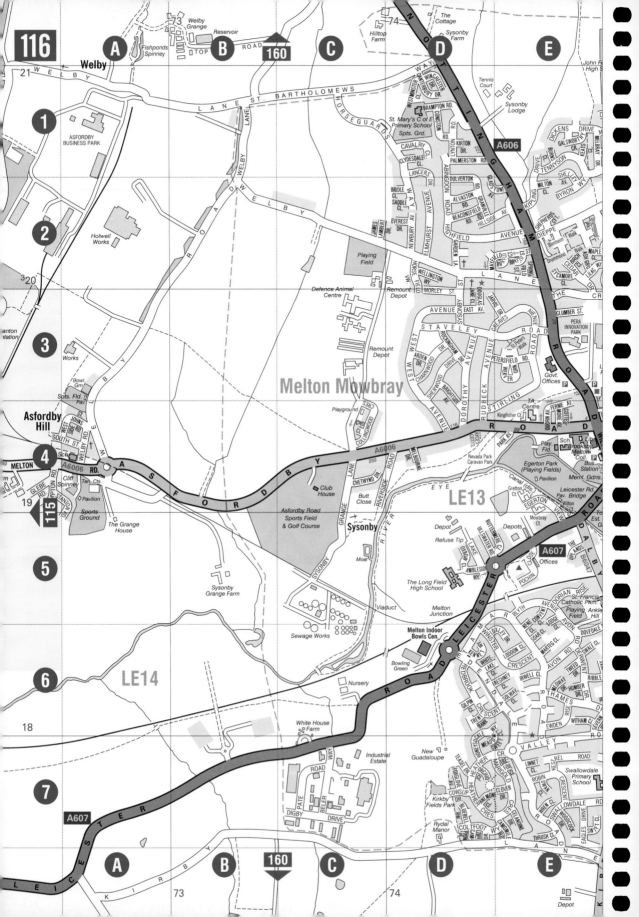

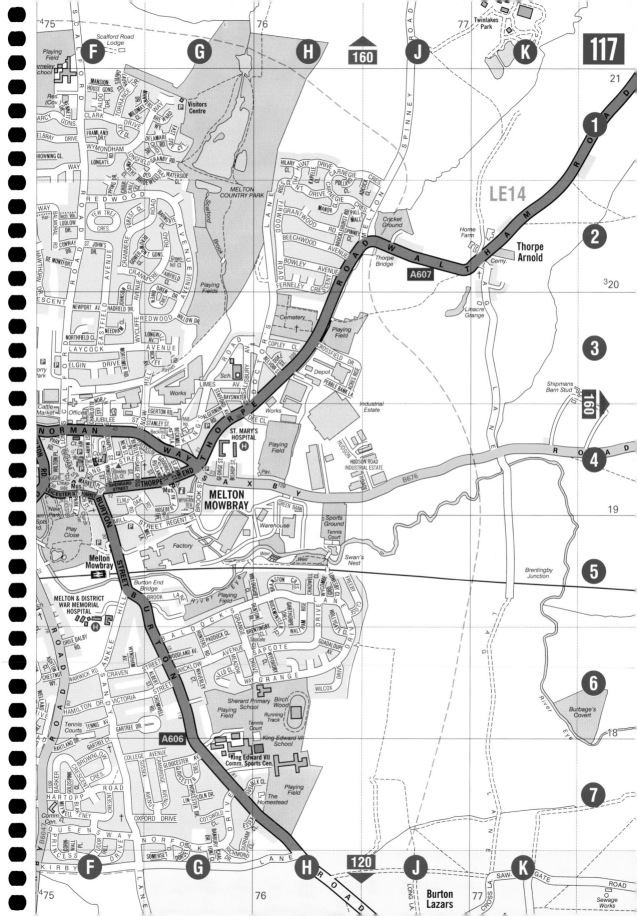

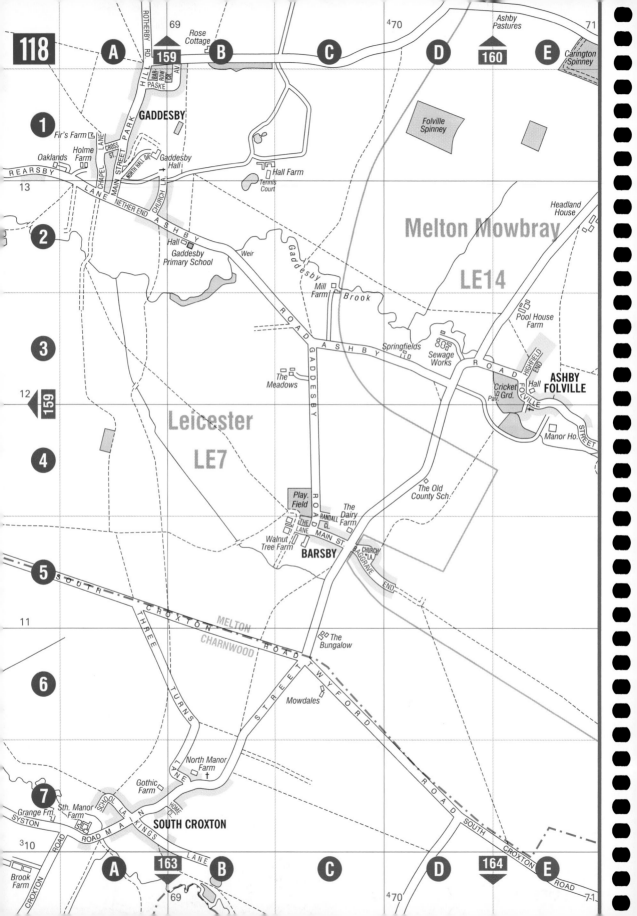

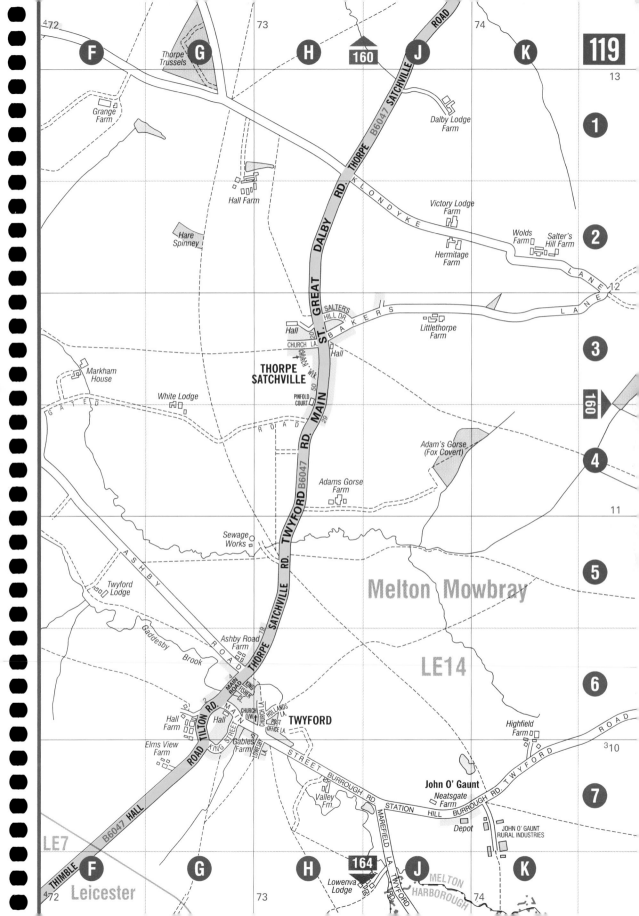

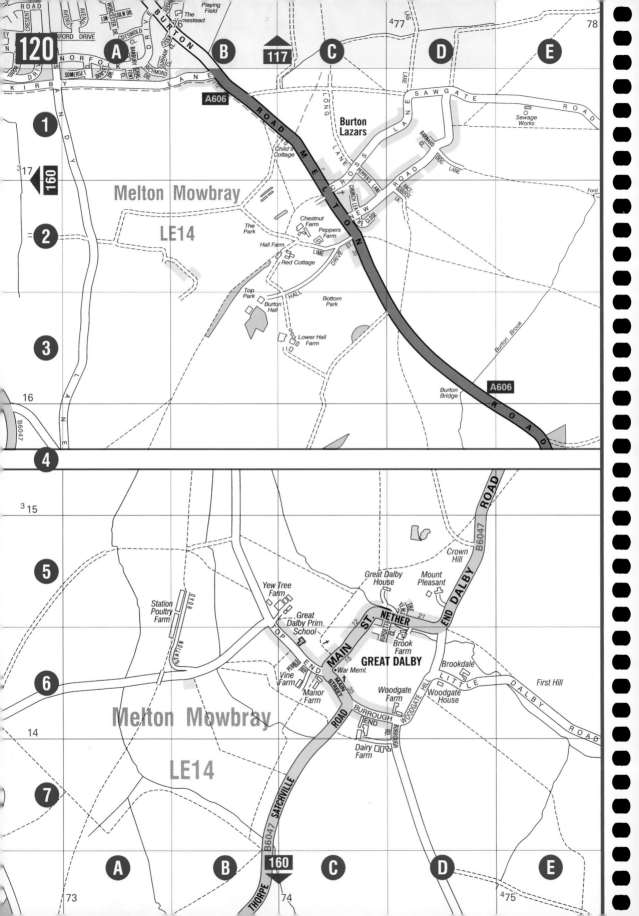

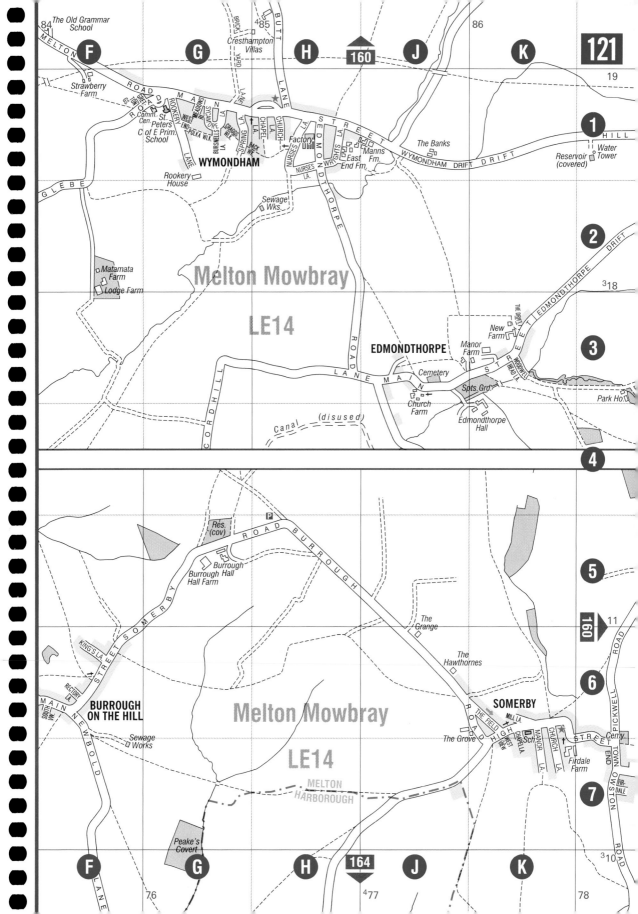

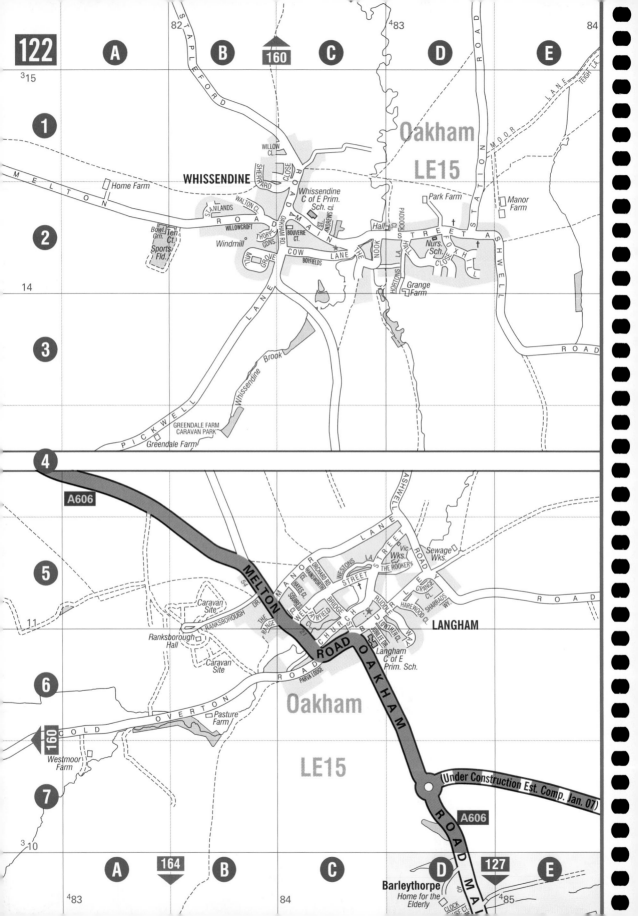

**A** · 82 **B** 160 **C** · 83 **D** · 84 **E**

³15

Oakham
LE15

1

WHISSENDINE

Home Farm

WILLOW CL.

MELTON

WALTON CL.

Park Farm

Manor Farm

Whissendine
C of E Prim.
Sch.

14

2

SCANILANDS

WILLOWCROFT

Bowl.
Grn.
Ten.
Ct.
Sports
Fld.

Windmill

THORPE
GDNS.

GROVE
MILL

COW LANE
BOYFIELDS

BOUVERIE CT.

Hall

THE NOOK

PADDOCK
HALL
HORTON CL.

FOXHILL CLOSE

Nurs.
Sch.

Grange
Farm

ASHWELL

STREET

ROAD
MAIN

OAKHAM RD.

SHERRARD
CLOSE

ST.
ANDREWS CL.

3

Whissendine
Brook

PICKWELL

GREENDALE FARM
CARAVAN PARK

Greendale Farm

ROAD

4

A606

Oakham
LE15

5

11

MELTON

ROAD

Caravan
Site

RANKSBOROUGH DR

Ranksborough
Hall

Caravan
Site

THE GRANGE

MANOR

ORCHARD RD.

HANSBOROUGH

HAYES CL.

WELL CROSS

BRIDGE
FIELD

CHURCH
STREET

WESTONS LA.
WESTON
STREET

STREET

THE ROOKERY

LANGHAM

ASHWELL
LANE

ROAD

Vic.

Sewage
Wks.

Wks.

GRANGE
CL.

HAREWOOD CL.

SHARRADS
WT.

ROAD

RUDDLE
LOWTHER CL.
JUBILEE TER.
WAY

Langham
C of E
Prim. Sch.

6

160
COLD
OVERTON
ROAD

Westmoor
Farm

Pasture
Farm

PARVA LODGE

OAKHAM

ROAD

7

Under Construction Est. Comp. Jan. 07

A606

³10

Barleythorpe
Home for the
Elderly

CLOCK
40

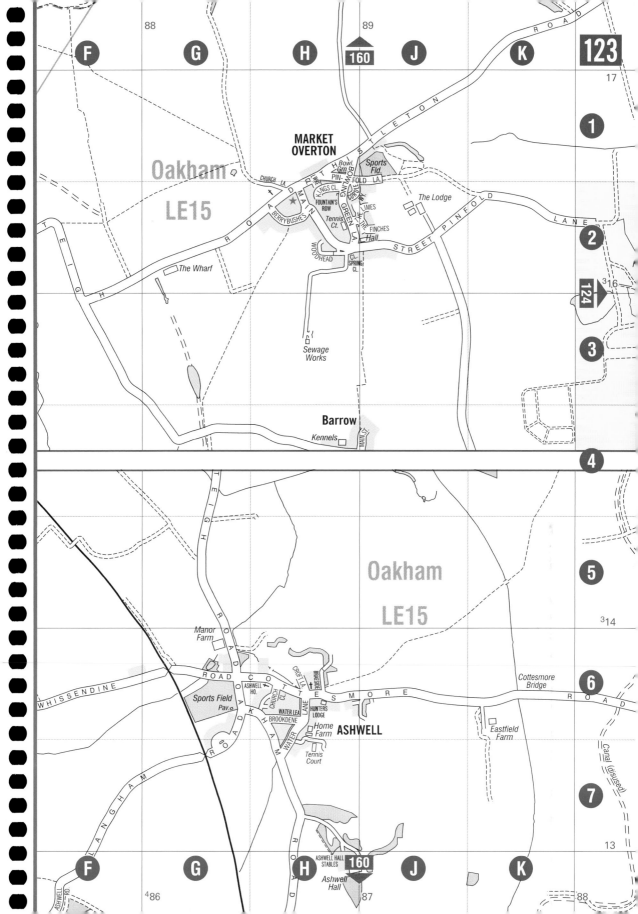

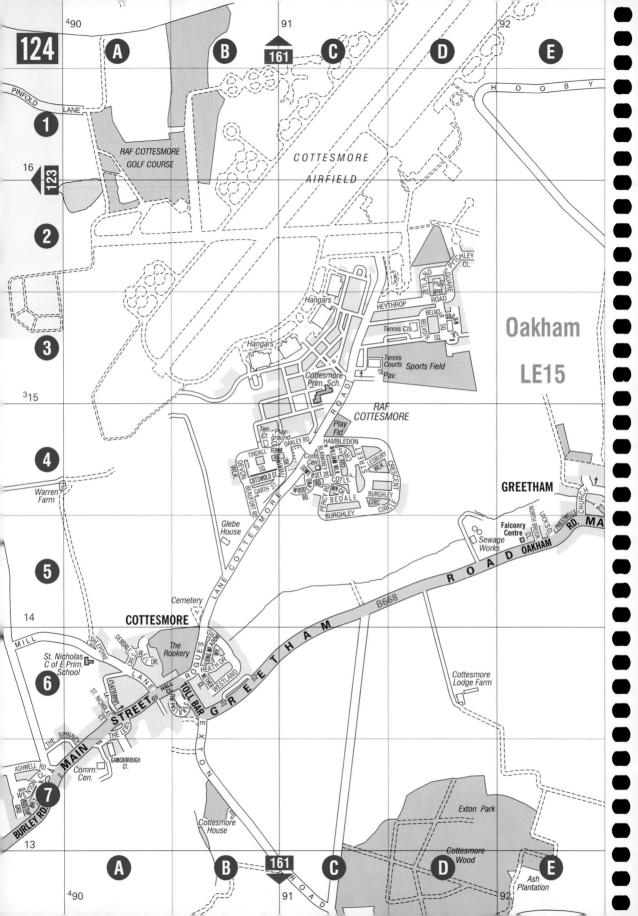

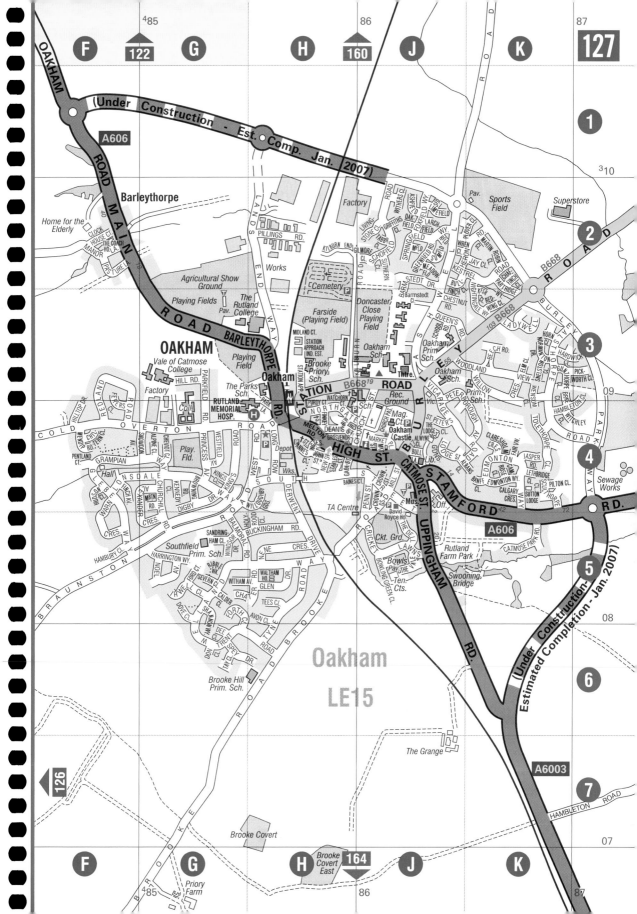

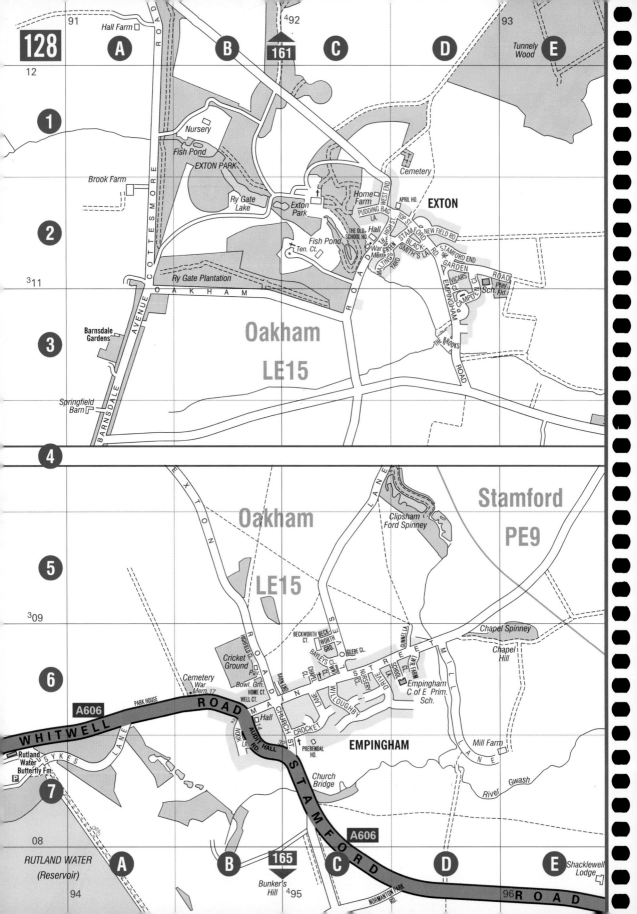

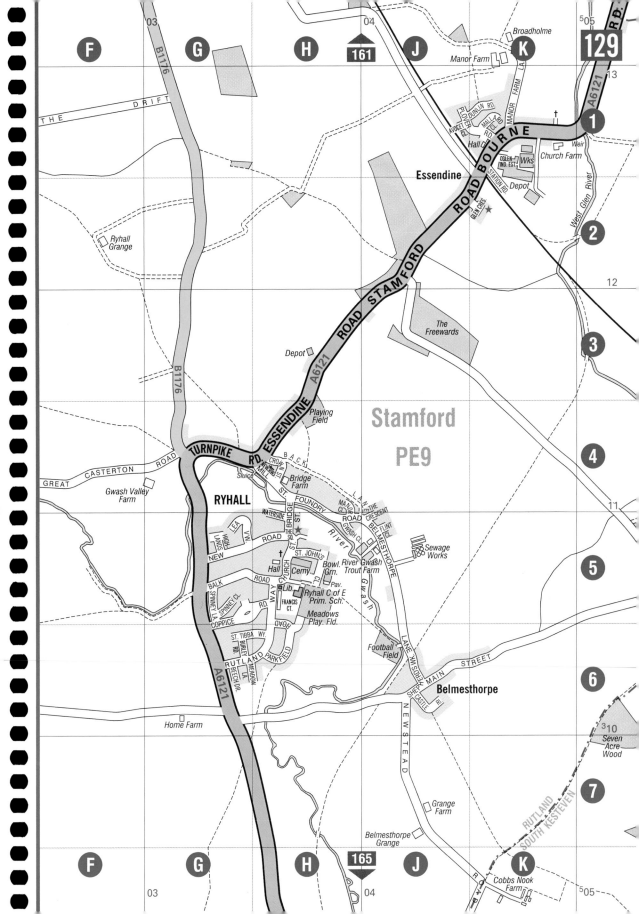

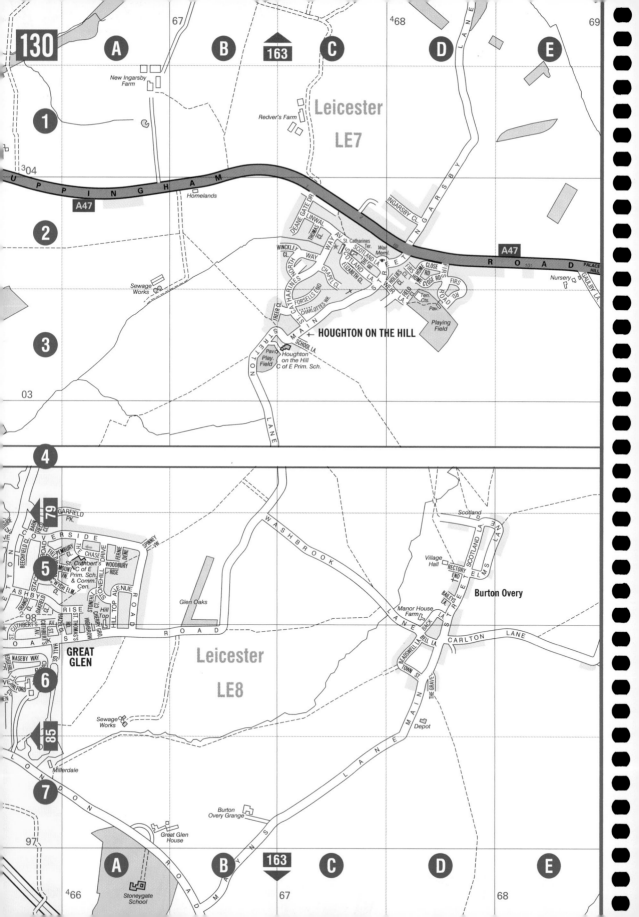

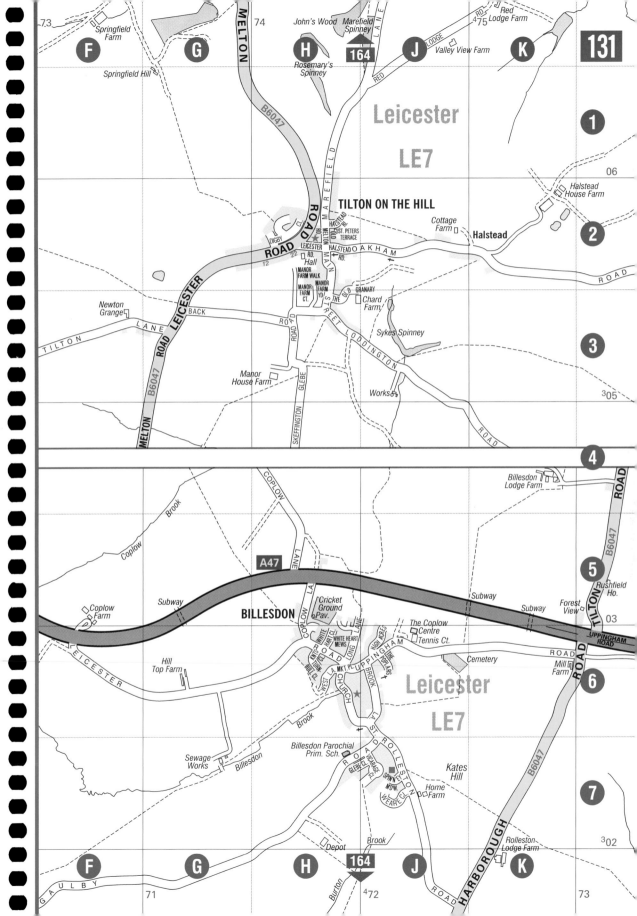

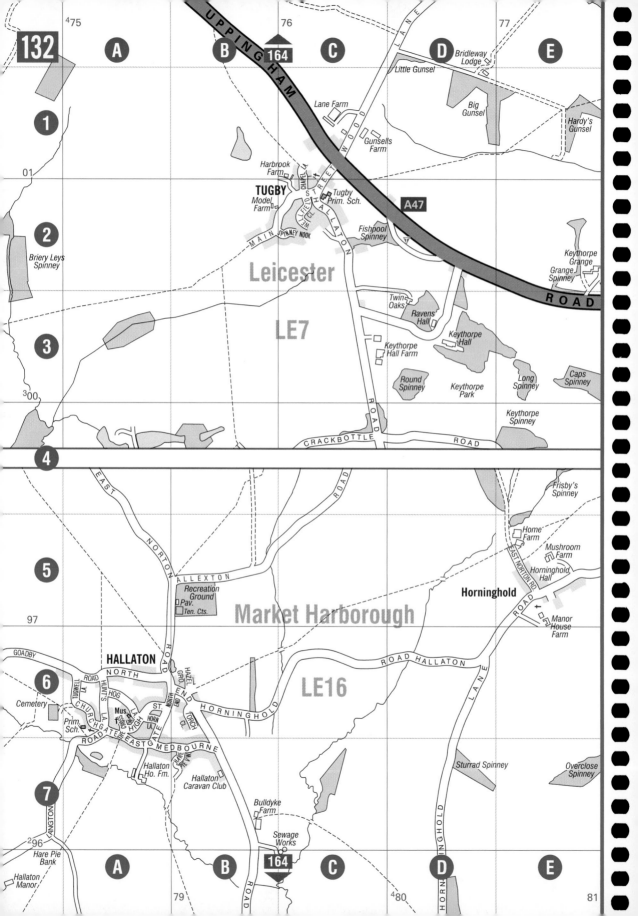

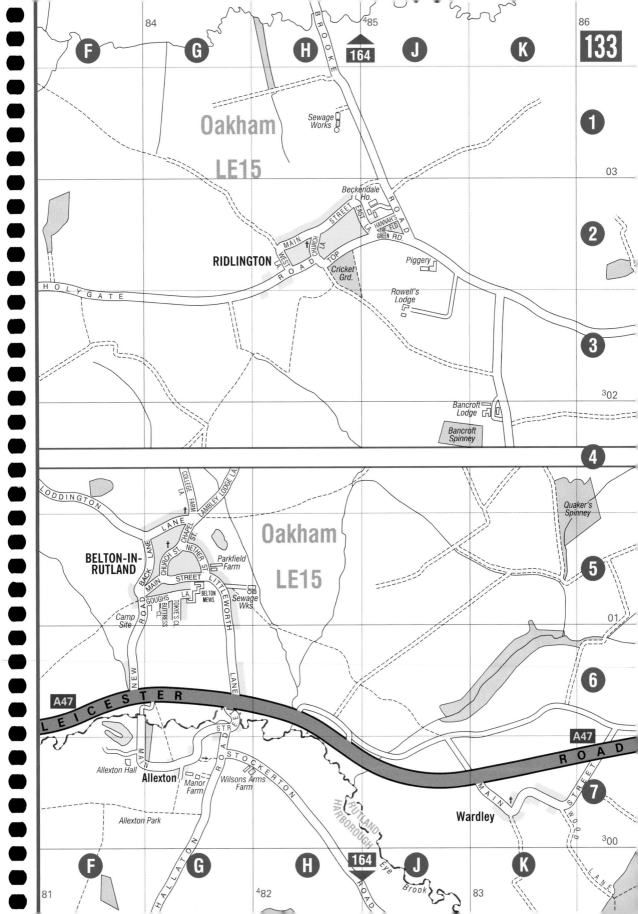

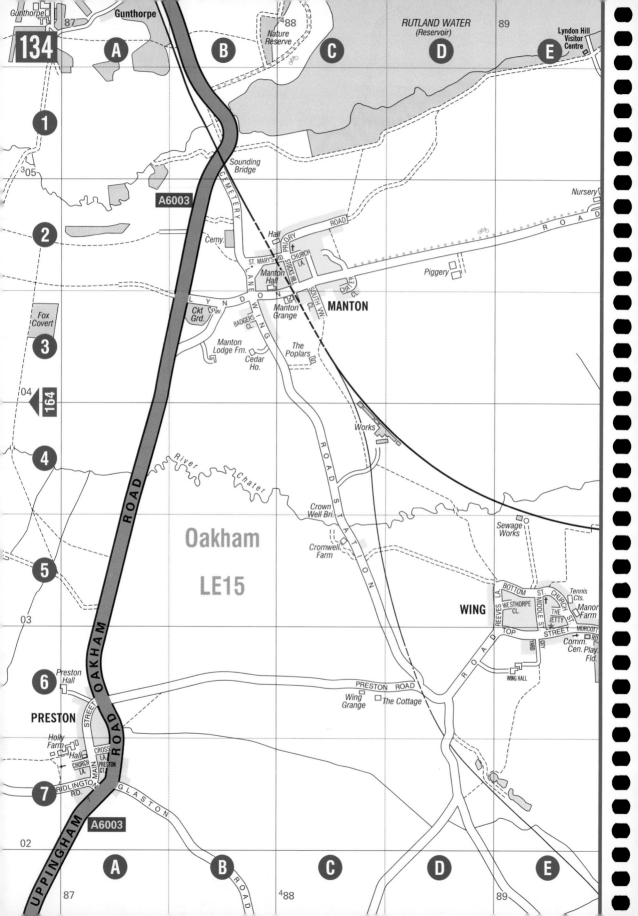

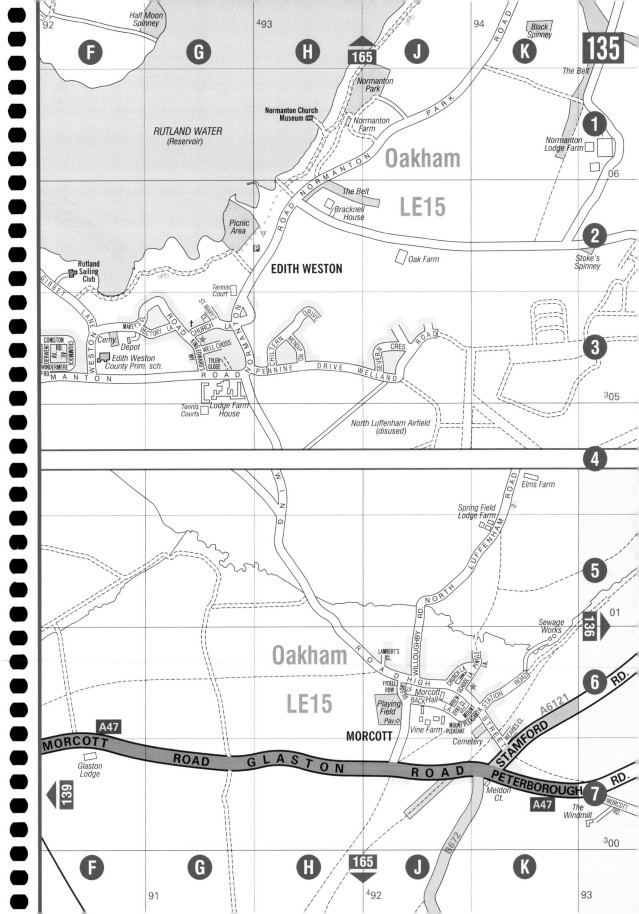

**F** **G** **H** **165** **J** **K**

92 93 94

Half Moon Spinney

Black Spinney

The Belt

**1**

Normanton Lodge Farm

06

Normanton Park

Normanton Church Museum

Normanton Farm

RUTLAND WATER
(Reservoir)

**Oakham**

**LE15**

The Belt

Bracknell House

NORMANTON PARK ROAD

NORMANTON ROAD

**2**

Oak Farm

Stoke's Spinney

Picnic Area

P

**EDITH WESTON**

Rutland Sailing Club

GIBBET LANE

Tennis Court

ST MARYS CL.

CHURCH LA.

NORMANTON ROAD

CHILTERN

MENDIP RD.

DRIVE

SEVERN

CRES.

WELLAND ROAD

**3**

305

CONISTON RD. AV.

DERWENT AV.

GRINWICK

WINDERMERE RD.

Cemy.

Depot

Edith Weston County Prim. sch.

WELL CROSS

KING EDWARDS WY.

TYLER CLOSE

MAKEY'S CL.

RECTORY LA.

ROAD

NORMANTON ROAD

PENNINE DRIVE

WELLAND

Tennis Courts

Lodge Farm House

North Luffenham Airfield
(disused)

**4**

WING

**Oakham**

**LE15**

Elms Farm

Spring Field Lodge Farm

NORTH LUFFENHAM ROAD 2

**5**

01

Sewage Works

**136**

ROAD

HIGH

WILLOUGHBY RD.

LAMBERT'S CL.

FYDELL ROW

SIMS CL.

BACK

Morcott Hall

VICH LA.

FYKE CL.

CHURCH LA.

SCHOOL LA.

PINGLE LA.

MOUNT

STATION ROAD

STREET

WEARES CL.

**6** RD.

A6121

STAMFORD

Playing Field

Pav.

**MORCOTT**

Vine Farm

MOUNT PLEASANT

PLEASANT

Cemetery

**A47**

**MORCOTT**

ROAD

GLASTON

ROAD

PETERBOROUGH

**7** RD.

MORCOTT RD.

Glaston Lodge

**139**

Meldon Ct.

**A47**

The Windmill

300

B672

**F** **G** **H** **165** **J** **K**

91 92 93

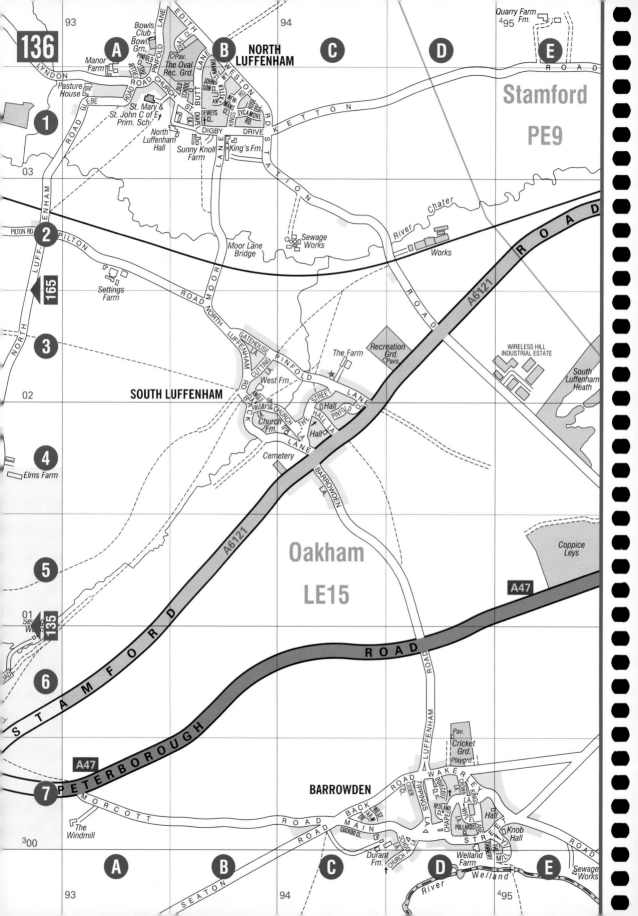

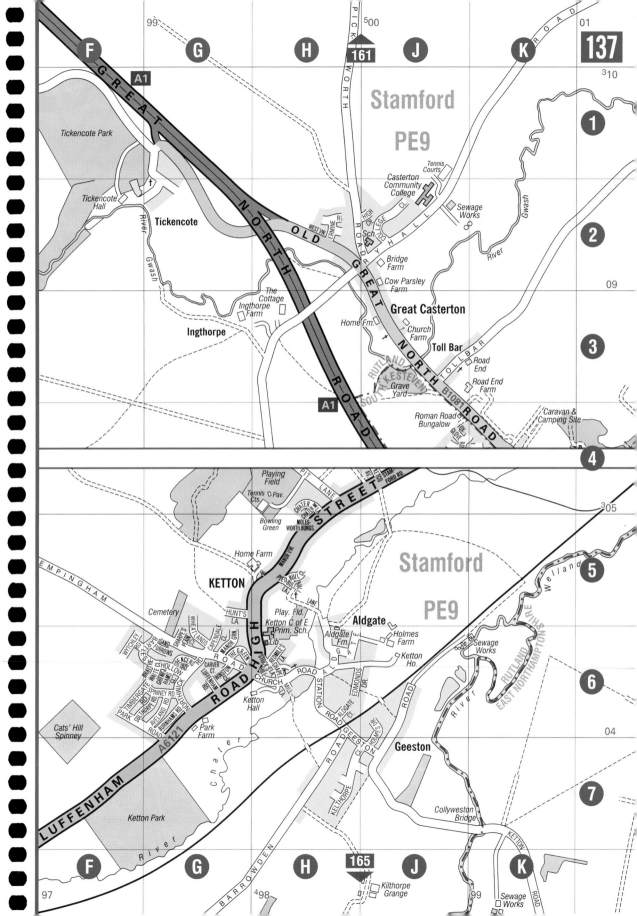

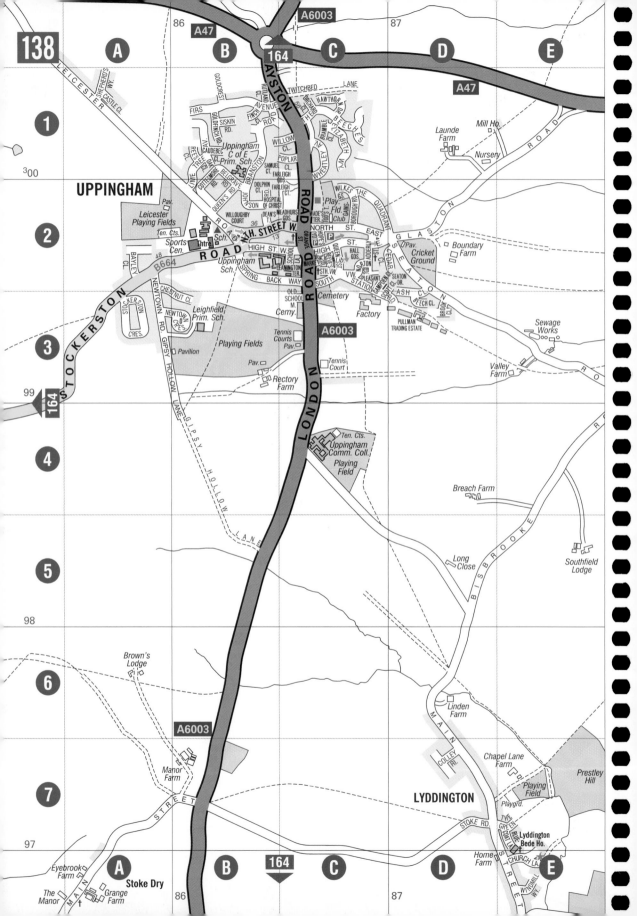

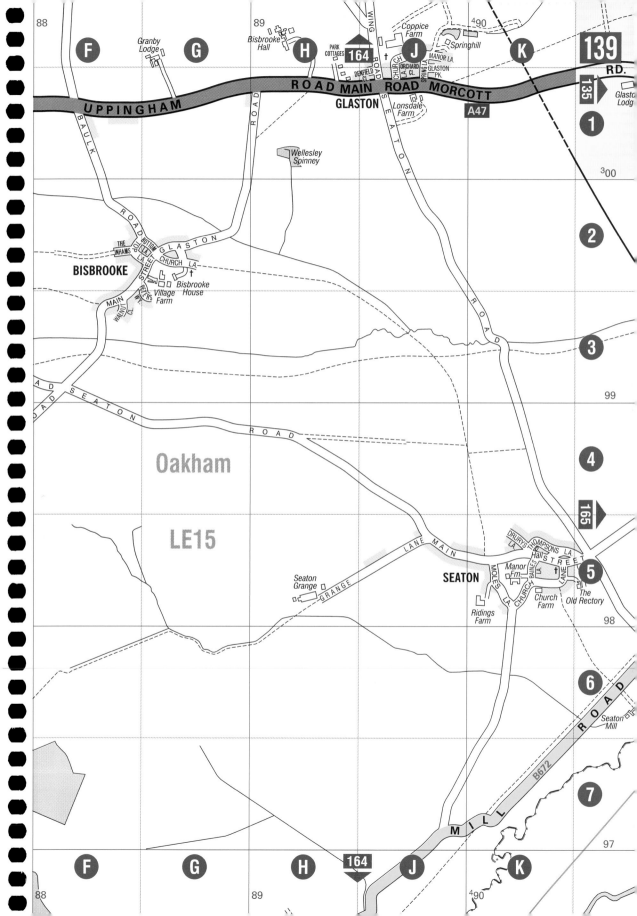

F  G  H  J  K

88  89  490

Granby Lodge

Bisbrooke Hall

Park Cottages

164

DENFIELD CL.

WING ROAD

Coppice Farm

Springhill

ORCHARD CL.

MANOR LA.

SPRING LA.

GLASTON PK.

CHURCH LA.

GLASTON

Lonsdale Farm

ROAD MAIN  ROAD MORCOTT

UPPINGHAM

A47

135

RD.

Glaston Lodge

1

300

Wellesley Spinney

SEATON ROAD

2

ROAD

BOTTOM LA.

GLASTON

CHURCH LA.

THE INHAMS

JOLLY

STREET

BISBROOKE

Bisbrooke House

Village Farm

MAIN

ST. PETERS WAY

WALNUT CL.

ROAD

99

3

ROAD SEATON

ROAD

Oakham

LE15

4

165

DRURYS LA.

THOMPSONS LA.

Hall

STREET

BANKS LA.

Manor Fm.

LANE MAIN

GRANGE

Seaton Grange

SEATON

MOLES LA.

CHURCH LA.

Church Farm

The Old Rectory

5

98

Ridings Farm

6

ROAD

Seaton Mill

B672

MILL

7

97

F  G  H  J  K

88  89  490

164

164

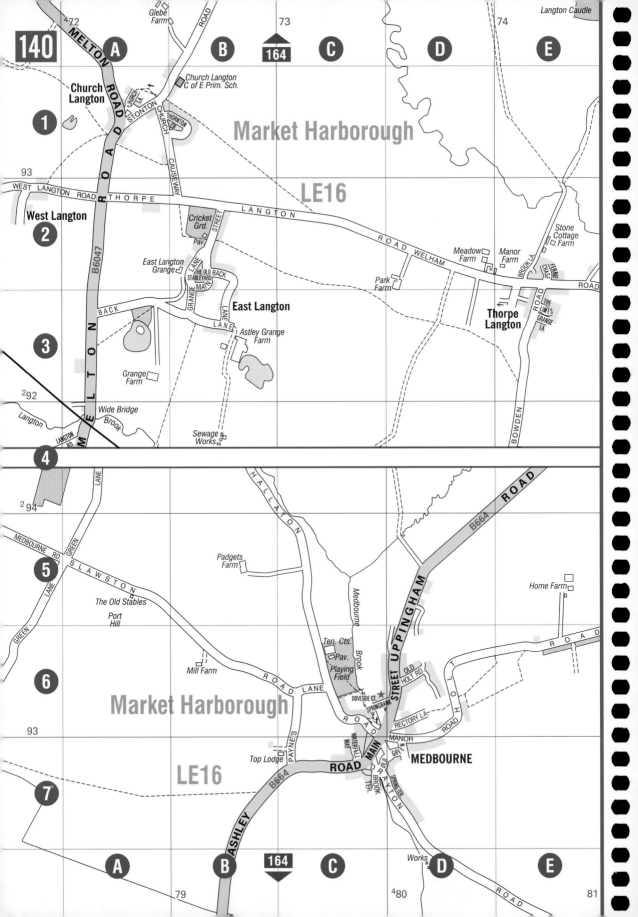

**A** **B** **C** **D** **E**

472    73    ▲ 164    74    *Langton Caudle*

*Glebe Farm*

**1**

Church Langton

*Church Langton C of E Prim. Sch.*

**Market Harborough**

THORNTON CR.

CHURCH LA.

STONTON LA.

CHURCH

CAUSEWAY

MELTON ROAD

93

WEST LANGTON ROAD    THORPE

**LE16**

**2**

West Langton

B6047

*Cricket Grd.*

*Pav.*

STREET

LANGTON

ROAD

WELHAM

*Meadow Farm*

*Manor Farm*

*Stone Cottage Farm*

BROOK LA.

FERNIE CHASE

*East Langton Grange*

GRANGE LANE

THE OLD STABLEYARD

BACK

MAIN

**East Langton**

*Park Farm*

ROAD

**Thorpe Langton**

THE LIMES

GRANGE LA.

**3**

BACK LANE

LANE

*Astley Grange Farm*

*Grange Farm*

BOWDEN

292

*Langton*

**Wide Bridge**

*Brook*

LANGTON RD.

MELTON

*Sewage Works*

**4**

294

LANE

HALLATON

LANE

MEDBOURNE RD.

GREEN

SLAWSTON

*Padgets Farm*

ROAD

B664

ROAD

**5**

GREEN LANE

*The Old Stables*

*Port Hill*

*Medbourne Brook*

*Home Farm*

STREET    UPPINGHAM

OLD HOLT RD.

ROAD

**6**

*Mill Farm*

ROAD LANE

*Ten. Cts.*
*Pav.*

*Playing Field*

DOVESIDE CT. ★

SPRINGBANK

RECTORY LA.

HOLT ROAD

**Market Harborough**

93

PAYNE'S

ROAD

WATERFALL WAY

MAIN

STREET

MANOR

GREEN

DRAYTON

**MEDBOURNE**

**LE16**

*Top Lodge*

B664    ROAD

BROOK TER.

OLD DRAYTON

SPRING TER.

**7**

**A** **B** ▼ 164 **C** *Works* **D** **E**

79    480    ROAD    81

ASHLEY

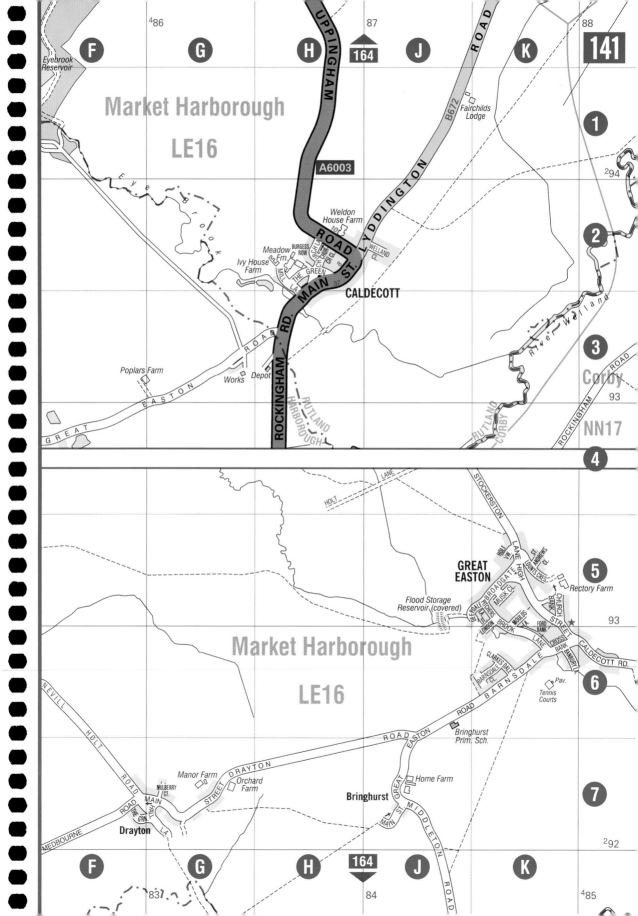

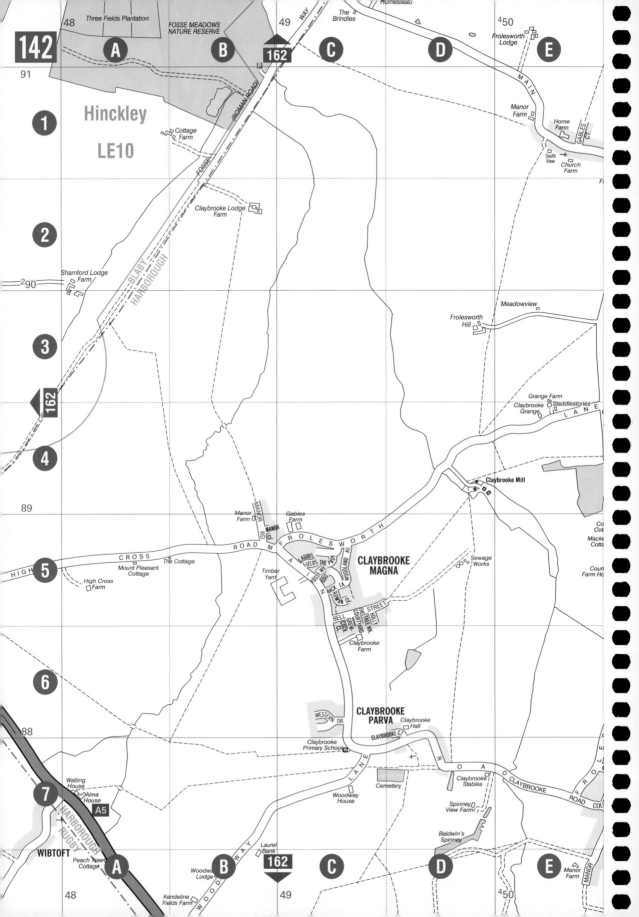

**142**

A    B    162    C    D    E

48    Three Fields Plantation    49    WAY    The Brindles    ⁴50

FOSSE MEADOWS NATURE RESERVE    Homestead    Frolesworth Lodge

91

**1**

**Hinckley**

**LE10**

Cottage Farm

(ROMAN ROAD)    FOSSE    MAIN

Manor Farm    Home Farm    GABLES CT.

South View    Church Farm

Claybrooke Lodge Farm

**2**

Sharnford Lodge Farm

²90

BLABY    HARBOROUGH

Meadowview

Frolesworth Hill

**3**

162

Grange Farm

Claybrooke Grange    Staddlestones

LANE

**4**

162

Claybrooke Mill

89

Manor Farm    Gables Farm

MANOR RD.    MANOR CL.

Sewage Works

**5**

HIGH    CROSS    Mount Pleasant Cottage    The Cottage    ROAD

FROLESWORTH AV.

CLAYBROOKE MAGNA

High Cross Farm    Timber Yard

LAUREL FIELDS    THE PADK    FOSSE WY.    NEW TOWN

BACK LA.    BROWN CL.

BELL    STREET    HILL    MAPLE TREE WK.    COURTYARD    ORCH- ARD CL.    GREN- GRECK CL.

Claybrooke Farm

**6**

WESTERN DR.

CLAYBROOKE PARVA

Claybrooke Hall

CLAYBROOKE CL.

Claybrooke Primary School

88

Watling House    Alma House

**7**    A5

Cemetery    Woodway House

Claybrooke Stables

Spinney View Farm

R O A D    CLAYBROOKE    ROAD    FROLE    COL

HARBOROUGH    RUGBY

**WIBTOFT**

Peach Tree Cottage

Baldwin's Spinney

LANE

A    Woodway Lodge    B    Laurel Bank    162    C    D    Manor Farm    E

MANOR

WOODWAY

48    Kendeline Fields Farm    49    ⁴50

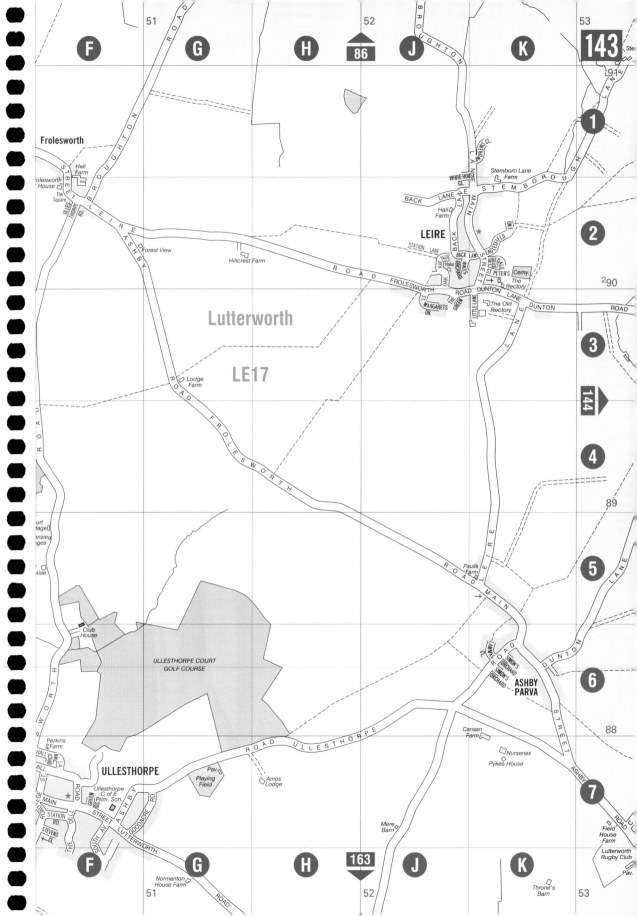

F G H 86 J K

51 52 53

1

Ste

91

Frolesworth

Hall
Farm

Frolesworth
House

The
Square

BROUGHTON

STREET

LEIRE

ASHBY

RD.

STREET

FROLESWORTH

Forest View

Hillcrest Farm

ROAD

FROLESWORTH

LEIRE

WHITE HOUSE
CL.

BACK LANE

Hall
Farm

STATION LANE

BACK LANE

LANE

MAIN

STEMBORO LANE
Farm

STEMBOROUGH LANE

ST. PETER'S
CL.

AVE.

OAK

AVENUE

DONISTHORPE

BROCK

BACK LANE

STREET

DUNTON

NIRED CL.

ENDLESFIELD
END

Cemy.

The
Rectory

LANE

LANE

DUNTON

ROAD

290

MARGARETS
DR.

ST.

THE
GREEN

LITTLE LANE

ROAD

The Old
Rectory

2

3

144

4

89

Lutterworth

LE17

Lodge
Farm

ROAD

FROLESWORTH

ROAD

ROAD

MAIN

LEIRE

Pauls
Farm

5

DUNTON

LANE

Club
House

ULLESTHORPE COURT
GOLF COURSE

urt
ttage

onzie
ges

ouse

WORTH

SIMON'S
ORCHARD

SIMON'S ORCHARD

LAWN

ASHBY
PARVA

6

STREET

ASHBY

88

Perkins
Farm

HALL

ORCH.

MILL

ST.

ULLESTHORPE

ROAD

ULLESTHORPE

Pav
Playing
Field

Amos
Lodge

Canaan
Farm

Nurseries

Pykes House

Ullesthorpe
C of E
Prim. Sch.

GREEN

ASHBY

GOODACRE RD.

STREET

LUTTERWORTH

BRIDGE

MAIN

ROAD

STATION
RD.

STEVENS
DL.

SOUTH AV.

THE

7

ROAD

ASHBY

Field
House
Farm

Lutterworth
Rugby Club

Mere
Barn

Pav.

F G H 163 J K

51 52 53

Normanton
House Farm

ROAD

Throne's
Barn

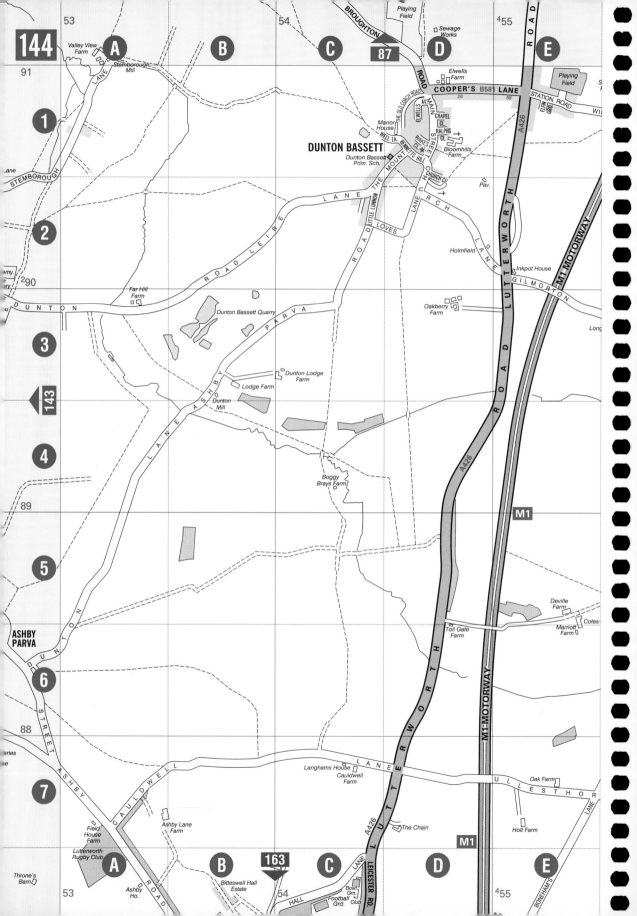

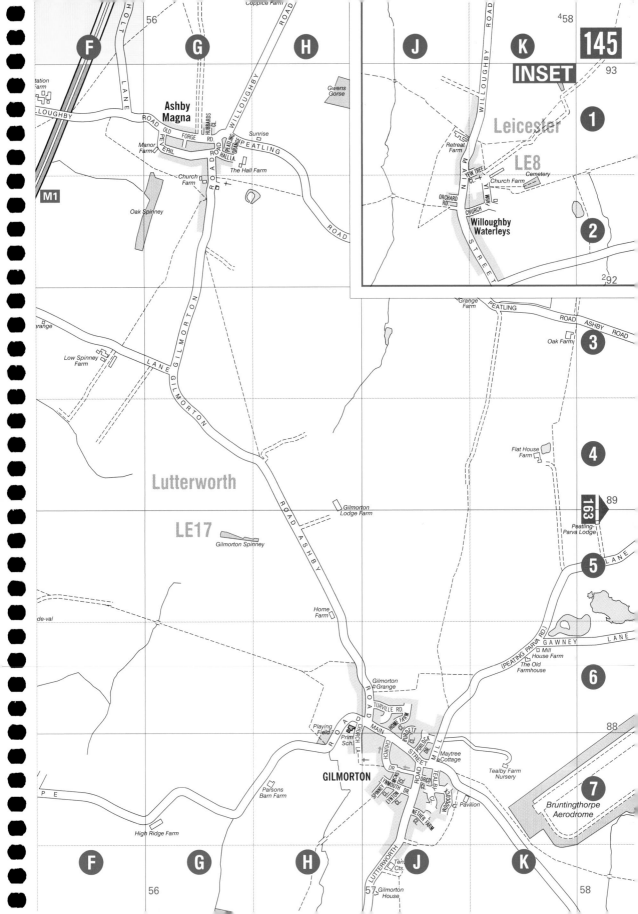

**INSET**

F G H J K

1 2 3 4 5 6 7

Coppice Farm

Gwens Gorse

Station Farm

WILLOUGHBY

**Ashby Magna**

Manor Farm

FORGE RD.

OLD PEVERIL

HUBBARDS CL.

HALL LA.

PEATLING GRANGE

Sunrise

PEATLING

The Hall Farm

Church Farm

Oak Spinney

M1

ROAD

WILLOUGHBY

ROAD

Leicester

LE8

Retreat Farm

YEW TREE CL.

MAIN

MILL LA.

CHURCH

ORCHARD RD.

Church Farm

Cemetery

**Willoughby Waterleys**

STREET

Grange Farm

PEATLING

ROAD

ASHBY

ROAD

Oak Farm

Grange

Low Spinney Farm

GILMORTON

LANE

GILMORTON

**Lutterworth**

**LE17**

Gilmorton Spinney

Gilmorton Lodge Farm

ROAD

ASHBY

Home Farm

Flat House Farm

163

89

Peatling Parva Lodge

LANE

de-val

(PEATLING PARVA RD.)

GAWNEY

LANE

Mill

House Farm

The Old Farmhouse

88

Gilmorton Grange

TURVILLE RD.

ROAD

MAIN

HOME FARM

STREET

MILL

Maytree Cottage

Playing Field

CHURCH LA.

Prim. Sch.

BURBETT CL.

POLLOCK DR.

Tealby Farm Nursery

Parsons Barn Farm

**GILMORTON**

CHURCH DR.

SPINNEY CL.

LYNMOUTH DR.

LYNTON CL.

NETHER FARM CL.

TEALBY CL.

ORCD. CL.

SCHOOL WK.

Pavilion

7

**Bruntingthorpe Aerodrome**

High Ridge Farm

PE

LUTTERWORTH

Tenn. Cts.

Gilmorton House

F G H J K

56 57 58

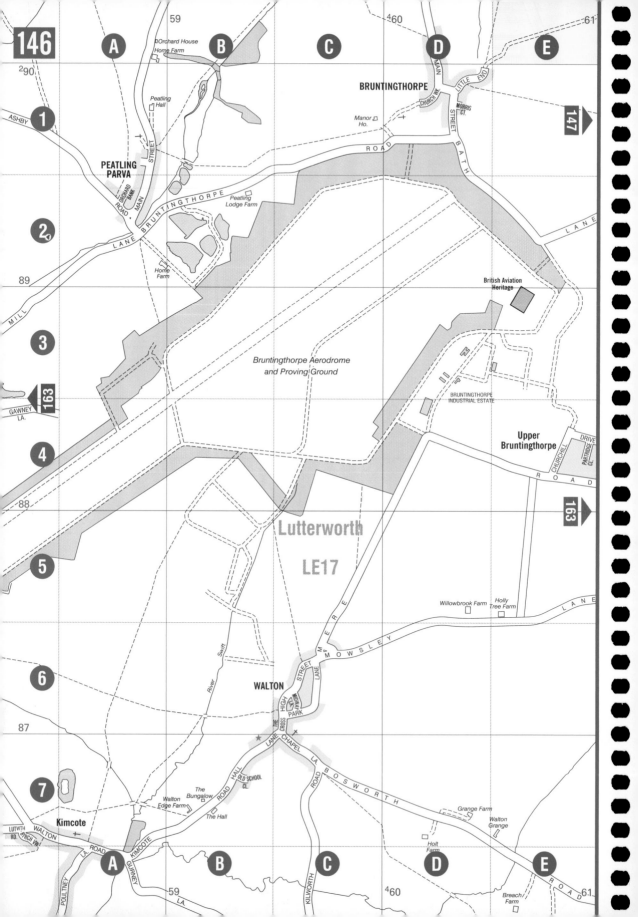

A  B  C  D  E

59  460  61

**BRUNTINGTHORPE**

Orchard House
Home Farm

Peatling
Hall

Manor
Ho.

1

ASHBY

CHURCH WK.

LITTLE END

MAIN

MORRIS
CT.

STREET

BATH

ROAD

147

**PEATLING
PARVA**

ORCHARD
BANK

MAIN

LANE

ROAD

STREET

BRUNTINGTHORPE

Peatling
Lodge Farm

LANE

2

89

Home
Farm

**British Aviation
Heritage**

3

MILL

*Bruntingthorpe Aerodrome
and Proving Ground*

BRUNTINGTHORPE
INDUSTRIAL ESTATE

163

GAWNEY
LA.

**Upper
Bruntingthorpe**

DRIVE

PARTRIDGE
CL.

4

CHURCHILL

ROAD

88

163

Willowbrook Farm

Holly
Tree Farm

LANE

**Lutterworth**

5

**LE17**

River

Swift

MERE

MOWSLEY

6

STREET

LANE

87

**WALTON**

HIGH

PARK

Willowbrook Farm

THE
CROSS

LANE

CHAPEL

7

The
Bungalow

HALL

ROAD

OLD SCHOOL
CL.

LA.

BOSWORTH

Grange Farm

Walton
Grange

**Kimcote**

Walton
Edge Farm

The Hall

KIMCOTE

ROAD

KILWORTH

ROAD

Holt
Farm

LUTWTH
RD.

WALTON

POULTNEY LA.

GURNEY

ORCH. WK.

ROAD

Breach
Farm

A  B  C  D  E

59  460  61

LA.

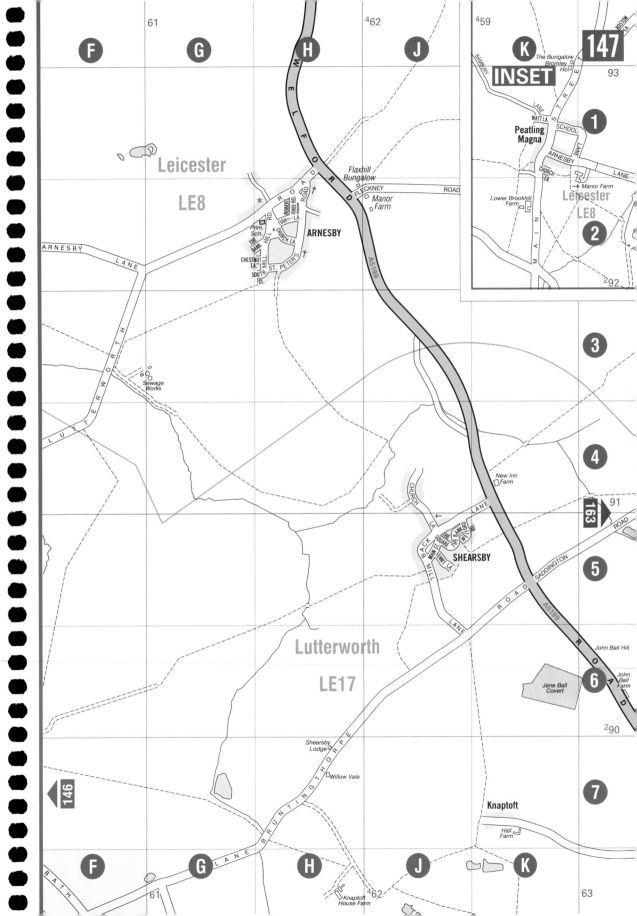

**F** **G** **H** **J**

61 ⁴62 ⁴59 **K** **147**

**INSET**

The Bungalow
Bromley
Ho.

Peatling
Magna

**1**

WATT LA.

SCHOOL LANE

ARNESBY LANE

BOSTON LA.

BANBURY LANE

STREET

93

Leicester
LE8

**2**

Lower Brookhill
Farm

CHURCH LA.

Manor Farm

MAIN

²92

Leicester

LE8

Flaxhill
Bungalow

FLECKNEY ROAD

Manor
Farm

ROAD

WELFORD ROAD

Prim.
Sch.

ROBERT HALL RD.

MILL HILL RD.

OAK LA.

CHURCH LA.

**ARNESBY**

THE BANK

CHESTNUT LA.

ST. PETER'S

SOUTH CL.

ARNESBY LANE

LUTTERWORTH ROAD

Sewage
Works

A5199

**3**

**4**

New Inn
Farm

CHURCH LA.

LANE

**163** 91

ROAD

**5**

BACK LANE

MILL LANE

SQUARE

MAIN ST.

FENNY LA.

THE BANK

MILL RD.

WELFORD RD.

**SHEARSBY**

SADDINGTON ROAD

A5199 ROAD

Lutterworth

LE17

John Ball Hill

**6**

Jane Ball
Covert

John
Ball
Farm

²90

**146**

BRUNTINGTHORPE

Shearsby
Lodge

Willow Vale

Knaptoft

**7**

Hall
Farm

**F** **G** **H** **J** **K**

BATH

LANE

61 ⁴62

Knaptoft
House Farm

63

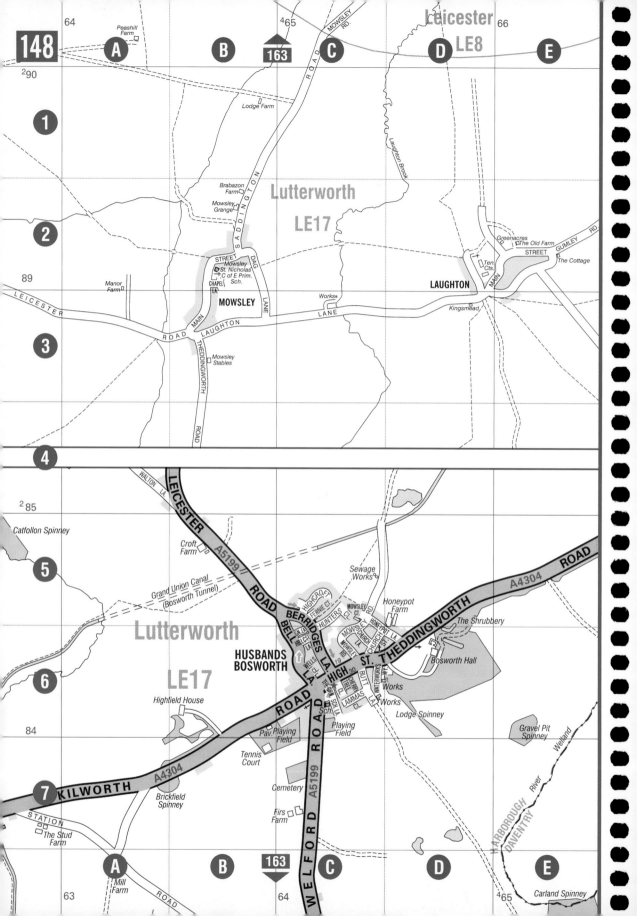

64

²90

A    B    163    C    Leicester    D    LE8    E

465    Mowsley Rd.

1

Peashill Farm

Lodge Farm

Brabazon Farm

Mowsley Grange

**Lutterworth**

**LE17**

Laughton Brook

2

89

Manor Farm

STREET

Mowsley St. Nicholas C of E Prim. Sch.

CHAPEL LA.

**MOWSLEY**

SADDINGTON

DAG LANE

Works

LANE

Laughton

Greenacres

The Old Farm

STREET

GUMLEY RD.

Ten Cts.

The Cottage

**LAUGHTON**

Kingsmead

LEICESTER

3

ROAD

MAIN

LAUGHTON

Mowsley Stables

THEDDINGWORTH

ROAD

4

²85

Catfollon Spinney

WALTON LA.

LEICESTER

5

Croft Farm

A5199

Grand Union Canal (Bosworth Tunnel)

ROAD

Sewage Works

HIGHCROFT

MOWSLEY CT.

FERNIE CT.

HUNTERS

Honeypot Farm

A4304

ROAD

The Shrubbery

**Lutterworth**

BERRIDGES LA.

BELL

GN.LA.

HILL CT.

MOWSLEY LA.

MOWSLEY CL.

HONEYPOT LA.

CHURCH

ST. THEDDINGWORTH

Bosworth Hall

6

**HUSBANDS BOSWORTH**

**LE17**

Highfield House

WELLS CL.

HIGH

ST.

A5199

CHERRY TREE

CL.

BUTT

LAMMAS CL.

WATERWORKS

Works

Works

Lodge Spinney

Gravel Pit Spinney

Weland

84

Pav. Playing Field

ROAD

WELFORD

Sch.

30

Playing Field

River

HARBOROUGH

DAVENTRY

Tennis Court

Cemetery

7

**KILWORTH**

A4304

Brickfield Spinney

Firs Farm

STATION

The Stud Farm

A    B    163    C    D    E

63

Mill Farm

ROAD

64

465

Carland Spinney

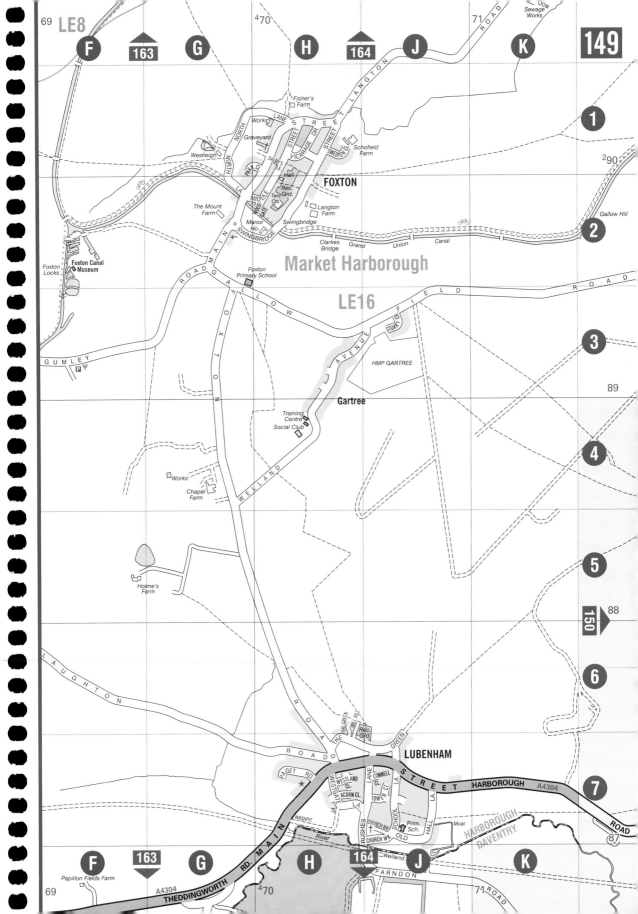

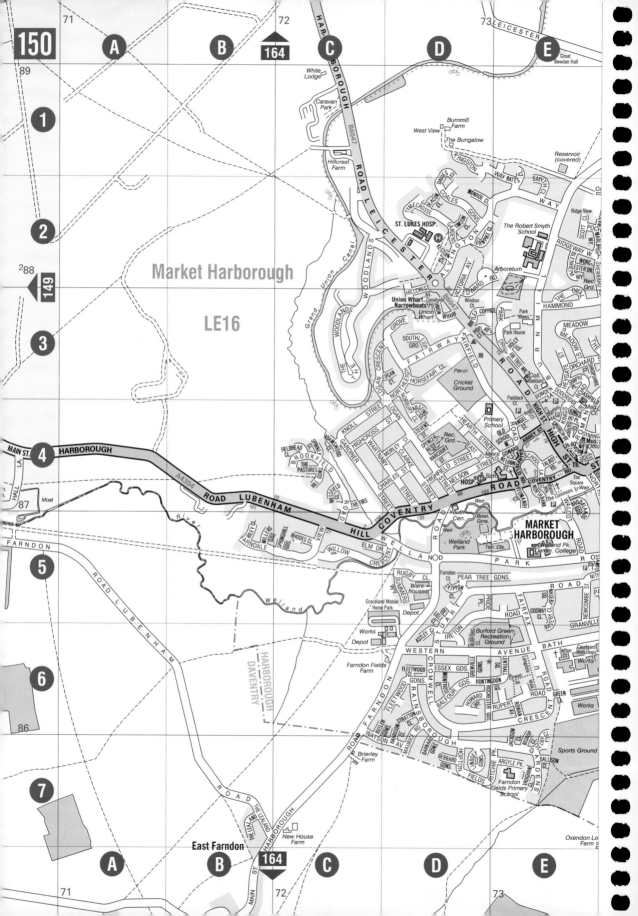

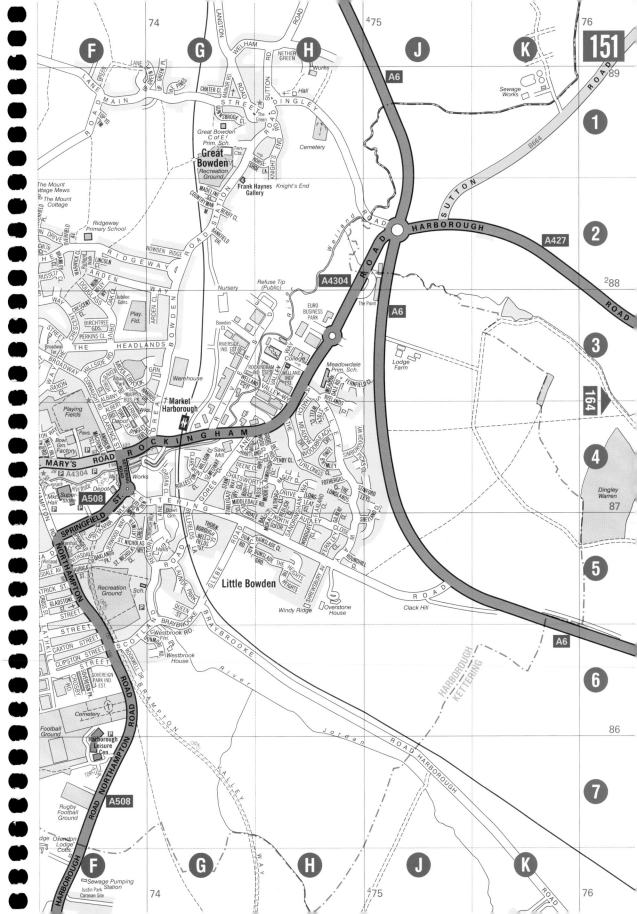

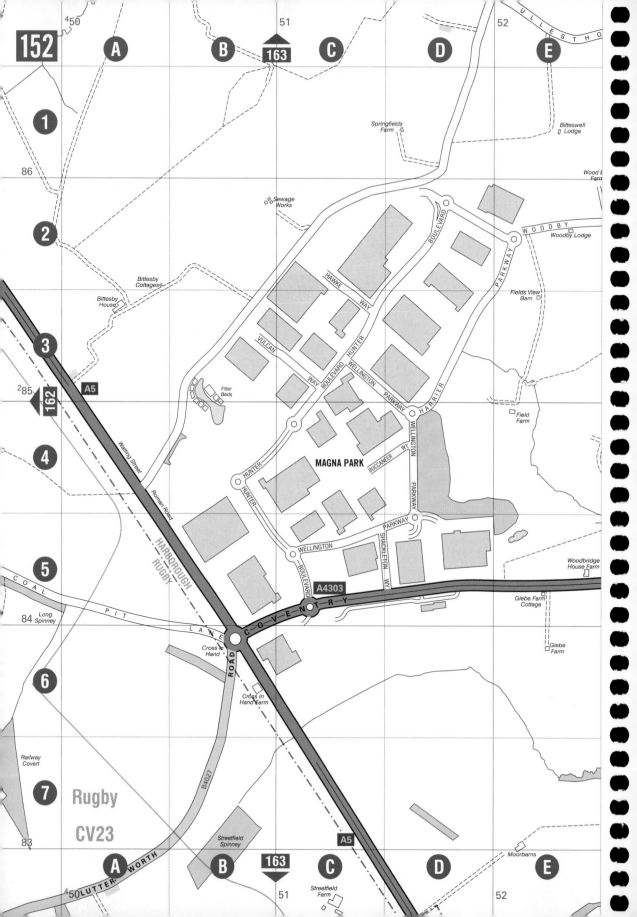

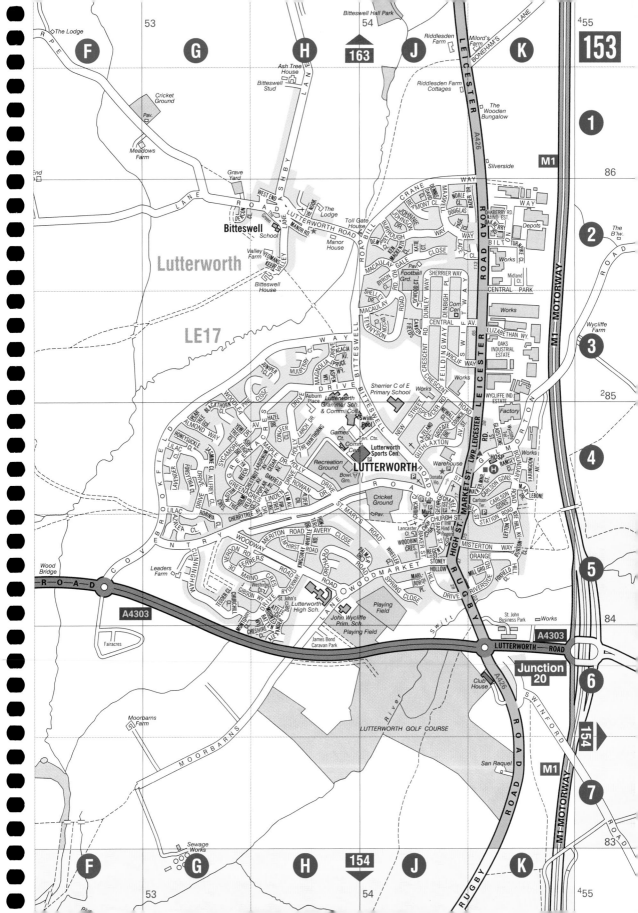

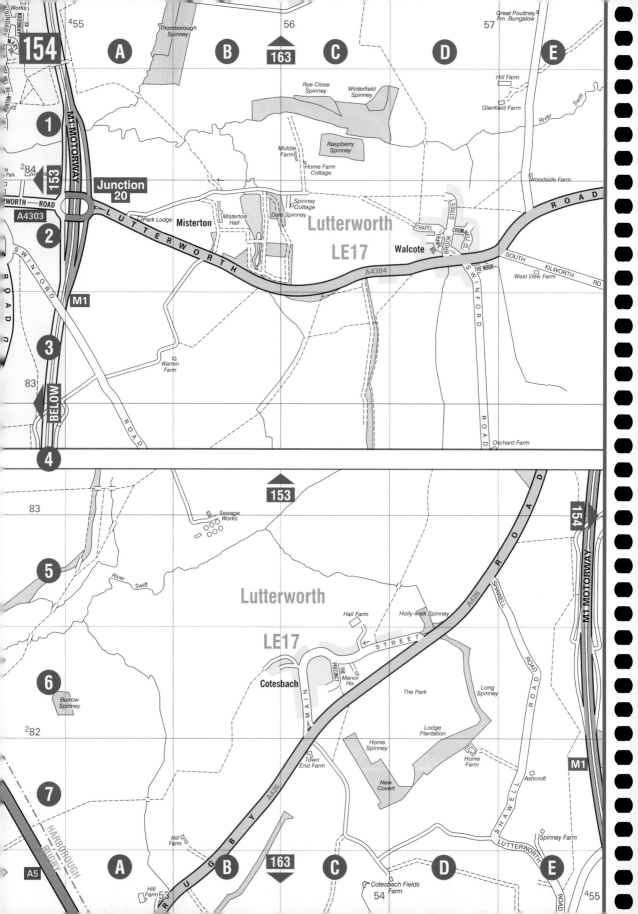

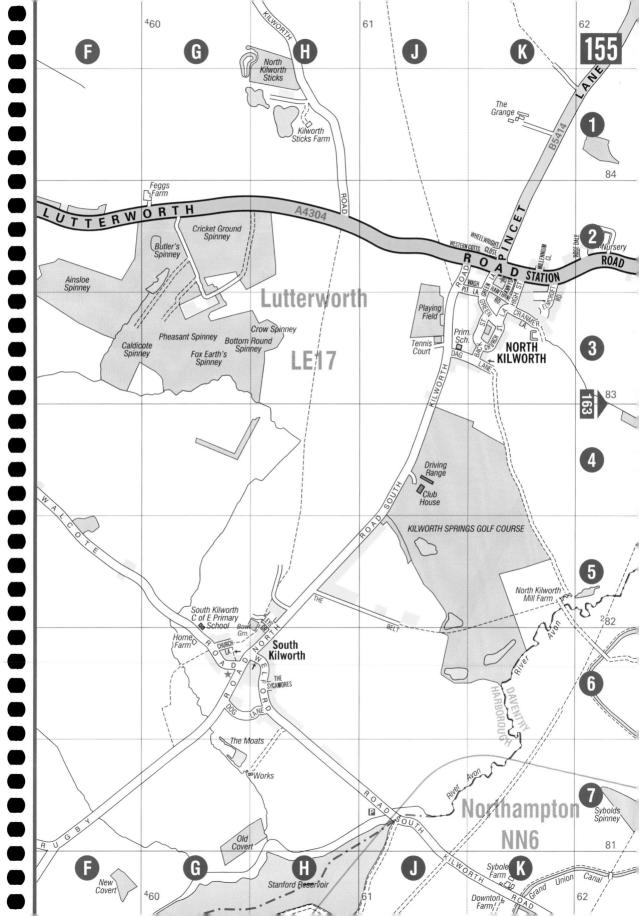

F  G  H  J  K

460  61  62

North Kilworth Sticks

Kilworth Sticks Farm

The Grange

1

84

Feggs Farm

LUTTERWORTH  A4304  ROAD

Cricket Ground Spinney

Butler's Spinney

Ainsloe Spinney

Lutterworth

Pheasant Spinney

Caldicote Spinney

Crow Spinney

Bottom Round Spinney

Fox Earth's Spinney

LE17

WHEELWRIGHT CLOSE
WESTERN COTTS.
Millennium Cl.
ROSE DALE

ROAD STATION ROAD

Nursery

2

WASH PIT LA.
HAWTHORNE RD.
GREEN LA.
HIGH ST.
PARKWAY
CRANMER LA.
ELMCROFT RD.

Playing Field

Tennis Court

Prim. Sch.

BACK LA.
CHURCH ST.

NORTH KILWORTH

3

DAG LANE

163  83

Driving Range

Club House

KILWORTH SPRINGS GOLF COURSE

4

WALCOTE

ROAD SOUTH
KILWORTH

North Kilworth Mill Farm

5

282

South Kilworth C of E Primary School

Home Farm

Bowl. Grn.

CHURCH LA.

South Kilworth

THE SYCAMORES

THE BELT

River Avon

HARBOROUGH
DAVENTRY

6

ROAD

NORTH WELFORD LANE

DOG LANE

The Moats

Works

ROAD SOUTH

P

River Avon

Northampton NN6

7

Sybolds Spinney

81

RUGBY

F  G  H  J  K

New Covert

Old Covert

Stanford Reservoir

460  61

KILWORTH ROAD SOUTH

Sybole Farm

Downton Farm

Grand Union Canal

62

B5414
PINCET LANE

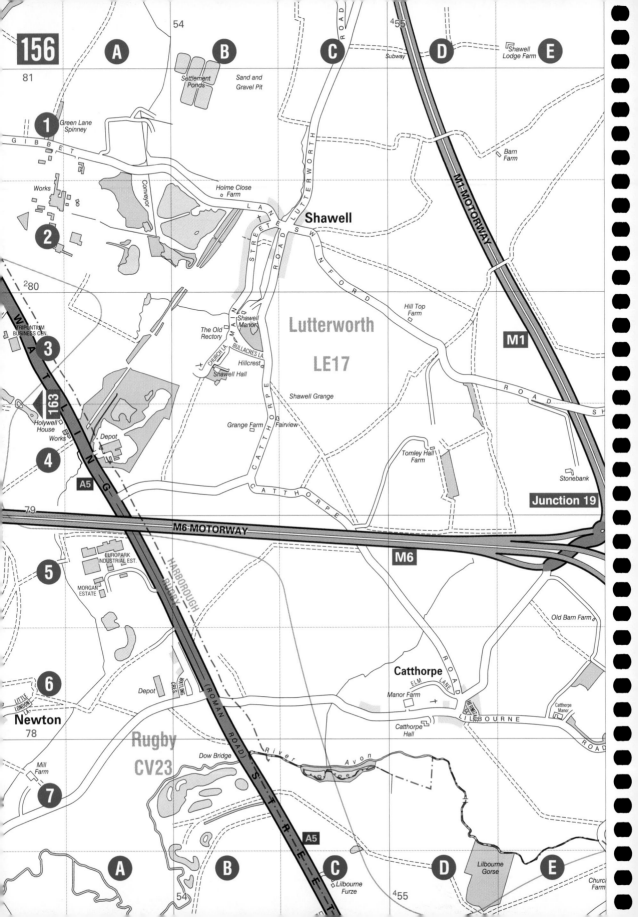

**A**    **B**    **C**    **D**    **E**

81

54    455

Settlement Ponds

Sand and Gravel Pit

Subway

Shawell Lodge Farm

**1**

Green Lane Spinney

GIBBET

Barn Farm

Works

Conveyor

Holme Close Farm

Shawell

**2**

LANE

STREET

SWINFORD

LUTTERWORTH

ROAD

M1-MOTORWAY

280

WATLING

TRIPONTIUM BUSINESS CEN.

The Old Rectory

CHURCH LA.

MAIN

Shawell Manor

BULLACRES LA.

Hillcrest

Shawell Hall

**Lutterworth**

**LE17**

Hill Top Farm

**M1**

**3**

163

Holywell House

Works

Depot

Shawell Grange

Grange Farm

Fairview

CATTHORPE

ROAD

SH

**4**

A5

Tomley Hall Farm

Stonebank

CATTHORPE

**Junction 19**

79

**M6-MOTORWAY**

**5**

EUROPARK INDUSTRIAL EST.

MORGAN ESTATE

HARBOROUGH

RUGBY

**M6**

Old Barn Farm

**6**

LITTLE LONDON LA.

Depot

WATLING

CRES.

**Newton**

78

**Rugby**

**CV23**

Catthorpe

ELM

Manor Farm

ROAD

LANE

HEMPLO...

Catthorpe Manor

LILBOURNE

Mill Farm

Dow Bridge

(ROMAN ROAD)

S·T·R·E·E·T

River

Avon

Catthorpe Hall

ROAD

**7**

A5

Lilbourne Furze

Lilbourne Gorse

Church Farm

**A**    **B**    **C**    **D**    **E**

54    455

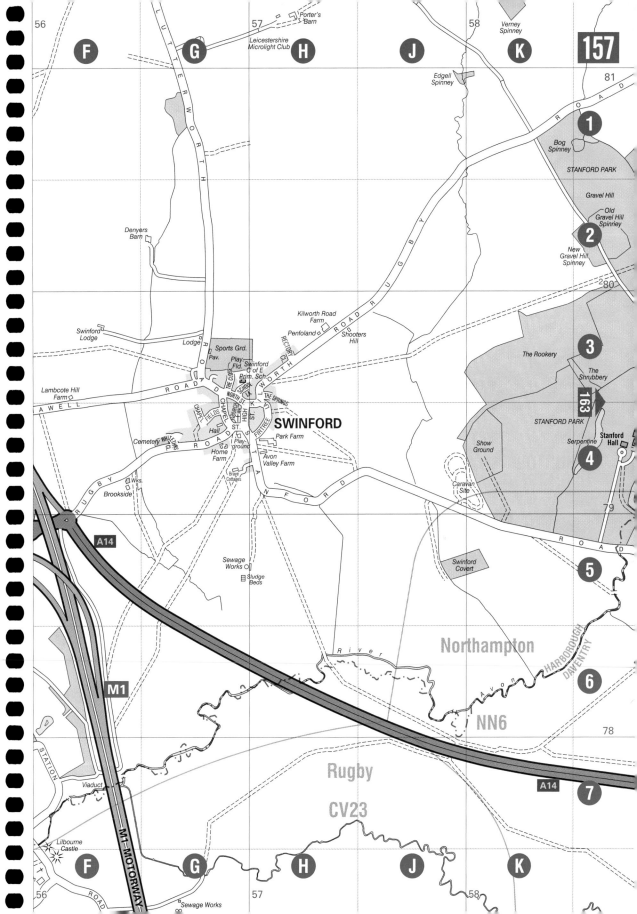

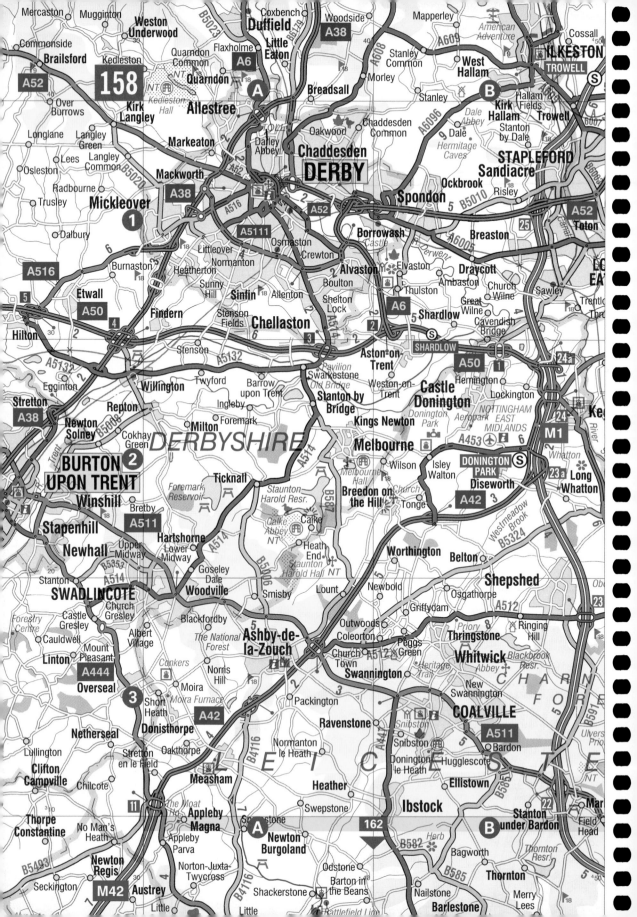

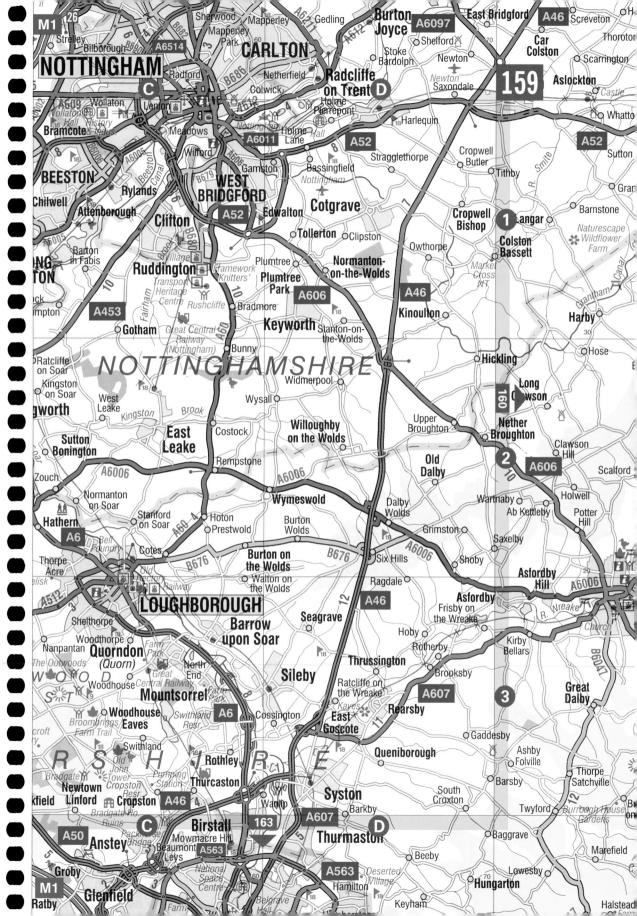

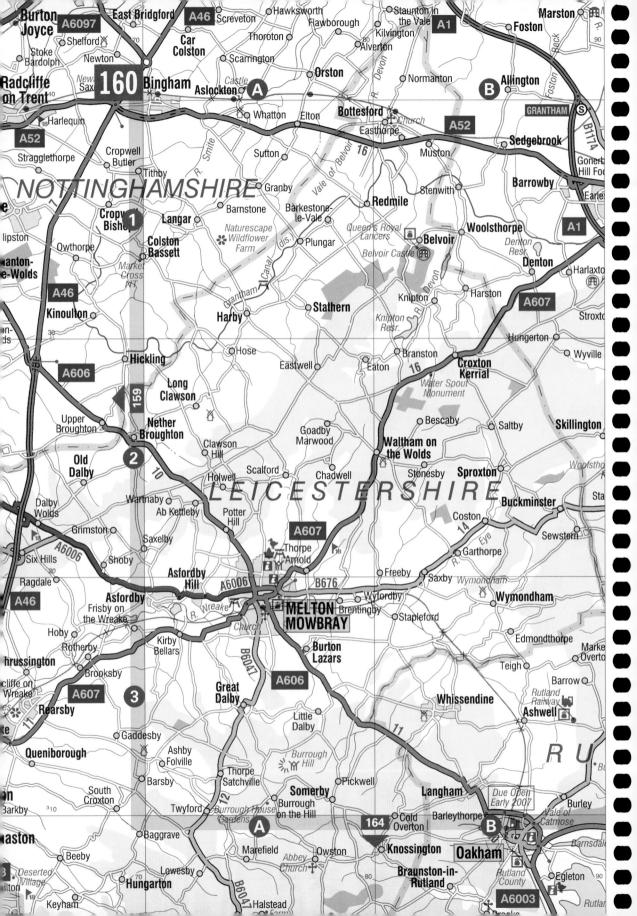

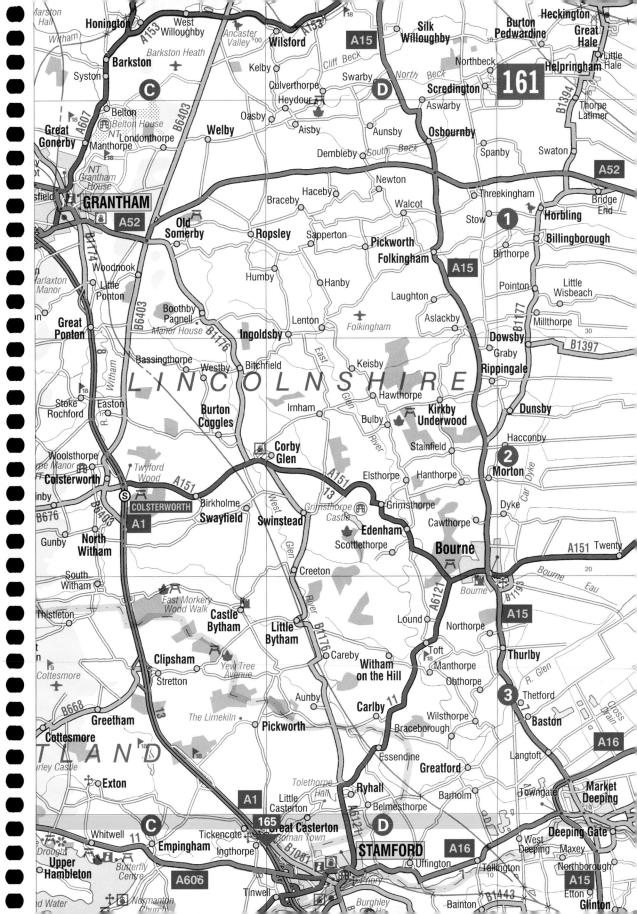

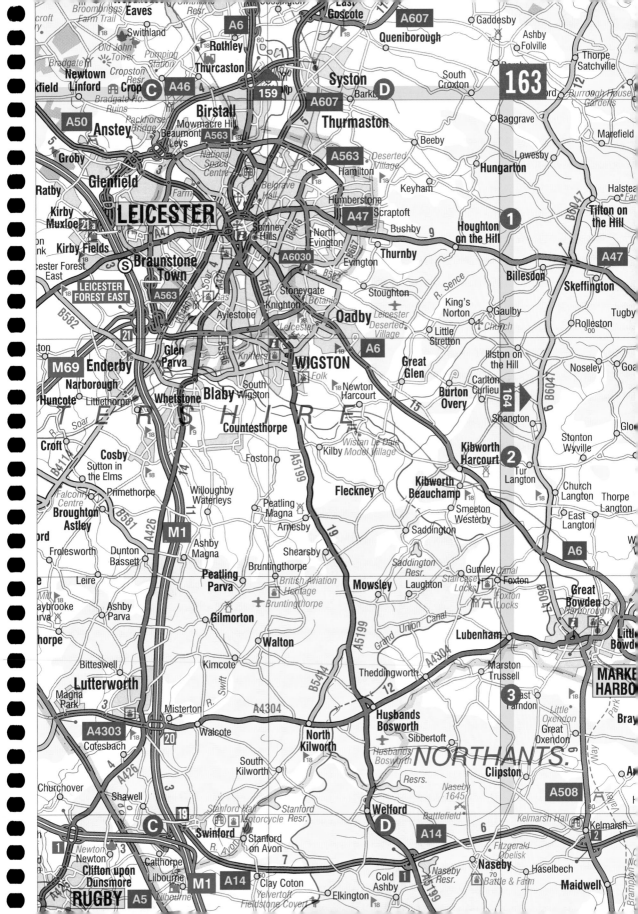

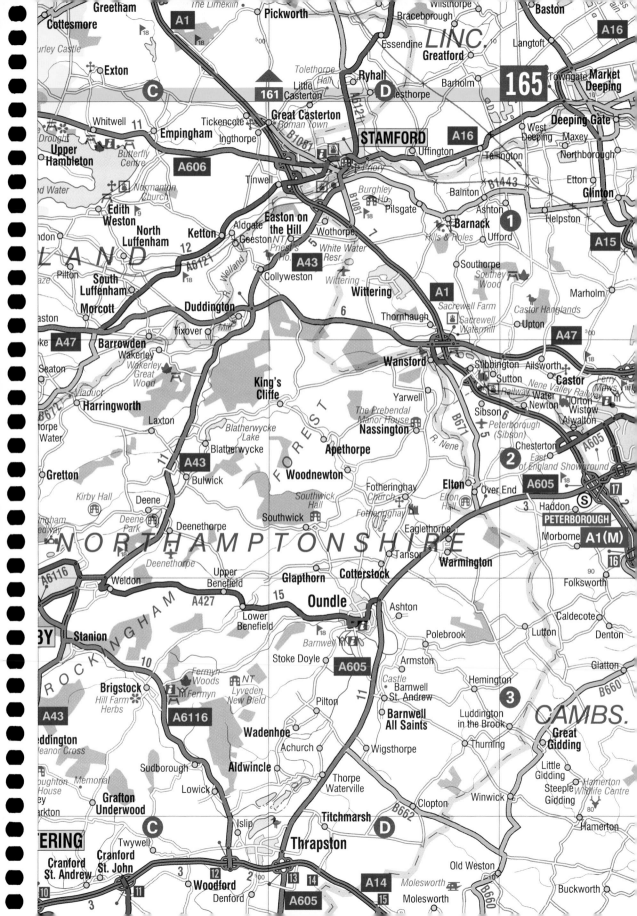

# INDEX

Including Streets, Places & Areas, Industrial Estates,
Flats & Walkways, Stations and Places of Interest.

## HOW TO USE THIS INDEX

1. Each street name is followed by its Postcode District and then by its Locality abbreviation(s) and then by its map reference;
   e.g. **Abberton Way** LE11: Lou . . . .1J **29** is in the LE11 Postcode District and the Loughborough Locality and is to be found in square 1J on page **29**. The page number is shown in bold type.

2. A strict alphabetical order is followed in which Av., Rd., St., etc. (though abbreviated) are read in full and as part of the street name;
   e.g. **Abbeycourt Rd.** appears after **Abbey Ct.** but before **Abbey Dr.**

3. Streets and a selection of flats and walkways too small to be shown on street map pages **4-157**, appear in the index with the thoroughfare to which it is connected shown in brackets; e.g. **Aldwinckles Yd.** LE16: Mkt H . . . . 4E **150** (off Church St.)

4. Addresses that are in more than one part are referred to as not continuous.

5. Places and areas are shown in the index in **BLUE TYPE** and the map reference is to the actual map square in which the town centre or area is located and not to the place name shown on the map. Map references for entries that appear on street map pages **4-157** are shown first, with references to road map pages **158-165** shown in brackets; e.g. **AB KETTLEBY** . . . .7H 111 (2A 160)

6. An example of a selected place of interest is Ashby-de-la-Zouch Mus. . . . . 5K 23

7. An example of a station is **Barrow upon Soar Station (Rail)** . . . . 4D 32. Included are Rail **(Rail)** and Park & Ride **(Park & Ride)**.

8. Map references for entries that appear on large scale pages **4-5** are shown first, with small scale map references shown in brackets;
   e.g. **Abbey Bus. Pk.** LE1: Leic . . . .1B **4** (7E **64**)

## GENERAL ABBREVIATIONS

**App.** : Approach
**Arc.** : Arcade
**Av.** : Avenue
**Bk.** : Back
**Blvd.** : Boulevard
**Bri.** : Bridge
**Bldg.** : Building
**Bldgs.** : Buildings
**Bungs.** : Bungalows
**Bus.** : Business
**Cvn.** : Caravan
**C'way.** : Causeway
**Cen.** : Centre
**Chu.** : Church
**Circ.** : Circle
**Cl.** : Close
**Comn.** : Common
**Cnr.** : Corner
**Cott.** : Cottage
**Cotts.** : Cottages
**Ct.** : Court
**Cres.** : Crescent
**Cft.** : Croft
**Dr.** : Drive
**E.** : East

**Ent.** : Enterprise
**Est.** : Estate
**Fld.** : Field
**Flds.** : Fields
**Gdn.** : Garden
**Gdns.** : Gardens
**Gth.** : Garth
**Ga.** : Gate
**Gt.** : Great
**Grn.** : Green
**Gro.** : Grove
**Hgts.** : Heights
**Ho.** : House
**Ho's.** : Houses
**Ind.** : Industrial
**Info.** : Information
**Junc.** : Junction
**La.** : Lane
**Lit.** : Little
**Lwr.** : Lower
**Mnr.** : Manor
**Mkt.** : Market
**Mdw.** : Meadow
**Mdws.** : Meadows
**M.** : Mews

**Mt.** : Mount
**Mus.** : Museum
**Nth.** : North
**Pde.** : Parade
**Pk.** : Park
**Pas.** : Passage
**Pl.** : Place
**Prom.** : Promenade
**Ri.** : Rise
**Rd.** : Road
**Rdbt.** : Roundabout
**Shop.** : Shopping
**Sth.** : South
**Sq.** : Square
**St.** : Street
**Ter.** : Terrace
**Twr.** : Tower
**Trad.** : Trading
**Up.** : Upper
**Va.** : Vale
**Vw.** : View
**Vis.** : Visitors
**Wlk.** : Walk
**W.** : West
**Yd.** : Yard

## LOCALITY ABBREVIATIONS

Ab K : **Ab Kettleby**
Acre : **Acresford**
A Vil : **Albert Village**
Alle : **Allexton**
Anst : **Anstey**
A Mag : **Appleby Magna**
A Par : **Appleby Parva**
Arne : **Arnesby**
Ash : **Asfordby**
Ash H : **Asfordby Hill**
Ash Z : **Ashby-de-la-Zouch**
Ash F : **Ashby Folville**
Ash M : **Ashby Magna**
Ash P : **Ashby Parva**
A'll : **Ashwell**
A Fla : **Aston Flamville**
A Tre : **Aston-on-Trent**
Ath : **Atherstone**
Att : **Atterton**
Bag : **Bagworth**
Bar : **Bardon Hill**
Bark : **Barkby**
Bark T : **Barkby Thorpe**
Bark V : **Barkestone-le-Vale**
B'one : **Barlestone**
Barl : **Barleythorpe**
Barr : **Barrow**
B'den : **Barrowden**
Bar S : **Barrow upon Soar**
Bars : **Barsby**
B Bea : **Barton in the Beans**
Barw : **Barwell**
Beau L : **Beaumont Leys**
Bee : **Beeby**
Belm : **Belmesthorpe**
Belt : **Belton**
Bel R : **Belton-in-Rutland**
Besc : **Bescaby**

Bill : **Billesdon**
Bils : **Bilstone**
Birs : **Birstall**
Bisb : **Bisbrooke**
Bitt : **Bitteswell**
Bla : **Blaby**
Blac : **Blackfordby**
Blas : **Blaston**
Boot : **Boothorpe**
Bott : **Bottesford**
Boun : **Boundary**
Bran : **Branston**
Brau : **Braunstone**
B Rut : **Braunston-in-Rutland**
Bray : **Braybrooke**
B Hil : **Breedon on the Hill**
Bren : **Brentingby**
Brin : **Bringhurst**
B Ast : **Broughton Astley**
Brun : **Bruntingthorpe**
Buck : **Buckminster**
Bur : **Burbage**
Bur H : **Burrough on the Hill**
Bur L : **Burton Lazars**
Bur W : **Burton on the Wolds**
Bur O : **Burton Overy**
Bush : **Bushby**
Cad : **Cadeby**
Cald : **Caldecote**
C'ott : **Caldecott**
Calk : **Calke**
Carl : **Carlton**
C Don : **Castle Donington**
Cat : **Catthorpe**
Char : **Charley**
Chell : **Chellaston**
C Gre : **Church Gresley**
C Lan : **Church Langton**

C Mag : **Claybrooke Magna**
C Par : **Claybrooke Parva**
C Dus : **Clifton upon Dusmore**
Coal : **Coalville**
C Ove : **Cold Overton**
Cole : **Coleorton**
Coll : **Collyweston**
Con : **Congerstone**
C Oak : **Copt Oak**
Cosb : **Cosby**
Coss : **Cossington**
Cote : **Cotes**
C'ach : **Cotesbach**
Cott : **Cottesmore**
Count : **Countesthorpe**
Crof : **Croft**
Crop : **Cropston**
Crox : **Croxton Kerrial**
Dadl : **Dadlington**
Des : **Desford**
Din : **Dingley**
Dis : **Diseworth**
D Hea : **Donington le Heath**
Don : **Donisthorpe**
Dray : **Drayton**
D Bas : **Dunton Bassett**
Earl S : **Earl Shilton**
East F : **East Farndon**
East G : **East Goscote**
East L : **East Langton**
East : **Easthorpe**
Eat : **Eaton**
E Wes : **Edith Weston**
Edm : **Edmondthorpe**
Ell : **Ellistown**
Elm : **Elmesthorpe**
Emp : **Empingham**
End : **Enderby**

Ess : **Essendine**
Ext : **Exton**
F Dray : **Fenny Drayton**
Flec : **Fleckney**
Fost : **Foston**
Fox : **Foxton**
F Wre : **Frisby on the Wreake**
Frol : **Frolesworth**
Gad : **Gaddesby**
Gar : **Gartree**
Gilm : **Gilmorton**
Glas : **Glaston**
Glen : **Glenfield**
G Par : **Glen Parva**
Goa : **Goadby**
G Bow : **Great Bowden**
G Cas : **Great Casterton**
G Dal : **Great Dalby**
G Eas : **Great Easton**
G Gle : **Great Glen**
G Ox : **Great Oxendon**
Gt Stret : **Great Stretton**
Gree : **Greetham**
Grif : **Griffydam**
Groby : **Groby**
Hall : **Hallaton**
Hals : **Halstead**
Ham : **Hamilton**
Harb : **Harby**
H'hill : **Hartshill**
Harts : **Hartshorne**
Hat : **Hathern**
Hea : **Heather**
Hem : **Hemington**
H Hill : **Higham-on-the-Hill**
Hinc : **Hinckley**
Hob : **Hoby**
Hol : **Holwell**
Horn : **Horninghold**
Hos : **Hose**
Hot : **Hoton**
Hou H : **Houghton on the Hill**
Hug : **Hugglescote**
Hun : **Huncote**
H Bos : **Husbands Bosworth**
Ibs : **Ibstock**
I Wal : **Isley Walton**
J O'Ga : **John O'Gaunt**
Keg : **Kegworth**
Ket : **Ketton**
Keyh : **Keyham**
Keyt : **Keythorpe**
K Bea : **Kibworth Beauchamp**
Kib H : **Kibworth Harcourt**
Kilby : **Kilby**
Kim : **Kimcote**
K New : **King's Newton**
King S : **Kingston on Soar**
K Bel : **Kirby Bellars**
K Mux : **Kirby Muxloe**
K Mal : **Kirkby Mallory**
Knap : **Knaptoft**
Knip : **Knipton**
Knos : **Knossington**
Lan : **Langar**
L'ham : **Langham**
L'ton : **Laughton**
Leic : **Leicester**
Leic E : **Leicester Forest East**
Leire : **Leire**
Lilb : **Lilbourne**
L Bow : **Little Bowden**
Litt : **Littlethorpe**
Lock : **Lockington**
L Cla : **Long Clawson**
L Wha : **Long Whatton**
Lou : **Loughborough**
Low : **Lowesby**
Lub : **Lubenham**
Lut : **Lutterworth**
Lyd : **Lyddington**
Manc : **Mancetter**
Mant : **Manton**

Mare : **Marefield**
Mkt B : **Market Bosworth**
Mkt H : **Market Harborough**
Mkt O : **Market Overton**
Mark : **Markfield**
Mea : **Measham**
Med : **Medbourne**
Mel : **Melbourne**
Mel M : **Melton Mowbray**
Mist : **Misterton**
Moi : **Moira**
Mor : **Morcott**
Moun : **Mountsorrel**
Mows : **Mowsley**
Mus : **Muston**
Nail : **Nailstone**
Nan : **Nanpantan**
Nar : **Narborough**
N Bro : **Nether Broughton**
New : **Newbold**
N Ver : **Newbold Verdon**
N'ton : **Newton**
N Bur : **Newton Burgoland**
New H : **Newton Harcourt**
New L : **Newtown Linford**
Norm : **Normanton**
Nor H : **Normanton le Heath**
Nor S : **Normanton on Soar**
N Kil : **North Kilworth**
N Luf : **North Luffenham**
N Twy : **Norton-Juxta-Twycross**
N Air : **Nottingham East Midlands Airpo**
Nun : **Nuneaton**
Oad : **Oadby**
O'ham : **Oakham**
Oak : **Oakthorpe**
Ods : **Odstone**
O Dal : **Old Dalby**
O Hil : **Orton-on-the-Hill**
Osb : **Osbaston**
Osg : **Osgathorpe**
Over : **Overseal**
Pac : **Packington**
Peat M : **Peatling Magna**
P Par : **Peatling Parva**
Peck : **Peckleton**
Pin : **Pinwall**
Plun : **Plungar**
Pott M : **Potters Marston**
Pres : **Preston**
P'old : **Prestwold**
Quen : **Queniborough**
Quo : **Quorn**
Ratby : **Ratby**
Rat S : **Ratcliffe on Soar**
Rat W : **Ratcliffe on the Wreake**
Rav : **Ravenstone**
Rear : **Rearsby**
Red : **Redmile**
Rid : **Ridlington**
Roth : **Rotherby**
R'ley : **Rothley**
Ryh : **Ryhall**
Sad : **Saddington**
Sap : **Sapcote**
Scal : **Scalford**
Scra : **Scraptoft**
Sea : **Seagrave**
Seat : **Seaton**
Sew : **Sewstern**
S'one : **Shackerstone**
Shar : **Shardlow**
S'ord : **Sharnford**
Shaw : **Shawell**
Shea : **Shearsby**
S Mag : **Sheepy Magna**
S Par : **Sheepy Parva**
Shep : **Shepshed**
Sileby : **Sileby**
Slaw : **Slawston**
Smee W : **Smeeton Westerby**
Smis : **Smisby**
Snar : **Snarestone**

Som : **Somerby**
S Cro : **South Croxton**
S Kil : **South Kilworth**
S Luf : **South Luffenham**
Spro : **Sproxton**
Stam : **Stamford**
Stan S : **Stanford on Soar**
S Bar : **Stanton under Bardon**
Stap : **Stapleton**
Sta : **Stathern**
Stau H : **Staunton Harold**
S Dry : **Stoke Dry**
S Gol : **Stoke Golding**
Ston : **Stonesby**
S Stan : **Stoney Stanton**
S'ton : **Stoughton**
Stre : **Stretton**
Sut Bon : **Sutton Bonington**
S Che : **Sutton Cheney**
Swad : **Swadlincote**
Swan : **Swannington**
Swark : **Swarkestone**
Swep : **Swepstone**
Swin : **Swinford**
Swith : **Swithland**
Sys : **Syston**
Thor : **Thornton**
T Arn : **Thorpe Arnold**
T Wat : **Thorpe by Water**
T Lan : **Thorpe Langton**
T Sat : **Thorpe Satchville**
Thrin : **Thringstone**
Thru : **Thrussington**
Thul : **Thulston**
Thurc : **Thurcaston**
Thurl : **Thurlaston**
Thurm : **Thurmaston**
Thurn : **Thurnby**
Tick : **Tickencote**
T Hil : **Tilton on the Hill**
Ton : **Tonge**
Tug : **Tugby**
Twy : **Twycross**
T'ord : **Twyford**
Ull : **Ullesthorpe**
Ulv : **Ulverscroft**
Up Bro : **Upper Broughton**
U Bru : **Upper Bruntingthorpe**
Upp : **Uppingham**
Wal : **Walcote**
W Wol : **Waltham on the Wolds**
Walt : **Walton**
Walt W : **Walton on the Wolds**
Wan : **Wanlip**
Ward : **Wardley**
Wart : **Wartnaby**
Welb : **Welby**
Welf : **Welford**
W Lan : **West Langton**
W Tre : **Weston-on-Trent**
Whet : **Whetstone**
Whis : **Whissendine**
Whit : **Whitwick**
Wig : **Wigston**
W'ley : **Willesley**
Will : **Willey**
Will W : **Willoughby Waterleys**
Wils : **Wilson**
Win : **Wing**
Wist : **Wistow**
With : **Witherley**
Wood : **Woodhouse**
W Eav : **Woodhouse Eaves**
W'orpe : **Woodthorpe**
W'lle : **Woodville**
Wort : **Worthington**
Wyc : **Wycomb**
Wyk : **Wykin**
Wym : **Wymeswold**
W'ham : **Wymondham**

---

## A

**Abberton Way** LE11: Lou . . . . . . . . . . . . . . . .1J **29**
**Abbey Bus. Pk.** LE1: Leic . . . . . . . . . . .1B **4** (7E **64**)
**Abbey Cl.** LE12: Shep . . . . . . . . . . . . . . . . . . . .2C **28**
  LE65: Ash Z . . . . . . . . . . . . . . . . . . . . . . .5H **23**
**Abbey Ct.** LE4: Leic . . . . . . . . . . . . . . . . . . . . .4F **65**
**Abbeycourt Rd.** LE4: Leic . . . . . . . . . . . . . . . .3F **65**
**Abbey Dr.** LE4: Leic . . . . . . . . . . . . . . . . . . . . .3F **65**
  LE65: Ash Z . . . . . . . . . . . . . . . . . . . . . . .5H **23**
**Abbey Ga.** LE4: Leic . . . . . . . . . . . . . . . . . . . . .7E **64**
**Abbey Ho.** LE3: Leic . . . . . . . . . . . . . . . . . . . .6B **64**

**Abbey La.** LE4: Leic . . . . . . . . . . . . . . . . . . . . .5E **64**
**Abbey Mdws.** LE4: Leic . . . . . . . . . . . . . . . . . .5F **65**
**Abbeymead Rd.** LE4: Leic . . . . . . . . . . . . . . . .3F **65**
**Abbey Pk. Rd.** LE4: Leic . . . . . . . . . . . . . . . . .5E **64**
**Abbey Pk. St.** LE4: Leic . . . . . . . . . . . . . . . . . .6G **65**
Abbey Pumping Station . . . . . . . . . . . . . . . . . .4F **65**
**Abbey Ri.** LE4: Leic . . . . . . . . . . . . . . . . . . . . .3F **65**
**Abbey Rd.** LE19: End . . . . . . . . . . . . . . . . . . . .7H **75**
  LE67: Char, Coal . . . . . . . . . . . . . . . . . . .1K **39**
**Abbey St.** LE1: Leic . . . . . . . . . . . . . . .1D **4** (7F **65**)
  LE16: Mkt H . . . . . . . . . . . . . . . . . . . . . . .4E **150**
**Abbey Wlk.** LE1: Leic . . . . . . . . . . . . .1C **4** (7F **65**)
**Abbots Cl.** LE5: Leic . . . . . . . . . . . . . . . . . . . .6D **66**

**Abbots Ct.** LE5: Leic . . . . . . . . . . . . . . . . . . . .6D **66**
**Abbotsford Cl.** LE7: Scra . . . . . . . . . . . . . . . . .6H **67**
**Abbotsford Rd.** LE5: Leic . . . . . . . . . . . . . . . . .7B **66**
  LE65: Ash Z . . . . . . . . . . . . . . . . . . . . . . .6A **24**
**Abbots Rd. Nth.** LE5: Leic . . . . . . . . . . . . . . . .6D **66**
**Abbots Rd. Sth.** LE5: Leic . . . . . . . . . . . . . . . .6E **66**
**Abbotts Cl.** LE7: Sys . . . . . . . . . . . . . . . . . . . .2B **60**
**Abbotts Grn.** LE10: Bur . . . . . . . . . . . . . . . . . .6J **103**
**Abbott's Oak Dr.**
  LE67: Coal . . . . . . . . . . . . . . . . . . . . . . . .2H **39**
**Aberdale Rd.** LE2: Leic . . . . . . . . . . . . . . . . . . .3H **77**
**Aber Rd.** LE2: Leic . . . . . . . . . . . . . . . . . . . . . .5K **71**
**Aber Wlk.** LE2: Leic . . . . . . . . . . . . . . . . . . . . .5K **71**

Abingdon Rd. LE2: Leic . . . . . . . . . . . . . . . . . . .3H 71
   LE13: Mel M . . . . . . . . . . . . . . . . . . . .1D 116
Abingfon Wlk. LE2: Leic . . . . . . . . . . . . . . . . .4H 71
AB KETTLEBY . . . . . . . . . . . . .7H 111 (2A 160)
Abney Cres. DE12: Mea . . . . . . . . . . . . . . . .1E 48
Abney Dr. DE12: Mea . . . . . . . . . . . . . . . . . .1E 48
Abney St. LE5: Leic . . . . . . . . . . . . . . . . . . .3J 71
Abney Wlk. DE12: Mea . . . . . . . . . . . . . . . . .1E 48
Acacia Av. LE4: Birs . . . . . . . . . . . . . . . . . . .5H 59
   LE17: Lut . . . . . . . . . . . . . . . . . . . . . .3H 153
Acacia Cl. LE3: Leic E . . . . . . . . . . . . . . . . .5D 68
Acan Way LE19: Nar . . . . . . . . . . . . . . . . . .2E 80
Acer Cl. LE4: Leic . . . . . . . . . . . . . . . . . . . .2C 64
   LE11: Lou . . . . . . . . . . . . . . . . . . . . . .4E 30
   LE19: Nar . . . . . . . . . . . . . . . . . . . . . .2E 80
ACHURCH . . . . . . . . . . . . . . . . . . . . . . . . .3D 165
Achurch Cl. LE9: S Stan . . . . . . . . . . . . . . .7J 101
Acorn Cl. LE4: Birs . . . . . . . . . . . . . . . . . . .7G 59
   LE16: Lub . . . . . . . . . . . . . . . . . . . . . .7H 149
Acorn St. LE4: Leic . . . . . . . . . . . . . . . . . . .4H 65
Acorn Way LE18: Wig . . . . . . . . . . . . . . . . .6A 78
Acre La. DE72: A Tre . . . . . . . . . . . . . . . . . .1E 6
Acresford Rd. DE12: Acre, Don . . . . . . . . . .5A 34
Acres Ri. LE3: Mel M . . . . . . . . . . . . . . . . .3H 117
Acres Rd. LE3: Leic E . . . . . . . . . . . . . . . . .4E 68
Adam & Eve St. LE16: Mkt H . . . . . . . . . . .4E 150
Adam Dale LE11: Lou . . . . . . . . . . . . . . . . .7D 18
Adamswood Cl. LE16: Mkt H . . . . . . . . . . .4C 150
Adcock Cl. LE13: Mel M . . . . . . . . . . . . . . .2J 117
Adcock Rd. LE3: Leic . . . . . . . . . . . . . . . . .7B 64
Adcocks Cl. LE11: Lou . . . . . . . . . . . . . . . . .5F 19
Adcocks Yd. DE12: Mea . . . . . . . . . . . . . . .7E 34
Adcote Cl. LE9: Barw . . . . . . . . . . . . . . . . .4K 99
Adderley Rd. LE2: Leic . . . . . . . . . . . . . . . .5G 71
Adderly St. LE15: Upp . . . . . . . . . . . . . . . .2C 138
Adelaide Cl. LE4: Beau L . . . . . . . . . . . . . . .6C 58
Adkins Ct. LE12: Bar S . . . . . . . . . . . . . . . .3C 32
Adlington Rd. LE2: Oad . . . . . . . . . . . . . . . .2E 78
Admiral Ct. LE16: Mkt H . . . . . . . . . . . . . . .4D 150
Adrian Dr. LE9: Barw . . . . . . . . . . . . . . . . .3K 99
Afton Cl. LE11: Lou . . . . . . . . . . . . . . . . . . .7K 17
AGAR NOOK . . . . . . . . . . . . . . . . . . . . . . . .3J 39
Agar Nook Ct. LE67: Coal . . . . . . . . . . . . . .3J 39
Agar Nook La. LE67: Coal . . . . . . . . . . . . . .2K 39
Agar St. LE4: Leic . . . . . . . . . . . . . . . . . . . .5H 65
Aikman Av. LE3: Leic . . . . . . . . . . . . . . . . . .6K 63
Aikman Cl. LE3: Leic . . . . . . . . . . . . . . . . . .7A 64
AILSWORTH . . . . . . . . . . . . . . . . . . . . . . . .2D 165
Aingarth LE11: Lou . . . . . . . . . . . . . . . . . . .7G 19
Ainsdale LE8: Flec . . . . . . . . . . . . . . . . . . .4C 88
Ainsdale Rd. LE3: Leic . . . . . . . . . . . . . . . .2A 70
Ainsworth Dr. LE12: Sileby . . . . . . . . . . . . .7K 33
Ainsworth Wlk. LE3: Leic . . . . . . . . . . . . . .2A 70
Aintree Cl. LE5: Leic . . . . . . . . . . . . . . . . . .3F 73
Aintree Cres. LE2: Oad . . . . . . . . . . . . . . . .2B 78
Airedale Cl. LE17: Leire . . . . . . . . . . . . . . .2K 143
AISBY . . . . . . . . . . . . . . . . . . . . . . . . . . . .1D 161
Aisne Rd. LE18: Wig . . . . . . . . . . . . . . . . . .5E 76
Akbert St. NG13: Bott . . . . . . . . . . . . . . . . .2G 107
Alan Bray Cl. LE10: Hinc . . . . . . . . . . . . . . .4A 102
Alan Cl. LE4: Leic . . . . . . . . . . . . . . . . . . . .2H 65
Aland Gdns. LE9: B Ast . . . . . . . . . . . . . . . .4E 86
Alan Moss Rd. LE11: Lou . . . . . . . . . . . . . . .6B 18
Alans Way LE9: N Ver . . . . . . . . . . . . . . . . .6H 93
Albany, The LE2: Leic . . . . . . . . . . . . . . . . .4J 71
Albany Pk. LE16: Mkt H . . . . . . . . . . . . . . . .3F 151
Albany Rd. LE16: Mkt H . . . . . . . . . . . . . . . .3F 151
Albany St. LE11: Lou . . . . . . . . . . . . . . . . . .5C 18
Albemarle Hall LE5: Leic . . . . . . . . . . . . . . .6C 66
Alberta St. LE5: Leic . . . . . . . . . . .2G 4 (1H 71)
Albert Av. LE12: Sileby . . . . . . . . . . . . . . . .7K 33
Albert Ct. LE2: Leic . . . . . . . . . . . . . . . . . . .5K 71
   LE8: Whet . . . . . . . . . . . . . . . . . . . . .1K 81
Albert Hall LE67: Coal . . . . . . . . . . . . . . . . .3K 39
Albert Pl. LE11: Lou . . . . . . . . . . . . . . . . . .7F 19
Albert Prom. LE11: Lou . . . . . . . . . . . . . . . .7G 19
Albert Rd. LE2: Leic . . . . . . . . . . . . . . . . . .5J 71
   LE10: Hinc . . . . . . . . . . . . . . . . . . . .2G 103
   LE16: Mkt H . . . . . . . . . . . . . . . . . . .4F 151
   LE67: Coal . . . . . . . . . . . . . . . . . . . .3D 38
Albert St. LE7: Sys . . . . . . . . . . . . . . . . . . .2D 60
   LE8: Flec . . . . . . . . . . . . . . . . . . . . . .3B 88
   LE8: Kib H . . . . . . . . . . . . . . . . . . . . .1J 89
   LE11: Lou . . . . . . . . . . . . . . . . . . . . .7F 19
   LE13: Mel M . . . . . . . . . . . . . . . . . . .6G 117
   LE67: Ibs . . . . . . . . . . . . . . . . . . . . . .3K 51
ALBERT VILLAGE . . . . . . . . . . .2A 22 (3A 158)
Albion Cl. DE12: Moi . . . . . . . . . . . . . . . . . .7C 22
Albion Ct. LE2: Oad . . . . . . . . . . . . . . . . . . .3C 78
Albion Pde. LE7: Sys . . . . . . . . . . . . . . . . . .2D 60
Albion Rd. LE12: Sileby . . . . . . . . . . . . . . . .1J 45
Albion St. LE1: Leic . . . . . . . . . .5D 4 (2F 71)
   LE2: Oad . . . . . . . . . . . . . . . . . . . . . .3C 78
   LE7: Anst . . . . . . . . . . . . . . . . . . . . . .7J 57
   LE7: Sys . . . . . . . . . . . . . . . . . . . . . . .2D 60
   LE18: Wig . . . . . . . . . . . . . . . . . . . . .6F 77
Alcester Dr. LE5: Leic . . . . . . . . . . . . . . . . .3F 73

Alcott Cl. LE3: Leic . . . . . . . . . . . . . . . . . . .3A 70
Aldeby Cl. LE2: Leic . . . . . . . . . . . . . . . . . .4B 76
   LE19: End . . . . . . . . . . . . . . . . . . . . .6J 75
Alder Cl. LE3: Leic E . . . . . . . . . . . . . . . . . .5D 68
Alder Cres. LE17: Lut . . . . . . . . . . . . . . . . .4H 153
Alder Gro. Est. LE19: Nar . . . . . . . . . . . . . .6D 74
Alderleigh Rd. LE2: G Par . . . . . . . . . . . . . .7E 76
Alderstone Cl. LE18: Wig . . . . . . . . . . . . . . .1J 83
Alderton Cl. LE4: Leic . . . . . . . . . . . . . . . . .1J 65
ALDGATE . . . . . . . . . . . . . . . .6H 137 (1C 165)
Aldgate PE9: Ket . . . . . . . . . . . . . . . . . . . .6H 137
Aldgate Av. LE5: Leic . . . . . . . . . . . . . . . . .4D 72
Aldgate Ct. PE9: Ket . . . . . . . . . . . . . . . . .6H 137
Aldin Way LE10: Hinc . . . . . . . . . . . . . . . . .7D 98
Aldridge Rd. LE10: Bur . . . . . . . . . . . . . . . .5G 103
Aldwinckles Yd. *LE16: Mkt H* . . . . . . . . . . .*4E 150*
   *(off Church St.)*
ALDWINCLE . . . . . . . . . . . . . . . . . . . . . . . .3D 165
Alesworth Dr. LE10: Bur . . . . . . . . . . . . . . .7J 103
Alexander Av. LE9: Earl S . . . . . . . . . . . . . .2E 100
   LE19: End . . . . . . . . . . . . . . . . . . . . .5E 74
Alexander Cres. LE15: O'ham . . . . . . . . . . .4G 127
Alexander Dr. LE17: Lut . . . . . . . . . . . . . . .6H 153
Alexander Gdns. LE10: Hinc . . . . . . . . . . . .1F 103
Alexander Rd. LE12: Quo . . . . . . . . . . . . . . .4K 31
Alexander St. LE3: Leic . . . . . . . .3A 4 (1E 70)
Alexandra Ct. LE2: Oad . . . . . . . . . . . . . . . .3D 78
Alexandra Rd. DE11: Swad . . . . . . . . . . . . .1A 22
   LE2: Leic . . . . . . . . . . . . . . . . . . . . .6K 71
Alexandra St. LE4: Thurm . . . . . . . . . . . . . .5A 60
   LE19: Nar . . . . . . . . . . . . . . . . . . . . .1G 81
Alfred Pl. LE1: Leic . . . . . . . . . . .4E 4 (2G 71)
Alfred St. LE11: Lou . . . . . . . . . . . . . . . . . .5F 19
Alfreton Cl. LE10: Bur . . . . . . . . . . . . . . . . .6J 103
Alfreton Rd. LE18: Wig . . . . . . . . . . . . . . . . .4J 77
Algernon Rd. LE13: Mel M . . . . . . . . . . . . .4G 117
Alice Gdns. LE8: Whet . . . . . . . . . . . . . . . . .4K 81
Allandale Rd. LE2: Leic . . . . . . . . . . . . . . . .6A 72
Allen Av. LE12: Quo . . . . . . . . . . . . . . . . . . .4K 31
Allendale Rd. LE11: Lou . . . . . . . . . . . . . . . .4F 31
ALLENTON . . . . . . . . . . . . . . . . . . . . . . . . .1A 158
Allenwood Rd. LE2: Leic . . . . . . . . . . . . . . . .4E 76
Allerton Dr. LE3: Leic . . . . . . . . . . . . . . . . .5A 64
ALLESLEY . . . . . . . . . . . . . . . . . . . . . . . . .3A 162
ALLESTREE . . . . . . . . . . . . . . . . . . . . . . . .1A 158
ALLEXTON . . . . . . . . . . . . . .7G 133 (1B 164)
Allexton Gdns. LE3: Leic . . . . . . . . . . . . . . .7H 63
Allexton Rd. LE16: Hall . . . . . . . . . . . . . . . .5B 132
Allfrey Cl. LE17: Lut . . . . . . . . . . . . . . . . . .4G 153
Alliance Rd. LE3: Glen . . . . . . . . . . . . . . . . .7G 63
ALLINGTON . . . . . . . . . . . . . . . . . . . . . . . . .1B 160
Allington Dr. LE4: Birs . . . . . . . . . . . . . . . . .4H 59
Allington St. LE4: Leic . . . . . . . . . . . . . . . . .6H 65
Allinson Ct. LE5: Leic . . . . . . . . . . . . . . . . .1C 72
Allison Cl. LE65: Ash Z . . . . . . . . . . . . . . . .3K 23
Allotment La. CV13: S'one . . . . . . . . . . . . . .3H 91
Alloway Cl. LE4: Leic . . . . . . . . . . . . . . . . . .2K 65
All Saints Cl. LE9: Sap . . . . . . . . . . . . . . . . .4J 105
   LE14: Ash . . . . . . . . . . . . . . . . . . . . .3G 115
All Saints Open LE1: Leic . . . . . . .2A 4 (1E 70)
All Saints Rd. LE3: Leic . . . . . . . . .3A 4 (1E 70)
   *(not continuous)*
   LE7: Thurc . . . . . . . . . . . . . . . . . . . . .3B 58
Allsopp's La. LE11: Lou . . . . . . . . . . . . . . . .5H 19
Alma Rd. LE10: Hinc . . . . . . . . . . . . . . . . . .2G 103
Alma St. LE3: Leic . . . . . . . . . . . . . . . . . . . .7C 64
Almeys La. LE9: Earl S . . . . . . . . . . . . . . . .2E 100
Almond Cl. LE8: Count . . . . . . . . . . . . . . . . .5E 82
   LE11: Lou . . . . . . . . . . . . . . . . . . . . .5E 30
Almond Rd. LE2: Leic . . . . . . . . . .9C 5 (4F 71)
   LE17: Lut . . . . . . . . . . . . . . . . . . . . .4G 153
   LE67: Bag . . . . . . . . . . . . . . . . . . . . .7G 53
Almond Way LE9: Earl S . . . . . . . . . . . . . . .4D 100
Alpine Cl. LE15: O'ham . . . . . . . . . . . . . . . .4G 127
Alport Way LE18: Wig . . . . . . . . . . . . . . . . .6A 78
Alsthorpe Rd. LE15: O'ham . . . . . . . . . . . . .3K 127
Alston Dr. LE11: Lou . . . . . . . . . . . . . . . . . .4B 18
Altar Stones La. LE67: Mark . . . . . . . . . . . . .3E 54
Althorp Cl. LE2: Leic . . . . . . . . . . . . . . . . . .3B 76
   LE16: L Bow . . . . . . . . . . . . . . . . . . .4H 151
Althorpe Dr. LE11: Lou . . . . . . . . . . . . . . . .5A 18
Alton Hill LE67: Rav . . . . . . . . . . . . . . . . . . .2E 36
Alton Rd. LE2: Leic . . . . . . . . . . . . . . . . . . .3E 76
Alton Way LE65: Ash Z . . . . . . . . . . . . . . . .6A 24
ALVASTON . . . . . . . . . . . . . . . . . . . . . . . . .1A 158
Alvaston Rd. LE3: Leic . . . . . . . . . . . . . . . . .6B 70
   LE13: Mel M . . . . . . . . . . . . . . . . . .1A 158
ALVECOTE . . . . . . . . . . . . . . . . . . . . . . . . .1A 162
Alvecote Rd. LE2: Leic . . . . . . . . . . . . . . . . .3D 76
ALVERTON . . . . . . . . . . . . . . . . . . . . . . . . .1A 160
Alvington Way LE16: Mkt H . . . . . . . . . . . . .2D 150
Alvis Dale LE7: R'ley . . . . . . . . . . . . . . . . . .4F 45
ALWALTON . . . . . . . . . . . . . . . . . . . . . . . . .2D 165
Alwyne Cl. LE15: O'ham . . . . . . . . . . . . . . .4J 127
   *(not continuous)*
Alyssum Way LE19: Nar . . . . . . . . . . . . . . .7D 74
Amadis Rd. LE4: Beau L . . . . . . . . . . . . . . .2A 64

Amanda Rd. LE2: Leic . . . . . . . . . . . . . . . . .4B 76
Ambassador Rd. DE74: N Air . . . . . . . . . . . .1K 11
   LE5: Leic . . . . . . . . . . . . . . . . . . . . .1C 72
Ambassador Wlk. LE5: Leic . . . . . . . . . . . . .1C 72
AMBASTON . . . . . . . . . . . . . . . . . . . . . . . .1B 158
Ambergate Cl. LE9: B Ast . . . . . . . . . . . . . .5E 86
Ambergate Dr. LE4: Birs . . . . . . . . . . . . . . .5F 59
Amberley Cl. LE4: Thurm . . . . . . . . . . . . . . .7A 60
Ambion Ct. CV13: Mkt B . . . . . . . . . . . . . . .2C 94
Ambion Ri. CV13: Mkt B . . . . . . . . . . . . . . .3B 94
Ambion Way LE10: Hinc . . . . . . . . . . . . . . .2J 103
Ambler Cl. LE18: Wig . . . . . . . . . . . . . . . . .7K 77
Ambleside LE9: Barw . . . . . . . . . . . . . . . . .3B 100
Ambleside Cl. LE2: Leic . . . . . . . . . . . . . . . .5C 76
   LE11: Lou . . . . . . . . . . . . . . . . . . . . .3B 30
Ambleside Dr. LE2: Leic . . . . . . . . . . . . . . . .4C 76
Ambleside Way LE2: Leic . . . . . . . . . . . . . . .5C 76
   LE3: Mel M . . . . . . . . . . . . . . . . . . .5D 116
Ambrose Cl. LE3: Leic . . . . . . . . . . . . . . . . .1B 70
Amersham Rd. LE4: Leic . . . . . . . . . . . . . . .5D 64
Amersham Way DE12: Mea . . . . . . . . . . . . .6D 34
Amesbury Ct. LE18: Wig . . . . . . . . . . . . . . . .1J 83
Amesbury Rd. LE18: Wig . . . . . . . . . . . . . . .1J 83
Amhurst Cl. LE3: Leic . . . . . . . . . . . . . . . . .5K 63
Amis Cl. LE11: Lou . . . . . . . . . . . . . . . . . . .5A 18
Amos Rd. LE3: Leic . . . . . . . . . . . . . . . . . . .1H 69
Amsden Ri. LE9: B Ast . . . . . . . . . . . . . . . . .3C 86
Amyson Rd. LE5: Leic . . . . . . . . . . . . . . . . .1E 72
Amy St. LE3: Brau . . . . . . . . . . . . . . . . . . . .1A 76
Ancaster Way LE15: N Luf . . . . . . . . . . . . .1B 136
Anchor Cl. LE12: Hat . . . . . . . . . . . . . . . . . .2J 17
Anchor La. LE12: Hat . . . . . . . . . . . . . . . . . .1J 17
   LE67: Cole . . . . . . . . . . . . . . . . . . . . .3A 26
Andover St. LE2: Leic . . . . . . . . . .5F 4 (2G 71)
Andrew Av. LE9: Cosb . . . . . . . . . . . . . . . . .5H 81
Andrew Cl. CV13: S Gol . . . . . . . . . . . . . . . .3A 98
Andrew Cl. LE2: Leic . . . . . . . . . . .6G 5 (3H 71)
Andrewes Cl. LE3: Leic . . . . . . . . . . . . . . . .2D 70
Andrewes St. LE3: Leic . . . . . . . . . . . . . . . .2D 70
Andrewes Wlk. LE3: Leic . . . . . . . . . . . . . . .2D 70
Andrew Macdonald Cl. LE16: Mkt H . . . . . .4F 151
Andrew Rd. LE7: Anst . . . . . . . . . . . . . . . . .7J 57
Andrews Cl. LE17: Leire . . . . . . . . . . . . . . .1K 143
Aneford Rd. LE4: Leic . . . . . . . . . . . . . . . . .5A 66
Anemone Cl. LE13: Mel M . . . . . . . . . . . . . .7D 116
Angela Dr. LE5: Leic . . . . . . . . . . . . . . . . . .3D 72
Angel Cl. LE16: Mkt H . . . . . . . . . . . . . . . . .4E 150
Angel St. LE16: Mkt H . . . . . . . . . . . . . . . . .4E 150
Angel Yd. LE11: Lou . . . . . . . . . . . . . . . . . .6F 19
Angle La. LE15: S Luf . . . . . . . . . . . . . . . . .3B 136
Anglesey Rd. LE18: Wig . . . . . . . . . . . . . . . .5F 77
Angus Cl. LE7: Thurn . . . . . . . . . . . . . . . . . .1H 73
Angus Dr. LE11: Lou . . . . . . . . . . . . . . . . . .6B 18
Angus Rd. LE9: Barw . . . . . . . . . . . . . . . . . .4K 99
Ankle Hill LE13: Mel M . . . . . . . . . . . . . . . .6F 117
Annies Wharf LE11: Lou . . . . . . . . . . . . . . . .5F 19
Ann St. LE1: Leic . . . . . . . . . . . . .3F 4 (1G 71)
Ann's Way LE2: Oad . . . . . . . . . . . . . . . . . .4E 78
Annwell La. LE65: Smis . . . . . . . . . . . . . . . .2G 23
ANSLEY . . . . . . . . . . . . . . . . . . . . . . . . . . .2A 162
Anson Rd. DE74: N Air . . . . . . . . . . . . . . . . .1J 11
   LE12: Shep . . . . . . . . . . . . . . . . . . . .7B 16
ANSTEY . . . . . . . . . . . . . . . . .7J 57 (1C 163)
Anstey Frith LE3: Glen . . . . . . . . . . . . . . . . .4J 63
Anstey La. LE4: Leic . . . . . . . . . . . . . . . . . .3A 64
   LE6: Groby . . . . . . . . . . . . . . . . . . . .3E 62
   *(not continuous)*
   LE7: Anst . . . . . . . . . . . . . . . . . . . . . .2J 63
   LE7: Thurc . . . . . . . . . . . . . . . . . . . . .5K 57
ANSTY . . . . . . . . . . . . . . . . . . . . . . . . . . . .3A 162
Anthony Cl. LE7: Sys . . . . . . . . . . . . . . . . . .3A 60
Anthony Dr. LE7: Thurn . . . . . . . . . . . . . . . .2H 73
Anthony Rd. LE4: Leic . . . . . . . . . . . . . . . . .5D 64
Anthony St. LE7: R'ley . . . . . . . . . . . . . . . . .6E 44
Antill Cl. LE14: Ash . . . . . . . . . . . . . . . . . . .2G 115
Antringham Cl. LE5: Ham . . . . . . . . . . . . . . .4E 66
APETHORPE . . . . . . . . . . . . . . . . . . . . . . . .2D 165
Apiary Ga. DE74: C Don . . . . . . . . . . . . . . . .5K 7
Apollo Cl. LE2: Leic . . . . . . . . . . .4G 4 (2H 71)
Apollo Ct. LE2: Leic . . . . . . . . . . .5G 4 (2H 71)
Applebee Rd. LE10: Bur . . . . . . . . . . . . . . . .5F 103
Applebees Mdw. LE10: Hinc . . . . . . . . . . . . .5B 102
Applebees Wlk. LE10: Hinc . . . . . . . . . . . . .5C 102
Appleby Cl. LE3: Leic . . . . . . . . . . . . . . . . . .2G 69
Appleby Ho. LE10: Hinc . . . . . . . . . . . . . . . .2H 103
Appleby La. DE12: Snar . . . . . . . . . . . . . . . .6F 49
APPLEBY MAGNA . . . . . . . . . .5B 48 (1A 162)
APPLEBY PARVA . . . . . . . . . . .7A 48 (1A 162)
Appleby Rd. LE4: Thurm . . . . . . . . . . . . . . .6C 60
Applegate LE1: Leic . . . . . . . . . . .4B 4 (2E 70)
Appleton Av. LE4: Leic . . . . . . . . . . . . . . . . .2D 64
Appleton Dr. LE12: Wym . . . . . . . . . . . . . . . .2J 21
Apple Tree Cl. CV13: Nail . . . . . . . . . . . . . . .2C 92
   LE9: Barw . . . . . . . . . . . . . . . . . . . . .1A 100
Approach, The LE5: Leic . . . . . . . . . . . . . . . .3B 72
April Ho. LE15: Ext . . . . . . . . . . . . . . . . . . .2D 128

Aqueduct Rd. LE67: Cole . . . . . .3J 25
Aquitance Ct. LE19: End . . . . . .5E 74
Arbor Ct. LE2: Leic . . . . . .3H 71
Arbor Rd. LE9: Crof . . . . . .5A 80
Arbour Rd. LE4: Leic . . . . . .4H 65
Arbury Dale LE12: Shep . . . . . .1E 28
Arcade, The LE18: Wig . . . . . .5K 77
Archdale St. LE7: Sys . . . . . .2B 60
Archdeacon La. LE1: Leic . . . . . .1D 4 (7F 65)
Archer Cl. LE4: Leic . . . . . .2K 65
LE11: Lou . . . . . .4K 17
Archers Grn. LE7: East G . . . . . .5F 47
Archers La. LE9: Peck . . . . . .5H 95
Archers Rdbt. LE8: G Gle . . . . . .2J 85
Archery Cl. LE8: Count . . . . . .5F 83
Archway Rd. LE5: Leic . . . . . .5G 67
Ardath Rd. LE4: Leic . . . . . .5J 65
Arden Av. LE3: Brau . . . . . .6K 69
Arden Cl. LE16: Mkt H . . . . . .3G 151
Arden Dr. LE13: Mel M . . . . . .3D 116
Arden Ter. LE3: Leic . . . . . .5B 70
Arden Way LE16: Mkt H . . . . . .2F 151
Argents Mead LE10: Hinc . . . . . .3G 103
Argent's Mead Wlk. LE10: Hinc . . . . . .3G 103
Argosy Rd. DE74: N Air . . . . . .1B 12
Arguile Pl. LE10: Hinc . . . . . .2F 103
Argyle Pk. LE16: Mkt H . . . . . .7E 150
Argyle St. LE67: Ibs . . . . . .3K 51
Arkwright Cotts. LE9: B Ast . . . . . .5D 86
Arkwright Ho. LE9: B Ast . . . . . .3C 86
Armada Ct. LE10: Hinc . . . . . .4E 102
Armadale Cl. LE10: Hinc . . . . . .2D 102
Armadale Dr. LE5: Leic . . . . . .6E 66
Armadale Grn. LE5: Leic . . . . . .6E 66
Armetts La. LE12: Osg . . . . . .6D 14
Armitage Cl. LE11: Lou . . . . . .6E 18
Armour Cl. LE10: Bur . . . . . .6G 103
Armson Av. LE9: K Mux . . . . . .2C 68
ARMSTON . . . . . .3D 165
Armston Rd. LE9: Cosb . . . . . .6H 81
LE12: Quo . . . . . .6A 32
Arncliffe Rd. LE5: Leic . . . . . .6E 66
Arndale LE18: Wig . . . . . .7B 78
ARNESBY . . . . . .2H 147 (2D 163)
Arnesby Cres. LE2: Leic . . . . . .3F 77
Arnesby La. LE8: Peat M . . . . . .1K 147 & 2F 147
Arnesby Rd. LE8: Flec . . . . . .6A 88
Arnhem St. LE1: Leic . . . . . .5E 4 (2G 71)
Arnold Av. LE18: Wig . . . . . .7G 77
Arnold Cl. LE9: Cosb . . . . . .7H 81
Arnold Rd. CV13: S Gol . . . . . .4A 98
Arnold's Cres. LE9: N Ver . . . . . .7H 93
Arnold Smith Ho. LE12: Shep . . . . . .6D 16
(off Bridge St.)
Arnold St. LE1: Leic . . . . . .1G 4 (7H 65)
Arnside Cl. DE11: C Gre . . . . . .2A 22
Arran Rd. LE4: Leic . . . . . .2K 65
Arran Way LE8: Count . . . . . .6F 83
LE10: Hinc . . . . . .2E 102
Arreton Ct. LE2: Leic . . . . . .1J 77
ARTHINGWORTH . . . . . .3A 164
Arthur St. LE9: Barw . . . . . .3A 100
LE11: Lou . . . . . .7E 18
Artisan Rd. LE14: O Dal . . . . . .6D 110
Arum Way LE3: Leic . . . . . .1H 69
Arundel Cl. LE12: Moun . . . . . .4C 44
Arundel Gro. LE12: Shep . . . . . .1C 28
Arundel St. LE3: Leic . . . . . .2D 70
Ascot Dr. LE67: Coal . . . . . .4G 39
Ascot Rd. LE4: Leic . . . . . .4H 65
ASFORDBY . . . . . .2G 115 (3A 160)
Asfordby Bus. Pk.
LE14: Welb . . . . . .1A 116
ASFORDBY HILL . . . . . .4A 116 (3A 160)
Asfordby Pl. LE14: Ash . . . . . .3G 115
Asfordby Rd. LE13: Mel M . . . . . .4A 116
LE14: Ash H . . . . . .4A 116
LE14: Hob . . . . . .1C 114
Asfordby St. LE5: Leic . . . . . .1K 71
Asha Margh LE4: Leic . . . . . .4G 65
Ashbourne Rd. LE18: Wig . . . . . .4J 77
Ashbourne St. LE2: Leic . . . . . .2J 71
Ashburton Cl. LE10: Bur . . . . . .5K 103
Ashburton Rd. LE67: Hug . . . . . .5B 38
Ashby Ct. LE10: Hinc . . . . . .7G 99
Ashby Cres. LE11: Lou . . . . . .7B 18
ASHBY-DE-LA-ZOUCH . . . . . .5K 23 (3A 158)
Ashby-de-la-Zouch By-Pass
DE11: Boun . . . . . .1F 23
LE65: Ash Z, Smis . . . . . .1F 23
Ashby-de-la-Zouch Mus. . . . . . .5K 23
ASHBY FOLVILLE . . . . . .3E 118 (3A 160)
Ashby Grange LE10: Hinc . . . . . .5H 99
Ashby La. DE11: Blac . . . . . .2E 22
LE17: Bitt . . . . . .2H 153
LE67: Swep . . . . . .2B 50
ASHBY MAGNA . . . . . .1G 145 (2C 163)

Ashby Pk. LE65: Ash Z . . . . . .4C 24
ASHBY PARVA . . . . . .6K 143 (3C 163)
Ashby Parva Rd. LE17: D Bas . . . . . .3B 144
Ashby Ri. LE8: G Gle . . . . . .7K 79
Ashby Rd. CV9: Twy . . . . . .2C 90
CV13: Cad . . . . . .4B 94
DE12: W'lle . . . . . .1C 22
DE12: Don . . . . . .3C 34
DE12: Mea . . . . . .6F 35
DE12: Moi . . . . . .7B 22
DE73: B Hil . . . . . .7A 10
DE74: Keg . . . . . .2D 12
LE7: Gad . . . . . .2A 118
LE9: Barw, Stap . . . . . .4H 99
LE9: Stap . . . . . .1J 99
LE10: Hinc . . . . . .1G 103
LE11: Lou . . . . . .6C 18
LE12: Belt, Grif, Osg . . . . . .6D 14
LE12: Belt, L Wha . . . . . .3A 16
LE14: Ash F . . . . . .3C 118
LE14: T'ord . . . . . .5F 119
LE17: Bitt . . . . . .7A 144
LE17: Frol . . . . . .2F 143
LE17: Gilm . . . . . .5H 145
LE17: P Par . . . . . .3K 145 & 1A 146
LE17: Ull . . . . . .7F 143
LE65: Ash Z, Cole . . . . . .4D 24
(not continuous)
LE65: Pac . . . . . .2A 36
LE67: Coal . . . . . .1H 37
LE67: Cole . . . . . .4G 25
LE67: Grif . . . . . .7A 14
LE67: Ibs . . . . . .3J 51
(not continuous)
LE67: Mark . . . . . .3F 55
LE67: New . . . . . .1H 25
LE67: Rav . . . . . .2G 37
LE67: Thrin . . . . . .2C 26
Ashby Rd. Central LE12: Shep . . . . . .2D 28
Ashby Rd. E. LE12: Shep . . . . . .2E 28
Ashby Rd. W.
LE12: Belt, Shep . . . . . .2J 27
Ashby Sq. LE11: Lou . . . . . .6E 18
Ash Cl. DE72: A Tre . . . . . .1D 6
LE6: Ratby . . . . . .5A 62
LE12: Bar S . . . . . .2D 32
LE15: Upp . . . . . .3D 138
Ashclose Av. LE2: Leic . . . . . .1J 77
Ash Ct. LE2: Leic . . . . . .8C 5
LE6: Groby . . . . . .4C 62
Ash Cft. CV9: S Mag . . . . . .6C 90
Ash Dale LE67: Thrin . . . . . .4D 26
Ashdale LE67: Ibs . . . . . .4J 51
Ashdown Av. LE3: Leic . . . . . .1B 70
Ashdown Cl. LE11: Lou . . . . . .5A 18
Ashdown Rd. LE18: Wig . . . . . .4K 77
Ash Dr. DE12: Mea . . . . . .6E 34
LE7: Sys . . . . . .3D 60
Ashfield LE15: O'ham . . . . . .2J 127
Ashfield Dr. DE12: Moi . . . . . .5D 22
LE7: Anst . . . . . .1H 63
Ashfield Rd. LE2: Leic . . . . . .4J 71
LE4: Thurm . . . . . .5B 60
LE16: Mkt H . . . . . .3E 150
Ashford Ct. LE2: Leic . . . . . .6K 71
Ashford Rd. LE2: Leic . . . . . .6G 71
LE10: Hinc . . . . . .4E 102
LE67: Whit . . . . . .6D 26
ASH GREEN . . . . . .3A 162
Ash Gro. LE8: Bla . . . . . .1B 82
LE12: Hat . . . . . .7K 13
LE12: Moun . . . . . .3E 44
LE13: Mel M . . . . . .2E 116
NG13: Bott . . . . . .1F 107
Ashington Cl. LE3: Leic . . . . . .6B 64
Ashland Dr. LE67: Coal . . . . . .2A 38
Ashlands Way LE19: Nar . . . . . .7D 74
Ashlar Dr. DE12: Don . . . . . .3B 34
Ashleigh Ct. LE3: Glen . . . . . .6G 63
LE3: Leic . . . . . .4C 70
Ashleigh Dr. LE11: Lou . . . . . .1C 30
LE17: Lut . . . . . .4G 153
Ashleigh Gdns. LE3: Leic . . . . . .4C 70
LE9: Barw . . . . . .2B 100
Ashleigh Rd. LE3: Glen . . . . . .6G 63
LE3: Leic . . . . . .3B 70
ASHLEY . . . . . .2A 164
Ashley Rd. LE16: Med . . . . . .7B 140
Ashley Way LE16: L Bow . . . . . .3H 151
Ashlyns Ri. LE3: Leic . . . . . .2J 69
Ashmead Cres. LE4: Birs . . . . . .4J 59
Ashover Cl. LE9: Cosb . . . . . .5H 81
Ashover Rd. LE5: Leic . . . . . .3K 71
Ash Rd. LE9: Crof . . . . . .6B 80
Ash St. LE5: Leic . . . . . .7J 65
Ashthorpe Rd. LE3: Leic . . . . . .3A 70

ASHTON
Peterborough . . . . . .3D 165
Stamford . . . . . .1D 165
Ashton Cl. LE2: Oad . . . . . .5C 78
LE13: Mel M . . . . . .6F 117
LE18: Wig . . . . . .7J 77
Ash Tree Cl. LE2: Oad . . . . . .4D 78
Ash Tree Rd. LE2: Oad . . . . . .4D 78
LE9: Cosb . . . . . .6H 81
LE67: Hug . . . . . .5B 38
Ashtree Rd. LE5: Ham . . . . . .4E 66
Ashurst Cl. LE18: Wig . . . . . .1A 84
Ashurst Rd. LE3: Brau . . . . . .7K 69
Ashville Trad. Est. LE8: Whet . . . . . .5J 81
Ashville Way LE8: Whet . . . . . .4J 81
Ash Way LE14: F Wre . . . . . .5H 115
ASHWELL . . . . . .6H 123 (3B 160)
Ashwell Hall Stables
LE15: A'll . . . . . .7H 123
Ashwell Ho. LE15: A'll . . . . . .6G 123
Ashwell Rd. LE15: A'll . . . . . .7F 123
(not continuous)
LE15: Cott . . . . . .7A 124
LE15: L'ham . . . . . .4D 122
LE15: O'ham . . . . . .3J 127
LE15: Whis . . . . . .2E 122
Ashwell St. LE1: Leic . . . . . .6E 5 (3G 71)
Askrigg Way LE18: Wig . . . . . .6A 78
ASLACKBY . . . . . .1D 161
ASLOCKTON . . . . . .1A 160
Aspen Av. LE11: Lou . . . . . .4E 30
Aspen Cl. DE12: Mea . . . . . .6E 34
LE67: Rav . . . . . .2A 38
Aspen Dr. LE8: Count . . . . . .5E 82
Aspens Hollow LE67: Thrin . . . . . .4D 26
Aspen Way LE17: Lut . . . . . .3H 153
Asplin Rd. LE2: Leic . . . . . .3E 76
Asquith Blvd. LE2: Leic . . . . . .3G 77
(not continuous)
Asquith Way LE2: Leic . . . . . .3G 77
Assheton La. CV9: Twy . . . . . .2C 90
Assured Cl. LE4: Thurm . . . . . .6K 59
Aster Cl. LE10: Bur . . . . . .5H 103
Aster Way LE10: Bur . . . . . .5G 103
Astill Cl. LE6: Ratby . . . . . .6C 62
Astill Dr. LE4: Leic . . . . . .2F 65
Astill Lodge Rd. LE4: Beau L . . . . . .7A 58
ASTLEY . . . . . .3A 162
Astley Cl. LE3: Leic . . . . . .4B 70
LE16: Mkt H . . . . . .6D 150
Astley Rd. LE9: Earl S . . . . . .2E 100
Astley Way LE65: Ash Z . . . . . .4B 24
ASTON FLAMVILLE . . . . . .5D 104 (2B 162)
Aston Flamville Rd. LE10: Bur . . . . . .4B 104
Aston Hall Dr. DE72: A Tre . . . . . .1C 6
Aston Hill LE2: Leic . . . . . .7G 71
Aston La. DE72: A Tre . . . . . .1E 6
(not continuous)
LE10: A Fla . . . . . .4B 104
LE10: Bur . . . . . .5K 103
LE67: S'ord . . . . . .6F 105
ASTON-ON-TRENT . . . . . .1C 6 (2B 158)
ASWARBY . . . . . .1D 161
ATHERSTONE . . . . . .2A 162
Atherstone By-Pass CV9: Ath . . . . . .5A 96
Atherstone Cl. LE2: Oad . . . . . .3F 79
Atherstone Rd. CV13: Att, F Dray . . . . . .4H 97
DE12: A Mag, A Par . . . . . .5A 48
DE12: Mea . . . . . .1E 48
LE11: Lou . . . . . .4D 30
Atkinson Rd. LE65: Ash Z . . . . . .4H 23
Atkinson St. LE5: Leic . . . . . .1K 71
(not continuous)
Atkins St. LE2: Leic . . . . . .6C 5 (3F 71)
Atkins Way LE10: Bur . . . . . .1H 103
Atlas Cl. LE2: Leic . . . . . .4G 4 (2H 71)
Atlas Ct. LE67: Coal . . . . . .2D 38
Atlas Ho. LE67: Coal . . . . . .3C 38
Atlas Rd. LE67: Coal . . . . . .2D 38
ATTENBOROUGH . . . . . .1C 159
Attenborough Cl. LE3: Brau . . . . . .6H 69
LE18: Wig . . . . . .4A 78
Atterbury Cl. LE12: Bar S . . . . . .4D 32
Atterton La. CV9: With . . . . . .5B 96
Attfield Dr. LE8: Whet . . . . . .2K 81
Attingham Cl. LE4: Leic . . . . . .5K 65
ATTLEBOROUGH . . . . . .2A 162
Attlebridge Cl. LE5: Ham . . . . . .4D 66
Attlee Cl. LE17: Lut . . . . . .5H 153
Attlee Way LE17: Lut . . . . . .3E 76
Auburn Ho. LE3: Leic . . . . . .7A 64
LE8: Bla . . . . . .1A 82
Auburn Pl. LE17: Lut . . . . . .3H 153
Auburn Rd. LE8: Bla . . . . . .1A 82
Auden Cl. LE4: Leic . . . . . .4B 64
Audit Hall Rd. LE15: Emp . . . . . .7B 128
Audley Cl. LE16: L Bow . . . . . .5H 151

Audley End LE3: Leic . . . . . . . . . . . . . . .6B **70**
Augusta Cl. LE3: Leic . . . . . . . . . . . . .1G **69**
Augustus Cl. LE7: Sys . . . . . . . . . . . .3B **60**
Aulton Cres. LE10: Hinc . . . . . . . . .2E **102**
Aulton Way LE10: Hinc . . . . . . . . . .2E **102**
Aumberry Gap LE11: Lou . . . . . . . . . .6F **19**
AUNBY . . . . . . . . . . . . . . . . . . . . . . . .3D **161**
AUNSBY . . . . . . . . . . . . . . . . . . . . . . .1D **161**
Auriga St. LE16: Mkt H . . . . . . . . . . .5F **151**
Auster Ind. Est. LE4: Thurm . . . . . .7B **60**
Austhorp Gro. LE15: Cott . . . . . . . .7A **124**
Austin Ri. LE5: Leic . . . . . . . . . . . . . .5E **66**
Austins Cl. LE16: Mkt H . . . . . . . . .4D **150**
AUSTREY . . . . . . . . . . . . . . . . . . . . . .1A **162**
Austrey La. LE8: Count . . . . . . . . . . .7F **83**
Austrey Rd. DE12: A Par . . . . . . . . .7A **48**
Austwick Cl. LE4: Leic . . . . . . . . . . .3C **64**
Autumn Rd. LE2: Leic . . . . . . . . . . .5C **76**
Avalon Way LE7: Anst . . . . . . . . . . . .1J **63**
Avebury Av. LE4: Leic . . . . . . . . . . .5C **64**
Aveland Rd. PE9: Ket . . . . . . . . . . .6G **137**
Avenue, The DE72: W Tre . . . . . . . . .3B **6**
  LE2: Leic . . . . . . . . . . . . . . . . . . . .5J **71**
  LE2: Oad . . . . . . . . . . . . . . . . . . . .4J **79**
  LE3: Glen . . . . . . . . . . . . . . . . . . .5F **63**
  LE8: Bla . . . . . . . . . . . . . . . . . . . .1A **82**
  LE9: B Ast . . . . . . . . . . . . . . . . . .3C **86**
Avenue Cl. LE7: Quen . . . . . . . . . . .7F **47**
Avenue Gdns. LE2: Leic . . . . . . . . .6J **71**
Avenue Nth. LE9: Earl S . . . . . . . . .2F **101**
Avenue Rd. LE2: Leic . . . . . . . . . . .6J **71**
  LE7: Quen . . . . . . . . . . . . . . . . . .7G **47**
  LE12: Sileby . . . . . . . . . . . . . . . . .1K **45**
  LE65: Ash Z . . . . . . . . . . . . . . . . .6J **23**
  LE67: Coal . . . . . . . . . . . . . . . . . .4D **38**
Avenue Rd. Extension LE2: Leic . . .6G **71**
Avenue Sth. LE9: Earl S . . . . . . . . .2F **101**
Averil Rd. LE5: Leic . . . . . . . . . . . . .7D **66**
Avery Cl. LE17: Lut . . . . . . . . . . . . .5H **153**
Avery Dr. LE7: Sys . . . . . . . . . . . . . .7D **46**
  LE67: Mark . . . . . . . . . . . . . . . . . .4F **55**
Avery Hill LE3: Leic . . . . . . . . . . . . .3H **69**
Avington Cl. LE3: Leic . . . . . . . . . . .4A **64**
Avoca Cl. LE5: Leic . . . . . . . . . . . . .1D **72**
Avocet Cl. PE9: Ess . . . . . . . . . . . .1J **129**
Avon Cl. LE2: Oad . . . . . . . . . . . . . .3E **78**
  LE15: O'ham . . . . . . . . . . . . . . . .5H **127**
Avondale Rd. CV13: B'one . . . . . . .6B **92**
  LE18: Wig . . . . . . . . . . . . . . . . . . .5K **77**
Avon Dr. LE8: Whet . . . . . . . . . . . . .2K **81**
Avon Rd. LE3: Brau . . . . . . . . . . . . .5J **69**
  LE12: Bar S . . . . . . . . . . . . . . . . .5D **32**
  LE13: Mel M . . . . . . . . . . . . . . . .5E **116**
Avonside Dr. LE5: Leic . . . . . . . . . .2B **72**
Avon St. LE2: Leic . . . . . . . . . . . . . .3H **71**
Avon Va. Rd. LE11: Lou . . . . . . . . . .2G **31**
Avon Wlk. LE10: Hinc . . . . . . . . . . .3D **102**
Axbridge Cl. LE4: Leic . . . . . . . . . . .5D **64**
Ayces Cotts. LE13: Mel M . . . . . . . .4D **116**
AYLESTONE . . . . . . . . . . . .2C **76** (1C **163**)
Aylestone Dr. LE2: Leic . . . . . . . . . .3D **76**
Aylestone La. LE18: Wig . . . . . . . . .4G **77**
Aylestone Leisure Cen. . . . . . . . . . .7F **71**
AYLESTONE PARK . . . . . . . . . . . . .1F **77**
Aylestone Rd. LE2: Leic . . . .10B **5** (2C **76**)
Aylestone Wlk. LE2: Leic . . .9C **5** (4F **71**)
Aylmer Rd. LE3: Leic . . . . . . . . . . . .3K **69**
Ayrshire Cl. LE9: Barw . . . . . . . . . .4K **99**
Aysgarth Rd. LE4: Leic . . . . . . . . . .3C **64**
AYSTON . . . . . . . . . . . . . . . . . . . . . . .1B **164**
Ayston Rd. LE3: Brau . . . . . . . . . . .6A **70**
  LE15: Upp . . . . . . . . . . . . . . . . . .1B **138**
Azalea Cl. LE10: Bur . . . . . . . . . . . .6H **103**
  LE17: Lut . . . . . . . . . . . . . . . . . . .5G **153**
Azalea Dr. LE10: Bur . . . . . . . . . . . .5H **103**
Azalea Wlk. LE10: Bur . . . . . . . . . . .6H **103**

### B

Babelake St. LE65: Pac . . . . . . . . . .4K **35**
Babingley Dr. LE4: Leic . . . . . . . . . .4D **64**
Babington Ct. LE7: R'ley . . . . . . . . .6E **44**
Babington Rd. LE7: R'ley . . . . . . . . .6E **44**
  LE12: Bar S . . . . . . . . . . . . . . . . .3D **32**
Babington Row LE2: Leic . . . . . . . .3G **77**
Back La. CV13: Mkt B . . . . . . . . . . .2C **94**
  DE72: Shar . . . . . . . . . . . . . . . . . .1J **7**
  DE74: C Don . . . . . . . . . . . . . . . . .3J **7**
  LE7: Coss . . . . . . . . . . . . . . . . . . .5K **45**
  LE7: Thru . . . . . . . . . . . . . . . . . . .7B **114**
  LE8: Bur O . . . . . . . . . . . . . . . . . .6D **130**
  LE12: Cote . . . . . . . . . . . . . . . . . .4K **19**
  LE12: Sileby . . . . . . . . . . . . . . . . .1J **45**
  LE14: Hob . . . . . . . . . . . . . . . . . .2B **114**
  LE14: L Cla . . . . . . . . . . . . . . . . .2H **111**
  LE15: Bel R . . . . . . . . . . . . . . . . .5G **133**

Back La. LE15: Mor . . . . . . . . . . . . .6J **135**
  LE15: S Luf . . . . . . . . . . . . . . . . .4B **136**
  LE16: East L . . . . . . . . . . . . . . . .3A **140**
  LE17: C Mag . . . . . . . . . . . . . . . .5C **142**
  LE17: Leire . . . . . . . . . . . . . . . . .2J **143**
  LE17: Shea . . . . . . . . . . . . . . . . .5J **147**
  NG33: Sew . . . . . . . . . . . . . . . . .7J **113**
  PE9: Ryh . . . . . . . . . . . . . . . . . .4H **129**
Back Rd. LE7: T Hil . . . . . . . . . . . . .3G **131**
  LE15: B'den . . . . . . . . . . . . . . . . .7C **136**
Back St. LE17: N Kil . . . . . . . . . . . .3K **155**
  NG33: Buck . . . . . . . . . . . . . . . . .5G **113**
Back Wlk. LE14: W'ham . . . . . . . . .1H **121**
Badcock Way LE8: Flec . . . . . . . . . .5C **88**
Baddeley Dr. LE18: Wig . . . . . . . . . .4H **77**
BADDESLEY ENSOR . . . . . . . . . . .2A **162**
Baden Rd. LE5: Leic . . . . . . . . . . . .4A **72**
Badger Cl. LE8: Flec . . . . . . . . . . . .5C **88**
Badger Ct. LE11: Lou . . . . . . . . . . . .3B **30**
Badger Dr. LE8: Whet . . . . . . . . . . .4K **81**
Badgers Bank LE7: R'ley . . . . . . . . .5E **44**
Badgers Cl. LE4: Leic . . . . . . . . . . .3B **64**
  LE15: Mant . . . . . . . . . . . . . . . . .3B **134**
  LE19: Nar . . . . . . . . . . . . . . . . . . .2E **80**
Badger's Cnr. LE7: East G . . . . . . . .4F **47**
Badgers Holt LE2: Oad . . . . . . . . . .4C **78**
Badgers Mead LE9: K Mux . . . . . . .2A **68**
Badgers Wlk. LE12: Quo . . . . . . . . .6J **31**
Badminton Rd. LE4: Leic . . . . . . . .1K **65**
  LE7: Sys . . . . . . . . . . . . . . . . . . . .7D **46**
BAGGRAVE . . . . . . . . . . . . . . . . . . .1D **163**
Baggrave End LE14: Bars . . . . . . . .5C **118**
Baggrave St. LE5: Leic . . . . . . . . . .1K **71**
Bagley Cl. LE11: Lou . . . . . . . . . . . .4A **18**
BAGWORTH . . . . . . . . . .1F **93** (1B **162**)
Bagworth La. LE67: Thor . . . . . . . . .1H **93**
Bagworth Rd. CV13: B'one . . . . . . .5C **92**
  CV13: Nail . . . . . . . . . . . . . . . . . .2C **92**
Bailey Cl. LE11: Lou . . . . . . . . . . . .3B **30**
Baileys La. LE8: Bur O . . . . . . . . . .5D **130**
Bainbridge Rd. LE3: Leic . . . . . . . .6B **70**
  LE11: Lou . . . . . . . . . . . . . . . . . . .2G **31**
  LE18: Wig . . . . . . . . . . . . . . . . . . .7A **78**
Baines Ct. LE15: O'ham . . . . . . . . .4H **127**
Baines La. LE3: Leic E . . . . . . . . . .4F **69**
  LE10: Hinc . . . . . . . . . . . . . . . . . .2G **103**
  LE15: Seat . . . . . . . . . . . . . . . . .5K **139**
BAINTON . . . . . . . . . . . . . . . . . . . . .1D **165**
Bakehouse La. LE8: Sad . . . . . . . . .7D **88**
Baker Av. LE65: Ash Z . . . . . . . . . . .6H **23**
Bakers La. LE14: T Sat . . . . . . . . . .3H **119**
  NG13: Red . . . . . . . . . . . . . . . . .1E **106**
Baker St. DE11: Swad . . . . . . . . . . .1A **42**
  LE17: Lut . . . . . . . . . . . . . . . . . . .5J **153**
  LE67: Coal . . . . . . . . . . . . . . . . . .2C **38**
Bakers Way LE5: Ham . . . . . . . . . . .3F **67**
Bakery Cl. LE9: Cosb . . . . . . . . . . .7H **81**
Bakery Ct. LE65: Ash Z . . . . . . . . . .5K **23**
Bakewell Ct. LE67: Coal . . . . . . . . .3E **38**
Bakewell Dr. DE74: C Don . . . . . . . .6J **7**
Bakewell Rd. LE11: Lou . . . . . . . . . .3C **18**
  LE18: Wig . . . . . . . . . . . . . . . . . . .4J **77**
Bakewells La. LE67: Cole . . . . . . . .4K **25**
Bakewell St. LE2: Leic . . . . . . . . . . .2J **71**
  LE67: Coal . . . . . . . . . . . . . . . . . .3E **38**
Bala Rd. LE9: Crof . . . . . . . . . . . . . .5B **80**
Balcombe Av. LE3: Leic . . . . . . . . . .1B **70**
Balderstone Cl. LE5: Leic . . . . . . . .2C **72**
Baldock's La. LE13: Mel M . . . . . . .6G **117**
Baldwin Av. LE18: Wig . . . . . . . . . . .7G **77**
Baldwin Ri. LE9: B Ast . . . . . . . . . . .3B **86**
Baldwin Rd. LE2: Leic . . . . . . . . . . .3H **77**
Bale Rd. LE4: Leic . . . . . . . . . . . . . .5A **66**
Balfour Cl. LE10: Hinc . . . . . . . . . . .4H **103**
Balfour Gdns. LE16: Mkt H . . . . . . .6D **150**
Balfour St. LE3: Leic . . . . . . . . . . . .7D **64**
Balisfire Gro. LE4: Leic . . . . . . . . . .3B **64**
Balk, The LE3: Glen . . . . . . . . . . . . .5F **63**
Balk Rd. PE9: Ryh . . . . . . . . . . . . . .5G **129**
Balladine Rd. LE7: Anst . . . . . . . . . .6J **57**
Ballards Cl. LE4: Leic . . . . . . . . . . .3B **64**
Ballater Cl. LE5: Leic . . . . . . . . . . . .4F **73**
Balliol Av. LE7: Sys . . . . . . . . . . . . .3E **60**
Balliol Rd. LE10: Bur . . . . . . . . . . . .5J **103**
Balmoral Av. LE12: Shep . . . . . . . . .1C **28**
Balmoral Cl. LE2: Leic . . . . . . . . . . .1J **77**
  LE16: L Bow . . . . . . . . . . . . . . . .5H **151**
Balmoral Ct. DE74: Hem . . . . . . . . .3B **8**
Balmoral Dr. LE3: Brau . . . . . . . . . .5J **69**
Balmoral Rd. LE9: Earl S . . . . . . . .3C **100**
  LE12: Moun . . . . . . . . . . . . . . . . .3D **44**
  LE13: Mel M . . . . . . . . . . . . . . . .2F **117**
  LE15: O'ham . . . . . . . . . . . . . . . .5G **127**
  LE67: Coal . . . . . . . . . . . . . . . . . .4F **39**
Bambrook Cl. LE9: Des . . . . . . . . . .2J **95**
Bamburgh Cl. LE16: L Bow . . . . . . .4H **151**
  LE65: Ash Z . . . . . . . . . . . . . . . . .6K **23**

Bambury La. LE8: Count . . . . . . . . .7D **82**
  LE8: Peat M . . . . . . . . . . . . . . . . .1K **147**
Bambury Way LE2: Leic . . . . . . . . . .2G **77**
Bampton Cl. LE18: Wig . . . . . . . . . .1K **83**
Bampton St. LE11: Lou . . . . . . . . . .7F **19**
  LE13: Mel M . . . . . . . . . . . . . . . .7G **117**
Banbury Dr. LE12: Shep . . . . . . . . .7B **16**
Banbury La. LE16: G Eas . . . . . . . .6K **141**
Bandalls La. LE12: Bar S . . . . . . . . .5A **20**
Banff Cl. LE15: O'ham . . . . . . . . . . .4K **127**
Bank, The LE8: Arne . . . . . . . . . . . .2H **147**
  LE8: Count . . . . . . . . . . . . . . . . . .5F **83**
  LE8: K Bea . . . . . . . . . . . . . . . . . .3J **89**
  LE17: Shea . . . . . . . . . . . . . . . . .5J **147**
Bankart Av. LE2: Leic . . . . . . . . . . .6A **72**
Bankfield Dr. LE16: G Bow . . . . . . .2G **151**
Banks, The LE7: Quen . . . . . . . . . . .7G **47**
  LE9: Cosb . . . . . . . . . . . . . . . . . .7H **81**
  LE12: Bar S . . . . . . . . . . . . . . . . .3D **32**
  LE12: Sea . . . . . . . . . . . . . . . . . .3K **33**
  LE12: Sileby . . . . . . . . . . . . . . . . .1J **45**
Banks Cl., The LE12: Sileby . . . . . .1J **45**
Bankside LE5: Leic . . . . . . . . . . . . .6G **67**
Banks Rd. LE2: Leic . . . . . . . . . . . .1D **76**
Banks Sports Club . . . . . . . . . . . . .1D **76**
Bank St. LE17: Lut . . . . . . . . . . . . .5J **153**
Bank Ter. LE9: Barw . . . . . . . . . . . .4K **99**
Banky Mdw. LE10: Bur . . . . . . . . . .4K **103**
Bannerman Rd. LE5: Leic . . . . . . . .4K **71**
Bannister Rd. LE3: Brau . . . . . . . . .2K **75**
Bantlam La. LE19: End . . . . . . . . . .5F **75**
Baptist M., The LE8: Bla . . . . . . . . .7C **76**
Baptist Wlk. LE10: Hinc . . . . . . . . . .2G **103**
Barbara Av. LE5: Leic . . . . . . . . . . .7D **66**
  LE9: Leic E . . . . . . . . . . . . . . . . .4C **68**
  LE9: N Ver . . . . . . . . . . . . . . . . . .7H **93**
Barbara Cl. LE19: End . . . . . . . . . . .5E **74**
Barbara Rd. LE3: Leic . . . . . . . . . . .6B **70**
Barclay St. LE3: Leic . . . . . . . . . . . .3C **70**
Barden Cl. LE11: Lou . . . . . . . . . . . .7K **17**
Bardolph St. LE4: Leic . . . . . . . . . .6H **65**
Bardolph St. E. LE4: Leic . . . . . . . .6J **65**
BARDON . . . . . . . . . . . . . .5G **39** (3B **158**)
Bardon 22 Ind. Pk. LE67: Bar . . . . .1H **53**
Bardon Cl. LE3: Leic . . . . . . . . . . . .3K **63**
  LE67: Coal . . . . . . . . . . . . . . . . . .5G **39**
BARDON HILL . . . . . . . . . . . . . . . . .1J **53**
Bardon Rd. LE9: Barw . . . . . . . . . .2A **100**
  LE67: Coal . . . . . . . . . . . . . . . . . .4F **39**
Bardsey Cl. LE10: Hinc . . . . . . . . . .2E **102**
Barfoot Cl. LE8: Flec . . . . . . . . . . . .2A **88**
Barford Rd. LE2: Leic . . . . . . . . . . .3F **77**
Barford Cl. LE18: Wig . . . . . . . . . . .1J **83**
Barge Cl. LE18: Wig . . . . . . . . . . . .1G **83**
BARHOLM . . . . . . . . . . . . . . . . . . . .3D **161**
BARKBY . . . . . . . . . . . . . .5F **61** (3D **159**)
Barkby Holt La. LE7: Bark . . . . . . . .5F **61**
Barkby La. LE7: Sys . . . . . . . . . . . .3B **60**
Barkby Rd. LE4: Leic . . . . . . . . . . . .4K **65**
  LE7: Bee . . . . . . . . . . . . . . . . . . . .1K **67**
  LE7: Quen . . . . . . . . . . . . . . . . . .2G **61**
  LE7: Sys . . . . . . . . . . . . . . . . . . . .1D **60**
BARKBY THORPE . . . . . . . . . . . . . .6E **60**
Barkby Thorpe La. LE4: Thurm . . . .4A **60**
  LE7: Bark T . . . . . . . . . . . . . . . . .4C **60**
Barkbythorpe Rd. LE4: Leic . . . . . . .2B **66**
  LE7: Bark T . . . . . . . . . . . . . . . . .2B **66**
Barker Cres. LE13: Mel M . . . . . . . .7F **117**
Barker Fld. LE14: L Cla . . . . . . . . . .2H **111**
Barker St. LE5: Leic . . . . . . . . . . . .7K **65**
Barkestone La. NG13: Bott . . . . . . .4F **107**
  NG13: Plun . . . . . . . . . . . . . . . . .6C **106**
  NG13: Red . . . . . . . . . . . . . . . . .2B **106**
BARKESTONE-LE-VALE . . . .3B **106** (1A **160**)
Barkford Cl. LE17: Scra . . . . . . . . . .5G **67**
Barklam Cl. DE12: Don . . . . . . . . . .3A **34**
BARKSTON . . . . . . . . . . . . . . . . . . . .1C **161**
BARLESTONE . . . . . . . . . .5C **92** (1B **162**)
Barlestone Dr. LE10: Hinc . . . . . . . .2D **102**
Barlestone Rd. LE9: N Ver . . . .6E **92** & 4G **93**
  LE67: Bag . . . . . . . . . . . . . . . . . .2F **93**
  LE13: Glen . . . . . . . . . . . . . . . . . .6G **63**
Barleyfield LE10: Hinc . . . . . . . . . . .7F **99**
Barley La. LE8: Fost . . . . . . . . . . . .7J **83**
Barleyman Cl. LE5: Leic . . . . . . . . .3E **66**
BARLEYTHORPE . . . . . . . .2F **127** (1B **164**)
Barleythorpe Rd.
  LE15: O'ham . . . . . . . . . . . . . . . .3G **127**
Barley Way LE7: R'ley . . . . . . . . . . .5E **44**
Barling Rd. LE5: Leic . . . . . . . . . . . .6B **66**
Barlow Rd. LE15: O'ham . . . . . . . . .4H **127**
Barmouth Av. LE2: Leic . . . . . . . . . .2G **77**
Barmstedt Cl. LE15: O'ham . . . . . . .3J **127**
  (not continuous)
Barmstedt Dr. LE15: O'ham . . . . . . .2J **127**
BARNACK . . . . . . . . . . . . . . . . . . . .1D **165**
BARNACLE . . . . . . . . . . . . . . . . . . . .3A **162**

Barnard Cl. LE2: Leic . . . . . . . . . . . .5G **4** (2H **71**)
LE14: Bur L . . . . . . . . . . . . . . . . . . .1D **120**
Barnard Gdns. LE16: Mkt H . . . . . . . .7D **150**
Barnards Dr. LE12: Sileby . . . . . . . . . .7K **33**
Barnard Way LE12: Moun . . . . . . . . . .3D **44**
Barnby Av. LE18: Wig . . . . . . . . . . . . .4J **77**
Barn Cl. DE74: C Don . . . . . . . . . . . . .5K **7**
LE18: Wig . . . . . . . . . . . . . . . . . . . .1A **84**
Barn End LE15: Emp . . . . . . . . . . . . .6B **128**
(not continuous)
Barnes Cl. LE4: Leic . . . . . . . . . . . . . .1A **66**
LE8: K Bea . . . . . . . . . . . . . . . . . . .3H **89**
Barnes Heath Rd. LE5: Leic . . . . . . . . .2C **72**
Barnet Cl. LE2: Oad . . . . . . . . . . . . . .5C **78**
Barnett Cl. LE7: Coss . . . . . . . . . . . . .5K **45**
Barnfield Cl. LE8: G Gle . . . . . . . . . . .7K **79**
LE12: L Wha . . . . . . . . . . . . . . . . . .5F **13**
Barngate Cl. LE4: Birs . . . . . . . . . . . . .5F **59**
LE13: Mel M . . . . . . . . . . . . . . . . . .2G **117**
Barnley Cl. LE8: Count . . . . . . . . . . . .5E **82**
Barns Cl. LE9: K Mux . . . . . . . . . . . . .2A **68**
Barnsdale LE16: G Eas . . . . . . . . . . . .6K **141**
Barnsdale Av. LE15: Ext . . . . . . . . . . .4A **128**
Barnsdale Cl. LE11: Lou . . . . . . . . . . .5E **18**
LE16: G Eas . . . . . . . . . . . . . . . . . .6K **141**
Barnsdale Gardens . . . . . . . . . . . . . .3A **128**
Barnsdale Rd. LE4: Beau L . . . . . . . . . .1K **63**
Barnsdale Way LE19: End . . . . . . . . . .3H **75**
Barnstaple Cl. LE18: Wig . . . . . . . . . . .1K **83**
Barnstaple Rd. LE5: Leic . . . . . . . . . . .4F **73**
BARNSTONE . . . . . . . . . . . . . . . . . .1A **160**
Barns Way LE9: Des . . . . . . . . . . . . . .1J **95**
Barn Way LE67: Mark . . . . . . . . . . . . .5G **55**
BARNWELL ALL SAINTS . . . . . . . . . . .3D **165**
Barnwell Av. LE4: Leic . . . . . . . . . . . .2F **65**
BARNWELL ST ANDREW . . . . . . . . . .3D **165**
Baronet Way LE5: Leic . . . . . . . . . . . .5G **67**
Barons Cl. LE9: K Mux . . . . . . . . . . . .2A **68**
Barons Ct. LE12: Moun . . . . . . . . . . .1E **44**
Baron St. LE1: Leic . . . . . . . .4F **4** (2G **71**)
Barons Way LE12: Moun . . . . . . . . . . .1E **44**
Barrack Row LE11: Lou . . . . . . . . . . . .5F **19**
Barracks, The LE9: Barw . . . . . . . . . . .4K **99**
Barradale Av. LE12: Sileby . . . . . . . . . .7J **33**
Barratt Cl. LE2: Leic . . . . . . . . . . . . . .5K **71**
Barrie Rd. LE10: Hinc . . . . . . . . . . . . .7G **99**
Barrington Pk. Ind. Est.
LE4: Beau L . . . . . . . . . . . . . . . . .1B **64**
Barrington Rd. LE2: Leic . . . . . . . . . . .6A **72**
Barr La. CV13: H Hill . . . . . . . . . . . . . .6H **97**
Barroon DE74: C Don . . . . . . . . . . . . .5K **7**
BARROW . . . . . . . . . . . . . .4H **123** (3B **160**)
BARROWBY . . . . . . . . . . . . . . . . . . .1B **160**
Barrowcliffe Cl. LE12: Bar S . . . . . . . . .3C **32**
Barrow Cres. LE7: Gad . . . . . . . . . . . .1A **118**
BARROWDEN . . . . . . . . . . .7D **136** (1C **165**)
Barrowden La. LE15: S Luf . . . . . . . . . .4C **136**
Barrowden Rd. PE9: Ket . . . . . . . . . . .7G **137**
Barrow Rd. LE12: Bur W . . . . . . . . . . .5E **20**
LE12: Cote . . . . . . . . . . . . . . . . . . .4K **19**
LE12: Quo . . . . . . . . . . . . . . . . . . .5K **31**
LE12: Sileby . . . . . . . . . . . . . . . . . .6G **33**
Barrow Rd. Bus. Pk. LE12: Sileby . . . . . .1J **45**
Barrow St. LE11: Lou . . . . . . . . . . . . .7F **19**
BARROW UPON SOAR . . . . . . . . .4D **32** (3C **159**)
Barrow upon Soar Station (Rail) . . . . . .4D **32**
BARROW UPON TRENT . . . . . . . . . . .2A **158**
Barry Cl. LE9: Leic E . . . . . . . . . . . . . .4C **68**
Barry Dr. LE7: Sys . . . . . . . . . . . . . . .1D **60**
LE9: Leic E . . . . . . . . . . . . . . . . . . .4C **68**
Barry Rd. LE5: Leic . . . . . . . . . . . . . .5F **67**
BARSBY . . . . . . . . . . . . . . .5C **118** (3D **159**)
Barsby Dr. LE11: Lou . . . . . . . . . . . . .4B **18**
Barsby Wlk. LE4: Leic . . . . . . . . . . . . .2D **64**
Barshaw Pk. Ind. Est. LE4: Beau L . . . . .1C **64**
Bartholomew St. LE2: Leic . . . . . . . . . .3J **71**
Bartles Hollow PE9: Ket . . . . . . . . . . .6G **137**
Barton Cl. LE6: Ratby . . . . . . . . . . . . .7B **62**
LE18: Wig . . . . . . . . . . . . . . . . . . .7J **77**
BARTON IN FABIS . . . . . . . . . . . . . .1C **159**
BARTON IN THE BEANS . . . . . . . . . . .1A **162**
Barton La. CV13: Con . . . . . . . . . . . . .4J **91**
CV13: Nail . . . . . . . . . . . . . . . . . . .3A **92**
Barton Rd. CV13: Con . . . . . . . . . . . .6G **91**
CV13: Mkt B . . . . . . . . . . . . . . . . . .1C **94**
CV13: Osb . . . . . . . . . . . . . . . . . . .5A **92**
LE3: Leic . . . . . . . . . . . . . . . . . . . .6C **64**
BARTON SEAGRAVE . . . . . . . . . . . . .3B **164**
BARWELL . . . . . . . . . . . . . .4K **99** (2B **162**)
Barwell Bus. Cen. LE9: Barw . . . . . . . .4A **100**
Barwell La. LE9: Barw . . . . . . . . . . . . .5K **99**
LE10: Hinc . . . . . . . . . . . . . . . . . . .7H **99**
Barwell Path LE10: Hinc . . . . . . . . . . .1H **103**
Barwell Rd. LE9: K Mux . . . . . . . . . . .2B **68**
Basin Bri. La. CV13: S Gol . . . . . . . . . .4K **97**

Baslow Rd. LE5: Leic . . . . . . . . . . . . .3K **71**
Bassett Av. LE8: Count . . . . . . . . . . . .6E **82**
Bassett La. LE9: Sap . . . . . . . . . . . . .4J **105**
Bassett St. LE3: Leic . . . . . . . . . . . . .7D **64**
LE18: Wig . . . . . . . . . . . . . . . . . . .7F **77**
BASSINGFIELD . . . . . . . . . . . . . . . . .1D **159**
BASSINGTHORPE . . . . . . . . . . . . . . .2C **161**
BASTON . . . . . . . . . . . . . . . . . . . . .3D **161**
Batchelor Rd. LE8: Flec . . . . . . . . . . . .3B **88**
Bateman Rd. LE3: Leic . . . . . . . . . . . .7A **64**
Bates Cl. LE16: Mkt H . . . . . . . . . . . .2E **150**
Bath Cl. LE9: Sap . . . . . . . . . . . . . . .3J **105**
Bath La. DE12: Moi . . . . . . . . . . . . . .7A **22**
LE3: Leic . . . . . . . . . . . . . .3A **4** (1E **70**)
LE17: Brun . . . . . . . . . . . . . . . . . . .1D **146**
Bath St. LE4: Leic . . . . . . . . . . . . . . .3G **65**
(not continuous)
LE7: Sys . . . . . . . . . . . . . . . . . . . .1C **60**
LE16: Mkt H . . . . . . . . . . . . . . . . . .6E **150**
LE65: Ash Z . . . . . . . . . . . . . . . . . .5K **23**
Bathurst Rd. LE5: Leic . . . . . . . . . . . .3F **73**
Battenberg Rd. LE3: Leic . . . . . . . . . .1C **70**
Battersbee Rd. LE3: Leic . . . . . . . . . . .6E **70**
Battersbee Rd. LE3: Leic . . . . . . . . . . .6J **63**
Battersbee Wlk. LE3: Leic . . . . . . . . . .6J **63**
Battersbee Way LE3: Leic . . . . . . . . . .6J **63**
Battledown Cl. LE10: Hinc . . . . . . . . . .1E **102**
Battlefield Line
Shackerstone Station . . . . . . . . . .3J **91**
Battlefield of Bosworth Country Pk. . . . .1B **162**
Battleflat Dr. LE67: Ell . . . . . . . . . . . .2E **52**
Battleflat La. LE67: Ell . . . . . . . . . . . .3H **53**
BATTRAM . . . . . . . . . . . . . . . . . . . .6D **52**
Battram Rd. LE67: Ell . . . . . . . . . . . . .6D **52**
Baulk Rd. LE15: Bisb . . . . . . . . . . . . .1F **139**
Baxter Ga. LE11: Lou . . . . . . . . . . . . .6F **19**
BAXTERLEY . . . . . . . . . . . . . . . . . . .2A **162**
Baxters Cl. LE4: Leic . . . . . . . . . . . . . .3B **64**
Bayberry Gdns. LE2: Leic . . . . . . . . . . .4E **76**
Baycliff Cl. LE3: Leic . . . . . . . . . . . . . .6B **64**
Bayham Cl. LE5: Leic . . . . . . . . . . . . .2D **72**
Bayley Cl. LE15: Upp . . . . . . . . . . . . .2A **138**
Bayleys Cl. LE15: Emp . . . . . . . . . . . .6C **128**
Bayliss Cl. LE12: Quo . . . . . . . . . . . . .4K **31**
Baysdale LE18: Wig . . . . . . . . . . . . . .6B **78**
Baysdale Rd. LE2: Leic . . . . . . .8B **5** (4E **70**)
Bay St. LE1: Leic . . . . . . . . . .1B **4** (7E **64**)
Bayswater LE13: Mel M . . . . . . . . . . .3G **117**
Bayswater Dr. LE2: G Par . . . . . . . . . .7D **76**
Beacon Av. LE4: Thurm . . . . . . . . . . .6B **60**
LE11: Lou . . . . . . . . . . . . . . . . . . .2D **30**
LE12: Quo . . . . . . . . . . . . . . . . . . .6J **31**
Beacon Cl. LE4: Beau L . . . . . . . . . . . .7A **58**
LE6: Groby . . . . . . . . . . . . . . . . . . .4D **62**
LE67: Mark . . . . . . . . . . . . . . . . . .4G **55**
Beacon Ct. LE3: Glen . . . . . . . . . . . . .5H **63**
Beacon Cres. LE67: Coal . . . . . . . . . . .4H **39**
Beacon Dr. LE11: Lou . . . . . . . . . . . . .2E **30**
Beacon Rd. LE11: Lou . . . . . . . . . . . . .3D **30**
LE12: W Eav . . . . . . . . . . . . . . . . . .3K **41**
Beaconsfield Rd. LE3: Leic . . . . . . . . . .3C **70**
LE13: Mel M . . . . . . . . . . . . . . . . .2D **116**
Beacon Vw. LE67: Bag . . . . . . . . . . . .6G **53**
NG13: Bott . . . . . . . . . . . . . . . . . .1H **107**
Beadmans Cnr. LE67: Rav . . . . . . . . . .3K **37**
Beadswell La. LE8: Bur O . . . . . . . . . .6D **130**
Beaker Cl. LE8: Smee W . . . . . . . . . . .5H **89**
Beale's Cl. LE9: Stap . . . . . . . . . . . . .1H **99**
Beal St. LE2: Leic . . . . . . . . .3G **4** (1H **71**)
Beamont Cl. LE17: Lut . . . . . . . . . . . .2J **153**
Beams Mdw. LE10: Hinc . . . . . . . . . . .5C **102**
Beardsley Rd. LE12: Quo . . . . . . . . . . .5K **31**
Bearsdon Cres. LE10: Hinc . . . . . . . . . .1E **102**
Bear Yd. LE15: Upp . . . . . . . . . . . . . .2C **138**
(off Orange St., not continuous)
Beatrice Rd. LE3: Leic . . . . . . . . . . . . .7B **64**
Beatty Av. LE5: Leic . . . . . . . . . . . . . .7A **66**
Beatty Cl. LE10: Hinc . . . . . . . . . . . . .7G **99**
Beatty Rd. LE5: Leic . . . . . . . . . . . . . .7A **66**
LE7: Sys . . . . . . . . . . . . . . . . . . . .1D **60**
Beauchamp Gdns. LE8: K Bea . . . . . . . .4J **89**
Beauchamp Rd. LE8: K Bea . . . . . . . . .3H **89**
Beaufort Av. LE11: Lou . . . . . . . . . . . .3E **30**
Beaufort Cl. LE2: Oad . . . . . . . . . . . . .4F **79**
LE9: Des . . . . . . . . . . . . . . . . . . . .3H **95**
LE10: Bur . . . . . . . . . . . . . . . . . . .7H **103**
Beaufort Rd. LE3: Leic . . . . . . . . . . . .6A **70**
LE15: Cott . . . . . . . . . . . . . . . . . . .4B **124**
Beaufort Way LE2: Oad . . . . . . . . . . . .4F **79**
Beaumanor Dr. LE12: Wood . . . . . . . . .7G **31**
Beaumanor Gdns. LE12: Wood . . . . . . .7G **31**
Beaumanor Rd. LE4: Leic . . . . . . . . . . .4F **65**
Beaumaris Cres. LE12: Shep . . . . . . . . .1C **28**
Beaumaris Rd. LE12: Moun . . . . . . . . .4C **44**
Beaumont Av. LE10: Hinc . . . . . . . . . .4D **102**
LE65: Ash Z . . . . . . . . . . . . . . . . . .5H **23**
Beaumont Ct. LE11: Lou . . . . . . . . . . .4E **18**

Beaumont Gdns. LE13: Mel M . . . . . . .2F **117**
Beaumont Grn. LE6: Groby . . . . . . . . .4D **62**
LE67: Cole . . . . . . . . . . . . . . . . . . .3J **25**
Beaumont Hall LE2: Leic . . . . . . . . . . .7B **72**
BEAUMONT LEYS . . . . . . . . .2A **64** (1C **163**)
Beaumont Leys Cl. LE4: Leic . . . . . . . . .3D **64**
Beaumont Leys La. LE4: Beau L . . . . . . .1C **64**
Beaumont Leys Ter. LE4: Leic . . . . . . . .3A **64**
Beaumont Lodge Rd.
LE4: Beau L . . . . . . . . . . . . . . . . .7B **58**
Beaumont Pk. Sports Pavilion . . . . . . . .1B **64**
Beaumont Rd. LE5: Leic . . . . . . . . . . .1J **71**
LE11: Lou . . . . . . . . . . . . . . . . . . .3F **31**
LE12: Bar S . . . . . . . . . . . . . . . . . .3C **32**
LE67: Whit . . . . . . . . . . . . . . . . . . .7G **27**
Beaumont St. LE2: Oad . . . . . . . . . . . .2C **78**
Beaumont Wlk. LE4: Leic . . . . . . . . . . .3A **64**
Beaumont Way LE4: Beau L . . . . . . . . .1A **64**
Beauville Dr. LE4: Leic . . . . . . . . . . . .3A **64**
Beaver Cen., The LE2: Leic . . .10C **5** (5F **71**)
Beaver Cl. LE8: Whet . . . . . . . . . . . . .4K **81**
Bebby Rd. LE7: Scra . . . . . . . . . . . . . .6H **67**
Beck Cl. LE2: G Par . . . . . . . . . . . . . .5A **76**
Beckett Av. CV13: Mkt B . . . . . . . . . . .3C **94**
Beckett Rd. LE5: Leic . . . . . . . . . . . . .6A **66**
Beckingham Rd. LE2: Leic . . . . . . . . . .4J **71**
Beckingthorpe Dr. NG13: Bott . . . . . . .1H **107**
Beckmill Ct. LE13: Mel M . . . . . . . . . .4G **117**
Beckmill La. LE13: Mel M . . . . . . . . . .4G **117**
Beckworth Ct. LE15: Emp . . . . . . . . . .6C **128**
Beckworth Gro. LE15: Emp . . . . . . . . .6C **128**
Bedale Av. LE10: Hinc . . . . . . . . . . . . .1J **103**
Bedale Cl. LE67: Coal . . . . . . . . . . . . .4C **38**
Bedale Dr. LE4: Leic . . . . . . . . . . . . . .1C **64**
Bedale St. LE15: Cott . . . . . . . . . . . . .4C **124**
Bede Hall LE2: Leic . . . . . . . . .7A **5** (3E **70**)
Bede Island Rd. LE2: Leic . . . . .6A **5** (3E **70**)
Bede St. LE3: Leic . . . . . . . . . .6A **5** (2D **70**)
Bedford Cl. DE74: Keg . . . . . . . . . . . . .7H **9**
LE9: Des . . . . . . . . . . . . . . . . . . . .2H **95**
LE10: Hinc . . . . . . . . . . . . . . . . . . .7H **99**
Bedford Dr. LE6: Groby . . . . . . . . . . . .4D **62**
Bedford Rd. LE18: Wig . . . . . . . . . . . .5G **77**
Bedford Sq. LE11: Lou . . . . . . . . . . . .7F **19**
Bedford St. LE11: Lou . . . . . . . . . . . . .7F **19**
Bedford St. Nth. LE1: Leic . . . . .1E **4** (7G **65**)
Bedford St. Sth. LE1: Leic . . . . .2D **4** (1F **71**)
BEDWORTH . . . . . . . . . . . . . . . . . . .3A **162**
BEEBY . . . . . . . . . . . . . . . . .1K **67** (1D **163**)
Beeby Cl. LE7: Sys . . . . . . . . . . . . . . .2E **60**
Beeby Rd. LE5: Leic . . . . . . . . . . . . . .1K **71**
LE7: Bark, Bee . . . . . . . . . . . . . . . .5F **61**
LE7: Scra . . . . . . . . . . . . . . . . . . . .4J **67**
Beech Av. LE6: Groby . . . . . . . . . . . . .5C **62**
LE17: Lut . . . . . . . . . . . . . . . . . . .4G **153**
LE67: Rav . . . . . . . . . . . . . . . . . . .4J **37**
Beech Cl. LE12: Shep . . . . . . . . . . . . .6E **16**
LE67: Mark . . . . . . . . . . . . . . . . . .5G **55**
Beech Ct. LE2: Leic . . . . . . . . . . . . . . .8C **5**
LE18: Wig . . . . . . . . . . . . . . . . . . .5J **77**
Beechcroft Av. LE3: Brau . . . . . . . . . . .7A **70**
Beechcroft Rd. LE2: Leic . . . . . . . . . . .6J **71**
Beech Dr. DE11: W'lle . . . . . . . . . . . . .1D **22**
LE3: Brau . . . . . . . . . . . . . . . . . . . .4H **69**
LE7: Sys . . . . . . . . . . . . . . . . . . . .3D **60**
LE67: Thor . . . . . . . . . . . . . . . . . . .2J **93**
NG13: Bott . . . . . . . . . . . . . . . . . .2H **107**
PE9: Ryh . . . . . . . . . . . . . . . . . . . .6G **129**
Beeches, The LE9: Earl S . . . . . . . . . . .1E **100**
LE15: Upp . . . . . . . . . . . . . . . . . . .1C **138**
Beeches Av. LE12: Moun . . . . . . . . . . .2E **44**
Beeches Rd. LE11: Lou . . . . . . . . . . . .1G **31**
Beechfield Av. LE4: Birs . . . . . . . . . . . .6G **59**
Beechfield Cl. LE8: G Gle . . . . . . . . . . .7K **79**
Beechings Cl. LE8: Count . . . . . . . . . . .6D **82**
Beech Rd. LE2: Oad . . . . . . . . . . . . . .3C **78**
LE8: Bla . . . . . . . . . . . . . . . . . . . . .2B **82**
LE15: O'ham . . . . . . . . . . . . . . . . .3K **127**
Beech St. LE5: Leic . . . . . . . . . . . . . . .7J **65**
Beech Tree Cl. LE8: Kib H . . . . . . . . . .1J **89**
Beech Tree Rd. LE67: Coal . . . . . . . . . .4G **39**
Beech Wlk. LE67: Mark . . . . . . . . . . . .5G **55**
Beech Way LE9: Des . . . . . . . . . . . . . .2G **95**
LE65: Ash Z . . . . . . . . . . . . . . . . . .5B **24**
LE67: Ibs . . . . . . . . . . . . . . . . . . . .3J **51**
Beechwood Av. LE3: Leic E . . . . . . . . . .4E **68**
LE4: Thurm . . . . . . . . . . . . . . . . . .7A **60**
LE7: Quen . . . . . . . . . . . . . . . . . . .7F **47**
LE10: Bur . . . . . . . . . . . . . . . . . . .7G **103**
LE13: Mel M . . . . . . . . . . . . . . . . .2H **117**
Beechwood Cl. LE5: Leic . . . . . . . . . . .2E **72**
Beechwood Rd. LE19: Litt . . . . . . . . . .3F **81**
Beehive Av. DE12: Moi . . . . . . . . . . . .7C **22**
Bee Hive La. LE11: Lou . . . . . . . . . . . .7F **19**
BEESTON . . . . . . . . . . . . . . . . . . . . .1C **159**
Beggar's La. LE3: End, Leic E . . . . . . . .5C **68**
LE19: End . . . . . . . . . . . . . . . . . . .1C **74**

**Begonia Cl.** LE3: Leic E . . . . . . . . . . . . .5D **68**
LE10: Bur . . . . . . . . . . . . . . . . . .6H **103**
**Begonia Dr.** LE10: Bur . . . . . . . . . . . .5H **103**
**Belcher Cl.** LE67: Hea . . . . . . . . . . . .3F **51**
**BELCHER'S BAR** . . . . . . . . . . . . . . .7K **51**
**Belfry Cl.** LE10: Bur . . . . . . . . . . . . .7G **103**
**Belfry Dr.** LE3: Leic . . . . . . . . . . . . .2G **69**
**BELGRAVE** . . . . . . . . . . . . . . . . . . .5H **65**
**Belgrave Av.** LE4: Leic . . . . . . . . . . .3G **65**
**Belgrave Blvd.** LE4: Leic . . . . . . . . . .1C **64**
(Beaumont Leys La.)
LE4: Leic . . . . . . . . . . . . . . . . .2E **64**
(Woodstock Rd.)
**Belgrave Circ.** LE1: Leic . . . . . . . . . .6G **65**
**Belgrave Cl.** LE67: Coal . . . . . . . . . . .3J **39**
**Belgrave Flyover** LE1: Leic . . . . . . . .7G **65**
LE4: Leic . . . . . . . . . . . . . . . . .6G **65**
**Belgrave Ga.** LE1: Leic . . . . . .3D **4** (1F **71**)
*Belgrave Hall (Mus.)* . . . . . . . . . . . . .3G **65**
**Belgrave Ind. Cen.** LE4: Leic . . . . . . .5G **65**
**Belgrave Rd.** LE4: Leic . . . . . . . . . . .6G **65**
LE15: Upp . . . . . . . . . . . . . . .1B **138**
**Bellamy Cl.** LE2: G Par . . . . . . . . . . .5A **76**
**Bell Av.** DE72: A Tre . . . . . . . . . . . . .1C **6**
**Bell Cen., The** LE13: Mel M . . . . . . . .4F **117**
**Bell Cl.** LE6: Ratby . . . . . . . . . . . . . .6B **62**
LE9: B Ast . . . . . . . . . . . . . . . .6E **86**
LE67: S Bar . . . . . . . . . . . . . . .3B **54**
**Belldrome, The** *LE17: C Mag* . . . . . . .5C **142**
(off Roman Cl.)
**Beller Way** LE13: Mel M . . . . . . . . . .7C **116**
**Belleville Dr.** LE2: Oad . . . . . . . . . . .2E **78**
**Belle Vue Av.** LE4: Leic . . . . . . . . . . .4E **64**
*Belle-Vue Cinema* . . . . . . . .1D **4** (1F **71**)
**Belle Vue Rd.** LE9: Earl S . . . . . . . . .2B **100**
**Bellfields La.** LE16: L Bow . . . . . . . .5G **151**
**Bellfields St.** LE16: L Bow . . . . . . . .5G **151**
**Bellflower Rd.** LE5: Ham . . . . . . . . . .3D **66**
*Bell Foundry Mus.* . . . . . . . . . . . . . .6G **19**
**Bellholme Cl.** LE4: Leic . . . . . . . . . . .3H **65**
**Bell La.** LE5: Leic . . . . . . . . .2G **4** (1H **71**)
LE8: Bur O . . . . . . . . . . . . . . .6D **130**
LE17: H Bos . . . . . . . . . . . . . .6C **148**
LE19: Nar . . . . . . . . . . . . . . . .2G **81**
**Bells La.** LE9: N Ver . . . . . . . . . . . . .6G **93**
**Bell St.** LE17: C Mag . . . . . . . . . . . .5C **142**
LE17: Lut . . . . . . . . . . . . . . . .4K **153**
LE18: Wig . . . . . . . . . . . . . . . .5K **77**
**Bell Vw.** LE19: Nar . . . . . . . . . . . . . .1G **81**
**BELMESTHORPE** . . . . . . . .6J **129** (3D **161**)
**Belmesthorpe La.** PE9: Ryh . . . . . . . .5J **129**
**Belmont Dr.** LE67: Coal . . . . . . . . . . .2A **38**
**Belmont St.** LE2: Leic . . . . . . . . . . . .1D **76**
**Belmont Way** LE11: Lou . . . . . . . . . . .1J **29**
**Belper Cl.** LE2: Oad . . . . . . . . . . . . . .5C **78**
LE18: Wig . . . . . . . . . . . . . . . .1G **83**
**Belper St.** LE4: Leic . . . . . . . . . . . . .5H **65**
**Belt, The** LE17: S Kil . . . . . . . . . . . . .5H **155**
**BELTON**
Grantham . . . . . . . . . . . . . . . .1C **161**
Loughborough . . . . . . . . . .4H **15** (2B **158**)
**Belton Cl.** LE2: Leic . . . . . . . . . . . . .3F **77**
LE67: Coal . . . . . . . . . . . . . . . .3J **39**
**BELTON-IN-RUTLAND** . . . . . .5G **133** (1B **164**)
**Belton M.** LE15: Bel R . . . . . . . . . . . .5G **133**
**Belton Pk.** LE11: Lou . . . . . . . . . . . . .4E **18**
**Belton Rd.** LE3: Brau . . . . . . . . . . . .7A **70**
LE11: Lou . . . . . . . . . . . . . . . .5D **18**
**Belton Rd. W.** LE11: Lou . . . . . . . . . .4C **18**
**Belton Rd. W. Extension** LE11: Lou . . . .4D **18**
**Belton St.** LE12: Shep . . . . . . . . . . . .6D **16**
**Belton Wlk.** LE2: Leic . . . . . . . . . . . .3F **77**
**BELVOIR** . . . . . . . . . . . . . . . . . . . .1B **160**
**Belvoir Av.** LE14: Ab K . . . . . . . . . . .7H **111**
NG13: Bott . . . . . . . . . . . . . . .3G **107**
*Belvoir Castle* . . . . . . . . . . . . . . . . .1B **160**
**Belvoir Cl.** LE2: Oad . . . . . . . . . . . . .4E **78**
LE9: Des . . . . . . . . . . . . . . . . .2H **95**
LE12: Moun . . . . . . . . . . . . . . .4D **44**
**Belvoir Dr.** LE2: Leic . . . . . . . . . . . .2C **76**
LE7: Sys . . . . . . . . . . . . . . . . .1E **60**
LE11: Lou . . . . . . . . . . . . . . . .3D **30**
LE65: Ash Z . . . . . . . . . . . . . . .6K **23**
**Belvoir Dr. E.** LE2: Leic . . . . . . . . . . .2D **76**
**Belvoir Rd.** LE67: Coal . . . . . . . . . . .3C **38**
NG13: Bott . . . . . . . . . . . . . . .4G **107**
(not continuous)
NG13: Red . . . . . . . . . . . . . . .2E **106**
**Belvoir Sq.** LE15: Cott . . . . . . . . . . . .3D **124**
(not continuous)
**Belvoir St.** LE1: Leic . . . . . . .5D **4** (2F **71**)
LE13: Mel M . . . . . . . . . . . . . .3H **117**
**Belvoir Way** LE12: Shep . . . . . . . . . .1C **28**
**Beman Cl.** LE4: Leic . . . . . . . . . . . . .1A **66**
**Bembridge Cl.** LE3: Leic . . . . . . . . . .6D **64**
**Bembridge Rd.** LE3: Leic . . . . . . . . . .6C **64**
**Benbow Cl.** LE10: Hinc . . . . . . . . . . .6G **99**

**Bencroft Cl.** LE7: Anst . . . . . . . . . . . .7H **57**
**Bendbow Ri.** LE3: Leic . . . . . . . . . . . .4H **69**
**Benenden Way** LE65: Ash Z . . . . . . . .4J **23**
**Benford Gdns.** LE9: B Ast . . . . . . . . .6D **86**
**Benjamin Russell Ct.** LE2: Leic . . . .7A **5** (3E **70**)
**Bennet Ri.** LE9: Hun . . . . . . . . . . . . .1C **80**
**Bennett Cl.** CV13: S Gol . . . . . . . . . .3A **98**
**Bennett Dr.** LE13: Mel M . . . . . . . . . .1F **117**
**Bennetts Hill** LE17: D Bas . . . . . . . . .1D **144**
**Bennett's La.** LE7: Coss . . . . . . . . . .4K **45**
**Bennett Wlk.** LE3: Leic . . . . . . . . . . .3K **69**
**Bennett Way** LE18: Wig . . . . . . . . . . .7G **77**
**Bennion Rd.** LE4: Beau L . . . . . . . . . .1A **64**
LE7: Bush . . . . . . . . . . . . . . . .3J **73**
**Benscliffe Dr.** LE11: Lou . . . . . . . . . .1C **30**
**Benscliffe Gdns.** LE2: Leic . . . . . . . .5D **76**
**Benscliffe Rd.** LE6: New L . . . . . . . . .5A **42**
LE67: New L . . . . . . . . . . . . . .5A **42**
**Benskins Oval** LE4: Beau L . . . . . . . .6C **58**
**Benskin Wlk.** LE4: Leic . . . . . . . . . . .4B **64**
**Benskyn Cl.** LE8: Count . . . . . . . . . . .5D **82**
**Benson St.** LE5: Leic . . . . . . . . . . . . .2A **72**
**Bens Way** LE5: Leic . . . . . . . . . . . . .2D **72**
**Bentburn Ho.** LE3: Leic . . . . . . . . . . .7A **64**
**Bentinghouse Gdns.** LE2: Leic . . . . . .4D **76**
**Bentinghouse Rd.** LE2: Leic . . . . . . . .4D **76**
**BENTLEY** . . . . . . . . . . . . . . . . . . . .2A **162**
**Bentley Cl.** LE11: Lou . . . . . . . . . . . .7G **19**
**Bentley Pl.** LE13: Mel M . . . . . . . . . .4F **117**
**Bentley Rd.** DE74: C Don . . . . . . . . . .4H **7**
LE4: Birs . . . . . . . . . . . . . . . . .5G **59**
**Beresford Ct.** LE12: Shep . . . . . . . . . .6E **16**
**Beresford Dr.** LE2: Leic . . . . . . . . . . .7K **71**
**Berford Cl.** LE9: B Ast . . . . . . . . . . . .5D **86**
**Bergen Dr.** LE2: Oad . . . . . . . . . . . . .4D **78**
**Berkeley Cl.** LE2: Oad . . . . . . . . . . . .3F **79**
LE12: Moun . . . . . . . . . . . . . . .3E **44**
**Berkeley Cl. Pk. Homes** LE12: Moun . . .3E **44**
**Berkeley Rd.** LE11: Lou . . . . . . . . . . .3A **30**
**Berkley St.** LE1: Leic . . . . . . .1A **4** (7E **64**)
**Berkshire Rd.** LE2: Leic . . . . . . . . . . .1D **76**
**BERKSWELL** . . . . . . . . . . . . . . . . . .3A **162**
**Bernard Cl.** LE67: Ibs . . . . . . . . . . . .5K **51**
**Bernard St.** DE11: W'lle . . . . . . . . . . .1B **22**
**Berners St.** LE2: Leic . . . . . . . .3G **4** (1H **71**)
**Berridge Dr.** LE2: Oad . . . . . . . . . . . .4D **78**
**Berridge La.** LE4: Leic . . . . . . . . . . . .3H **65**
**Berridges La.** LE17: H Bos . . . . . . . . .5C **148**
**Berridge St.** LE1: Leic . . . . . . .4C **4** (2F **71**)
**Berridge Wlk.** LE4: Leic . . . . . . . . . . .3H **65**
**Berrington Cl.** LE5: Leic . . . . . . . . . . .6A **66**
**Berrisford St.** LE67: Coal . . . . . . . . . .4C **38**
**Berry Av.** DE73: B Hil . . . . . . . . . . . .6C **10**
**Berrybushes** LE15: Mkt O . . . . . . . . .2H **123**
**Berry Cl.** LE16: G Bow . . . . . . . . . . .2G **151**
LE67: Rav . . . . . . . . . . . . . . . .2A **38**
**Berrycott La.** LE12: Sea . . . . . . . . . . .3K **33**
**Berryhill La.** LE67: D Hea . . . . . . . . . .6B **38**
**Berry's La.** LE6: Ratby . . . . . . . . . . . .6A **62**
(not continuous)
**Berwick Rd.** LE65: Ash Z . . . . . . . . . .5B **24**
**Beryl Av.** LE10: Hinc . . . . . . . . . . . . .1D **102**
**BESCABY** . . . . . . . . . . . . . . . . . . . .2B **160**
**Bescaby La.** LE14: W Wol . . . . . . . . . .2D **112**
**Bessingham Cl.** LE5: Ham . . . . . . . . . .4E **66**
**Best Cl.** LE18: Wig . . . . . . . . . . . . . . .7F **77**
**Bestwood Cl.** LE3: Leic . . . . . . . . . . .5B **64**
**Beth-El** LE18: Wig . . . . . . . . . . . . . . .1J **83**
**Betty Henser's La.** LE12: Moun . . . . . .7D **32**
**Bevan Rd.** LE4: Leic . . . . . . . . . . . . .5C **58**
**Beveridge La.** LE67: Bar, Ell . . . . . . . .2E **52**
**Beveridge St.** LE12: Bar S . . . . . . . . .4D **32**
**Beverley Av.** LE4: Leic . . . . . . . . . . . .5H **65**
**Beverley Cl.** LE4: Thurm . . . . . . . . . . .6A **60**
**Beverley Dr.** LE9: B Ast . . . . . . . . . . .3C **86**
**Beverley Rd.** DE74: N Air . . . . . . . . . .1B **12**
**Bevington Cl.** LE6: Ratby . . . . . . . . . .5A **62**
**Bewcastle Gro.** LE4: Leic . . . . . . . . . .1D **64**
**Bewcastle Ho.** LE4: Leic . . . . . . . . . .1D **64**
**Bewicke Rd.** LE3: Leic . . . . . . . . . . . .5B **70**
**Bexhill Ri.** LE5: Leic . . . . . . . . . . . . .7G **67**
**Biam Way** LE3: Brau . . . . . . . . . . . . .7A **70**
**Bickley Av.** LE13: Mel M . . . . . . . . . .3G **117**
**Biddle Rd.** LE3: Leic . . . . . . . . . . . . .7B **64**
LE19: Litt . . . . . . . . . . . . . . . .2G **81**
**Biddulph Av.** LE2: Leic . . . . . . . . . . . .3J **71**
**Biddulph St.** LE2: Leic . . . . . . . . . . . .3J **71**
**Bideford Cl.** LE18: Wig . . . . . . . . . . . .2K **83**
**Bideford Rd.** LE5: Leic . . . . . . . . . . . .4F **73**
**Bidford Cl.** LE3: Brau . . . . . . . . . . . .5J **69**
**Bidford Ct.** LE3: Brau . . . . . . . . . . . .5J **69**
**Bidford Rd.** LE3: Brau . . . . . . . . . . . .5J **69**
**Biggin, The** DE74: C Don . . . . . . . . . .5K **7**
**Biggin Hill Rd.** LE5: Leic . . . . . . . . . .5D **72**
**Biggin St.** LE11: Lou . . . . . . . . . . . . .6F **19**
**Biggs Cl.** LE8: Whet . . . . . . . . . . . . . .4A **82**
**Big La.** LE12: Bar S, Sea . . . . . . . . . . .1J **33**
**Bignal Dr.** LE3: Leic E . . . . . . . . . . . .4F **69**

**Bilberry Cl.** LE3: Brau . . . . . . . . . . . .2A **76**
**BILBOROUGH** . . . . . . . . . . . . . . . . .1C **159**
**Billa Barra La.** LE67: S Bar . . . . . . . . .2A **54**
**Bill Crane Way** LE17: Lut . . . . . . . . . .2J **153**
**BILLESDON** . . . . . . . . . . .6H **131** (1A **164**)
**Billesdon Cl.** LE3: Leic . . . . . . . . . . . .3J **63**
**BILLINGBOROUGH** . . . . . . . . . . . . .1D **161**
**Billington Cl.** LE4: Leic . . . . . . . . . . . .3E **64**
**Billington Rd. E.** LE9: Elm . . . . . . . . . .5C **100**
**Billington Rd. W.** LE9: Elm . . . . . . . . .5C **100**
**Bilsdale Rd.** LE18: Wig . . . . . . . . . . . .7B **78**
**BILSTONE** . . . . . . . . . . . . .6F **91** (1A **162**)
**Bilstone Rd.** CV9: Twy . . . . . . . . . . . .2C **90**
CV13: Bils, Con . . . . . . . . . . . .6F **91**
**Bilton Way** LE17: Lut . . . . . . . . . . . . .2K **153**
**Bindleys La.** LE8: G Gle . . . . . . . . . . .7K **79**
**BINGHAM** . . . . . . . . . . . . . . . . . . . .1A **160**
**Bingley Cl.** LE19: Litt . . . . . . . . . . . . .3G **81**
**Bingley Rd.** LE19: Litt . . . . . . . . . . . .3G **81**
**BINLEY** . . . . . . . . . . . . . . . . . . . . . .3A **162**
**Bintree Cl.** LE5: Ham . . . . . . . . . . . . .4D **66**
**Birch Av.** LE12: Bar S . . . . . . . . . . . . .2D **32**
LE67: Whit . . . . . . . . . . . . . . . .7G **27**
**Birch Cl.** LE4: Leic . . . . . . . . . . . . . . .5K **65**
LE9: Earl S . . . . . . . . . . . . . . .4C **100**
LE11: Lou . . . . . . . . . . . . . . . .5E **30**
LE13: Mel M . . . . . . . . . . . . . .2E **116**
LE67: Mark . . . . . . . . . . . . . . .7G **55**
**Birch Ct.** LE2: G Par . . . . . . . . . . . . . .5A **76**
**Birches, The** LE9: Barw . . . . . . . . . . . .4K **99**
**Birchfield Av.** LE67: Mark . . . . . . . . . .1F **55**
**BIRCHLEY HEATH** . . . . . . . . . . . . . . .2A **162**
**BIRCHMOOR** . . . . . . . . . . . . . . . . . .1A **162**
**Birch Tree Av.** LE4: Birs . . . . . . . . . . .4G **59**
**Birchtree Gdns.** LE16: Mkt H . . . . . . . .3F **151**
**Birchtree Rd.** LE18: Wig . . . . . . . . . . .4K **77**
**Birch Vw.** LE17: Kim . . . . . . . . . . . . .7A **146**
**Birchwood Cl.** LE3: Leic E . . . . . . . . . .5D **68**
LE7: Sys . . . . . . . . . . . . . . . . .2E **60**
LE67: Cole . . . . . . . . . . . . . . . .1H **37**
**BIRD HILL** . . . . . . . . . . . . . . . . . . . .3D **42**
**Bird Hill Rd.** LE12: W Eav . . . . . . . . . .2D **42**
**Birdie Cl.** LE8: K Bea . . . . . . . . . . . . .3K **89**
**Birds La.** LE14: Sta . . . . . . . . . . . . . .2H **109**
**Birds Nest Av.** LE3: Leic . . . . . . . . . . .6K **63**
**Birkby Cl.** LE5: Ham . . . . . . . . . . . . . .3E **66**
**Birkdale Av.** LE2: Leic . . . . . . . . . . . .6K **71**
**Birkdale Rd.** LE7: Anst . . . . . . . . . . . .7H **57**
**Birkenshaw Rd.** LE3: Leic . . . . . . . . . .5A **64**
**Birkenshaw Wlk.** LE5: Leic . . . . . . . . .2D **72**
**BIRKHOLME** . . . . . . . . . . . . . . . . . . .2C **161**
**Birsmore Av.** LE4: Leic . . . . . . . . . . . .2K **65**
**BIRSTALL** . . . . . . . . . . . . . .6G **59** (1C **163**)
**Birstall Rd.** LE4: Birs . . . . . . . . . . . . .7H **59**
**Birstall St.** LE1: Leic . . . . . . . . . . . . .7H **65**
**Birstow Cres.** LE4: Leic . . . . . . . . . . .1D **64**
**BIRTHORPE** . . . . . . . . . . . . . . . . . . .1D **161**
**Birtley Coppice** LE16: Mkt H . . . . . . . .3D **150**
**BISBROOKE** . . . . . . . . . .2G **139** (2B **164**)
**Bisbrooke Rd.** LE15: Lyd . . . . . . . . . . .5D **138**
(not continuous)
**Bishop Cl.** LE16: Mkt H . . . . . . . . . . . .7E **150**
**Bishop Dale** LE67: Thrin . . . . . . . . . . .4D **26**
**Bishopdale Rd.** LE4: Leic . . . . . . . . . .3C **64**
**Bishop Mdw. Rd.** LE11: Lou . . . . . . . .2C **18**
**Bishopston Wlk.** LE4: Leic . . . . . . . . .3F **65**
**Bishop St.** LE1: Leic . . . . . . . .4D **4** (2F **71**)
LE11: Lou . . . . . . . . . . . . . . . .6G **19**
LE13: Mel M . . . . . . . . . . . . . .4G **117**
**Bisley St.** LE3: Leic . . . . . . . . . . . . . .4D **70**
**BITCHFIELD** . . . . . . . . . . . . . . . . . . .2C **161**
**BITTESWELL** . . . . . . . . . .2H **153** (3C **163**)
**Bitteswell Rd.** LE17: Lut . . . . . . . . . . .3H **153**
**BLABY** . . . . . . . . . . . . . . . . .1B **82** (2C **163**)
**Blaby By-Pass** LE8: Bla . . . . . . . . . . .2A **82**
**Blaby Ind. Est.** LE8: Bla . . . . . . . . . . .7A **76**
**Blaby Rd.** LE18: Wig . . . . . . . . . . . . .7F **77**
LE19: End . . . . . . . . . . . . . . . .5F **75**
**Blackberry La.** LE7: Coss . . . . . . . . . .4A **46**
LE67: Ibs . . . . . . . . . . . . . . . . .1K **51**
**Blackbird Av.** LE4: Leic . . . . . . . . . . . .6D **64**
**Blackbird Rd.** LE4: Leic . . . . . . . . . . .6D **64**
**Blackbrook Cl.** LE12: Shep . . . . . . . . .7C **16**
**Blackbrook Ct.** LE11: Lou . . . . . . . . . .4C **18**
LE67: Coal . . . . . . . . . . . . . . . .4H **39**
**Blackbrook Dr.** LE67: Coal . . . . . . . . .4H **39**
**Blackbrook Rd.** LE11: Lou . . . . . . . . . .7A **18**
**Blackbrook Way** LE11: Lou . . . . . . . . .5K **17**
**Blackburn Rd.** LE9: Barw . . . . . . . . . .4K **99**
**Blackett Av.** LE3: Leic . . . . . . . . . . . .6A **64**
**Blackett Dr.** LE67: Hea . . . . . . . . . . . .3F **51**
**BLACKFORDBY** . . . . . . . . .3D **22** (3A **158**)
**Blackfordby La.** DE12: Moi . . . . . . . . . .4D **22**
**BLACK FRIARS** . . . . . . . . . . . . . . . . .1D **70**
**Blackfriars St.** LE3: Leic . . . . . . .3A **4** (1E **70**)
**Blackham Rd.** LE11: Lou . . . . . . . . . . .2E **30**
**Black Horse Hill** DE12: A Mag . . . . . . .5B **48**

Black Horse Yd. LE10: Hinc . . . . . . . . . . .2G **103**
Black La. LE12: Walt W . . . . . . . . . . . . . . .6G **21**
Blackmore Dr. LE3: Leic . . . . . . . . . . . . . .2A **70**
Blacksmith Cl. LE14: N Bro . . . . . . . . . . . .2C **110**
Blacksmith End LE14: Sta . . . . . . . . . . . .2H **109**
Blacksmith Pl. LE5: Ham . . . . . . . . . . . . . .3E **66**
Blacksmiths Av. LE12: Shep . . . . . . . . . . .5E **16**
Blacksmiths Cl. LE7: Thru . . . . . . . . . . . .7B **114**
   LE15: Ext . . . . . . . . . . . . . . . . . . . . . .2D **128**
Blacksmiths Yd. CV13: S Gol . . . . . . . . . .3A **98**
Blackthorn Cl. LE17: Lut . . . . . . . . . . . . .4G **153**
Blackthorn Dr. LE4: Beau L . . . . . . . . . . .7A **58**
   LE7: Sys . . . . . . . . . . . . . . . . . . . . . . .2B **60**
Blackthorn La. LE2: Oad . . . . . . . . . . . . .1D **78**
Blackthorn Rd. LE3: Glen . . . . . . . . . . . . .7F **63**
   (not continuous)
Blackthorn Way DE12: Mea . . . . . . . . . . .6E **34**
Blackwell Cl. LE18: Wig . . . . . . . . . . . . . .7A **78**
Blackwood LE67: Coal . . . . . . . . . . . . . . .3H **39**
Bladen Cl. LE8: Count . . . . . . . . . . . . . . .5D **82**
Blair Cl. LE12: Moun . . . . . . . . . . . . . . . .4C **44**
Blairmore Rd. LE3: Leic . . . . . . . . . . . . . .1G **69**
Blaise Gro. LE4: Leic . . . . . . . . . . . . . . . .5K **65**
Blake Cl. LE10: Hinc . . . . . . . . . . . . . . . .6G **99**
Blake Ct. LE19: End . . . . . . . . . . . . . . . .5E **74**
Blake Dr. LE11: Lou . . . . . . . . . . . . . . . . .5B **18**
Blakeney Cres. LE13: Mel M . . . . . . . . . . .7F **117**
Blakenhall Cl. LE19: Nar . . . . . . . . . . . . .1D **80**
Blakenhall Rd. LE5: Leic . . . . . . . . . . . . .2C **72**
Blakeshay Cl. LE3: Leic . . . . . . . . . . . . . .4K **63**
Blakesley Rd. LE18: Wig . . . . . . . . . . . . .5B **78**
Blakesley Wlk. LE4: Leic . . . . . . . . . . . . .4B **64**
Blake St. LE1: Leic . . . . . . . . . . . .2C **4** (1F **71**)
Blake Wlk. LE1: Leic . . . . . . . . . . .2C **4** (1F **71**)
Bland Rd. LE3: Leic . . . . . . . . . . . . . . . . .6K **63**
Blankley Dr. LE2: Leic . . . . . . . . . . . . . . .6K **71**
Blanklyn Av. LE5: Leic . . . . . . . . . . . . . . .2K **71**
Blankney Rd. LE15: Cott . . . . . . . . . . . . .4C **124**
BLASTON . . . . . . . . . . . . . . . . . . . . . . . .2B **164**
BLATHERWYCKE . . . . . . . . . . . . . . . . . .2C **165**
Blaydon Cl. LE3: Leic . . . . . . . . . . . . . . . .6B **64**
Bleach Mill DE12: Mea . . . . . . . . . . . . . .2E **48**
Bleakmoor Cl. LE7: Rear . . . . . . . . . . . . . .1J **47**
Bleasby Cl. LE4: Leic . . . . . . . . . . . . . . . .2C **66**
Blenheim Cl. LE10: Hinc . . . . . . . . . . . . .6J **99**
   LE11: Lou . . . . . . . . . . . . . . . . . . . . . .6A **18**
   LE18: Wig . . . . . . . . . . . . . . . . . . . . . .1F **83**
Blenheim Cres. LE9: B Ast . . . . . . . . . . . .3B **86**
Blenheim Rd. LE4: Birs . . . . . . . . . . . . . .5H **59**
Blenheim Wlk. LE13: Mel M . . . . . . . . . . .2E **116**
Blenheim Way LE4: Leic . . . . . . . . . . . . .2E **64**
   LE16: Mkt H . . . . . . . . . . . . . . . . . . . .2E **150**
Blickling Wlk. LE5: Leic . . . . . . . . . . . . . .6A **66**
Blissett Rd. LE3: Leic . . . . . . . . . . . . . . . .7A **64**
Blithfield Av. LE11: Lou . . . . . . . . . . . . . .7A **18**
Blockleys Yd. LE10: Hinc . . . . . . . . . . . . .3F **103**
Bloom Cl. LE67: Rav . . . . . . . . . . . . . . . .2A **38**
Bloomfield Rd. LE2: Leic . . . . . . . . . . . . .2F **77**
Blossom Rd. LE3: Leic . . . . . . . . . . . . . . .3A **70**
Blossoms, The LE67: Mark . . . . . . . . . . . .7G **55**
Blount Rd. LE4: Thurm . . . . . . . . . . . . . .7B **60**
Bloxham Rd. LE3: Leic . . . . . . . . . . . . . . .7B **64**
Bloxoms Cl. LE3: Brau . . . . . . . . . . . . . . .2K **75**
Bloxsom Cl. LE67: Bag . . . . . . . . . . . . . . .6G **53**
Blubell Dr. LE6: Groby . . . . . . . . . . . . . . .3E **62**
Blue Banks Av. LE2: G Par . . . . . . . . . . . .5A **76**
Bluebell Cl. DE12: Don . . . . . . . . . . . . . .3A **34**
   LE2: Oad . . . . . . . . . . . . . . . . . . . . . . .3G **79**
   LE7: Quen . . . . . . . . . . . . . . . . . . . . . .6G **47**
   LE9: K Mux . . . . . . . . . . . . . . . . . . . . .1C **68**
Bluebell Dr. LE2: Leic . . . . . . . . . . . . . . .4F **77**
   LE11: Lou . . . . . . . . . . . . . . . . . . . . . .2D **30**
Bluebell Row LE13: Mel M . . . . . . . . . . . .7D **116**
Blue Boar Yd. LE10: Hinc . . . . . . . . . . . . .3F **103**
Bluecoat La. LE15: Lyd . . . . . . . . . . . . . .7E **138**
Blue Gates Rd. LE4: Beau L . . . . . . . . . . .1K **63**
Blue Granite Pk. LE12: Moun . . . . . . . . . .2E **44**
Blue Pots Cl. LE3: Leic E . . . . . . . . . . . . .5D **68**
Blue Pots La. NG32: Eat . . . . . . . . . . . . .6G **109**
Blundell Rd. LE5: Leic . . . . . . . . . . . . . . .4C **72**
Blunt's La. LE18: Wig . . . . . . . . . . . . . . . .6J **77**
Blyth Av. LE13: Mel M . . . . . . . . . . . . . . .5E **116**
Bob Trewick Ho. LE1: Leic . . . . . .6E **5** (3G **71**)
Bodenham Cl. LE18: Wig . . . . . . . . . . . . .1J **83**
Bodicoat Cl. LE8: Whet . . . . . . . . . . . . . .4K **81**
Bodkin Row DE12: Oak . . . . . . . . . . . . . .6D **34**
Bodkin Wlk. LE4: Leic . . . . . . . . . . . . . . .3B **64**
Bodmin Av. LE18: Wig . . . . . . . . . . . . . . .1J **83**
Bodmin Cl. LE10: Hinc . . . . . . . . . . . . . . .6H **99**
Bodnant Av. LE5: Leic . . . . . . . . . . . . . . .4A **72**
Bodycote Cl. LE9: B Ast . . . . . . . . . . . . . .5D **86**
Bofols Rd. LE14: O Dal . . . . . . . . . . . . . .6C **110**
Boilerhouse Rd. LE14: O Dal . . . . . . . . . .7C **110**
Bollington Rd. LE2: Oad . . . . . . . . . . . . .2E **78**
Bolsover St. LE5: Leic . . . . . . . . . . . . . . .1A **72**
Bolton La. LE14: Hos . . . . . . . . . . . . . . . .6B **108**

Bolton Rd. LE3: Leic . . . . . . . . . . . . . . . .2C **70**
Bolus Rd. LE3: Brau . . . . . . . . . . . . . . . .5G **69**
Bombard Rd. LE14: O Dal . . . . . . . . . . . .6C **110**
Bonchurch Cl. LE67: Whit . . . . . . . . . . . .6F **27**
Bonchurch Rd. LE67: Whit . . . . . . . . . . . .6F **27**
Bonchurch St. LE3: Leic . . . . . . . . . . . . . .7D **64**
Boncroft Gdns. DE12: Oak . . . . . . . . . . . .5C **34**
Bond Cl. LE11: Lou . . . . . . . . . . . . . . . . . .2G **31**
Bondgate DE74: C Don . . . . . . . . . . . . . . .5J **7**
Bond La. LE12: Moun . . . . . . . . . . . . . . . .2C **44**
Bondman Cl. LE4: Leic . . . . . . . . . . . . . . .1E **64**
Boneham's La. LE17: Lut, Gilm . . .1K **153** & 7E **144**
Bonner Cl. LE2: Oad . . . . . . . . . . . . . . . .4F **79**
Bonners La. LE2: Leic . . . . . . . . . .6B **5** (3E **70**)
Bonney Rd. LE3: Leic . . . . . . . . . . . . . . . .5K **63**
Bonnington Rd. LE2: Leic . . . . . . . . . . . . .6H **71**
Bonsall St. LE5: Leic . . . . . . . . . . . . . . . .3J **71**
Bonville Pl. LE3: Leic . . . . . . . . . . . . . . . .6B **70**
BOOTHBY PAGNELL . . . . . . . . . . . . . . .1C **161**
Booth Cl. LE5: Leic . . . . . . . . . . . . . . . . .2D **72**
Boothorpe La. DE11: Boot . . . . . . . . . . . .3C **22**
Booth Rd. LE67: Thrin . . . . . . . . . . . . . . .3D **26**
Bordeaux Cl. LE19: End . . . . . . . . . . . . . .5E **74**
Border Dr. LE4: Leic . . . . . . . . . . . . . . . . .1D **64**
Borlace St. LE3: Leic . . . . . . . . . . . . . . . .1D **70**
Borough, The LE10: Hinc . . . . . . . . . . . . .3G **103**
Borough St. DE74: C Don . . . . . . . . . . . . .5K **7**
   DE74: Keg . . . . . . . . . . . . . . . . . . . . . .6H **9**
BORROWASH . . . . . . . . . . . . . . . . . . . . .1B **158**
Borrowcup Cl. LE8: Count . . . . . . . . . . . . .5C **82**
Borrowdale Cl. LE9: Earl S . . . . . . . . . . . .3E **100**
Borrowdale Way LE5: Leic . . . . . . . . . . . .4F **73**
   LE11: Lou . . . . . . . . . . . . . . . . . . . . . .2B **30**
Borrowell DE74: Keg . . . . . . . . . . . . . . . . .5G **9**
Bostock Cl. LE9: Elm . . . . . . . . . . . . . . . .6F **101**
Boston La. LE8: Peat M, Fost . . . . . . . . . .1K **147**
Boston Rd. LE4: Beau L . . . . . . . . . . . . . .2K **63**
Boston Way LE9: Barw . . . . . . . . . . . . . . .4J **99**
Boswell St. LE19: Nar . . . . . . . . . . . . . . . .7E **74**
Bosworth Battlefield Vis. Cen. . . . . . . . . .1B **162**
Bosworth Cl. LE10: Hinc . . . . . . . . . . . . .2D **102**
   LE65: Ash Z . . . . . . . . . . . . . . . . . . . .4A **24**
Bosworth Grn. LE9: Earl S . . . . . . . . . . . .1G **101**
Bosworth Ho. LE2: Leic . . . . . . . . . . . . . . .5B **4**
   LE10: Hinc . . . . . . . . . . . . . . . . . . . . .2H **103**
   (off Priory Wlk.)
Bosworth La. LE9: Osb . . . . . . . . . . . . . . .5F **93**
Bosworth Rd. CV13: B'one, Osb . . . . . . . .6B **92**
   CV13: Carl, Con . . . . . . . . . . . . . . . . . .6G **91**
   DE12: Mea, Snar . . . . . . . . . . . . . . . . .7E **34**
   DE74: C Don . . . . . . . . . . . . . . . . . . . . .5H **7**
   LE9: K Mal . . . . . . . . . . . . . . . . . . . . .6F **95**
   LE17: Walt . . . . . . . . . . . . . . . . . . . . .7C **146**
Bosworth St. LE3: Leic . . . . . . . . . . . . . . .1D **70**
Bosworth Water Trust . . . . . . . . . . . . . . .1A **162**
BOTCHESTON . . . . . . . . . . . . . . . . . . . .1B **162**
Botley Wlk. LE5: Leic . . . . . . . . . . . . . . . .1C **72**
BOTTESFORD . . . . . . . . . . . . . .2G **107** (3B **160**)
Bottesford Station (Rail) . . . . . . . . . . . . .1J **107**
Bottleacre La. LE11: Lou . . . . . . . . . . . . . .3E **18**
Bottom Grn. LE14: Up Bro . . . . . . . . . . . .1A **110**
Bottom La. LE15: Bisb . . . . . . . . . . . . . . .2G **139**
Bottom Rd. LE67: Grif . . . . . . . . . . . . . . . .2A **26**
Bottom St. LE15: Win . . . . . . . . . . . . . . .5E **134**
Bott's La. DE12: A Mag . . . . . . . . . . . . . . .5B **48**
Botts Way LE67: Coal . . . . . . . . . . . . . . . .5F **39**
Boulder La. LE2: Leic . . . . . . . . . . . . . . . .2F **77**
Boulter Cres. LE18: Wig . . . . . . . . . . . . . .5K **77**
BOULTON . . . . . . . . . . . . . . . . . . . . . . .1A **158**
Boulton Cl. LE9: B Ast . . . . . . . . . . . . . . .6D **86**
Boulton Ct. LE2: Oad . . . . . . . . . . . . . . . .4G **79**
BOUNDARY . . . . . . . . . . . . . . . . . . . . . .1E **22**
Boundary Ct. DE74: C Don . . . . . . . . . . . .2K **7**
Boundary Rd. LE2: Leic . . . . . . . . . . . . . .6D **70**
   LE12: Moun . . . . . . . . . . . . . . . . . . . . .3D **44**
   LE17: Lut . . . . . . . . . . . . . . . . . . . . . .4K **153**
Boundary Way LE12: Shep . . . . . . . . . . . .5E **16**
BOURNE . . . . . . . . . . . . . . . . . . . . . . . . .2D **161**
Bourne Mall LE4: Beau L . . . . . . . . . . . . .2A **64**
Bourne Rd. PE9: Ess . . . . . . . . . . . . . . . .1K **129**
Bourton Cres. LE2: Oad . . . . . . . . . . . . . .3E **78**
Bouverie Ct. LE15: Whis . . . . . . . . . . . . . .2C **122**
Bowbridge Gdns. NG13: Bott . . . . . . . . . .1F **107**
Bowbridge La. NG13: Bott . . . . . . . . . . . .1F **107**
Bowden Ct. LE16: Mkt H . . . . . . . . . . . . .3G **151**
Bowden La. LE16: Mkt H . . . . . . . . . . . . .3E **150**
Bowden Ridge LE16: Mkt H . . . . . . . . . . .2G **151**
Bowden Rd. LE16: T Lan . . . . . . . . . . . . .4E **140**
Bowhill Gro. LE5: Leic . . . . . . . . . . . . . . .1G **73**
Bowhill Way LE5: Leic . . . . . . . . . . . . . . .7G **67**
Bowker Cres. LE65: Ash Z . . . . . . . . . . . .6H **23**
Bowler Ct. LE11: Lou . . . . . . . . . . . . . . . .6H **17**
Bowler Way LE11: Lou . . . . . . . . . . . . . . .6C **18**
Bowley, The DE74: Dis . . . . . . . . . . . . . . .4K **11**
Bowley Av. LE13: Mel M . . . . . . . . . . . . .2H **117**
Bowley Ct. LE13: Mel M . . . . . . . . . . . . . .4F **117**
Bowleys La. DE12: A Mag . . . . . . . . . . . .5A **48**

Bowling Grn. Cl. LE12: Sileby . . . . . . . . . .7K **33**
   LE15: O'ham . . . . . . . . . . . . . . . . . . . .5J **127**
Bowling Grn. La. LE15: Mkt O . . . . . . . . .1H **123**
Bowling Grn. Rd. LE10: Hinc . . . . . . . . . .2H **103**
Bowling Grn. St. LE1: Leic . . . . . .4D **4** (2F **71**)
Bowman Grn. LE10: Bur . . . . . . . . . . . . . .5J **103**
Bowmans Way LE3: Glen . . . . . . . . . . . . .6F **63**
Bowman's La. LE3: Leic . . . . . . . .1A **4** (7E **64**)
Boyers Orchard LE14: Harb . . . . . . . . . . .2D **108**
Boyer St. LE11: Lou . . . . . . . . . . . . . . . . .6G **19**
Boyers Wlk. LE3: Leic E . . . . . . . . . . . . . .4D **68**
Boyfields LE15: Whis . . . . . . . . . . . . . . . .2C **122**
Boynton Rd. LE3: Leic . . . . . . . . . . . . . . .3A **70**
Boyslade Rd. LE10: Bur . . . . . . . . . . . . . .6J **103**
Boyslade Rd. E. LE10: Bur . . . . . . . . . . . .6J **103**
Brabazon Rd. LE2: Oad . . . . . . . . . . . . . .2B **78**
BRACEBOROUGH . . . . . . . . . . . . . . . . . .3D **161**
BRACEBY . . . . . . . . . . . . . . . . . . . . . . . .1D **161**
Bracken Cl. LE3: Leic E . . . . . . . . . . . . . . .5D **68**
   LE5: Leic . . . . . . . . . . . . . . . . . . . . . . .3D **72**
   LE67: Hug . . . . . . . . . . . . . . . . . . . . . .6C **38**
Bracken Dale LE7: East G . . . . . . . . . . . .5G **47**
Brackenfield Way LE4: Thurm . . . . . . . . . .5C **60**
Bracken Hill LE6: New L . . . . . . . . . . . . . .5C **56**
Brackenthwaite LE4: Leic . . . . . . . . . . . . .3K **65**
Bracken Wlk. LE67: Mark . . . . . . . . . . . . .4G **55**
   (Bracken Way)
   LE67: Mark . . . . . . . . . . . . . . . . . . . . .5G **55**
   (Oakleaf Av.)
Bracken Way LE67: Mark . . . . . . . . . . . . .4G **55**
Brackley Cl. LE4: Leic . . . . . . . . . . . . . . . .5A **66**
Bradbourne Rd. LE5: Leic . . . . . . . . . . . . .2K **71**
Bradbury Cl. LE9: Cosb . . . . . . . . . . . . . .7H **81**
Braddon Rd. LE11: Lou . . . . . . . . . . . . . .4A **18**
Bradfield Cl. LE5: Leic . . . . . . . . . . . . . . .2A **72**
Bradfords La. LE67: Cole . . . . . . . . . . . . .4J **25**
Bradgate Av. LE4: Thurm . . . . . . . . . . . . .6B **60**
Bradgate Cl. LE7: Thurn . . . . . . . . . . . . . .2G **73**
   LE12: Moun . . . . . . . . . . . . . . . . . . . . .7D **32**
   LE12: Sileby . . . . . . . . . . . . . . . . . . . . .1J **45**
Bradgate Country Pk. . . . . . . . . . . . . . . .5D **56**
Bradgate Country Pk. Vis. Cen. . . . . . . . . .4F **57**
Bradgate Dr. LE6: Ratby . . . . . . . . . . . . .5A **62**
   LE18: Wig . . . . . . . . . . . . . . . . . . . . . .4H **77**
   LE67: Coal . . . . . . . . . . . . . . . . . . . . . .4J **39**
Bradgate Flats LE14: Ash . . . . . . . . . . . .2G **115**
Bradgate Hill LE6: Groby . . . . . . . . . . . . .7K **55**
Bradgate La. LE14: Ash . . . . . . . . . . . . . .2G **115**
Bradgate Mall LE4: Beau L . . . . . . . . . . .2B **64**
Bradgate Rd. LE6: New L . . . . . . . . . . . . .5C **56**
   LE7: Anst . . . . . . . . . . . . . . . . . . . . . .6F **57**
   LE7: Crop . . . . . . . . . . . . . . . . . . . . . .2H **57**
   LE9: Barw . . . . . . . . . . . . . . . . . . . . . .2A **100**
   LE10: Hinc . . . . . . . . . . . . . . . . . . . . .1J **103**
   LE11: Lou . . . . . . . . . . . . . . . . . . . . . .3C **30**
   LE67: Mark . . . . . . . . . . . . . . . . . . . . .4G **55**
Bradgate St. LE4: Leic . . . . . . . . . . . . . . .6D **64**
Brading Rd. LE3: Leic . . . . . . . . . . . . . . . .6C **64**
BRADLEY GREEN . . . . . . . . . . . . . . . . . .1A **162**
BRADMORE . . . . . . . . . . . . . . . . . . . . . .1C **159**
Bradshaw Av. LE2: G Par . . . . . . . . . . . . .5C **76**
Bradshaw Ct. LE2: G Par . . . . . . . . . . . . .5C **76**
Bradstone Cl. LE9: B Ast . . . . . . . . . . . . .5F **87**
Bradston Rd. LE2: Leic . . . . . . . . . . . . . . .3E **76**
Braemar Cl. LE4: Leic . . . . . . . . . . . . . . . .2J **65**
   LE12: Moun . . . . . . . . . . . . . . . . . . . . .4D **44**
Braemar Dr. LE4: Leic . . . . . . . . . . . . . . .2J **65**
Braeside LE15: A'll . . . . . . . . . . . . . . . . . .6H **123**
BRAILSFORD . . . . . . . . . . . . . . . . . . . . .1A **158**
Brailsford Rd. LE3: Leic . . . . . . . . . . . . . .2K **69**
   LE18: Wig . . . . . . . . . . . . . . . . . . . . . .4H **77**
Braithewaite Cl. PE9: Ket . . . . . . . . . . . . .6G **137**
Bramall Ct. LE5: Leic . . . . . . . . . . . . . . . .7A **66**
Bramall Rd. LE5: Leic . . . . . . . . . . . . . . . .7A **66**
Bramber Cl. LE4: Thurm . . . . . . . . . . . . . .7A **60**
Bramble Cl. LE3: Glen . . . . . . . . . . . . . . .7H **63**
   LE5: Ham . . . . . . . . . . . . . . . . . . . . . . .4F **67**
   LE11: Lou . . . . . . . . . . . . . . . . . . . . . .5C **18**
   LE15: Upp . . . . . . . . . . . . . . . . . . . . . .1C **138**
Bramble Dr. LE9: N Ver . . . . . . . . . . . . . .6H **93**
Brambles Rd. LE67: Hug . . . . . . . . . . . . .6C **38**
Bramble Wlk. LE9: Cosb . . . . . . . . . . . . . .5H **81**
Bramble Way LE3: Brau . . . . . . . . . . . . . .6A **70**
Brambling Rd. LE5: Leic . . . . . . . . . . . . . .7K **65**
Brambling Way LE2: Oad . . . . . . . . . . . . .3C **78**
BRAMCOTE
   Nottingham . . . . . . . . . . . . . . . . . . . . .3B **162**
   Nuneaton . . . . . . . . . . . . . . . . . . . . . .1C **159**
Bramcote Cl. LE10: Hinc . . . . . . . . . . . . .7J **99**
Bramcote Rd. LE3: Leic . . . . . . . . . . . . . .7B **70**
   LE11: Lou . . . . . . . . . . . . . . . . . . . . . .4D **30**
   LE18: Wig . . . . . . . . . . . . . . . . . . . . . .5J **77**
Brame Rd. LE10: Hinc . . . . . . . . . . . . . . .1F **103**
Bramham Cl. LE3: Leic . . . . . . . . . . . . . . .5B **64**
Bramley Cl. DE12: Moi . . . . . . . . . . . . . . .7C **22**
   LE9: B Ast . . . . . . . . . . . . . . . . . . . . . .3C **86**
   LE12: Sileby . . . . . . . . . . . . . . . . . . . . .7K **33**

Bramley Cl.—Brooksby Rd.

**Bramley Cl.** LE12: Wym ... 2K **21**
LE16: Mkt H ... 2F **151**
**Bramley Ct.** LE3: Glen ... 6F **63**
**Bramley Orchard** LE7: Bush ... 2J **73**
**Bramley Rd.** LE3: Leic ... 1C **70**
LE4: Birs ... 6H **59**
**BRAMPTON ASH** ... 3A **164**
**Brampton Av.** LE3: Leic ... 1B **70**
**Brampton Rd.** LE13: Mel M ... 1D **116**
**Brampton Valley Way** LE16: Mkt H, G Ox ... 6F **151**
**Brampton Way** LE2: Oad ... 2B **78**
**Brancaster Cl.** LE4: Leic ... 4D **64**
**Brand Hill** LE12: W Eav ... 4E **42**
**Brand La.** LE12: Wood, W Eav ... 2F **43**
**BRANDON** ... 3B **162**
**Brandon Ct.** LE8: Bla ... 7B **76**
**Brandon Rd.** LE10: Hinc ... 4E **102**
**Brandon St.** LE4: Leic ... 6G **65**
**Bransdale Rd.** LE18: Wig ... 6B **78**
**Branson Ct.** *LE9: S Stan ... 1K **105***
*(off Church St.)*
**BRANSTON** ... 6J **109** (2B **160**)
**Branston Av.** LE12: Bar S ... 3E **32**
**Branston Cres.** LE13: Mel M ... 5H **117**
**Branston Ho.** LE18: Wig ... 4G **77**
**Branston Rd.** LE15: Upp ... 1B **138**
**Branting Hill** LE6: Groby ... 3F **63**
**Branting Hill Av.** LE3: Glen ... 4F **63**
**Branting Hill Gro.** LE3: Glen ... 3F **63**
**BRASCOTE** ... 7G **93**
**Brascote La.** CV13: Cad ... 5C **94**
LE9: N Ver ... 7G **93**
**Brascote Rd.** LE10: Hinc ... 3C **102**
**Bratmyr** LE8: Flec ... 2B **88**
**Braunstone Av.** LE3: Leic ... 5K **69**
**Braunstone Cl.** LE3: Brau ... 6K **69**
**BRAUNSTONE FRITH** ... 1H **69**
**Braunstone Frith Ind. Est.** LE3: Leic ... 2F **69**
**Braunstone Ga.** LE3: Leic ... 5A **4** (2D **70**)
**Braunstone La.** LE3: Brau ... 4G **69**
(not continuous)
**Braunstone La. E.** LE3: Leic ... 7B **70**
**Braunstone Leisure Cen.** ... 3K **69**
**Braunstone Recreation Cen.** ... 3H **69**
**BRAUNSTONE TOWN** ... 6J **69** (1C **163**)
**Braunstone Way** LE3: Leic ... 4J **69**
**BRAUNSTON-IN-RUTLAND** ... 6C **126** (1B **164**)
**Braunston Rd.** LE15: B Rut, O'ham. . 4E **126** & 5F **127**
LE15: Knos ... 2C **126**
**BRAYBROOKE** ... 3A **164**
**Braybrooke Rd.** LE4: Leic ... 5A **66**
LE16: L Bow, Mkt H ... 5G **151**
**Braye Cotts.** LE17: Swin ... 4G **157**
**Braymish Cl.** LE8: Kib H ... 3K **89**
**Brazil St.** LE2: Leic ... 9B **5** (4E **70**)
**Breachfield Rd.** LE12: Bar S ... 4D **32**
**BREACH HILL** ... 1D **36**
**Breach La.** LE9: Earl S ... 3D **100**
**Breach Rd.** LE67: Coal ... 5D **38**
**Breadcroft La.** LE12: Bar S ... 3D **32**
**BREADSALL** ... 1A **158**
**Breakback Rd.** LE12: W Eav ... 1B **42**
**BREASTON** ... 1B **158**
**Brechin Cl.** LE10: Hinc ... 3D **102**
**Brecon Cl.** LE18: Wig ... 6F **77**
**Breech Hedge** LE7: R'ley ... 5E **44**
**Breedon Av.** LE18: Wig ... 5J **77**
**Breedon Brand** DE73: B Hil ... 1C **14**
**Breedon La.** LE12: Osg ... 4B **14**
LE65: Wort ... 2B **14**
**BREEDON ON THE HILL** ... 7A **10** (2B **158**)
**Breedon St.** LE2: Leic ... 2J **71**
**Brendon Cl.** LE12: Shep ... 2E **28**
**Brendon Way** LE65: Ash Z ... 6K **23**
**Brenfield Dr.** LE10: Hinc ... 3D **102**
**Brent Ct.** LE3: Brau ... 1K **75**
**BRENTINGBY** ... 3A **160**
**Brentingby Cl.** LE13: Mel M ... 6G **117**
**Brent Knowle Gdns.** LE5: Leic ... 2F **73**
**Brentwood Rd.** LE2: Leic ... 6G **71**
**BRETBY** ... 2A **158**
**Bretby Rd.** LE2: Leic ... 2E **76**
**BRETFORD** ... 3B **162**
**Breton Cl.** LE18: Kilby ... 6C **84**
**Brettell Rd.** LE2: Leic ... 4D **76**
**Bretton Cl.** LE4: Leic ... 3E **64**
**Bretton Wlk.** LE4: Leic ... 3E **64**
**Breward Way** LE13: Mel M ... 1G **117**
**Brewer Cl.** LE4: Leic ... 1A **66**
**Brex Ri.** LE3: Leic ... 1H **69**
**Brian Rd.** LE4: Leic ... 5D **64**
**Brians Cl.** LE7: Sys ... 1E **60**
**Brianway, The** LE5: Leic ... 7B **66**
**Briar Cl.** DE11: Blac ... 3D **22**
LE2: Oad ... 4D **78**
LE10: Bur ... 5J **103**
LE67: Hug ... 5C **38**
**Briarfield Dr.** LE5: Leic ... 5G **67**
**Briargate Dr.** LE4: Birs ... 5E **58**
**Briarmead** LE10: Bur ... 7H **103**
**Briar Meads** LE2: Oad ... 5C **78**
**Briar Rd.** LE5: Leic ... 7F **67**
**Briar Wlk.** LE2: Oad ... 4D **78**
**Brick Kiln Cft.** DE12: Mea ... 7F **35**
**Brick Kiln La.** LE12: Shep ... 2C **28**
LE67: Ibs ... 5K **51**
**Brick Kiln St.** LE10: Hinc ... 3F **103**
**Brickman Cl.** LE3: Leic E ... 5C **68**
**Brickwood Pl.** LE12: Bur W ... 3F **21**
**Brick Yd. La.** LE14: W'ham ... 1G **121**
**Bridevale Rd.** LE2: Leic ... 3E **76**
**Bridge Bus. Pk.** LE4: Thurm ... 6K **59**
**Bridge Cl.** DE11: C Gre ... 1A **22**
LE4: Thurm ... 5B **60**
**BRIDGE END** ... 1D **161**
**Bridge Flds.** DE74: Keg ... 5J **9**
**Bridgeland Rd.** LE11: Lou ... 6G **19**
**Bridge La.** CV9: With ... 6B **96**
DE72: W Tre ... 4A **6**
LE15: Gree ... 5G **125**
**Bridgemere Cl.** LE2: Leic ... 4B **76**
**Bridge M.** LE67: Whit ... 1D **38**
**Bridge Pk. Rd.** LE4: Thurm ... 6K **59**
**Bridge Pl.** LE65: Ash Z ... 4K **23**
**Bridge Rd.** LE5: Leic ... 1K **71**
LE10: Bur ... 4G **103**
LE67: Coal ... 4D **38**
**Bridgeside Cotts.** LE11: Lou ... 5E **18**
**Bridge St.** DE11: C Gre ... 1A **22**
LE11: Lou ... 6E **18**
LE12: Bar S ... 4C **32**
LE12: Shep ... 6D **16**
LE15: L'ham ... 5C **122**
LE65: Pac ... 3A **36**
PE9: Ryh ... 5H **129**
**Bridgewater Dr.** LE8: G Gle ... 7K **79**
**Bridge Way** LE8: Whet ... 3K **81**
**Bridle, The** LE2: G Par ... 4B **76**
**Bridle Cl.** LE9: Crof ... 6A **80**
LE13: Mel M ... 2D **116**
**Bridle Path Rd.** LE9: Elm ... 6C **100**
**Bridle Rd.** LE67: Coal ... 1C **38**
**Bridlespur Way** LE4: Leic ... 1E **64**
**Bridport Cl.** LE18: Wig ... 7K **77**
**Brierfield Rd.** LE9: Cosb ... 7H **81**
**Briers Cl.** LE19: Nar ... 2F **81**
**Briers Way** LE67: Whit ... 6E **26**
**Briggins Wlk.** *LE15: L'ham ... 5C **122***
*(off Burley Rd.)*
**Brighton Av.** LE7: Sys ... 1E **60**
LE18: Wig ... 3J **77**
**Brighton Cl.** LE18: Wig ... 3J **77**
**Brighton Rd.** LE5: Leic ... 6K **65**
**Brightside Av.** LE13: Mel M ... 3D **116**
**Brightside Rd.** LE5: Leic ... 3A **72**
**Brightwell Dr.** LE3: Leic E ... 3F **69**
**BRIGSTOCK** ... 3C **165**
**Brindley Ri.** LE5: Leic ... 5G **67**
**Brindley Rd.** LE10: Hinc ... 3B **102**
LE67: Coal ... 2A **38**
**BRINGHURST** ... 7J **141** (2B **164**)
**Bringhurst Grn.** LE3: Leic ... 7J **63**
**Bringhurst Rd.** LE3: Leic ... 7H **63**
**Brington Cl.** LE18: Wig ... 6A **78**
**BRINKLOW** ... 3B **162**
**Brinks, The** LE12: Quo ... 6B **32**
**Brinsmead Rd.** LE2: Leic ... 1H **77**
**Brisco Av.** LE11: Lou ... 4D **18**
**Briscoe La.** LE12: Wood ... 7F **31**
**Bristol Av.** LE4: Leic ... 5D **64**
LE65: Ash Z ... 7J **23**
**Britannia Rd.** LE10: Bur ... 6K **103**
**Britannia Shop. Cen.** LE10: Hinc ... 2G **103**
**Britannia St.** LE1: Leic ... 1E **4** (7G **65**)
LE12: Shep ... 6D **16**
**Britannia Wlk.** LE16: Mkt H ... 5F **151**
**Britannia Way** LE4: Thurm ... 4A **60**
**Britannia Works** LE4: Thurm ... 4A **60**
**Britford Av.** LE18: Wig ... 1J **83**
**British Aviation Heritage** ... 2D **146**
**British School Gdns.** *LE13: Mel M ... 4F **117***
*(off Chapel St.)*
**Briton Lodge Cl.** DE12: Moi ... 7B **22**
**Briton St.** LE3: Leic ... 3D **70**
**Brittany Av.** LE65: Ash Z ... 4J **23**
**Brixham Dr.** LE2: Leic ... 3G **77**
LE18: Wig ... 3G **77**
**Brixworth Ri.** LE5: Leic ... 1G **73**
**Broad Av.** LE5: Leic ... 1B **72**
**Broadbent Cl.** LE8: Whet ... 2K **81**
**Broadfield Way** LE8: Count ... 5D **82**
**Broadford Cl.** LE4: Leic ... 2K **65**
**Broadgate** LE16: G Eas ... 5K **141**
**Broadgate Cl.** LE4: Birs ... 5G **59**
**BROAD HILL** ... 2C **44**
**Broadhill Rd.** DE74: Keg ... 6G **9**
**Broadhurst St.** LE4: Leic ... 4H **65**
**Broad La.** LE67: Mark ... 6C **54**
**Broad Mdw.** LE18: Wig ... 7A **78**
**Broadmead Rd.** LE8: Bla ... 3A **82**
**Broadnook Cl.** LE3: Leic ... 3J **63**
**Broad Rushes** DE74: C Don ... 2K **7**
**Broad St.** LE7: Sys ... 2C **60**
LE11: Lou ... 6E **18**
LE19: End ... 5F **75**
LE67: Coal ... 4D **38**
**Broadsword Way** LE10: Bur ... 7G **103**
**Broadway** LE7: Sys ... 2C **60**
LE11: Lou ... 3E **30**
**Broadway, The** LE2: Oad ... 6B **72**
LE16: Mkt H ... 3E **150**
**Broadway Furlong** LE7: Anst ... 6J **57**
**Broadway Rd.** LE5: Leic ... 5K **71**
**Broadway Ter.** LE16: Mkt H ... 3F **151**
**Brockenhurst Dr.** LE3: Brau ... 7J **69**
**BROCKEY, THE** ... 2A **100**
**Brockey Cl.** LE9: Barw ... 3A **100**
**Brockhurst Av.** LE10: Bur ... 7G **103**
**Brocklehurst Rd.** LE13: Mel M ... 2H **117**
**Brocklesby Way** LE5: Leic ... 6G **67**
**Brocks Hill Cl.** LE2: Oad ... 4D **78**
**Brocks Hill Country Pk.** ... 5B **78**
**Brocks Hill Dr.** LE2: Oad ... 3D **78**
**Brocks Hill Environment Cen.** ... 4B **78**
**Broctone Cl.** LE9: B Ast ... 5F **87**
**Broctone Dr.** LE9: B Ast ... 3C **86**
**Brodick Cl.** LE10: Hinc ... 3D **102**
**Brodick Rd.** LE10: Hinc ... 3C **102**
**Brodick Wlk.** LE5: Leic ... 6K **65**
**Bromhead St.** LE11: Lou ... 5G **19**
**Bromley La.** LE12: Belt ... 4H **15**
**Brompton Rd.** LE5: Ham ... 3E **66**
**Bromwich Cl.** LE3: Brau ... 5G **69**
**Bronte Cl.** LE3: Leic ... 3A **70**
**Bronze Barrow Cl.** LE18: Wig ... 7B **78**
**Brook Bank** LE5: Leic ... 7B **66**
**Brook Cl.** LE15: Upp ... 3D **138**
LE65: Pac ... 3K **35**
**Brook Ct.** LE8: Count ... 5F **83**
**Brook Cres.** LE14: Ash ... 2J **115**
**Brookdale** LE10: Hinc ... 3E **102**
**Brookdale Rd.** LE3: Leic ... 2H **69**
**Brookdene** LE15: A'll ... 6H **123**
**Brook Dr.** LE6: Ratby ... 6A **62**
**BROOKE** ... 1B **164**
**Brooke Cl.** LE15: O'ham ... 3K **127**
**Brooke Rd.** LE15: B Rut, O'ham ... 6D **126** & 7G **127**
LE15: Rid ... 1H **133**
**Brookes Av.** LE9: Crof ... 6A **80**
**Brookes Ho.** LE9: Crof ... 6A **80**
**Brookes's Yard** *LE10: Hinc ... 2G **103***
*(off King St.)*
**Brook Farm Ct.** LE12: Hot ... 1D **20**
**Brookfield** LE8: G Gle ... 1J **85**
LE10: S'ord ... 6H **105**
**Brookfield Av.** LE7: Sys ... 2D **60**
LE11: Lou ... 2C **30**
**Brookfield Bowling Club** ... 4K **71**
**Brookfield Ct.** LE13: Mel M ... 2E **116**
**Brookfield Ri.** LE2: Leic ... 2F **77**
**Brookfield Rd.** LE10: Bur ... 5F **103**
LE16: Mkt H ... 4C **150**
**Brookfield St.** LE7: Sys ... 2D **60**
LE13: Mel M ... 2E **116**
**Brookfield Way** LE8: K Bea ... 3K **89**
LE17: Lut ... 5G **153**
**Brook Gdns.** LE2: G Par ... 5B **76**
**Brookhouse Av.** LE2: Leic ... 6G **5** (3H **71**)
**Brook Ho. Cl.** LE7: Rear ... 3J **47**
**Brookhouse St.** LE2: Leic ... 6G **5** (3H **71**)
**Brookland Rd.** LE2: Leic ... 6G **71**
**Brooklands Cl.** LE8: Whet ... 2K **81**
LE9: B Ast ... 4D **86**
**Brooklands Gdns.** LE16: Mkt H ... 4E **150**
**Brooklands Rd.** LE9: Cosb ... 5H **81**
**Brookland Way** LE12: Moun ... 4E **44**
**Brook La.** LE7: Bill ... 6J **131**
LE9: Peck ... 5J **95**
LE11: Lou ... 3B **30**
LE12: Bar S ... 3D **32**
LE13: Mel M ... 5G **117**
LE14: Ash ... 3G **115**
LE16: T Lan ... 2E **140**
LE67: Thrin ... 4D **26**
**Brook Rd.** LE5: Leic ... 7F **67**
LE12: W Eav ... 7B **30**
**Brooks, The** LE15: Ext ... 3D **128**
**BROOKSBY** ... 3D **159**
**Brooksby Cl.** LE2: Oad ... 2C **78**
**Brooksby Dr.** LE2: Oad ... 2C **78**
**Brooksby Rd.** LE14: Hob ... 4B **114**

Brooksby St. LE2: Leic . . . . . . . . . . . . . . . . . .6E 70
Brook Side LE65: Ash Z . . . . . . . . . . . . . . . . .5K 23
(off Brook St.)
Brookside CV13: B'one . . . . . . . . . . . . . . . . . .6C 92
DE74: Dis . . . . . . . . . . . . . . . . . . . . . . .4A 12
LE5: Leic . . . . . . . . . . . . . . . . . . . . . . .4K 71
LE7: Bark . . . . . . . . . . . . . . . . . . . . . . .5F 61
LE7: Rear . . . . . . . . . . . . . . . . . . . . . . .2J 47
LE7: Sys . . . . . . . . . . . . . . . . . . . . . . . .1C 60
(not continuous)
LE8: Whet . . . . . . . . . . . . . . . . . . . . . . .3K 81
LE10: Bur . . . . . . . . . . . . . . . . . . . . . . .5G 103
Brookside Cl. LE12: Bar S . . . . . . . . . . . . . . .2D 32
LE12: Shep . . . . . . . . . . . . . . . . . . . . . . .1E 28
Brookside Cres. LE67: Ibs . . . . . . . . . . . . . . .3K 51
Brookside Dr. LE2: Oad . . . . . . . . . . . . . . . . .3E 78
Brookside Gdns. LE8: Flec . . . . . . . . . . . . . . .4B 88
Brookside Pl. CV9: S Mag . . . . . . . . . . . . . . . .5C 90
Brookside Rd. LE11: Lou . . . . . . . . . . . . . . . .3B 30
Brooks La. LE67: Whit . . . . . . . . . . . . . . . . . .6D 26
Brook St. LE4: Thurm . . . . . . . . . . . . . . . . . .6K 59
LE7: Rear . . . . . . . . . . . . . . . . . . . . . . .3J 47
LE7: Sys . . . . . . . . . . . . . . . . . . . . . . . .1C 60
LE8: Whet . . . . . . . . . . . . . . . . . . . . . . .2K 81
LE9: Hun . . . . . . . . . . . . . . . . . . . . . . . .2B 80
LE12: Bur W . . . . . . . . . . . . . . . . . . . . . . .3F 21
LE12: Shep . . . . . . . . . . . . . . . . . . . . . . .6D 16
LE12: Sileby . . . . . . . . . . . . . . . . . . . . . . .1J 45
LE12: Wym . . . . . . . . . . . . . . . . . . . . . . .2K 21
LE13: Mel M . . . . . . . . . . . . . . . . . . . . . .4G 117
LE17: Wal . . . . . . . . . . . . . . . . . . . . . . .2D 154
LE19: End . . . . . . . . . . . . . . . . . . . . . . .5F 75
LE65: Ash Z . . . . . . . . . . . . . . . . . . . . . .5K 23
Brook Ter. LE16: Med . . . . . . . . . . . . . . . . . .7C 140
Broom Av. LE11: Lou . . . . . . . . . . . . . . . . . .4E 30
Broombriggs Rd. LE3: Leic . . . . . . . . . . . . . . .3J 63
Broome Av. LE7: East G . . . . . . . . . . . . . . . . .4G 47
Broome La. LE7: East G, Rat W . . . . . . . . . . . .3D 46
Broomfield LE7: East G . . . . . . . . . . . . . . . . .5G 47
Broomhills Rd. LE19: Nar . . . . . . . . . . . . . . . .1D 80
Broomleys LE8: Count . . . . . . . . . . . . . . . . . .5D 82
Broom Leys Av. LE67: Coal . . . . . . . . . . . . . . .4F 39
Broom Leys Rd. LE67: Coal . . . . . . . . . . . . . . .4E 38
Broom Way LE19: Nar . . . . . . . . . . . . . . . . . .7D 74
Brosdale Dr. LE10: Hinc . . . . . . . . . . . . . . . .2D 102
Brougham St. LE1: Leic . . . . . . . . . . .2F 4 (1G 71)
BROUGHTON . . . . . . . . . . . . . . . . . . . . . .3B 164
BROUGHTON ASTLEY . . . . . . . . . .5E 86 (2C 163)
Broughton Cl. LE7: Anst . . . . . . . . . . . . . . . . .6J 57
LE11: Lou . . . . . . . . . . . . . . . . . . . . . . .6A 18
Broughton La. LE8: Will W . . . . . . . . . . . . . . .4K 87
LE9: B Ast . . . . . . . . . . . . . . . . . . . . . . .6C 86
LE9: Cosb . . . . . . . . . . . . . . . . . . . . . . .4K 87
LE14: L Cla . . . . . . . . . . . . . . . . . . . . . . .3F 111
LE9: Leire . . . . . . . . . . . . . . . . . . . . . . .6C 86
BROUGHTON LODGES . . . . . . . . . . . . . . . . .4D 110
Broughton Rd. LE2: Leic . . . . . . . . . . . . . . . .3E 76
LE9: Cosb . . . . . . . . . . . . . . . . . . . . . . .2F 87
LE9: Crof . . . . . . . . . . . . . . . . . . . . . . .5A 80
LE9: S Stan . . . . . . . . . . . .1K 105 & 2A 86
LE17: D Bas . . . . . . . . . . . . . . . . . . . . . .7F 87
LE17: Frol . . . . . . . . . . . . . . . . . . . . . . .1F 143
Broughtons Fld. LE18: Wig . . . . . . . . . . . . . . .1A 84
Broughton St. LE67: Coal . . . . . . . . . . . . . . . .4D 38
Broughton Way LE9: B Ast . . . . . . . . . . . . . . .2B 86
Brown Av. LE12: Quo . . . . . . . . . . . . . . . . . .5A 32
Brown Ct. LE65: Ash Z . . . . . . . . . . . . . . . . .4H 23
Brownhill Cres. LE7: R'ley . . . . . . . . . . . . . . . .7B 44
Browning Cl. LE13: Mel M . . . . . . . . . . . . . . . .1F 117
Browning Dr. DE12: Mea . . . . . . . . . . . . . . . .2D 48
LE10: Hinc . . . . . . . . . . . . . . . . . . . . . . .2F 103
Browning Rd. LE11: Lou . . . . . . . . . . . . . . . . .6B 18
LE15: O'ham . . . . . . . . . . . . . . . . . . . . . .4G 127
Browning St. LE3: Leic . . . . . . . . . . . . . . . . .3C 70
LE19: Nar . . . . . . . . . . . . . . . . . . . . . . .7E 74
Brownlow Cres. LE13: Mel M . . . . . . . . . . . . . .7F 117
Brown's Cl. LE9: Sap . . . . . . . . . . . . . . . . . .3K 105
Browns La. LE11: Lou . . . . . . . . . . . . . . . . . .7E 18
Browns Way LE8: Whet . . . . . . . . . . . . . . . . .4K 81
Broxburn Cl. LE4: Leic . . . . . . . . . . . . . . . . .2K 65
Broxfield Cl. LE2: Oad . . . . . . . . . . . . . . . . .5C 78
Bruces La. LE14: Som . . . . . . . . . . . . . . . . . .1A 126
LE15: Knos . . . . . . . . . . . . . . . . . . . . . . .1A 126
Bruce St. LE3: Leic . . . . . . . . . . . . . . . . . . .4D 70
Bruce Way LE8: Whet . . . . . . . . . . . . . . . . . .4J 81
Bruin St. LE4: Leic . . . . . . . . . . . . . . . . . . .5G 65
Bruins Wlk. LE2: Oad . . . . . . . . . . . . . . . . . .3B 78
Brunel Av. LE3: Leic . . . . . . . . . . . . . . . . . .6A 64
Brunel Rd. LE10: Hinc . . . . . . . . . . . . . . . . . .3F 103
Brunel Way LE67: Coal . . . . . . . . . . . . . . . . . .1B 38
Brunswick St. LE1: Leic . . . . . . . . . .2G 4 (1H 71)
BRUNTINGTHORPE . . . . . . .1D 146 (2D 163)
Bruntingthorpe Aerodrome and Proving Ground
. . . . . . . . . . . . . . . . . . . . . . . . . . . . .3B 146
Bruntingthorpe Ind. Est. LE17: U Bru . . . . . . .3D 146
Bruntingthorpe Rd. LE17: P Par . . . . . . . . . . .2A 146
LE17: Shea . . . . . . . . . . . . . . . . . . . . . . .7H 147

Brush Dr. LE11: Lou . . . . . . . . . . . . . . . . . . .4F 19
Brushfield Av. LE12: Sileby . . . . . . . . . . . . . . .7K 33
Bruxby St. LE7: Sys . . . . . . . . . . . . . . . . . . .2B 60
Bryan Cl. LE12: Bar S . . . . . . . . . . . . . . . . . .3D 32
Bryan's Cl. LE67: Whit . . . . . . . . . . . . . . . . .5F 27
Bryar's Cl. LE8: Sad . . . . . . . . . . . . . . . . . .7D 88
Bryngarth Cres. LE5: Leic . . . . . . . . . . . . . . .7D 66
Bryony Rd. LE5: Ham . . . . . . . . . . . . . . . . . .4F 67
Buccaneer Way LE17: Lut . . . . . . . . . . . . . . .4C 152
Buchan Wlk. LE3: Leic . . . . . . . . . . . . . . . . .2A 70
Buckfast Cl. LE5: Leic . . . . . . . . . . . . . . . . .4B 72
LE18: Wig . . . . . . . . . . . . . . . . . . . . . . .7J 77
Buckhaven Cl. LE4: Leic . . . . . . . . . . . . . . . .2K 65
Buckhorn Sq. LE11: Lou . . . . . . . . . . . . . . . .6G 19
Buckingham Cl. LE6: Groby . . . . . . . . . . . . . .4C 62
LE10: Hinc . . . . . . . . . . . . . . . . . . . . . . .6H 99
Buckingham Dr. LE2: Leic . . . . . . . . . . . . . . .3B 76
LE11: Lou . . . . . . . . . . . . . . . . . . . . . . .5A 18
Buckingham Rd. LE8: Count . . . . . . . . . . . . . .5F 83
LE15: O'ham . . . . . . . . . . . . . . . . . . . . . .5H 127
LE67: Coal . . . . . . . . . . . . . . . . . . . . . . .3F 39
Buckinghams Way LE10: S'ord . . . . . . . . . . . .7G 105
Buckland Rd. LE5: Leic . . . . . . . . . . . . . . . . .6K 65
Buckley Cl. DE12: Mea . . . . . . . . . . . . . . . . .1E 48
BUCKMINSTER . . . . . . . . . . . . .5G 113 (2B 160)
Buckminster Cl. LE13: Mel M . . . . . . . . . . . . .5H 117
Buckminster Pk. . . . . . . . . . . . . . . . . . . . . .3K 113
Buckminster Rd. LE3: Leic . . . . . . . . . . . . . . .6C 64
LE14: Spro . . . . . . . . . . . . . . . . . . . . . . .2H 113
NG33: Buck . . . . . . . . . . . . . . . . . . . . . . .2H 113
Bucksburn Wlk. LE4: Leic . . . . . . . . . . . . . . .2K 65
Buckwell Rd. LE9: Sap . . . . . . . . . . . . . . . . .3J 105
BUCKWORTH . . . . . . . . . . . . . . . . . . . . . . .3D 165
Buddon Cl. LE3: Leic . . . . . . . . . . . . . . . . . .3J 63
Buddon Ct. LE12: Moun . . . . . . . . . . . . . . . . .3E 44
Buddon La. LE12: Quo . . . . . . . . . . . . . . . . .7J 31
Bude Dr. LE3: Glen . . . . . . . . . . . . . . . . . . .5G 63
Bude Rd. LE18: Wig . . . . . . . . . . . . . . . . . . .7K 77
BULBY . . . . . . . . . . . . . . . . . . . . . . . . . .2D 161
BULKINGTON . . . . . . . . . . . . . . . . . . . . . . .3A 162
Bullacres La. LE17: Shaw . . . . . . . . . . . . . . .3B 156
Buller Rd. LE4: Leic . . . . . . . . . . . . . . . . . . .5G 65
Buller St. LE8: K Bea . . . . . . . . . . . . . . . . . .3H 89
Bullfield Cl. LE15: Gree . . . . . . . . . . . . . . . . .4F 125
Bullfinch Cl. LE15: O'ham . . . . . . . . . . . . . . .2J 127
Bullfurlong La. LE10: Bur . . . . . . . . . . . . . . .6J 103
Bull Head St. LE18: Wig . . . . . . . . . . . . . . . .4K 77
Bull Hill LE12: Osg . . . . . . . . . . . . . . . . . . .3B 14
LE65: Wort . . . . . . . . . . . . . . . . . . . . . . .3B 14
Bull La. LE15: O'ham . . . . . . . . . . . . . . . . . .4J 127
PE9: Ket . . . . . . . . . . . . . . . . . . . . . . . .5H 137
Bull Ring LE12: Shep . . . . . . . . . . . . . . . . . .7D 16
Bull's Head Row DE73: Wils . . . . . . . . . . . . . .3A 10
Bulrush Cl. LE12: Moun . . . . . . . . . . . . . . . . .3F 45
Bulstrode Pl. DE74: Keg . . . . . . . . . . . . . . . .6G 9
Bulwer Rd. LE2: Leic . . . . . . . . . . . . . . . . . .6H 71
(not continuous)
BULWICK . . . . . . . . . . . . . . . . . . . . . . . . .2C 165
Bumble Bee Gdns. LE10: S'ord . . . . . . . . . . . .7H 105
Bungalows, The LE9: N Ver . . . . . . . . . . . . . .6H 93
BUNKER HILL . . . . . . . . . . . . . . . . . . . . . . .6F 17
Bunneys Mdw. LE10: Hinc . . . . . . . . . . . . . . .5C 102
BUNNY . . . . . . . . . . . . . . . . . . . . . . . . . .2C 159
BURBAGE . . . . . . . . . . . . . . . . .5K 103 (2B 162)
Burbage Cl. LE11: Lou . . . . . . . . . . . . . . . . . .4C 18
Burbage Common Country Pk. . . . . . . . . . . . .7A 100
Burbage Common Country Pk. Vis. Cen.
. . . . . . . . . . . . . . . . . . . . . . . . . . . . .7A 100
Burbage Comn. Rd. LE9: Elm . . . . . . . . . . . . .1D 104
LE10: Elm . . . . . . . . . . . . . . . . . . . . . . .7A 100
Burbage Rd. LE10: Bur . . . . . . . . . . . . . . . . .3J 103
Burbage Wood Country Pk. . . . . . . . . . . . . . .2A 104
Burchnall Rd. LE3: Brau . . . . . . . . . . . . . . . .6G 69
Burden La. LE14: Harb . . . . . . . . . . . . . . . . .2D 108
Burder St. LE11: Lou . . . . . . . . . . . . . . . . . .4F 19
Burdett Cl. LE3: Brau . . . . . . . . . . . . . . . . . .6J 69
Burdett Cl. LE17: Gilm . . . . . . . . . . . . . . . . .7J 145
Burdetts Cl. LE14: G Dal . . . . . . . . . . . . . . . .6C 120
Burdett Way LE4: Leic . . . . . . . . . . . . . . . . .2D 64
Burditt Cl. LE67: Bag . . . . . . . . . . . . . . . . . .6F 53
Burdock Cl. LE5: Ham . . . . . . . . . . . . . . . . . .4F 67
Burfield Av. LE11: Lou . . . . . . . . . . . . . . . . . .7E 18
Burfield St. LE4: Leic . . . . . . . . . . . . . . . . . .6H 65
Burford Cl. LE16: Mkt H . . . . . . . . . . . . . . . .6D 150
Burgess Rd. LE2: Leic . . . . . . . . . . . . . . . . .2E 76
LE67: Coal . . . . . . . . . . . . . . . . . . . . . . .4C 38
Burgess Row LE16: C'ott . . . . . . . . . . . . . . . .2H 141
Burgess St. LE1: Leic . . . . . . . . .1B 4 (1E 70)
LE18: Wig . . . . . . . . . . . . . . . . . . . . . . .5K 77
Burghley Circ. LE15: Cott . . . . . . . . . . . . . . .4C 124
Burghley Cl. LE16: L Bow . . . . . . . . . . . . . . .4G 151
Burgin Rd. LE7: Anst . . . . . . . . . . . . . . . . . .1H 63
Burgins La. LE14: W Wol . . . . . . . . . . . . . . . .1C 112
Burleigh Av. LE18: Wig . . . . . . . . . . . . . . . . .4H 77
Burleigh Rd. LE10: Hinc . . . . . . . . . . . . . . . .1F 103
LE11: Lou . . . . . . . . . . . . . . . . . . . . . . .6E 18
BURLEY . . . . . . . . . . . . . . . . . . . . . . . . . .3B 160

Burley Cl. LE9: Cosb . . . . . . . . . . . . . . . . . .6H 81
LE9: Des . . . . . . . . . . . . . . . . . . . . . . . .2H 95
Burley Homes LE4: Birs . . . . . . . . . . . . . . . . .1F 65
Burley Parkway LE15: O'ham . . . . . . . . . . . . .3K 127
Burley Ri. DE74: Keg . . . . . . . . . . . . . . . . . .7H 9
Burley Rd. LE15: Cott . . . . . . . . . . . . . . . . . .7A 124
(not continuous)
LE15: L'ham . . . . . . . . . . . . . . . . . . . . . .5C 122
LE15: O'ham . . . . . . . . . . . . . . . . . . . . . .4J 127
PE9: Ryh . . . . . . . . . . . . . . . . . . . . . . . .6G 129
Burleys Flyover LE1: Leic . . . . . .1D 4 (7F 65)
Burleys Way LE1: Leic . . . . . . . .1C 4 (7F 65)
Burlington Rd. LE2: Leic . . . . . . . . . . . . . . . .6J 71
Burnaby Av. LE5: Leic . . . . . . . . . . . . . . . . .1K 71
Burnaby Pl. LE14: Ash . . . . . . . . . . . . . . . . .2G 115
BURNASTON . . . . . . . . . . . . . . . . . . . . . . .1A 158
Burnaston Rd. LE2: Leic . . . . . . . . . . . . . . . .2E 76
Burnaston Way LE11: Lou . . . . . . . . . . . . . . .4G 31
Burnell Rd. LE3: Leic . . . . . . . . . . . . . . . . . .5B 70
Burneston Way LE18: Wig . . . . . . . . . . . . . . .6A 78
Burnet Cl. LE5: Ham . . . . . . . . . . . . . . . . . . .4E 66
Burney La. DE73: Mel . . . . . . . . . . . . . . . . . .7A 10
Burnham Cl. LE18: Wig . . . . . . . . . . . . . . . . .2K 83
Burnham Ct. LE9: Cosb . . . . . . . . . . . . . . . . .7H 81
Burnham Dr. LE4: Leic . . . . . . . . . . . . . . . . .4D 64
LE8: Whet . . . . . . . . . . . . . . . . . . . . . . .3K 81
Burnhams Rd. PE9: Ket . . . . . . . . . . . . . . . . .6G 137
Burnmill Rd. LE16: G Bow, Mkt H . . . . . . . . . .3E 150
Burnmoor St. LE2: Leic . . . . . . . . .10B 5 (5E 70)
LE13: Mel M . . . . . . . . . . . . . . . . . . . . . .1E 116
Burns Cl. DE12: Mea . . . . . . . . . . . . . . . . . .2D 48
Burnside Rd. LE2: Leic . . . . . . . . . . . . . . . . .2G 77
LE9: B Ast . . . . . . . . . . . . . . . . . . . . . . .5D 86
Burns Rd. LE11: Lou . . . . . . . . . . . . . . . . . . .5B 18
Burns St. LE2: Leic . . . . . . . . . . . . . . . . . . .7G 71
LE19: Nar . . . . . . . . . . . . . . . . . . . . . . .7F 75
Burnsway LE10: Hinc . . . . . . . . . . . . . . . . . .2F 103
Burrough End LE14: G Dal . . . . . . . . . . . . . . .6C 120
Burrough Hill Country Pk. . . . . . . . . . . . . . . .3A 160
BURROUGH ON THE HILL . . . . . .6F 121 (3A 160)
Burrough Rd. LE14: G Dal . . . . . . . . . . . . . . .6D 120
LE14: J O'Ga . . . . . . . . . . . . . . . . . . . . .7H 119
(not continuous)
LE14: Som . . . . . . . . . . . . . . . . . . . . . . .5H 121
Burroughs Rd. LE6: Ratby . . . . . . . . . . . . . . .6A 62
Burrough Way LE17: Lut . . . . . . . . . . . . . . . .2J 153
Burrow Cl. LE3: Leic . . . . . . . . . . . . . . . . . .3J 63
Burrows, The LE19: Nar . . . . . . . . . . . . . . . .1D 80
Burrows Cl. LE19: Nar . . . . . . . . . . . . . . . . .2F 81
Bursdon Cl. LE3: Leic . . . . . . . . . . . . . . . . . .1H 69
Bursdon Ct. LE3: Leic . . . . . . . . . . . . . . . . .1H 69
Bursnells La. LE14: W'ham . . . . . . . . . . . . . .1G 121
Bursom Ind. Est. LE4: Beau L . . . . . . . . . . . . .7C 58
Bursom Rd. LE4: Beau L . . . . . . . . . . . . . . . .7B 58
BURTON BANDALLS . . . . . . . . . . . . . . . . . . .5A 20
Burton Cl. LE2: Oad . . . . . . . . . . . . . . . . . . .4F 79
LE14: Harb . . . . . . . . . . . . . . . . . . . . . . .2C 108
LE17: Lut . . . . . . . . . . . . . . . . . . . . . . . .5K 153
BURTON COGGLES . . . . . . . . . . . . . . . . . . .2C 161
Burton Hall LE12: Bur W . . . . . . . . . . . . . . . .4F 21
BURTON HASTINGS . . . . . . . . . . . . . . . . . . .3B 162
BURTON JOYCE . . . . . . . . . . . . . . . . . . . . .1D 159
Burton La. LE12: Bur W . . . . . . . . . . . . . . . . .4B 20
LE12: Wym . . . . . . . . . . . . . . . . . .2J 21 & 1H 31
BURTON LAZARS . . . . . . . . . . . .2C 120 (3A 160)
BURTON ON THE WOLDS . . . . . . . .3G 21 (2C 159)
BURTON OVERY . . . . . . . . . . . . . .5D 130 (2D 163)
BURTON PEDWARDINE . . . . . . . . . . . . . . . . .1D 161
Burton Rd. CV9: N Twy, Twy . . . . . . . . . . . . .1A 90
CV13: F Dray . . . . . . . . . . . . . . . . . . . . . .4H 97
DE12: Mea . . . . . . . . . . . . . . . . . . . . . . .7C 34
LE12: Sileby . . . . . . . . . . . . . . . . . . . . . .1J 45
LE13: Mel M . . . . . . . . . . . . . . . . . . . . . .5F 117
LE65: Ash Z . . . . . . . . . . . . . . . . . . . . . .2G 23
Burtons La. LE67: Swan . . . . . . . . . . . . . . . . .6A 26
Burton St. LE1: Leic . . . . . . . . . .3F 4 (1G 71)
LE11: Lou . . . . . . . . . . . . . . . . . . . . . . .1F 31
LE13: Mel M . . . . . . . . . . . . . . . . . . . . . .4F 117
BURTON UPON TRENT . . . . . . . . . . . . . . . . .2A 158
Burton Wlk. LE12: Sileby . . . . . . . . . . . . . . . .7J 33
Burton Walks LE11: Lou . . . . . . . . . . . . . . . . .1F 31
BURTON WOLDS . . . . . . . . . . . . . . . . . . . . .2D 159
Buscot Cl. LE4: Leic . . . . . . . . . . . . . . . . . . .6K 65
BUSHBY . . . . . . . . . . . . . . . . . . .3J 73 (1D 163)
Bushby Rd. LE5: Leic . . . . . . . . . . . . . . . . . .7K 65
Bush Lock Cl. LE18: Wig . . . . . . . . . . . . . . . .1G 83
Bushloe Ct. LE18: Wig . . . . . . . . . . . . . . . . .6J 77
Bushloe End LE18: Wig . . . . . . . . . . . . . . . . .6J 77
Bushnell Cl. LE9: B Ast . . . . . . . . . . . . . . . . .6E 86
Bushy Cl. LE19: Nar . . . . . . . . . . . . . . . . . . .1F 81
BUSM Business Pk. LE4: Leic . . . . . . . . . . . . .5G 65
Butcher's La. LE12: Sea . . . . . . . . . . . . . . . . .3K 33
Butcombe Rd. LE4: Leic . . . . . . . . . . . . . . . . .5D 64
Bute Cl. LE10: Hinc . . . . . . . . . . . . . . . . . . .2F 103
Bute Way LE8: Count . . . . . . . . . . . . . . . . . .6F 83
Butler Cl. LE4: Leic . . . . . . . . . . . . . . . . . . .2A 66
LE6: Ratby . . . . . . . . . . . . . . . . . . . . . . .6B 62

Butler Gdns. LE16: Mkt H .............6C 150
Butler Way LE12: Sileby ...............2K 45
Butt Cl. CV13: B'one ..................5C 92
   LE18: Wig .........................7A 78
Butt Cl. La. LE1: Leic ........2C 4 (1F 71)
Buttercup Av. DE12: Don ...............3A 34
Buttercup Cl. LE6: Groby ..............3E 62
   LE12: Moun ........................2F 45
   LE19: Nar .........................7E 74
Buttercup Dr. LE67: Coal ..............4G 39
Buttercup Rd. LE11: Lou ...............5E 30
Butterley Dr. LE11: Lou ...............1K 29
Buttermere Cl. LE13: Mel M ...........5D 116
Buttermere St. LE2: Leic .......8A 5 (4E 70)
Buttermere Way LE12: Bar S ............2C 32
Butterwick Dr. LE4: Leic ..............2C 64
Butthole La. LE11: Lou ................5G 17
   LE12: Shep ........................6E 16
Butt La. DE11: W'lle ..................1C 22
   LE10: Hinc .......................2H 103
   LE14: W'ham ......................1H 121
   LE15: N Luf .......................1B 136
   LE17: H Bos .......................6C 148
Butt La. Cl. LE10: Hinc ...............2H 103
Buttress Cl. LE15: Bel R ..............5G 133
Buxton Cl. LE8: Whet ..................2A 82
Buxton St. LE2: Leic ..................1J 71
Buzzard Cl. DE12: Mea .................1D 48
   LE9: B Ast ........................3D 86
Byfield Dr. LE18: Wig .................5A 78
Byford Rd. LE4: Leic ..................4E 64
Byford Way LE4: Leic ..................5E 64
Byland Way LE11: Lou ..................5K 17
Bypass Rd. LE14: Ash .................2F 115
Byre Cres. LE9: B Ast .................5D 86
Byron Cl. LE8: Flec ...................4C 88
   LE17: Lut .........................2J 153
   LE19: End .........................6E 74
Byron Ct. LE8: Flec ...................4B 88
Byron Cres. DE12: Mea .................2E 48
Byron St. LE1: Leic ...........2E 4 (1G 71)
   LE9: Barw .........................2A 100
   LE9: Earl S .......................3D 100
   LE11: Lou .........................5C 18
Byron St. Extension LE11: Lou .........5C 18
Byron Way LE13: Mel M ................2E 116
Byrton Dr. LE67: Ell ..................1C 52
Byway Rd. LE5: Leic ...................5A 72

## C

Cabin Leas LE11: Lou ..................4F 19
CADEBY .....................6C 94 (1B 162)
Cadeby Cl. LE10: Hinc ................1E 102
Cadeby La. CV13: Cad ..................2E 94
Cademan Cl. LE2: Leic .................1H 77
Cademan St. LE67: Whit ................6F 27
Cadle Cl. LE9: S Stan .................7J 101
Cadle St. LE9: N Ver ..................5H 93
Caernarvon Cl. LE12: Moun .............4D 44
   LE12: Shep ........................1C 28
Cairngorm Cl. LE2: Leic ...............1F 77
Cairns Cl. LE3: Brau ..................1K 75
Cairnsford Rd. LE2: Leic ..............2H 77
Calais Hill LE1: Leic .........5E 4 (2G 71)
Calais St. LE1: Leic ..........5E 4 (2G 71)
CALDECOTE
   Nuneaton .........................2A 162
   Peterborough .....................3D 165
Caldecote Rd. LE3: Leic ...............6A 70
CALDECOTT ...................2H 141 (2B 164)
Caldecott Cl. LE18: Wig ...............6A 78
Caldecott Rd. LE16: G Eas ............6K 141
Calder Cl. LE15: O'ham ...............5G 127
   (not continuous)
Calder Rd. LE4: Leic ..................3C 64
Caldon Cl. LE10: Hinc .................3E 102
Caldwell St. LE11: Lou ................6E 18
Caledine Rd. LE3: Leic ................6A 64
Calgary Cres. LE15: O'ham ............4K 127
Calgary Rd. LE1: Leic ..........1F 4 (7G 65)
CALKE ...............................2A 158
Calke Cl. LE11: Lou ...................5E 30
Callan Cl. LE19: Nar ..................1E 80
Callis, The LE65: Ash Z ...............4K 23
Caloe Cl. LE12: Sileby ................1A 46
Calver Cres. LE9: Sap ................4K 105
Calver Hey Rd. LE4: Leic ..............3A 64
Calverton Av. LE18: Wig ...............4J 77
Calverton Cl. LE6: Ratby ..............6B 62
Camborne Cl. LE18: Wig ................7J 77
Cambourne Rd. LE10: Bur ..............5K 103
Cambrian Cl. LE9: Cosb ................7H 81
Cambrian Way LE65: Ash Z ..............6K 23
Cambridge Av. LE13: Mel M ............7G 117
Cambridge Cl. LE7: Sys ................2E 60

Cambridge Dr. LE9: Des ................2G 95
Cambridge Rd. LE8: Whet ...............3K 81
   LE9: Cosb .........................6H 81
Cambridge St. LE3: Leic ...............3C 70
   LE11: Lou .........................5F 19
   LE12: Shep ........................1D 28
Camborne Cl. LE67: Coal ...............3E 38
Camden Rd. LE3: Brau .................6A 70
Camden St. LE1: Leic ..........2E 4 (1G 71)
Camelford Rd. LE67: Hug ...............5C 38
Camella Cl. LE19: Nar .................7D 74
Camelot Way LE19: Nar .................7E 74
Cameron Av. LE4: Leic .................3H 65
Camfield Ri. LE2: Leic ................4D 76
Camomile Rd. LE13: Mel M ............7E 116
Campbell Av. LE4: Thurm ...............7A 60
Campbell St. LE1: Leic .........5F 4 (2G 71)
Campden Cl. LE15: Ext .................3D 128
   LE15: Upp ........................2C 138
Campion Cl. LE19: Nar .................1E 80
Campion Hill DE74: C Don ..............4J 7
Campion Pl. LE13: Mel M ..............7D 116
Campion Wlk. LE4: Leic ................3B 64
Campton Cl. LE10: Bur ................4H 103
Campus Cen. Bldg. LE2: Leic ...........6B 5
   (off Gosling St.)
Camrose Cl. LE15: O'ham ..............4K 127
Camville Rd. LE3: Leic ................3K 69
Canada Flds. LE17: Lut ...............3J 153
Canal Bank LE11: Lou ..................5E 18
Canal La. LE14: Hos ..................5A 108
   LE14: L Cla .......................1J 111
   LE14: Sta ........................1F 109
Canalside LE16: Mkt H .................3D 150
Canal St. DE12: Oak ...................5C 34
   LE2: Leic .........................1C 76
   LE4: Thurm ........................5K 59
   LE18: Wig .........................1F 83
Canal Way LE10: Hinc .................4C 102
Canberra Way LE10: Bur ...............7H 103
Candle La. LE9: Earl S ................2E 100
Cank St. LE1: Leic ............4C 4 (2F 71)
CANLEY .............................3A 162
Cannam Cl. LE8: Whet ..................4A 82
Canning Pl. LE1: Leic ..........1C 4 (7F 65)
Canning St. LE1: Leic ..........1C 4 (7F 65)
   LE10: Hinc .......................2F 103
Canning Way LE11: Lou .................4A 18
Cannock Cl. LE67: Ell .................1D 52
Cannock St. LE4: Leic .................2C 66
Canon Cl. LE2: Oad ....................3D 78
Canons Cl. LE19: Nar ..................1F 81
Canonsleigh Rd. LE4: Leic .............3E 64
Canonsleigh Wlk. LE4: Leic ............3E 64
Canon St. LE4: Leic ...................5H 65
Canterbury Dr. LE13: Mel M ...........1D 116
   LE65: Ash Z .......................4J 23
Canterbury Ter. LE3: Leic .............4B 70
Cantrell Rd. LE3: Leic ................4H 69
Canvey Cl. LE18: Wig ..................5B 78
Capendale Cl. PE9: Ket ...............6G 137
Capers Cl. LE19: End ..................5E 74
Capesthorne Cl. LE5: Leic .............6K 65
Captains La. LE67: Mark ...............5F 55
Cara Cl. LE2: Leic ....................7J 71
Carbery Cl. LE2: Oad ..................4F 79
CAR COLSTON .........................1A 160
Cardigan Dr. LE18: Wig ................6F 77
Cardinal Cl. LE6: Ratby ...............6B 62
Cardinals Wlk. LE5: Leic ..............6E 66
CAREBY .............................3D 161
Carey Cl. LE18: Wig ...................1K 83
Carey Dr. LE9: Hun ....................2B 80
Carey Gdns. LE9: K Mux ................2B 68
Carey Hill Rd. LE9: S Stan ...........1J 105
Carey's Cl. LE1: Leic .........4B 4 (2E 70)
Carfax Av. LE2: Oad ...................1B 78
Carillon & War Memorial ...............7E 18
Carillon Ct. LE11: Lou ................6F 19
Carington St. LE11: Lou ...............5D 18
Carisbrooke Av. LE2: Leic .............1J 77
Carisbrooke Ct. LE2: Leic .............1J 77
Carisbrooke Gdns. LE2: Leic ...........7J 71
Carisbrooke Lawn Tennis Club .........1H 77
Carisbrooke Pk. LE2: Leic .............1J 77
Carisbrooke Rd. LE2: Leic .............7J 71
   LE12: Moun ........................4C 44
CARLBY .............................3D 161
Carlisle St. LE3: Leic ................2B 70
Carlson Gdns. LE17: Lut ..............4K 153
   (not continuous)
Carlson Ter. LE17: Lut ...............4K 153
Carl St. LE2: Leic ....................2C 76
CARLTON
   Nottingham .......................1C 159
   Nuneaton .........................1A 162
Carlton Av. LE19: Nar .................1G 81

Carlton Cl. LE11: Lou .................5D 18
   LE13: Glen ........................6G 63
CARLTON CURLIEU ......................2D 163
Carlton Dr. LE18: Wig .................5J 77
Carlton Gdns. LE8: G Gle ..............2K 85
Carlton La. LE8: Bur O ...............6D 130
Carlton Pk. LE8: Bur O ................7F 75
Carlton Rd. CV13: Carl, Mkt B ...7K 91 & 1A 94
   LE8: Kib H ........................1J 89
Carlton St. LE1: Leic .........6C 5 (3F 71)
Carlyon Ct. LE9: K Mux ................2C 68
Carlyon Rd. CV9: Ath ..................5A 96
Carlyon Rd. Ind. Est. CV9: Ath ........4A 96
   (not continuous)
Carmen Gro. LE6: Groby ................3B 62
Carnation Cl. LE3: Leic E .............5D 68
Carnation St. LE4: Leic ...............4F 65
Carnegie Cres. LE13: Mel M ...........1H 117
Carnival Way DE74: C Don ..............4K 7
Carnoustie Rd. LE3: Leic ..............2H 69
CAROL GREEN ........................3A 162
Caroline Ct. LE2: Leic ................2E 76
Carousel Pk. LE9: Barw ................2J 99
Carpenters Cl. LE3: Glen ..............7F 63
   LE10: Bur ........................6J 103
Carpe Rd. LE4: Leic ...................5K 65
Carrfields La. LE14: F Wre ...........5H 115
CARR HILL ..........................6C 16
Carr Hill Rd. LE67: Whit ..............4E 26
Carriageway, The LE15: Knos ..........2C 126
Carrington Rd. LE5: Ham ...............3E 66
Carrow Rd. LE3: Leic ..................2F 69
Carrs Cl. DE74: C Don .................5J 7
Carr's Dr. LE9: Earl S ................2E 100
Carrs Hill LE9: Barw ..................4B 100
Carr's Rd. LE9: Earl S ................2E 100
Carter Cl. LE19: End ..................5E 74
Carter Dale LE67: Whit ................5D 26
Carter St. LE4: Leic ..................6J 65
Cartland Dr. LE11: Lou ................4A 18
Carts La. LE1: Leic ...........3C 4 (1F 71)
Cartwright Dr. LE2: Oad ...............3B 78
Cartwright St. LE11: Lou ..............5F 19
Cartwright Way LE67: Bar ..............1K 53
Carty Rd. LE5: Ham ....................3E 66
Carver Ct. PE9: Ket ..................6G 137
Carvers Cnr. LE2: G Par ...............5B 76
Carver's Path LE7: East G .............5G 47
Cashmore Vw. LE4: Leic ................2D 64
Castell Dr. LE6: Groby ................3D 62
CASTLE BYTHAM ......................3C 161
Castle Cl. LE9: Earl S ................1E 100
   LE9: Sap .........................4J 105
   LE15: Upp ........................1A 138
   NG13: Bott .......................2K 107
Castle Ct. LE10: Bur .................5G 103
Castledine Av. LE12: Quo ..............4A 32
Castledine St. LE11: Lou ..............1F 31
   LE12: Quo .........................5K 31
Castledine St. Extension LE11: Lou ....1F 31
CASTLE DONINGTON ............5K 7 (2B 158)
Castle Donington Mus. .................5K 7
Castle Flds. LE3: Brau ................7J 69
Castle Flds. LE4: Beau L ..............1A 64
Castlegate Av. LE4: Birs ..............5F 59
Castle Ga. Ho. LE65: Ash Z ............5K 23
CASTLE GRESLEY .....................3A 158
Castle Hill DE74: C Don ...............4K 7
   LE12: Moun ........................2E 44
   (not continuous)
   LE67: Whit ........................6F 27
Castlemaine Dr. LE10: Hinc ...........7H 99
Castle Ri. LE6: Groby .................4D 62
   PE9: Belm ........................6J 129
Castle Rd. LE9: K Mux .................2B 68
   LE12: Moun ........................3D 44
Castle Rock Dr. LE67: Coal ............2H 39
Castle St. LE1: Leic ..........4B 4 (2E 70)
   LE10: Hinc .......................3G 103
   LE67: Whit ........................6F 27
Castleton Rd. LE18: Wig ...............4J 77
Castle Vw. LE1: Leic ..........5B 4 (2E 70)
Castle Vw. Rd. NG13: East ............3J 107
   (not continuous)
Castle Way LE65: Ash Z .................7J 23
Castle Wood Mobile Home Pk. LE9: Sap ..3C 104
CASTOR .............................2D 165
Caswell Cl. LE4: Leic .................2D 64
Caters Cl. LE4: Anst ..................7H 57
Catesby St. LE3: Leic .................2D 70
Catherines Cl. LE12: Quo ..............5B 32
Catherine St. LE4: Leic ...............6H 65
Catherine St. Ind. Est. LE4: Leic .....4K 65
Cathkin Cl. LE3: Leic .................2H 69
Catmose Pk. LE15: O'ham ..............5K 127
Catmose St. LE15: O'ham ..............4J 127
CATTHORPE ..................6D 156 (3C 163)

**Catthorpe Mnr.** LE17: Cat . . . . . . . . . . . . . . . .6E **156**
**Catthorpe Rd.** LE17: Cat, Shaw . . . . . . . . . . .4B **156**
**Cattle Mkt.** LE11: Lou . . . . . . . . . . . . . . . . . . .7F **19**
**Cauby Cl.** LE12: Sileby . . . . . . . . . . . . . . . . . .1A **46**
**Caudebec Cl.** LE15: Upp . . . . . . . . . . . . . . . .1B **138**
**Caudle Cl.** LE7: Crop . . . . . . . . . . . . . . . . . . .2K **57**
**CAULDWELL** . . . . . . . . . . . . . . . . . . . . . . . . .3A **158**
**Cauldwell La.** LE17: Ash P, Lut . . . . . . . . . . .7A **144**
**Causeway** LE12: Quo . . . . . . . . . . . . . . . . . . .4C **32**
**Causeway La.** LE1: Leic . . . . . . . . .2B **4** (1E **70**)
  LE7: Crop . . . . . . . . . . . . . . . . . . . . . . . . . . .3J **57**
**Cavalry Cl.** LE13: Mel M . . . . . . . . . . . . . . . .1D **116**
**CAVENDISH BRIDGE** . . . . . . . . . .1K **7** (1B **158**)
**Cavendish Cl.** DE74: C Don . . . . . . . . . . . . . .6J **7**
**Cavendish Cres.** LE67: Hug . . . . . . . . . . . . . .5C **38**
**Cavendish M.** LE2: Leic . . . . . . . . . . . . . . . . .7E **70**
**Cavendish Rd.** LE2: Leic . . . . . . . . . . . . . . . .6E **70**
**Cavendish Tennis Club** . . . . . . . . . . . . . . . .6B **76**
**Cave Rd.** LE12: Bar S . . . . . . . . . . . . . . . . . .3D **32**
**Caversham Rd.** LE2: Leic . . . . . . . . . . . . . . .5C **76**
**Cawdell Dr.** LE12: L Wha . . . . . . . . . . . . . . .7H **13**
**Cawsand Rd.** LE18: Wig . . . . . . . . . . . . . . . . .7J **77**
**Cawston Cl.** LE5: Ham . . . . . . . . . . . . . . . . . .4D **66**
**CAWTHORPE** . . . . . . . . . . . . . . . . . . . . . . . . .2D **161**
**Caxton Pl.** LE12: Bar S . . . . . . . . . . . . . . . . .4D **32**
**Caxton St.** LE16: Mkt H . . . . . . . . . . . . . . . . .6F **151**
**Cecil Gdns.** LE2: Leic . . . . . . . . . . . . . . . . . .1J **71**
**Cecilia Rd.** LE2: Leic . . . . . . . . . . . . . . . . . . .5H **71**
**Cecil Rd.** LE2: Leic . . . . . . . . . . . . . . . . . . . . .1H **71**
**Cedar Av.** LE4: Birs . . . . . . . . . . . . . . . . . . . .6G **59**
  LE17: Lut . . . . . . . . . . . . . . . . . . . . . . . . . . .4H **153**
  LE18: Wig . . . . . . . . . . . . . . . . . . . . . . . . . .6K **77**
**Cedar Cl.** LE3: Glen . . . . . . . . . . . . . . . . . . . .5J **63**
  LE8: K Bea . . . . . . . . . . . . . . . . . . . . . . . . . .3H **89**
  LE15: Upp . . . . . . . . . . . . . . . . . . . . . . . . . .2D **138**
  LE65: Ash Z . . . . . . . . . . . . . . . . . . . . . . . . .5B **24**
**Cedar Ct.** LE2: Leic . . . . . . . . . . . . . . . . . . . .8C **5**
  LE5: Leic . . . . . . . . . . . . . . . . . . . . . . . . . . .6C **66**
  LE6: Groby . . . . . . . . . . . . . . . . . . . . . . . . . .4D **62**
  LE10: Bur . . . . . . . . . . . . . . . . . . . . . . . . . .5K **103**
**Cedar Cres.** LE19: Nar . . . . . . . . . . . . . . . . . .2F **81**
**Cedar Cft.** DE72: A Tre . . . . . . . . . . . . . . . . .1C **6**
**Cedar Dr.** CV13: Mkt B . . . . . . . . . . . . . . . . .3D **94**
  LE7: Sys . . . . . . . . . . . . . . . . . . . . . . . . . . .3D **60**
  LE13: Mel M . . . . . . . . . . . . . . . . . . . . . . . .2E **116**
  LE67: Ibs . . . . . . . . . . . . . . . . . . . . . . . . . . .3J **51**
**Cedar Gro.** DE12: Moi . . . . . . . . . . . . . . . . . .5D **22**
  LE12: Moun . . . . . . . . . . . . . . . . . . . . . . . . .3E **44**
**Cedar Rd.** DE74: C Don . . . . . . . . . . . . . . . . .6K **7**
  LE2: Leic . . . . . . . . . . . . . . . . . . . . . . . . . . .3J **71**
  LE8: Bla . . . . . . . . . . . . . . . . . . . . . . . . . . . .3B **82**
  LE9: Earl S . . . . . . . . . . . . . . . . . . . . . . . . .3C **100**
  LE11: Lou . . . . . . . . . . . . . . . . . . . . . . . . . . .2G **31**
**Cedars, The** LE2: Leic . . . . . . . . . . . . . . . . . .1H **77**
**Cedars Ct.** LE2: Leic . . . . . . . . . . . . . . . . . . .4J **71**
**Cedar St.** LE15: B Rut . . . . . . . . . . . . . . . . . .6C **126**
**Cedarwood Cl.** LE4: Leic . . . . . . . . . . . . . . . .5K **65**
**Celandine Cl.** LE2: Oad . . . . . . . . . . . . . . . . .4G **79**
  LE12: Moun . . . . . . . . . . . . . . . . . . . . . . . . .2F **45**
**Celandine Dr.** LE13: Mel M . . . . . . . . . . . . . .7E **116**
**Celandine Rd.** LE5: Ham . . . . . . . . . . . . . . . .4E **66**
**Cello Cl.** LE67: Whit . . . . . . . . . . . . . . . . . . . .6E **26**
**Celt St.** LE3: Leic . . . . . . . . . . . . . . . . . . . . . .3D **70**
**Cemetery La.** LE15: Mant . . . . . . . . . . . . . . . .2B **134**
**Cemetery Rd.** LE8: Whet . . . . . . . . . . . . . . . .2K **81**
  LE12: Sileby . . . . . . . . . . . . . . . . . . . . . . . . .1K **45**
**Central Av.** LE2: Leic . . . . . . . . . . . . . . . . . . .5J **71**
  LE7: Sys . . . . . . . . . . . . . . . . . . . . . . . . . . .1D **60**
  LE12: Shep . . . . . . . . . . . . . . . . . . . . . . . . . .7D **16**
  LE17: Lut . . . . . . . . . . . . . . . . . . . . . . . . . . .3J **153**
  LE18: Wig . . . . . . . . . . . . . . . . . . . . . . . . . .6H **77**
  LE67: Ibs . . . . . . . . . . . . . . . . . . . . . . . . . . .4K **51**
**Central Cl.** LE8: Whet . . . . . . . . . . . . . . . . . .1K **81**
**Central Ct.** LE67: Coal . . . . . . . . . . . . . . . . . .4D **38**
**Central Pk.** LE17: Lut . . . . . . . . . . . . . . . . . . .2K **153**
**Central Pas.** LE67: Ibs . . . . . . . . . . . . . . . . . .4K **51**
**Central Rd.** LE3: Leic . . . . . . . . . . . . . . . . . . .7D **64**
  LE67: Hug . . . . . . . . . . . . . . . . . . . . . . . . . .5D **38**
**Central St.** LE8: Count . . . . . . . . . . . . . . . . . .5F **83**
**Centre Ct.** LE19: Brau . . . . . . . . . . . . . . . . . .1H **75**
**Centurion Ct.** LE6: Ratby . . . . . . . . . . . . . . . .7B **62**
  LE19: Brau . . . . . . . . . . . . . . . . . . . . . . . . . .7H **69**
**Centurion Way** LE19: Brau . . . . . . . . . . . . . . .6G **69**
**Century Cl.** LE5: Leic . . . . . . . . . . . . . . . . . . .1E **72**
**Chadderton Cl.** LE2: Leic . . . . . . . . . . . . . . . .1G **77**
**CHADDESDEN** . . . . . . . . . . . . . . . . . . . . . . .1A **158**
**CHADDESDEN COMMON** . . . . . . . . . . . . . . .1A **158**
**CHADWELL** . . . . . . . . . . . . . . . . . . . . . . . . . .2A **160**
**Chadwell Cl.** LE13: Mel M . . . . . . . . . . . . . . .5H **117**
  LE14: Ash . . . . . . . . . . . . . . . . . . . . . . . . . . .3F **115**
**Chadwell Rd.** LE3: Leic . . . . . . . . . . . . . . . . .7J **63**
**Chadwick Cl.** LE9: N Ver . . . . . . . . . . . . . . . .6H **93**
**Chadwick Wlk.** LE4: Leic . . . . . . . . . . . . . . . .3D **64**
**Chaffinch Cl.** LE4: Beau L . . . . . . . . . . . . . . . .7B **58**
  LE15: O'ham . . . . . . . . . . . . . . . . . . . . . . . . .2K **127**
**Chainama Cl.** LE3: Leic . . . . . . . . . . . . . . . . .1G **69**
**Chainbridge Cl.** LE11: Lou . . . . . . . . . . . . . . .5E **18**

**Chale Rd.** LE4: Leic . . . . . . . . . . . . . . . . . . . .4F **65**
**Chalfont Cl.** LE13: Mel M . . . . . . . . . . . . . . . .1A **120**
**Chalfont Dr.** LE12: Sileby . . . . . . . . . . . . . . . .3J **45**
**Chalgrove Wlk.** LE5: Leic . . . . . . . . . . . . . . . .1C **72**
**Challottee** LE12: Shep . . . . . . . . . . . . . . . . . .7E **16**
**Chalmondley Dr.**
  LE13: Mel M . . . . . . . . . . . . . . . . . . . . . . . . .1G **117**
**Chalvington Cl.** LE5: Leic . . . . . . . . . . . . . . . .4E **72**
**Chambers Cl.** LE67: Mark . . . . . . . . . . . . . . . .4H **55**
**Champion Cl.** LE5: Leic . . . . . . . . . . . . . . . . .2D **72**
**Chancel Rd.** LE4: Leic . . . . . . . . . . . . . . . . . .5D **58**
**Chancery St.** LE1: Leic . . . . . . . . . . .5C **4** (2F **71**)
**Chandlers Cft.** LE67: Ibs . . . . . . . . . . . . . . . . .2J **51**
**Chandler Way** LE9: B Ast . . . . . . . . . . . . . . . .5F **87**
**Chandos St.** LE2: Leic . . . . . . . . . . . . . . . . . .3J **71**
**Channing Way** LE67: Ell . . . . . . . . . . . . . . . . .1C **52**
**Chantrell Cl.** LE67: Bag . . . . . . . . . . . . . . . . . .1F **93**
**Chantry Cl.** LE9: Hun . . . . . . . . . . . . . . . . . . .2B **80**
**Chapel Bar** LE12: Wym . . . . . . . . . . . . . . . . . .2K **21**
**Chapel Cl.** DE11: A Vil . . . . . . . . . . . . . . . . . .2A **22**
  LE7: Hou H . . . . . . . . . . . . . . . . . . . . . . . . . .2C **130**
  LE7: Sys . . . . . . . . . . . . . . . . . . . . . . . . . . .1D **60**
  LE7: Thurc . . . . . . . . . . . . . . . . . . . . . . . . . .2B **58**
  LE14: Ab K . . . . . . . . . . . . . . . . . . . . . . . . . .7H **111**
  LE15: Emp . . . . . . . . . . . . . . . . . . . . . . . . . .6C **128**
                          (not continuous)
  LE17: D Bas . . . . . . . . . . . . . . . . . . . . . . . . .1D **144**
  LE18: Kilby . . . . . . . . . . . . . . . . . . . . . . . . . .6B **84**
  LE67: Rav . . . . . . . . . . . . . . . . . . . . . . . . . . .3K **37**
**Chapel Ct.** LE5: Leic . . . . . . . . . . . . . . . . . . .5D **72**
  LE12: Shep . . . . . . . . . . . . . . . . . . . . . . . . . .5D **16**
**Chapel Flds.** LE17: Swin . . . . . . . . . . . . . . . . .4G **157**
**CHAPEL GREEN** . . . . . . . . . . . . . . . . . . . . . .3A **162**
**Chapel Grn.** LE3: Leic E . . . . . . . . . . . . . . . . .4F **69**
**Chapel Hill** LE6: Groby . . . . . . . . . . . . . . . . . .3C **62**
**Chapel La.** CV9: With . . . . . . . . . . . . . . . . . . .5B **96**
  CV13: Con . . . . . . . . . . . . . . . . . . . . . . . . . .5G **91**
  LE2: Leic . . . . . . . . . . . . . . . . . . . . . . . . . . .7H **71**
  LE6: Ratby . . . . . . . . . . . . . . . . . . . . . . . . . .6A **62**
  LE7: Gad . . . . . . . . . . . . . . . . . . . . . . . . . . .2A **118**
  LE7: Tug . . . . . . . . . . . . . . . . . . . . . . . . . . .2C **132**
  LE9: Cosb . . . . . . . . . . . . . . . . . . . . . . . . . .7H **81**
  LE9: Des . . . . . . . . . . . . . . . . . . . . . . . . . . .1H **95**
  LE10: S'ord . . . . . . . . . . . . . . . . . . . . . . . . .7H **105**
  LE12: Osg . . . . . . . . . . . . . . . . . . . . . . . . . .7E **14**
  LE14: Ab K . . . . . . . . . . . . . . . . . . . . . . . . . .7H **111**
  LE14: Hob . . . . . . . . . . . . . . . . . . . . . . . . . .1B **114**
  LE14: Hos . . . . . . . . . . . . . . . . . . . . . . . . . .5B **108**
  LE14: N Bro . . . . . . . . . . . . . . . . . . . . . . . . .2C **110**
  LE14: O Dal . . . . . . . . . . . . . . . . . . . . . . . . .7A **110**
  LE14: Som . . . . . . . . . . . . . . . . . . . . . . . . . .6K **121**
  LE14: Sta . . . . . . . . . . . . . . . . . . . . . . . . . . .2H **109**
  LE14: Up Bro . . . . . . . . . . . . . . . . . . . . . . . .1A **110**
  LE14: W'ham . . . . . . . . . . . . . . . . . . . . . . . .1H **121**
  LE15: B'den . . . . . . . . . . . . . . . . . . . . . . . . .7D **136**
  LE15: N Luf . . . . . . . . . . . . . . . . . . . . . . . . .1B **136**
  LE17: Mows . . . . . . . . . . . . . . . . . . . . . . . . .2B **148**
  LE17: Wal . . . . . . . . . . . . . . . . . . . . . . . . . .2D **154**
  LE17: Walt . . . . . . . . . . . . . . . . . . . . . . . . . .7C **146**
  LE18: Wig . . . . . . . . . . . . . . . . . . . . . . . . . .6K **77**
  LE67: Cole . . . . . . . . . . . . . . . . . . . . . . . . . .3J **25**
  NG32: Crox . . . . . . . . . . . . . . . . . . . . . . . . .6G **107**
  PE9: Ket . . . . . . . . . . . . . . . . . . . . . . . . . . . .6H **137**
**Chapel M.** LE9: Barw . . . . . . . . . . . . . . . . . . .4A **100**
**Chapel Ri.** LE65: Wort . . . . . . . . . . . . . . . . . .2B **14**
**Chapel St.** CV13: B'one . . . . . . . . . . . . . . . . .5C **92**
  DE12: Don . . . . . . . . . . . . . . . . . . . . . . . . . .3A **34**
  DE12: Mea . . . . . . . . . . . . . . . . . . . . . . . . . .7E **34**
  DE12: Oak . . . . . . . . . . . . . . . . . . . . . . . . . .6B **34**
  LE2: Oad . . . . . . . . . . . . . . . . . . . . . . . . . . .3C **78**
  LE7: Sys . . . . . . . . . . . . . . . . . . . . . . . . . . .1C **60**
  LE8: Bla . . . . . . . . . . . . . . . . . . . . . . . . . . . .7B **76**
  LE9: Barw . . . . . . . . . . . . . . . . . . . . . . . . . .4K **99**
  LE9: Earl S . . . . . . . . . . . . . . . . . . . . . . . . .1F **101**
  LE9: Stap . . . . . . . . . . . . . . . . . . . . . . . . . . .1J **99**
  LE10: S'ord . . . . . . . . . . . . . . . . . . . . . . . . .7H **105**
  LE12: Shep . . . . . . . . . . . . . . . . . . . . . . . . . .5D **16**
  LE13: Mel M . . . . . . . . . . . . . . . . . . . . . . . .4F **117**
  LE15: Bel R . . . . . . . . . . . . . . . . . . . . . . . . .5G **133**
  LE17: Lut . . . . . . . . . . . . . . . . . . . . . . . . . . .4J **153**
  LE17: Swin . . . . . . . . . . . . . . . . . . . . . . . . . .4G **157**
  LE19: End . . . . . . . . . . . . . . . . . . . . . . . . . . .5E **74**
  LE65: Smis . . . . . . . . . . . . . . . . . . . . . . . . . .1H **23**
  LE67: Ibs . . . . . . . . . . . . . . . . . . . . . . . . . . .3K **51**
  NG13: Bark V . . . . . . . . . . . . . . . . . . . . . . . .3A **106**
  NG13: Bott . . . . . . . . . . . . . . . . . . . . . . . . . .1G **107**
  NG32: Eat . . . . . . . . . . . . . . . . . . . . . . . . . .7G **109**
**Chapel Yd.** LE10: Hinc . . . . . . . . . . . . . . . . . .3G **103**
**Chaplin Cl.** LE12: Sileby . . . . . . . . . . . . . . . . .1J **45**
**Chaplin Ct.** LE3: Brau . . . . . . . . . . . . . . . . . . .4H **69**
**Chapman Cl.** CV13: B'one . . . . . . . . . . . . . . . .5C **92**
**Chapmans Mdws.** LE65: Ash Z . . . . . . . . . . . .7A **24**
**Chapman St.** LE11: Lou . . . . . . . . . . . . . . . . . .6G **19**
**Chappell Cl.** LE4: Thurm . . . . . . . . . . . . . . . . .6A **60**
**Charlecote Av.** LE3: Brau . . . . . . . . . . . . . . . .6K **69**
**Charles Dr.** LE7: Anst . . . . . . . . . . . . . . . . . . .7J **57**
**Charles Hall Cl.** LE12: Shep . . . . . . . . . . . . . .6E **16**

**Charles Mall** LE1: Leic . . . . . . . . . . . . . . . . . .1F **71**
                      (off Haymarket Cen.)
**Charles Rd.** CV9: Manc . . . . . . . . . . . . . . . . . .6A **96**
**Charles St.** LE1: Leic . . . . . . . . . . . . . .2D **4** (1F **71**)
  LE10: Hinc . . . . . . . . . . . . . . . . . . . . . . . . . .2H **103**
  LE11: Lou . . . . . . . . . . . . . . . . . . . . . . . . . . .5F **19**
  LE12: Sileby . . . . . . . . . . . . . . . . . . . . . . . . .2J **45**
  LE16: Mkt H . . . . . . . . . . . . . . . . . . . . . . . . .4D **150**
**Charles St.** LE67: Coal . . . . . . . . . . . . . . . . . .2A **38**
**Charleston Cres.** LE9: Barw . . . . . . . . . . . . . .4K **99**
**Charles Way** LE2: Oad . . . . . . . . . . . . . . . . . .3E **78**
  LE8: Whet . . . . . . . . . . . . . . . . . . . . . . . . . . .4A **82**
**Charley Dr.** LE11: Lou . . . . . . . . . . . . . . . . . . .1C **30**
**Charley Rd.** LE12: Char, Nan . . . . . . . . . . . . . .1F **41**
  LE12: Char, Shep . . . . . . . . . . . . . . . . . . . . . .2A **28**
**Charlock Rd.** LE5: Ham . . . . . . . . . . . . . . . . . .4F **67**
**Charlotte St.** LE13: Mel M . . . . . . . . . . . . . . . .4F **117**
**Charlottes Wlk.** LE7: Hou H . . . . . . . . . . . . . .3C **130**
**Charlton Cl.** LE8: Whet . . . . . . . . . . . . . . . . . .3A **82**
**Charnborough Ct.** LE67: Coal . . . . . . . . . . . . .4H **39**
**Charnborough Rd.** LE67: Coal . . . . . . . . . . . . .3H **39**
**Charnia Gro.** LE12: Swith . . . . . . . . . . . . . . . .6K **43**
**Charnor Rd.** LE3: Leic . . . . . . . . . . . . . . . . . .7J **63**
**Charnwood** LE6: Ratby . . . . . . . . . . . . . . . . . .5A **62**
**Charnwood Av.** DE74: C Don . . . . . . . . . . . . . .5A **8**
  LE4: Thurm . . . . . . . . . . . . . . . . . . . . . . . . . .5B **60**
  LE8: Whet . . . . . . . . . . . . . . . . . . . . . . . . . . .1K **81**
  LE14: Ash . . . . . . . . . . . . . . . . . . . . . . . . . . .2G **115**
**Charnwood Cl.** LE3: Leic E . . . . . . . . . . . . . . .3E **68**
  LE4: Thurm . . . . . . . . . . . . . . . . . . . . . . . . . .5B **60**
  LE10: Hinc . . . . . . . . . . . . . . . . . . . . . . . . . .1H **103**
**Charnwood Dr.** LE3: Leic E . . . . . . . . . . . . . . .4E **68**
  LE7: Thurn . . . . . . . . . . . . . . . . . . . . . . . . . .2H **73**
  LE13: Mel M . . . . . . . . . . . . . . . . . . . . . . . .3D **116**
  LE67: Mark . . . . . . . . . . . . . . . . . . . . . . . . . .5H **55**
**Charnwood Ind. Units** LE2: Leic . . . . . . . . . . .1H **71**
**Charnwood Leisure Cen.** . . . . . . . . . . . . . . . .7E **18**
**Charnwood Mnr.** LE19: Nar . . . . . . . . . . . . . . .1G **81**
**Charnwood Mus.** . . . . . . . . . . . . . . . . . . . . . .7E **18**
**Charnwood Ri.** LE12: W Eav . . . . . . . . . . . . . .4D **42**
**Charnwood Rd.** LE7: Anst . . . . . . . . . . . . . . . .6H **57**
  LE9: Barw . . . . . . . . . . . . . . . . . . . . . . . . . . .2A **100**
  LE10: Hinc . . . . . . . . . . . . . . . . . . . . . . . . . .1G **103**
  LE11: Lou . . . . . . . . . . . . . . . . . . . . . . . . . . .1F **31**
  LE12: Shep . . . . . . . . . . . . . . . . . . . . . . . . . .2D **28**
**Charnwood St.** LE5: Leic . . . . . . . . . . . . . . . . .1J **71**
  LE67: Coal . . . . . . . . . . . . . . . . . . . . . . . . . .4E **38**
**Charnwood Wlk.** LE5: Leic . . . . . . . . . . . . . . . .7J **65**
**Charteris Cl.** LE11: Lou . . . . . . . . . . . . . . . . . .4B **18**
**Charter St.** LE1: Leic . . . . . . . . . . . .1D **4** (7F **65**)
**Chartley Rd.** LE3: Leic . . . . . . . . . . . . . . . . . .4C **70**
**Chartwell Dr.** LE18: Wig . . . . . . . . . . . . . . . . .5G **77**
**Chartwell Dr. Ind. Est.** LE18: Wig . . . . . . . . . .5G **77**
**Chartwell Point** LE18: Wig . . . . . . . . . . . . . . .5H **77**
**Chase, The** LE3: Brau . . . . . . . . . . . . . . . . . . .1K **75**
  LE7: East G . . . . . . . . . . . . . . . . . . . . . . . . . .4F **47**
  LE8: G Gle . . . . . . . . . . . . . . . . . . . . . . . . . .5A **130**
  LE67: Mark . . . . . . . . . . . . . . . . . . . . . . . . . .5G **55**
**Chater Cl.** LE5: Leic . . . . . . . . . . . . . . . . . . . .7F **67**
  LE15: Mant . . . . . . . . . . . . . . . . . . . . . . . . . .2C **134**
  LE16: G Bow . . . . . . . . . . . . . . . . . . . . . . . . .1G **151**
**Chater La.** PE9: Ket . . . . . . . . . . . . . . . . . . . .4H **137**
**Chater M.** PE9: Ket . . . . . . . . . . . . . . . . . . . . .4H **137**
**Chater Rd.** LE15: O'ham . . . . . . . . . . . . . . . . .5G **127**
**Chatham St.** LE1: Leic . . . . . . . . . . . .5D **4** (2F **71**)
**Chatsworth Cl.** LE10: Bur . . . . . . . . . . . . . . . . .5J **103**
  LE12: Shep . . . . . . . . . . . . . . . . . . . . . . . . . .7C **16**
**Chatsworth Dr.** LE7: Sys . . . . . . . . . . . . . . . . .2B **60**
  LE16: L Bow . . . . . . . . . . . . . . . . . . . . . . . . .4G **151**
**Chatsworth Rd.** LE11: Lou . . . . . . . . . . . . . . . .5B **18**
**Chatsworth St.** LE2: Leic . . . . . . . . . . . . . . . . .2J **71**
**Chatteris Av.** LE5: Leic . . . . . . . . . . . . . . . . . .4F **73**
**Chatworth Av.** LE18: Wig . . . . . . . . . . . . . . . . .7G **77**
**Chaucer St.** LE2: Leic . . . . . . . . . . . . . . . . . . .4J **71**
  LE19: Nar . . . . . . . . . . . . . . . . . . . . . . . . . . .7E **74**
**Chaveney Ct.** LE12: Quo . . . . . . . . . . . . . . . . .6J **31**
**Chaveney Rd.** LE12: Quo . . . . . . . . . . . . . . . . .6J **31**
**Chaveney Wlk.** LE12: Quo . . . . . . . . . . . . . . . .6J **31**
**Cheapside** LE1: Leic . . . . . . . . . . . . .3C **4** (1F **71**)
  LE13: Mel M . . . . . . . . . . . . . . . . . . . . . . . .4F **117**
**Checketts Cl.** LE4: Leic . . . . . . . . . . . . . . . . . .4H **65**
**Checketts Rd.** LE4: Leic . . . . . . . . . . . . . . . . .3G **65**
**Checkland Rd.** LE4: Thurm . . . . . . . . . . . . . . . .5A **60**
**Cheddar Rd.** LE18: Wig . . . . . . . . . . . . . . . . . .5A **78**
**Cheer Cl.** LE8: Whet . . . . . . . . . . . . . . . . . . . .5K **81**
**Chelker Way** LE11: Lou . . . . . . . . . . . . . . . . . .7A **18**
**CHELLASTON** . . . . . . . . . . . . . . . . . . . . . . . . .1A **158**
**Chellaston La.** DE72: Chell . . . . . . . . . . . . . . . .1B **6**
**Chellaston Rd.** LE18: Wig . . . . . . . . . . . . . . . .4J **77**
**Chelsea Cl.** LE2: G Par . . . . . . . . . . . . . . . . . .7D **76**
**Cheltenham Dr.** LE65: Ash Z . . . . . . . . . . . . . .4J **23**
**Cheltenham Rd.** LE4: Leic . . . . . . . . . . . . . . . .4C **64**
**Cheney Cl.** LE9: Hun . . . . . . . . . . . . . . . . . . . .2B **80**
**Cheney End** LE9: Hun . . . . . . . . . . . . . . . . . . .2B **80**
**Cheney Rd.** LE4: Leic . . . . . . . . . . . . . . . . . . .2C **66**
**Chepstow Rd.** LE2: Leic . . . . . . . . . . . . . . . . .4J **71**

Cheribough Rd. DE74: C Don . . . . . . . . . . . . . .5J 7
Cheriton Rd. LE2: Leic . . . . . . . . . . . . . . . .3D 76
Cherrybrook Cl. LE4: Beau L . . . . . . . . . . . .6B 58
Cherry Cl. LE11: Lou . . . . . . . . . . . . . . . . .4E 30
Cherry Dr. LE7: Sys . . . . . . . . . . . . . . . . .3D 60
Cherry Gro. LE8: G Gle . . . . . . . . . . . . . . .5A 130
Cherry Hills Rd. LE3: Leic . . . . . . . . . . . . . .1G 69
Cherryleas Dr. LE3: Leic . . . . . . . . . . . . . . .3C 70
Cherry Orchard Est.
 CV13: H Hill . . . . . . . . . . . . . . . . . . . .6G 97
Cherry Rd. LE8: Bla . . . . . . . . . . . . . . . . .2B 82
Cherry St. LE18: Wig . . . . . . . . . . . . . . . . .6H 77
Cherry Tree Av. LE9: Leic E . . . . . . . . . . . . .4C 68
Cherrytree Av. LE17: Lut . . . . . . . . . . . . . .5G 153
Cherry Tree Cl. LE8: Count . . . . . . . . . . . . .5E 82
 LE17: H Bos . . . . . . . . . . . . . . . . . . .6C 148
Cherrytree Cl. LE7: Anst . . . . . . . . . . . . . . .1H 63
Cherry Tree Ct. DE12: Moi . . . . . . . . . . . . . .5D 22
 LE9: Leic E . . . . . . . . . . . . . . . . . . . .4C 68
Cherry Tree Dr. LE9: Barw . . . . . . . . . . . . .2A 100
 NG13: Plun . . . . . . . . . . . . . . . . . . . .5D 106
Cherry Tree Gro. LE19: End . . . . . . . . . . . . .5E 74
Cherwell Cl. LE10: Hinc . . . . . . . . . . . . . . .3D 102
Cherwell Rd. LE12: Bar S . . . . . . . . . . . . . .4D 32
Cheshire Cl. LE17: Lut . . . . . . . . . . . . . . .6H 153
Cheshire Dr. LE18: Wig . . . . . . . . . . . . . . .5F 77
Cheshire Gdns. LE2: Leic . . . . . . . . . . . . . .1D 76
Cheshire Rd. LE2: Leic . . . . . . . . . . . . . . .1D 76
Chesnut Cl. LE19: Litt . . . . . . . . . . . . . . . .3F 81
Chessher St. LE10: Hinc . . . . . . . . . . . . . . .2F 103
Chester Cl. LE1: Leic . . . . . . . . . . . . .1G 4 (7H 65)
 LE8: Bla . . . . . . . . . . . . . . . . . . . . . .2C 82
 LE11: Lou . . . . . . . . . . . . . . . . . . . . .7D 18
Chesterfield Rd. LE5: Leic . . . . . . . . . . . . . .3K 71
Chesterfield Way LE9: Barw . . . . . . . . . . . .3B 100
Chester Rd. LE8: Bla . . . . . . . . . . . . . . . . .2C 82
CHESTERTON . . . . . . . . . . . . . . . . . . . .2D 165
Chesterton Ct. LE19: End . . . . . . . . . . . . . .6E 74
Chesterton Wlk. LE3: Leic . . . . . . . . . . . . . .2A 70
 (off Gaskell Wlk.)
Chestnut Av. LE2: Oad . . . . . . . . . . . . . . . .3B 78
 LE5: Leic . . . . . . . . . . . . . . . . . . . . .5E 66
 LE17: Lut . . . . . . . . . . . . . . . . . . . . .4G 153
Chestnut Cl. CV13: Mkt B . . . . . . . . . . . . . .3D 94
 DE12: Moi . . . . . . . . . . . . . . . . . . . .6D 22
 LE7: Quen . . . . . . . . . . . . . . . . . . . .7F 47
 LE7: Sys . . . . . . . . . . . . . . . . . . . . .3D 60
 LE9: B Ast . . . . . . . . . . . . . . . . . . . .5E 86
 LE12: Quo . . . . . . . . . . . . . . . . . . . .7J 31
 LE12: Shep . . . . . . . . . . . . . . . . . . . .7E 16
 LE15: Upp . . . . . . . . . . . . . . . . . . . .2A 138
 LE67: Ibs . . . . . . . . . . . . . . . . . . . . .4J 51
 NG13: Bott . . . . . . . . . . . . . . . . . . . .1J 107
Chestnut Ct. LE12: Moun . . . . . . . . . . . . . .2E 44
Chestnut Dr. LE2: Oad . . . . . . . . . . . . . . . .4J 79
 LE7: Bush . . . . . . . . . . . . . . . . . . . . .3J 73
Chestnut Grange LE9: B Ast . . . . . . . . . . . .5D 86
Chestnut Grn. DE11: C Gre . . . . . . . . . . . . .1A 22
Chestnut Gro. LE67: Coal . . . . . . . . . . . . . .4H 39
Chestnut La. LE8: Arne . . . . . . . . . . . . . . .2G 147
Chestnut Pl. LE12: Bar S . . . . . . . . . . . . . .4D 32
Chestnut Rd. LE3: Glen . . . . . . . . . . . . . . .6G 63
 LE15: O'ham . . . . . . . . . . . . . . . . . . .3J 127
Chestnuts, The LE8: Count . . . . . . . . . . . . .5E 82
Chestnuts Cl. LE12: Sut Bon . . . . . . . . . . . . .6K 9
Chestnut St. LE11: Lou . . . . . . . . . . . . . . . .6E 18
Chestnut Wlk. LE6: Groby . . . . . . . . . . . . . .4D 62
 LE67: Mark . . . . . . . . . . . . . . . . . . . .7G 55
Chestnut Way LE7: East G . . . . . . . . . . . . . .5G 47
 LE13: Mel M . . . . . . . . . . . . . . . . . . .6F 117
Chettle Rd. LE3: Leic . . . . . . . . . . . . . . . .7A 64
Chetwynd Dr. LE13: Mel M . . . . . . . . . . . . .4C 116
Chevin Av. LE3: Leic . . . . . . . . . . . . . . . . .2H 69
Cheviot Cl. LE15: O'ham . . . . . . . . . . . . . .4G 127
 LE16: Mkt H . . . . . . . . . . . . . . . . . . .2F 151
Chiltern Dr. LE15: E Wes . . . . . . . . . . . . . .3H 135
Chiltern Grn. LE2: Leic . . . . . . . . . . . . . . .2G 77
Chiltern Ri. LE65: Ash Z . . . . . . . . . . . . . . .6A 24
CHILWELL . . . . . . . . . . . . . . . . . . . . . .1C 159
Chislehurst Av. LE3: Brau . . . . . . . . . . . . . .7J 69
Chiswick Dr. LE11: Lou . . . . . . . . . . . . . . . .6A 18
Chiswick Rd. LE2: Leic . . . . . . . . . . . . . . . .6F 71
Chitterman Way LE67: Mark . . . . . . . . . . . . .5G 55
Chorley Wood Rd. LE5: Leic . . . . . . . . . . . . .3F 73
Chrisett Cl. LE5: Leic . . . . . . . . . . . . . . . .1D 72
Christie Dr. LE11: Lou . . . . . . . . . . . . . . . .4B 18
Cheviot Dr. LE12: Shep . . . . . . . . . . . . . . .7E 16
Cheviot Rd. LE2: Leic . . . . . . . . . . . . . . . .2F 77
Chichester Cl. LE11: Lou . . . . . . . . . . . . . . .3A 30
 LE67: Ell . . . . . . . . . . . . . . . . . . . . . .1C 52
Chilcombe Cl. LE4: Leic . . . . . . . . . . . . . . .3E 64
Chilcombe Wlk. LE4: Leic . . . . . . . . . . . . . .3E 64
CHILCOTE . . . . . . . . . . . . . . . . . . . . . .3A 158
Chilcott Cl. LE67: Coal . . . . . . . . . . . . . . . .3F 39
Chiltern Av. LE9: Cosb . . . . . . . . . . . . . . . .7H 81
 LE12: Shep . . . . . . . . . . . . . . . . . . . .7F 17
Chiltern Cl. LE15: O'ham . . . . . . . . . . . . . .4F 127

Christopher Cl. LE8: Count . . . . . . . . . . . . .6E 82
 LE67: Ibs . . . . . . . . . . . . . . . . . . . . .2K 51
Christopher Dr. LE4: Leic . . . . . . . . . . . . . .2B 66
Christow St. LE1: Leic . . . . . . . . . . .1F 4 (7G 65)
Church Av. LE3: Leic . . . . . . . . . . . . . . . . .2C 70
Church Bank LE16: G Eas . . . . . . . . . . . . . .5K 141
Churchbell Way LE4: Beau L, Leic . . . . . . . . .6B 58
 (not continuous)
Church C'way. LE16: C Lan . . . . . . . . . . . . .1A 140
Church Cl. CV13: S Gol . . . . . . . . . . . . . . . .3A 98
 DE11: Blac . . . . . . . . . . . . . . . . . . . .2D 22
 LE7: Sys . . . . . . . . . . . . . . . . . . . . . .1D 60
 LE8: K Bea . . . . . . . . . . . . . . . . . . . .2J 89
 LE9: B Ast . . . . . . . . . . . . . . . . . . . . .4D 86
 LE9: Barw . . . . . . . . . . . . . . . . . . . . .4K 99
 LE10: Bur . . . . . . . . . . . . . . . . . . . . .6K 103
 LE14: Hos . . . . . . . . . . . . . . . . . . . . .6B 108
 LE15: A'll . . . . . . . . . . . . . . . . . . . . .6H 123
 LE16: C'ott . . . . . . . . . . . . . . . . . . . .2H 141
 LE17: D Bas . . . . . . . . . . . . . . . . . . . .1D 144
 LE17: Lut . . . . . . . . . . . . . . . . . . . . .4J 153
Church Cnr. NG13: Red . . . . . . . . . . . . . . .1E 106
Church Ct. LE19: Nar . . . . . . . . . . . . . . . . .2G 81
 (off Church La.)
Church Cft. CV9: S Mag . . . . . . . . . . . . . . .6C 90
Church Dr. LE17: Gilm . . . . . . . . . . . . . . . .7J 145
 LE67: Mark . . . . . . . . . . . . . . . . . . . .5F 55
CHURCH END . . . . . . . . . . . . . . . . . . . .2A 162
Church Farm Ct. LE10: A Fla . . . . . . . . . . . .5D 104
Church Farm La. LE8: Will W . . . . . . . . . . . .2K 145
Church Fld. CV13: Con . . . . . . . . . . . . . . . .5G 91
Church Ga. DE74: Keg . . . . . . . . . . . . . . . . .6H 9
 LE1: Leic . . . . . . . . . . . . . . . .2C 4 (1F 71)
 LE11: Lou . . . . . . . . . . . . . . . . . . . . .6F 19
 LE12: Shep . . . . . . . . . . . . . . . . . . . .6E 16
 LE17: Lut . . . . . . . . . . . . . . . . . . . . .5J 153
Churchgate LE16: Hall . . . . . . . . . . . . . . . .6A 132
Church Ga. M. LE11: Lou . . . . . . . . . . . . . . .6F 19
 (off Church Ga.)
CHURCH GRESLEY . . . . . . . . . . .2A 22 (3A 158)
Church Hill LE4: Birs . . . . . . . . . . . . . . . . .7H 59
 LE7: Scra . . . . . . . . . . . . . . . . . . . . .6H 67
 LE12: W Eav . . . . . . . . . . . . . . . . . . . .3E 42
 LE67: Bag . . . . . . . . . . . . . . . . . . . . .2F 93
 LE67: Swan . . . . . . . . . . . . . . . . . . . .4B 26
Church Hill Rd. LE4: Thurm . . . . . . . . . . . . .6A 60
 LE12: Moun . . . . . . . . . . . . . . . . . . . .3D 44
Church Ho. M. CV9: S Mag . . . . . . . . . . . . .6C 90
Churchill Cl. LE2: Oad . . . . . . . . . . . . . . . .3C 78
 LE13: Mel M . . . . . . . . . . . . . . . . . . .2F 117
 LE17: Lut . . . . . . . . . . . . . . . . . . . . .5G 153
 LE65: Ash Z . . . . . . . . . . . . . . . . . . . .5H 23
Churchill Dr. LE3: Leic E . . . . . . . . . . . . . . .3F 69
 LE17: U Bru . . . . . . . . . . . . . . . . . . . .4E 146
Churchill Rd. LE15: O'ham . . . . . . . . . . . . .4G 127
Churchill St. LE2: Leic . . . . . . . . . . . .7G 5 (3H 71)
Churchill Way LE8: Flec . . . . . . . . . . . . . . .4C 88
Church Lands LE11: Lou . . . . . . . . . . . . . . .4F 19
Church La. CV9: S Mag . . . . . . . . . . . . . . . .6C 90
 CV13: Cad . . . . . . . . . . . . . . . . . . . . .6C 94
 CV13: F Dray . . . . . . . . . . . . . . . . . . .2G 97
 DE74: C Don . . . . . . . . . . . . . . . . . . .5K 7
 DE74: Hem, Lock . . . . . . . . . . . . . . . . .4B 8
 DE74: Lock . . . . . . . . . . . . . . . . . . . . .4D 8
 LE2: Leic . . . . . . . . . . . . . . . . . . . . .1H 71
 LE2: S'ton . . . . . . . . . . . . . . . . . . . . .6G 73
 LE4: Thurm . . . . . . . . . . . . . . . . . . . .6A 60
 LE6: Ratby . . . . . . . . . . . . . . . . . . . .6A 62
 LE7: Anst . . . . . . . . . . . . . . . . . . . . .7H 57
 LE7: Gad . . . . . . . . . . . . . . . . . . . . .2A 118
 LE7: Rat W . . . . . . . . . . . . . . . . . . . .2E 46
 LE7: Rear . . . . . . . . . . . . . . . . . . . . .2J 47
 LE7: Thru . . . . . . . . . . . . . . . . . . . . .7B 114
 LE7: Thurn . . . . . . . . . . . . . . . . . . . .3H 73
 LE8: Arne . . . . . . . . . . . . . . . . . . . . .2H 147
 LE8: Flec . . . . . . . . . . . . . . . . . . . . .3B 88
 LE8: Peat M . . . . . . . . . . . . . . . . . . . .1K 147
 LE8: Whet . . . . . . . . . . . . . . . . . . . . .1K 81
 LE9: Barw . . . . . . . . . . . . . . . . . . . . .4K 99
 LE9: Des . . . . . . . . . . . . . . . . . . . . .2H 95
 LE9: Stap . . . . . . . . . . . . . . . . . . . . .1H 99
 LE12: Bar S . . . . . . . . . . . . . . . . . . . .3D 32
 LE12: Osg . . . . . . . . . . . . . . . . . . . . .6E 14
 LE12: Quo . . . . . . . . . . . . . . . . . . . . .5K 31
 LE14: Ab K . . . . . . . . . . . . . . . . . . . .7H 111
 LE14: Ash . . . . . . . . . . . . . . . . . . . . .3G 115
 LE14: Bars . . . . . . . . . . . . . . . . . . . .5C 118
 LE14: F Wre . . . . . . . . . . . . . . . . . . . .5H 115
 LE14: Hob . . . . . . . . . . . . . . . . . . . . .1B 114
 LE14: L Cla . . . . . . . . . . . . . . . . . . . .2H 111
 LE14: N Bro . . . . . . . . . . . . . . . . . . . .1D 110
 LE14: O Dal . . . . . . . . . . . . . . . . . . . .7A 110
 LE14: Som . . . . . . . . . . . . . . . . . . . . .6K 121
 LE14: Spro . . . . . . . . . . . . . . . . . . . .1H 113
 LE14: Sta . . . . . . . . . . . . . . . . . . . . .3H 109
 LE14: T Sat . . . . . . . . . . . . . . . . . . . .3H 119
 LE14: T'ord . . . . . . . . . . . . . . . . . . . .6H 119

Church La. LE14: Up Bro . . . . . . . . . . . . . . .1A 110
 LE14: W Wol . . . . . . . . . . . . . . . . . . . .1C 112
 LE14: Wart . . . . . . . . . . . . . . . . . . . .6F 111
 LE14: W'ham . . . . . . . . . . . . . . . . . . .1H 121
 LE15: B'den . . . . . . . . . . . . . . . . . . . .7D 136
 LE15: Bisb . . . . . . . . . . . . . . . . . . . . .2G 139
 LE15: E Wes . . . . . . . . . . . . . . . . . . . .3G 135
 LE15: Glas . . . . . . . . . . . . . . . . . . . . .1J 139
 LE15: Gree . . . . . . . . . . . . . . . . . . . .4E 124
 LE15: Lyd . . . . . . . . . . . . . . . . . . . . .7E 138
 LE15: Mant . . . . . . . . . . . . . . . . . . . .2C 134
 LE15: Mkt O . . . . . . . . . . . . . . . . . . .1H 123
 LE15: Mor . . . . . . . . . . . . . . . . . . . . .6J 135
 LE15: Pres . . . . . . . . . . . . . . . . . . . . .7A 134
 LE15: Rid . . . . . . . . . . . . . . . . . . . . .2H 133
 LE15: S Luf . . . . . . . . . . . . . . . . . . . .4C 136
 LE15: Seat . . . . . . . . . . . . . . . . . . . .5K 139
 LE15: Stre . . . . . . . . . . . . . . . . . . . . .2K 125
 LE16: C Lan . . . . . . . . . . . . . . . . . . . .1A 140
 LE16: C'ott . . . . . . . . . . . . . . . . . . . .2H 141
 LE17: D Bas . . . . . . . . . . . . . . . . . . . .2D 144
 LE17: Gilm . . . . . . . . . . . . . . . . . . . .6H 145
 LE17: H Bos . . . . . . . . . . . . . . . . . . . .6C 148
 LE17: S Kil . . . . . . . . . . . . . . . . . . . .6G 155
 LE17: Shaw . . . . . . . . . . . . . . . . . . . .3B 156
 LE17: Shea . . . . . . . . . . . . . . . . . . . .4J 147
 LE19: Nar . . . . . . . . . . . . . . . . . . . . .1G 81
 LE67: Rav . . . . . . . . . . . . . . . . . . . . .4J 37
 LE67: Swan, Whit . . . . . . . . . . . . . . . . .6B 26
 LE67: Thor . . . . . . . . . . . . . . . . . . . .2K 93
 NG13: Bott . . . . . . . . . . . . . . . . . . . .1H 107
 NG13: Plun . . . . . . . . . . . . . . . . . . . .5C 106
 NG13: Red . . . . . . . . . . . . . . . . . . . .2E 106
 NG32: Crox . . . . . . . . . . . . . . . . . . . .6H 107
 NG32: Eat . . . . . . . . . . . . . . . . . . . . .6G 109
 NG33: Sew . . . . . . . . . . . . . . . . . . . .7J 113
CHURCH LANGTON . . . . . . . . . .1A 140 (2A 164)
CHURCH LAWFORD . . . . . . . . . . . . . . . . .3B 162
Church Lea LE14: Bur L . . . . . . . . . . . . . . . .2C 120
Church Leys Av.
 LE7: Rear . . . . . . . . . . . . . . . . . . . . .2J 47
Church Nook LE18: Wig . . . . . . . . . . . . . . . .5K 77
CHURCHOVER . . . . . . . . . . . . . . . . . . . .3C 163
Church Pas. LE15: O'ham . . . . . . . . . . . . . .4J 127
Church Ponds Cl.
 LE6: Ratby . . . . . . . . . . . . . . . . . . . .6B 62
Church Rd. CV9: With . . . . . . . . . . . . . . . . .5B 96
 CV13: B'one . . . . . . . . . . . . . . . . . . . .5C 92
 CV13: Nail . . . . . . . . . . . . . . . . . . . . .2C 92
 CV13: S'one . . . . . . . . . . . . . . . . . . . .3H 91
 LE2: Leic . . . . . . . . . . . . . . . . . . . . . .2C 76
 LE3: Glen . . . . . . . . . . . . . . . . . . . . .5F 63
 LE4: Leic . . . . . . . . . . . . . . . . . . . . .3G 65
 LE5: Leic . . . . . . . . . . . . . . . . . . . . .5D 72
 LE7: Wan . . . . . . . . . . . . . . . . . . . . .3J 59
 LE8: G Gle . . . . . . . . . . . . . . . . . . . .1J 85
 LE8: K Bea . . . . . . . . . . . . . . . . . . . .3J 89
 LE9: K Mal . . . . . . . . . . . . . . . . . . . .6F 95
 LE9: K Mux . . . . . . . . . . . . . . . . . . . .2B 68
 LE9: Peck . . . . . . . . . . . . . . . . . . . . .6K 95
 PE9: Ket . . . . . . . . . . . . . . . . . . . . . .6H 137
Church Side LE12: Shep . . . . . . . . . . . . . . .6E 16
Church Sq. LE16: Mkt H . . . . . . . . . . . . . . .4E 150
Church St. CV9: Twy . . . . . . . . . . . . . . . . .3C 90
 CV13: Mkt B . . . . . . . . . . . . . . . . . . .2D 94
 DE12: A Mag . . . . . . . . . . . . . . . . . . .6A 48
 DE12: Don . . . . . . . . . . . . . . . . . . . .4A 34
 DE74: Lock . . . . . . . . . . . . . . . . . . . . .4D 8
 LE1: Leic . . . . . . . . . . . . . . . .4E 4 (2G 71)
 LE2: Oad . . . . . . . . . . . . . . . . . . . . . .3C 78
 LE4: Thurm . . . . . . . . . . . . . . . . . . . .7K 59
 LE7: Bill . . . . . . . . . . . . . . . . . . . . . .6H 131
 LE7: R'ley . . . . . . . . . . . . . . . . . . . . .6F 45
 LE8: Bla . . . . . . . . . . . . . . . . . . . . . .1B 82
 LE8: Count . . . . . . . . . . . . . . . . . . . . .6F 83
 LE9: Earl S . . . . . . . . . . . . . . . . . . . .1E 100
 LE9: S Stan . . . . . . . . . . . . . . . . . . . .1K 105
 LE9: Sap . . . . . . . . . . . . . . . . . . . . .4J 105
 LE9: Thurl . . . . . . . . . . . . . . . . . . . . .2C 96
 LE10: Bur . . . . . . . . . . . . . . . . . . . . .5K 103
 LE12: Bar S . . . . . . . . . . . . . . . . . . . .3D 32
 LE12: Belt . . . . . . . . . . . . . . . . . . . . .4H 15
 LE12: Hat . . . . . . . . . . . . . . . . . . . . .1J 17
 LE12: Sea . . . . . . . . . . . . . . . . . . . . .3K 33
 LE12: Shep . . . . . . . . . . . . . . . . . . . .6D 16
 LE12: Wym . . . . . . . . . . . . . . . . . . . .2K 21
 LE13: Mel M . . . . . . . . . . . . . . . . . . .4F 117
 LE14: Scal . . . . . . . . . . . . . . . . . . . . .6C 112
 LE15: B Rut . . . . . . . . . . . . . . . . . . . .6C 136
 LE15: Bel R . . . . . . . . . . . . . . . . . . . .5G 133
 LE15: Emp . . . . . . . . . . . . . . . . . . . . .6B 128
 LE15: L'ham . . . . . . . . . . . . . . . . . . . .6C 122
 LE15: N Luf . . . . . . . . . . . . . . . . . . . .1A 136
 LE15: O'ham . . . . . . . . . . . . . . . . . . .4J 127
 LE15: Win . . . . . . . . . . . . . . . . . . . . .5E 134
 LE16: Mkt H . . . . . . . . . . . . . . . . . . .4E 150
 LE17: H Bos . . . . . . . . . . . . . . . . . . . .6C 148

Church St.—Common Side


**Church St.** LE17: Lut 5J 153
LE17: N Kil 3K 155
LE65: Wort 2B 14
LE67: Swep 4B 50
NG13: Bott 1H 107
PE9: Ryh 5H 129
**Church Ter.** CV13: B'one 5C 92
LE13: Mel M 4F 117
CHURCH TOWN 5G 25 (3A 158)
**Church Vw.** LE9: N Ver 6G 93
LE14: T'ord 6G 119
LE19: Nar 1G 81
LE67: Ibs 5J 51
NG13: Bott 1G 107
**Church Wlk.** CV9: Ath, Manc 6A 96
CV13: S'one 3H 91
*DE12: Don 4A 34*
*(off Church St.)*
LE4: Leic 3G 65
LE8: Bla 1B 82
LE9: Sap 4J 105
LE10: Hinc 3G 103
LE14: Hos 6B 108
LE14: Sta 3H 109
LE14: T Sat 3H 119
LE16: L Bow 5G 151
LE16: Lub 7J 149
LE17: Brun 1D 146
LE17: Swin 4G 157
**Church Walks** CV13: S Gol 3A 98
**Churchward Av.** LE4: Leic 2C 64
CHURCH WILNE 1B 158
**Churchyard** *LE65: Ash Z 5A 24*
*(off Lwr. Church St.)*
**Cider Cl.** LE15: B'den 7D 136
**Circle, The** LE5: Leic 2B 72
**Citrus Gro.** DE74: Keg 5G 9
**City, The** LE8: Kib H 1J 89
City Gallery 4E 4 (2G 71)
**City Hgts.** LE11: Lou 6F 19
**City of Dan** LE67: Whit 7F 27
**City of Three Waters**
LE67: Whit 5E 26
**City Rd.** LE14: Sta 2G 109
**City Yd.** LE15: Win 6E 134
**Claire Ct.** LE12: Sileby 1A 46
**Clapgun St.** DE74: C Don 5K 7
**Clarefield Rd.** LE3: Leic 2B 70
**Clare Gro.** LE3: Brau 5H 69
**Clare Ho's.** LE2: Leic 7K 71
**Claremont Dr.** LE16: L Bow 4G 151
LE67: Rav 2K 37
(not continuous)
**Claremont St.** LE4: Leic 3G 65
**Clarence Ct.** LE10: Hinc 3H 103
**Clarence Dr.** LE67: Coal 4F 39
**Clarence Rd.** LE10: Hinc 3H 103
LE19: End 6H 75
**Clarence St.** LE1: Leic 2D 4 (1F 71)
LE11: Lou 5F 19
LE16: Mkt H 4F 151
**Clarendon Ho.** LE10: Hinc 4E 102
CLARENDON PARK 6H 71
**Clarendon Pk. Rd.** LE2: Leic 6G 71
**Clarendon Rd.** LE10: Hinc 4F 103
**Clarendon St.** LE2: Leic 7B 5 (3E 70)
**Claresholm Cres.**
LE15: O'ham 4K 127
**Claridge Pl.** LE65: Ash Z 5K 23
**Clark Dr.** LE13: Mel M 1F 117
**Clarke Cl.** LE67: Whit 7F 27
**Clarke Gro.** LE4: Birs 7G 59
**Clarke Rd.** LE67: Coal 4J 39
**Clarkesdale** LE16: G Eas 6K 141
**Clarkes La.** DE72: A Tre 1D 6
**Clarkes Rd.** LE18: Wig 6H 77
**Clarke St.** LE4: Leic 3H 65
LE16: Mkt H 4D 150
**Clark Gdns.** LE8: Bla 1A 82
**Clatterpot La.** LE15: Cott 6A 124
**Clawson Cl.** LE11: Lou 4B 18
CLAWSON HILL 2A 160
**Clawson La.** LE14: Ab K 6J 111
LE14: N Bro 1D 110
**Claxton Ri.** LE14: L Cla 3H 111
**Claybrook Av.** LE3: Brau 7A 70
**Claybrooke Ct.** LE17: C Par 6C 142
CLAYBROOKE MAGNA 5C 142 (3B 162)
Claybrooke Mill 4D 142
CLAYBROOKE PARVA 6C 142 (3B 162)
**Claybrooke Rd.** LE17: Ull 7E 142
CLAY COTON 3C 163
**Claydon Rd.** LE5: Leic 6A 66
**Clay La.** LE67: Cole 3A 26
LE67: Ell 3E 52
**Claymill Rd.** LE4: Leic 2B 66
**Clay St.** LE12: Wym 2K 21
**Clayton Dr.** LE4: Thurm 7B 60
**Clearview Cres.** LE9: Earl S 1E 100
**Cleeve Mt.** LE11: Lou 6A 18
**Clematis Cl.** LE4: Beau L 1A 64
**Clement Av.** LE4: Leic 3G 65
**Clements Ga.** DE74: Dis 3A 12
**Clephan Bldg.** *LE2: Leic 5B 4*
*(off Oxford St.)*
**Clevedon Cres.** LE4: Leic 6A 66
**Cleveland Rd.** LE10: Hinc 3F 103
LE11: Lou 4D 30
LE18: Wig 4K 77
**Cleveleys Av.** LE3: Brau 7A 70
**Cliff Av.** LE11: Lou 5D 18
**Cliffe Hill Rail Terminal** LE67: Bar 1G 53
**Cliffe Hill Rd.** LE67: S Bar 3B 54
**Cliffe Ho. M.** LE8: Whet 1K 81
**Cliffe La.** LE67: Mark 2E 54
LE67: S Bar 4D 54
(not continuous)
**Cliffe Rd.** LE4: Birs 7F 59
**Clifford Rd.** LE11: Lou 5D 18
**Clifford St.** LE3: Leic 2D 70
LE18: Wig 6F 77
**Cliffwood Av.** LE4: Birs 6F 59
CLIFTON 1C 159
**Clifton Av.** LE65: Ash Z 3K 23
CLIFTON CAMPVILLE 3A 158
**Clifton Ct.** LE10: Hinc 2E 102
**Clifton Dr.** LE18: Wig 1G 83
LE65: Ash Z 4J 23
**Clifton Rd.** LE2: Leic 7E 70
**Clifton Thorpe Mdws.** LE65: Ash Z 2K 23
CLIFTON UPON DUNSMORE 3C 163
**Clifton Way** LE10: Hinc 1D 102
**Clink La.** LE67: Swan 7A 26
**Clint Hill Dr.** LE9: S Stan 7K 101
**Clipper Rd.** LE4: Leic 3B 66
CLIPSHAM 3C 161
**Clipsham Rd.** LE15: Stre 1K 125
CLIPSTON
Keyworth 1D 159
Market Harborough 3A 164
**Clipstone Cl.** LE18: Wig 6A 78
**Clipstone Gdns.** LE18: Wig 6A 78
**Clipstone Ho.** LE2: Leic 2H 71
**Clipston St.** LE16: Mkt H 6F 151
**Clives Way** LE10: Hinc 1F 103
**Clock Ho. Ct.** LE15: Barl 2F 127
Clock Tower 3D 4
**Clock Twr. Mall** LE1: Leic 3D 4
**Cloisters, The** LE9: Earl S 2D 100
CLOPTON 3D 165
**Close, The** DE11: A Vil 3B 22
LE6: Ratby 5A 62
LE7: Anst 6H 57
LE8: Bla 7B 76
LE9: Barw 3A 100
LE9: K Mal 6G 95
LE10: S'ord 7G 105
LE14: Bur L 2C 120
LE17: Swin 3G 157
LE19: End 6E 74
**Cloud Hill Vw.** LE67: New 1G 25
**Cloud Lea** LE12: Moun 4E 44
**Cloud Trail** DE73: Wils 4C 10
**Cloud Way Ct.** LE11: Lou 4E 18
**Clovelly Rd.** LE3: Glen 5H 63
LE5: Leic 3B 72
**Clover Cl.** LE19: Nar 1E 80
**Cloverdale Rd.** LE5: Ham 3E 66
**Clover Dr.** LE13: Mel M 7E 116
**Clover Fld.** LE10: Hinc 7F 99
**Clover La.** LE12: Moun 3F 45
**Clover Pk. Trad. Est.** LE10: Hinc 7E 98
**Clover Pl.** LE67: Thrin 3D 26
**Clover Wlk.** LE7: East G 5G 47
**Clowbridge Dr.** LE11: Lou 7A 18
**Clumber Cl.** LE7: Sys 7D 46
LE11: Lou 5E 30
**Clumber Rd.** LE5: Leic 2A 72
**Clumber St.** LE13: Mel M 3E 116
**Clutsom Rd.** LE67: Coal 5C 38
**Clyde Ct.** LE67: Thrin 3D 26
**Clydesdale Cl.** LE13: Mel M 1D 116
**Clyde St.** LE1: Leic 2F 4 (1G 71)
**Coach Ho., The** LE15: Barl 2F 127
**Coach Ho. Ct.** *LE11: Lou 7F 19*
*(off Woodgate)*
**Coachmans Ct.** LE12: Shep 5E 16
**Coach Rd.** LE12: Shep 7E 16
(not continuous)
**Coalbourn Cl.** LE4: Leic 2E 64
**Coales Av.** LE8: Whet 4A 82
**Coales Gdns.** LE16: Mkt H 2D 150
**Coalfield Way** LE65: Ash Z 5B 24
**Coal La.** LE14: Hos 5B 108
**Coal Pit La.** CV23: Will 5A 152
LE17: Will 5A 152
COALVILLE 4C 38 (3B 158)
**Coalville Bus. Cen.** LE67: Coal 2D 38
**Coalville Bus. Pk.** LE67: Coal 3C 38
**Coalville La.** LE67: Coal, Rav 3K 37
**Coatbridge Av.** LE4: Leic 2K 65
**Coates Av.** LE3: Leic 7A 64
**Cobbett Rd.** LE3: Brau 5H 69
**Cobden St.** LE1: Leic 1G 4 (6H 65)
LE11: Lou 6G 19
(Freehold St.)
LE11: Lou 6G 19
(Moor La.)
**Cobden St. Ind. Est.** LE4: Leic 6H 65
**Cobwells Cl.** LE8: Flec 4C 88
**Coe Av.** LE11: Lou 5K 17
**Cokayne Rd.** LE3: Leic 1H 69
COKHAY GREEN 2A 158
**Colbert Dr.** LE3: Brau 1A 76
**Colbrook Wlk.** LE5: Leic 4A 72
**Colby Dr.** LE4: Thurm 1B 66
**Colby Rd.** LE4: Thurm 1B 66
**Colchester Rd.** LE5: Leic 1D 72
COLD ASHBY 3D 163
COLD OVERTON 3B 160
**Cold Overton Rd.** LE15: C Ove, Knos 2C 126
LE15: L'ham 6A 122
LE15: O'ham 4F 127
**Coldstream Cl.** LE10: Hinc 2D 102
**Colebrook Cl.** LE5: Leic 4A 72
**Coleford Rd.** LE4: Leic 1C 66
**Coleman Cl.** LE5: Leic 7B 66
**Coleman Ct.** LE5: Leic 7B 66
**Coleman Rd.** LE5: Leic 7B 66
LE8: Flec 3A 88
COLEORTON 4J 25 (3B 158)
**Coleorton Hall** LE67: Cole 4G 25
**Coleorton La.** LE65: Pac 2A 36
COLEORTON MOOR 4J 25
**Coleridge Dr.** LE19: End 6E 74
**Coles Cl.** LE4: Leic 1K 65
**Coley Cl.** LE10: Hinc 4G 103
**Colgrove Rd.** LE11: Lou 1E 30
**Colindale Av.** LE4: Birs 5G 59
**Colin Grundy Dr.** LE5: Leic 5D 66
**Collaton Rd.** LE18: Wig 6J 77
**College Av.** LE2: Leic 6G 5 (3H 71)
LE13: Mel M 7F 117
**College Cl.** LE67: Coal 4C 38
PE9: G Cas 2J 137
**College Farm La.** LE15: Bel R 4G 133
**College Hall** LE2: Leic 7H 71
**College Ho.** LE8: Whet 1K 81
**College La.** LE10: Hinc 2H 103
**College Rd.** LE7: Sys 3D 60
LE8: Whet 1K 81
**College St.** LE2: Leic 5G 4 (3H 71)
LE17: Ull 7E 142
**Collett Rd.** LE4: Leic 2C 64
**Colley Ri.** LE15: Lyd 7D 138
**Colliers Way** LE67: Ell 2E 52
**Collingham Rd.** LE3: Leic 5C 70
**Collingwood Cl.** LE13: Mel M 4C 116
**Collingwood Cres.** LE13: Mel M 4C 116
**Collingwood Dr.** LE12: Sileby 7K 33
**Collin Pl.** LE4: Leic 4J 65
**Collins Cl.** LE3: Brau 5H 69
COLLYWESTON 1C 165
**Colne Cl.** LE2: Oad 3F 79
**Colonel's La.** LE14: Up Bro 1A 110
**Colsterdale Cl.** LE4: Leic 1D 64
COLSTERWORTH 2C 161
COLSTON BASSETT 1D 159
**Colston La.** LE14: Harb, Lan 1A 108
**Coltbeck Av.** LE19: Nar 1E 80
**Coltfoot Way** LE13: Mel M 7D 116
**Colthurst Way** LE5: Leic 1G 73
**Colton St.** LE1: Leic 4E 4 (2G 71)
**Colts Cl.** LE10: Bur 7G 103
**Coltsfoot Way** LE9: B Ast 6E 86
**Coltsford Rd.** LE5: Ham 4E 66
**Columbia Cl.** LE19: End 5E 74
**Columbine Cl.** LE3: Brau 5J 69
**Columbine Rd.** LE5: Ham 3D 66
**Colwell Rd.** LE3: Leic 6D 64
COLWICK 1C 159
**Combe Cl.** LE3: Leic 6C 64
**Comet Cl.** LE3: Leic 7B 64
**Comet Way** LE67: Coal 2C 38
**Commercial Sq.** LE2: Leic 5F 71
**Common, The** LE5: Leic 4C 72
LE9: Barw 4A 100
**Common Rd.** DE11: C Gre 2A 22
**Commons, The** LE16: Mkt H 4E 150
COMMONSIDE 1A 158
**Common Side** DE11: C Gre 1A 22

Compass Rd. LE5: Leic . . . . . . . . . . . . . . .7E **66**
Compton Av. DE72: A Tre . . . . . . . . . . . . . . .1C **6**
Compton Cl. LE11: Lou . . . . . . . . . . . . . . .3A **30**
Compton Dr. LE9: Hun . . . . . . . . . . . . . . .1B **80**
Compton Rd. LE3: Leic . . . . . . . . . . . . . . .5C **70**
Conaglen Rd. LE2: Leic . . . . . . . . . . . . . . .2B **76**
Condon Rd. LE12: Bar S . . . . . . . . . . . . . . .4E **32**
Condor Cl. LE9: B Ast . . . . . . . . . . . . . . .3D **86**
Conduit St. LE2: Leic . . . . . . . .5F **4** (2G **71**)
Cone La. LE2: Leic . . . . . . . . . . . . . . .5J **71**
Coneries, The LE11: Lou . . . . . . . . . . . . . . .6F **19**
Conery, The LE4: Leic . . . . . . . . . . . . . . .4G **65**
Conery La. LE12: Sea . . . . . . . . . . . . . . .2K **33**
                (not continuous)
   LE19: End . . . . . . . . . . . . . . .4E **74**
Coneygrey LE8: Flec . . . . . . . . . . . . . . .2A **88**
CONGERSTONE . . . . . . . . . . . .6G **91** (1A **162**)
Congerstone La. CV13: B Bea . . . . . . . . . . . . . . .4K **91**
   CV13: S'one . . . . . . . . . . . . . . .4H **91**
Conifer Cl. LE2: Leic . . . . . . . . . . . . . . .3J **71**
   LE17: Lut . . . . . . . . . . . . . . .4H **153**
Conifers Mobile Home Pk. LE6: Ratby . . . . . .7B **62**
Coninsby Cl. LE3: Leic . . . . . . . . . . . . . . .6B **70**
Coniston Av. LE2: Leic . . . . . . . .8A **5** (4E **70**)
Coniston Cl. LE9: Earl S . . . . . . . . . . . . . . .2E **100**
Coniston Ct. LE9: Earl S . . . . . . . . . . . . . . .2E **100**
Coniston Cres. LE11: Lou . . . . . . . . . . . . . . .2B **30**
Coniston Gdns. LE65: Ash Z . . . . . . . . . . . . . . .6A **24**
Coniston Rd. LE12: Bar S . . . . . . . . . . . . . . .3D **32**
   LE13: Mel M . . . . . . . . . . . . . . .1D **116**
   LE15: E Wes . . . . . . . . . . . . . . .3F **135**
Coniston Way LE9: Crof . . . . . . . . . . . . . . .5B **80**
Conkers . . . . . . . . . . . . . . .6A **22**
Conkers Waterside Cen. . . . . . . . . . . . . . . .7A **22**
Connaught Ho. LE11: Lou . . . . . . . . . . . . . . .7F **19**
Connaught Rd. LE16: Mkt H . . . . . . . . . . . . . . .3F **151**
Connaught St. LE2: Leic . . . . . . . . . . . . . . .3H **71**
Connell Cl. LE16: Lub . . . . . . . . . . . . . . .7J **149**
Constable Av. LE4: Leic . . . . . . . . . . . . . . .6H **65**
Constance Rd. LE5: Leic . . . . . . . . . . . . . . .2K **71**
Constitution Hill LE1: Leic . . . . . .4F **4** (2G **71**)
Convent Cl. LE13: Mel M . . . . . . . . . . . . . . .5E **116**
Convent Dr. LE67: Coal . . . . . . . . . . . . . . .4D **38**
Conway Cl. LE11: Lou . . . . . . . . . . . . . . .5A **18**
Conway Dr. LE12: Shep . . . . . . . . . . . . . . .1B **28**
   LE13: Mel M . . . . . . . . . . . . . . .2F **117**
Conway Rd. LE2: Leic . . . . . . . . . . . . . . .4K **71**
   LE12: Moun . . . . . . . . . . . . . . .3D **44**
Cooden Av. LE3: Leic . . . . . . . . . . . . . . .3B **70**
Cooke Cl. LE3: Brau . . . . . . . . . . . . . . .5H **69**
   LE4: Thurm . . . . . . . . . . . . . . .6B **60**
Cooke's Dr. LE9: B Ast . . . . . . . . . . . . . . .4C **86**
Cooks Dr. DE74: C Don . . . . . . . . . . . . . . .5J **7**
Cooks La. LE9: Sap . . . . . . . . . . . . . . .4J **105**
   LE18: Wig . . . . . . . . . . . . . . .1A **84**
Cookson Pl. LE11: Lou . . . . . . . . . . . . . . .4A **18**
Cookson Rd. LE4: Leic . . . . . . . . . . . . . . .1C **66**
Cooks Wlk. LE3: Glen . . . . . . . . . . . . . . .6G **63**
Coombe Pl. LE12: Shep . . . . . . . . . . . . . . .1E **28**
Coombe Pl. LE2: Oad . . . . . . . . . . . . . . .4D **78**
Coombe Ri. LE2: Oad . . . . . . . . . . . . . . .4E **78**
Co-operation St. LE19: End . . . . . . . . . . . . . . .5F **75**
Cooper Cl. LE2: Leic . . . . . . . . . . . . . . .5E **72**
   LE9: Hun . . . . . . . . . . . . . . .1C **80**
   LE67: Whit . . . . . . . . . . . . . . .6D **26**
Cooper Ct. LE11: Lou . . . . . . . . . . . . . . .1H **31**
Cooper Gdns. LE2: Oad . . . . . . . . . . . . . . .4F **79**
Cooper La. LE6: Ratby . . . . . . . . . . . . . . .6B **62**
Cooper's La. LE17: D Bas . . . . . . . . . . . . . . .1D **144**
Cooper's Nook LE7: East G . . . . . . . . . . . . . . .5F **47**
Cooper St. LE4: Leic . . . . . . . . . . . . . . .5G **65**
Copdale Rd. LE5: Leic . . . . . . . . . . . . . . .2A **72**
Cope Dale Cl. CV13: B'one . . . . . . . . . . . . . . .5B **92**
Copeland Av. LE3: Leic . . . . . . . . . . . . . . .5A **64**
Copeland Cres. LE11: Lou . . . . . . . . . . . . . . .5B **18**
Copeland Rd. LE4: Birs . . . . . . . . . . . . . . .7F **59**
Copgrove Cl. LE5: Ham . . . . . . . . . . . . . . .2F **67**
Cophills Cl. DE12: Mea . . . . . . . . . . . . . . .1E **48**
Copinger Rd. LE2: Leic . . . . . . . . . . . . . . .1F **77**
Copley Cl. LE13: Mel M . . . . . . . . . . . . . . .3H **117**
Coplow Av. LE5: Leic . . . . . . . . . . . . . . .5A **72**
Coplow Cres. LE7: Sys . . . . . . . . . . . . . . .3C **60**
Coplow La. LE7: Bill . . . . . . . . . . . . . . .4H **131**
                (not continuous)
Coppice, The CV9: Manc . . . . . . . . . . . . . . .7A **96**
   LE2: Oad . . . . . . . . . . . . . . .7B **72**
   LE4: Thurm . . . . . . . . . . . . . . .6C **60**
   LE8: Count . . . . . . . . . . . . . . .5E **82**
   LE10: Bur . . . . . . . . . . . . . . .3J **103**
   LE12: Quo . . . . . . . . . . . . . . .7B **32**
   LE19: Nar . . . . . . . . . . . . . . .1E **80**
   LE67: Mark . . . . . . . . . . . . . . .5G **55**
Coppice Cl. LE10: Hinc . . . . . . . . . . . . . . .7J **99**
   LE67: Rav . . . . . . . . . . . . . . .2K **37**
Coppice Ct. LE4: Thurm . . . . . . . . . . . . . . .6C **60**
Coppice La. LE7: Quen . . . . . . . . . . . . . . .7H **47**
Coppice Rd. PE9: Ryh . . . . . . . . . . . . . . .5G **129**

Coppice Side DE11: Swad . . . . . . . . . . . . . . .1A **22**
Coppice Wlk. LE10: Hinc . . . . . . . . . . . . . . .7J **99**
Copse, The LE2: Oad . . . . . . . . . . . . . . .4J **79**
   LE7: Bush . . . . . . . . . . . . . . .3K **73**
Copse Cl. LE2: Leic . . . . . . . . . . . . . . .5C **76**
   LE2: Oad . . . . . . . . . . . . . . .1E **78**
   LE3: Leic E . . . . . . . . . . . . . . .6D **68**
   LE67: Hug . . . . . . . . . . . . . . .5C **38**
Copse Gro. LE11: Lou . . . . . . . . . . . . . . .5E **30**
Copson St. LE67: Ibs . . . . . . . . . . . . . . .4K **51**
COPSTON MAGNA . . . . . . . . . . . . . . .3B **162**
Copthall Ho. LE18: Wig . . . . . . . . . . . . . . .5F **77**
Copthorne Cl. LE3: Leic . . . . . . . . . . . . . . .1H **69**
COPT OAK . . . . . . . . . . . . . . .6E **40**
Copt Oak Ct. LE19: Nar . . . . . . . . . . . . . . .1E **80**
Copt Oak Rd. LE12: Nan . . . . . . . . . . . . . . .4F **41**
   LE19: Nar . . . . . . . . . . . . . . .7D **74**
   LE67: C Oak . . . . . . . . . . . . . . .1C **54**
Corah St. LE3: Leic . . . . . . . .5A **4** (2E **70**)
Coral Cl. LE10: Bur . . . . . . . . . . . . . . .7J **103**
Coral St. LE4: Leic . . . . . . . . . . . . . . .5G **65**
Corbet Cl. LE4: Leic . . . . . . . . . . . . . . .3B **64**
CORBY . . . . . . . . . . . . . . .3B **164**
CORBY GLEN . . . . . . . . . . . . . . .2D **161**
Cordelia Cl. LE5: Leic . . . . . . . . . . . . . . .5A **66**
Cordell Rd. LE11: Lou . . . . . . . . . . . . . . .4B **18**
Cordery Rd. LE5: Leic . . . . . . . . . . . . . . .3D **72**
Cordhill La. LE14: Edm . . . . . . . . . . . . . . .4G **121**
Cordle Way LE15: Mkt O . . . . . . . . . . . . . . .2H **123**
Cordonnier Cl. LE9: B Ast . . . . . . . . . . . . . . .6E **86**
Cordwell Cl. DE74: C Don . . . . . . . . . . . . . . .4H **7**
Corfield Ri. LE3: Leic . . . . . . . . . . . . . . .4J **69**
Coriander Rd. LE2: Leic . . . . . . . .7A **5** (3D **70**)
Cork La. LE2: G Par . . . . . . . . . . . . . . .6A **76**
Corkscrew La. LE65: Pac . . . . . . . . . . . . . . .7C **24**
   LE67: Cole . . . . . . . . . . . . . . .5D **24**
Cork St. LE5: Leic . . . . . . . . . . . . . . .2J **71**
CORLEY . . . . . . . . . . . . . . .3A **162**
CORLEY ASH . . . . . . . . . . . . . . .3A **162**
CORLEY MOOR . . . . . . . . . . . . . . .3A **162**
Cornfield LE10: Hinc . . . . . . . . . . . . . . .6F **99**
Cornfield Cl. LE19: Litt . . . . . . . . . . . . . . .2G **81**
Cornwallis Av. LE4: Leic . . . . . . . . . . . . . . .4B **64**
Cornwall Pl. LE13: Mel M . . . . . . . . . . . . . . .7F **117**
Cornwall Rd. LE4: Leic . . . . . . . . . . . . . . .5D **64**
   LE18: Wig . . . . . . . . . . . . . . .6F **77**
Cornwall St. LE19: End . . . . . . . . . . . . . . .5F **75**
Cornwall Way LE10: Hinc . . . . . . . . . . . . . . .6H **99**
Coronation Av. LE9: B Ast . . . . . . . . . . . . . . .4C **86**
   LE14: L Cla . . . . . . . . . . . . . . .3G **111**
   LE18: Wig . . . . . . . . . . . . . . .6H **77**
Coronation Dr. DE12: Moi . . . . . . . . . . . . . . .6B **34**
Coronation Rd. LE9: Earl S . . . . . . . . . . . . . . .4C **100**
Coronet Cl. LE7: Anst . . . . . . . . . . . . . . .7J **57**
Corporation Rd. LE4: Leic . . . . . . . . . . . . . . .4F **65**
Corshaw Wlk. LE5: Leic . . . . . . . . . . . . . . .6K **65**
Cort Cres. LE3: Leic . . . . . . . . . . . . . . .3J **69**
Corydalis Cl. LE11: Lou . . . . . . . . . . . . . . .5E **30**
COSBY . . . . . . . . . . . .7H **81** (2C **163**)
Cosby Hill LE9: Cosb . . . . . . . . . . . . . . .4K **87**
Cosby Rd. LE8: Count . . . . . . . . . . . . . . .6B **82**
   LE9: B Ast . . . . . . . . . . . . . . .4D **86**
   LE19: Litt . . . . . . . . . . . . . . .3G **81**
COSSALL . . . . . . . . . . . . . . .1B **158**
COSSINGTON . . . . . . . .4K **45** (3D **159**)
Cossington La. LE7: Coss . . . . . . . . . . . . . . .5B **46**
   LE7: R'ley . . . . . . . . . . . . . . .6G **45**
Cossington Rd. LE12: Sileby . . . . . . . . . . . . . . .2J **45**
Cossington St. LE4: Leic . . . . . . . . . . . . . . .5H **65**
Cossington Street Sports Cen. . . . . . . . . . . .5H **65**
Costello Cl. LE67: Ibs . . . . . . . . . . . . . . .2K **51**
COSTOCK . . . . . . . . . . . . . . .2C **159**
COSTON . . . . . . . . . . . . . . .2B **160**
Coston Rd. LE14: Spro . . . . . . . . . . . . . . .4G **113**
   NG33: Buck . . . . . . . . . . . . . . .6F **113**
COTES . . . . . . . . . . . .4K **19** (2C **159**)
COTESBACH . . . . . . . .6C **154** (3C **163**)
Cotes Dr. LE11: Lou . . . . . . . . . . . . . . .4F **19**
Cotes Rd. LE10: Bur . . . . . . . . . . . . . . .6J **103**
   LE12: Bar S, Cote . . . . . . . . . . . . . . .5K **19**
COTGRAVE . . . . . . . . . . . . . . .1D **159**
Cothelstone Av. LE11: Lou . . . . . . . . . . . . . . .5A **18**
Cotley Cres. LE15: Cott . . . . . . . . . . . . . . .4C **124**
Cotley Rd. LE4: Leic . . . . . . . . . . . . . . .1C **64**
Cotman Dr. LE10: Hinc . . . . . . . . . . . . . . .7D **98**
Cotman Wlk. LE4: Leic . . . . . . . . . . . . . . .6H **65**
Cotsmore Cl. LE67: Hea . . . . . . . . . . . . . . .3F **51**
Cotswold Cl. LE11: Lou . . . . . . . . . . . . . . .7B **18**
   LE13: Mel M . . . . . . . . . . . . . . .7G **117**
Cotswold Grn. LE4: Leic . . . . . . . . . . . . . . .1C **64**
Cotswold St. LE15: Cott . . . . . . . . . . . . . . .4B **124**
Cotswold Wlk.
   *LE15: O'ham* . . . . . . . . . . . . . . .4F **127**
            *(off Grampian Way)*
Cotswold Way LE65: Ash Z . . . . . . . . . . . . . . .6A **24**
Cottage, The LE15: B Rut . . . . . . . . . . . . . . .6D **126**

Cottage Cl. LE6: Ratby . . . . . . . . . . . . . . .5A **62**
Cottage Farm Cl. LE3: Brau . . . . . . . . . . . . . . .2K **75**
   LE12: Osg . . . . . . . . . . . . . . .6E **14**
Cottage Gdns. LE9: Earl S . . . . . . . . . . . . . . .2E **100**
Cottage Gdns. Cl. LE12: Hat . . . . . . . . . . . . . . .1J **17**
Cottage La. LE9: B Ast . . . . . . . . . . . . . . .4E **86**
   LE9: Des . . . . . . . . . . . . . . .1H **95**
   LE67: Ulv . . . . . . . . . . . . . . .2E **54**
Cottage La. Ind. Est. LE9: B Ast . . . . . . . . . . . . . . .4E **86**
Cottage Rd. LE18: Wig . . . . . . . . . . . . . . .7A **78**
Cottage Row LE3: Brau . . . . . . . . . . . . . . .7B **70**
Cottagers Cl. LE2: Leic . . . . . . . . . . . . . . .3E **76**
COTTERSTOCK . . . . . . . . . . . . . . .2D **165**
COTTESMORE . . . . . . . . .6A **124** (3C **161**)
Cottesmore Av. LE2: Oad . . . . . . . . . . . . . . .4F **79**
   LE13: Mel M . . . . . . . . . . . . . . .4E **116**
Cottesmore Dr. LE11: Lou . . . . . . . . . . . . . . .3D **30**
Cottesmore Rd. LE5: Leic . . . . . . . . . . . . . . .7K **65**
   LE15: A'll . . . . . . . . . . . . . . .6H **123**
   LE15: Ext . . . . . . . . . . . . . . .2A **128**
   LE15: Upp . . . . . . . . . . . . . . .2B **138**
COTTINGHAM . . . . . . . . . . . . . . .2B **164**
Cotton Cl. LE4: Leic . . . . . . . . . . . . . . .1K **65**
   LE9: B Ast . . . . . . . . . . . . . . .5E **86**
Cotton Cft. LE9: Earl S . . . . . . . . . . . . . . .2E **100**
Cotton Cft. LE12: Shep . . . . . . . . . . . . . . .1D **28**
Cotton M. LE9: Earl S . . . . . . . . . . . . . . .3E **100**
Cotton Way LE11: Lou . . . . . . . . . . . . . . .3C **18**
Coulson Cl. LE8: Whet . . . . . . . . . . . . . . .3A **82**
Council Rd. LE10: Hinc . . . . . . . . . . . . . . .2G **103**
Council St. LE17: Lut . . . . . . . . . . . . . . .4J **153**
COUNTESTHORPE . . . . . . . .6E **82** (2C **163**)
Countesthorpe Rd. LE8: Bla . . . . . . . . . . . . . . .3F **83**
   LE8: Whet . . . . . . . . . . . . . . .7H **81**
   LE9: Cosb . . . . . . . . . . . . . . .7H **81**
   LE18: Wig . . . . . . . . . . . . . . .7H **77**
             (not continuous)
Counting Ho. Rd. LE2: Leic . . . . . .10D **5** (5F **71**)
Countryman M. LE16: G Bow . . . . . . . . . . . . . . .2G **151**
Countrymans Way LE7: East G . . . . . . . . . . . . . . .4F **47**
   LE12: Shep . . . . . . . . . . . . . . .5E **16**
Countryman Way LE67: Mark . . . . . . . . . . . . . . .5G **55**
County Bri. Mobile Home Pk. LE12: Hat . . . . . .6K **13**
Court Cl. LE9: K Mux . . . . . . . . . . . . . . .2C **68**
Courtenay Rd. LE3: Leic . . . . . . . . . . . . . . .5C **64**
Courtney Cl. LE67: Whit . . . . . . . . . . . . . . .1E **38**
Court Rd. LE2: G Par . . . . . . . . . . . . . . .6B **76**
   LE7: Thurn . . . . . . . . . . . . . . .3H **73**
Courtyard, The CV13: S Gol . . . . . . . . . . . . . . .3A **98**
   LE10: Hinc . . . . . . . . . . . . . . .2G **103**
   LE14: W Wol . . . . . . . . . . . . . . .1C **112**
   LE17: C Mag . . . . . . . . . . . . . . .5C **142**
   LE67: Coal . . . . . . . . . . . . . . .2D **38**
Courtyard Workshops LE16: Mkt H . . . . . .6E **150**
COVENTRY . . . . . . . . . . . . . . .3A **162**
Coventry Rd. LE9: Sap, B Ast, Crof . . . . . .6J **105**
   LE10: Bur . . . . . . . . . . . . . . .7H **103**
   LE10: Hinc . . . . . . . . . . . . . . .4B **102**
   LE10: S'ord . . . . . . . . . . . . . . .7G **105**
   LE16: Mkt H . . . . . . . . . . . . . . .5D **150**
   LE17: Lut . . . . . . . . . . . . . . .6B **152**
   LE19: Nar . . . . . . . . . . . . . . .4D **80**
Coverack Wlk. LE5: Leic . . . . . . . . . . . . . . .3B **72**
Coverdale LE67: Whit . . . . . . . . . . . . . . .5E **26**
Coverdale Rd. LE18: Wig . . . . . . . . . . . . . . .7B **78**
Coverside Rd. LE8: G Gle . . . . . . . . . . . . . . .7K **79**
Covert, The LE7: East G . . . . . . . . . . . . . . .4F **47**
Covert Cl. LE2: Oad . . . . . . . . . . . . . . .2E **78**
   LE7: Sys . . . . . . . . . . . . . . .2A **60**
Covert La. LE7: Scra . . . . . . . . . . . . . . .7H **67**
Covert Pl. DE11: A Vil . . . . . . . . . . . . . . .3A **22**
Covett Way LE3: Leic . . . . . . . . . . . . . . .2J **69**
Cowdall Rd. LE3: Leic . . . . . . . . . . . . . . .4J **69**
Cowdray Cl. LE11: Lou . . . . . . . . . . . . . . .2E **30**
COW HILL . . . . . . . . . . . . . . .2F **29**
Cow La. LE15: Whis . . . . . . . . . . . . . . .2C **122**
Cowley Way LE5: Leic . . . . . . . . . . . . . . .7G **67**
Cowman Cl. LE14: Ash . . . . . . . . . . . . . . .2H **115**
Cowper Rd. LE10: Bur . . . . . . . . . . . . . . .5G **103**
Cow Row NG33: Buck . . . . . . . . . . . . . . .5G **113**
Cowslip Cl. DE12: Don . . . . . . . . . . . . . . .3A **34**
   LE19: Nar . . . . . . . . . . . . . . .1D **80**
Cowslip Dr. LE13: Mel M . . . . . . . . . . . . . . .7D **116**
COXBENCH . . . . . . . . . . . . . . .1A **158**
Cox Dr. NG13: Bott . . . . . . . . . . . . . . .1F **107**
Crabtree Cl. DE74: C Don . . . . . . . . . . . . . . .6J **7**
Crabtree Cnr. LE2: Leic . . . . . . . . . . . . . . .3G **77**
Crabtree Rd. LE9: Barw . . . . . . . . . . . . . . .5J **99**
Crackbottle Rd. LE7: Goa, Keyt . . . . . .4C **132**
Craddock Dr. LE12: Quo . . . . . . . . . . . . . . .6K **31**
Craddock St. LE11: Lou . . . . . . . . . . . . . . .6F **19**
Cradock Rd. LE2: Leic . . . . . . . . . . . . . . .5H **71**
Cradock St. LE5: Leic . . . . . . . .2G **4** (1H **71**)
Crafton St. E. LE1: Leic . . . . . . . .2F **4** (1H **71**)
Crafton St. W. LE1: Leic . . . . . . . .2E **4** (1G **71**)
Craftsmans Way LE7: East G . . . . . . . . . . . . . . .5F **47**

Cragdale—Danehurst Av.

Cragdale LE67: Whit 4D 26
Craggs Wlk. LE14: W'ham 1G 121
Craig Gdns. LE3: Leic 1H 69
Craighill Rd. LE2: Leic 7H 71
Craighill Wlk. LE2: Leic 7H 71
Crammond Cl. LE10: Hinc 3E 102
Cramps Cl. LE12: Bar S 4D 32
Cranberry Cl. LE3: Brau 5H 69
Cranborne Gdns. LE2: Oad 7D 72
Cranbrook Rd. LE7: Thurn 1H 73
Crane Ley Rd. LE6: Groby 3C 62
Cranesbill Rd. LE5: Ham 5E 66
Crane St. LE1: Leic 1C 4 (7F 65)
Cranfield Rd. LE2: Leic 2D 76
CRANFORD ST ANDREW 3C 165
CRANFORD ST JOHN 3C 165
Cranmer Cl. LE8: Bla 3A 82
Cranmer Dr. LE7: Sys 2B 60
Cranmere Rd. LE13: Mel M 2F 117
Cranmer La. LE17: N Kil 3K 155
Cranmer St. LE3: Leic 3D 70
CRANOE 2A 164
Cranshaw Cl. LE12: L Wha 6G 13
Cransley Cl. LE5: Ham 3E 66
Cranstone Cres. LE3: Glen 7G 63
Crantock Cl. LE5: Leic 4F 73
Cranwell Cl. LE5: Leic 5D 72
Craven Cl. LE11: Lou 4D 30
Craven's Rough LE67: Ulv 1K 55
Craven St. LE1: Leic 1B 4 (7E 64)
LE13: Mel M 6F 117
Crawford Cl. LE3: Leic 1B 70
Crawford Ho. LE18: Wig 5G 77
Crayburn Ho. LE3: Leic 6A 64
Crayford Way LE5: Leic 5F 67
Craythorne Way LE18: Wig 6B 78
Creaton Ct. LE18: Wig 6A 78
Creaton Rd. LE18: Wig 6A 78
Crediton Cl. LE18: Wig 1K 83
CREETON 2D 161
Crescent, The DE73: B Hil 7A 10
LE1: Leic 6D 5 (3F 71)
LE7: R'ley 4E 44
LE8: Bla 2B 82
LE9: Elm 5C 100
LE13: Mel M 3E 116
LE14: Ash 2H 115
LE14: O Dal 4B 110
LE14: Sta 3H 109
LE16: Mkt H 3F 151
LE18: Wig 4J 77
NG33: Buck 5G 113
PE9: Ryh 4J 129
Crescent Cl. LE16: Mkt H 3F 151
Crescent Rd. LE17: Lut 3J 153
LE67: Hug 5C 38
Crescent St. LE1: Leic 6D 5 (3F 71)
Cressida Ct. LE3: Brau 5J 69
Cressida Pl. LE3: Leic 5J 69
Cresswell Cl. LE4: Thurm 7C 60
Cresswell Dr. LE15: Cott 6A 124
Crestway, The LE8: Whet 1K 81
Creswell Dr. LE67: Rav 4J 37
Crete Av. LE18: Wig 6E 76
CREWTON 1A 158
Cricketers Dr. LE11: Lou 4E 18
Cricket La. LE11: Lou 3B 30
Cricket Lawns LE15: O'ham 5J 127
Crick's Retreat LE8: G Gle 7H 79
Critchlow Rd. LE9: Hun 1B 80
Crocket La. LE15: Emp 6C 128
CROFT 5A 80 (2C 163)
Croft, The CV9: Twy 3C 90
DE12: Mea 7D 34
DE74: Keg 6H 9
LE9: K Mux 2C 68
LE65: Ash Z 6B 24
LE67: Rav 4K 37
Croft Av. LE2: Leic 2C 76
Croft Cl. LE9: Barw 4A 100
Croft Dr. LE18: Wig 3H 77
Crofters Cl. LE3: Glen 6E 62
Crofters Dr. LE5: Leic 7C 66
Crofters Va. Pk. CV13: B'one 5C 92
Croft Gdns. LE14: O Dal 7A 110
Croft Glebe Nature Reserve 4A 80
Cft. Hill Rd. LE9: Hun 3A 80
Croft La. LE15: A'll 6H 123
Croft Rd. LE4: Beau L 6C 58
LE9: Cosb 5D 80
LE9: Thurl 4C 96
Crofts, The LE67: Mark 4F 55
Croft Way LE9: B Ast 4E 86
LE67: Mark 5F 55
Cromarty Cl. LE4: Leic 3K 65
Cromarty Dr. LE10: Hinc 2C 102
Cromer St. LE2: Leic 4J 71
Cromford Av. LE18: Wig 7G 77
Cromford Rd. LE9: Cosb 5H 81
Cromford St. LE2: Leic 1J 71
Cromford Way LE9: B Ast 4F 87
Cromore Cl. LE67: Coal 3J 39
Crompton Rd. LE14: Ash H 2K 115
Cromwell Cl. LE17: Wal 2D 154
LE65: Ash Z 4B 24
Cromwell Cres. LE16: Mkt H 6D 150
Cromwell Ho. LE2: Leic 7F 71
Cromwell Rd. LE8: G Gle 1K 85
LE12: Moun 4D 44
LE13: Mel M 6G 117
Croome Cl. LE11: Lou 2G 31
CROPSTON 3J 57 (3C 159)
Cropston Av. LE11: Lou 1K 29
Cropston Cl. LE3: Leic 1H 69
Cropston Dr. LE67: Coal 4G 39
Cropston Pump Station 2H 57
Cropston Rd. LE7: Anst, Crop 3J 57
Cropthorne Av. LE5: Leic 2B 72
CROPWELL BISHOP 1D 159
CROPWELL BUTLER 1D 159
Crosby Rd. LE16: Mkt H 6F 151
Cross, The LE16: Hall 6A 132
LE17: Walt 6C 146
LE19: End 5F 75
Cross Bank LE16: G Eas 6K 141
Cross Farm Ct. LE9: S Stan 1K 105
Crossfield Dr. LE13: Mel M 3H 117
Cross Grn. LE7: R'ley 6E 44
Cross Hedge LE7: R'ley 5E 44
Cross Hedge Cl. LE4: Leic 2C 64
Cross Hill Cl. LE12: Wym 2K 21
Cross Hill La. LE11: Lou 3D 30
(not continuous)
Cross Keys Grn. LE5: Leic 7G 67
Crosskirk Rd. LE10: Hinc 2C 102
Crossland Row LE10: Bur 5K 103
Cross La. LE12: Moun 4D 44
LE14: Bur L 2C 120
LE15: Pres 7A 134
Crossley Cl. LE12: Bar S 4C 32
Crossleys LE8: Flec 4B 88
Crossley St. LE3: Glen 6G 63
Cross Rd. LE2: Leic 5J 71
Cross St. DE73: B Hil 7B 10
LE2: Oad 1C 78
LE4: Leic 5G 65
LE7: Gad 1A 118
LE7: Sys 2D 60
LE8: Bla 1B 82
LE11: Lou 5G 19
LE12: Hat 1J 17
LE16: Mkt H 5F 151
LE18: Wig 6K 77
LE19: End 5F 75
Cross Wlk. LE5: Leic 1C 72
Crossway, The LE2: Leic 2F 77
LE3: Brau 7A 70
Crossways LE10: Bur 6J 103
Crossways, The LE4: Birs 6G 59
Crossways Farm Cvn. Site LE10: Bur 7A 104
Crossways Ho's. LE8: Bla 1B 82
Crosswood Cl. LE11: Lou 7A 18
Crowan Dr. LE18: Wig 1J 83
Crowfoot Way LE9: B Ast 6D 86
Crowhurst Dr. LE3: Brau 7J 69
Crow La. LE3: Leic 4D 70
Crown & Anchor Yd. LE10: Hinc 2G 103
Crown Bldg. LE1: Leic 5C 4
(off Newarke St.)
Crown Bus. Pk. LE14: O Dal 6D 110
Crown Cotts. CV13: Ods 7F 51
Crown Ct. LE10: Hinc 2G 103
Crown Gdns. LE15: O'ham 4J 127
Crown Hill Cl. CV13: S Gol 3A 98
Crown Hill Rd. LE10: Bur 7G 103
CROWN HILLS 1C 72
Crown Hills Av. LE5: Leic 2A 72
Crown Hills Ri. LE5: Leic 2A 72
Crown La. LE12: Moun 1D 44
LE15: B'den 7D 136
Crown Mdw. CV13: Con 6G 91
Crown St. LE15: O'ham 4J 127
PE9: Ryh 4H 129
Crowson Cl. LE12: Shep 2D 28
CROXTON KERRIAL 6H 107 (2B 160)
Croxton Kerrial Water Spout 2B 160
Croxton Rd. LE7: S Cro 7A 118
Croyde Cl. LE5: Leic 3B 72
Croyland Grn. LE5: Leic 1G 73
Crummock Av. LE15: E Wes 3F 135
Crusader Cl. LE67: Whit 6F 27
Cuckoo Cl. LE15: B'den 7C 136
(not continuous)
Cufflin Cl. LE6: Ratby 6B 62
Cuffling Cl. LE3: Leic 1H 69
Cuffling Dr. LE3: Leic 1H 69
Culham Av. LE5: Leic 6K 65
Culver Rd. LE3: Leic 6C 64
CULVERTHORPE 1D 161
Culworth Dr. LE18: Wig 6A 78
Cumberland Rd. LE11: Lou 6D 18
LE18: Wig 5E 76
LE67: Ell 1D 52
Cumberland St. LE1: Leic 2A 4 (1E 70)
Cumberland Trad. Est. LE11: Lou 6C 18
Cumberland Wlk. LE15: Cott 4C 124
(off Oakley Rd.)
Cumberland Way LE9: Barw 3K 99
Cumberwell Dr. LE19: End 7H 75
Cumbrae Dr. LE10: Hinc 2E 102
Cumbrian Way LE12: Shep 7E 16
Cunnery Cl. CV13: B'one 5B 92
Cunningham Dr. LE17: Lut 5G 153
Curlew Cl. LE7: Sys 1B 60
LE12: Moun 7C 32
LE67: Coal 4G 39
Curlew Wlk. LE5: Leic 7J 65
Curteys Cl. LE3: Leic 6B 70
Curtis Cl. LE8: Whet 2A 82
Curtis Way CV13: Osb 5A 92
Curzon Av. LE4: Birs 7G 59
LE18: Wig 7G 77
Curzon Cinema
Loughborough 7F 19
Curzon Cl. LE7: Quen 7F 47
LE10: Bur 4J 103
Curzon Rd. LE2: Leic 1E 76
Curzon St. LE1: Leic 1G 4 (7H 65)
LE11: Lou 6E 18
LE67: Ibs 4K 51
Cutchel, The LE17: Lut 5J 153
(off Church Ga.)
Cuthberts Yd. CV13: B'one 5C 92
Cutters Cl. LE19: Nar 2F 81
Cutting La. LE15: S Luf 3B 136
Cuttings, The LE7: Thurn 1H 73
Cygnet Cl. LE7: Sys 1B 60
LE12: Sileby 1J 45
Cypress Cl. LE11: Lou 4E 30
Cyprus Rd. LE2: Leic 2E 76
Cyril St. LE3: Brau 7A 70

## D

Dabey Cl. LE67: Mark 5F 55
DADLINGTON 1B 98 (2B 162)
Dadlington La. LE9: Stap 1E 98
Dadlington Rd. CV13: S Gol 2C 98
Dag La. LE17: Mows 2B 148
LE17: N Kil 3J 155
Dahlia Cl. LE10: Bur 5H 103
Dairy La. LE14: Hos 6B 108
LE14: N Bro 2D 110
Daisy Cl. DE12: Don 3A 34
LE6: Groby 3E 62
LE67: Bag 6G 53
LE67: Coal 4G 39
Dakota Rd. DE74: N Air 1K 11
Dakyn Rd. LE5: Leic 1F 73
DALBURY 1A 158
Dalby Av. LE4: Birs 5H 59
LE7: Bush 2J 73
Dalby Cl. LE13: Mel M 5E 116
Dalby Dr. LE6: Groby 3D 62
Dalby End LE14: G Dal 5D 120
Dalby Rd. LE7: Anst 6H 57
Dalby's La. LE16: Fox 1H 149
DALBY WOLDS 2D 159
DALE 1B 158
Dale Acre LE8: Count 5F 83
Daleacre Av. DE74: Lock 3D 8
Dale Av. LE18: Wig 4G 77
Dale End Cl. LE10: Hinc 4D 102
Dale Gdns. DE12: Mea 7F 35
Dales, The LE8: Count 5C 82
Dale St. LE2: Leic 2J 71
Dalgliesh Way LE14: Ash 3F 115
Dalkeith Rd. LE4: Leic 2K 65
Dalkeith Wlk. LE67: Thrin 3D 26
Dalley Cl. LE7: Sys 3D 60
Dallison Cl. LE16: Mkt H 7E 150
Dalliwell LE14: Sta 3H 109
Dalton Rd. LE5: Ham 3F 67
Dames La. LE67: N Bur 7B 50
Damson Ct. LE10: Hinc 4E 102
Danbury Dr. LE4: Leic 4D 64
Dandees Cl. LE67: Mark 4G 55
Danehill LE6: Ratby 5A 62
DANE HILLS 1B 70
Danehurst Av. LE3: Leic 1B 70

Daneshill Rd. LE3: Leic . . . . . . . . . . . . . . .2C 70
Dane St. LE3: Leic . . . . . . . . . . . . . . . . . .2D 70
Daniel Rd. CV9: Manc . . . . . . . . . . . . . . . .6A 96
Dan Maskell Tennis & Netball Cen. . . .1D 30
Dannett St. LE3: Leic . . . . . . . . . . . . . . . .1D 70
Dannett Wlk. LE3: Leic . . . . . . . . . . . . . . .2D 70
Danvers La. LE12: Shep . . . . . . . . . . . . . .6E 16
Danvers Rd. LE3: Leic . . . . . . . . . . . . . . . .4C 70
   LE12: Moun . . . . . . . . . . . . . . . . . . . . .3E 44
Darby Way LE19: Nar . . . . . . . . . . . . . . . .2E 80
Darcy Gdns. LE13: Mel M . . . . . . . . . . . .1F 117
Darenth Dr. LE4: Leic . . . . . . . . . . . . . . . .3A 64
Dares Wlk. LE10: Hinc . . . . . . . . . . . . . . .2G 103
Darien Way LE3: Brau . . . . . . . . . . . . . . .5G 69
Darker St. LE1: Leic . . . . . . . . . .2C 4 (1F 71)
DARLEY ABBEY . . . . . . . . . . . . . . . . . .1A 158
Darley Av. LE18: Wig . . . . . . . . . . . . . . . .7G 77
Darley Rd. LE8: Bla . . . . . . . . . . . . . . . . .2A 82
   LE10: Bur . . . . . . . . . . . . . . . . . . . . . .5H 103
Darley St. LE2: Leic . . . . . . . . . . . . . . . . .2J 71
Darlington Rd. LE3: Leic . . . . . . . . . . . . .6A 64
Darnall Rd. LE2: Leic . . . . . . . . .8A 5 (4D 70)
Darsway DE74: C Don . . . . . . . . . . . . . . .4H 7
Dart Cl. LE2: Oad . . . . . . . . . . . . . . . . . . .3E 78
   LE10: Hinc . . . . . . . . . . . . . . . . . . . . .3D 102
Dartford Rd. LE2: Leic . . . . . . . . . . . . . . .6D 70
Darwen Cl. LE3: Leic . . . . . . . . . . . . . . . .6B 64
Darwin Cl. LE3: Brau . . . . . . . . . . . . . . . .6G 69
   LE9: B Ast . . . . . . . . . . . . . . . . . . . . . .5D 86
   LE10: Hinc . . . . . . . . . . . . . . . . . . . . .7H 99
Dashwood Rd. LE2: Leic . . . . . . . . . . . . .4J 71
Dauphine Cl. LE67: Coal . . . . . . . . . . . . .3K 39
Davenport Av. LE2: Oad . . . . . . . . . . . . .3B 78
Davenport Rd. LE5: Leic . . . . . . . . . . . . .2D 72
   LE18: Wig . . . . . . . . . . . . . . . . . . . . . .7J 77
Davenport Ter. LE10: Hinc . . . . . . . . . . .3H 103
Davett Cl. LE5: Leic . . . . . . . . . . . . . . . . .1D 72
David Av. LE4: Leic . . . . . . . . . . . . . . . . .1E 64
David Lees Cl. LE67: Ell . . . . . . . . . . . . . .2E 52
David Lloyd Leisure
   Leicester . . . . . . . . . . . . . . . . . . . . . .7J 69
David Royce Ho. LE15: O'ham . . . . . . . .5J 127
                             (not continuous)
Davies La. LE16: Mkt H . . . . . . . . . . . . . .2D 150
Davison Cl. LE5: Leic . . . . . . . . . . . . . . . .1C 72
Dawkins Rd. DE12: Don . . . . . . . . . . . . . .3A 34
Dawlish Cl. LE5: Leic . . . . . . . . . . . . . . . .2F 73
Dawson Rd. LE12: Osg . . . . . . . . . . . . . . .6D 14
Dawsons La. LE9: Barw . . . . . . . . . . . . . .4A 100
Day Bell Cl. NG13: Bott . . . . . . . . . . . . . .1H 107
Daybell Cl. LE8: Whet . . . . . . . . . . . . . . .7K 75
Daybell Rd. DE12: Moi . . . . . . . . . . . . . . .7C 22
Day St. LE4: Leic . . . . . . . . . . . . . . . . . . .3G 65
Dayton Cl. LE67: Coal . . . . . . . . . . . . . . .2A 38
Deacon Av. CV13: B'one . . . . . . . . . . . . .5B 92
Deacon Cl. LE12: Shep . . . . . . . . . . . . . .7E 16
   LE16: Mkt H . . . . . . . . . . . . . . . . . . . .2D 150
   LE17: Bitt . . . . . . . . . . . . . . . . . . . . . .2G 153
Deacon Rd. LE4: Leic . . . . . . . . . . . . . . . .5D 58
Deacon St. LE2: Leic . . . . . . . . . .7B 5 (3E 70)
Dead La. LE11: Lou . . . . . . . . . . . . . . . . .6F 19
Dean Cl. LE10: Hinc . . . . . . . . . . . . . . . .1H 103
Deancourt Rd. LE2: Leic . . . . . . . . . . . . .2H 77
Deane Ga. Dr. LE7: Hou H . . . . . . . . . . . .2C 130
Deanery Cres. LE4: Leic . . . . . . . . . . . . .5D 58
Deane St. LE11: Lou . . . . . . . . . . . . . . . .5C 18
Dean Rd. LE4: Leic . . . . . . . . . . . . . . . . .5J 65
   LE10: Hinc . . . . . . . . . . . . . . . . . . . . .1H 103
Dean Rd. W. LE10: Hinc . . . . . . . . . . . . .1H 103
Deansburn Ho. LE3: Leic . . . . . . . . . . . .6K 63
Deanside Dr. LE11: Lou . . . . . . . . . . . . . .4B 18
Dean's La. LE12: W Eav . . . . . . . . . . . . . .1J 41
Dean's St. LE15: O'ham . . . . . . . . . . . . .4H 127
Dean's Ter. LE15: Upp . . . . . . . . . . . . . . .2B 138
Debdale LE15: Cott . . . . . . . . . . . . . . . . .6A 124
Debdale Hill LE14: O Dal . . . . . . . . . . . . .7A 110
Debdale La. LE8: Smee W . . . . . . . . . . . .5J 89
Debdale Pl. LE14: Ash . . . . . . . . . . . . . . .3F 115
Dee Cl. LE13: Mel M . . . . . . . . . . . . . . . .4G 117
   LE15: O'ham . . . . . . . . . . . . . . . . . . .6G 127
Deeming Dr. LE12: Quo . . . . . . . . . . . . . .4K 31
DEENE . . . . . . . . . . . . . . . . . . . . . . . . . .2C 165
Deene Cl. LE16: L Bow . . . . . . . . . . . . . .4G 151
DEENETHORPE . . . . . . . . . . . . . . . . . . .2C 165
Deepdale LE5: Leic . . . . . . . . . . . . . . . . .1B 72
   LE16: G Eas . . . . . . . . . . . . . . . . . . . .5K 141
Deepdale Cl. LE67: Ibs . . . . . . . . . . . . . .3K 51
Deepdene Cl. DE11: C Gre . . . . . . . . . . . .2A 22
DEEPING GATE . . . . . . . . . . . . . . . . . . .1D 165
Deepway, The LE12: Quo . . . . . . . . . . . . .6J 31
Deer Acre LE11: Lou . . . . . . . . . . . . . . . .4F 19
Degens Way LE67: Hug . . . . . . . . . . . . . .5B 38
De Havilland Way LE10: Bur . . . . . . . . . .7H 103
Deighton Way LE11: Lou . . . . . . . . . . . . .4A 18
De-la-Bere Cres. LE10: Bur . . . . . . . . . .5K 103
Delamare Rd. LE13: Mel M . . . . . . . . . . .1G 117
Delaware Rd. LE5: Leic . . . . . . . . . . . . . .3G 73

De Lisle Cl. LE16: Mkt H . . . . . . . . . . . . .5D 150
Delisle Ct. LE11: Lou . . . . . . . . . . . . . . . .1K 29
Dell, The LE15: O'ham . . . . . . . . . . . . . . .5J 127
   LE17: Ull . . . . . . . . . . . . . . . . . . . . . .7F 143
Delph, The DE73: B Hil . . . . . . . . . . . . . .7B 10
Delven La. DE74: C Don . . . . . . . . . . . . . .5J 7
DEMBLEBY . . . . . . . . . . . . . . . . . . . . . .1D 161
De Montfort LE13: Mel M . . . . . . . . . . . .2F 117
De Montfort Cl. LE11: Lou . . . . . . . . . . . .5A 18
DeMontfort Ct. LE7: Anst . . . . . . . . . . . .7H 57
De Montfort Hall . . . . . . . . . . . .8G 5 (4H 71)
De Montfort Ho. LE1: Leic . . . . . . .6C 5 (3F 71)
De Montfort M. LE1: Leic . . . . . . .6F 5 (3G 71)
De Montfort Pl. LE1: Leic . . . . . . .6F 5 (3G 71)
De Montfort Rd. LE10: Hinc . . . . . . . . . .1H 103
De Montfort Sq. LE1: Leic . . . . . . .7E 5 (3G 71)
De Montfort St. LE1: Leic . . . . . . .8E 5 (4G 71)
De Montfort University . . . . . . . . . . . . .5B 4
Dempsey Cl. LE17: Lut . . . . . . . . . . . . . .2J 153
Denacre Av. LE18: Wig . . . . . . . . . . . . . .7G 77
Denbigh Pl. LE17: Lut . . . . . . . . . . . . . . .3J 153
Denbydale LE18: Wig . . . . . . . . . . . . . . .7B 78
Denegate Av. LE4: Birs . . . . . . . . . . . . . .5F 59
Denfield Cl. LE15: Glas . . . . . . . . . . . . . .1J 139
                             (not continuous)
DENFORD . . . . . . . . . . . . . . . . . . . . . . .3C 165
Denham Cl. LE3: Leic . . . . . . . . . . . . . . . .1G 69
Denis Cl. LE3: Leic . . . . . . . . . . . . . . . . .1B 70
Denis Rd. LE10: Bur . . . . . . . . . . . . . . . .6F 103
Deniston Av. LE9: B Ast . . . . . . . . . . . . . .3B 86
Denman La. LE9: Hun . . . . . . . . . . . . . . .1B 80
Denmark Rd. LE2: Leic . . . . . . . . . . . . . .7E 70
Denmead Av. LE18: Wig . . . . . . . . . . . . .5J 77
Dennis David Cl. LE17: Lut . . . . . . . . . . .2J 153
Dennis St. LE67: Hug . . . . . . . . . . . . . . .6D 38
Denstone Cl. LE65: Ash Z . . . . . . . . . . . .3J 23
DENTON
   Grantham . . . . . . . . . . . . . . . . . . . . .1B 160
   Peterborough . . . . . . . . . . . . . . . . . .3D 165
Denton Ri. LE13: Mel M . . . . . . . . . . . . .5H 117
Denton St. LE3: Leic . . . . . . . . . . . . . . . .2B 70
Denton Wlk. LE18: Wig . . . . . . . . . . . . . .6A 78
DERBY . . . . . . . . . . . . . . . . . . . . . . . . . .1A 158
Derby Cl. LE9: B Ast . . . . . . . . . . . . . . . .5E 86
Derby La. CV13: S'one . . . . . . . . . . . . . . .1F 91
   DE12: Snar . . . . . . . . . . . . .6J 49 & 1F 91
Derby Rd. : Smis . . . . . . . . . . . . . . . . . . .1J 23
   DE11: Swad . . . . . . . . . . . . . . . . . . . .1B 22
   DE72: Thul . . . . . . . . . . . . . . . . . . . . .1D 6
   DE74: Keg . . . . . . . . . . . . . . . . . . . . .5G 9
   LE10: Hinc . . . . . . . . . . . . . . . . . . . .1G 103
   LE11: Lou . . . . . . . . . . . . . . . . . . . . .3A 18
   LE12: Hat . . . . . . . . . . . . . . . . . . . . .6K 13
   LE65: Ash Z . . . . . . . . . . . . . . . . . . . .4K 23
Derby Southern By-Pass DE73 . . . . . . . .5E 8
Derby Sq. LE11: Lou . . . . . . . . . . . . . . . .6F 19
Derry's Hollow LE67: Ell . . . . . . . . . . . . .2E 52
Derry Wlk. LE4: Leic . . . . . . . . . . . . . . . .2E 64
Dersingham Rd. LE4: Leic . . . . . . . . . . . .4D 64
De Ruthyn Cl. DE12: Moi . . . . . . . . . . . . .7C 22
Derwent Av. LE15: E Wes . . . . . . . . . . . .3F 135
Derwent Cl. LE9: Earl S . . . . . . . . . . . . . .3E 100
Derwent Dr. LE11: Lou . . . . . . . . . . . . . .2B 30
                             (not continuous)
   LE13: Mel M . . . . . . . . . . . . . . . . . . .6E 116
   LE15: O'ham . . . . . . . . . . . . . . . . . . .4H 127
Derwent Gdns. LE65: Ash Z . . . . . . . . . .7A 24
Derwent Rd. LE12: Bar S . . . . . . . . . . . . .2D 32
Derwent St. LE2: Leic . . . . . . . . . . . . . . .2J 71
Derwent Wlk. LE2: Oad . . . . . . . . . . . . . .3E 78
DESBOROUGH . . . . . . . . . . . . . . . . . . . .3B 164
DESFORD . . . . . . . . . . . . . . . .2H 95 (1B 162)
Desford Hill LE9: Des . . . . . . . . . . . . . . . .1F 95
Desford La. LE6: Ratby . . . . . . . . . . . . . .7A 62
   LE9: K Mal . . . . . . . . . . . . . . . . . . . . .6G 95
   LE9: K Mux . . . . . . . . . . . . . . . . . . . . .1A 68
   LE9: Peck . . . . . . . . . . . . . . . . . . . . . .5K 95
Desford Rd. LE9: Des, Thurl . . . . . . . . . . .7A 68
   LE9: N Ver . . . . . . . . . . . . . . . . . . . . .6J 93
   LE9: Thurl . . . . . . . . . . . . . . . . . . . . .1A 96
   LE19: End, Thurl . . . . . . . . . . . . . . . . .2B 74
   LE19: Nar . . . . . . . . . . . . . . . . . . . . . .1F 81
Devana Av. LE67: Coal . . . . . . . . . . . . . . .4F 39
Devana Rd. LE2: Leic . . . . . . . . . . . . . . . .4J 71
Devenports Hill LE7: Bush . . . . . . . . . . . .2K 73
De Verdon Rd. LE17: Lut . . . . . . . . . . . . .5G 153
De Verdun Av. LE12: Belt . . . . . . . . . . . . .5H 15
Deveron Cl. LE67: Coal . . . . . . . . . . . . . .3J 39
Deveron Cl. LE10: Hinc . . . . . . . . . . . . . .2E 102
Deveron Way LE10: Hinc . . . . . . . . . . . . .2E 102
DEVITTS GREEN . . . . . . . . . . . . . . . . . .2A 162
Devitt Way LE9: B Ast . . . . . . . . . . . . . . .6D 86
Devon Cl. DE12: Moi . . . . . . . . . . . . . . . .5E 22
Devonia Rd. LE2: Oad . . . . . . . . . . . . . . .4F 79
Devon La. NG13: Bott . . . . . . . . . . . . . . .1H 107
Devonshire Av. LE18: Wig . . . . . . . . . . . .7G 77
Devonshire Ct. LE2: Oad . . . . . . . . . . . . .4D 78

Devonshire La. LE11: Lou . . . . . . . . . . . .7F 19
Devonshire Rd. LE4: Leic . . . . . . . . . . . . .5E 64
Devonshire Sq. LE11: Lou . . . . . . . . . . . .7F 19
Devonshire Wlk. LE2: Oad . . . . . . . . . . . .5E 78
Devon Wlk. LE15: Cott . . . . . . . . . . . . . .4B 124
Devon Way LE5: Leic . . . . . . . . . . . . . . . .2B 72
Deweys Cl. LE5: N Luf . . . . . . . . . . . . . . .1B 136
Dexters Cl. LE12: Quo . . . . . . . . . . . . . . .4A 32
Dicken, The LE8: Whet . . . . . . . . . . . . . .2K 81
Dickens Cl. LE12: Sileby . . . . . . . . . . . . .7K 33
Dickens Ct. LE3: Leic . . . . . . . . . . . . . . . .2A 70
Dickens Dr. LE13: Mel M . . . . . . . . . . . .1E 116
Dickinson Way LE4: Thurm . . . . . . . . . . .6B 60
Dickmans La. LE14: Harb . . . . . . . . . . . .2D 108
Didcott Way DE12: A Mag . . . . . . . . . . . .5B 48
Didsbury St. LE3: Leic . . . . . . . . . . . . . . .3J 69
Dieppe Way LE13: Mel M . . . . . . . . . . . .2E 116
Digby Cl. LE3: Leic . . . . . . . . . . . . . . . . .4B 70
   LE7: T Hil . . . . . . . . . . . . . . . . . . . . . .2H 131
Digby Dr. LE13: Mel M . . . . . . . . . . . . . .7C 116
   LE5: N Luf . . . . . . . . . . . . . . . . . . . . .1B 136
   LE15: O'ham . . . . . . . . . . . . . . . . . . .4G 127
Digby Hall LE2: Leic . . . . . . . . . . . . . . . .1B 78
Dillon Grn. LE3: Leic . . . . . . . . . . . . . . . .5K 63
Dillon Ri. LE3: Leic . . . . . . . . . . . . . . . . .6K 63
Dillon Rd. LE3: Leic . . . . . . . . . . . . . . . . .6K 63
Dillon Way LE3: Leic . . . . . . . . . . . . . . . .5K 63
Dimmingsdale Cl. LE7: Anst . . . . . . . . . . .6J 57
DINGLEY . . . . . . . . . . . . . . . . . . . . . . . .3A 164
Dingley Av. LE4: Leic . . . . . . . . . . . . . . . .5J 65
Dingley Link LE18: Wig . . . . . . . . . . . . . .5B 78
Dingley Rd. LE16: G Bow . . . . . . . . . . . .1H 151
Dingley Ter. LE16: Mkt H . . . . . . . . . . . . .4F 151
Discovery Way LE65: Ash Z . . . . . . . . . . .4B 24
DISEWORTH . . . . . . . . . . . .4A 12 (2B 158)
Diseworth Rd. DE74: C Don . . . . . . . . . . .6J 7
Diseworth St. LE2: Leic . . . . . . . . . . . . . .2J 71
DISHLEY . . . . . . . . . . . . . . . . . . . . . . . . .4A 18
Disney Cl. LE9: S Stan . . . . . . . . . . . . . . .1J 105
Disraeli Cl. LE8: K Bea . . . . . . . . . . . . . . .3H 89
Disraeli St. LE2: Leic . . . . . . . . . . . . . . . .1C 76
   LE12: Quo . . . . . . . . . . . . . . . . . . . . .5A 32
Ditchling Av. LE3: Leic . . . . . . . . . . . . . . .1A 70
Dixon Dr. LE2: Leic . . . . . . . . . . . . . . . . .4J 71
Dobney Av. LE7: Quen . . . . . . . . . . . . . . .6E 46
Doctor Cookes Cl. LE9: Barw . . . . . . . . . .4K 99
Doctors Flds. LE9: Earl S . . . . . . . . . . . . .3C 100
Doctor's La. DE73: B Hil . . . . . . . . . . . . .7B 10
   LE13: Mel M . . . . . . . . . . . . . . . . . . .3H 117
Doctor's Wlk., The DE12: Mea . . . . . . . . .7E 34
Doddridge Rd. LE16: Mkt H . . . . . . . . . .3E 150
Dodgeford La. LE12: Osg . . . . . . . . . . . . .5F 15
Dodwells Bri. Ind. Est. LE10: Hinc . . . . . .3A 102
Dodwells Rd. LE10: Hinc . . . . . . . . . . . . .4A 102
Dog and Gun La. LE8: Whet . . . . . . . . . . .4K 81
Dog La. DE73: Wils . . . . . . . . . . . . . . . . .3A 10
   LE14: Bur L . . . . . . . . . . . . . . . . . . . .1D 120
   LE35: S Kil . . . . . . . . . . . . . . . . . . . . .6G 155
Dogwood Ct. LE2: Oad . . . . . . . . . . . . . .2C 78
Dolphin Ct. LE15: Upp . . . . . . . . . . . . . .2B 138
Dolphin Sq. LE1: Leic . . . . . . . . . . . . . . . .4D 4
Dominion Rd. LE3: Glen . . . . . . . . . . . . . .6G 63
Dominus Way LE3: Brau . . . . . . . . . . . . . .7H 69
Domont Cl. LE12: Shep . . . . . . . . . . . . . .7D 16
Donald Cl. LE4: Leic . . . . . . . . . . . . . . . . .2B 66
Donaldson Rd. LE4: Leic . . . . . . . . . . . . .6G 65
Donata Ho. LE17: Lut . . . . . . . . . . . . . . .4J 153
Doncaster Rd. LE4: Leic . . . . . . . . . . . . . .5B 64
Don Cl. LE15: O'ham . . . . . . . . . . . . . . . .6G 127
Donington Grand Prix Collection (Mus.) . . . . .1F 11
Donington Dr. LE65: Ash Z . . . . . . . . . . . .6J 23
Donington La. DE72: Shar . . . . . . . . . . . . .1A 8
   DE74: C Don . . . . . . . . . . . . . . . . . . . .1A 8
DONINGTON LE HEATH . . . .6C 38 (3B 158)
Donington le Heath Manor House . . . . . .6C 38
Donington Pk. Exhibition Cen. . . . . . . . . .1E 10
Donington Pk. Motor Racing Circuit . . . . .7E 6
DONISTHORPE . . . . . . . . . . . . .3A 34 (3A 158)
Donisthorpe La. DE12: Moi . . . . . . . . . . . .1A 34
Donkey La. LE9: Sap . . . . . . . . . . . . . . . .5H 105
Donnett Cl. LE5: Leic . . . . . . . . . . . . . . . .1D 72
Donnington St. LE2: Leic . . . . . . . . . . . . .2J 71
Dorchester Cl. LE8: Bla . . . . . . . . . . . . . .3C 82
   LE18: Wig . . . . . . . . . . . . . . . . . . . . . .1K 83
Dorchester Rd. LE3: Leic . . . . . . . . . . . . .2A 70
   LE10: Bur . . . . . . . . . . . . . . . . . . . . .4A 104
DORDON . . . . . . . . . . . . . . . . . . . . . . . .1A 162
Dore Rd. LE5: Leic . . . . . . . . . . . . . . . . . .3J 71
Dorfold Wlk. LE4: Leic . . . . . . . . . . . . . . .5K 65
Dorian Ri. LE13: Mel M . . . . . . . . . . . . . .5E 116
Dormer Ct. LE12: Hat . . . . . . . . . . . . . . . .1J 17
Dorothy Av. LE2: G Par . . . . . . . . . . . . . .5B 76
   LE4: Thurm . . . . . . . . . . . . . . . . . . . . .7K 59
   LE13: Mel M . . . . . . . . . . . . . . . . . . .4D 116
Dorothy Rd. LE5: Leic . . . . . . . . . . . . . . .2K 71
Dorset Av. LE3: Glen . . . . . . . . . . . . . . . .5G 63
   LE18: Wig . . . . . . . . . . . . . . . . . . . . . .5E 76

Dorset Dr. DE12: Moi ....5E 22
LE13: Mel M ....1A 120
Dorset St. LE4: Leic ....6G 65
Double Rail Cl. LE18: Wig ....7G 77
Doudney Cl. LE9: S Stan ....2J 105
Douglas Bader Dr. LE17: Lut ....2J 153
Douglas Ct. LE2: Leic ....8B 5
Douglas Dr. LE67: Ibs ....5K 51
Douglas Jane Cl. LE13: Mel M ....3D 116
Douglass Dr. LE16: Mkt H ....2F 151
Dove Cl. LE10: Hinc ....3D 102
LE15: O'ham ....5G 127
Dovecote, The ....6E 16
Dovecote DE73: Ton ....6D 10
DE74: C Don ....5K 7
LE12: Shep ....6E 16
Dovecote, The DE73: B Hil ....7B 10
Dovecote Cl. LE9: Sap ....4J 105
LE15: B'den ....7D 136
Dovecote Rd. LE9: Crof ....4A 80
Dovecotes, The LE7: Quen ....7J 47
Dovecote St. LE12: Hat ....1J 17
Dovecote Way LE9: Barw ....4A 100
Dovedale Av. LE8: Bla ....2B 82
Dovedale Cl. LE13: Mel M ....6E 116
Dovedale Cl. LE2: Leic ....6A 72
Dovedale Rd. LE2: Leic ....6A 72
LE4: Thurm ....6A 60
Dover Cl. LE12: Moun ....4D 44
Dover Ho. LE1: Leic ....5E 4 (2G 71)
Dove Ri. LE2: Oad ....2E 78
Dove Rd. DE74: N Air ....1A 12
LE67: Coal ....5G 39
Dover St. LE1: Leic ....5E 4 (2G 71)
LE8: K Bea ....3H 89
Doveside Ct. LE16: Med ....6C 140
Dower Ho. Gdns. LE12: Quo ....5A 32
Downham Av. LE4: Leic ....4E 64
Downing Dr. LE5: Leic ....4E 72
Downside Dr. LE65: Ash Z ....4J 23
Down St. LE4: Leic ....5H 65
DOWSBY ....2D 161
Doyle Cl. LE11: Lou ....4B 18
Dragon La. LE9: N Ver ....6G 93
Dragwell DE74: Keg ....6H 9
Drake Way LE10: Hinc ....6G 99
Draper St. LE2: Leic ....4J 71
DRAUGHTON ....3A 164
DRAYCOTT ....1B 158
DRAYTON ....7G 141 (2B 164)
Drayton Cl. CV13: F Dray ....2G 97
Drayton La. CV13: F Dray ....7D 96
Drayton Rd. LE3: Leic ....7J 63
LE16: Brin ....7G 141
LE16: Med ....7C 140
Dribdale LE8: Flec ....4C 88
Drift, The LE14: Edm ....3K 121
NG33: Buck, Sew ....4J 113
NG33: Sew ....7K 113
PE9: Ess ....1F 129
Drift Cl. DE11: Blac ....3D 22
Drift Hill LE14: W'ham ....1K 121
NG13: Red ....1E 106
Drift Side DE11: Blac ....4D 22
Drinkstone Rd. LE5: Leic ....2A 72
Drive, The LE4: Birs ....7G 59
LE7: Scra ....6H 67
LE8: Count ....6B 82
LE8: K Bea ....3K 89
LE9: Barw ....2A 100
LE12: W Eav ....3D 42
Drive Dalby Rd. LE13: Mel M ....6F 117
Driveway, The LE7: Bush ....2J 73
Drome Cl. LE67: Coal ....3K 39
Dromintee Rd. LE67: Bar ....1H 53
Dronfield St. LE5: Leic ....2J 71
Drovers Ct. LE9: Des ....2H 95
Drovers Way LE9: Des ....2J 95
LE19: Nar ....2F 81
Druids Pl. LE10: Hinc ....2G 103
Druid St. LE10: Hinc ....2G 103
Drumcliff Rd. LE5: Leic ....1G 73
Drummond Rd. LE4: Leic ....3F 65
LE19: End ....5E 74
Drummond Wlk. LE13: Mel M ....2E 116
Drury La. LE2: Oad ....2B 78
Drurys La. LE15: Seat ....5K 139
Dryden Cl. DE12: Mea ....1E 48
Dryden St. LE1: Leic ....2E 4 (7G 65)
Dryer Cl. LE67: Ibs ....5K 51
Dry Pot La. LE12: L Wha ....7C 12
Duck La. DE12: A Mag ....5B 48
DUDDINGTON ....1C 165
Dudleston Cl. LE5: Leic ....2C 72
Dudley Av. LE5: Leic ....1E 72
Dudley Cl. LE5: Leic ....1E 72
Dudley Ct. LE12: Sileby ....1J 45

Dudley Ri. LE10: Bur ....5G 103
Dudley Whenham Cl. LE7: Sys ....1C 60
DUFFIELD ....1A 158
Duffield Av. LE18: Wig ....4H 77
Duffield St. LE2: Leic ....2J 71
Dukes Cl. LE4: Thurm ....6B 60
LE18: Wig ....5H 77
Dukes Dr. LE2: Leic ....5J 71
Dukes Dr. Flats LE2: Leic ....5J 71
Dukes Rd. LE14: O Dal ....5D 110
Duke St. LE1: Leic ....6D 5 (3F 71)
LE11: Lou ....5F 19
LE13: Mel M ....3H 117
Dulverton Cl. LE11: Lou ....3A 30
LE18: Wig ....1K 83
Dulverton Rd. LE3: Leic ....3C 70
LE13: Mel M ....2D 116
Dumbleton Cl. LE3: Leic ....6C 70
Dumps Rd. LE67: Whit ....5E 26
Dunbar Rd. LE4: Leic ....4A 66
LE67: Coal ....4J 39
Dunbar Way LE65: Ash Z ....5A 24
Dunblane Av. LE4: Leic ....2K 65
Dunblane Way LE10: Hinc ....1D 102
Duncan Av. LE9: Hun ....1B 80
Duncan Rd. LE2: Leic ....1D 76
Duncan Way LE11: Lou ....4A 18
Duncombe Rd. LE3: Leic ....5A 64
Dundee Rd. LE8: Bla ....3B 82
Dundonald Rd. LE4: Leic ....5G 65
Dunholme Av. LE11: Lou ....6K 17
Dunholme Rd. LE4: Leic ....5A 66
Dunire Cl. LE4: Leic ....3C 64
Dunkirk St. LE1: Leic ....6E 5 (2G 71)
Dunley Way LE17: Lut ....3J 153
Dunlin Rd. LE5: Leic ....7J 65
PE9: Ess ....1K 129
Dunmore Rd. LE16: L Bow ....6G 151
DUNSBY ....2D 161
Dunslade Cl. LE16: L Bow ....5H 151
Dunslade Gro. LE16: L Bow ....5H 151
Dunslade Rd. LE16: L Bow ....5G 151
Duns La. LE3: Leic ....5A 4 (2E 70)
Dunsmore Cl. LE11: Lou ....3B 30
Dunstall Av. LE3: Brau ....5H 69
Dunster Cl. LE12: Moun ....3D 44
Dunster St. LE3: Leic ....2B 70
Dunsville Wlk. LE4: Leic ....3K 65
DUNTON BASSETT ....1D 144 (2C 163)
Dunton La. LE17: Ash P ....6K 143
LE17: Leire ....3K 143
Dunton Rd. LE9: B Ast ....6F 87
LE17: Leire ....3K 143
Dunton St. LE3: Leic ....7D 64
LE18: Wig ....7F 77
Dupont Cl. LE3: Glen ....7H 63
Dupont Gdns. LE3: Glen ....7H 63
Duport Cl. LE10: Bur ....4J 103
Durban Rd. LE4: Beau L ....6C 58
Durham Cl. LE13: Mel M ....7G 117
LE67: Bag ....7G 53
Durham Dr. LE18: Wig ....4G 77
Durham Rd. LE11: Lou ....4C 18
Durham Wlk. LE67: Bag ....7G 53
Durnford Rd. LE18: Wig ....1J 83
Durrell Cl. LE11: Lou ....4A 18
Durris Cl. LE67: Coal ....3J 39
Durston Cl. LE5: Leic ....3F 73
Duxbury Rd. LE5: Leic ....7A 66
Dwyer Cl. LE7: Sys ....3B 60
Dwyers Cl. LE14: Asfo ....2H 115
Dyers Ct. LE11: Lou ....5G 19
(off Mill La.)
DYKE ....2D 161
Dysart Way LE1: Leic ....1G 4 (7G 65)
Dyson Cl. LE17: Lut ....3J 153
Dyson's Cl. DE12: Mea ....1D 48

E

Eagle Cl. DE12: Mea ....1D 48
LE9: B Ast ....3C 86
Eagles Dr. LE13: Mel M ....7E 116
Eaglesfield End LE17: Leire ....2K 143
EAGLETHORPE ....2D 165
Eales Yd. LE10: Hinc ....3G 103
Ealing Rd. LE2: Leic ....6F 71
Eamont Cl. LE2: Leic ....5D 76
Eamont Grn. LE2: Leic ....5D 76
EARLESFIELD ....1C 161
Earle Smith Cl. LE8: Whet ....2K 81
Earl Howe St. LE2: Leic ....3H 71
Earl Howe Ter. LE3: Leic ....5A 4 (2D 70)
Earl Russell St. LE2: Leic ....2C 76
Earls Cl. LE4: Thurm ....6B 60
Earls Cl. Ind. Est. LE4: Thurm ....6B 60

EARLSDON ....3A 162
EARL SHILTON ....2D 100 (2B 162)
Earl Shilton Rd. LE9: Thurl ....3A 96 & 1H 101
Earls Rd. LE14: O Dal ....5D 110
Earl St. LE1: Leic ....2E 4 (1G 71)
LE9: Earl S ....2F 101
Earl's Way LE4: Thurm ....6B 60
Earlswood Rd. LE5: Leic ....4F 73
Easby Cl. LE11: Lou ....5K 17
EASENHALL ....3B 162
East Av. LE2: Leic ....5J 71
LE7: Sys ....1E 60
LE8: Whet ....1K 81
LE13: Mel M ....3D 116
E. Bond St. LE1: Leic ....2C 4 (1F 71)
EAST BRIDGFORD ....1D 159
EAST CARLTON ....3B 164
East Cl. LE10: Bur ....4G 103
Eastcourt Rd. LE2: Leic ....2J 77
East Cres. LE67: Ell ....3E 52
East End LE14: L Cla ....2J 111
Eastern Blvd. LE2: Leic ....8A 5 (4E 70)
EAST FARNDON ....7B 150 (3A 164)
Eastfield Av. LE13: Mel M ....3F 117
Eastfield Ct. LE3: Leic ....2A 70
Eastfield Rd. LE3: Leic ....2B 70
LE4: Thurm ....5B 60
Eastgate LE16: Hall ....7A 132
East Gates LE1: Leic ....3C 4 (1F 71)
EAST GOSCOTE ....5G 47 (3D 159)
E. Goscote Ind. Est. LE7: East G ....5E 46
East Grn. LE9: Barw ....4K 99
EASTHORPE ....2J 107 (1B 160)
Easthorpe La. NG13: Mus ....3K 107
NG13: Red ....1E 106
Easthorpe Rd. NG13: Bott ....2H 107
Easthorpe Vw. NG13: Bott ....2J 107
East La. LE15: Rid ....2H 133
LE67: Bar ....1K 53
EAST LANGTON ....2B 140 (2A 164)
EAST LEAKE ....2C 159
Eastleigh Rd. LE3: Leic ....4C 70
East Link LE19: Brau ....1J 75
Eastmere Rd. LE18: Wig ....5B 78
EAST NORTON ....1A 164
E. Norton Rd. LE16: Hall ....4A 132
LE16: Horn ....5E 132
EASTON ....2C 161
EASTON ON THE HILL ....1D 165
E. Orchard LE12: Sileby ....3J 45
East Pk. Rd. LE5: Leic ....3J 71
East Rd. LE4: Birs ....1G 65
LE12: Wym ....1K 21
E. Side Cft. LE13: Mel M ....1G 117
East St. LE1: Leic ....5E 4 (2G 71)
LE2: Oad ....2C 78
LE16: Mkt H ....4D 150
East Wlk. LE6: Ratby ....5A 62
LE67: Ibs ....4K 51
Eastway DE74: C Don ....5K 7
Eastway Rd. LE18: Wig ....4K 77
EASTWELL ....2A 160
Eastwood Rd. LE2: Leic ....3D 76
Eastwoods Rd. LE10: Hinc ....1J 103
EATON ....6G 109 (2A 160)
Eaton Cl. NG32: Eat ....6G 109
Eaton Rd. DE74: C Don ....5K 7
EAVES GREEN ....3A 162
Ebchester Cl. LE2: Leic ....5C 76
Ebchester Rd. LE2: Leic ....5C 76
Ebenezer Cotts. CV13: Osb ....5A 92
Ecohouse ....2K 69
Edale Cl. LE3: Leic ....4J 69
Edale Grn. LE10: Bur ....5J 103
Eddystone Rd. LE5: Leic ....7G 67
Edelin Rd. LE11: Lou ....2F 31
Eden Cl. LE2: Oad ....2E 78
LE11: Lou ....5A 18
Edendale Dr. LE10: Hinc ....7H 99
Edendale Rd. LE13: Mel M ....6D 116
Eden Gdns. LE4: Beau L ....6C 58
Edenhall Cl. LE2: Oad ....2E 78
LE4: Leic ....3K 65
EDENHAM ....2D 161
Edenhurst Av. LE3: Brau ....1K 75
Eden Rd. LE2: Oad ....2E 78
Edensor St. LE4: Leic ....3J 65
Eden Way LE2: Leic ....6D 76
Edgbaston Cl. LE4: Beau L ....6D 58
Edgecote Cl. LE5: Leic ....5C 76
Edgefield Cl. LE5: Ham ....3D 66
Edghill Cl. LE8: G Gle ....1K 85
Edgehill Rd. LE4: Leic ....4A 66
Edgeley Cl. LE3: Leic ....5A 64
Edgeley Rd. LE8: Count ....5E 82
Edinburgh Cl. LE16: Mkt H ....3F 151
Edinburgh Rd. LE9: Earl S ....3C 100

Edinburgh Way LE12: Moun . . . . . . . . . . . . . .3C **44**
Edith Av. LE3: Brau . . . . . . . . . . . . . . . . . .1A **76**
EDITH WESTON . . . . . . . . . . . . . . .3G **135** (1C **165**)
Edith Weston Rd. LE15: N Luf . . . . . . . .1B **136**
Edmonds Dr. PE9: Ket . . . . . . . . . . . . . .6H **137**
EDMONDTHORPE . . . . . . . . . . . .3K **121** (3B **160**)
Edmondthorpe Drift LE14: Edm . . . . . . .3K **121**
Edmondthorpe Rd. LE14: Edm, W'ham . . .1H **121**
Edmonton Rd. LE1: Leic . . . . . . . . .1F **4** (7G **65**)
Edmonton Way LE15: O'ham . . . . . . . . .4K **127**
EDWALTON . . . . . . . . . . . . . . . . . . . . .1D **159**
Edward Av. LE3: Brau . . . . . . . . . . . . . . .7K **69**
Edward Cl. LE2: Oad . . . . . . . . . . . . . . . .3E **78**
Edward Dr. LE2: G Par . . . . . . . . . . . . . .7E **76**
Edward Rd. LE2: Leic . . . . . . . . . . . . . . .5H **71**
  LE8: Flec . . . . . . . . . . . . . . . . . . . . . .4B **88**
  LE16: Mkt H . . . . . . . . . . . . . . . . . . . .3D **150**
Edwards Cen. LE10: Hinc . . . . . . . . . . .3G **103**
                                    (off The Horsefair)
Edward St. DE11: A Vil . . . . . . . . . . . . . .2A **22**
  LE5: Leic . . . . . . . . . . . . . . . . . . . . . .7J **65**
  LE7: Anst . . . . . . . . . . . . . . . . . . . . . .7J **57**
  LE10: Hinc . . . . . . . . . . . . . . . . . . . . .1F **103**
  LE11: Lou . . . . . . . . . . . . . . . . . . . . . .5E **18**
Egerton Av. LE4: Leic . . . . . . . . . . . . . . .4E **64**
Egerton Rd. LE13: Mel M . . . . . . . . . . . .4G **117**
Egerton Vw. LE13: Mel M . . . . . . . . . . . .4E **116**
EGGINGTON . . . . . . . . . . . . . . . . . . . .2A **158**
Egginton St. LE5: Leic . . . . . . . . . . . . . .3J **71**
Eglantine Cl. LE2: Oad . . . . . . . . . . . . . .1C **78**
EGLETON . . . . . . . . . . . . . . . . . . . . . .1B **164**
Eider Cl. LE8: Whet . . . . . . . . . . . . . . . .5K **81**
Eileen Av. LE4: Leic . . . . . . . . . . . . . . . .4E **64**
Elbow La. LE1: Leic . . . . . . . . . . .2B **4** (1E **70**)
  LE67: S Bar . . . . . . . . . . . . . . . . . . . .3B **54**
Elder Cl. LE3: Leic . . . . . . . . . . . . . . . . .3K **63**
Elder La. LE67: Grif . . . . . . . . . . . . . . . .1A **26**
Eldon St. LE1: Leic . . . . . . . . . . .2E **4** (1G **71**)
Elfed Thomas Bldg. LE1: Leic . . . . . . . . .5C **4**
Elfin Gro. LE17: D Bas . . . . . . . . . . . . . .1E **144**
Elford St. LE65: Ash Z . . . . . . . . . . . . . .5K **23**
Elgin Av. LE3: Leic . . . . . . . . . . . . . . . . .6K **63**
Elgin Dr. LE13: Mel M . . . . . . . . . . . . . .3F **117**
Elgin Wlk. LE67: Thrin . . . . . . . . . . . . . .3D **26**
Eliot Cl. LE11: Lou . . . . . . . . . . . . . . . . .4K **17**
Elisha Cl. LE9: S Stan . . . . . . . . . . . . . .1K **105**
Elizabethan Way LE17: Lut . . . . . . . . . . .3K **153**
Elizabeth Av. LE67: Ibs . . . . . . . . . . . . . .3K **51**
Elizabeth Cl. LE7: Hou H . . . . . . . . . . . .2C **130**
  LE8: Flec . . . . . . . . . . . . . . . . . . . . . .5B **88**
Elizabeth Ct. LE3: Glen . . . . . . . . . . . . . .5F **63**
  LE18: Wig . . . . . . . . . . . . . . . . . . . . . .6J **77**
Elizabeth Cres. LE18: Wig . . . . . . . . . . . .4H **77**
Elizabeth Dr. LE2: Oad . . . . . . . . . . . . . .4E **78**
  LE4: Thurm . . . . . . . . . . . . . . . . . . . .5A **60**
Elizabeth Gdns. LE8: Whet . . . . . . . . . . .2K **81**
Elizabeth Ho. LE3: Leic . . . . . . . . . . . . . .7A **64**
Elizabeth Pk. Sports & Community Cen. . . . . .5A **60**
Elizabeth Pl. LE8: Flec . . . . . . . . . . . . . .5B **88**
  LE10: Hinc . . . . . . . . . . . . . . . . . . . . .7G **99**
Elizabeth St. LE5: Leic . . . . . . . . . . . . . .2A **72**
Elizabeth Way LE15: Upp . . . . . . . . . . . .1C **138**
ELKINGTON . . . . . . . . . . . . . . . . . . . .3D **163**
Ellaby Rd. LE11: Lou . . . . . . . . . . . . . . .4B **18**
Elland Rd. LE3: Leic . . . . . . . . . . . . . . . .2F **69**
Ellesmere Pl. LE3: Leic . . . . . . . . . . . . . .5B **70**
Ellesmere Rd. LE3: Leic . . . . . . . . . . . . .5B **70**
Elliot Cl. LE2: Oad . . . . . . . . . . . . . . . . .4F **79**
  LE8: K Bea . . . . . . . . . . . . . . . . . . . . .3J **89**
  LE8: Whet . . . . . . . . . . . . . . . . . . . . .5A **82**
Elliots Yd. LE8: Count . . . . . . . . . . . . . . .6F **83**
Elliott Dr. LE3: Leic E . . . . . . . . . . . . . . .4F **69**
  LE4: Thurm . . . . . . . . . . . . . . . . . . . .7C **60**
Elliott Rd. LE4: Leic . . . . . . . . . . . . . . . .2D **64**
Elliott's La. LE67: Mark . . . . . . . . . . . . . .4C **54**
Ellis Av. LE4: Leic . . . . . . . . . . . . . . . . .5G **65**
Ellis Cl. LE3: Glen . . . . . . . . . . . . . . . . .6F **63**
  LE12: Bar S . . . . . . . . . . . . . . . . . . . .3E **32**
  LE12: Quo . . . . . . . . . . . . . . . . . . . . .5K **31**
  LE67: Ell . . . . . . . . . . . . . . . . . . . . . .2E **52**
Ellis Dr. LE9: Leic E . . . . . . . . . . . . . . . .4D **68**
Ellis Flds. LE2: Oad . . . . . . . . . . . . . . . .5G **79**
Ellison Av. DE72: A Tre . . . . . . . . . . . . . .1C **6**
Ellison Cl. LE9: S Stan . . . . . . . . . . . . . .7J **105**
  LE18: Wig . . . . . . . . . . . . . . . . . . . . .1F **83**
Ellis St. LE7: Anst . . . . . . . . . . . . . . . . .7H **57**
ELLISTOWN . . . . . . . . . . . . . . .3E **52** (3B **158**)
Ellistown La. LE67: Ell . . . . . . . . . . . . . . .4H **53**
Ellistown Ter. Rd. LE67: Ell . . . . . . . . . . . .3E **52**
Ellwood Cl. LE5: Leic . . . . . . . . . . . . . . .3D **72**
Elm Av. LE17: Lut . . . . . . . . . . . . . . . . .4H **153**
  LE65: Ash Z . . . . . . . . . . . . . . . . . . . .4B **24**
Elm Cl. LE6: Groby . . . . . . . . . . . . . . . . .4D **62**
  LE12: Moun . . . . . . . . . . . . . . . . . . . .2E **44**
  LE15: O'ham . . . . . . . . . . . . . . . . . . . .3K **127**
  LE67: Ibs . . . . . . . . . . . . . . . . . . . . . .4J **51**
Elm Ct. LE2: Leic . . . . . . . . . . . . . . . . . .8B **5**

Elmcroft Av. LE5: Leic . . . . . . . . . . . . . . .7D **66**
Elmcroft Rd. LE17: N Kil . . . . . . . . . . . . .3K **155**
Elmdale Rd. LE9: Earl S . . . . . . . . . . . . . .4C **100**
Elmdale St. LE4: Leic . . . . . . . . . . . . . . .4G **65**
Elm Dr. LE16: Mkt H . . . . . . . . . . . . . . . .5C **150**
ELMESTHORPE . . . . . . . . . .5D **100** (2B **162**)
Elmesthorpe Est. LE9: Elm . . . . . . . . . . .5D **100**
Elmesthorpe La. LE9: Earl S, Elm . . . . . . .3B **100**
Elmfield Av. LE2: Leic . . . . . . . . . . . . . . .4J **71**
  LE4: Birs . . . . . . . . . . . . . . . . . . . . . .6F **59**
Elmfield Gdns. LE2: Leic . . . . . . . . . . . . .4J **71**
Elm Gdns. LE12: Moun . . . . . . . . . . . . . .3E **44**
Elm Gro. DE12: Moi . . . . . . . . . . . . . . . .5D **22**
Elmhirst Rd. LE17: Lut . . . . . . . . . . . . . .5H **153**
Elmhurst Av. LE13: Mel M . . . . . . . . . . . .2D **116**
Elmhurst Cl. LE19: Nar . . . . . . . . . . . . . .2E **80**
Elm La. LE17: Cat . . . . . . . . . . . . . . . . .6D **156**
  NG32: Sap . . . . . . . . . . . . . . . . . . . . .7G **109**
Elms, The LE8: Bla . . . . . . . . . . . . . . . . .2B **82**
  LE8: Count . . . . . . . . . . . . . . . . . . . . .5E **82**
  LE11: Lou . . . . . . . . . . . . . . . . . . . . . .7G **19**
  LE67: Mark . . . . . . . . . . . . . . . . . . . . .3F **55**
  LE67: Whit . . . . . . . . . . . . . . . . . . . . .6D **26**
Elms Cl. LE2: Oad . . . . . . . . . . . . . . . . .4D **78**
Elms Ct. LE2: Leic . . . . . . . . . . . . . . . . .7J **71**
  LE7: Anst . . . . . . . . . . . . . . . . . . . . . .7J **57**
Elms Dr. LE9: Peck . . . . . . . . . . . . . . . . .5K **95**
  LE12: Quo . . . . . . . . . . . . . . . . . . . . .6K **31**
Elms Gro. LE11: Lou . . . . . . . . . . . . . . . .7G **19**
  LE12: Bar S . . . . . . . . . . . . . . . . . . . .2D **32**
Elms La. LE8: Bur O . . . . . . . . . . . . . . . .5D **130**
Elmsleigh Av. LE2: Leic . . . . . . . . . . . . . .6K **71**
Elms Rd. LE2: Leic . . . . . . . . . . . . . . . . .6J **71**
  LE13: Mel M . . . . . . . . . . . . . . . . . . . .4F **117**
Elms Rd. Ho's. LE2: Leic . . . . . . . . . . . . .7K **71**
Elmsthorpe Ri. LE3: Leic . . . . . . . . . . . . .4A **70**
Elm Tree Av. LE3: Glen . . . . . . . . . . . . . .6E **62**
Elmtree Cl. LE5: Ham . . . . . . . . . . . . . . .4E **66**
Elm Tree Dr. LE10: Bur . . . . . . . . . . . . . .3J **103**
Elm Tree Rd. LE9: Cosb . . . . . . . . . . . . .7G **81**
Elmwood Row LE2: Leic . . . . . . . . . . . . .4G **77**
Elsadene Av. LE4: Leic . . . . . . . . . . . . . .3H **65**
Elsadene Ct. LE2: Leic . . . . . . . . . . . . . .6K **71**
Elsadene Wlk. LE4: Leic . . . . . . . . . . . . .2G **65**
Elsalene Cl. LE6: Groby . . . . . . . . . . . . . .1A **62**
Elsalene Dr. LE6: Groby . . . . . . . . . . . . .1A **62**
Elsdon Cl. LE67: Whit . . . . . . . . . . . . . . .6D **26**
Elsham Cl. LE3: Leic . . . . . . . . . . . . . . . .2H **69**
Elstead La. DE11: Blac . . . . . . . . . . . . . .2D **22**
ELSTHORPE . . . . . . . . . . . . . . . . . . . .2D **161**
Elston Flds. LE2: Leic . . . . . . . . . . . . . . .2F **77**
Elstree Av. LE5: Leic . . . . . . . . . . . . . . . .6G **67**
Elsworthy Wlk. LE3: Leic . . . . . . . . . . . . .1H **69**
ELTON
  Nottingham . . . . . . . . . . . . . . . . . . . . .1A **160**
  Peterborough . . . . . . . . . . . . . . . . . . . .2D **165**
Elton Way LE67: Ell . . . . . . . . . . . . . . . .3E **52**
ELVASTON . . . . . . . . . . . . . . . . . . . . .1B **158**
Elvaston Ct. LE65: Ash Z . . . . . . . . . . . . .6A **24**
Elwell Av. LE9: Barw . . . . . . . . . . . . . . . .1A **100**
Elwells Av. LE17: D Bas . . . . . . . . . . . . .1D **144**
Elwin Av. LE18: Wig . . . . . . . . . . . . . . . .4K **77**
Emberton Cl. LE18: Wig . . . . . . . . . . . . . .5B **78**
Embleton Cl. LE10: Hinc . . . . . . . . . . . . .2E **102**
Emburn Ho. LE3: Leic . . . . . . . . . . . . . . .6K **63**
Emerson Cl. LE4: Leic . . . . . . . . . . . . . . .3A **64**
Emperor Way LE8: Whet . . . . . . . . . . . . .5K **81**
EMPINGHAM . . . . . . . . . . .6C **128** (1C **165**)
Empingham Rd. LE15: Ext . . . . . . . . . . . .2D **128**
  PE9: Ket . . . . . . . . . . . . . . . . . . . . . .5F **137**
Empire Rd. LE3: Leic . . . . . . . . . . . . . . .7D **64**
Empress Rd. LE11: Lou . . . . . . . . . . . . . .6G **19**
ENDERBY . . . . . . . . . . . . .5F **75** (2C **163**)
Enderby La. LE19: End, Leic E . . . . . . . . .7D **68**
Enderby Leisure Cen. . . . . . . . . . . . . . . .6F **75**
Enderby Rd. LE8: Whet . . . . . . . . . . . . . .7J **75**
  LE9: Thurl . . . . . . . . . . . . . . . . . . . . .2C **96**
Enderby Rd. Ind. Est. LE8: Whet . . . . . . . .7K **75**
Englefield Rd. LE5: Leic . . . . . . . . . . . . . .2F **73**
Englewood Cl. LE4: Leic . . . . . . . . . . . . .5D **64**
Ennerdale Gdns. LE65: Ash Z . . . . . . . . .6B **24**
Ennerdale Rd. LE12: Bar S . . . . . . . . . . .3D **32**
Ensbury Gdns. LE4: Leic . . . . . . . . . . . . .4D **72**
Enston St. LE9: N Ver . . . . . . . . . . . . . . .6H **93**
Enterprise Ho. LE9: K Mux . . . . . . . . . . .2B **68**
Epinal Ct. LE11: Lou . . . . . . . . . . . . . . . .5B **18**
Epinal Way LE11: Lou . . . . . . . . . . . . . . .5B **18**
  LE12: Lou, Quo . . . . . . . . . . . . . . . . . .2F **31**
Epping Dr. LE13: Mel M . . . . . . . . . . . . .2F **117**
Epping Way LE2: Leic . . . . . . . . . . . . . . .5C **76**
Epsom Rd. LE4: Leic . . . . . . . . . . . . . . . .4H **65**
Equity Rd. LE3: Leic . . . . . . . . . . . . . . . .3D **70**
  LE9: Earl S . . . . . . . . . . . . . . . . . . . . .3D **100**
  LE19: End . . . . . . . . . . . . . . . . . . . . .5E **74**
Equity Rd. E. LE9: Earl S . . . . . . . . . . . . .2D **100**
Erdyngton Rd. LE3: Leic . . . . . . . . . . . . .3K **69**

Eric Wood Bldg. LE2: Leic . . . . . . . . .6B **5** (3E **70**)
Erith Rd. LE2: Leic . . . . . . . . . . . . . . . . .6D **70**
Ermine Ri. PE9: G Cas . . . . . . . . . . . . . .2H **137**
Ernee Cl. LE3: Glen . . . . . . . . . . . . . . . .7H **63**
Erringtons Cl. LE2: Oad . . . . . . . . . . . . . .6G **79**
Erskine Cl. LE10: Hinc . . . . . . . . . . . . . .1D **102**
Erskine St. LE1: Leic . . . . . . . . . . .2E **4** (1G **71**)
Ervington Ct. LE19: Brau . . . . . . . . . . . . .2H **75**
Ervin's Lock Rd. LE18: Wig . . . . . . . . . . .1G **83**
Ervin Way LE7: Quen . . . . . . . . . . . . . . .6G **47**
Eskdale Cl. LE2: Oad . . . . . . . . . . . . . . .4F **79**
Eskdale Rd. LE4: Leic . . . . . . . . . . . . . . .3D **64**
  LE10: Hinc . . . . . . . . . . . . . . . . . . . . .3D **102**
ESSENDINE . . . . . . . . . . . . . .1K **129** (3D **161**)
Essendine Rd. PE9: Ryh . . . . . . . . . . . . . .4H **129**
Essex Cl. LE9: Des . . . . . . . . . . . . . . . . .2H **95**
  LE13: Mel M . . . . . . . . . . . . . . . . . . . .7G **117**
Essex Gdns. LE16: Mkt H . . . . . . . . . . . .6D **150**
Essex Rd. LE4: Leic . . . . . . . . . . . . . . . .5A **66**
  LE18: Wig . . . . . . . . . . . . . . . . . . . . .5F **77**
Estelle Ho. LE4: Thurm . . . . . . . . . . . . . .5A **60**
Estima Cl. LE2: Leic . . . . . . . . . . . . . . . .7J **71**
Estley Rd. LE9: B Ast . . . . . . . . . . . . . . .3C **86**
Estoril Av. LE18: Wig . . . . . . . . . . . . . . . .4A **78**
Ethel Rd. LE5: Leic . . . . . . . . . . . . . . . . .3A **72**
Eton Cl. LE2: Leic . . . . . . . . . . . . . . . . . .7H **71**
  LE65: Ash Z . . . . . . . . . . . . . . . . . . . .3J **23**
ETTON . . . . . . . . . . . . . . . . . . . . . . . .1D **165**
ETWALL . . . . . . . . . . . . . . . . . . . . . . .1A **158**
Eunice Av. LE9: Hun . . . . . . . . . . . . . . . .2B **80**
Euro Bus. Pk. LE16: L Bow . . . . . . . . . . .3H **151**
Europark Ind. Est. CV23: C Dus . . . . . . . .5A **156**
Euston St. LE2: Leic . . . . . . . . . . . . . . . .6F **71**
Evelyn Dr. LE3: Leic . . . . . . . . . . . . . . . .5C **70**
Evelyn Rd. LE3: Brau . . . . . . . . . . . . . . . .5J **69**
Everard Cres. LE67: S Bar . . . . . . . . . . . .4B **54**
Everard Way LE19: End . . . . . . . . . . . . . .3K **75**
  LE67: S Bar . . . . . . . . . . . . . . . . . . . .4B **54**
Everest Ct. LE1: Leic . . . . . . . . . . .1G **4** (7H **65**)
Everest Dr. LE13: Mel M . . . . . . . . . . . . .2D **116**
Everett Cl. LE4: Thurm . . . . . . . . . . . . . .7C **60**
Everson Cl. LE9: B Ast . . . . . . . . . . . . . .5D **86**
Every St. LE1: Leic . . . . . . . . . . . .4D **4** (2F **71**)
Evesham Rd. LE3: Leic . . . . . . . . . . . . . .5C **70**
EVINGTON . . . . . . . . . . . . . . . .5D **72** (1D **163**)
Evington Cl. LE5: Leic . . . . . . . . . . . . . . .3A **72**
Evington Cr. LE5: Leic . . . . . . . . . . . . . . .4C **72**
Evington Dr. LE5: Leic . . . . . . . . . . . . . . .4K **71**
Evington Footway LE2: Leic . . . . . . .7G **5** (3H **71**)
Evington La. LE5: Leic . . . . . . . . . . . . . . .4K **71**
Evington M. LE5: Leic . . . . . . . . . . . . . . .4D **72**
Evington Parks Rd. LE2: Leic . . . . . . . . . .4K **71**
Evington Pl. LE2: Leic . . . . . . . . . . . . . . .3J **71**
Evington Pool . . . . . . . . . . . . . . . . . . . .4E **72**
Evington Rd. LE2: Leic . . . . . . . . . .7G **5** (3H **71**)
Evington St. LE2: Leic . . . . . . . . . .6G **5** (2H **71**)
Evington Valley Rd. LE5: Leic . . . . . . . . . .4K **71**
Ewden Ri. LE13: Mel M . . . . . . . . . . . . . .6E **116**
Excalibur Cl. LE3: Leic E . . . . . . . . . . . . .5E **68**
Exchange, The LE2: Leic . . . . . . . . . . . . .4E **76**
Exeter Rd. LE18: Wig . . . . . . . . . . . . . . .5H **77**
Exmoor Av. LE4: Leic . . . . . . . . . . . . . . .6D **64**
Exmoor Cl. LE11: Lou . . . . . . . . . . . . . . .3B **30**
  LE18: Wig . . . . . . . . . . . . . . . . . . . . .7K **77**
  LE67: Ell . . . . . . . . . . . . . . . . . . . . . .1D **52**
Exploration Dr. LE4: Leic . . . . . . . . . . . . .4F **65**
EXTON . . . . . . . . . . . . . . . .2D **128** (3C **161**)
Exton Rd. LE5: Leic . . . . . . . . . . . . . . . .7A **66**
  LE15: Cott . . . . . . . . . . . . . . . . . . . . .7B **124**
  LE15: Emp . . . . . . . . . . . . . . . . . . . . .4B **128**
Eye Brook Cl. LE11: Lou . . . . . . . . . . . . .1K **29**
Eyebrook Cl. LE5: Ham . . . . . . . . . . . . . .3E **66**
Eynsford Cl. LE2: Leic . . . . . . . . . . . . . . .7A **72**
EYRES MONSELL . . . . . . . . . . . . . . . . .5D **76**

## F

Fabius Cl. LE10: Hinc . . . . . . . . . . . . . . .4F **103**
Factory La. LE16: Mkt H . . . . . . . . . . . . . .4E **150**
Factory Rd. LE10: Hinc . . . . . . . . . . . . . .2G **103**
Factory St. LE11: Lou . . . . . . . . . . . . . . .7G **19**
  LE12: Shep . . . . . . . . . . . . . . . . . . . . .6D **16**
Fair Acre Rd. LE9: Barw . . . . . . . . . . . . . .4K **99**
Fairacres LE17: Lut . . . . . . . . . . . . . . . . .6F **153**
Fairbourne Rd. LE3: Brau . . . . . . . . . . . . .6A **70**
Fairburn Ho. LE3: Leic . . . . . . . . . . . . . . .6K **63**
Faircharm Trad. Est. LE3: Leic . . . . . . . . .5D **70**
Fairefield Cres. LE3: Glen . . . . . . . . . . . . .4H **63**
Faire Rd. LE3: Glen . . . . . . . . . . . . . . . . .5H **63**
Fairestone Av. LE3: Glen . . . . . . . . . . . . .6G **63**
Fairfax Cl. LE4: Leic . . . . . . . . . . . . . . . .4A **66**
  LE65: Ash Z . . . . . . . . . . . . . . . . . . . .4B **24**
Fairfax Ct. LE8: G Gle . . . . . . . . . . . . . . .1K **85**
Fairfax Rd. LE4: Leic . . . . . . . . . . . . . . . .4A **66**
  LE16: Mkt H . . . . . . . . . . . . . . . . . . . .5E **150**
Fair Fld. LE14: W Wol . . . . . . . . . . . . . . .2C **112**

Fairfield—Flesh Hovel La.


Fairfield LE67: Ibs 4K 51
Fairfield Cl. LE13: Mel M 2G 117
LE15: L'ham 5C 122
Fairfield Ct. LE11: Lou 7G 19
LE67: Hug 6C 38
Fairfield Rd. LE2: Oad 2D 78
LE16: Mkt H 3D 150
LE67: Hug 6C 38
Fairfield St. LE5: Leic 2J 71
LE18: Wig 6F 77
Fairford Av. LE5: Leic 4D 72
Fairhaven Rd. LE7: Anst 5J 57
Fairholme Rd. LE2: Leic 2H 77
Fairisle Way LE8: Count 6F 83
Fair Mead LE12: Moun 4E 44
Fairmeadows Way LE11: Lou 4D 30
Fairmount Dr. LE11: Lou 1C 30
Fairstone Hill LE2: Oad 4D 78
Fair Vw. LE15: O'ham 4K 127
Fairview Av. LE8: Whet 2K 81
Fairway LE8: K Bea 3K 89
LE16: Mkt H 3D 150
Fairway, The LE2: Leic 2E 76
LE2: Oad 6B 72
LE8: Bla 2A 82
LE9: K Mux 3D 68
LE10: Bur 4J 103
Fairway Dr. LE7: R'ley 7C 44
Fairway Rd. LE12: Shep 7E 16
Fairway Rd. Sth. LE12: Shep 2E 28
Fairways Ct. LE10: Hinc 7K 99
Falcon Bus. Pk. LE11: Lou 4G 19
Falcon Cl. LE3: Leic E 5C 68
LE9: B Ast 3C 86
Falconer Cres. LE3: Leic 6J 63
Falconers Grn. LE10: Bur 5J 103
Falcon Rd. LE7: Anst 1G 63
Falconry Cen. 5E 124
Falcon St. LE11: Lou 5G 19
Faldo Cl. LE4: Leic 1A 66
Faldo Dr. LE13: Mel M 1F 117
Fallow Cl. LE8: Whet 4K 81
LE9: B Ast 5D 86
Fallowfield Rd. LE5: Leic 3F 73
Falmouth Dr. LE10: Hinc 6H 99
LE18: Wig 7J 77
Falmouth Rd. LE5: Leic 3B 72
Faraday Cl. LE9: B Ast 6D 86
Faraday Rd. LE10: Hinc 4B 102
Far Coton CV13: Mkt B 4A 94
Faringdon Av. LE17: Lut 4K 153
Far Lash LE10: Bur 4J 103
Far Lash Extension
LE10: Bur 4J 103
Farleigh Av. LE18: Wig 4K 77
Farleigh Cl. LE9: B Ast 3C 86
Farleigh Ct. LE15: Upp 2B 138
Farleigh Gdns. LE15: Upp 1B 138
(not continuous)
Farley Rd. LE2: Leic 7K 71
Farley Way LE9: K Mux 1D 68
LE12: Quo 5J 31
Farm Cl. LE4: Birs 6H 59
LE19: Litt 2G 81
Farm Cl., The LE2: Leic 3F 77
Farm Dr. LE12: Bar S 3E 32
Farmers Cl. LE3: Glen 6E 62
Farm Ho. Cl. NG13: Bott 1G 107
Farm La. LE67: D Hea 6B 38
Farm Rd. LE9: Barw 2B 100
LE10: Bur 5H 103
FARM TOWN 5F 25
Farm Town La. LE67: Cole 5F 25
Farmway LE3: Brau 2J 75
Farndale LE18: Wig 6B 78
LE67: Whit 5D 26
Farndale Cl. LE2: Leic 8B 5 (4E 70)
Farndale Dr. LE11: Lou 3D 30
Farndale Vw. LE16: Mkt H 5B 150
Farndon Ct. LE16: Mkt H 5D 150
Farndon Dr. LE9: S Stan 1H 105
Farndon Rd. LE16: Lub 7J 149 & 5A 150
LE16: Mkt H 6C 150
Farneway LE10: Hinc 2E 102
Farnham Cl. LE7: R'ley 5E 44
Farnham Ct. LE12: Moun 1D 44
Farnham Rd. LE11: Lou 2F 31
Farnham St. LE5: Leic 1J 71
LE12: Quo 5K 31
Farnworth Cl. LE4: Leic 3K 65
Farrier La. LE4: Leic 3B 64
Farriers Cl. DE12: Snar 6G 49
Farriers Ga. CV13: F Dray 2H 97
Farriers Way LE7: East G 5F 47
LE10: Bur 6J 103
LE14: Sta 2H 109
Farringdon St. LE5: Leic 7J 65
Farringdon Wlk. LE5: Leic 7J 65
(off Farringdon St.)
Farr Wood Cl. LE6: Groby 3C 62
Far St. LE12: Wym 1J 21
Farthings, The LE12: Hat 1J 17
Fastnet Rd. LE5: Leic 7G 67
Fathingdale Cl. LE9: Cosb 6J 81
Faversham Cl. LE3: Leic 1G 69
Fayrhurst Rd. LE2: Leic 2E 76
Fearon St. LE11: Lou 6D 18
Featherbed La. LE65: Ash Z 4B 24
Featherby Dr. LE2: G Par 5A 76
Featherston Dr. LE10: Bur 4G 103
Featherstone Dr. LE2: Leic 6C 76
Feature Rd. LE4: Thurm 4A 60
Federation St. LE19: End 5E 74
Feildingway LE17: Lut 3J 153
Feldspar Cl. LE19: End 3E 74
Fell Cl. LE8: Flec 5C 88
Felley Way LE3: Leic 6C 64
Felstead Rd. LE4: Leic 2D 64
Fencote Rd. LE5: Ham 2E 66
Fennel St. LE11: Lou 6F 19
Fenners Cl. LE4: Beau L 6C 58
Fenn Lanes
CV13: Dadl, F Dray, S Gol 1H 97 & 1A 98
FENNY DRAYTON 2H 97 (2A 162)
Fenny La. LE17: Shea 5J 147
Fenton Av. DE11: Blac 2D 22
Fenton Cl. DE12: Mea 2D 48
LE2: Oad 5C 78
Fenton Cres. DE12: Mea 2E 48
Fenwick Rd. LE2: Oad 4G 79
Ferers Cl. LE15: O'ham 4F 127
Fermain Cl. LE5: Leic 2F 73
Fern Bank LE5: Leic 1J 71
Fern Cl. LE7: Thurn 2G 73
Fern Cres. LE6: Groby 2B 62
Ferndale LE67: Ibs 4J 51
Ferndale Dr. LE6: Ratby 6B 62
Ferndale Gro. LE10: Hinc 4D 102
Ferndale Rd. LE2: Leic 2H 77
LE4: Thurm 7A 60
Ferndown Cl. LE3: Leic 1G 69
Ferneley Av. LE10: Hinc 7D 98
Ferneley Cres.
LE13: Mel M 2H 117
Ferneley Ri. LE7: Thru 7B 114
Ferness Cl. LE10: Hinc 1E 102
Ferness Rd. LE10: Hinc 1E 102
Fernfield Cl. LE16: L Bow 3H 151
Fernhurst Rd. LE3: Brau 7K 69
Fernie Av. LE13: Mel M 4E 116
Fernie Chase LE16: T Lan 2E 140
Fernie Cl. LE2: Oad 4E 78
Fernie Ct. LE17: H Bos 5C 148
Fernie Dene LE8: G Gle 5A 130
Fernie Rd. LE5: Leic 7K 65
LE16: Mkt H 4F 151
Fernie Sq. LE15: Cott 4B 124
Fernlea LE19: Nar 7D 74
Fernley Cl. LE16: L Bow 5H 151
Fernleys Cl. LE4: Leic 3B 64
Fern Ri. LE5: Leic 5E 66
Ferrars Ct. LE3: Brau 6H 69
Ferrers Cl. DE74: C Don 5J 7
LE65: Ash Z 6H 23
Ferrers Cft. CV13: B'one 6C 92
Ferrers Ri. LE6: Groby 3C 62
Ferrers Rd. LE17: Lut 5G 153
LE67: Whit 7F 27
Ferrers St. LE2: Leic 3F 77
Ferrous Cl. LE4: Leic 6J 65
Ferryman Rd. LE11: Lou 5G 19
Festival Av. LE4: Thurm 7K 59
Festival Dr. LE11: Lou 4E 18
Festival Way LE11: Lou 4E 18
Fettes Cl. LE65: Ash Z 3J 23
Field, The LE14: Som 6K 121
Field Av. LE12: Shep 4E 16
Field Cl. LE7: Hou H 3D 130
LE10: Hinc 7J 99
LE13: Mel M 6G 117
LE19: Litt 2G 81
LE67: Thrin 4D 26
Field Ct. Rd. LE6: Groby 3D 62
Field Crest LE12: Moun 4D 44
Fieldfare Wlk. LE5: Leic 7J 65
Fieldgate Cres. LE4: Birs 5E 58
FIELD HEAD 5H 55 (1B 162)
Fieldhead Cl. LE16: Mkt H 4C 150
Fieldhead Rd. LE67: Mark 2E 54
Field Ho. LE11: Lou 6C 18
Fieldhouse Rd. LE4: Leic 3H 65
Fieldhurst Av. LE3: Brau 7J 69
Fielding Ct. LE11: Lou 6G 19
Fielding Rd. LE4: Birs 6F 59
Field La. DE11: Boun 1E 22
DE73: Ton 6D 10
Field St. LE12: Shep 6D 16
Field Vw. LE4: Thurm 6C 60
LE7: Sys 2A 60
LE67: Whit 6D 26
Field Way LE9: Earl S 2C 100
Fieldway, The LE9: B Ast 5D 86
Fieldway Cres. LE8: G Gle 7K 79
Field Work Rd. LE14: O Dal 6C 110
Filbert St. LE2: Leic 8A 5 (4E 70)
Filbert St. E. LE2: Leic 8C 5 (4F 71)
Filbert Way LE2: Leic 8A 5 (4E 70)
Fillingate LE7: Wan 1H 59
FILLONGLEY 3A 162
Finch Av. LE15: O'ham 4F 127
Finch Cl. LE3: Leic 2J 69
LE15: Upp 1B 138
Finches, The LE9: Des 3H 95
LE15: Mkt O 2J 123
Finch Wlk. LE14: Ash 2F 115
Finch Way LE19: Nar 2E 80
FINDERN 1A 158
Findley Cl. CV9: Manc 7A 96
Fineshade Av. LE3: Leic 6C 64
Finkey St. LE15: O'ham 4H 127
Finney Cl. DE12: Don 3A 34
Finney Spring Towermill 2A 28
Finsbury Av. LE11: Lou 7G 19
LE12: Sileby 1A 46
Finsbury Rd. LE4: Leic 5J 65
Finson Cl. LE18: Wig 5K 77
Fiona Dr. LE7: Thurn 2H 73
Firdale LE14: Som 7K 121
Firestone Cl. LE3: Leic 1G 69
Firfield Av. LE4: Birs 6G 59
Firs, The LE7: Sys 3C 60
LE16: Mkt H 4C 150
Firs Av. LE15: Upp 1B 138
Firs Cl. LE7: Hou H 2D 130
Firs Rd. LE7: Hou H 2D 130
Fir Tree Av. LE8: Count 5E 82
LE17: Lut 4H 153
Fir Tree Cl. LE9: Barw 2A 100
LE18: Wig 3J 77
Fir Tree La. LE6: Groby 2C 62
Firtree La. LE17: Swin 4H 157
Fir Tree Wlk. DE12: Moi 5D 22
(off Ashfield Dr.)
LE16: Mkt H 3E 150
Firtree Wlk. LE6: Groby 3C 62
Firwood Rd. LE13: Mel M 2H 117
Fisher Cl. LE7: Coss 4K 45
LE9: S Stan 1H 105
Fishley Cl. LE3: Glen 7F 63
Fishpond La. NG13: Bark V 3B 106
Fishponds Cl. LE3: Glen 6F 63
Fishpond Way LE11: Lou 5E 30
Fishpools LE3: Brau 1J 75
Fishpool Way LE12: Bar S 2E 32
Fitzroy St. LE3: Leic 2D 70
Fitzwilliam Cl. LE2: Oad 4F 79
Fitzwilliam Wlk. LE15: Cott 4C 124
Five Foot LE10: Hinc 1G 103
Flagstaff 42 Bus. Pk. LE65: Ash Z 3B 24
Flagstaff Rd. LE14: O Dal 6D 110
Flamborough Rd. LE5: Leic 7F 67
Flamingo Dr. LE8: Whet 5K 81
Flamville Rd. LE10: Bur 6A 104
Flatholme Rd. LE5: Leic 6G 67
Flatten Way LE7: Sys 1C 60
Flatts Cl. LE67: Ibs 2K 51
FLAWBOROUGH 1A 160
Flaxfield Cl. LE6: Groby 3D 62
FLAXHOLME 1A 158
Flaxland LE7: R'ley 5E 44
Flaxland Cl. LE16: L Bow 4H 151
Flaxland Cres. LE12: Sileby 2J 45
Flax La. CV9: Twy 3C 90
Flax Rd. LE4: Leic 4H 65
FLECKNEY 4B 88 (2D 163)
Fleckney Ind. Est. LE8: Flec 4C 88
Fleckney Rd. LE8: Arne, Flec 2J 147
LE8: K Bea 3F 89
LE8: Sad 5C 88
LE18: Kilby 7C 84
Fleckney Sports & Leisure Cen. 2B 88
Fleet, The LE9: S Stan 6K 101
Fleet St. LE1: Leic 2E 4 (1G 71)
Fleetwood Cl. LE16: Mkt H 6D 150
Fleetwood Ct. LE2: Leic 6G 71
Fleetwood Gdns. LE16: Mkt H 6D 150
Fleetwood Rd. LE2: Leic 6G 71
Fleming Av. NG13: Bott 1J 107
Fleming Cl. LE11: Lou 4B 18
Fleming Rd. LE10: Hinc 4B 102
Flesh Hovel La. LE12: Quo 2A 32

Fletcher Bldg. LE2: Leic . . . . . . . . . . . . . . . .6A 5
Fletcher Mall LE4: Beau L . . . . . . . . . . . . . . .2A 64
Fletcher Rd. LE9: S Stan . . . . . . . . . . . . . .7K 101
    LE10: Bur . . . . . . . . . . . . . . . . . . . . . . . .4H 103
Fletchers Cl. LE19: Nar . . . . . . . . . . . . . . . .2F 81
Fletchers Way LE7: East G . . . . . . . . . . . . . .5F 47
Fletcher Way LE7: East G . . . . . . . . . . . . . . .5F 47
Flint Cl. PE9: Ryh . . . . . . . . . . . . . . . . . . .5J 129
Flora St. LE3: Leic . . . . . . . . . . . . . . . . . . . .2D 70
Florence Av. LE18: Wig . . . . . . . . . . . . . . . .7G 77
Florence Rd. LE5: Leic . . . . . . . . . . . . . . . . .1J 71
Florence St. LE2: Leic . . . . . . . . . . . . . . . . .1E 76
Florence Wragg Way LE2: Oad . . . . . . . . .4F 79
Floret Cl. LE67: Rav . . . . . . . . . . . . . . . . . . .2A 38
Florian Way LE10: Hinc . . . . . . . . . . . . . . .2C 102
Floyd Cl. LE4: Leic . . . . . . . . . . . . . . . . . . .1A 66
Fludes Ct. LE2: Oad . . . . . . . . . . . . . . . . . . .3E 78
Fludes La. LE2: Oad . . . . . . . . . . . . . . . . . . .3E 78
Foan Hill LE67: Swan . . . . . . . . . . . . . . . . . .7B 26
FOLESHILL . . . . . . . . . . . . . . . . . . . . . . . . .3A 162
FOLKINGHAM . . . . . . . . . . . . . . . . . . . . . . .1D 161
FOLKSWORTH . . . . . . . . . . . . . . . . . . . . . .2D 165
Folville Ri. LE3: Leic . . . . . . . . . . . . . . . . . .5A 70
Folville St. LE14: Ash F . . . . . . . . . . . . . . . .3E 118
Fontwell Dr. LE2: Leic . . . . . . . . . . . . . . . . .3B 76
Forbes Cl. LE3: Glen . . . . . . . . . . . . . . . . . .7G 63
Ford, The LE2: G Par . . . . . . . . . . . . . . . . . .1C 82
    LE8: Bla . . . . . . . . . . . . . . . . . . . . . . . . . .1C 82
Ford Bank LE16: G Eas . . . . . . . . . . . . . . . .5K 141
Ford Cl. LE2: Leic . . . . . . . . . . . . . . . . . . . .5C 76
Fordice Cl. LE67: Hug . . . . . . . . . . . . . . . . . .5C 38
Ford Ri. LE2: Leic . . . . . . . . . . . . . . . . . . . .5C 76
Fordview Cl. LE8: G Gle . . . . . . . . . . . . . . . .7J 79
FOREMARK . . . . . . . . . . . . . . . . . . . . . . . . .2A 158
Forest Av. LE4: Thurm . . . . . . . . . . . . . . . . .5K 59
Forest Bus. Pk. LE67: Bar . . . . . . . . . . . . . .1J 53
Forest Cl. LE6: Groby . . . . . . . . . . . . . . . . . .3B 62
    LE13: Mel M . . . . . . . . . . . . . . . . . . . . . . .2F 117
Forest Ct. LE2: Leic . . . . . . . . . . . . . . . . . . .8B 5
    LE11: Lou . . . . . . . . . . . . . . . . . . . . . . . . . .7E 18
Forest Dr. LE9: K Mux . . . . . . . . . . . . . . . . .3C 68
    LE12: Sileby . . . . . . . . . . . . . . . . . . . . . . . .7J 33
Foresters Cl. LE3: Glen . . . . . . . . . . . . . . . .6F 63
Foresters Row LE7: East G . . . . . . . . . . . . . .5F 47
Forest Ga. LE7: Anst . . . . . . . . . . . . . . . . . .7H 57
Forest Ho. La. LE3: Leic E . . . . . . . . . . . . . .6C 68
Forest La. LE12: Belt . . . . . . . . . . . . . . . . . .5H 15
Forest Lea DE12: Moi . . . . . . . . . . . . . . . . . .7A 22
Forest Ri. LE2: Oad . . . . . . . . . . . . . . . . . . .2E 78
    LE6: Groby . . . . . . . . . . . . . . . . . . . . . . . . .3B 62
    LE7: Thurn . . . . . . . . . . . . . . . . . . . . . . . . .2H 73
    LE9: Des . . . . . . . . . . . . . . . . . . . . . . . . . .2J 95
    LE9: Leic E . . . . . . . . . . . . . . . . . . . . . . . .4D 68
Forest Rd. LE5: Leic . . . . . . . . . . . . . . . . . .6J 65
    LE10: Hinc . . . . . . . . . . . . . . . . . . . . . . . .3J 103
    LE11: Lou . . . . . . . . . . . . . . . . . . . . . . . . . .2C 30
    LE12: Quo . . . . . . . . . . . . . . . . . . . . . . . . .6J 31
    LE12: Wood, W Eav . . . . . . . . . . . . . . . . . .2D 42
    LE19: End, Nar . . . . . . . . . . . . . . . . . . . . . .3D 74
    LE67: Coal . . . . . . . . . . . . . . . . . . . . . . . . .5D 38
    LE67: Mark . . . . . . . . . . . . . . . . . . . . . . . . .4E 54
Forest St. LE12: Shep . . . . . . . . . . . . . . . . .7E 16
Forest Vw. LE6: Groby . . . . . . . . . . . . . . . . .3B 62
Forest Vw. Rd. LE9: Barw . . . . . . . . . . . . . .3A 100
Forest Way LE3: Leic . . . . . . . . . . . . .2A 4 (6B 64)
    LE9: Des . . . . . . . . . . . . . . . . . . . . . . . . . .2H 95
Forge Cl. LE3: Glen . . . . . . . . . . . . . . . . . . .6E 62
    LE8: Flec . . . . . . . . . . . . . . . . . . . . . . . . . .3B 88
Forge Cnr. LE8: Bla . . . . . . . . . . . . . . . . . . .1B 82
Forge Ct. LE7: Sys . . . . . . . . . . . . . . . . . . . .1D 60
Forge End LE7: R'ley . . . . . . . . . . . . . . . . . . .7E 44
Forg La. NG13: Plun . . . . . . . . . . . . . . . . . .6C 106
Forman Rd. LE12: Shep . . . . . . . . . . . . . . . .1D 28
Formans Way LE67: Rav . . . . . . . . . . . . . . .2A 38
Formula One Indoor Karting . . . . . . . . . . .1G 21
Forrester Av. DE72: W Tre . . . . . . . . . . . . . .3B 6
Forrester Cl. LE67: Cole . . . . . . . . . . . . . . . .7H 25
Forresters Cl. LE10: Bur . . . . . . . . . . . . . . .5J 103
Forresters Rd. LE10: Bur . . . . . . . . . . . . . .5J 103
Forryan Cl. LE9: Cosb . . . . . . . . . . . . . . . . . .7H 81
Forryan Rd. LE10: Bur . . . . . . . . . . . . . . . .4J 103
Forryans Cl. LE18: Wig . . . . . . . . . . . . . . . . .1A 84
Forsells End LE7: Hou H . . . . . . . . . . . . . . .3C 130
Forsyth Cl. LE11: Lou . . . . . . . . . . . . . . . . . .4K 17
Forsythia Cl. LE17: Lut . . . . . . . . . . . . . . . .4G 153
Forth Cl. LE15: O'ham . . . . . . . . . . . . . . . . .5G 127
Forties La. LE65: Smis . . . . . . . . . . . . . . . . .1H 23
Fort Rd. LE12: Moun . . . . . . . . . . . . . . . . . .3D 44
Forty Foot La. DE73: Wils . . . . . . . . . . . . . .3A 10
Fosbrook Dr. DE74: C Don . . . . . . . . . . . . . .4H 7
Fosbrooke Cl. LE67: Rav . . . . . . . . . . . . . . .4J 37
Fosse Cl. LE10: Bur . . . . . . . . . . . . . . . . . .6A 104
    LE10: S'ord . . . . . . . . . . . . . . . . . . . . . . .7G 105
    LE19: End . . . . . . . . . . . . . . . . . . . . . . . . .6H 75
Fosse La. LE3: Leic . . . . . . . . . . . . . . . . . . .7C 64
Fosse Meadows Nature Reserve . . . . . . . .1B 142
Fosse Pk. Av. LE19: Brau . . . . . . . . . . . . . . .3K 75

Fosse Pk. Shop. Cen. LE19: Brau . . . . . . . . .3K 75
Fosse Pk. Sth. LE19: End . . . . . . . . . . . . . . .3K 75
Fosse Plaza LE19: End . . . . . . . . . . . . . . . . .3K 75
Fosse Rd. LE3: Leic . . . . . . . . . . . . . . . . . . .2C 70
Fosse Rd. Nth. LE3: Leic . . . . . . . . . . . . . . .1C 70
Fosse Rd. Sth. LE3: Leic . . . . . . . . . . . . . . . .5B 70
Fosse Way LE7: Rat W, Sys . . . . . . . . . . . . . .3B 60
Fosseway Gdns. LE17: C Mag . . . . . . . . . . .5C 142
FOSTON
    Grantham . . . . . . . . . . . . . . . . . . . . . . .1B 160
    Leicester . . . . . . . . . . . . . . . . . .7J 83 (2D 163)
Foston La. LE8: Fost . . . . . . . . . . . . . . . . . . .6J 83
Foston Rd. LE8: Count, Fost . . . . . . . . . . . . .5F 83
Fothergill Cl. LE16: L Bow . . . . . . . . . . . . . .4H 151
FOTHERINGHAY . . . . . . . . . . . . . . . . . . . . .2D 165
Foulds La. LE8: Bla . . . . . . . . . . . . . . . . . . .7A 76
Foundry La. LE1: Leic . . . . . . . . . . . . . . . . .7G 65
    LE7: Sys . . . . . . . . . . . . . . . . . . . . . . . . . .2B 60
Foundry Rd. PE9: Ryh . . . . . . . . . . . . . . . . .4H 129
Foundry Sq. LE1: Leic . . . . . . . . . . . . .1E 4 (7F 65)
Fountains Av. LE2: Leic . . . . . . . . . . . . . . . .5D 76
Fountains Row LE15: Mkt O . . . . . . . . . . . . .2H 123
                                (not continuous)
FOUR OAKS . . . . . . . . . . . . . . . . . . . . . . . . .3A 162
Fowke St. LE7: R'ley . . . . . . . . . . . . . . . . . . .6F 45
Fowler Cl. LE4: Leic . . . . . . . . . . . . . . . . . . .2C 64
Foxbank Ind. Est. LE9: S Stan . . . . . . . . . .7J 101
Fox Cl. LE8: Flec . . . . . . . . . . . . . . . . . . . . . .5C 88
Foxcote Dr. LE11: Lou . . . . . . . . . . . . . . . . . .1J 29
Fox Covert LE8: Whet . . . . . . . . . . . . . . . . . .4K 81
    LE11: Lou . . . . . . . . . . . . . . . . . . . . . . . . . .4F 19
Fox Covert Cl. LE7: Thurc . . . . . . . . . . . . . . .4C 58
Foxcroft Cl. LE3: Leic . . . . . . . . . . . . . . . . . .7C 70
Fox End LE9: Thurl . . . . . . . . . . . . . . . . . . . .2C 96
Foxfield Cl. LE17: Lut . . . . . . . . . . . . . . . . . .5K 153
Foxfield Way LE15: O'ham . . . . . . . . . . . . . .2J 127
    LE13: Mel M . . . . . . . . . . . . . . . . . . . . . . .7D 116
Foxglove Av. DE12: Don . . . . . . . . . . . . . . . .3A 34
Foxglove Cl. LE7: East G . . . . . . . . . . . . . . . .5G 47
    LE9: B Ast . . . . . . . . . . . . . . . . . . . . . . . . .6E 86
    LE12: Moun . . . . . . . . . . . . . . . . . . . . . . . .2F 45
    LE19: Nar . . . . . . . . . . . . . . . . . . . . . . . . . .1E 80
Foxglove Dr. LE6: Groby . . . . . . . . . . . . . . . .3E 62
Foxglove Rd. LE5: Ham . . . . . . . . . . . . . . . . .4E 66
    LE67: Coal . . . . . . . . . . . . . . . . . . . . . . . . .4G 39
    PE9: Stam . . . . . . . . . . . . . . . . . . . . . . . .4J 137
Foxhill LE15: Whis . . . . . . . . . . . . . . . . . . . .2D 122
Foxhill Dr. LE2: G Par . . . . . . . . . . . . . . . . . .5A 76
Foxhills DE74: Keg . . . . . . . . . . . . . . . . . . . .7G 9
Foxholes Rd. LE3: Leic . . . . . . . . . . . . . . . . .3H 69
Fox Hollies LE10: S'ord . . . . . . . . . . . . . . . .7G 105
Fox Hollow LE2: Oad . . . . . . . . . . . . . . . . . .4F 79
    LE7: Crop . . . . . . . . . . . . . . . . . . . . . . . . . .3K 57
    LE7: East G . . . . . . . . . . . . . . . . . . . . . . . .4F 47
Foxhunter Dr. LE2: Oad . . . . . . . . . . . . . . . .2B 78
Foxhunter Rdbt. LE19: End . . . . . . . . . . . . . .6H 75
Fox La. LE1: Leic . . . . . . . . . . . . . . . . .3D 4 (1F 71)
    LE9: K Mux . . . . . . . . . . . . . . . . . . . . . . . .2B 68
Foxon St. LE3: Leic . . . . . . . . . . . . . .5A 4 (2D 70)
Foxon Way LE3: Brau . . . . . . . . . . . . . . . . . .6H 69
Fox Pk. Mobile Homes LE12: Bar S . . . . . . . .3D 32
Fox Pond La. LE2: Oad . . . . . . . . . . . . . . . . .7G 79
Fox Rd. DE74: C Don . . . . . . . . . . . . . . . . . .5H 7
Fox's Covert CV13: F Dray . . . . . . . . . . . . . .2G 97
Fox St. LE1: Leic . . . . . . . . . . . . . . . . .2G 4 (2G 71)
FOXTON . . . . . . . . . . . . . . . . . . . .1H 149 (3D 163)
Foxton Canal Mus. . . . . . . . . . . . . . . . . . . .2F 149
Foxton Lock Cl. LE18: Wig . . . . . . . . . . . . . . .1G 83
Foxton Locks Country Pk. . . . . . . . . . . . . . .3D 163
Foxton Rd. LE16: Lub . . . . . . . . . . . . . . . . .3G 149
Frain Gdns. DE73: B Hil . . . . . . . . . . . . . . . .7B 10
Framework Knitters Cotts. LE2: Oad . . . . . .2C 78
Framland Dr. LE13: Mel M . . . . . . . . . . . . . .1F 117
Framland Ho. LE2: Leic . . . . . . . .4G 4 (2H 71)
Frampton Av. LE3: Leic . . . . . . . . . . . . . . . . .2B 70
Franche Rd. LE3: Leic . . . . . . . . . . . . . . . . . .1C 70
Francis Cl. LE3: Brau . . . . . . . . . . . . . . . . . .1K 75
Francis Ct. LE2: Leic . . . . . . . . . . . . . . . . . .2C 76
    PE9: Ryh . . . . . . . . . . . . . . . . . . . . . . . . .5H 129
Francis Dr. LE11: Lou . . . . . . . . . . . . . . . . . .4A 18
Francis La. LE67: N Bur . . . . . . . . . . . . . . . .6B 50
Francis St. LE2: Leic . . . . . . . . . . . . . . . . . . .6K 71
Francis Wlk. LE2: Leic . . . . . . . . . . . . . . . . . .5A 72
Francis Way LE67: Ell . . . . . . . . . . . . . . . . . .2E 52
Frank Booton Cl. LE9: Earl S . . . . . . . . . . . .2G 101
Frank Haynes Gallery . . . . . . . . . . . . . . . . .2G 151
Franklin Way LE8: Whet . . . . . . . . . . . . . . . .4K 81
Franklyn Rd. LE2: Leic . . . . . . . . . . . . . . . . .2B 76
Frank's La. LE17: Wal . . . . . . . . . . . . . . . . .2D 154
Frankson Av. LE3: Brau . . . . . . . . . . . . . . . .6A 70
Franks Rd. LE67: Bar . . . . . . . . . . . . . . . . . .1J 53
Fraser Cl. LE2: Leic . . . . . . . . . . . . . .1F 4 (7G 65)
Frearson Rd. LE67: Hug . . . . . . . . . . . . . . . .5B 38
Frederick Cl. DE74: Keg . . . . . . . . . . . . . . . . .5G 9
    LE10: Hinc . . . . . . . . . . . . . . . . . . . . . . . .1D 102
Frederick Cl. LE7: Quen . . . . . . . . . . . . . . . .6G 47

Frederick Rd. LE5: Leic . . . . . . . . . . . . . . . . .1J 71
Frederick St. LE11: Lou . . . . . . . . . . . . . . . . .7E 18
    LE18: Wig . . . . . . . . . . . . . . . . . . . . . . . . . .5K 77
Fredscott Cl. LE5: Leic . . . . . . . . . . . . . . . . .7G 67
Freeboard Rd. LE3: Brau . . . . . . . . . . . . . . .1K 75
FREEBY . . . . . . . . . . . . . . . . . . . . . . . . . . . .2B 160
Freeby Cl. LE13: Mel M . . . . . . . . . . . . . . . .5H 117
Freehold Rd. LE4: Birs . . . . . . . . . . . . . . . . .1G 65
Freehold St. LE1: Leic . . . . . . . . . . . .1G 4 (7H 65)
    LE11: Lou . . . . . . . . . . . . . . . . . . . . . . . . . .6G 19
    LE12: Quo . . . . . . . . . . . . . . . . . . . . . . . . .5B 32
    LE12: Shep . . . . . . . . . . . . . . . . . . . . . . . . .7E 16
Free La. LE1: Leic . . . . . . . . . . . . . . .3D 4 (1F 71)
Freeman Rd. Nth. LE5: Leic . . . . . . . . . . . . .7B 66
Freemans Common Nature Reserve . . . . . . .5F 71
Freemans Ct. LE6: Ratby . . . . . . . . . . . . . . . .6B 62
Freemans La. LE10: Bur . . . . . . . . . . . . . . . .6K 103
Freeman's Way LE7: East G . . . . . . . . . . . . .4G 47
Freemantle Rd. LE2: Leic . . . . . . . . . . . . . . .6A 72
Freeman Way LE12: Quo . . . . . . . . . . . . . . . .4K 31
Freemen's Comn. Ho's. LE2: Leic . . . . . . . . .5G 71
Freemen's Comn. Rd. LE2: Leic . . . . .10C 5 (5F 71)
Freemen's Comn. Trad. Est. LE2: Leic . . . . .5F 71
Freemen's Holt LE2: Leic . . . . . . . . . . . . . . .1C 76
Freer Cl. LE7: Hou H . . . . . . . . . . . . . . . . . . .3B 130
    LE8: Bla . . . . . . . . . . . . . . . . . . . . . . . . . .1B 82
    LE18: Wig . . . . . . . . . . . . . . . . . . . . . . . . . .1A 84
Freeschool La. LE1: Leic . . . . . . . . . .3B 4 (1E 70)
Freesia Cl. LE11: Lou . . . . . . . . . . . . . . . . . .5E 30
French Rd. LE5: Leic . . . . . . . . . . . . . . . . . .7A 66
Frensham Cl. LE2: Oad . . . . . . . . . . . . . . . . .4C 78
Freshney Cl. LE13: Mel M . . . . . . . . . . . . . .6E 116
Freshwater Cl. LE18: Wig . . . . . . . . . . . . . . .2K 83
Freswick Cl. LE10: Hinc . . . . . . . . . . . . . . . .2C 102
Frewen Dr. LE9: Sap . . . . . . . . . . . . . . . . . . .3J 105
Frewin St. LE5: Leic . . . . . . . . . . . . . . . . . . .7A 66
Friar La. LE1: Leic . . . . . . . . . . . . . . .5B 4 (2E 70)
Friars C'way. LE1: Leic . . . . . . . . . . . .3A 4 (1E 70)
Friary Cl. LE10: Hinc . . . . . . . . . . . . . . . . . .2H 103
Friday St. LE1: Leic . . . . . . . . . . . . . .1B 4 (7E 64)
Friendship Ho. LE4: Leic . . . . . . . . . . . . . . . .6H 65
Frinton Av. LE5: Leic . . . . . . . . . . . . . . . . . . .3F 73
Frisby La. LE15: S Luf . . . . . . . . . . . . . . . . .4B 136
FRISBY ON THE WREAKE . . . . . . .5H 115 (3D 159)
Frisby Rd. LE5: Leic . . . . . . . . . . . . . . . . . . .6J 65
    LE9: Barw . . . . . . . . . . . . . . . . . . . . . . . . .3A 100
Friswell La. LE9: Barw . . . . . . . . . . . . . . . . . .3K 99
Fritchley Cl. LE9: Hun . . . . . . . . . . . . . . . . . .2C 80
Frith Cl. LE3: Glen . . . . . . . . . . . . . . . . . . . .6G 63
Frith Way LE10: Hinc . . . . . . . . . . . . . . . . . .7D 98
Froanes Cl. LE19: End . . . . . . . . . . . . . . . . . .4E 74
Frobisher Cl. LE10: Hinc . . . . . . . . . . . . . . . .6G 99
FROG ISLAND . . . . . . . . . . . . . . . . . .1A 4 (7E 64)
Frog Island LE3: Leic . . . . . . . . . . . . .1A 4 (7E 64)
FROLESWORTH . . . . . . . . . . . . . .1E 142 (2C 163)
Frolesworth La. LE17: C Mag . . . . . . . . . . . . .5C 142
Frolesworth Rd. LE3: Leic . . . . . . . . . . . . . . .1J 69
    LE9: B Ast . . . . . . . . . . . . . . . . . . . . . . . . .6B 86
    LE10: S'ord . . . . . . . . . . . . . . . . . . . . . . . .6J 105
    LE17: Ash P . . . . . . . . . . . . . . . . . . . . . . . .4G 143
    LE17: Leire . . . . . . . . . . . . . . . . . . . . . . . . .2J 143
    LE17: S'ord . . . . . . . . . . . . . . . . . . . . . . . .6J 105
    LE17: Ull . . . . . . . . . . . . . . . . . . . . . . . . . .7E 142
Frolesworth Way LE3: Leic . . . . . . . . . . . . . .1J 69
Frome Av. LE2: Oad . . . . . . . . . . . . . . . . . . .2F 79
Front St. LE4: Birs . . . . . . . . . . . . . . . . . . . .6H 59
Fulbeck Av. LE5: Leic . . . . . . . . . . . . . . . . . .3F 73
Fulford Rd. LE3: Leic . . . . . . . . . . . . . . . . . .2G 69
Fuller Cl. LE9: Des . . . . . . . . . . . . . . . . . . . .1J 95
Fullhurst Av. LE3: Leic . . . . . . . . . . . . . . . . .4B 70
Fulmar Rd. LE7: Anst . . . . . . . . . . . . . . . . . .7H 57
Fulton Dr. LE67: Coal . . . . . . . . . . . . . . . . . .2A 38
Furley Ct. LE15: O'ham . . . . . . . . . . . . . . . .3H 127
                        (off Station Rd., not continuous)
Furlong Cl. LE7: Sys . . . . . . . . . . . . . . . . . . .2E 60
Furlongs, The LE16: L Bow . . . . . . . . . . . . . .4H 151
Furnace La. DE12: Moi . . . . . . . . . . . . . . . . .1A 34
Furnace La. Ind. Est. DE12: Moi . . . . . . . . . .1A 34
Furnival Cl. LE8: Flec . . . . . . . . . . . . . . . . . .3A 88
Furrow Cl. LE7: R'ley . . . . . . . . . . . . . . . . . . .6E 44
Furrows Cl. LE19: Litt . . . . . . . . . . . . . . . . . .2G 81
Fydell Row LE15: Mor . . . . . . . . . . . . . . . . . .6J 135

# G

Gables, The LE65: Ash Z . . . . . . . . . . . . . . . .7A 24
Gables Ct. LE17: Frol . . . . . . . . . . . . . . . . . .1E 142
Gables Hall, The LE2: Leic . . . . . . . . . . . . . .7B 72
GADDESBY . . . . . . . . . . . . . . . . . .1A 118 (3D 159)
Gaddesby Av. LE3: Leic . . . . . . . . . . . . . . . .4C 70
Gaddesby La. LE7: Rear . . . . . . . . . . . . . . . .3J 47
                                (not continuous)
    LE14: F Wre . . . . . . . . . . . . . . . . . . . . . . .6J 115
    LE14: Roth . . . . . . . . . . . . . . . . . . . . . . . .3D 114
Gaddesby La. LE7: Bars . . . . . . . . . . . . . . . .3C 118
Gainsborough Av. LE10: Hinc . . . . . . . . . . . .7D 98

Gainsborough Ct. LE15: Cott . . . . . . . . . . . .7A **124**
Gainsborough Rd. LE2: Leic . . . . . . . . . . . . .7G **71**
   LE8: Kib H . . . . . . . . . . . . . . . . . . . . .2J **89**
   LE15: Upp . . . . . . . . . . . . . . . . . . . .2C **138**
Galahad Cl. LE3: Leic E . . . . . . . . . . . . . . .5E **68**
Galaxy Wlk. LE2: Leic . . . . . . . . . . . . . . . .2J **71**
Galby St. LE5: Leic . . . . . . . . . . . . . . . . . .7K **65**
Galdstone M. *LE9: B Ast* . . . . . . . . . . . . .3C **86**
                     (off Estley Rd.)
Gale Cl. LE17: Lut . . . . . . . . . . . . . . . . . .2J **153**
Gallards Hill LE3: Leic . . . . . . . . . . . . . . . .4H **69**
             (not continuous)
GALLEY COMMON . . . . . . . . . . . . . . . .2A **162**
Galleywood Dr. LE4: Leic . . . . . . . . . . . . . .4D **64**
Gallico Cl. LE11: Lou . . . . . . . . . . . . . . . . .5B **18**
Gallimore Cl. LE3: Glen . . . . . . . . . . . . . . .5J **63**
Galloway Cl. LE9: Barw . . . . . . . . . . . . . . .4J **99**
Gallow Fld. Rd. LE16: Fox, Gar, Mkt H . . .2G **149**
Gallows La. DE12: Mea . . . . . . . . . . . . . . .3F **49**
Gallowtree Ga. LE1: Leic . . . . . . . .3D **4** (1F **71**)
Gallus Dr. LE10: Hinc . . . . . . . . . . . . . . . .2D **102**
Galsworthy Ct. LE3: Leic . . . . . . . . . . . . . .2A **70**
Galsworthy Cres. LE13: Mel M . . . . . . . . . .1E **116**
Galway Rd. LE4: Leic . . . . . . . . . . . . . . . .1E **64**
Gamble Cl. LE67: Ibs . . . . . . . . . . . . . . . . .2K **51**
Gamble Way LE12: Quo . . . . . . . . . . . . . . .4K **31**
Gamekeepers Ct. LE5: Ham . . . . . . . . . . . .3E **66**
Gamel Rd. LE5: Leic . . . . . . . . . . . . . . . . .2D **72**
Gamel Wlk. LE5: Leic . . . . . . . . . . . . . . . .2D **72**
GAMSTON . . . . . . . . . . . . . . . . . . . . . .1D **159**
Ganton Rd. LE3: Leic . . . . . . . . . . . . . . . . .1G **69**
Gaol St. LE15: O'ham . . . . . . . . . . . . . . . .4H **127**
Garat's Hay LE12: Wood . . . . . . . . . . . . . .1F **43**
Garden Cl. LE2: Oad . . . . . . . . . . . . . . . . .3C **78**
   LE10: Bur . . . . . . . . . . . . . . . . . . .5G **103**
Garden Cres. DE74: C Don . . . . . . . . . . . . .5K **7**
Gardenfield Rd. LE4: Leic . . . . . . . . . . . . . .2B **66**
Garden La. LE13: Mel M . . . . . . . . . . . . . .2D **116**
   LE67: Ibs . . . . . . . . . . . . . . . . . . . . .5K **51**
Garden Rd. LE10: Hinc . . . . . . . . . . . . . . .2G **103**
   LE15: Ext . . . . . . . . . . . . . . . . . . . .2D **128**
   LE67: Coal . . . . . . . . . . . . . . . . . . . .2E **38**
Garden Row DE74: Keg . . . . . . . . . . . . . . . .5H **9**
Garden St. LE1: Leic . . . . . . . . . .1D **4** (7F **65**)
   LE4: Thurm . . . . . . . . . . . . . . . . . . .6A **60**
   LE18: Wig . . . . . . . . . . . . . . . . . . . .7F **77**
Gardiner St. LE16: Mkt H . . . . . . . . . . . . .4C **150**
Gardner Cl. LE11: Lou . . . . . . . . . . . . . . . .4A **18**
Garendon Av. LE12: Hat . . . . . . . . . . . . . . .2J **17**
Garendon Cl. LE12: Shep . . . . . . . . . . . . . .7E **16**
Garendon Grn. LE11: Lou . . . . . . . . . . . . . .7B **18**
Garendon Pk. . . . . . . . . . . . . . . . . . . . . .6J **17**
Garendon Rd. LE11: Lou . . . . . . . . . . . . . .6B **18**
   LE12: Shep . . . . . . . . . . . . . . . . . . .7D **16**
   LE67: Coal . . . . . . . . . . . . . . . . . . . .4H **39**
Garendon St. LE2: Leic . . . . . . . . . . . . . . .1H **71**
Garendon Way LE6: Groby . . . . . . . . . . . . .4C **62**
Garfield Pk. LE8: G Gle . . . . . . . . . . . . . . .6K **79**
Garfield Rd. LE67: Hug . . . . . . . . . . . . . . .5C **38**
Garfield St. LE4: Leic . . . . . . . . . . . . . . . .6G **65**
Garfit Rd. LE9: K Mux . . . . . . . . . . . . . . . .2C **68**
Garganey Cl. LE67: Coal . . . . . . . . . . . . . .4G **39**
Garland LE7: R'ley . . . . . . . . . . . . . . . . . .5E **44**
Garland Cres. LE3: Leic . . . . . . . . . . . . . . .6B **64**
Garnett Cres. LE2: Leic . . . . . . . . . . . . . . .4C **76**
Garratt Sq. LE8: Whet . . . . . . . . . . . . . . . .2K **81**
Garrick Wlk. LE1: Leic . . . . . . . . . . . . . . . . .3D **4**
Garsdale LE18: Wig . . . . . . . . . . . . . . . . .6B **78**
Garsington Wlk. LE5: Leic . . . . . . . . . . . . .1C **72**
Garth Av. LE4: Leic . . . . . . . . . . . . . . . . .2E **64**
GARTHORPE . . . . . . . . . . . . . . . . . . . . .2B **160**
Garthorpe Dr. LE13: Mel M . . . . . . . . . . . .5H **117**
Garthorpe La. LE14: W Wol . . . . . . . . . . . .2D **112**
Garth St. LE15: Cott . . . . . . . . . . . . . . . . .2D **124**
Garton Cl. DE12: A Mag . . . . . . . . . . . . . . .5B **48**
Garton Rd. LE11: Lou . . . . . . . . . . . . . . . .7F **19**
GARTREE . . . . . . . . . . . . . . . . . . . . . . .4H **149**
Gartree Ct. LE13: Mel M . . . . . . . . . . . . . .7F **117**
Gartree Cres. LE9: Earl S . . . . . . . . . . . . . .2C **100**
Gartree Dr. LE13: Mel M . . . . . . . . . . . . . .6F **117**
Gartree Rd. LE2: Leic . . . . . . . . . . . . . . . .6B **72**
Gascoigne Av. LE7: Quen . . . . . . . . . . . . . .7G **47**
Gaskell Wlk. LE3: Leic . . . . . . . . . . . . . . . .2A **70**
Gas La. LE18: Wig . . . . . . . . . . . . . . . . . .7J **77**
Gasny Av. DE74: C Don . . . . . . . . . . . . . . . .3K **7**
Gas St. LE1: Leic . . . . . . . . . . . .1D **4** (7F **65**)
Gas Wlk. LE14: Harb . . . . . . . . . . . . . . . .2D **108**
Gatcombe Dr. LE67: Coal . . . . . . . . . . . . . .4G **39**
Gated Rd. LE14: T Sat . . . . . . . . . . . . . . .4F **119**
Gatehouse La. LE15: S Luf . . . . . . . . . . . . .3B **136**
Gateway, The LE2: Leic . . . . . . . . .6B **5** (3E **70**)
Gateway Bldg. LE2: Leic . . . . . . . . .6B **5** (3E **70**)
Gateway St. LE2: Leic . . . . . . . . . .6B **5** (3E **70**)
GAULBY . . . . . . . . . . . . . . . . . . . . . . . .1D **163**
Gaulby La. LE2: S'ton . . . . . . . . . . . . . . . .7F **73**
   LE7: Hou H . . . . . . . . . . . . . . . . . .2E **130**
Gaulby Rd. LE7: Bill . . . . . . . . . . . . . . . . .7F **131**

Gaul St. LE3: Leic . . . . . . . . . . . . . . . . . . .3D **70**
Gavin Cl. LE3: Brau . . . . . . . . . . . . . . . . . .5G **69**
Gavin Dr. LE11: Lou . . . . . . . . . . . . . . . . . .4B **18**
Gawney La. LE17: Gilm . . . . . . .6K **145** & 4A **146**
Gayhurst Cl. LE3: Brau . . . . . . . . . . . . . . . .1K **75**
   LE18: Wig . . . . . . . . . . . . . . . . . . . .6A **78**
Gayton Av. LE4: Leic . . . . . . . . . . . . . . . . .5J **65**
Gayton Hgts. LE19: End . . . . . . . . . . . . . . .4E **74**
Geary Cl. LE6: Ratby . . . . . . . . . . . . . . . . .6C **62**
   LE19: Nar . . . . . . . . . . . . . . . . . . . . .2F **81**
   LE67: Whit . . . . . . . . . . . . . . . . . . . .6D **26**
Geary's Cl. LE67: Thor . . . . . . . . . . . . . . . .3K **93**
GEC Ind. Est. LE8: Whet . . . . . . . . . . . . . . .3J **81**
Gedding Rd. LE5: Leic . . . . . . . . . . . . . . . .2A **72**
GEDDINGTON . . . . . . . . . . . . . . . . . . . .3B **164**
Geddington Cl. LE18: Wig . . . . . . . . . . . . . .6A **78**
Gedge Way LE2: Leic . . . . . . . . . . . . . . . . .2E **76**
GEDLING . . . . . . . . . . . . . . . . . . . . . . .1D **159**
Gee La. LE67: Coal . . . . . . . . . . . . . . . . . .2E **38**
             (not continuous)
Gees Lock Cl. LE2: Leic . . . . . . . . . . . . . . . .4B **76**
GEESTON . . . . . . . . . . . . . . .7J **137** (1C **165**)
Geeston PE9: Ket . . . . . . . . . . . . . . . . . . .6H **137**
Gelders Hall Ind. Est. LE12: Shep . . . . . . . .2C **28**
Gelders Hall Rd. LE12: Shep . . . . . . . . . . . .1C **28**
Gelert Av. LE5: Leic . . . . . . . . . . . . . . . . . .1F **73**
Gelscoe La. LE12: Belt . . . . . . . . . . . . . . . .1D **14**
GELSMOOR . . . . . . . . . . . . . . . . . . . . . .2J **25**
Gelsmoor Rd. LE67: Cole . . . . . . . . . . . . . .2J **25**
George Deacon Ct. *LE11: Lou* . . . . . . . . . .6E **18**
            (off Ashby Rd.)
George Foster Cl. LE9: Earl S . . . . . . . . . . . .1F **101**
George Fox La. CV13: F Dray . . . . . . . . . . . .2H **97**
George Geary Cl. LE9: Barw . . . . . . . . . . . . .3B **100**
Georgeham Cl. LE18: Wig . . . . . . . . . . . . . .7K **77**
George Hill Cl. LE9: S Stan . . . . . . . . . . . . .7J **101**
George Marriott Cl. LE9: S Stan . . . . . . . . . .2H **105**
George St. LE1: Leic . . . . . . . . . . .1E **4** (7G **65**)
   LE7: Anst . . . . . . . . . . . . . . . . . . . .7H **57**
   LE9: Barw . . . . . . . . . . . . . . . . . . .4A **100**
   LE10: Hinc . . . . . . . . . . . . . . . . . . .3G **103**
   LE11: Lou . . . . . . . . . . . . . . . . . . . .6D **18**
   LE13: Mel M . . . . . . . . . . . . . . . . .4G **117**
   LE17: Lut . . . . . . . . . . . . . . . . . . . .4J **153**
   LE19: End . . . . . . . . . . . . . . . . . . . .5E **74**
   LE67: Whit . . . . . . . . . . . . . . . . . . . .7F **27**
George Toon Ct. LE7: Sys . . . . . . . . . . . . . .1C **60**
George Ward Ct. LE9: Barw . . . . . . . . . . . . .3A **100**
George Yd. LE11: Lou . . . . . . . . . . . . . . . . .6F **19**
Georgina Ct. DE74: C Don . . . . . . . . . . . . . .4K **7**
Gerrard Cres. DE74: Keg . . . . . . . . . . . . . . .7H **9**
Gerrard Gdns. LE16: Mkt H . . . . . . . . . . . .7D **150**
Gervas Rd. LE5: Leic . . . . . . . . . . . . . . . . .7E **66**
Geveze Way LE9: B Ast . . . . . . . . . . . . . . . .6E **86**
Gibbet La. CV13: Bils . . . . . . . . . . . . . . . . .7F **91**
   LE15: E Wes . . . . . . . . . . . . . . . . . .2F **135**
   LE17: Shaw . . . . . . . . . . . . . . . . . .1A **156**
Gibbon's Cl. LE4: Leic . . . . . . . . . . . . . . . .6G **65**
Gibson Cl. LE18: Wig . . . . . . . . . . . . . . . . .5K **77**
Gibson Rd. LE12: Sileby . . . . . . . . . . . . . . .7K **33**
Gibson's La. LE14: O Dal . . . . . . . . . . . . . .7A **110**
Gibson Way LE17: Lut . . . . . . . . . . . . . . . .5G **153**
Gifford Cl. LE5: Leic . . . . . . . . . . . . . . . . . .4D **72**
Gilbert Cl. LE4: Leic . . . . . . . . . . . . . . . . . .2A **66**
   LE16: L Bow . . . . . . . . . . . . . . . . . .5H **151**
Gilbert Murray Hall LE2: Oad . . . . . . . . . . . .7C **72**
Gilbert's Dr. LE9: N Ver . . . . . . . . . . . . . . .6G **93**
Giles Cl. LE12: Quo . . . . . . . . . . . . . . . . . .7B **32**
Gillam Butts LE8: Count . . . . . . . . . . . . . . .6E **82**
Gillamore Dr. LE67: Whit . . . . . . . . . . . . . .2G **39**
Gillbank Dr. LE6: Ratby . . . . . . . . . . . . . . .6A **62**
Gilliver St. LE2: Leic . . . . . . . . . . . . . . . . . .7H **71**
   LE9: N Ver . . . . . . . . . . . . . . . . . . .5H **93**
Gilmore Cl. LE15: O'ham . . . . . . . . . . . . . .2J **127**
GILMORTON . . . . . . . . . . . . . .7J **145** (3C **163**)
Gilmorton Av. LE2: Leic . . . . . . . . . . . . . . .4A **76**
Gilmorton Cl. LE2: Leic . . . . . . . . . . . . . . . .4B **76**
Gilmorton La.
   LE17: Ash M, D Bas . . . . . . . . . . . . .2E **144**
Gilmorton Rd. LE17: Ash M . . . . . . . . . . . . .3G **145**
   LE17: Lut . . . . . . . . . . . . . . . . . . . .4K **153**
Gilmour Cl. LE4: Beau L . . . . . . . . . . . . . . .1B **64**
Gilpin Cl. LE13: Mel M . . . . . . . . . . . . . . .6D **116**
Gilroes Crematorium LE3: Leic . . . . . . . . . . .4A **64**
Gilson's Cl. LE15: Mor . . . . . . . . . . . . . . . .6J **135**
Gilstead Cl. LE7: Thurn . . . . . . . . . . . . . . .3H **73**
Gimson Av. LE9: Cosb . . . . . . . . . . . . . . . .6H **81**
Gimson Cl. LE5: Leic . . . . . . . . . . . . . . . . .5C **66**
Gimson Rd. LE3: Leic . . . . . . . . . . . . . . . . .1B **70**
Gipsy Hollow La. LE15: Upp . . . . . . . . . . . .3A **138**
Gipsy La. LE4: Leic . . . . . . . . . . . . . . . . . .4J **65**
   LE5: Leic . . . . . . . . . . . . . . . . . . . .5B **66**
   LE7: R'ley . . . . . . . . . . . . . . . . . . . .4C **44**
   LE12: Bar S . . . . . . . . . . . . . . . . . . .2H **33**
Gipsy Rd. LE4: Leic . . . . . . . . . . . . . . . . . .4H **65**
Gisborough Way LE11: Lou . . . . . . . . . . . . .5K **17**

Gisbourne Ct. LE5: Leic . . . . . . . . . . . . . . . .5C **72**
Glade, The LE3: Brau . . . . . . . . . . . . . . . . .1K **75**
Gladstone Av. LE11: Lou . . . . . . . . . . . . . . .5E **18**
   LE13: Mel M . . . . . . . . . . . . . . . . .2D **116**
Gladstone Cl. LE10: Hinc . . . . . . . . . . . . . .7H **103**
Gladstone St. LE1: Leic . . . . . . . . . .2E **4** (1G **71**)
   LE7: Anst . . . . . . . . . . . . . . . . . . . .7J **57**
   LE8: Flec . . . . . . . . . . . . . . . . . . . . .4B **88**
   LE8: K Bea . . . . . . . . . . . . . . . . . . .3H **89**
   LE11: Lou . . . . . . . . . . . . . . . . . . . .5F **19**
   LE12: Hat . . . . . . . . . . . . . . . . . . . . .1J **17**
   LE16: Mkt H . . . . . . . . . . . . . . . . . .5F **151**
   LE17: Lut . . . . . . . . . . . . . . . . . . . .4K **153**
   LE18: Wig . . . . . . . . . . . . . . . . . . . .5K **77**
   LE67: Ibs . . . . . . . . . . . . . . . . . . . . .4K **51**
Gladstone Ter. LE10: Hinc . . . . . . . . . . . . . .3H **103**
Glaisdale Cl. LE4: Leic . . . . . . . . . . . . . . . .3C **64**
Glaisdale Rd. LE18: Wig . . . . . . . . . . . . . . .7A **78**
Glamis Cl. LE12: Moun . . . . . . . . . . . . . . . .4C **44**
Glamorgan Av. LE18: Wig . . . . . . . . . . . . . .6F **77**
GLAPTHORN . . . . . . . . . . . . . . . . . . . . .2D **165**
GLASTON . . . . . . . . . . . . . . .1J **139** (1B **164**)
Glaston Pk. LE15: Glas . . . . . . . . . . . . . . . .1J **139**
Glaston Rd. LE15: Bisb . . . . . . . . . . . . . . . .2G **139**
   LE15: Mor . . . . . . . . . . . . . . . . . . . .7H **135**
   LE15: Pres . . . . . . . . . . . . . . . . . . .7A **134**
   LE15: Upp . . . . . . . . . . . . . . . . . . .2D **138**
GLATTON . . . . . . . . . . . . . . . . . . . . . . .3D **165**
Glazebrook Rd. LE3: Leic . . . . . . . . . . . . . .5K **63**
Glazebrook Sq. LE3: Leic . . . . . . . . . . . . . .6A **64**
Glean Cl. LE9: B Ast . . . . . . . . . . . . . . . . .6D **86**
Glebe, The CV13: B'one . . . . . . . . . . . . . . .5B **92**
Glebe Cl. LE2: Leic . . . . . . . . . . . . . . . . . .1A **78**
   LE3: Glen . . . . . . . . . . . . . . . . . . . .6F **63**
   LE7: Bill . . . . . . . . . . . . . . . . . . . . .7H **131**
   LE12: Moun . . . . . . . . . . . . . . . . . . .2D **44**
   LE15: Emp . . . . . . . . . . . . . . . . . . .6C **128**
   LE18: Wig . . . . . . . . . . . . . . . . . . . .5K **77**
Glebe Dr. LE8: Count . . . . . . . . . . . . . . . . .6D **82**
Glebe Gdns. LE2: Leic . . . . . . . . . . . . . . . .7B **72**
Glebe Ho. LE8: Bla . . . . . . . . . . . . . . . . . .1C **82**
Glebeland Cl. LE7: Thru . . . . . . . . . . . . . . .6B **114**
Glebelands, The LE8: G Gle . . . . . . . . . . . . .1J **85**
Glebelands Rd. LE4: Leic . . . . . . . . . . . . . .5D **58**
Glebe Rd. LE2: Leic . . . . . . . . . . . . . . . . . .1A **78**
   LE6: Groby . . . . . . . . . . . . . . . . . . .3C **62**
   LE7: Quen . . . . . . . . . . . . . . . . . . .7G **47**
   LE9: B Ast . . . . . . . . . . . . . . . . . . .4C **86**
   LE10: Hinc . . . . . . . . . . . . . . . . . . .3J **103**
   LE14: Ash H . . . . . . . . . . . . . . . . . .2K **105**
   LE14: W'ham . . . . . . . . . . . . . . . . .2F **121**
   LE15: N Luf . . . . . . . . . . . . . . . . . .1A **136**
   LE16: L Bow . . . . . . . . . . . . . . . . . .5G **151**
   LE67: Thrin . . . . . . . . . . . . . . . . . . .3C **26**
Glebe St. LE2: Leic . . . . . . . . . . . .5F **4** (3G **71**)
   LE11: Lou . . . . . . . . . . . . . . . . . . . .5G **19**
Glebe Vw. LE67: Coal . . . . . . . . . . . . . . . . .2K **37**
Glebe Way LE7: Sys . . . . . . . . . . . . . . . . . .1A **60**
   LE15: O'ham . . . . . . . . . . . . . . . . .4F **127**
Glenalmond Cl. LE65: Ash Z . . . . . . . . . . . .4J **23**
Glen Av. LE67: Ibs . . . . . . . . . . . . . . . . . . .5A **52**
Glen Bank LE10: Hinc . . . . . . . . . . . . . . . .2H **103**
Glenbarr Av. LE4: Leic . . . . . . . . . . . . . . . .6D **64**
Glenbarr Cl. LE10: Hinc . . . . . . . . . . . . . . .3D **102**
Glenbarr Dr. LE10: Hinc . . . . . . . . . . . . . . .3D **102**
Glenborne Rd. LE2: Leic . . . . . . . . . . . . . . .4G **77**
Glencoe Av. LE4: Leic . . . . . . . . . . . . . . . . .2J **65**
Glen Cres. PE9: Ess . . . . . . . . . . . . . . . . .2K **129**
Glencroft LE2: G Par . . . . . . . . . . . . . . . . .7D **76**
Glendale Av. LE3: Glen . . . . . . . . . . . . . . . .3F **63**
Glendon Cl. LE14: Ash . . . . . . . . . . . . . . . .3F **115**
Glendon St. LE4: Leic . . . . . . . . . . . . . . . . .5H **65**
Glendower Cl. LE5: Leic . . . . . . . . . . . . . . .1D **72**
Glen Dr. LE15: O'ham . . . . . . . . . . . . . . . .5H **127**
Gleneagles Av. LE4: Leic . . . . . . . . . . . . . . .2K **65**
Gleneagles Cl. LE10: Bur . . . . . . . . . . . . . .7G **103**
Gleneagles Wlk. LE4: Leic . . . . . . . . . . . . . .2J **65**
GLENFIELD . . . . . . . . . . . . . . . .5F **63** (1C **163**)
Glenfield Cres. LE3: Leic . . . . . . . . . . . . . . .6G **63**
Glenfield Frith Dr. LE3: Glen . . . . . . . . . . . .5G **63**
Glenfield La. LE9: K Mux . . . . . . . . . . . . . . .1C **68**
Glenfield Rd. LE3: Leic . . . . . . . . . . . . . . . .7J **63**
Glenfield Rd. E. LE3: Leic . . . . . . . . . . . . . .2C **70**
Glenfields LE12: Shep . . . . . . . . . . . . . . . . .7C **16**
Glenfrith Cl. LE3: Leic . . . . . . . . . . . . . . . .3K **63**
   LE12: Moun . . . . . . . . . . . . . . . . . . .3F **45**
Glenfrith Gdns. LE3: Leic . . . . . . . . . . . . . .3F **45**
Glenfrith Way LE3: Leic . . . . . . . . . . . . . . . .5K **63**
Glengarry Cl. LE3: Leic . . . . . . . . . . . . . . . .7A **64**
Glengarry Ct. LE3: Leic . . . . . . . . . . . . . . . .7K **63**
Glengarry Way LE3: Leic . . . . . . . . . . . . . . .6K **63**
Glengate LE18: Wig . . . . . . . . . . . . . . . . . .6F **77**
Glen Gorse Rdbt. LE2: Oad . . . . . . . . . . . . .6G **79**
Glenhills Blvd. LE2: Leic . . . . . . . . . . . . . . .3C **76**
             (not continuous)
Glenhills Way LE2: Leic . . . . . . . . . . . . . . . .3C **76**
Glen Ind. Est. PE9: Ess . . . . . . . . . . . . . . .1K **129**

Glenmore Av.—Green, The


Glenmore Av. LE12: Shep .6C 16
Glenmore Rd. LE4: Leic .3K 65
Glen Pk. Av. LE3: Glen .4F 63
GLEN PARVA .5A 76 (2C 163)
Glen Ri. LE2: G Par .4B 76
LE2: Oad .6G 79
Glen Rd. LE2: Oad .3E 78
LE8: New H .3E 84
Glenrothes Cl. LE3: Leic .2G 69
Glen St. LE4: Leic .4H 65
Glenville Av. LE2: G Par .6B 76
LE3: Glen .4G 63
Glen Way LE2: Oad .4E 78
LE67: Coal .5F 39
Glenwood Cl. LE2: Leic .6K 71
GLINTON .1D 165
GLOOSTON .2A 164
Glossop St. LE5: Leic .3J 71
Gloucester Av. LE7: Sys .1E 60
LE13: Mel M .7G 117
Gloucester Cl. LE9: Des .3H 95
Gloucester Cres. LE13: Mel M .7G 117
LE18: Wig .5E 76
Glover Ct. LE2: Leic .2C 76
Glover Rd. DE74: C Don .4K 7
Glovers Wlk. LE4: Leic .2C 64
Glyn Cl. LE9: Barw .3K 99
GOADBY .2A 164
GOADBY MARWOOD .2A 160
Goadby Rd. LE14: W Wol .1B 112
LE16: Hall .6A 132
Goals Soccer Cen.
Leicester .3B 72
Goatham La. CV13: Osb .7C 92
Goddard Cl. LE7: Bush .2J 73
Goddard Ct. LE16: Mkt H .3E 150
Goddards Cl. LE2: Oad .3B 78
LE4: Leic .4B 64
LE18: Kilby .6C 84
Goddards Slang LE2: Oad .3B 78
Godfrey Cl. LE4: Beau L .7A 58
Godsons Hill CV13: Mkt B .2B 94
Godstow Wlk. LE5: Leic .1C 72
Godwin Av. LE18: Wig .6A 78
Godwin Ct. LE18: Wig .6K 77
Goldcrest LE15: Upp .1B 138
Golden Sq. LE12: Hat .2H 17
Goldfinch Cl. LE11: Lou .7D 18
Goldfinch Rd. LE15: Upp .1B 138
Goldhill LE2: Leic .3G 77
Goldhill Gdns. LE2: Leic .1K 77
Goldhill Rd. LE2: Leic .1K 77
Golding Cl. LE11: Lou .4K 17
Goldsmith Rd. LE3: Leic .3A 70
Goldspink Cl. LE13: Mel M .7F 117
Golf Course La. LE3: Leic .2G 69
Goliath Rd. LE67: Coal .2D 38
GONERBY HILL FOOT .1C 161
Goodacre Rd. LE17: Ull .7F 143
Goode's Av. LE7: Sys .3D 60
Goode's La. LE7: Sys .2C 60
Goodheart Way LE3: Brau .5G 69
Gooding Av. LE3: Leic .3K 69
(not continuous)
Gooding Cl. LE3: Leic .4B 70
Goodriche Ho. *LE13: Mel M* .4G 117
*(off St Johns Ct.)*
Goodriche St. LE13: Mel M .4G 117
Goods Yd. Cl. LE11: Lou .6D 18
GOODWOOD .2D 72
Goodwood Bowling Club .7C 66
Goodwood Cl. LE16: L Bow .4H 151
Goodwood Cres. LE5: Leic .2D 72
Goodwood Rd. LE5: Leic .1D 72
Goosehills Rd. LE10: Bur .6H 103
Goose La. LE9: Barw .5K 99
Gopsall Rd. CV13: Con .5F 91
LE10: Hinc .1G 103
Gopsall St. LE2: Leic .3H 71
Gordon Av. LE2: Leic .7G 5 (3H 71)
Gordon Ho. LE2: Leic .4G 4 (2H 71)
Gordon Rd. LE11: Lou .4F 19
Gores La. LE16: L Bow .4G 151
Gorham Ri. LE9: B Ast .3B 86
Gorseburn Ho. LE3: Leic .6K 63
Gorse Hill LE7: Anst .1J 63
(not continuous)
Gorse Hill City Farm .5B 64
Gorse Hill Ind. Est. LE4: Beau L .2A 64
Gorse La. DE12: Moi .5A 22
LE2: Oad .5F 79
LE7: Sys .2B 60
Gorse Rd. LE67: Hug .6C 38
Gorsty Cl. LE4: Leic .3B 64
Goscote Dr. LE17: Lut .4J 153
Goscote Hall Rd. LE4: Birs .7F 59
Goscote Ho. LE2: Leic .5G 4 (2H 71)
GOSELEY DALE .2A 158
Gosford Dr. LE10: Hinc .2D 102
Goshawk Cl. LE9: B Ast .3C 86
Gosling Ct. LE2: Leic .6B 5
Gosling St. LE2: Leic .6B 5 (3E 70)
GOTHAM .1C 159
Gotham St. LE2: Leic .6G 5 (3H 71)
Gough Rd. LE5: Leic .1A 72
Goughs La. LE15: Bel R .5G 133
Goward St. LE16: Mkt H .4E 150
Gower St. LE1: Leic .1D 4 (7G 65)
Gowrie Cl. LE10: Hinc .1E 102
GRABY .2D 161
Grace Ct. LE2: Leic .7E 70
Gracedieu LE67: Whit .2F 27
Gracedieu La. LE12: Belt .7F 15
Gracedieu Rd. LE11: Lou .7A 18
LE67: Whit .4D 26
Grace Gdns. LE2: Leic .1E 76
Graceland Mobile Home Pk. LE16: Mkt H .5C 150
Grace Rd. LE2: Leic .7E 70
LE9: Des .2H 95
LE9: Sap .3K 105
Grafton Dr. LE18: Wig .6B 78
Grafton Pl. LE1: Leic .1C 4 (7F 65)
Grafton Rd. LE11: Lou .4C 18
GRAFTON UNDERWOOD .3C 165
Graham Ri. LE11: Lou .4B 18
Graham St. LE5: Leic .2G 4 (1H 71)
Gramer Ct. CV9: Manc .7A 96
Grampian Cl. LE2: Leic .1F 77
Grampian Way LE15: O'ham .4F 127
Granary Cl. LE3: Glen .7F 63
LE8: K Bea .4J 89
Granary M. LE1: Leic .2C 4
GRANBY .1A 160
Granby Av. LE5: Leic .1K 71
Granby Bldgs. LE1: Leic .4D 4
Granby Cl. LE10: Hinc .4F 103
Granby Dr. NG13: Bott .2G 107
Granby Ho. *LE13: Mel M* .4F 117
*(off Greenslade)*
Granby La. NG13: Plun .5C 106
Granby Pl. LE1: Leic .4D 4 (2F 71)
Granby Rd. LE2: Leic .1D 76
LE10: Hinc .4F 103
LE13: Mel M .1G 117
Granby St. LE1: Leic .4D 4 (2F 71)
LE11: Lou .6E 18
Grange, The LE9: Earl S .3D 100
LE19: Nar .2G 81
LE65: Pac .2A 36
Grange Av. LE3: Leic E .4F 69
LE7: Rear .4H 47
Grange Bus. Pk. LE8: Whet .7K 75
Grange Cl. LE2: Leic .5C 76
LE3: Glen .6F 63
LE6: Ratby .6B 62
LE8: G Gle .7K 79
LE9: N Ver .6H 93
LE15: L'ham .5D 122
LE65: Ash Z .6J 23
Grange Ct. LE2: Leic .8B 5
LE9: Des .1H 95
Grange Dr. DE74: C Don .5J 7
LE2: G Par .5B 76
LE8: Whet .1K 81
LE10: Bur .6H 103
LE13: Mel M .5G 117
Grange Farm Bus. Pk. LE67: Hug .7E 38
Grange Farm Cl. DE74: Hem .3A 8
Grangefields Dr. LE7: R'ley .6F 45
Grange La. CV13: Nail .7A 52 & 1D 92
LE2: Leic .6B 5 (3F 71)
LE7: Thurn .3H 73
LE12: Moun .4D 44
LE15: Seat .5H 139
LE16: East L .3B 140
LE16: T Lan .3E 140
Grange Pk. LE7: Thurn .3G 73
Granger Ct. LE11: Lou .6E 18
Grange Rd. CV13: Nail .7A 52
LE9: B Ast .4C 86
LE12: Shep .7C 16
LE18: Wig .3J 77
LE67: Hug .6D 38
LE67: Ibs .4K 51
Grange St. LE11: Lou .5E 18
Grange Vw. LE67: Ell .5E 52
Grangeway Rd. LE18: Wig .4K 77
Granite Cl. LE19: End .4E 74
Granite Way LE7: Sys .3A 60
LE12: Moun .7C 32
GRANTHAM .1C 161
Grantham Av. LE9: B Ast .2B 86
Grantham Rd. LE5: Leic .6E 66
NG13: Bott .2H 107
Grant Way LE2: Leic .4E 76
Grantwood Rd. LE13: Mel M .2H 117
Granville Av. LE2: Oad .2B 78
Granville Cres. LE18: Wig .3H 77
Granville Gdns. LE10: Hinc .3F 103
Granville Ind. Est.
DE11: W'lle .1B 22
Granville Rd. LE1: Leic .8G 5 (4H 71)
LE10: Hinc .3F 103
LE13: Mel M .2D 116
LE18: Wig .3H 77
Granville St. LE11: Lou .6E 18
LE16: Mkt H .5E 150
Grapes Gdn. Cl. LE12: Moun .1E 44
Grape St. LE1: Leic .2B 4 (1E 70)
Grasmere LE67: Coal .2H 39
Grasmere Cl. LE12: Bar S .3D 32
Grasmere Rd. LE11: Lou .4D 30
LE18: Wig .5B 78
Grasmere St. LE2: Leic .6A 5 (3E 70)
Grass Acres LE3: Brau .1J 75
Grassholme Dr. LE11: Lou .1J 29
Grassington Cl. LE4: Leic .2C 64
Grassy La. DE12: Mea .6F 35
LE67: Mark .5C 54
Gravel, The LE8: Bur O .6D 130
Gravel St. LE1: Leic .2C 4 (1F 71)
Gray La. LE12: Sileby .2K 45
Graylyn Ct. LE4: Thurm .7A 60
Grays Cl. DE74: C Don .5K 7
Grays Ct. LE12: Bar S .3D 32
LE19: End .5E 74
Gray St. LE11: Lou .1F 31
Grayswood Dr. LE4: Beau L .6A 58
Gt. Arler Rd. LE2: Leic .7G 71
GREAT BOWDEN .1H 151 (3A 164)
Gt. Bowden Hall LE16: G Bow .1E 150
Gt. Bowden Rd. LE16: Mkt H .4G 151
GREAT CASTERTON .2J 137 (1D 165)
Gt. Casterton Rd. PE9: Ryh .4F 129
Great Central Railway
Leicester North Station .1F 65
Loughborough Central Station .7G 19
Quorn & Woodhouse Station .6H 31
Rothley Station .7B 44
Great Central Railway Mus. .7G 19
Gt. Central Rd. LE11: Lou .7G 19
Gt. Central St. LE1: Leic .2A 4 (1E 70)
Gt. Central Way LE3: Leic .6A 5 (5D 70)
GREAT CRANSLEY .3B 164
GREAT DALBY .6C 120 (3A 160)
Gt. Dalby Rd. LE14: T Sat .3H 119
GREAT EASTON .5K 141 (2B 164)
Gt. Easton Rd. LE16: Brin .7J 141
LE16: C'ott, G Eas .4F 141
GREATFORD .3D 161
GREAT GIDDING .3D 165
GREAT GLEN .1K 85 (2D 163)
Gt. Glen By-Pass LE2: Oad .6G 79
LE8: G Gle .6G 79
GREAT GONERBY .1C 161
GREAT HALE .1D 161
GREAT HEATH .3A 162
Great La. LE14: F Wre .5H 115
LE15: Gree .4F 125
Great Mdw. Rd. LE4: Leic .3B 64
Great Nth. Rd. LE15: Gree, Stre .1K 125
PE9: G Cas, Stam, Tick .1F 137
GREAT OAKLEY .3B 164
GREAT OXENDON .3A 164
GREAT PONTON .1C 161
GREAT STRETTON .3K 79
GREAT WILNE .1B 158
Greaves Av. LE13: Mel M .3E 116
LE14: O Dal .4C 110
Grebe Cl. LE12: Bar S .3E 32
Grebe Way LE8: Whet .4K 81
Greedon Ri. LE12: Sileby .7J 33
Green, The CV9: Manc .7A 96
CV13: Dadl .1B 98
DE12: Don .3A 34
DE72: A Tre .1D 6
DE72: W Tre .3A 6
DE73: B Hil .7A 10
DE74: C Don .5H 7
DE74: Dis .4K 11
(not continuous)
LE7: Anst .7G 57
LE7: Sys .1D 60
LE7: Thru .7B 114
LE8: Bla .1C 82
LE8: K Bea .3H 89
LE9: Crof .4A 80
LE9: Hun .2B 80
LE10: S'ord .7H 105
LE12: Hat .1J 17
LE12: L Wha .6G 13


188 A-Z Leicestershire Atlas

Green, The LE12: Moun . . . . . . . . . . . . . .2E **44**
(not continuous)
LE12: Walt W . . . . . . . . . . . . . . . . . .6G **21**
LE14: Hos . . . . . . . . . . . . . . . . . . . .6B **108**
LE14: Sta . . . . . . . . . . . . . . . . . . . .2H **109**
LE15: Ext . . . . . . . . . . . . . . . . . . . .2C **128**
LE15: Lyd . . . . . . . . . . . . . . . . . . . .7E **138**
LE15: Rid . . . . . . . . . . . . . . . . . . . .2J **133**
LE16: C'ott . . . . . . . . . . . . . . . . . . .2H **141**
LE16: Dray . . . . . . . . . . . . . . . . . . .7F **141**
LE16: G Bow . . . . . . . . . . . . . . . . . .1H **151**
LE16: Lub . . . . . . . . . . . . . . . . . . . .7H **149**
LE17: Bitt . . . . . . . . . . . . . . . . . . . .2H **153**
LE17: H Bos . . . . . . . . . . . . . . . . . .6C **148**
LE17: Leire . . . . . . . . . . . . . . . . . . .3J **143**
LE65: Ash Z . . . . . . . . . . . . . . . . . . .5K **23**
LE67: D Hea . . . . . . . . . . . . . . . . . .7C **38**
LE67: Mear . . . . . . . . . . . . . . . . . . .4F **55**
LE67: N Bur . . . . . . . . . . . . . . . . . . .7C **50**
LE67: Thrin . . . . . . . . . . . . . . . . . . .4D **26**
NG11: King S . . . . . . . . . . . . . . . . . . .4K **9**
NG13: Bark V . . . . . . . . . . . . . . . . . .3A **106**
PE9: Ket . . . . . . . . . . . . . . . . . . . .6G **137**
Greenacre Dr. LE5: Leic . . . . . . . . . . .2D **72**
Greenacres LE67: Coal . . . . . . . . . . . .3H **39**
Greenacres Dr. LE17: Leic . . . . . . . . . .4G **153**
Green Bank LE13: Mel M . . . . . . . . . . .4H **117**
Greenbank Dr. LE2: Oad . . . . . . . . . . .3D **78**
Greenbank Rd. LE5: Leic . . . . . . . . . . .5F **67**
Greenclose La. LE11: Lou . . . . . . . . . . .6E **18**
Greencoat Ct. LE3: Leic . . . . . . . . . . . .7J **63**
Greencoat Rd. LE3: Leic . . . . . . . . . . . .7J **63**
Greencroft LE9: S Stan . . . . . . . . . . . .2J **105**
Greendale Farm Cvn. Pk. LE15: Whis . . .4B **122**
(not continuous)
Greendale Rd. LE2: G Par . . . . . . . . . . .5B **76**
GREEN END . . . . . . . . . . . . . . . . . .3A **162**
Greenfield Rd. DE12: Mea . . . . . . . . . .7F **35**
LE15: O'ham . . . . . . . . . . . . . . . . .2J **127**
Green Flds. LE8: Whet . . . . . . . . . . . . .2K **81**
Greenfields Dr. LE67: Coal . . . . . . . . . .3G **39**
Green Gdns. LE17: Ull . . . . . . . . . . . . .7F **143**
Greengate La. LE4: Leic . . . . . . . . . . . .6D **58**
GREENHILL . . . . . . . . . . . . . . . . . . .4G **39**
Greenhill LE12: Hat . . . . . . . . . . . . . . .1J **17**
Greenhill Cl. LE13: Mel M . . . . . . . . . . .2G **117**
LE19: Nar . . . . . . . . . . . . . . . . . . .2E **80**
Greenhill Dr. LE9: Barw . . . . . . . . . . . .3A **100**
Green Hill Ri. LE12: Hat . . . . . . . . . . . .7K **13**
Greenhill Rd. CV13: S Gol . . . . . . . . . . .3A **98**
LE2: Leic . . . . . . . . . . . . . . . . . . . .6G **71**
LE67: Coal . . . . . . . . . . . . . . . . . . .3G **39**
Greenhithe Rd. LE2: Leic . . . . . . . . . . .6D **70**
Greenhithe Wlk. LE2: Leic . . . . . . . . . .6E **70**
Greenland Av. LE5: Leic . . . . . . . . . . . .6C **66**
Greenland Dr. LE5: Leic . . . . . . . . . . . .6C **66**
Green La. CV13: Nail . . . . . . . . . . . . . .2A **92**
DE12: Snar . . . . . . . . . . . . . . . . . . .7H **49**
DE73: B Hil . . . . . . . . . . . . . . . . . . .5A **10**
DE74: Dis . . . . . . . . . . . . . . . . . . . .3K **11**
LE8: Count . . . . . . . . . . . . . . . . . . .5F **83**
LE9: Earl S . . . . . . . . . . . . . . . . . . .1E **100**
LE9: Stap . . . . . . . . . . . . . . . . . . . .1H **99**
LE12: Sea . . . . . . . . . . . . . . . . . . . .3K **33**
LE14: Harb . . . . . . . . . . . . . . . . . . .3D **108**
LE16: G Bow . . . . . . . . . . . . . . . . . .1F **151**
LE16: Mkt H . . . . . . . . . . . . . . . . . .6E **150**
LE16: Slaw . . . . . . . . . . . . . . . . . . .6A **140**
LE17: H Bos . . . . . . . . . . . . . . . . . .6C **148**
LE17: N Kil . . . . . . . . . . . . . . . . . . .2K **155**
LE67: Whit . . . . . . . . . . . . . . . . . . .2E **38**
NG13: East . . . . . . . . . . . . . . . . . . .3J **107**
Green La. Cl. LE5: Leic . . . . . . . . . . . .1B **72**
LE12: Sea . . . . . . . . . . . . . . . . . . . .3K **33**
Green La. Rd. LE5: Leic . . . . . . . . . . . .7K **65**
Greenlawn Wlk. LE4: Leic . . . . . . . . . .6D **64**
Green Leas DE72: A Tre . . . . . . . . . . . .1C **6**
Greenmoor Rd. LE10: Bur . . . . . . . . . .6G **103**
Green Rd. LE9: B Ast . . . . . . . . . . . . . .3C **86**
Greens Health & Fitness Cen.
Leicester . . . . . . . . . . . . . . . . .5E **64**
Greenside Cl. DE12: Don . . . . . . . . . . .3A **34**
Greenside Pl. LE2: Leic . . . . . . . . . . . .3F **77**
Greenslade LE13: Mel M . . . . . . . . . . .4F **117**
Greensward LE7: East G . . . . . . . . . . . .4G **47**
Green Wlk. LE3: Leic . . . . . . . . . . . . . .2J **69**
Greenway LE8: K Bea . . . . . . . . . . . . .3K **89**
Greenway, The LE4: Leic . . . . . . . . . . .4G **65**
Greenway Cl. LE7: R'ley . . . . . . . . . . . .6E **44**
Greenwich Cl. LE3: Leic . . . . . . . . . . . .5B **64**
LE19: Nar . . . . . . . . . . . . . . . . . . . .1F **81**
Greenwood Cl. LE4: Thurm . . . . . . . . . .7C **60**
Greenwood Rd. CV13: S Gol . . . . . . . . .3B **98**
LE5: Leic . . . . . . . . . . . . . . . . . . . .1B **72**
GREETHAM . . . . . . . . . . . .5F **125** (3C **161**)
Greetham Rd. LE15: Cott, Gree . . . . . . .6B **124**
LE15: Stre . . . . . . . . . . . . . . . . . . .2K **125**

Gregory Cl. CV13: B'one . . . . . . . . . . . .5B **92**
LE4: Thurm . . . . . . . . . . . . . . . . . . .6C **60**
Gregory Rd. CV13: B'one . . . . . . . . . . . .5B **92**
Gregorys Cl. LE3: Brau . . . . . . . . . . . . .6H **69**
Gregory St. LE11: Lou . . . . . . . . . . . . . .7F **19**
Gregson Cl. LE4: Leic . . . . . . . . . . . . . .1K **65**
GRENDON . . . . . . . . . . . . . . . . . . .2A **162**
Grendon Cl. LE18: Wig . . . . . . . . . . . . .5A **78**
GRENDON COMMON . . . . . . . . . . . . .2A **162**
Grenehams Cl. PE9: Ket . . . . . . . . . . . .6G **137**
Grenfell Rd. LE2: Leic . . . . . . . . . . . . . .7A **72**
Grenfell Wlk. LE2: Leic . . . . . . . . . . . . .7A **72**
Grenville Gdns. LE16: Mkt H . . . . . . . . .6D **150**
Gresley Cl. LE4: Leic . . . . . . . . . . . . . .2C **64**
LE7: Thurn . . . . . . . . . . . . . . . . . . .1H **73**
Gretna Way LE5: Leic . . . . . . . . . . . . . .7G **67**
GRETTON . . . . . . . . . . . . . . . . . . . .2C **165**
Gretton Ct. LE13: Mel M . . . . . . . . . . . .4E **116**
Gretton Gdns. LE14: W'ham . . . . . . . . .1F **121**
Grewcock Cl. LE17: C Mag . . . . . . . . . .5C **142**
Grey Cl. LE6: Groby . . . . . . . . . . . . . . .3D **62**
Grey Cres. LE6: New L . . . . . . . . . . . . . .4B **56**
Grey Friars LE1: Leic . . . . . . . . . .4C **4** (2F **71**)
Greylag Cl. LE8: Whet . . . . . . . . . . . . . .5K **81**
Greylands Paddock LE6: Groby . . . . . . . .3D **62**
Greys Dr. LE6: Groby . . . . . . . . . . . . . .4C **62**
Greystoke Cl. LE4: Leic . . . . . . . . . . . . .3E **64**
Greystoke Wlk. LE4: Leic . . . . . . . . . . . .3E **64**
Greystone Av. LE5: Leic . . . . . . . . . . . . .1D **72**
GRIFF . . . . . . . . . . . . . . . . . . . . . . .3A **162**
Griffin Cl. LE4: Thurm . . . . . . . . . . . . . .1C **66**
LE12: Shep . . . . . . . . . . . . . . . . . . .7C **16**
Griffith Gdns. LE65: Ash Z . . . . . . . . . . .6H **23**
Griffiths Cl. LE15: O'ham . . . . . . . . . . . .2J **127**
GRIFFYDAM . . . . . . . . . . .2A **26** (3B **158**)
Griggs Rd. LE11: Lou . . . . . . . . . . . . . . .3F **31**
Grimes Ga. DE74: Dis . . . . . . . . . . . . . .2A **12**
GRIMSTHORPE . . . . . . . . . . . . . . . . .2D **161**
GRIMSTON . . . . . . . . . . . . . . . . . . .2D **159**
Grimston Cl. LE4: Leic . . . . . . . . . . . . . .2C **66**
Grisedale Cl. LE2: Leic . . . . . . . . .8B **5** (4E **70**)
Grittar Cl. LE18: Wig . . . . . . . . . . . . . . .5A **78**
Grizedale Gro. LE19: Nar . . . . . . . . . . . .7D **74**
GROBY . . . . . . . . . . . . . . .3D **62** (1C **163**)
Groby By-Pass LE6: Groby . . . . . . . . . . .2D **62**
Groby La. LE6: New L . . . . . . . . . . . . . .6B **56**
Groby Rd. LE3: Glen . . . . . . . . . . . . . . .3F **63**
LE3: Leic . . . . . . . . . . . . . . . . . . . . .5J **63**
LE6: Ratby, Groby . . . . . . . . . . . . . . .5A **62**
(not continuous)
LE7: Anst . . . . . . . . . . . . . . . . . . . .2G **63**
Groby Trad. Est. LE6: Groby . . . . . . . . . .2C **62**
Grocot Rd. LE5: Leic . . . . . . . . . . . . . . .4C **72**
Grosvenor Cl. LE2: G Par . . . . . . . . . . . .7D **76**
Grosvenor Cres. LE2: Oad . . . . . . . . . . .1B **78**
LE10: Bur . . . . . . . . . . . . . . . . . . . .5K **103**
Grosvenor Ho. LE1: Leic . . . . . . . . . . . . .5C **4**
LE15: O'ham . . . . . . . . . . . . . . . . . .4H **127**
Grosvenor St. LE1: Leic . . . . . . . .1E **4** (7G **65**)
Grove, The LE9: Des . . . . . . . . . . . . . . .2G **95**
LE10: Hinc . . . . . . . . . . . . . . . . . . .3F **103**
LE11: Lou . . . . . . . . . . . . . . . . . . . .6C **18**
LE15: Ash . . . . . . . . . . . . . . . . . . . .2F **115**
Grovebury Rd. LE4: Leic . . . . . . . . . . . . .3E **64**
Grovebury Wlk. LE4: Leic . . . . . . . . . . . .3F **65**
Grove Farm Triangle LE19: End . . . . . . . .3J **75**
Grove La. LE12: Bar S . . . . . . . . . . . . . .4D **32**
Grove Pk. LE10: Bur . . . . . . . . . . . . . . .5K **103**
LE19: End . . . . . . . . . . . . . . . . . . . .3J **75**
Grove Rd. LE5: Leic . . . . . . . . . . . . . . . .1J **71**
LE8: Whet . . . . . . . . . . . . . . . . . . . .3K **81**
LE10: Bur . . . . . . . . . . . . . . . . . . . .6J **103**
LE11: Lou . . . . . . . . . . . . . . . . . . . .7C **18**
LE67: Whit . . . . . . . . . . . . . . . . . . . .7E **26**
Grove Way LE19: End . . . . . . . . . . . . . . .4K **75**
Guadaloupe Av. LE13: Mel M . . . . . . . . .6H **117**
Guestwick Grn. LE5: Ham . . . . . . . . . . . .4E **66**
Guild Cl. LE7: Crop . . . . . . . . . . . . . . . .2K **57**
Guildford Way LE11: Lou . . . . . . . . . . . .3A **30**
Guildhall . . . . . . . . . . . . . . . . . . . . .2E **70**
(off Guildhall La.)
Guildhall La. LE1: Leic . . . . . . . . .4B **4** (2E **70**)
Guilford Dr. LE18: Wig . . . . . . . . . . . . . .3H **77**
Guildford Rd. LE2: Leic . . . . . . . . . . . . .7K **71**
Guilford St. LE2: Leic . . . . . . . . . . . . . . .3J **71**
Guinevere Way LE3: Leic E . . . . . . . . . . .5E **68**
Gullet La. LE9: K Mux . . . . . . . . . . . . . .3A **68**
GUMLEY . . . . . . . . . . . . . . . . . . . . .2D **163**
Gumley Rd. LE8: Smee W . . . . . . . . . . . .5H **89**
LE16: Fox . . . . . . . . . . . . . . . . . . . .3F **149**
LE17: L'ton . . . . . . . . . . . . . . . . . . .2E **148**
Gumley Sq. LE19: End . . . . . . . . . . . . . .5F **75**
GUNBY . . . . . . . . . . . . . . . . . . . . . .2C **161**
Gunby Rd. NG33: Sew . . . . . . . . . . . . . .7K **113**
Gunnel La. LE15: Emp . . . . . . . . . . . . . .6D **128**
Gunsbrook Cl. LE16: G Bow . . . . . . . . . .1G **151**
GUNTHORPE . . . . . . . . . . . . . . . . . .1A **134**

Gunthorpe Cl. LE15: O'ham . . . . . . . . . .3K **127**
Gunthorpe Rd. LE3: Leic . . . . . . . . . . . . .3H **69**
Gurnall Rd. LE4: Beau L . . . . . . . . . . . . .2A **64**
Gurney Cres. LE19: Litt . . . . . . . . . . . . . .3G **81**
Gurney La. LE17: Kim . . . . . . . . . . . . . . .7A **146**
Guru Nanak Sikh Mus. & Temple . . . . .3A **4** (1E **70**)
Guscott Rd. LE67: Coal . . . . . . . . . . . . .3E **38**
Guthlaxton Av. LE2: Leic . . . . . . . .5G **4** (2H **71**)
LE17: Lut . . . . . . . . . . . . . . . . . . . .4J **153**
Guthlaxton Gap LE9: Crof . . . . . . . . . . . .5C **80**
Guthlaxton St. LE2: Leic . . . . . . . . .5G **4** (2H **71**)
Guthlaxton Way LE18: Wig . . . . . . . . . . .1A **84**
Guthridge Cres. LE3: Leic . . . . . . . . . . . .4B **70**
Gutteridge St. LE67: Coal . . . . . . . . . . . .3C **38**
Gwash Cl. PE9: Ryh . . . . . . . . . . . . . . . .5H **129**
Gwencole Av. LE3: Brau . . . . . . . . . . . . .7A **70**
Gwencole Cres. LE3: Brau . . . . . . . . . . . .1A **76**
Gwendolen Rd. LE5: Leic . . . . . . . . . . . .2K **71**
(not continuous)
Gwendolen Rd. Gdns. LE5: Leic . . . . . . . .2A **72**
Gwendolin Av. LE4: Birs . . . . . . . . . . . . .6H **59**
Gwendoline Av. LE10: Hinc . . . . . . . . . . .1D **102**
Gwendoline Dr. LE8: Count . . . . . . . . . . .6D **82**
Gynsill Cl. LE7: Anst . . . . . . . . . . . . . . . .1J **63**
Gynsill La. LE7: Anst . . . . . . . . . . . . . . .3H **63**
Gynsills Hall LE3: Glen . . . . . . . . . . . . . .3H **63**

## H

HACCONBY . . . . . . . . . . . . . . . . . . .2D **161**
HACEBY . . . . . . . . . . . . . . . . . . . . .1D **161**
Hackett Cl. LE65: Ash Z . . . . . . . . . . . . .5K **23**
Hackett Rd. LE3: Leic . . . . . . . . . . . . . . .6K **63**
Haddenham Rd. LE3: Leic . . . . . . . . . . . .5C **70**
HADDON . . . . . . . . . . . . . . . . . . . . .2D **165**
Haddon Cl. LE7: Sys . . . . . . . . . . . . . . .2B **60**
Haddon St. LE2: Leic . . . . . . . . . . . . . . .2J **71**
Haddon Way LE11: Lou . . . . . . . . . . . . . .5E **30**
Hadfield Dr. LE13: Mel M . . . . . . . . . . . .3F **117**
Hadrian Cl. LE7: Sys . . . . . . . . . . . . . . .3A **60**
LE10: Hinc . . . . . . . . . . . . . . . . . . . .2C **102**
Hadrian Rd. LE4: Leic . . . . . . . . . . . . . .1D **64**
LE4: Thurm . . . . . . . . . . . . . . . . . . .6A **60**
Hagley Cl. LE16: L Bow . . . . . . . . . . . . .4H **151**
Haig Pl. LE3: Leic . . . . . . . . . . . . . . . . .5A **70**
Haileybury Av. LE65: Ash Z . . . . . . . . . . .4J **23**
Hailey Av. LE11: Lou . . . . . . . . . . . . . . .5A **18**
Hainsworth Cl. LE15: L'ham . . . . . . . . . .5C **122**
Halberd Cl. LE10: Bur . . . . . . . . . . . . . .7G **103**
Halcroft Ri. LE18: Wig . . . . . . . . . . . . . .7K **77**
Half Cft., The LE7: Sys . . . . . . . . . . . . . .1C **60**
Half Moon Cres. LE2: Oad . . . . . . . . . . .1E **78**
Halford Cl. LE8: G Gle . . . . . . . . . . . . . .1K **85**
LE8: Whet . . . . . . . . . . . . . . . . . . . .3K **81**
Halford Ho. LE8: G Gle . . . . . . . . . . . . . .7K **79**
Halford Rd. LE8: K Bea . . . . . . . . . . . . .3H **89**
Halford St. LE1: Leic . . . . . . . . . .4D **4** (7A **71**)
LE7: Sys . . . . . . . . . . . . . . . . . . . . .2C **60**
Halifax Rd. LE4: Leic . . . . . . . . . . . . . . .3E **64**
Halkin St. LE4: Leic . . . . . . . . . . . . . . . .5H **65**
Hallam Av. LE4: Birs . . . . . . . . . . . . . . .6F **59**
Hallam Cl. LE9: Earl S . . . . . . . . . . . . . .2F **101**
Hallam Cres. E. LE3: Leic . . . . . . . . . . . .5K **69**
HALLAM FIELDS . . . . . . . . . . . . . . . .1B **158**
Hallam Flds. DE74: C Don . . . . . . . . . . . .6J **7**
Hallamford Rd. LE12: Shep . . . . . . . . . . .3B **16**
HALLATON . . . . . . . . . . . .6A **132** (2A **164**)
Hallaton Mus. . . . . . . . . . . . . . . . . . .6A **132**
Hallaton Rd. LE5: Leic . . . . . . . . . . . . . .6B **66**
LE7: Tug . . . . . . . . . . . . . . . . . . . . .2C **132**
LE15: Alle . . . . . . . . . . . . . . . . . . . .7G **133**
LE16: Horn . . . . . . . . . . . . . . . . . . .6D **132**
LE16: Med . . . . . . . . . . . . . . . . . . . .4B **140**
Hallaton St. LE2: Leic . . . . . . . . . . . . . .1E **76**
Hallbrook Rd. LE9: B Ast . . . . . . . . . . . .6D **86**
Hall Cl. DE11: Blac . . . . . . . . . . . . . . . .3E **22**
LE2: G Par . . . . . . . . . . . . . . . . . . . .5B **76**
LE7: Coss . . . . . . . . . . . . . . . . . . . .4K **45**
LE8: Kib H . . . . . . . . . . . . . . . . . . . .2H **89**
LE15: Cott . . . . . . . . . . . . . . . . . . .6A **124**
LE15: Whis . . . . . . . . . . . . . . . . . . .2D **122**
Hall Cft. LE12: Shep . . . . . . . . . . . . . . .6D **16**
Hallcroft Av. LE8: Count . . . . . . . . . . . . .6E **82**
Hallcroft Gdns. LE8: Count . . . . . . . . . . .6E **82**
Hall Dr. CV13: S Gol . . . . . . . . . . . . . . .3B **98**
LE2: Oad . . . . . . . . . . . . . . . . . . . .2D **78**
LE12: Bur W . . . . . . . . . . . . . . . . . . .3F **21**
LE14: Ash . . . . . . . . . . . . . . . . . . .3F **115**
LE14: Bur L . . . . . . . . . . . . . . . . . . .3C **120**
Halley Cl. LE4: Beau L . . . . . . . . . . . . . .7A **58**
Hall Farm Cl. DE74: C Don . . . . . . . . . . . .5J **7**
LE7: Quen . . . . . . . . . . . . . . . . . . . .7H **47**
Hall Farm Ct. LE12: Sea . . . . . . . . . . . . .4K **33**
Hall Farm Cres. LE9: B Ast . . . . . . . . . . .5E **86**
Hall Farm Rd. LE7: Thurc . . . . . . . . . . . .3B **58**
Hallfield Cl. CV9: Twy . . . . . . . . . . . . . . .2B **90**

Hallfields—Hawthorne Rd.

**Hallfields** CV9: Twy 2B **90**
**Hallfields La.** LE7: R'ley 6E **44**
**Hall Gdns.** CV9: With 5A **96**
DE74: Hem 4B **8**
LE8: G Gle 1K **85**
LE15: Upp 2C **138**
(not continuous)
LE67: Rav 4H **37**
**Hall Ga.** DE74: Dis 4K **11**
LE67: Coal 4J **39**
**Hallgate Dr.** LE3: Leic 3K **63**
**Hall La.** CV9: With 5B **96**
CV13: Osb 7B **92**
DE12: Don 4A **34**
LE2: Leic 1C **76**
LE15: S Luf 4C **136**
LE16: Dray 7G **141**
**Hall La.** LE17: Ash M 1G **145**
LE17: Bitt 7C **144**
LE17: Ull 7F **143**
LE17: Walt 7B **146**
LE65: Pac 2K **35**
LE67: Whit 7F **27**
**Hall Leys** LE12: Quo 6A **32**
**Hall Leys La.** DE73: K New 6A **6**
**Hall Orchard La.** LE14: F Wre 5H **115**
**Hall Rd.** LE7: Scra 6H **67**
LE10: Bur 5G **103**
**Halls Ct.** LE9: S Stan 1K **105**
**Halls Cres.** LE10: S'ord 6H **105**
(not continuous)
**Hall St.** LE67: Ibs 5J **51**
**Hall Wlk.** LE19: End 4F **75**
**Halsbury St.** LE2: Leic 4K **71**
HALSTEAD 2K **131** (1A **164**)
**Halstead Ri.** LE7: T Hil 2H **131**
**Halstead Rd.** LE7: T Hil 2H **131**
LE12: Moun 3C **44**
**Halstead St.** LE5: Leic 1K **71**
**Halter Slade** LE18: Wig 7A **78**
**Halywell Nook** LE7: R'ley 4F **45**
**Hamble Cl.** LE9: Des 2H **95**
**Hambledon Cres.** LE11: Lou 3D **30**
LE15: Cott 4C **124**
**Hambledon Grn.** LE4: Leic 1D **64**
**Hamble Rd.** LE2: Oad 2E **78**
**Hambleton Cl.** LE3: Leic E 4D **68**
LE15: O'ham 4K **127**
**Hambleton Rd.** LE15: O'ham 7K **127**
**Hambury Cl.** LE15: O'ham 5F **127**
**Hamelin Rd.** LE3: Leic 3K **69**
HAMERTON 3D **165**
**Hamilford Cl.** LE7: Scra 5G **67**
HAMILTON 3E **66** (1D **163**)
**Hamilton Bus. Pk.** LE5: Ham 2D **66**
**Hamilton Circ.** LE5: Ham 3F **67**
**Hamilton Cl.** LE10: Hinc 1D **102**
**Hamilton Dr.** LE13: Mel M 6F **117**
**Hamilton La.** LE7: Bark T, Scra 4G **67**
**Hamilton Rd.** LE67: Coal 4J **39**
**Hamilton St.** LE2: Leic 3H **71**
**Hamilton Way** LE5: Leic 4D **66**
**Hammercliffe Rd.** LE5: Leic 6J **65**
**Hammond Way** LE16: Mkt H 3E **150**
**Hampden Rd.** LE4: Leic 4A **66**
**Hampshire Rd.** LE2: Leic 1D **76**
**Hampton Cl.** LE2: G Par 7D **76**
LE18: Wig 6A **78**
LE67: Coal 4F **39**
**Hamstead Cl.** LE19: Nar 1F **81**
**Hams Way** LE10: S'ord 7G **105**
**Hanbury Gdns.** LE15: B Rut 6C **126**
**Hanbury Rd.** LE5: Leic 3F **73**
HANBY 1D **161**
**Hand Av.** LE3: Leic 3J **69**
(not continuous)
**Hand Cl.** LE3: Leic 3J **69**
**Handley St.** LE2: Leic 1E **76**
**Hand's Wlk.** NG13: Bott 2G **107**
**Hanford Way** LE11: Lou 5F **19**
**Hangmans La.** LE10: Hinc 7H **99**
**Hannah Pde.** LE4: Birs 6G **59**
**Hannah's Fld.** LE15: Rid 2J **133**
**Hannam Ct.** LE1: Leic 2D **4** (1F **71**)
**Hanover Cl.** LE5: Leic 5D **66**
**Hanover Ct.** LE10: Bur 5H **103**
LE11: Lou 5B **18**
**Hanover Dr.** LE12: Sileby 1K **45**
**Hansen Ct.** LE18: Wig 6G **77**
**Hansom Ct.** LE10: Hinc 3G **103**
**Hansom Rd.** LE10: Hinc 1J **103**
HANTHORPE 2D **161**
**Hanworth Cl.** LE5: Ham 4E **66**
**Haramead Bus. Cen.** LE1: Leic 7H **65**
**Haramead Rd.** LE1: Leic 7H **65**
Harborough Leisure Cen. 7F **151**
HARBOROUGH MAGNA 3B **162**
Harborough Mus. 4E **150**
**Harborough Rd.** LE2: Oad 2C **78**
LE7: Bill 7K **131**
LE8: Kib H 2K **89**
LE16: Bray 7J **151**
LE16: Din 2J **151**
LE16: East F 7B **150**
LE16: G Ox 7F **151**
LE16: Lub 7K **149**
LE16: Mkt H 1C **150**
Harborough Theatre 4E **150**
HARBY 2D **108** (1A **160**)
**Harby La.** LE14: Hos 6B **108**
LE14: Sta 2F **109**
NG13: Plun 7B **106**
Harby Nature Reserve 2E **108**
**Harcourt Cl.** LE7: Sys 1C **60**
**Harcourt Est.** LE8: Kib H 2J **89**
**Harcourt Pl.** DE74: C Don 4K **7**
**Harcourt Rd.** LE8: K Bea 3H **89**
LE18: Wig 7A **78**
**Harcourt Spinney** CV13: Mkt B 1C **94**
**Harcourt St.** LE16: Mkt H 4D **150**
**Harcourt Way** LE19: Brau 2H **75**
**Hardie Cres.** LE3: Brau 5H **69**
**Harding St.** LE1: Leic 1A **4** (7E **64**)
**Hardwick Cl.** LE15: O'ham 3K **127**
**Hardwick Ct.** LE3: Leic 4C **70**
**Hardwick Cres.** LE7: Sys 2B **60**
**Hardwick Dr.** LE11: Lou 6A **18**
**Hardwicke Rd.** LE19: Nar 1D **80**
**Hardwick Rd.** LE5: Leic 3G **73**
**Hardy Cl.** LE10: Hinc 6G **99**
**Hardy's Av.** LE4: Leic 2J **65**
**Harebell Cl.** LE5: Ham 3D **66**
**Harebell Dr.** LE13: Mel M 7D **116**
**Harecroft Cres.** LE9: Sap 3K **105**
**Harefield Av.** LE3: Leic 7B **70**
**Harene Cres.** LE3: Leic E 4C **68**
**Hare Pie Vw.** LE16: Hall 7B **132**
**Harewood Cl.** LE15: L'ham 5D **122**
**Harewood St.** LE5: Leic 7K **65**
**Harford Way** LE10: Bur 4H **103**
**Harland Cl.** LE9: Cosb 6H **81**
LE14: Ash 3G **115**
HARLAXTON 1B **160**
**Harlaxton St.** LE3: Leic 5B **70**
**Harlaxton Wlk.** LE3: Leic 5C **70**
**Harlech Cl.** LE11: Lou 5C **18**
**Harlech Wlk.** LE13: Mel M 2F **117**
HARLEQUIN 1D **159**
**Harlequin Rd.** LE12: Sileby 2J **45**
**Harlequin Way** LE8: Whet 5K **81**
**Harley Cl.** LE12: Shep 1D **28**
**Harold's La.** LE19: End 4F **75**
**Harold St.** LE2: Leic 7E **70**
**Harper's La.** CV9: Manc 7A **96**
**Harratts Cl.** LE67: Ibs 4K **51**
**Harrier Cl.** LE9: B Ast 3C **86**
**Harrier Parkway** LE17: Lut 4D **152**
**Harriman Cl.** LE12: Shep 6D **16**
HARRINGTON 3A **164**
**Harrington Cl.** LE12: Quo 5A **32**
**Harrington Cres.** *LE15: Ext 3D 128*
*(off Campden Cl.)*
**Harrington Rd.** LE12: Shep 7E **16**
LE18: Wig 5A **78**
**Harrington St.** LE4: Leic 6J **65**
**Harrington Way** LE15: O'ham 5G **127**
HARRINGWORTH 2C **165**
**Harringworth Rd.** LE5: Leic 3D **72**
**Harris Cl.** LE9: B Ast 5D **86**
**Harris Grn.** LE3: Brau 4G **69**
**Harrison Cl.** LE3: Glen 6G **63**
LE8: Whet 4A **82**
LE9: Earl S 2E **100**
LE16: Mkt H 7D **150**
LE18: Wig 7H **77**
**Harrison Pl.** LE67: Coal 4C **38**
**Harrison Rd.** LE4: Leic 6H **65**
**Harrison's Row** LE7: Sys 1D **60**
**Harrison St.** LE4: Thurm 5A **60**
**Harris Rd.** LE4: Leic 3B **64**
**Harrod Dr.** LE16: Mkt H 3G **151**
**Harrogate Rd.** LE4: Leic 5J **65**
**Harrogate Way** LE18: Wig 6A **78**
**Harrop Cl.** LE8: Bla 1A **82**
**Harrowbrook Ind. Est.** LE10: Hinc 4B **102**
**Harrowbrook Rd.** LE10: Hinc 4B **102**
**Harrow Cl.** LE3: Leic E 6D **68**
LE65: Ash Z 3J **23**
**Harrowden Ct.** LE5: Leic 1C **72**
**Harrowden Ri.** LE5: Leic 1C **72**
**Harrowgate Dr.** LE4: Birs 4E **58**
**Harrow Rd.** LE3: Leic 3C **70**
**Harry French Ct.** LE11: Lou 6C **18**
HARSTON 1B **160**
**Hart Cl.** LE8: Whet 4K **81**
**Hartfield Rd.** LE5: Leic 6F **67**
**Hartington Grn.** LE10: Bur 5H **103**
**Hartington Rd.** LE2: Leic 1J **71**
**Hartland Dr.** LE13: Mel M 7F **117**
LE16: L Bow 4G **151**
**Hartopp Cl.** LE7: Bush 2J **73**
**Hartopp Rd.** LE2: Leic 5H **71**
LE13: Mel M 7F **117**
**Hart Rd.** LE5: Leic 1J **71**
HARTSHILL 2A **162**
**Hartshorn Cl.** LE4: Thurm 7B **60**
HARTSHORNE 2A **158**
**Harvard Cl.** LE2: Oad 2D **78**
**Harvest Cl.** LE4: Leic 3B **64**
LE19: Litt 3H **81**
**Harvester Cl.** LE3: Leic E 6D **68**
**Harvesters Cnr.** LE7: East G 5G **47**
**Harvest Gro.** DE12: Moi 6C **22**
**Harvest Way** LE9: B Ast 6D **86**
**Harvey Cl.** LE8: Bla 7B **76**
**Harvey Ct.** DE74: C Don 5K **7**
**Harvey Rd.** DE74: C Don 6K **7**
**Harveys Cl.** LE9: Sap 4J **105**
**Harvey Wlk.** LE1: Leic 4A **4** (2E **70**)
**Harwin Rd.** LE5: Leic 3D **72**
**Harwood Dr.** LE10: Hinc 6J **99**
HASELBECH 3A **164**
**Haskell Cl.** LE3: Brau 5H **69**
**Haslyn Wlk.** LE67: Coal 4H **39**
(not continuous)
**Hassal Rd.** LE3: Leic 6J **63**
**Hassell M.** LE7: Rear 3H **47**
**Hastings, The** LE3: Brau 6H **69**
LE67: Ibs 3K **51**
**Hastings Av.** LE67: Whit 7G **27**
**Hastings Cl.** DE73: B Hil 7A **10**
LE8: Flec 5C **88**
**Hastings Dr.** LE9: Barw 3A **100**
**Hastings Hollow** DE12: Mea 1E **48**
**Hastings Rd.** DE11: Swad 1A **22**
LE5: Leic 6K **65**
LE9: K Mux 3C **68**
LE12: W Eav 4D **42**
**Hastings St.** DE74: C Don 6K **7**
LE11: Lou 6E **18**
**Hastings Wlk.** LE3: Brau 6J **69**
**Hastings Way** LE65: Ash Z 6A **24**
**Hathaway Av.** LE3: Brau 6K **69**
**Hatherleigh Rd.** LE5: Leic 4B **72**
HATHERN 1J **17** (2C **159**)
**Hathern Dr.** LE11: Lou 4H **17**
LE12: Hat 3J **17**
**Hathern Rd.** LE12: L Wha 6H **13**
LE12: Shep 5E **16**
**Hathern Turn** LE12: Hat 7K **13**
**Hat Rd.** LE3: Brau 1J **75**
**Hattern Av.** LE4: Leic 2D **64**
**Haulton Dr.** DE74: C Don 4J **7**
**Havelock St.** LE2: Leic 7B **5** (3E **70**)
LE11: Lou 6D **18**
**Haven, The** LE11: Lou 5B **18**
**Haven Cl.** LE3: Leic E 5D **68**
LE12: Belt 4H **15**
**Havencrest Dr.** LE5: Leic 7D **66**
**Haven Rd.** CV13: Mkt B 3C **94**
**Haven Wlk.** LE5: Leic 1G **73**
**Hawarden Av.** LE5: Leic 7B **66**
**Hawcliffe Rd.** LE12: Moun 1C **44**
**Hawk Cl.** LE9: B Ast 3C **86**
**Hawker Rd.** LE2: Oad 4F **79**
**Hawkesbury Rd.** LE2: Leic 1E **76**
HAWKES END 3A **162**
**Hawkes Hill** LE2: Leic 3F **77**
**Hawke Way** LE17: Lut 2C **152**
**Hawkins Cl.** LE10: Hinc 6G **99**
HAWKSWORTH 1A **160**
**Hawley Cl.** LE67: Hug 6E **38**
**Hawley Rd.** LE10: Hinc 4F **103**
**Hawthorn Av.** LE4: Birs 5H **59**
**Hawthorn Bldg.** LE2: Leic 5B **4**
**Hawthorn Cl.** LE9: Leic E 5C **68**
LE14: O Dal 7A **110**
LE67: Coal 3E **38**
**Hawthorn Ct.** LE2: Leic 8B **5**
**Hawthorn Cres.** LE10: Bur 7H **103**
**Hawthorn Dr.** LE8: Bla 3B **82**
LE13: Mel M 2F **117**
LE15: Upp 1C **138**
**Hawthorne Av.** LE12: Hat 1J **17**
**Hawthorne Cl.** DE12: Mea 6E **34**
LE2: Oad 5J **79**
**Hawthorne Ct.** LE5: Leic 5C **72**
**Hawthorne Dr.** LE5: Leic 4C **72**
LE67: Ibs 5J **51**
LE67: Thor 2J **93**
**Hawthorne Rd.** LE17: N Kil 2K **155**

190 A-Z Leicestershire Atlas

Hawthorne St. LE3: Leic . . . . . . . . . . . . . . . .7B 64
Hawthorne Way LE9: Barw . . . . . . . . . . . . .4A 100
Hawthorn Gro. LE2: Oad . . . . . . . . . . . . . . .1D 78
Hawthorn Ri. LE6: Groby . . . . . . . . . . . . . . .3D 62
Hawthorn Rd. DE74: C Don . . . . . . . . . . . . . .3K 7
　LE12: Moun . . . . . . . . . . . . . . . . . . . . .2E 44
Hawthorns, The LE2: Leic . . . . . . . . . . . . . .6K 71
　LE8: Count . . . . . . . . . . . . . . . . . . . . .5E 82
　LE17: Lut . . . . . . . . . . . . . . . . . . . . . .4H 153
　LE67: Mark . . . . . . . . . . . . . . . . . . . . .5G 55
HAWTHORPE . . . . . . . . . . . . . . . . . . . . . .2D 161
Haybarn Cl. LE19: Litt . . . . . . . . . . . . . . . .3H 81
Haybrooke Rd. LE12: Sileby . . . . . . . . . . . . .7K 33
Hayden Av. LE2: Oad . . . . . . . . . . . . . . . . .4F 79
Hayden Cl. LE4: Leic . . . . . . . . . . . . . . . . .3E 64
Hayden Wlk. LE2: Oad . . . . . . . . . . . . . . . .4F 79
Haydon Rd. LE11: Lou . . . . . . . . . . . . . . . .6C 18
Hayes Cl. LE15: L'ham . . . . . . . . . . . . . . . .5C 122
　LE67: Whit . . . . . . . . . . . . . . . . . . . . . .7F 27
Hayes End LE9: Des . . . . . . . . . . . . . . . . .2H 95
Hayes Rd. LE18: Wig . . . . . . . . . . . . . . . . .5A 78
Hayfield Cl. LE3: Glen . . . . . . . . . . . . . . . .6F 63
Hay Hill LE12: Bar S . . . . . . . . . . . . . . . . .6G 33
Hayling Cres. LE5: Leic . . . . . . . . . . . . . . .6C 66
Haymarket LE1: Leic . . . . . . . . .3D 4 (1F 71)
Haymarket Cen. LE1: Leic . . . . . . .3D 4 (1F 71)
Haymarket Theatre . . . . . . . . . . . . .2D 4 (1F 71)
Haymeadow Cl. LE11: Lou . . . . . . . . . . . . . .3D 30
Haynes Rd. LE5: Leic . . . . . . . . . . . . . . . . .7A 66
Hays La. LE10: Hinc . . . . . . . . . . . . . . . . .4E 102
Hayward Av. LE11: Lou . . . . . . . . . . . . . . . .1G 31
Haywood Cl. LE5: Leic . . . . . . . . . . . . . . . .3D 72
Hazeland Ct. LE17: Lut . . . . . . . . . . . . . . . .4J 153
Hazelbank Cl. LE4: Leic . . . . . . . . . . . . . . .4D 64
Hazelbank Rd. LE8: Count . . . . . . . . . . . . . .5F 83
Hazel Cl. DE12: Mea . . . . . . . . . . . . . . . . .7E 34
　LE4: Birs . . . . . . . . . . . . . . . . . . . . . .5H 59
　LE8: G Gle . . . . . . . . . . . . . . . . . . . . .7K 79
　LE19: Litt . . . . . . . . . . . . . . . . . . . . . .3G 81
Hazeldene Rd. LE5: Ham . . . . . . . . . . . . . . .4F 67
Hazel Dr. LE3: Brau . . . . . . . . . . . . . . . . .2K 75
　LE17: Lut . . . . . . . . . . . . . . . . . . . . . .4H 153
Hazel Gro. DE12: Moi . . . . . . . . . . . . . . . . .5D 22
　LE16: Hall . . . . . . . . . . . . . . . . . . . . .6B 132
Hazelhead Rd. LE7: Anst . . . . . . . . . . . . . . .7H 57
Hazel Kaye's Garden Nursery . . . . . . . . . . . .3H 47
Hazelnut Cl. LE5: Leic . . . . . . . . . . . . . . . .3D 72
Hazelrigg Cl. DE74: C Don . . . . . . . . . . . . . .4H 7
Hazel Rd. LE11: Lou . . . . . . . . . . . . . . . . .3E 30
Hazel St. LE2: Leic . . . . . . . . . .9C 5 (4F 71)
　LE9: Des . . . . . . . . . . . . . . . . . . . . . .2G 95
Hazel Way LE9: Barw . . . . . . . . . . . . . . . . .3K 99
Hazelwood Cres. LE14: Ash . . . . . . . . . . . . .2F 115
Hazelwood Rd. LE5: Leic . . . . . . . . . . . . . . .4K 71
　LE18: Wig . . . . . . . . . . . . . . . . . . . . .1G 83
Hazlemere Cl. LE8: Bla . . . . . . . . . . . . . . . .2B 82
Heacham Dr. LE4: Leic . . . . . . . . . . . . . . . .3B 64
Headingley Cl. LE4: Beau L . . . . . . . . . . . . .6C 58
　LE67: Coal . . . . . . . . . . . . . . . . . . . . .5G 39
Headland, The LE7: East G . . . . . . . . . . . . . .4H 47
Headland Rd. LE5: Leic . . . . . . . . . . . . . . . .4C 72
Headlands, The LE16: Mkt H . . . . . . . . . . . . .3F 151
Headley Rd. LE3: Brau . . . . . . . . . . . . . . . .1K 75
Heafield Dr. DE74: Keg . . . . . . . . . . . . . . . .6H 9
Healey Cl. LE4: Leic . . . . . . . . . . . . . . . . .2D 64
Healey St. LE18: Wig . . . . . . . . . . . . . . . . .7F 77
Heanor St. LE1: Leic . . . . . . . . . .1B 4 (7E 64)
Heards Cl. LE18: Wig . . . . . . . . . . . . . . . . .1A 84
Heard Wlk. LE4: Leic . . . . . . . . . . . . . . . . .3B 64
Hearth St. LE16: Mkt H . . . . . . . . . . . . . . .4D 150
Heart of The National Forest Vis. Cen. . . . . . .7A 22
Heath Av. LE7: Sys . . . . . . . . . . . . . . . . . .2B 60
　LE19: End . . . . . . . . . . . . . . . . . . . . . .6J 75
Heathbrook Dr. LE6: Ratby . . . . . . . . . . . . . .6B 62
Heathcote Dr. LE12: Sileby . . . . . . . . . . . . .7K 33
Heathcote St. LE11: Lou . . . . . . . . . . . . . . .6E 18
Heathcott Rd. LE2: Leic . . . . . . . . . . . . . . .1E 76
Heath Ct. LE9: Earl S . . . . . . . . . . . . . . . .3C 100
Heath Dr. LE15: Cott . . . . . . . . . . . . . . . .6B 124
HEATH END . . . . . . . . . . . . . . . . . . . . . .2A 158
HEATHER . . . . . . . . . . . . . . . .3F 51 (3A 158)
Heatherbrook Rd. LE4: Beau L . . . . . . . . . . . .7A 58
Heather Cres. LE13: Mel M . . . . . . . . . . . . .7D 116
Heatherdale LE67: Ibs . . . . . . . . . . . . . . . .4J 51
Heather Ho. LE67: Hea . . . . . . . . . . . . . . . .3F 51
Heather La. LE65: Pac . . . . . . . . . . . . . . . .3A 36
　LE67: Nor H . . . . . . . . . . . . . . . . . . . .6D 36
　LE67: Rav . . . . . . . . . . . . . . . . . . . . . .7G 37
Heather Rd. LE2: Leic . . . . . . . . . . . . . . . .7G 71
HEATHERTON . . . . . . . . . . . . . . . . . . . . .1A 158
Heather Way LE8: Count . . . . . . . . . . . . . . .6F 83
Heathfield LE67: Thrin . . . . . . . . . . . . . . . .3E 26
Heathfield Rd. LE18: Wig . . . . . . . . . . . . . .3K 77
Heathgate Cl. LE4: Birs . . . . . . . . . . . . . . .5F 59
Heath La. DE11: Blac . . . . . . . . . . . . . . . . .2E 22
　　　　　　　　　　　(not continuous)
　LE9: Barw . . . . . . . . . . . . . . . . . . . . .2B 100

Heath La. Sth. LE9: Earl S . . . . . . . . . . . . .2C 100
Heathley Cl. LE3: Leic E . . . . . . . . . . . . . . .5D 68
Heathley Pk. Dr. LE3: Leic . . . . . . . . . . . . .5A 64
Heath Rd. CV13: Mkt B . . . . . . . . . . . . . . . .2B 94
　LE67: Bag . . . . . . . . . . . . . . . . . . . . .2G 93
Heawood Way LE3: Brau . . . . . . . . . . . . . . .6H 69
Heays Cl. LE3: Leic . . . . . . . . . . . . . . . . . .6J 63
Hebden Cl. LE2: Leic . . . . . . . . . . . . . . . . .6C 76
Hecadeck La. LE14: N Bro . . . . . . . . . . . . .2C 110
HECKINGTON . . . . . . . . . . . . . . . . . . . . .1D 161
Hector Rd. LE67: Coal . . . . . . . . . . . . . . . .2D 38
Heddington Cl. LE2: Leic . . . . . . . . . . . . . . .3G 77
Heddington Way LE2: Leic . . . . . . . . . . . . . .3G 77
Hedge Rd. LE67: Hug . . . . . . . . . . . . . . . . .5C 38
Hedgerow La. LE9: K Mux . . . . . . . . . . . . . .2B 68
Hedgerow Rd. LE3: Leic . . . . . . . . . . . . . . .3A 70
Hefford Gdns. LE4: Leic . . . . . . . . . . . . . . .2D 64
Heighton Cres. LE19: Litt . . . . . . . . . . . . . .3G 81
Heights, The LE16: L Bow . . . . . . . . . . . . . .5H 151
Helena Cres. LE4: Leic . . . . . . . . . . . . . . . .2E 64
Helmdon Rd. LE2: Leic . . . . . . . . .9A 5 (4D 70)
Helmsdale Cl. LE67: Coal . . . . . . . . . . . . . .3J 39
Helmsley Rd. LE2: Leic . . . . . . . . . . . . . . . .3F 77
HELPRINGHAM . . . . . . . . . . . . . . . . . . . .1D 161
HELPSTON . . . . . . . . . . . . . . . . . . . . . .1D 165
Helston Cl. LE18: Wig . . . . . . . . . . . . . . . .7J 77
HEMINGTON
　　Derby . . . . . . . . . . . . . . . .3B 8 (2B 158)
　　Peterborough . . . . . . . . . . . . . . . . . .3D 165
Hemington Ct. DE74: Hem . . . . . . . . . . . . . . .4A 8
Hemington Hill DE74: Hem . . . . . . . . . . . . . . .4A 8
Hemington La. DE74: Lock . . . . . . . . . . . . . . .3C 8
Hemington Rd. LE5: Leic . . . . . . . . . . . . . . .4F 73
Hemlock Cl. LE19: Nar . . . . . . . . . . . . . . . .7D 74
Hendon Grange LE2: Leic . . . . . . . . . . . . . . .7A 72
Henley Cres. LE3: Brau . . . . . . . . . . . . . . . .6K 69
Henley Rd. LE3: Leic . . . . . . . . . . . . . . . . .1C 70
Henray Av. LE2: Leic . . . . . . . . . . . . . . . . .6C 76
Henry Cl. LE3: Leic E . . . . . . . . . . . . . . . .5D 68
Henry Dane Way LE67: New . . . . . . . . . . . . .1G 25
Henry St. LE10: Hinc . . . . . . . . . . . . . . . .1D 102
Henshaw St. LE2: Leic . . . . . . . . .6C 5 (3F 71)
Hensman Cl. LE8: Flec . . . . . . . . . . . . . . . .5C 88
Henson Cl. LE4: Birs . . . . . . . . . . . . . . . . .7F 59
Henson's La. LE67: Thrin . . . . . . . . . . . . . . .3D 26
Henson Way LE10: S'ord . . . . . . . . . . . . . .6G 105
Henton Rd. LE3: Leic . . . . . . . . . . . . . . . . .2C 70
Herald Way LE10: Bur . . . . . . . . . . . . . . . .6G 103
Herbert Av. LE4: Leic . . . . . . . . . . . . . . . . .4H 65
Herbert Cl. LE8: Whet . . . . . . . . . . . . . . . .2A 82
Herbert St. LE11: Lou . . . . . . . . . . . . . . . . .5F 19
Herdsman Cl. LE19: Litt . . . . . . . . . . . . . . .2G 81
Hereford Cl. LE9: Barw . . . . . . . . . . . . . . . .3J 99
Hereford Rd. LE2: Leic . . . . . . . . . . . . . . . .1D 76
Hereward Dr. LE7: Thurn . . . . . . . . . . . . . . .2H 73
Herford Way LE10: Bur . . . . . . . . . . . . . . . .5J 103
Heritage Way LE5: Ham . . . . . . . . . . . . . . . .3F 67
Herle Av. LE3: Leic . . . . . . . . . . . . . . . . . .5K 69
Herle Wlk. LE3: Leic . . . . . . . . . . . . . . . . .5K 69
Hermitage Cl. LE2: Oad . . . . . . . . . . . . . . . .3C 78
　LE17: Cat . . . . . . . . . . . . . . . . . . . . .6D 156
Hermitage Ct. LE2: Oad . . . . . . . . . . . . . . . .3C 78
　LE67: Whit . . . . . . . . . . . . . . . . . . . . .1E 38
Hermitage Ind. Est., The LE67: Coal . . . . . . . .2C 38
Hermitage Leisure Cen. . . . . . . . . . . . . . . .7E 26
　LE11: Lou . . . . . . . . . . . . . . . . . . . . .1K 29
　LE67: Whit . . . . . . . . . . . . . . . . . . . . .1D 38
Heron Cl. LE8: G Gle . . . . . . . . . . . . . . . . .7K 79
　LE12: Moun . . . . . . . . . . . . . . . . . . . .2F 45
Herongate Rd. LE5: Leic . . . . . . . . . . . . . . .6B 66
Heron Rd. LE5: Leic . . . . . . . . . . . . . . . . . .7J 65
　LE12: Bar S . . . . . . . . . . . . . . . . . . . .3E 32
Herons Ct. LE10: Hinc . . . . . . . . . . . . . . . .4C 102
Heron's Way LE7: East G . . . . . . . . . . . . . .4G 47
Heron Way LE7: Sys . . . . . . . . . . . . . . . . . .1B 60
　LE19: End . . . . . . . . . . . . . . . . . . . . . .6H 75
　LE67: Coal . . . . . . . . . . . . . . . . . . . . .4F 39
Herrick Cl. LE12: Sileby . . . . . . . . . . . . . . .1H 45
　LE19: End . . . . . . . . . . . . . . . . . . . . . .5E 74
Herrick Dr. LE7: Thurn . . . . . . . . . . . . . . . .2H 73
Herrick Rd. LE2: Leic . . . . . . . . . . . . . . . . .7G 71
　LE11: Lou . . . . . . . . . . . . . . . . . . . . . .1E 30
　LE12: W Eav . . . . . . . . . . . . . . . . . . . .2D 42
Herricks Av. LE4: Leic . . . . . . . . . . . . . . . .1B 66
Herrick Way LE18: Wig . . . . . . . . . . . . . . . .1A 84
Herriot Way LE11: Lou . . . . . . . . . . . . . . . .5B 18
Herschell St. LE2: Leic . . . . . . . . . . . . . . . .4J 71
Herthull Rd. LE5: Leic . . . . . . . . . . . . . . . . .1E 72
Hervey Woods LE67: Whit . . . . . . . . . . . . . .6E 26
Hesilrige Wlk. LE5: Leic . . . . . . . . . . . . . . .6D 66
Hesketh Av. LE2: Leic . . . . . . . . . . . . . . . . .5C 76
Hesketh Cl. LE2: Leic . . . . . . . . . . . . . . . . .5C 76
Hewes Cl. LE2: G Par . . . . . . . . . . . . . . . . .5A 76
Hewett Cl. LE8: G Gle . . . . . . . . . . . . . . . . .1J 85
Hewitt Dr. LE9: K Mux . . . . . . . . . . . . . . . .3D 68

Hextall Rd. LE5: Leic . . . . . . . . . . . . . . . . .4C 72
Hextall St. LE67: Ibs . . . . . . . . . . . . . . . . .5K 51
Hexter Cl. LE8: Whet . . . . . . . . . . . . . . . . .5K 81
Heybridge Rd. LE5: Leic . . . . . . . . . . . . . . .6B 66
Heybrook Av. LE8: Bla . . . . . . . . . . . . . . . .2A 82
Heycock Cl. LE8: Flec . . . . . . . . . . . . . . . . .5C 88
HEYDOUR . . . . . . . . . . . . . . . . . . . . . . .1D 161
Heyford Rd. LE3: Leic . . . . . . . . . . . . . . . . .3H 69
Heygate St. LE16: Mkt H . . . . . . . . . . . . . . .3E 150
Heythrop Cl. LE2: Oad . . . . . . . . . . . . . . . .4F 79
Heythrop Rd. LE15: Cott . . . . . . . . . . . . . . .3C 124
　　　　　　　　　　　(not continuous)
Heyworth Rd. LE3: Leic . . . . . . . . . . . . . . . .6C 70
HICKLING . . . . . . . . . . . . . . . . . . . . . . .2D 159
Hickling Cl. LE7: R'ley . . . . . . . . . . . . . . . .6G 45
Hickling Ct. LE11: Lou . . . . . . . . . . . . . . . .6D 18
Hickling Dr. LE12: Sileby . . . . . . . . . . . . . .7K 33
Hickling La. LE14: L Cla . . . . . . . . . . . . . . .1F 111
　LE14: Up Bro . . . . . . . . . . . . . . . . . . .1A 110
Hidcote Rd. LE2: Oad . . . . . . . . . . . . . . . . .4C 78
Higgs Cl. LE5: Leic . . . . . . . . . . . . . . . . . .2C 72
High Acres LE7: Bill . . . . . . . . . . . . . . . . .6J 131
Higham La. CV11: Nun . . . . . . . . . . . . . . . .7G 97
　CV13: S Gol . . . . . . . . . . . . . . . . . . . .4A 98
　LE10: Wyk . . . . . . . . . . . . . . . . . . . . .7B 98
HIGHAM ON THE HILL . . . . . . . . .6H 97 (2A 162)
Higham Way LE10: Bur . . . . . . . . . . . . . . . .4H 103
Higham Way Ho. LE10: Bur . . . . . . . . . . . . .4H 103
Highbridge LE12: Sileby . . . . . . . . . . . . . . . .1J 45
Highbrow LE8: G Gle . . . . . . . . . . . . . . . . .5A 130
Highbury Rd. LE4: Leic . . . . . . . . . . . . . . . .6J 65
Highcliffe Rd. LE5: Ham . . . . . . . . . . . . . . .3C 66
High Cres. PE9: G Gas . . . . . . . . . . . . . . .2J 137
Highcroft Av. LE7: H Bos . . . . . . . . . . . . . . .5C 148
Highcroft Av. LE2: Oad . . . . . . . . . . . . . . . .3D 78
Highcroft Rd. LE2: Oad . . . . . . . . . . . . . . . .5F 79
High Cross Rd. LE17: C Mag . . . . . . . . . . . .5A 142
Highcross St. LE1: Leic . . . . . . . . .2A 4 (1E 70)
　　　　　　　　　　　(not continuous)
　LE16: Mkt H . . . . . . . . . . . . . . . . . . . .4C 150
Higher Grn. LE8: G Gle . . . . . . . . . . . . . . . .1K 85
Highfield Av. LE13: Mel M . . . . . . . . . . . . . .2D 116
Highfield Cl. CV9: S Mag . . . . . . . . . . . . . . .5C 90
　LE15: Emp . . . . . . . . . . . . . . . . . . . .6B 128
Highfield Ct. LE9: Earl S . . . . . . . . . . . . . .3D 100
Highfield Cres. LE18: Wig . . . . . . . . . . . . . .4K 77
　NG32: Crox . . . . . . . . . . . . . . . . . . . .6H 107
Highfield Dr. LE18: Wig . . . . . . . . . . . . . . . .4K 77
Highfield End LE14: Ash F . . . . . . . . . . . . .3E 118
Highfield Rd. DE11: Swad . . . . . . . . . . . . . .1A 22
　LE6: Groby . . . . . . . . . . . . . . . . . . . . .3C 62
HIGHFIELDS . . . . . . . . . . . . . . . . . . . . . .2J 71
Highfields LE12: Bar S . . . . . . . . . . . . . . . .3D 32
Highfields Adventure Playground . . . . . . . . . .1J 71
Highfields Cl. LE12: Shep . . . . . . . . . . . . . .5E 16
　LE65: Ash Z . . . . . . . . . . . . . . . . . . . .5H 23
Highfields Dr. LE11: Lou . . . . . . . . . . . . . . .1B 30
Highfields Farm Ent. Cen. LE9: S Stan . . . . . .6J 101
Highfields Rd. LE10: Hinc . . . . . . . . . . . . . .2H 103
　LE12: Moun . . . . . . . . . . . . . . . . . . . .3D 44
High Fld. St. LE9: S Stan . . . . . . . . . . . . . .7J 101
Highfield St. LE2: Leic . . . . . . . . .7G 5 (3H 71)
　LE7: Anst . . . . . . . . . . . . . . . . . . . . . .7J 57
　LE8: Flec . . . . . . . . . . . . . . . . . . . . . .3A 88
　LE9: Earl S . . . . . . . . . . . . . . . . . . . .3C 100
　LE16: Mkt H . . . . . . . . . . . . . . . . . . . .4D 150
　LE67: Coal . . . . . . . . . . . . . . . . . . . . .5B 38
　LE67: Thor . . . . . . . . . . . . . . . . . . . . .3K 93
Highgate LE2: Leic . . . . . . . . . . . . . . . . . .3G 77
　LE65: Ash Z . . . . . . . . . . . . . . . . . . . .3J 23
Highgate Av. LE4: Birs . . . . . . . . . . . . . . . .5E 58
Highgate Cl. NG13: Plun . . . . . . . . . . . . . .6C 106
Highgate Dr. LE2: Leic . . . . . . . . . . . . . . . .3H 77
Highgate La. NG13: Plun . . . . . . . . . . . . . .6C 106
Highgate Rd. LE12: Sileby . . . . . . . . . . . . . .1K 45
Highgrove Cl. LE67: Coal . . . . . . . . . . . . . . .4F 39
Highgrove Cres. LE2: Leic . . . . . . . . . . . . . .3B 76
Highland Av. LE9: Leic E . . . . . . . . . . . . . . .5C 68
Highland Dr. LE11: Lou . . . . . . . . . . . . . . . .4F 31
Highlands PE9: Ryh . . . . . . . . . . . . . . . . .5G 129
High Lees LE10: S'ord . . . . . . . . . . . . . . . .7G 105
High Leys Dr. LE2: Oad . . . . . . . . . . . . . . . .4C 78
High Mdw. LE12: Hat . . . . . . . . . . . . . . . . .1J 17
Highmeres Rd. LE4: Leic . . . . . . . . . . . . . . .3B 66
High St. CV13: S Gol . . . . . . . . . . . . . . . . .3A 98
　DE12: Mea . . . . . . . . . . . . . . . . . . . . .1E 48
　DE74: C Don . . . . . . . . . . . . . . . . . . . .6J 7
　DE74: Keg . . . . . . . . . . . . . . . . . . . . .6G 9
　LE1: Leic . . . . . . . . . . . . . . .3B 4 (1E 70)
　LE2: Oad . . . . . . . . . . . . . . . . . . . . . .2C 78
　LE5: Leic . . . . . . . . . . . . . . . . . . . . . .5D 72
　LE7: Sys . . . . . . . . . . . . . . . . . . . . . .1C 60
　LE8: Flec . . . . . . . . . . . . . . . . . . . . . .3B 88
　LE8: G Gle . . . . . . . . . . . . . . . . . . . . .1J 85
　LE8: K Bea . . . . . . . . . . . . . . . . . . . . .3H 89
　LE8: Whet . . . . . . . . . . . . . . . . . . . . .1K 81
　LE9: Barw . . . . . . . . . . . . . . . . . . . . .5K 99

High St. LE9: Des ............2H **95**
LE9: Earl S ..........2E **100**
LE11: Lou ..........6F **19**
LE12: Bar S ..........4D **32**
LE12: Quo ..........5K **31**
LE12: Sileby ..........1J **45**
LE13: Mel M ..........4F **117**
LE14: Som ..........6K **121**
LE14: W Wol ..........1C **112**
LE15: B Rut ..........6C **126**
LE15: Ext ..........2C **128**
LE15: Mor ..........6J **135**
LE15: O'ham ..........4H **127**
LE16: G Eas ..........5K **141**
LE16: Hall ..........6A **132**
LE16: Mkt H ..........4E **150**
LE17: H Bos ..........6C **148**
LE17: Lut ..........5J **153**
LE17: N Kil ..........3K **155**
LE17: Swin ..........4G **157**
LE17: Walt ..........6C **146**
LE19: End ..........5F **75**
LE65: Pac ..........2A **36**
LE67: Coal ..........3C **38**
LE67: Ibs ..........5J **51**
NG13: Bott ..........2G **107**
PE9: Ket ..........6H **137**
High St. E. LE15: Upp ..........2C **138**
High St. W. LE15: Upp ..........2B **138**
High Tor E. LE9: Earl S ..........1D **100**
High Tor W. LE9: Earl S ..........1D **100**
Highway Rd. LE4: Thurm ..........5B **60**
LE5: Leic ..........5A **72**
Hilary Bevins Cl. CV13: H Hill ..........5G **97**
Hilary Cl. LE13: Mel M ..........1H **117**
Hilary Cres. LE6: Groby ..........3B **62**
LE67: Whit ..........1G **39**
Hilcot Grn. LE3: Brau ..........6G **69**
(not continuous)
Hilders Rd. LE3: Leic ..........1A **70**
Hildyard Rd. LE4: Leic ..........5G **65**
Hillary Pl. LE3: Leic ..........5A **70**
Hillberry Cl. LE19: Nar ..........1E **80**
Hill Cl. LE9: Peck ..........5K **95**
Hill Ct. LE7: Thurn ..........3H **73**
Hillcrest Av. LE8: K Bea ..........2H **89**
LE16: Mkt H ..........3D **150**
Hillcrest Dr. LE11: Lou ..........4F **31**
Hillcrest La. LE17: H Bos ..........6C **148**
Hillcrest Rd. LE2: Leic ..........3H **77**
Hillcroft Cl. LE4: Thurm ..........5B **60**
Hillcroft Rd. LE5: Leic ..........2A **72**
Hill Dr. LE17: Lut ..........5J **153**
Hill Fld. LE2: Oad ..........4G **79**
Hill Gdns. LE16: Mkt H ..........4C **150**
Hillier Rd. LE5: Ham ..........3E **66**
Hill La. LE8: Count, Whet ..........6A **82**
LE67: Mark ..........4E **54**
Hill La. Cl. LE67: Mark ..........3F **55**
Hill Ri. DE12: Mea ..........6E **34**
LE4: Birs ..........5G **59**
LE4: Leic ..........1B **66**
LE12: W Eav ..........3D **42**
Hillrise LE10: Bur ..........3J **103**
Hillrise Av. LE3: Brau ..........7A **70**
Hill Rd. LE15: O'ham ..........3G **127**
Hillsborough Cl. LE2: G Par ..........6C **76**
Hillsborough Cres. LE2: G Par ..........6C **76**
Hillsborough Rd. LE2: G Par ..........6B **76**
Hillside CV13: Mkt B ..........2B **94**
DE12: A Mag ..........5B **48**
DE74: C Don ..........4K **7**
DE74: Keg ..........7H **9**
LE67: Mark ..........4F **55**
Hillside Av. LE13: Mel M ..........2D **116**
LE18: Wig ..........7K **77**
Hillside Ct. DE73: B Hil ..........7B **10**
Hillside Rd. LE10: Bur ..........5G **103**
LE16: Mkt H ..........3F **151**
Hillside Tennis Club ..........7C **66**
Hillside Way LE12: Shep ..........2C **28**
Hill St. DE12: Don ..........3A **34**
LE1: Leic ..........2E **4** (1G **71**)
LE9: Barw ..........4A **100**
LE9: Crof ..........5A **80**
LE9: N Ver ..........5H **93**
LE10: Hinc ..........3G **103**
LE65: Ash Z ..........5J **23**
Hill Top DE74: C Don ..........7H **7**
LE9: Earl S ..........1E **100**
Hill Top Av. LE8: G Gle ..........5A **130**
Hill Top Cvn. & Leisure Pk. LE7: Thru ..........5B **114**
Hilltop Dr. LE15: O'ham ..........4F **127**
Hilltop Ind. Est. LE67: Bar ..........1J **53**
Hill Top Rd. LE11: Lou ..........2C **30**
Hilltop Rd. LE5: Ham ..........3D **66**
Hill Vw. LE19: End ..........5J **75**


Hill Vw. Dr. LE9: Cosb ..........6H **81**
Hill Way LE2: Oad ..........4E **78**
HILTON ..........1A **158**
Hilton Gdns. DE72: A Tre ..........1C **6**
HINCKLEY ..........3G **103** (2B **162**)
Hinckley Bus. Pk. LE10: Hinc ..........3B **102**
Hinckley Concordia Theatre, The ..........2G **103**
Hinckley District Mus. ..........2G **103**
Hinckley Ent. Cen. *LE10: Hinc* ..........3G **103**
(off The Borough)
Hinckley Greyhound Stadium ..........5C **102**
Hinckley La. CV13: H Hill ..........6J **97**
Hinckley Leisure Cen. ..........3F **103**
Hinckley Rd. CV13: Dadl ..........2C **98**
CV13: Nail, Osb ..........3B **92** & 1D **92**
CV13: S Gol ..........3A **98**
LE3: Leic ..........3G **69**
LE3: Leic E ..........4E **68**
LE9: Barw ..........4H **99**
LE9: Des ..........6A **68**
LE9: Earl S ..........3B **100**
LE9: S Stan ..........2H **105**
LE9: Sap ..........3B **104**
LE9: Stap ..........1J **99**
LE10: A Fla ..........5D **104**
LE10: Bur ..........4K **103**
LE67: Ibs ..........5J **51**
Hinckley Station (Rail) ..........4G **103**
Hinckley United FC ..........7F **99**
Hincks Av. LE7: Scra ..........6H **67**
Hind Cl. LE8: Whet ..........3A **82**
Hind M., The LE17: Lut ..........5J **153**
Hindoostan Av. LE18: Wig ..........6E **76**
Hipwell Cres. LE4: Leic ..........3E **64**
HMP Gartree LE16: Gar ..........3J **149**
HMP Leicester LE1: Leic ..........7D **5** (3F **71**)
HMRC & Young Offenders Institute Glen Parva
LE2: G Par ..........6D **76**
Hoball Cl. LE3: Leic ..........6J **63**
Hobart St. LE2: Leic ..........5G **4** (2H **71**)
Hobbs Wick LE12: Sileby ..........1J **45**
Hobby Cl. LE9: B Ast ..........3D **86**
Hobill Cl. LE3: Leic E ..........5F **69**
LE9: Hun ..........1C **80**
Hobrook Rd. LE8: Flec ..........5C **88**
Hobson Rd. LE4: Leic ..........3F **65**
HOBY ..........2B **114** (3D **159**)
Hoby Rd. LE7: Thru ..........7B **114** & 4A **114**
LE14: Ash ..........5F **115** & 2F **115**
Hoby St. LE3: Leic ..........1D **70**
Hockey Cl. LE11: Lou ..........3E **18**
HOCKLEY ..........3A **162**
Hockley, The LE67: Whit ..........6F **27**
Hockley Farm Rd. LE3: Leic ..........3G **69**
Hodgson Cl. LE3: Leic ..........5A **64**
Hodson Cl. LE8: Whet ..........3K **81**
Hodson Ct. LE11: Lou ..........1F **31**
Hogarth Cl. LE10: Hinc ..........7D **98**
Hogarth Dr. LE10: Hinc ..........7D **98**
Hogarth Rd. LE4: Leic ..........4C **58**
LE67: Whit ..........6F **27**
Hog La. LE16: Hall ..........6A **132**
Hoke Ct. LE17: Leire ..........2J **143**
Holbeck Dr. LE9: B Ast ..........4E **86**
Holbein Cl. LE11: Lou ..........6G **19**
Holbourne Cl. LE12: Bar S ..........4C **32**
Holbrook Cl. LE2: Oad ..........4G **79**
Holbrook Rd. LE2: Leic ..........1A **78**
Holcombe Cl. LE67: Whit ..........5E **26**
Holden Av. DE72: A Tre ..........1C **6**
Holdenby Rd. LE7: L Bow ..........4H **151**
Holden Cl. LE8: Whet ..........4A **82**
Holden St. LE4: Leic ..........4G **65**
Holderness Rd. LE4: Leic ..........1D **64**
Holgate Cl. LE7: Anst ..........6J **57**
Holkham Av. LE4: Leic ..........5K **65**
Holland Cl. LE67: Whit ..........6E **26**
Holland Rd. LE2: Leic ..........1H **71**
Hollands La. LE14: T'ord ..........6H **119**
Holland Way LE19: Nar ..........1F **81**
Hollier's Wlk. LE10: Hinc ..........2G **103**
Holliers Way LE9: Oadby ..........5A **80**
Hollies Cl. LE7: Hou H ..........2D **130**
LE9: Thurl ..........2C **96**
Hollies Way LE7: Thurn ..........3H **73**
Hollingshead Yd. *LE13: Mel M* ..........4F **117**
(off Nottingham St.)
Hollington Rd. LE5: Leic ..........3K **71**
Hollins Rd. LE3: Leic ..........3J **69**
Hollinwell Cl. LE3: Leic ..........2G **69**
Hollow, The DE74: C Don ..........5K **7**
LE5: Leic ..........5D **72**
LE9: Earl S ..........2D **100**
LE15: Knos ..........2C **126**
LE67: Nor H ..........6D **36**
LE67: Thor ..........1H **93**
Hollow La. LE14: F Wre ..........5G **115**


Hollow Rd. DE73: B Hil ..........6A **10**
LE7: Anst ..........6H **57**
Hollowtree Rd. LE5: Ham ..........4E **66**
Holly Bank LE67: Hug ..........6D **38**
Hollybank Cl. LE5: Ham ..........4E **66**
Hollybank Ct. LE2: Leic ..........4H **71**
Hollybrook Cl. LE4: Thurm ..........7C **60**
Hollybush Cl. LE5: Leic ..........7F **67**
LE7: Sys ..........1B **60**
Holly Cl. DE12: Moi ..........5D **22**
LE10: Bur ..........6H **103**
LE16: Mkt H ..........3E **150**
Holly Cott. Farm LE15: Gree ..........4F **125**
Holly Ct. DE72: A Tre ..........1C **6**
LE2: Oad ..........1C **78**
HOLLYCROFT ..........2E **102**
Hollycroft LE10: Hinc ..........1E **102**
Hollycroft Cres. LE10: Hinc ..........2F **103**
Hollydene Cres. LE9: Earl S ..........3C **100**
Holly Dr. LE17: Lut ..........4H **153**
Hollygate Cl. LE13: Mel M ..........5H **117**
Holly Gro. LE8: Bla ..........1B **82**
Holly Hayes Environmental Resources Cen.
..........7G **59**
Holly Hayes Rd. LE67: Whit ..........7F **27**
Holly La. LE9: Barw ..........3A **100**
Holly Rd. DE12: Mea ..........7E **34**
Holly Tree Av. LE4: Birs ..........5G **59**
Hollytree Cl. LE11: Lou ..........4E **30**
LE12: Hot ..........1C **20**
Hollytree La. LE14: L Cla ..........2H **111**
Holly Tree Wlk. LE17: C Mag ..........5C **142**
Hollywood Bowl
Leicester ..........6J **69**
Holman Row LE5: Leic ..........1C **72**
Holmdale Rd. LE7: Sys ..........2C **60**
Holmden Av. LE18: Wig ..........6H **77**
Holme Dr. LE2: Oad ..........1D **78**
HOLME LANE ..........1D **159**
HOLME PIERREPONT ..........1D **159**
Holmes Cl. LE6: Groby ..........3C **62**
Holmes Ct. LE67: Hug ..........6D **38**
Holmes Dr. PE9: Ket ..........7J **137**
Holmewood Dr. LE9: K Mux ..........3D **68**
Holmfield LE14: Hob ..........2B **114**
Holmfield Av. LE2: Leic ..........5K **71**
LE11: Lou ..........4D **18**
Holmfield Av. E. LE3: Brau ..........4G **69**
Holmfield Av. W. LE3: Leic E ..........4G **69**
Holmfield Cl. LE17: Lut ..........4G **153**
Holmfield Rd. LE2: Leic ..........5J **71**
LE9: Des ..........2H **95**
Holmleigh Gdns. LE7: Thurn ..........3H **73**
Holmwood Ct. LE3: Leic ..........5J **63**
Holmwood Dr. LE3: Leic ..........5J **63**
Holt Cres. LE9: Thurl ..........2C **96**
Holt Dr. LE9: K Mux ..........3D **68**
LE11: Lou ..........1D **30**
Holt La. LE9: Cosb ..........4K **87**
LE16: G Eas ..........4H **141**
LE17: Ash M ..........7K **87**
Holt Ri. LE12: Shep ..........2E **28**
Holt Rd. LE4: Birs ..........7G **59**
LE10: Bur ..........4H **103**
LE16: Med ..........6D **140**
Holts Cl. LE2: Leic ..........4B **76**
Holts La. LE67: D Hea ..........6B **38**
Holt W. LE16: G Eas ..........5K **141**
HOLWELL ..........5K **111** (2A **160**)
Holy Bones LE1: Leic ..........3A **4** (1E **70**)
Holygate Rd. LE15: Rid ..........2F **133**
Holyoak Dr. LE10: S'ord ..........6G **105**
Holyoake Cres. LE67: Hea ..........3G **51**
Holyoake Dr. LE67: Hea ..........3G **51**
Holyoake St. LE19: End ..........6F **75**
Holyrood Cl. LE15: O'ham ..........5G **127**
Holyrood Dr. LE8: Count ..........5D **82**
Holywell Av. LE65: Ash Z ..........4K **23**
Holywell Dr. LE11: Lou ..........2A **30**
Holywell Rd. LE2: Leic ..........2C **76**
Holywell Way LE11: Lou ..........2A **30**
Home Av. LE3: Brau ..........6G **69**
Home Cl. LE7: S Cro ..........7B **118**
LE8: Bla ..........1B **82**
LE8: K Bea ..........3J **89**
Home Cl. Rd. LE7: Hou H ..........2D **130**
Home Ct. LE15: Emp ..........6B **128**
(not continuous)
Home Cft. Dr. LE65: Pac ..........2K **35**
Home Farm ..........5J **29**
Home Farm Barns LE67: Swep ..........4B **50**
Home Farm Cl. CV9: With ..........5B **96**
LE4: Leic ..........3C **64**
LE12: Wood ..........1G **43**
LE17: Gilm ..........6J **145**
Home Farm Ct. LE4: Leic ..........3C **64**
Home Farm M. CV13: Mkt B ..........2C **94**

Home Farm Sq. LE4: Leic . . . . . . . . . . . . . . . .3C 64
Home Farm Wlk. LE4: Leic . . . . . . . . . . . . . . .3C 64
Homefield La. LE7: R'ley . . . . . . . . . . . . . . . . .6F 45
Homefield Rd. LE12: Sileby . . . . . . . . . . . . . .7J 33
Homemead Av. LE4: Leic . . . . . . . . . . . . . . . . .6D 64
Home Pastures LE14: Hos . . . . . . . . . . . . . . .6B 108
Homer Dr. LE19: Nar . . . . . . . . . . . . . . . . . . . .1E 80
Homestead, The LE12: Moun . . . . . . . . . . . . .1E 44
Homestead Cl. LE7: Coss . . . . . . . . . . . . . . . .4K 45
Homestead Dr. LE18: Wig . . . . . . . . . . . . . . . .7K 77
Homestead Ho. LE9: Sap . . . . . . . . . . . . . . . .4J 105
Homestead Rd. LE67: Thrin . . . . . . . . . . . . . . .3D 26
Homestone Gdns. LE5: Leic . . . . . . . . . . . . . .1G 73
Homestone Ri. LE5: Leic . . . . . . . . . . . . . . . . .1G 73
Homeway Cl. LE12: Shep . . . . . . . . . . . . . . . .7E 16
Homeway Rd. LE5: Leic . . . . . . . . . . . . . . . . .4A 72
Homewelland Ho. LE16: Mkt H . . . . . . . . . . . .3D 150
                                        (off Poplars Ct.)
Honeybourne Cl. LE2: Oad . . . . . . . . . . . . . . .3C 78
Honeycomb Cl. LE19: Nar . . . . . . . . . . . . . . . .1E 80
Honeypot La. LE17: H Bos . . . . . . . . . . . . . . .5C 148
Honeysuckle Cl. LE7: East G . . . . . . . . . . . . . .5H 47
    LE17: Lut . . . . . . . . . . . . . . . . . . . . . . . .4G 153
    LE67: Coal . . . . . . . . . . . . . . . . . . . . . . . .4G 39
Honeysuckle Rd. LE5: Ham . . . . . . . . . . . . . . .4E 66
Honeysuckle Way LE11: Lou . . . . . . . . . . . . . .5E 30
    LE13: Mel M . . . . . . . . . . . . . . . . . . . . . .7D 116
Honeywell Cl. LE2: Oad . . . . . . . . . . . . . . . . .3C 78
HONINGTON . . . . . . . . . . . . . . . . . . . . . . . . .1C 161
Honiton Cl. LE18: Wig . . . . . . . . . . . . . . . . . . .7J 77
Hooby La. LE15: Gree, Stre . . . . . . . . . . . . . .1E 124
Hood Ct. LE65: Ash Z . . . . . . . . . . . . . . . . . . .5K 23
                                        (off North St.)
Hood Pk. Leisure Cen. . . . . . . . . . . . . . . . . . .4K 23
Hoods Cl. LE4: Leic . . . . . . . . . . . . . . . . . . . .7D 58
Hoopers Cl. NG13: Bott . . . . . . . . . . . . . . . . .2G 107
Hopefield Rd. LE3: Leic . . . . . . . . . . . . . . . . .5C 70
Hope's Yd. LE15: Upp . . . . . . . . . . . . . . . . . .2C 138
Hoppner Cl. LE4: Leic . . . . . . . . . . . . . . . . . .4D 58
Hopton Flds. LE16: Mkt H . . . . . . . . . . . . . . .7D 150
Hopwood Cl. LE4: Leic . . . . . . . . . . . . . . . . . .3B 64
Hopyard Cl. LE2: Leic . . . . . . . . . . . . . . . . . .4B 76
HORBLING . . . . . . . . . . . . . . . . . . . . . . . . . .1D 161
Hornbeam Cl. LE2: Oad . . . . . . . . . . . . . . . . .1C 78
    LE11: Lou . . . . . . . . . . . . . . . . . . . . . . . .5E 30
    LE19: Nar . . . . . . . . . . . . . . . . . . . . . . . .1E 80
Hornbeam Rd. LE9: N Ver . . . . . . . . . . . . . . . .6H 93
Hornby Rd. LE5: Ham . . . . . . . . . . . . . . . . . . .3E 66
Horn Cl. LE15: O'ham . . . . . . . . . . . . . . . . . .3K 127
Horndean Av. LE18: Wig . . . . . . . . . . . . . . . . .5J 77
Hornecroft LE7: R'ley . . . . . . . . . . . . . . . . . . .6E 44
HORNINGHOLD . . . . . . . . . . . . . .5D 132 (2B 164)
Horninghold La.
    LE16: Blas, Horn . . . . . . . . . . . . . . . . . . .7D 132
Horninghold Rd. LE16: Hall . . . . . . . . . . . . . . .6B 132
Horn La. LE16: Hall . . . . . . . . . . . . . . . . . . . .6A 132
Horsefair, The LE10: Hinc . . . . . . . . . . . . . . . .3G 103
Horsefair Cl. LE16: Mkt H . . . . . . . . . . . . . . .5C 150
Horsefair St. LE1: Leic . . . . . . . . . . .4C 4 (2F 71)
Horse Field Vw. LE13: Mel M . . . . . . . . . . . . . .2D 116
Horseguards Way LE13: Mel M . . . . . . . . . . . .1C 116
Horsepool LE10: Bur . . . . . . . . . . . . . . . . . . .6K 103
Horseshoe Cl. CV13: Mkt B . . . . . . . . . . . . . . .2A 94
    LE9: Cosb . . . . . . . . . . . . . . . . . . . . . . . .5H 81
Horseshoe La. LE16: G Bow . . . . . . . . . . . . . .1H 151
Horse Shoes, The DE74: Hem . . . . . . . . . . . . . .4A 8
Horses La. DE12: Mea . . . . . . . . . . . . . . . . . .1F 49
Horsewell La. LE18: Wig . . . . . . . . . . . . . . . . .1K 83
HORSTON HILL . . . . . . . . . . . . . . . . . . . . . . .4A 72
Horston Rd. LE5: Leic . . . . . . . . . . . . . . . . . . .4A 72
Horton Cl. LE8: Bla . . . . . . . . . . . . . . . . . . . . .1A 82
Horton's Cl. LE2: G Par . . . . . . . . . . . . . . . . . .5B 76
Hortons La. LE15: Whis . . . . . . . . . . . . . . . . .2D 122
Horwood Cl. LE18: Wig . . . . . . . . . . . . . . . . . .4A 78
HOSE . . . . . . . . . . . . . . . . . . . . . . . .6B 108 (2A 160)
Hose La. LE14: Harb, Hos . . . . . . . . . . . . . . . .5C 108
    LE14: Hos, L Cla . . . . . . . .1J 111 & 7A 108
Hoskins Cl. LE18: Wig . . . . . . . . . . . . . . . . . . .1A 84
Hospital Cl. LE5: Leic . . . . . . . . . . . . . . . . . . .3B 72
Hospital La. LE8: Bla . . . . . . . . . . . . . . . . . . . .2C 82
    LE67: Rav . . . . . . . . . . . . . . . . . . . . . . . . .4J 37
    LE67: Swan . . . . . . . . . . . . . . . . . . . . . . . .4B 26
Hospital of Christ LE15: Upp . . . . . . . . . . . . . .2B 138
Hospital Way LE11: Lou . . . . . . . . . . . . . . . . . .4H 31
Hotel St. LE1: Leic . . . . . . . . . . . . . .4C 4 (2F 71)
                                        (not continuous)
    LE67: Coal . . . . . . . . . . . . . . . . . . . . . . . .3D 38
Hotoft Rd. LE5: Leic . . . . . . . . . . . . . . . . . . . .6D 66
HOTON . . . . . . . . . . . . . . . . . . .1C 20 (2C 159)
Hoton Rd. LE12: Wym . . . . . . . . . . . . . . . . . . .2J 21
Hough Hill LE67: Swan . . . . . . . . . . . . . . . . . . .1A 38
Houghton La. LE7: Hou H . . . . . . . . . . . . . . . . .6H 73
HOUGHTON ON THE HILL . . . . . .2C 130 (1D 163)
Houghton St. LE5: Leic . . . . . . . . . . . . . . . . . .7K 65
Hough Windmill . . . . . . . . . . . . . . . . . . . . . . . .4B 26
Houlditch Rd. LE2: Leic . . . . . . . . . . . . . . . . . .7H 71
Housman Wlk. LE4: Leic . . . . . . . . . . . . . . . . .6H 65

Howard Cl. LE9: Barw . . . . . . . . . . . . . . . . . . .3K 99
    LE11: Lou . . . . . . . . . . . . . . . . . . . . . . . . .5A 18
Howard Rd. LE2: G Par . . . . . . . . . . . . . . . . . .6B 76
    LE2: Leic . . . . . . . . . . . . . . . . . .10G 5 (6G 71)
Howard St. LE11: Lou . . . . . . . . . . . . . . . . . . . .5F 19
Howard Way LE16: Mkt H . . . . . . . . . . . . . . . .6D 150
Howden Cl. LE11: Lou . . . . . . . . . . . . . . . . . . .7K 17
Howden Rd. LE2: Leic . . . . . . . . . . . . . . . . . . .4C 76
Howdon Rd. LE2: Oad . . . . . . . . . . . . . . . . . . .5D 78
Howe Cl. LE9: S Stan . . . . . . . . . . . . . . . . . . .2H 105
Howe Ct. LE67: Whit . . . . . . . . . . . . . . . . . . . .6D 26
HOWE GREEN . . . . . . . . . . . . . . . . . . . . . . . .3A 162
Howe La. LE7: R'ley . . . . . . . . . . . . . . . . . . . . .6E 44
Howe Rd. LE11: Lou . . . . . . . . . . . . . . . . . . . .2F 31
    LE67: Whit . . . . . . . . . . . . . . . . . . . . . . . .6D 26
Howitts Rd. NG13: Bott . . . . . . . . . . . . . . . . . .3G 107
Hoylake Cl. LE5: Leic . . . . . . . . . . . . . . . . . . . .5A 72
Hubbard Cl. LE8: Whet . . . . . . . . . . . . . . . . . .4A 82
Hubbards Cl. LE17: Ash M . . . . . . . . . . . . . . .1G 145
Hudson Cl. LE3: Leic . . . . . . . . . . . . . . . . . . . .6A 64
    LE15: O'ham . . . . . . . . . . . . . . . . . . . . . . .4F 127
Hudson Rd. LE12: Sileby . . . . . . . . . . . . . . . . .7J 33
    LE13: Mel M . . . . . . . . . . . . . . . . . . . . . . .4H 117
Hudson Rd. Ind. Est. LE13: Mel M . . . . . . . . . .4H 117
Hudson St. LE11: Lou . . . . . . . . . . . . . . . . . . .6G 19
Huggett Cl. LE4: Leic . . . . . . . . . . . . . . . . . . . .2A 66
HUGGLESCOTE . . . . . . . . . . .6D 38 (3B 158)
Hughenden Dr. LE2: Leic . . . . . . . . . . . . . . . . .6E 70
Humber Cl. LE5: Leic . . . . . . . . . . . . . . . . . . . .5D 66
Humber Dr. LE13: Mel M . . . . . . . . . . . . . . . . .6E 116
HUMBERSTONE . . . . . . . . . . .6D 66 (1D 163)
Humber Stone, The . . . . . . . . . . . . . . . . . . . . .3C 66
Humberstone Ct. LE5: Leic . . . . . . . . . . . . . . .6D 66
Humberstone Dr. LE5: Leic . . . . . . . . . . . . . . . .7B 66
HUMBERSTONE GARDEN CITY . . . . . . . . . . .5E 66
Humberstone Ga. LE1: Leic . . . . . . . .3D 4 (1F 71)
Humberstone La. LE4: Thurm, Leic . . . . . . . . . .7K 59
Humberstone Mall LE1: Leic . . . . . . . . . . . . . . .3D 4
                                        (off Haymarket Cen.)
Humberstone Rd. LE5: Leic . . . . . . . . .3E 4 (1G 71)
Humble La. LE7: Coss . . . . . . . . . . . . . . . . . . .4K 45
HUMBY . . . . . . . . . . . . . . . . . . . . . . . . . . . . .1D 161
Humes Cl. LE8: Whet . . . . . . . . . . . . . . . . . . . .5K 81
Hume St. LE11: Lou . . . . . . . . . . . . . . . . . . . . .6G 19
Humphrey Cl. LE11: Lou . . . . . . . . . . . . . . . . . .1G 31
Humphries Cl. LE5: Leic . . . . . . . . . . . . . . . . . .2C 72
HUNCOTE . . . . . . . . . . . . . . . .1B 80 (2C 163)
Huncote Leisure Cen. . . . . . . . . . . . . . . . . . . . .1A 80
Huncote Rd. LE9: Crof . . . . . . . . . . . . . . . . . . .3A 80
    LE9: S Stan . . . . . . . . . . . . . . . . . . . . . . . .7J 101
    LE19: Hun, Nar . . . . . . . . . . . . . . . . . . . . . .2C 80
HUNGARTON . . . . . . . . . . . . . . . . . . . . . . . . .1D 163
Hungarton Blvd. LE5: Leic . . . . . . . . . . . . . . . .6D 66
Hungarton Dr. LE7: Sys . . . . . . . . . . . . . . . . . .2E 60
HUNGERTON . . . . . . . . . . . . . . . . . . . . . . . . .1B 160
Hunt Dr. LE13: Mel M . . . . . . . . . . . . . . . . . . .1H 117
Hunter Blvd. LE17: Lut . . . . . . . . . . . . . . . . . . .4B 152
Hunter Rd. LE4: Leic . . . . . . . . . . . . . . . . . . . .5G 65
Hunters Cl. LE17: H Bos . . . . . . . . . . . . . . . . .5C 148
Hunters Dr. LE17: Lut . . . . . . . . . . . . . . . . . . .5H 153
Hunters La. CV13: F Dray . . . . . . . . . . . . . . . . .2H 97
Hunters Lodge LE15: A'll . . . . . . . . . . . . . . . . .6H 123
Hunters Rd. LE13: Mel M . . . . . . . . . . . . . . . . .6G 117
Hunter's Row LE9: Cosb . . . . . . . . . . . . . . . . . .5H 81
Hunters Wlk. CV9: With . . . . . . . . . . . . . . . . . .6B 96
Hunters Way LE2: Oad . . . . . . . . . . . . . . . . . . .4F 79
    LE3: Leic E . . . . . . . . . . . . . . . . . . . . . . . .5D 68
Huntingdon Cl. LE12: Bur W . . . . . . . . . . . . . . .3F 21
Huntingdon Ct. DE12: Mea . . . . . . . . . . . . . . . .7C 34
    LE11: Lou . . . . . . . . . . . . . . . . . . . . . . . . .6E 18
    LE65: Ash Z . . . . . . . . . . . . . . . . . . . . . . . .5K 23
Huntingdon Dr. DE74: C Don . . . . . . . . . . . . . . .4J 7
Huntingdon Gdns. LE16: Mkt H . . . . . . . . . . . .6D 150
Huntingdon Rd. LE4: Leic . . . . . . . . . . . . . . . . .4A 66
    LE65: Ash Z . . . . . . . . . . . . . . . . . . . . . . . .6H 23
Huntingdon Way DE12: Mea . . . . . . . . . . . . . . .7C 34
Huntings, The LE9: K Mux . . . . . . . . . . . . . . . . .2A 68
Hunt La. CV9: With . . . . . . . . . . . . . . . . . . . . .6B 96
HUNT'S LANE . . . . . . . . . . . . . . . . . . . . . . . . .6K 93
Hunts La. LE9: Des . . . . . . . . . . . .6K 93 & 1F 95
    LE16: Hall . . . . . . . . . . . . . . . . . . . . . . . . .6A 132
    PE9: Ket . . . . . . . . . . . . . . . . . . . . . . . . . .5G 137
Huntsman Cl. LE67: Mark . . . . . . . . . . . . . . . . .5G 55
Huntsmans Cl. LE12: Quo . . . . . . . . . . . . . . . . .4B 32
Huntsman's Dale LE7: East G . . . . . . . . . . . . . .4F 47
Huntsmans Way LE4: Leic . . . . . . . . . . . . . . . . .3K 65
Hunts Orchard LE12: Hat . . . . . . . . . . . . . . . . . .2J 17
Hurds Cl. LE7: Anst . . . . . . . . . . . . . . . . . . . . .7H 57
Hursley Cl. LE2: Oad . . . . . . . . . . . . . . . . . . . .3E 78
Hurst Ri. LE5: Leic . . . . . . . . . . . . . . . . . . . . . .2C 72
Hurst Rd. LE9: Earl S . . . . . . . . . . . . . . . . . . .3D 100
Hurstwood Rd. LE11: Lou . . . . . . . . . . . . . . . . .7K 17
HUSBANDS BOSWORTH . . . . . . . .6C 148 (3D 163)
Huston Cl. LE12: Bar S . . . . . . . . . . . . . . . . . . .5F 33
Huston Ct. LE11: Lou . . . . . . . . . . . . . . . . . . . .7E 18
                                        (off Wards End)

Hutchinson St. LE2: Leic . . . . . . . . . . . .4G 4 (2H 71)
Hutchinson Wlk. LE2: Leic . . . . . . . . . . .4G 4 (2H 71)
Hyacinth Way LE10: Bur . . . . . . . . . . . . . . . . .6G 103
Hyam's La. DE74: Dis . . . . . . . . . . . . . . . . . . . .3A 12
Hyde Cl. LE2: Oad . . . . . . . . . . . . . . . . . . . . . .5E 78
    LE3: Leic . . . . . . . . . . . . . . . . . . . . . . . . . .4B 64
    LE19: Nar . . . . . . . . . . . . . . . . . . . . . . . . .1F 81
Hydes La. LE10: Hinc . . . . . . . . . . . . . . . . . . .7B 102
Hydra Wlk. LE2: Leic . . . . . . . . . . . . . .4G 4 (2H 71)
Hylion Rd. LE2: Leic . . . . . . . . . . . . . . . . . . . . .2G 77

## I

Ibbetson Av. LE3: Glen . . . . . . . . . . . . . . . . . .7G 63
Ibsley Way LE2: Leic . . . . . . . . . . . . . . . . . . . .5D 76
IBSTOCK . . . . . . . . . . . . . . . . . . . .4J 51 (3B 158)
Ibstock Ind. Est. LE67: Ibs . . . . . . . . . . . . . . . .3A 52
Ibstock Rd. CV13: Nail . . . . . . . . . . .7K 51 & 1B 92
    LE67: Ell . . . . . . . . . . . . . . . . . . . . . . . . . .2C 52
    LE67: Rav . . . . . . . . . . . . . . . . . . . . . . . . .6K 37
Ickworth Cl. LE5: Leic . . . . . . . . . . . . . . . . . . .6A 66
Iffley Cl. LE5: Leic . . . . . . . . . . . . . . . . . . . . . .1C 72
Iffley Ct. LE5: Leic . . . . . . . . . . . . . . . . . . . . . .1C 72
Iliffe Av. LE2: Oad . . . . . . . . . . . . . . . . . . . . . .3B 78
Iliffe Rd. LE4: Leic . . . . . . . . . . . . . . . . . . . . . .5A 66
Iliffes Cl. LE12: Bar S . . . . . . . . . . . . . . . . . . . .3E 32
ILKESTON . . . . . . . . . . . . . . . . . . . . . . . . . . .1B 158
Illingworth Rd. LE5: Leic . . . . . . . . . . . . . . . . . .1C 72
Illston Gdns. LE12: Bar S . . . . . . . . . . . . . . . . .4E 32
ILLSTON ON THE HILL . . . . . . . . . . . . . . . . .2A 164
Ilmington Cl. LE3: Glen . . . . . . . . . . . . . . . . . . .5G 63
Ilminster Cl. LE10: Bur . . . . . . . . . . . . . . . . . .4A 104
Imperial Av. LE3: Leic . . . . . . . . . . . . . . . . . . . .4B 70
Imperial Rd. LE8: K Bea . . . . . . . . . . . . . . . . . .3H 89
Impey Cl. LE3: Brau . . . . . . . . . . . . . . . . . . . . .6G 69
Infirmary Cl. LE2: Leic . . . . . . . . . . . . .7C 5 (3F 71)
Infirmary Rd. LE1: Leic . . . . . . . . . . . .7C 5 (3F 71)
Infirmary Sq. LE1: Leic . . . . . . . . . . . .6C 5 (3F 71)
Ingarsby Cl. LE7: Hou H . . . . . . . . . . . . . . . . .2D 130
Ingarsby Dr. LE5: Leic . . . . . . . . . . . . . . . . . . .4E 72
Ingarsby La. LE7: Hou H . . . . . . . . . . . . . . . . .2D 130
Ingleberry Rd. LE12: Shep . . . . . . . . . . . . . . . .2E 28
INGLEBY . . . . . . . . . . . . . . . . . . . . . . . . . . . .2A 158
Ingleby Rd. LE18: Wig . . . . . . . . . . . . . . . . . . . .5J 77
Ingle Dr. LE6: Ratby . . . . . . . . . . . . . . . . . . . . .6A 62
    LE65: Ash Z . . . . . . . . . . . . . . . . . . . . . . . .4H 23
Inglenook Pk. Mobile Home Pk. LE4: Thurm . . .4B 60
Ingles Hill Cvn. Site LE65: Ash Z . . . . . . . . . . .3G 23
Ingle St. LE3: Leic . . . . . . . . . . . . . . . . . . . . . .7B 64
Ingold Av. LE4: Leic . . . . . . . . . . . . . . . . . . . . .3D 64
INGOLDSBY . . . . . . . . . . . . . . . . . . . . . . . . . .1D 161
Ingrams Way LE18: Wig . . . . . . . . . . . . . . . . . . .1A 84
INGTHORPE . . . . . . . . . . . . . . . .3G 137 (1C 165)
Inhams, The LE15: Bisb . . . . . . . . . . . . . . . . . . .2F 139
Inleys, The LE12: Shep . . . . . . . . . . . . . . . . . . .7F 17
Insley's La. CV13: S'one . . . . . . . . . . . . . . . . . .3H 91
Interlink Ind. Pk. LE67: Bar . . . . . . . . . . . . . . . .1H 53
Invergarry Cl. LE4: Leic . . . . . . . . . . . . . . . . . . .2K 65
Iona Cl. LE4: Leic . . . . . . . . . . . . . . . . . . . . . . .3B 64
Iona Rd. LE7: Sys . . . . . . . . . . . . . . . . . . . . . .1B 60
Iona Way LE8: Count . . . . . . . . . . . . . . . . . . . .6F 83
Ipswich Cl. LE4: Beau L . . . . . . . . . . . . . . . . . .7A 58
Irene Pollard Ho. LE4: Leic . . . . . . . . . . . . . . . .3H 65
Ireton Av. LE4: Leic . . . . . . . . . . . . . . . . . . . . .4B 66
Ireton Rd. LE4: Leic . . . . . . . . . . . . . . . . . . . . .5A 66
    LE16: Mkt H . . . . . . . . . . . . . . . . . . . . . . .6D 150
Iris Av. LE2: G Par . . . . . . . . . . . . . . . . . . . . . .5B 76
    LE4: Birs . . . . . . . . . . . . . . . . . . . . . . . . . .5H 59
Iris Cl. LE10: Bur . . . . . . . . . . . . . . . . . . . . . .6H 103
    LE12: Moun . . . . . . . . . . . . . . . . . . . . . . . .2F 45
Irlam St. LE18: Wig . . . . . . . . . . . . . . . . . . . . .1F 83
IRNHAM . . . . . . . . . . . . . . . . . . . . . . . . . . . . .2D 161
Ironworks Rd. LE4: Leic . . . . . . . . . . . . . . . . . .6J 65
Irwell Cl. LE13: Mel M . . . . . . . . . . . . . . . . . . .6E 116
    LE15: O'ham . . . . . . . . . . . . . . . . . . . . . . .5G 127
Irwin Av. LE11: Lou . . . . . . . . . . . . . . . . . . . . .4A 18
Isis Cl. LE2: Oad . . . . . . . . . . . . . . . . . . . . . . .2F 79
Island Cl. DE11: A Vil . . . . . . . . . . . . . . . . . . . .3A 22
    LE10: Hinc . . . . . . . . . . . . . . . . . . . . . . . .1H 103
ISLEY WALTON . . . . . . . . . . . .2F 11 (2B 158)
Islington St. LE2: Leic . . . . . . . . . . .10D 5 (5F 71)
ISLIP . . . . . . . . . . . . . . . . . . . . . . . . . . . . . . . .3C 165
Isobella Rd. LE3: Brau . . . . . . . . . . . . . . . . . . .6G 69
Ivanhoe Cl. LE3: Glen . . . . . . . . . . . . . . . . . . . .7G 63
Ivanhoe Dr. LE65: Ash Z . . . . . . . . . . . . . . . . . .5H 23
Ivanhoe Ind. Est. LE65: Ash Z . . . . . . . . . . . . . .3J 23
                                        (not continuous)
Ivanhoe Rd. LE18: Wig . . . . . . . . . . . . . . . . . . .6F 77
Ivanhoe St. LE3: Leic . . . . . . . . . . . . . . . . . . . .1C 70
Ivanhoe Way DE12: Moi . . . . . . . . . . . . . . . . . .1B 34
                                        (Measham Rd.)
    DE12: Moi . . . . . . . . . . . . . . . . . . . . . . . . .2A 34
                                        (Poplar Av.)
    LE65: Ash Z . . . . . . . . . . . . . . . . . . . . . . . .4A 24
    LE65: Ash Z, Calk . . . . . . . . . . . . . . . . . . . .1C 24
Ivatt Cl. LE7: Thurn . . . . . . . . . . . . . . . . . . . . .2J 73

Iveagh Cl.—Keyham Ct.


**Iveagh Cl.** DE12: Mea . . . 7F **35**
**Iveshead La.** LE12: Shep . . . 3C **28**
**Iveshead Rd.** LE12: Shep . . . 4C **28**
**Ivor Rd.** CV9: Ath . . . 6A **96**
**Ivychurch Cres.** LE5: Leic . . . 5F **67**
**Ivy Cl.** CV13: S Gol . . . 3A **98**
DE12: Don . . . 3A **34**
**Ivydale Cl.** LE4: Thurm . . . 7B **60**
**Ivydale Rd.** LE4: Thurm . . . 7B **60**
**Ivydene Cl.** LE9: Earl S . . . 2E **100**
**Ivy Ho. Cl.** LE12: Sea . . . 3K **33**
**Ivy Rd.** LE3: Leic . . . 4C **70**

## J

**Jacklin Dr.** LE4: Leic . . . 1K **65**
**Jacknell Cl.** LE10: Hinc . . . 3A **102**
**Jacknell Rd.** LE10: Hinc . . . 3A **102**
**Jackson Cl.** LE2: Oad . . . 3F **79**
LE16: Mkt H . . . 7E **150**
**Jackson Rd.** LE67: Bag . . . 6G **53**
**Jackson St.** LE4: Leic . . . 4H **65**
LE67: Coal . . . 3C **38**
**Jacks Wlk.** LE67: Hug . . . 5B **38**
**Jacob Cl.** LE19: End . . . 5E **74**
**Jacqueline Rd.** LE67: Mark . . . 5H **55**
**Jacquemart Cl.** LE67: Coal . . . 3K **39**
**Jacques Cl.** LE19: End . . . 5E **74**
**Jacques St.** LE67: Ibs . . . 3K **51**
**James Av.** LE11: Lou . . . 4A **18**
**James Bond Cvn. Pk.** LE17: Lut . . . 6H **153**
**James Gavin Way** LE2: Oad . . . 4G **79**
**James Lambert Dr.** LE13: Mel M . . . 2C **116**
**James St.** LE7: Anst . . . 6H **57**
LE8: Bla . . . 1A **82**
LE9: Earl S . . . 3D **100**
LE9: S Stan . . . 7J **101**
LE67: Coal . . . 4C **38**
**James Way** LE9: Cosb . . . 5H **81**
**James Went Bldg.** LE2: Leic . . . 5B **4**
**Janes Way** LE67: Mark . . . 5G **55**
**Japonica Cl.** LE11: Lou . . . 4E **30**
**Jarrett Cl.** LE19: End . . . 5E **74**
**Jarrom Ct.** LE2: Leic . . . 7B **5** (3E **70**)
**Jarrom St.** LE2: Leic . . . 8A **5** (4E **70**)
**Jarvis Cl.** LE10: Hinc . . . 6G **99**
**Jarvis Dr.** LE13: Mel M . . . 3D **116**
**Jarvis St.** LE3: Leic . . . 3A **4** (1E **70**)
**Jarvis Way** LE67: Whit . . . 6E **26**
**Jasmine Cl.** LE5: Ham . . . 3D **66**
LE11: Lou . . . 4E **30**
LE17: Lut . . . 4G **153**
**Jasmine Ct.** LE18: Wig . . . 6F **77**
LE19: Nar . . . 7D **74**
**Jasper Rd.** LE15: O'ham . . . 4K **127**
**Jay Cl.** LE15: O'ham . . . 2K **127**
**Jay's Cl.** NG13: Bott . . . 3G **107**
**Jean Dr.** LE4: Leic . . . 5D **64**
**Jeffares Cl.** DE74: Keg . . . 5G **9**
**Jeffcoats La.** LE67: Swan . . . 5B **26**
**Jeffries Cl.** LE10: Hinc . . . 1H **103**
**Jellicoe Rd.** LE5: Leic . . . 1A **72**
**Jellicoe Way** LE10: Hinc . . . 6G **99**
**Jenkins Rd.** LE67: Coal . . . 3E **38**
**Jennett Cl.** LE5: Leic . . . 1E **72**
**Jenny's La.** LE67: Rav . . . 4K **37**
**Jeremy Cl.** LE4: Leic . . . 4H **65**
**Jericho La.** NG13: Bark V . . . 2A **106**
**Jermyn St.** LE4: Leic . . . 4H **65**
**Jersey Rd.** LE4: Leic . . . 1D **64**
**Jersey Way** LE9: Barw . . . 4K **99**
**Jerwood Way** LE16: L Bow . . . 5F **151**
**Jessons Cl.** LE4: Leic . . . 3K **65**
**Jessop Cl.** LE3: Leic . . . 6A **64**
**Jetcott Av.** LE11: Lou . . . 4E **30**
**Jetties, The** LE15: N Luf . . . 1A **136**
**Jetty, The** LE1: Leic . . . 4C **4**
LE15: Win . . . 5E **134**
Jewry Wall Mus. and Vaughan College . . . 4A **4** (2E **70**)
**Jewsbury Av.** DE12: Mea . . . 7F **35**
**Jewsbury Way** LE3: Brau . . . 5G **69**
**Joe Moore's La.** LE12: W Eav . . . 5B **42**
**John Bold Av.** LE9: S Stan . . . 7K **101**
**John Minto Ho.** LE4: Leic . . . 6H **65**
**John Nichols St.** LE10: Hinc . . . 4E **102**
**Johnnie Johnson Dr.** LE17: Lut . . . 2J **153**
JOHN O' GAUNT . . . 7J **119**
**John O' Gaunt Rural Industries**
LE14: J O'Ga . . . 7K **119**
**John Phillips Cl.** LE11: Lou . . . 6C **18**
John Sandford Sports Cen. . . . 5A **4** (2E **70**)
**Johns Av.** LE12: Moun . . . 4E **44**
**Johns Cliffe Cl.** LE6: New L . . . 4B **56**
**John's Cl.** LE10: Bur . . . 6G **103**
**Johns Ct.** LE8: Bla . . . 1B **82**
**John's Lee Cl.** LE11: Lou . . . 2D **30**
**Johnson Cl.** LE8: Whet . . . 2A **82**
LE9: B Ast . . . 5E **86**
LE12: Bar S . . . 4D **32**
LE13: Mel M . . . 3F **117**
LE15: N Luf . . . 1B **136**
**Johnson Ri.** LE9: S Stan . . . 2K **105**
**Johnson Rd.** LE4: Birs . . . 6F **59**
LE15: Upp . . . 2B **138**
**Johnson St.** LE1: Leic . . . 1A **4** (7E **64**)
**John St.** DE11: C Gre . . . 1A **22**
LE10: Hinc . . . 2H **103**
LE15: O'ham . . . 4H **127**
LE19: End . . . 6F **75**
LE67: Thrin . . . 4D **26**
**Jolly Farmers La.** LE12: Shep . . . 3C **28**
**Jonathan Cl.** LE6: Groby . . . 3E **62**
**Jon Baker Ct.** LE10: Hinc . . . 3H **103**
**Jordan Av.** LE18: Wig . . . 7G **77**
**Jordan Cl.** LE3: Glen . . . 6G **63**
LE16: L Bow . . . 4G **151**
**Jordan Ct.** LE6: Ratby . . . 6B **62**
**Joseph Cl.** LE7: Crop . . . 3J **57**
LE12: Hot . . . 1C **20**
**Journeymans Grn.** LE6: Ratby . . . 6B **62**
**Jovian Dr.** LE10: Hinc . . . 2D **102**
**Jowett Cl.** LE3: Leic . . . 5A **64**
**Joyce Rd.** LE3: Leic . . . 6B **64**
**Jubilee Av.** LE12: Sileby . . . 6K **33**
LE14: Ash . . . 2H **115**
**Jubilee Cl.** LE7: Sys . . . 7D **46**
**Jubilee Ct.** *LE9: N Ver . . . 6H 93*
*(off Chadwick Cl.)*
*LE15: O'ham . . . 4H 127*
*(off Northgate, not continuous)*
**Jubilee Cres.** LE19: Nar . . . 2G **81**
**Jubilee Cft.** LE67: Swep . . . 3B **50**
**Jubilee Dr.** LE3: Glen . . . 7G **63**
LE9: Earl S . . . 3D **100**
LE11: Lou . . . 4E **18**
LE15: L'ham . . . 6C **122**
**Jubilee Gdns.** LE4: Leic . . . 6K **65**
LE16: Mkt H . . . 3F **151**
**Jubilee Ho.** LE9: K Mux . . . 2B **68**
**Jubilee Rd.** LE1: Leic . . . 1D **4** (7F **65**)
LE9: B Ast . . . 4C **86**
LE9: N Ver . . . 6H **93**
**Jubilee St.** LE13: Mel M . . . 4F **117**
**Jubilee Ter.** DE12: Don . . . 3A **34**
**Jubilee Way** LE14: Scal . . . 5C **112**
**Judges St.** LE11: Lou . . . 7G **19**
**Judith Dr.** LE5: Leic . . . 3D **72**
LE8: Count . . . 5F **83**
**Julian Rd.** LE2: Leic . . . 6C **76**
**Junction 21 App.** LE19: End . . . 2H **75**
**Junction Rd.** LE1: Leic . . . 1E **4** (7G **65**)
LE18: Wig . . . 5K **77**
**June Av.** LE4: Leic . . . 1B **66**
**Junior St.** LE1: Leic . . . 2B **4** (1E **70**)
**Juniper Cl.** LE3: Leic E . . . 5D **68**
LE17: Lut . . . 3H **153**
**Juniper Way** LE11: Lou . . . 4E **30**
**Juno Cl.** LE3: Glen . . . 7G **63**
**Jupiter Cl.** LE2: Leic . . . 3G **4** (1H **71**)
**Justin Pk. Cvn. Site** LE16: G Ox . . . 7F **151**

## K

**Kamloops Cres.** LE1: Leic . . . 1E **4** (7G **65**)
**Kane Cl.** LE67: Coal . . . 3B **38**
**Kapelle Cl.** LE13: Mel M . . . 1H **117**
**Kashmir Rd.** LE1: Leic . . . 1G **4** (7H **65**)
**Kate St.** LE3: Leic . . . 2D **70**
**Kay Rd.** LE3: Leic . . . 6K **63**
**Keats Cl.** LE9: Earl S . . . 1E **100**
LE13: Mel M . . . 1E **116**
LE19: End . . . 5E **74**
**Keats La.** LE9: Earl S . . . 1D **100**
**Keats Wlk.** LE4: Leic . . . 6H **65**
**Keays Way** LE7: Scra . . . 6H **67**
**Keble Dr.** LE7: Sys . . . 2D **60**
**Keble Rd.** LE2: Leic . . . 6G **71**
KEDLESTON . . . 1A **158**
**Kedleston Av.** LE4: Birs . . . 1G **65**
**Kedleston Rd.** LE5: Leic . . . 4K **71**
**Keel Dr.** NG13: Bott . . . 2G **107**
**Keenan Cl.** LE2: Leic . . . 3B **76**
**Keep, The** LE9: K Mux . . . 2B **68**
**Keepers Cl.** DE12: Moi . . . 7C **22**
LE12: Swith . . . 6J **43**
**Keepers' Cft.** LE7: East G . . . 5G **47**
**Keepers Wlk.** LE4: Leic . . . 3B **64**
KEGWORTH . . . 6H **9** (2B **158**)
**Kegworth Av.** LE5: Leic . . . 2B **72**
**Kegworth La.** LE12: L Wha . . . 5F **13**
Kegworth Mus. . . . 6G **9**
**Kegworth Rd.** NG11: King S, Rat S . . . 4K **9**
**Keightley Rd.** LE3: Leic . . . 5J **63**
**Keightley Wlk.** *LE3: Leic . . . 5K 63*
*(off Keightley Rd.)*
LE4: Thurm . . . 7B **60**
KEISBY . . . 2D **161**
**Kelbrook Cl.** LE4: Leic . . . 2C **64**
KELBY . . . 1D **161**
**Kelcey Rd.** LE12: Quo . . . 4K **31**
**Kelham Cl.** LE11: Lou . . . 5E **30**
**Kelham Gro.** LE67: Rav . . . 4J **37**
KELMARSH . . . 3A **164**
**Kelmarsh Av.** LE18: Wig . . . 6K **77**
**Kelso Cl.** DE12: Mea . . . 6E **34**
LE65: Ash Z . . . 5A **24**
**Kelso Ct.** LE67: Thrin . . . 3E **26**
**Kelso Grn.** LE2: Leic . . . 5D **76**
**Kelthorpe Cl.** PE9: Ket . . . 7H **137**
**Kelvon Cl.** LE3: Glen . . . 5H **63**
**Kemble Sq.** LE1: Leic . . . 3D **4**
**Kemp Rd.** LE3: Leic . . . 5J **63**
LE67: Coal . . . 5C **38**
**Kempson Rd.** LE2: Leic . . . 7E **70**
**Kendal Ct.** LE2: Leic . . . 8B **5** (4E **70**)
**Kendall's Av.** LE9: Crof . . . 5A **80**
**Kendal Pl.** LE67: Ell . . . 1D **52**
**Kendal Rd.** LE4: Leic . . . 3K **65**
LE12: Sileby . . . 2K **45**
LE67: Ell . . . 1D **52**
**Kendrick Cl.** LE67: Coal . . . 2B **38**
**Kendrick Dr.** LE2: Oad . . . 3D **78**
**Kenilworth Av.** LE11: Lou . . . 6A **18**
**Kenilworth Cl.** LE9: B Ast . . . 2C **86**
LE12: Moun . . . 3D **44**
**Kenilworth Dr.** LE2: Oad . . . 3B **78**
LE65: Ash Z . . . 6A **24**
**Kenilworth Rd.** LE18: Wig . . . 5F **77**
**Ken Mackenzie Cl.** LE17: Lut . . . 2J **153**
**Kenmore Cres.** LE67: Coal . . . 3J **39**
**Kenmore Dr.** LE10: Hinc . . . 1E **102**
**Kennedy Cl.** LE15: O'ham . . . 4G **127**
**Kennedy Way** LE3: Leic E . . . 5F **69**
**Kennel La.** CV9: With . . . 6B **96**
**Kenneth Gamble Ct.** LE18: Wig . . . 4H **77**
**Kenneth Holmes Hall** LE1: Leic . . . 6E **5**
**Kennet Way** LE13: Mel M . . . 6D **116**
**Kenny Cl.** LE8: Whet . . . 3A **82**
**Kensington Av.** LE11: Lou . . . 5A **18**
**Kensington Cl.** LE2: G Par . . . 7D **76**
LE2: Oad . . . 5E **78**
**Kensington Dr.** LE18: Wig . . . 3K **77**
**Kensington Rd.** LE67: Coal . . . 4G **39**
**Kensington St.** LE4: Leic . . . 5G **65**
**Kent Cres.** LE18: Wig . . . 5F **77**
**Kent Dr.** LE2: Oad . . . 3E **78**
LE10: Hinc . . . 6H **99**
**Kenton Av.** LE18: Wig . . . 7J **77**
**Kent St.** LE2: Leic . . . 2G **4** (1H **71**)
LE5: Leic . . . 2G **4** (1H **71**)
**Kenwood Rd.** LE2: Leic . . . 1J **77**
**Kepston Cl.** LE2: Leic . . . 4D **76**
KERESLEY . . . 3A **162**
KERESLEY NEWLAND . . . 3A **162**
**Kernan Dr.** LE11: Lou . . . 3D **18**
**Kerrial Gdns.** LE3: Leic . . . 7J **63**
**Kerrial Rd.** LE3: Leic . . . 7J **63**
**Kerry Cl.** LE9: Barw . . . 3J **99**
**Kerrysdale Av.** LE4: Leic . . . 4K **65**
**Kertley** LE8: Flec . . . 3B **88**
**Kestian Cl.** LE16: Mkt H . . . 2D **150**
**Kestral Rd.** LE13: Mel M . . . 7E **116**
**Kestrel Cl.** LE3: Leic E . . . 5C **68**
LE5: Leic . . . 7J **65**
LE7: Sys . . . 1B **60**
LE8: Flec . . . 5C **88**
LE9: B Ast . . . 3C **86**
LE10: Bur . . . 5J **103**
**Kestrel La.** LE5: Ham . . . 4D **66**
LE12: Moun . . . 2F **45**
**Kestrel Rd.** LE15: O'ham . . . 2J **127**
**Keswick Av.** LE11: Lou . . . 2B **30**
**Keswick Cl.** LE2: Leic . . . 5C **76**
LE4: Birs . . . 5H **59**
**Keswick Rd.** LE8: Bla . . . 2A **82**
**Ketco Av.** PE9: Ket . . . 4J **137**
KETTERING . . . 3B **164**
**Kettering Rd.** LE16: L Bow, Mkt H . . . 4F **151**
KETTON . . . 6H **137** (1C **165**)
**Ketton Rd.** LE15: N Luf . . . 1C **136**
PE9: Coll . . . 7K **137**
PE9: Ket . . . 1C **136**
**Kevern Cl.** LE18: Wig . . . 7J **77**
**Kew Dr.** LE2: Oad . . . 5E **78**
LE18: Wig . . . 3H **77**
KEYHAM . . . 1D **163**
**Keyham Cl.** LE5: Leic . . . 5D **66**
**Keyham Ct.** LE5: Leic . . . 6C **66**

**Keyham La.** LE5: Leic . . . . . . . . . . . . .5E **66**
   LE7: Bee, Keyh . . . . . . . . . . . . .2K **67**
**Keyham La. E.** LE7: Scra . . . . . . . . .4J **67**
**Keyham La. W.** LE5: Leic . . . . . . . .5F **67**
**Keythorpe St.** LE2: Leic . . . . . . . . .1H **71**
**KEYWORTH** . . . . . . . . . . . . . . . . .1D **159**
**Kham Rd.** LE15: A'll . . . . . . . . . . . .6H **123**
**KIBWORTH BEAUCHAMP** . . . . . . .3J **89** (2D **163**)
**Kibworth Ct.** LE8: K Bea . . . . . . . . .3J **89**
**KIBWORTH HARCOURT** . . . . . . .2J **89** (2D **163**)
**Kibworth Rd.** LE8: Flec . . . . . . . . . .4C **88**
   LE8: Sad, K Bea . . . . . . . . . . .6D **88**
*Kibworth Sports Cen.* . . . . . . . . . . .4J **89**
**Kidger Cl.** LE12: Shep . . . . . . . . . . .6E **16**
**Kielder Cl.** LE19: Nar . . . . . . . . . . .6D **74**
**Kilberry Cl.** LE10: Hinc . . . . . . . . . .2D **102**
**Kilbourne Cl.** LE12: Sileby . . . . . . . .2J **45**
**Kilburn Av.** LE2: Oad . . . . . . . . . . .2B **78**
**Kilburn End** LE15: O'ham . . . . . . . .2H **127**
**Kilburn Rd.** LE15: O'ham . . . . . . . . .3H **127**
**KILBY** . . . . . . . . . . . . . . . .6C **84** (2D **163**)
**Kilby Av.** LE4: Birs . . . . . . . . . . . . .1G **65**
**KILBY BRIDGE** . . . . . . . . . . . . . . .2K **83**
**Kilby Dr.** LE18: Wig . . . . . . . . . . . .7A **78**
**Kilby Grn.** LE10: Bur . . . . . . . . . . . .5J **103**
**Kilby Rd.** LE8: Flec . . . . . . . . . . . .3A **88**
   LE8: Wist . . . . . . . . . . . . . . . .5D **84**
**Kildare St.** LE1: Leic . . . . . . .3D **4** (1F **71**)
**Kildare Wlk.** LE1: Leic . . . . . . . . . . .3D **4**
**Kilmarie Cl.** LE10: Hinc . . . . . . . . . .2D **102**
**Kilmelford Ct.** LE4: Leic . . . . . . . . .2K **65**
**Kiln Av.** LE4: Thurm . . . . . . . . . . . .7B **60**
**Kiln Cl.** LE9: B Ast . . . . . . . . . . . . .5E **86**
**Kiln Gth.** LE7: R'ley . . . . . . . . . . . .4F **45**
**Kiln Way** DE11: W'lle . . . . . . . . . . .1B **22**
**Kilverstone Av.** LE5: Leic . . . . . . . .4F **73**
**KILVINGTON** . . . . . . . . . . . . . . . .1B **160**
**Kilwardby St.** LE65: Ash Z . . . . . . . .5J **23**
**Kilworth Dr.** LE5: Leic . . . . . . . . . .4A **72**
**Kilworth Rd.** LE17: H Bos . . . . . . . .7A **148**
   LE17: Kim, Walt . . . . . . . . . . .7C **146**
   LE17: N Kil . . . . . . . . . . . . . . .1H **155**
   LE17: Swin . . . . . . . . . . . . . . .3H **157**
**Kimberley Rd.** LE2: Leic . . . . . . . . .4J **71**
**Kimberley St.** LE8: K Bea . . . . . . . . .3H **89**
**KIMCOTE** . . . . . . . . . . . .7A **146** (3C **163**)
**Kimcote Rd.** LE17: Walt . . . . . . . . .7A **146**
**Kincaple Rd.** LE4: Leic . . . . . . . . . .2K **65**
**Kinchley Cl.** LE3: Leic . . . . . . . . . . .3K **63**
**Kinchley La.** LE7: R'ley . . . . . . . . . .3A **44**
**Kincraig Rd.** LE4: Leic . . . . . . . . . .2K **65**
**Kinder Cl.** LE8: Whet . . . . . . . . . . .4A **82**
**Kingcup Cl.** LE3: Leic E . . . . . . . . . .5D **68**
*King Edward VII Community College Sports Hall*
   . . . . . . . . . . . . . . . . . . . . . . .2J **39**
*King Edward VII Community Sports Cen.* . .7G **117**
**King Edward Av.** LE19: Nar . . . . . . .2F **81**
**King Edward Rd.** LE5: Leic . . . . . . . .7B **66**
   LE11: Lou . . . . . . . . . . . . . . . .7G **19**
**King Edward's Way** LE15: E Wes . . . .3G **135**
**Kingfisher Av.** LE5: Leic . . . . . . . . .7J **65**
**Kingfisher Cl.** LE3: Leic E . . . . . . . . .5C **68**
   LE7: Sys . . . . . . . . . . . . . . . . .1B **60**
   LE8: G Gle . . . . . . . . . . . . . . .7K **79**
   LE9: Des . . . . . . . . . . . . . . . .3H **95**
   LE12: Bar S . . . . . . . . . . . . . .3E **32**
   LE14: T'ord . . . . . . . . . . . . . .6G **119**
   LE15: O'ham . . . . . . . . . . . . .3K **127**
   LE67: Whit . . . . . . . . . . . . . .2H **39**
**Kingfisher Ct.** LE2: Leic . . . . . . . . . .6B **5**
   LE10: Hinc . . . . . . . . . . . . . .5C **102**
   LE11: Lou . . . . . . . . . . . . . . .1D **30**
   LE13: Mel M . . . . . . . . . . . . .4E **116**
**Kingfisher Rd.** LE12: Moun . . . . . . .2F **45**
**Kingfisher Wlk.** LE5: Leic . . . . . . . .7J **65**
**Kingfisher Way** CV9: S Par . . . . . . .6C **90**
   LE11: Lou . . . . . . . . . . . . . . .1D **30**
**King George Av.** LE11: Lou . . . . . . . .7H **19**
   LE65: Ash Z . . . . . . . . . . . . . .4J **23**
**King George Rd.** LE11: Lou . . . . . . . .7H **19**
**King George's Way** LE10: Hinc . . . . .4E **102**
**King John's Rd.** LE67: Whit . . . . . . . .5F **27**
**King Richard Rd.** LE10: Hinc . . . . . . .1F **103**
**King Richards Hill** LE9: Earl S . . . . . .1G **101**
   LE67: Whit . . . . . . . . . . . . . .6F **27**
**King Richards Rd.** LE3: Leic . . . . . . .2C **70**
**King Richard Way**
   LE65: Ash Z . . . . . . . . . . . . . .4B **24**
**Kings Av.** LE11: Lou . . . . . . . . . . . .4D **18**
**Kingsbridge Cl.** LE19: Nar . . . . . . . .1E **80**
**Kingsbridge Cres.** LE4: Beau L . . . . . .6B **58**
**Kingsbury Av.** LE5: Leic . . . . . . . . . .3E **72**
**KING'S CLIFFE** . . . . . . . . . . . . . . .2D **165**
**Kingscliffe Cres.** LE5: Leic . . . . . . . .3F **73**
**Kings Cl.** LE14: Scal . . . . . . . . . . . .6C **112**
   LE15: O'ham . . . . . . . . . . . . .4G **127**
**Kings Ct.** LE9: Barw . . . . . . . . . . . .3A **100**

**Kings Dr.** LE3: Leic E . . . . . . . . . . . .5E **68**
   LE18: Wig . . . . . . . . . . . . . . .5K **77**
**Kingsfield Rd.** LE9: Barw . . . . . . . . .3A **100**
   LE9: Cosb . . . . . . . . . . . . . . .7G **81**
**Kingsgate** DE74: Lock . . . . . . . . . . .4D **8**
**Kingsgate Av.** LE4: Birs . . . . . . . . . .5F **59**
**King's Head Pl.** LE16: Mkt H . . . . . .4E **150**
**Kings La.** LE7: S Cro . . . . . . . . . . . .7A **118**
   LE14: Bur H . . . . . . . . . . . . . .6F **121**
   LE15: B'den . . . . . . . . . . . . . .7D **136**
**Kingsley Cl.** LE19: Nar . . . . . . . . . . .7E **74**
**Kingsley St.** LE2: Leic . . . . . . . . . . .7G **71**
**Kings Lock Cl.** LE2: Leic . . . . . . . . .4B **76**
**Kingsmead Cl.** LE2: Leic . . . . . . . . . .2J **77**
**Kingsmead Rd.** LE2: Leic . . . . . . . . .1J **77**
**King's Mills La.** DE72: W Tre . . . . . . .3A **6**
**KING'S NEWNHAM** . . . . . . . . . . .3B **162**
**KINGS NEWTON** . . . . . . . . . . . . .2A **158**
**Kings Newton St.** LE2: Leic . . . . . . . .3J **71**
**KING'S NORTON** . . . . . . . . . . . . .1D **163**
**Kings Rd.** LE12: Shep . . . . . . . . . . .1D **28**
   LE13: Mel M . . . . . . . . . . . . .4G **117**
   LE14: L Cla . . . . . . . . . . . . . . .2H **111**
   LE15: O'ham . . . . . . . . . . . . .4G **127**
   LE16: Mkt H . . . . . . . . . . . . .4E **150**
**King's Row** LE9: Earl S . . . . . . . . . . .2D **100**
**Kingsthorpe Cl.** LE4: Leic . . . . . . . . .3F **65**
**Kingston Av.** LE18: Wig . . . . . . . . . .4H **77**
**Kingston Dr.** LE10: Hinc . . . . . . . . . .6H **99**
**Kingston La.** DE74: Keg . . . . . . . . . .6H **9**
**KINGSTON ON SOAR** . . . . . . .4K **9** (2C **159**)
**Kingston Rd.** LE2: Leic . . . . . . . . . . .4J **71**
**Kingston Way** LE16: Mkt H . . . . . . .4E **150**
**King St.** LE1: Leic . . . . . . . . .5D **4** (2F **71**)
   LE2: Oad . . . . . . . . . . . . . . . .3D **78**
   LE7: Bark T . . . . . . . . . . . . . . .6F **61**
   LE8: Whet . . . . . . . . . . . . . . .2K **81**
   LE9: Barw . . . . . . . . . . . . . . .4A **100**
   LE10: Hinc . . . . . . . . . . . . . .2G **103**
   LE11: Lou . . . . . . . . . . . . . . .7G **19**
   LE12: Sea . . . . . . . . . . . . . . .3K **33**
   LE12: Sileby . . . . . . . . . . . . . .1J **45**
   LE13: Mel M . . . . . . . . . . . . .4F **117**
   LE14: N Bro . . . . . . . . . . . . . .2D **110**
   LE14: Scal . . . . . . . . . . . . . . .6C **112**
   LE14: T'ord . . . . . . . . . . . . . .7G **119**
   LE19: End . . . . . . . . . . . . . . .5F **75**
   LE67: Coal . . . . . . . . . . . . . . .4D **38**
**Kings Wlk.** LE3: Leic E . . . . . . . . . . .4E **68**
   LE9: Earl S . . . . . . . . . . . . . . .2D **100**
**Kings Way** LE6: Groby . . . . . . . . . . .4D **62**
**Kingsway** LE3: Brau . . . . . . . . . . . .6K **69**
   LE17: Lut . . . . . . . . . . . . . . .5H **153**
**Kingsway Nth.** LE3: Brau . . . . . . . . .5J **69**
**Kingsway Rd.** LE5: Leic . . . . . . . . . .5A **72**
**Kingswood Av.** LE3: Leic . . . . . . . . .3B **70**
   LE11: Lou . . . . . . . . . . . . . . .5J **17**
**Kingswood Ct.** LE18: Wig . . . . . . . . .6J **77**
**King William's Way** LE7: Anst . . . . . .6J **57**
**Kinley Rd.** LE4: Leic . . . . . . . . . . . .2E **64**
**KINOULTON** . . . . . . . . . . . . . . . .1D **159**
**Kinross Av.** LE5: Leic . . . . . . . . . . .1G **73**
**Kinross Cres.** LE11: Lou . . . . . . . . . .5B **18**
**Kinross Way** LE10: Hinc . . . . . . . . . .2C **102**
**Kinsdale Dr.** LE5: Leic . . . . . . . . . . .7G **67**
**Kintyre Cl.** LE10: Hinc . . . . . . . . . .2E **102**
**Kintyre Dr.** LE4: Leic . . . . . . . . . . .2J **65**
**Kipling Dr.** LE13: Mel M . . . . . . . . .2E **116**
   LE19: End . . . . . . . . . . . . . . .6E **74**
**Kipling Gro.** LE4: Leic . . . . . . . . . . .4A **64**
**KIRBY BELLARS** . . . . . . . . . . . . . .3A **160**
**Kirby Cl.** LE9: Sap . . . . . . . . . . . . .3J **105**
   LE12: Moun . . . . . . . . . . . . .4D **44**
**Kirby Dr.** DE74: Keg . . . . . . . . . . . .7G **9**
**KIRBY FIELDS** . . . . . . . . . .3D **68** (1C **163**)
**Kirby La.** LE9: Leic E . . . . . . . . . . . .4D **68**
   LE13: Mel M . . . . . . . . . . . . .7F **117**
   LE14: Mel M . . . . . . . . . . . . .7A **116**
**KIRBY MUXLOE** . . . . . . . . .2B **68** (1C **163**)
*Kirby Muxloe Castle (remains of)* . . . . .1D **68**
**Kirby Rd.** LE3: Glen . . . . . . . . . . . .7D **62**
   LE3: Leic . . . . . . . . . . . . . . . .2C **70**
**Kirfield Dr.** LE10: Hinc . . . . . . . . . . .7J **99**
**Kirk Av.** DE74: Keg . . . . . . . . . . . . .6H **9**
**Kirkby La.** LE9: N Ver . . . . . . . . . . .7J **93**
   LE9: Peck . . . . . . . . . . . . . . .6H **95**
**KIRKBY MALLORY** . . . . . . .6G **95** (1B **162**)
**Kirkby Rd.** LE9: Barw . . . . . . . . . . .4K **99**
   LE9: Des . . . . . . . . . . . . . . . .3G **95**
   LE9: Earl S . . . . . . . . . . . . . . .1E **100**
**KIRKBY UNDERWOOD** . . . . . . . . .2D **161**
**Kirkdale Rd.** LE18: Wig . . . . . . . . . .6F **77**
**Kirke Wlk.** LE3: Leic . . . . . . . . . . . .1H **69**
**Kirkfield Rd.** LE8: Count . . . . . . . . . .5F **83**
**KIRK HALLAM** . . . . . . . . . . . . . . .1B **158**
**KIRK HILL** . . . . . . . . . . . . . . . . . .6E **16**

**Kirkhill** LE12: Shep . . . . . . . . . . . . .6E **16**
**Kirkhill Cl.** LE67: Coal . . . . . . . . . . .3K **39**
**Kirkland Cl.** DE74: C Don . . . . . . . . .5J **7**
**Kirkland Rd.** LE3: Brau . . . . . . . . . .7K **69**
**Kirk La.** LE19: End . . . . . . . . . . . . .5F **75**
**KIRK LANGLEY** . . . . . . . . . . . . . .1A **158**
**Kirkman Cl.** CV13: B'one . . . . . . . . .6B **92**
**Kirk's Cl.** LE15: Gree . . . . . . . . . . . .5F **125**
**Kirkscroft Wlk.** LE4: Leic . . . . . . . . .3F **65**
**Kirkstead Wlk.** LE4: Leic . . . . . . . . .3E **64**
**Kirkstone Cl.** LE3: Glen . . . . . . . . . .5H **63**
**Kirkstone Dr.** LE11: Lou . . . . . . . . . .2A **30**
**Kirkwall Cres.** LE5: Leic . . . . . . . . . .7G **67**
**Kirloe Av.** LE3: Leic E . . . . . . . . . . .4D **68**
**Kirminton Gdns.** LE5: Leic . . . . . . . .1E **72**
**Kirtley Way** LE9: B Ast . . . . . . . . . .4E **86**
**Kirton Dr.** LE13: Mel M . . . . . . . . . .1D **116**
**Kirton Rd.** LE67: Coal . . . . . . . . . . .3K **39**
**Kitchener Rd.** LE5: Leic . . . . . . . . . .7A **66**
   LE7: Anst . . . . . . . . . . . . . . . .6J **57**
**Kite Cl.** LE9: B Ast . . . . . . . . . . . . .2C **86**
**Klondyke La.** LE14: T Sat . . . . . . . . .2J **119**
**Klondyke Way** LE14: Ash . . . . . . . . .2F **115**
**KNAPTOFT** . . . . . . . . . . . . . . . . .7K **147**
**Knapton Cl.** LE10: Hinc . . . . . . . . . .7D **98**
**KNIGHTON** . . . . . . . . . . . . .1H **77** (1D **163**)
**Knighton Chu. Rd.** LE2: Leic . . . . . . .1J **77**
**Knighton Cl.** LE9: B Ast . . . . . . . . . .6E **86**
**Knighton Ct.** LE2: Leic . . . . . . . . . . .5J **71**
**Knighton Dr.** LE2: Leic . . . . . . . . . .7J **71**
**KNIGHTON FIELDS** . . . . . . . . . . . .6G **71**
**Knighton Flds. Rd. E.** LE2: Leic . . . . .7G **71**
**Knighton Flds. Rd. W.** LE2: Leic . . . .7F **71**
**Knighton Grange Rd.** LE2: Leic . . . . .7A **72**
**Knighton Hall** LE2: Leic . . . . . . . . . .7J **71**
**Knighton Junc. La.** LE2: Leic . . . . . . .6G **71**
**Knighton La.** LE2: Leic . . . . . . . . . . .7E **70**
**Knighton La. E.** LE2: Leic . . . . . . . . .7E **70**
**Knighton Lodge** LE2: Leic . . . . . . . . .7J **71**
**Knighton Pk. Rd.** LE2: Leic . . . . . . . .5H **71**
**Knighton Ri.** LE2: Leic . . . . . . . . . . .6A **72**
**Knighton Rd.** LE2: Leic . . . . . . . . . . .5H **71**
**Knighton St.** LE2: Leic . . . . . . . .7C **5** (3F **71**)
**Knighton Way** LE1: Leic . . . . . . .10F **5** (5G **71**)
**Knighton Yd.** LE17: N Kil . . . . . . . . .2K **155**
**Knights Cl.** LE4: Thurm . . . . . . . . . .6B **60**
   LE7: Bilth . . . . . . . . . . . . . . .6H **131**
   LE9: S Stan . . . . . . . . . . . . . .7J **101**
   LE10: Bur . . . . . . . . . . . . . . .7G **103**
   LE65: Ash Z . . . . . . . . . . . . . .4J **23**
**Knights Ct.** LE10: Hinc . . . . . . . . . . .3B **102**
**Knights Cres.** LE7: R'ley . . . . . . . . . .6E **44**
**Knight's End Rd.** LE16: G Bow . . . . .1H **151**
**Knights Gth.** LE67: Whit . . . . . . . . . .6F **27**
**Knights Link** LE9: Earl S . . . . . . . . . .1G **101**
**Knight's Rd.** LE4: Beau L . . . . . . . . .7C **58**
**Knightthorpe Ct.** LE11: Lou . . . . . . . .5B **18**
**Knightthorpe Lodge** *LE11: Lou* . . . . . .7K **17**
   *(off Windleden Rd.)*
**Knightthorpe Rd.** LE11: Lou . . . . . . .6B **18**
   *(not continuous)*
**KNIPTON** . . . . . . . . . . . . . . . . . .1B **160**
**Knipton Dr.** LE11: Lou . . . . . . . . . . .7A **18**
**Knipton Rd.** NG32: Bran . . . . . . . . .6K **109**
**Knollgate Cl.** LE4: Birs . . . . . . . . . . .5E **58**
**Knoll St.** LE16: Mkt H . . . . . . . . . . .4C **150**
**KNOSSINGTON** . . . . . . . . .2C **126** (1B **164**)
**Knossington Rd.** LE14: Som . . . . . . .1A **126**
   LE15: B Rut . . . . . . . . . . . . . .6B **126**
   LE15: Knos . . . . . . . . . . . . . .3A **126**
**Knowle, The** LE2: Leic . . . . . . . . . . .7J **71**
**Knowles Rd.** LE3: Leic . . . . . . . . . . .7J **63**
**Koppe Cl.** DE12: Moi . . . . . . . . . . . .5D **22**
**Krefeld Way** LE4: Leic . . . . . . . . . . .3A **64**

## L

**Labrador Cl.** LE1: Leic . . . . . . . .1F **4** (7G **65**)
**Laburnam Way** LE11: Lou . . . . . . . . .5E **30**
**Laburnum Av.** LE9: N Ver . . . . . . . . .6G **93**
   LE17: Lut . . . . . . . . . . . . . . .4H **153**
**Laburnum Cl.** LE12: Hat . . . . . . . . . .1J **17**
**Laburnum Dr.** LE9: Earl S . . . . . . . . .3C **100**
**Laburnum Rd.** LE5: Leic . . . . . . . . . .5E **66**
**Lacey Cl.** LE17: Lut . . . . . . . . . . . . .2J **153**
**Lacey Ct.** LE12: Shep . . . . . . . . . . . .7D **16**
**Ladbroke Gro.** LE8: Count . . . . . . . . .5F **83**
**Lady Ga.** DE74: Dis . . . . . . . . . . . . .4A **12**
**Lady Hay Rd.** LE3: Leic . . . . . . . . . . .3J **63**
**Lady Jane Mobile Home Pk.** LE6: New L . . .5C **56**
**Lady Leys** LE9: Cosb . . . . . . . . . . . .6G **81**
**Ladysmith Rd.** LE9: K Mux . . . . . . . .2B **68**
**Ladywell** LE15: O'ham . . . . . . . . . . .3K **127**
**Ladywood Ct.** LE17: Lut . . . . . . . . . .3J **153**

Lag La. LE14: Bur L ........5K 117
LE14: T Arn ........2K 117
Laithwaite Cl. LE4: Beau L ........7B 58
Lakeside Bus. Pk. LE4: Thurm ........7J 59
Lakeside Ct. LE7: Thurn ........3H 73
Lakeside Vw. LE67: Whit ........1E 38
Lake Ter. LE13: Mel M ........5D 116
Lakeview Chase LE5: Ham ........3E 66
Lakin Dr. LE3: Brau ........5G 69
Lakins, The DE12: Mea ........7F 35
Lambert Av. LE12: Shep ........7D 16
Lambert Cl. LE13: Mel M ........1F 117
Lambert Rd. LE3: Leic ........5C 70
Lambert's Cl. LE15: Mor ........6J 135
Lambley Lodge La. LE15: Bel R ........4G 133
Lamborne Rd. LE2: Leic ........3G 77
Lambourne Rd. LE4: Birs ........5H 59
Lamen Rd. LE3: Leic ........5J 63
Lamford Cl. LE10: Hinc ........2E 102
Lammas Cl. LE15: B Rut ........6D 126
LE17: Ash P ........6K 143
LE17: H Bos ........6C 148
Lamplighters LE8: Flec ........4B 88
Lamport Cl. LE11: Lou ........6A 18
LE18: Wig ........6B 78
Lancashire St. LE4: Leic ........3H 65
Lancaster Av. CV13: Mkt B ........3C 94
Lancaster Cl. LE9: Des ........2H 95
LE17: Lut ........5J 153
LE67: Coal ........3K 39
Lancaster Ct. LE6: Groby ........4C 62
Lancaster Pl. LE1: Leic ........8E 5 (4G 71)
Lancaster Rd. LE1: Leic ........7D 5 (3F 71)
LE10: Hinc ........3G 103
Lancaster St. LE5: Leic ........1K 71
Lancaster Wlk. LE1: Leic ........7D 5 (3F 71)
Lancaster Way LE2: G Par ........7E 76
Lance Cl. LE10: Bur ........6G 103
Lancelot Cl. LE3: Leic E ........5E 68
Lancers Dr. LE13: Mel M ........1D 116
Lancing Av. LE3: Leic ........1A 70
Landscape Dr. LE5: Leic ........3E 72
Landseer Dr. LE10: Hinc ........7E 98
Landseer Rd. LE2: Leic ........6H 71
Lands End Way LE15: O'ham ........2H 127
Land Society La. LE9: Earl S ........2D 100
Lane, The LE7: Bars ........5C 118
LE14: Roth ........3D 114
Lane Cl. LE3: Glen ........6G 63
Lanesborough Ct. LE11: Lou ........1E 30
Lanesborough Dr. LE7: Thurc ........2B 54
Lanesborough Rd. LE4: Leic ........2H 65
Lanes Cl. LE12: Sileby ........7K 33
Laneshaw Av. LE11: Lou ........1K 29
Lanes Hill Gro. LE9: S Stan ........2K 105
Laneside Dr. LE10: Hinc ........7J 99
Lanfear Ct. LE10: Hinc ........4F 103
Langabeer Ct. LE11: Lou ........6G 19
(off Nottingham Rd.)
LANGAR ........1A 160
Langar La. LE14: Harb ........1C 108
NG13: Lan ........1C 108
Langdale LE8: Flec ........3B 88
Langdale Av. LE11: Lou ........2B 30
Langdale Rd. LE4: Thurm ........6B 60
LE10: Hinc ........3C 102
Langdale Wlk. LE16: Mkt H ........6E 150
LANGHAM ........5C 122 (3B 160)
Langham Dr. LE19: Nar ........1E 80
Langham Rd. LE4: Leic ........3B 66
LE15: A'll ........7F 123
Langhill, The LE5: Leic ........1B 72
Langholm Rd. LE5: Leic ........1G 73
Langley Av. LE4: Leic ........3F 65
Langley Cl. LE9: Hun ........1C 80
LANGLEY COMMON ........1A 158
Langley Dr. DE74: Keg ........6G 9
LANGLEY GREEN ........1A 158
Langley Wlk. LE4: Leic ........3E 64
LANGTOFT ........3D 161
Langton Cl. LE67: Whit ........5E 26
Langton Rd. LE8: Kib H ........1J 89
LE16: Fox ........1H 149 & 4A 140
LE16: G Bow ........1G 151
LE16: Hall ........7A 132
LE18: Wig ........7K 77
Lansdowne Av. LE12: Shep ........5E 16
Lansdowne Dr. LE11: Lou ........2E 30
Lansdowne Gro. LE18: Wig ........1F 83
Lansdowne Rd. LE2: Leic ........7E 70
LE12: Shep ........5D 16
Lant, The LE12: Shep ........6E 16
Lapwing Cl. LE4: Beau L ........7B 58
Lapwing Ct. LE19: Nar ........2E 80
Larch Cl. LE17: Lut ........4H 153
Larchfield LE15: O'ham ........2J 127
Larch Gro. LE3: Brau ........4G 69

Larchmont Rd. LE4: Leic ........6D 64
Larch St. LE5: Leic ........7J 65
Larchwood Cl. LE8: Count ........5E 82
Larchwood Av. LE6: Groby ........3D 62
Larchwood Cl. LE2: Leic ........1G 77
Larchwood Ri. LE15: Knos ........2C 126
Larcot Gdn. Cl. LE12: Moun ........4E 44
Lark Cl. LE3: Leic E ........5D 68
Lark Ri. LE11: Lou ........5E 30
Larkspur Cl. LE5: Ham ........3D 66
Larkswood LE8: K Bea ........3K 89
LASH HILL ........3J 103
Lash Hill Path LE10: Bur ........3H 103
Lastingham Cl. LE2: Leic ........2G 77
Lathkill St. LE16: Mkt H ........6F 151
Latimer Cl. LE8: Bla ........3A 82
Latimer Ct. LE7: Anst ........7H 57
Latimer Cres. LE8: L Bow ........5F 151
Latimer Pl. LE4: Leic ........6G 65
Latimer Rd. LE7: Crop ........2K 57
Latimer St. LE3: Leic ........3D 70
LE7: Anst ........1J 63
Laud Cl. LE67: Ibs ........4J 51
LAUGHTON ........
Lutterworth ........2E 148 (3D 163)
Sleaford ........1D 161
Laughton La. LE17: L'ton, Mows ........3B 148
Laughton Rd. LE16: Lub ........6F 149
Launceston Dr. LE67: Hug ........5C 38
Launceston Ho. LE18: Wig ........1J 83
Launceston Rd. LE18: Wig ........7J 77
Launde Pk. LE16: L Bow ........5G 151
Launde Rd. LE2: Oad ........1E 78
LE67: Mark ........5H 55
Laundon Cl. LE6: Groby ........4D 62
Laundon Way LE6: Groby ........5C 62
LE8: Whet ........4A 82
Laundry La. LE4: Leic ........4H 65
Laura Davies Cl. LE13: Mel M ........1F 117
Laurel Cl. LE3: Glen ........6J 63
LE12: Moun ........2E 44
Laurel Dr. DE72: A Tre ........1C 6
LE2: Oad ........5F 79
LE8: Count ........5E 82
Laurel Flds. LE17: C Mag ........5C 142
Laurel Rd. LE2: Leic ........3J 71
LE8: Bla ........1B 82
LE11: Lou ........5E 30
Laurels, The LE67: Mark ........7G 55
Laurel Way NG13: Bott ........1F 107
Laureston Dr. LE2: Leic ........5K 71
Lavender Cl. LE8: Bla ........1A 82
LE11: Lou ........5E 30
Lavender Ho. LE13: Mel M ........4G 117
(off St Johns Ct.)
Lavender Rd. LE3: Leic ........4C 70
Lavershall Way LE19: Brau ........2J 75
Laverstock Rd. LE18: Wig ........1J 83
Lawford Rd. LE2: Leic ........4D 76
Lawn Av. LE4: Birs ........6H 59
Lawn Cl. LE4: Thurm ........6B 60
Lawn Cl. LE14: O Dal ........7A 110
Lawns, The LE2: Leic ........5J 71
LE10: Hinc ........3H 103
Lawns Wood LE10: Hinc ........3D 102
Lawnwood Rd. LE6: Groby ........3B 62
Lawrence Cl. LE4: Leic ........4C 58
LE15: Mkt O ........2H 123
LE67: Ell ........1C 52
Lawrence Wlk. LE3: Leic ........2A 70
Lawrence Way LE11: Lou ........3A 18
Lawson Cl. LE12: Sileby ........1J 45
Law St. LE4: Leic ........5G 65
Lawton Cl. LE10: Hinc ........3C 102
Lawyers La. LE2: Oad ........3C 78
(not continuous)
Laxford Cl. LE4: Leic ........4C 64
LE10: Hinc ........2C 102
LAXTON ........2C 165
Laxton Cl. LE4: Birs ........5H 59
LE18: Wig ........6B 78
Lay Cock Av. LE13: Mel M ........3F 117
Layton Rd. LE65: Leic ........7A 66
Lea, The LE8: K Bea ........3K 89
Lea Cl. LE4: Thurm ........6K 59
LE9: B Ast ........5E 86
Lea Dr. LE11: Lou ........4F 31
Leake La. LE12: Stan S ........1G 19
Lealand, The LE16: East F ........7B 150
Leamington Dr. LE8: Bla ........3B 82
Leamington Ter. LE15: Upp ........2C 138
Leas, The LE15: Cott ........6A 124
Leas Cl. LE7: Thurn ........1H 73
Leatherlands DE74: Keg ........5H 9
Lea Vw. PE9: Ryh ........5G 129
Leckhampton Rd. LE11: Lou ........6A 18

Leconfield Rd. LE11: Lou ........3A 30
Ledbury Cl. LE2: Oad ........4F 79
Ledbury Grn. LE4: Leic ........1D 64
Ledbury Rd. LE11: Lou ........4D 30
Ledbury Wlk. LE15: Cott ........4C 124
Ledwell Dr. LE3: Glen ........5G 63
Lee Circ. LE1: Leic ........2E 4 (1G 71)
Lee Cl. LE9: S Stan ........7K 101
Leecrofts, The LE9: Earl S ........2E 100
Lee Ri. LE6: Ratby ........6B 62
LEES ........1A 158
Lees Cres. LE67: Whit ........6G 27
Leeson St. LE2: Leic ........1E 76
Lee St. LE1: Leic ........2D 4 (1F 71)
Legion Dr. LE67: Ibs ........5K 51
Legion Way LE19: Brau ........7H 69
LEICESTER ........4D 4 (1C 163)
Leicester Bowling Club ........1J 77
Leicester City FC ........10A 5 (5E 70)
Leicester Comedy Festival, The ........4C 4
(off Hotel St.)
LEICESTER FOREST EAST ........5D 68 (1C 163)
Leicester Gas Mus. ........6E 70
Leicester La. LE9: Des ........2J 95
LE12: Swith ........7H 43
LE16: G Bow ........1D 150
LE19: End ........5F 75
Leicester Leys Leisure Cen. ........1A 64
Leicester Monarchs (Speedway) ........1A 4
(off St Margaret's Way)
Leicester Mus. of Technology ........4F 65
Leicester North Station
Great Central Railway ........1F 65
Leicester Outdoor Pursuits Cen. ........2G 65
Leicester Pl. LE13: Mel M ........4F 117
Leicester Racecourse ........3A 78
Leicester Rd. DE12: Mea ........7F 35
LE2: G Par ........7B 76
LE2: Leic ........1A 78
LE2: Oad ........3C 78
LE3: Glen ........4H 63
LE4: Leic ........4D 58
LE6: Groby ........3D 62
LE7: Anst ........7J 57
LE7: Bill ........6F 131
LE7: Crop, Thurc ........2A 58
LE7: T Hil ........3G 131
LE8: Bla ........7B 76
LE8: Count ........5F 83
LE8: Flec ........7G 85
LE8: Kib H ........1H 89
LE9: B Ast ........1B 86
(not continuous)
LE9: Barw ........5B 100
LE9: Earl S ........1E 100
LE9: Sap ........4J 105
LE10: Hinc ........2H 103
LE10: S'ord ........7G 105
LE11: Lou ........7F 19
LE12: Lou ........7F 19
LE12: Moun ........1E 44
LE12: Quo ........6A 32
LE12: Shep ........7E 16
LE13: Mel M ........6D 116
LE14: F Wre ........5J 115
LE14: F Wre, K Bel ........4D 114
LE14: K Bel, Mel M ........7A 116
LE15: Bel R, Ward ........6F 133
LE15: Upp ........1A 138
LE16: Mkt H ........2C 150
LE17: H Bos ........1J 153
LE17: Lut ........1J 153
LE17: Mows ........3A 148
LE18: Wig ........3J 77
LE19: End ........7H 75
LE65: Ash Z ........5A 24
LE67: Ibs ........3K 51
LE67: Mark ........4G 55
LE67: Rav ........1G 37
(not continuous)
LE67: Whit ........7F 27
Leicester Royal Infirmary Mus. ........8C 5 (4F 71)
Leicester St Martin's Cathedral ........4C 4 (2F 71)
Leicestershire County Cricket Ground ........1E 76
Leicestershire Lawn Tennis Club ........6J 71
Leicester Station (Rail) ........5F 4 (2G 71)
Leicester St. LE5: Leic ........1K 71
LE13: Mel M ........4F 117
Leicester Tigers RFC ........8D 5 (4F 71)
Leicester University ........10F 5 (5G 71)
Leicester Western By-Pass
LE4: Beau L, Leic ........2G 63
LE6: Groby ........7D 62
LE7: Anst ........2G 63
LE7: Sys, Wan ........3G 59
Leighton Av. LE11: Lou ........7K 17
Leighton Cres. LE9: Elm ........5E 100

LEIRE . . . . . . . . . . . . . . . . . .2K 143 (2C 163)
Leire La. LE9: B Ast . . . . . . . . . . . . . . . .6B 86
LE17: Ash P, Leire . . . . . . . . . . . .5K 143
LE17: D Bas . . . . . . . . . . . . . . .2B 144
Leire Rd. LE17: Frol, Leire . . . . . . . . .2F 143
Leire St. LE4: Leic . . . . . . . . . . . . . . . . .4H 65
Leith Cl. LE65: Ash Z . . . . . . . . . . . . . . .6B 24
Lema Cl. LE4: Leic . . . . . . . . . . . . . . . . .1A 66
Lemon Gro. DE11: C Gre, C Gre . . . . . . .2A 22
Lemontree Av. LE11: Lou . . . . . . . . . . . .4E 30
Lemyngton St. LE11: Lou . . . . . . . . . . . . .6F 19
Lena Dr. LE6: Groby . . . . . . . . . . . . . . . .1A 62
Len Hollis Ct. LE2: Leic . . . . . . . . . . . . . .5G 4
Lenthall Sq. LE16: Mkt H . . . . . . . . . . .6E 150
LENTON
    Grantham . . . . . . . . . . . . . . . . .1D 161
    Nottingham . . . . . . . . . . . . . . .1C 159
Leopold Cl. LE8: Count . . . . . . . . . . . . .5D 82
Leopold Rd. LE2: Leic . . . . . . . . . . . . . .6G 71
Leopold St. LE11: Lou . . . . . . . . . . . . . .6D 18
LE18: Wig . . . . . . . . . . . . . . . . . .6F 77
Leslie Cl. LE11: Lou . . . . . . . . . . . . . . . .4B 18
Lester Ct. LE12: L Wha . . . . . . . . . . . . .5E 12
Letchworth Rd. LE3: Leic . . . . . . . . . . . .1A 70
Lethbridge Cl. LE1: Leic . . . . . . .1F 4 (7G 65)
LE15: O'ham . . . . . . . . . . . . . .4K 127
Leven Cl. LE10: Hinc . . . . . . . . . . . . . .3E 102
Leveret Dr. LE8: Whet . . . . . . . . . . . . . .4K 81
Leveric Rd. LE5: Leic . . . . . . . . . . . . . . .6A 66
Lewis Cl. LE4: Leic . . . . . . . . . . . . . . . .4B 64
Lewisher Rd. LE4: Leic . . . . . . . . . . . . .3B 66
Lewis Rd. LE11: Lou . . . . . . . . . . . . . . .5B 18
Lewis Way LE8: Count . . . . . . . . . . . . . .6F 83
Lewitt Cl. LE4: Leic . . . . . . . . . . . . . . . .2D 64
Lexham St. LE4: Leic . . . . . . . . . . . . . . .4H 65
Leyburn Cl. DE11: C Gre . . . . . . . . . . . .2A 22
Leybury Way LE7: Scra . . . . . . . . . . . . .1H 73
Leycroft Rd. LE4: Beau L . . . . . . . . . . . .7B 58
Leyland Rd. LE3: Brau . . . . . . . . . . . . . .1K 75
Leys, The LE7: East G . . . . . . . . . . . . . .4G 47
LE8: Count . . . . . . . . . . . . . . . .6C 82
LE8: K Bea . . . . . . . . . . . . . . . .2J 89
LE12: Hat . . . . . . . . . . . . . . . . .2J 17
Leys Cl. LE2: Oad . . . . . . . . . . . . . . . . .2E 78
Leys Cres. LE17: S Kil . . . . . . . . . . . . .5H 155
Leysdale Cl. LE4: Leic . . . . . . . . . . . . . .3B 64
Leysland Av. LE8: Count . . . . . . . . . . . .5C 82
Leysmill Cl. LE10: Hinc . . . . . . . . . . . .2C 102
Leyton Cl. LE17: Lut . . . . . . . . . . . . . .5K 153
Liberty Pk. LE2: Leic . . . . . . . . .8A 5 (4E 70)
Liberty Rd. LE3: Leic . . . . . . . . . . . . . . .1H 69
Library Cl. LE10: Bur . . . . . . . . . . . . . .6K 103
Lichfield Av. LE9: B Ast . . . . . . . . . . . . .2C 86
Lichfield Dr. LE8: Bla . . . . . . . . . . . . . . .3B 82
Lichfield St. LE1: Leic . . . . . . . .1C 4 (7F 65)
Lidster Cl. LE5: Leic . . . . . . . . . . . . . . .6D 66
Lilac Av. LE5: Leic . . . . . . . . . . . . . . . .5E 66
Lilac Cl. LE10: Bur . . . . . . . . . . . . . . .5H 103
LE11: Lou . . . . . . . . . . . . . . . .4E 30
Lilac Dr. LE17: Lut . . . . . . . . . . . . . . .4G 153
Lilac Wlk. LE5: Leic . . . . . . . . . . . . . . .5E 66
Lilac Way LE7: East G . . . . . . . . . . . . . .5G 47
LE13: Mel M . . . . . . . . . . . . . .2E 116
LILBOURNE . . . . . . . . . . . . . . . . . .3C 163
Lilbourne Rd. LE17: Cat . . . . . . . . . . . .6D 156
Lilleshall Way LE11: Lou . . . . . . . . . . . .5K 17
Lily Bank LE67: Thrin . . . . . . . . . . . . . .2C 26
Limber Cres. LE3: Leic . . . . . . . . . . . . .4J 69
Limby Hall La. LE67: Swan . . . . . . . . . . .5K 25
Lime Av. DE12: Mea . . . . . . . . . . . . . . .6E 34
LE6: Groby . . . . . . . . . . . . . . . .4C 62
LE11: Lou . . . . . . . . . . . . . . . .7G 19
Lime Cl. LE7: Sys . . . . . . . . . . . . . . . . .2D 60
Lime Dr. LE7: Sys . . . . . . . . . . . . . . . . .3D 60
Limefield LE15: O'ham . . . . . . . . . . . . .2J 127
Lime Gro. LE8: Bla . . . . . . . . . . . . . . . .1B 82
LE9: Earl S . . . . . . . . . . . . . . .3D 100
LE9: K Mux . . . . . . . . . . . . . . .2B 68
LE67: Bag . . . . . . . . . . . . . . . .1F 93
NG13: Bott . . . . . . . . . . . . . . .2G 107
Lime Gro. Cl. LE4: Leic . . . . . . . . . . . . .2C 64
Limehurst Av. LE11: Lou . . . . . . . . . . . .5E 18
Limehurst Rd. LE5: Leic . . . . . . . . . . . . .5F 67
Limekiln, The DE73: B Hil . . . . . . . . . . . .7B 10
Lime Kilns LE18: Wig . . . . . . . . . . . . . . .1A 84
Lime Kilns, The LE12: Bar S . . . . . . . . . .3D 32
Limes, The LE15: Mkt O . . . . . . . . . . . .2J 123
LE16: T Lan . . . . . . . . . . . . . . .3E 140
LE67: Rav . . . . . . . . . . . . . . . .2A 38
Limes Av. LE13: Mel M . . . . . . . . . . . . .3G 117
Lime St. LE14: Bur L . . . . . . . . . . . . . .2C 120
Lime Tree Av. LE4: Birs . . . . . . . . . . . . .5G 59
LE15: Upp . . . . . . . . . . . . . . .2B 138
Limetree Gro. LE11: Lou . . . . . . . . . . . .7G 19
Lime Tree Rd. LE19: End . . . . . . . . . . . .6H 75
Linacres Rd. LE3: Leic . . . . . . . . . . . . . .4J 69
Lincoln Ct. LE16: Mkt H . . . . . . . . . . . .2F 151

Lincoln Dr. LE7: Sys . . . . . . . . . . . . . . .3E 60
LE8: Bla . . . . . . . . . . . . . . . . .3B 82
LE13: Mel M . . . . . . . . . . . . . .7G 117
LE18: Wig . . . . . . . . . . . . . . . . .6F 77
Lincoln Rd. LE9: Barw . . . . . . . . . . . . . .4K 99
Lincoln St. LE2: Leic . . . . . . . . .5G 4 (2H 71)
Linden Av. LE8: Count . . . . . . . . . . . . . .5C 82
Linden Cl. LE67: Ibs . . . . . . . . . . . . . . .3J 51
Linden Dr. LE5: Leic . . . . . . . . . . . . . . .4B 72
LE17: Lut . . . . . . . . . . . . . . . .4H 153
Linden Farm Dr. LE8: Count . . . . . . . . . .5D 82
Linden Gro. LE12: Moun . . . . . . . . . . . .3E 44
Linden La. LE9: K Mux . . . . . . . . . . . . . .3D 68
Linden Rd. LE10: Hinc . . . . . . . . . . . . .2F 103
LE11: Lou . . . . . . . . . . . . . . . .5E 18
Linden St. LE5: Leic . . . . . . . . . . . . . . .2K 71
Linden Way LE67: Coal . . . . . . . . . . . . .2C 38
Lindfield Rd. LE3: Leic . . . . . . . . . . . . . .7A 64
Lindisfarne Dr. LE11: Lou . . . . . . . . . . . .5J 17
Lindisfarne Rd. LE7: Sys . . . . . . . . . . . .2B 60
Lindrick Dr. LE5: Leic . . . . . . . . . . . . . .5A 72
Lindridge La. LE9: Des . . . . . . . . . . . . .1H 95
Lindsay Rd. LE5: Leic . . . . . . . . . . . . . .6B 70
Lindsey Gdns. LE16: Mkt H . . . . . . . . . .7D 150
Lindum Cl. LE7: Sys . . . . . . . . . . . . . . .3B 60
Lineker Way LE2: Leic . . . . . . . .9A 5 (4E 70)
Linford Cl. LE18: Wig . . . . . . . . . . . . . .6A 78
Linford Cres. LE67: Coal . . . . . . . . . . . .3H 39
LE67: Mark . . . . . . . . . . . . . . .5G 55
Linford Rd. LE11: Lou . . . . . . . . . . . . . .3C 30
Linford St. LE4: Leic . . . . . . . . . . . . . . .3G 65
Ling Av. LE11: Lou . . . . . . . . . . . . . . . .3F 31
Ling Dale LE7: East G . . . . . . . . . . . . . .5G 47
Lingdale Cl. LE11: Lou . . . . . . . . . . . . . .2F 31
Lingdale Lodge LE7: East G . . . . . . . . . .5G 47
Lings Cl. NG32: Eat . . . . . . . . . . . . . .6G 109
                        (not continuous)
Linkfield Av. LE12: Moun . . . . . . . . . . . .3E 44
Linkfield Rd. LE12: Moun . . . . . . . . . . . .3E 44
Link Ri. LE67: Mark . . . . . . . . . . . . . . .5H 55
Link Rd. LE2: Leic . . . . . . . . . . . . . . . .1A 78
LE7: Anst . . . . . . . . . . . . . . . .7G 57
LE7: Quen . . . . . . . . . . . . . . .7F 47
Links Cl. LE67: Hug . . . . . . . . . . . . . . .6D 38
Links Rd. LE8: K Bea . . . . . . . . . . . . . .3K 89
LE9: K Mux . . . . . . . . . . . . . . .3A 68
Linkway Gdns. LE3: Leic . . . . . . . . . . . .2C 70
Linley Av. LE12: Shep . . . . . . . . . . . . . .1E 28
Linley Grn. LE9: Cosb . . . . . . . . . . . . . .6H 81
Linnet Cl. LE13: Mel M . . . . . . . . . . . . .7E 116
Linnett Cl. LE19: Nar . . . . . . . . . . . . . .2E 80
Linney Rd. LE4: Leic . . . . . . . . . . . . . . .4C 64
Lintlaw Cl. LE4: Leic . . . . . . . . . . . . . . .2K 65
LINTON . . . . . . . . . . . . . . . . . . . . .3A 158
Linton St. LE5: Leic . . . . . . . . . . . . . . . .3J 71
Linwal Av. LE7: Hou H . . . . . . . . . . . . .2C 130
Linwood Cl. LE10: Hinc . . . . . . . . . . . .1E 102
Linwood La. LE2: Leic . . . . . . . . . . . . . .2F 77
Lipton Rd. LE4: Beau L . . . . . . . . . . . . .7A 58
Lisle St. LE11: Lou . . . . . . . . . . . . . . . .5E 18
Lismore Dr. LE10: Hinc . . . . . . . . . . . . .2E 102
Lismore Wlk. LE4: Leic . . . . . . . . . . . . .3B 64
Litelmede LE5: Leic . . . . . . . . . . . . . . .7A 66
Little Av. LE4: Leic . . . . . . . . . . . . . . . .3G 65
Lit. Barley Cl. LE4: Leic . . . . . . . . . . . . .3B 64
LITTLE BOWDEN . . . . . . . . .5G 151 (3A 164)
Lit. Bowden Mnr. LE16: L Bow . . . . . . . . .4F 151
LITTLE BYTHAM . . . . . . . . . . . . . . .3D 161
LITTLE CASTERTON . . . . . . . . . . . . .1D 165
Lit. Church La. LE12: Sileby . . . . . . . . . . .1J 45
LITTLE DALBY . . . . . . . . . . . . . . . . .3A 160
Lit. Dalby Rd. LE14: G Dal . . . . . . . . . .6D 120
Little Dale LE18: Wig . . . . . . . . . . . . . . .7A 78
Lit. Dunmow Rd. LE5: Leic . . . . . . . . . . .6B 66
LITTLE EATON . . . . . . . . . . . . . . . . .1A 158
Little End CV13: Cad . . . . . . . . . . . . . . .6C 94
LE17: Brun . . . . . . . . . . . . . . .1D 146
Littlefare, The LE3: Brau . . . . . . . . . . . .5H 69
Littlefield La. LE9: Des . . . . . . . . . . . . .2H 95
Littlegarth LE2: Leic . . . . . . . . . . . . . . .3F 77
LITTLE GIDDING . . . . . . . . . . . . . . . .3D 165
Lit. Glen Rd. LE2: G Par . . . . . . . . . . . . .7C 76
LITTLE HALE . . . . . . . . . . . . . . . . . .1D 161
Lit. Haw La. LE12: Shep . . . . . . . . . . . . .7C 16
LITTLE HEATH . . . . . . . . . . . . . . . . .3A 162
Little Hill DE74: C Don . . . . . . . . . . . . . .4K 7
LE18: Wig . . . . . . . . . . . . . . . . .6K 77
LITTLE HILL ESTATE, THE . . . . . . . . . . .7K 77
Lit. Holme St. LE3: Leic . . . . . . .5A 4 (2D 70)
Lit. John Rd. LE2: Leic . . . . . . . . . . . . . .4D 76
Little La. LE9: Des . . . . . . . . . . . . . . . .1H 95
LE12: Moun . . . . . . . . . . . . . . .2E 44
LE15: Gree . . . . . . . . . . . . . . .4F 125
LE17: Leire . . . . . . . . . . . . . . .3K 143
LE65: Pac . . . . . . . . . . . . . . . .2K 35
LITTLE LAWFORD . . . . . . . . . . . . . . .3B 162
Little London LE16: G Eas . . . . . . . . . . .5K 141

Lit. London La. CV23: N'ton . . . . . . . . . .6A 156
Little Lunnon LE17: D Bas . . . . . . . . . . .2C 144
Little Markfield LE67: Mark . . . . . . . . . . .5E 54
Lit. Masons Cl. LE3: Brau . . . . . . . . . . . .6H 69
Littlemeer Cl. LE3: Brau . . . . . . . . . . . . .6H 69
Lit. Mill Cl. CV13: B'one . . . . . . . . . . . . .5B 92
Lit. Moor La. LE11: Lou . . . . . . . . . . . . .7G 19
Littlemore Cl. LE5: Leic . . . . . . . . . . . . .1B 72
LITTLE OAKLEY . . . . . . . . . . . . . . . . .3B 164
LITTLE ORTON . . . . . . . . . . . . . . . . .1A 162
LITTLEOVER . . . . . . . . . . . . . . . . . .1A 158
LITTLE PONTON . . . . . . . . . . . . . . . .1C 161
Lit. Shaw La. LE67: C Oak . . . . . . . . . . .1C 54
LITTLE STRETTON . . . . . . . . . . . . . . .1D 163
Little Theatre . . . . . . . . . . . . . . . . . . .5E 4
LITTLETHORPE . . . . . . . . . .3F 81 (2C 163)
Littleton St. LE4: Leic . . . . . . . . . . . . . .7D 64
LITTLE TWYCROSS . . . . . . . . . .2C 90 (1A 162)
Littleway, The LE5: Leic . . . . . . . . . . . . .1B 72
                        (not continuous)
LITTLE WISBEACH . . . . . . . . . . . . . . .1D 161
Lit. Wood Cl. LE4: Leic . . . . . . . . . . . . .2C 64
Littleworth La. LE15: Bel R . . . . . . . . . . .5G 133
Livesey Ct. LE9: Sap . . . . . . . . . . . . . .4H 105
Livesey Dr. LE9: Sap . . . . . . . . . . . . . .4H 105
Livia Cl. LE10: Hinc . . . . . . . . . . . . . . .2C 102
Livingstone Cl. LE15: O'ham . . . . . . . . .2J 127
Livingstone St. LE3: Leic . . . . . . . . . . . .3C 70
Llewellyn Ct. LE2: Leic . . . . . . . . . . . . .6K 71
Lobbs Wood Cl. LE5: Leic . . . . . . . . . . .6D 66
Lobelia Cl. LE10: Bur . . . . . . . . . . . . . .6H 103
LE19: Nar . . . . . . . . . . . . . . . .1D 80
Lochmere Cl. LE10: Hinc . . . . . . . . . . . .3D 102
Lochmore Dr. LE10: Hinc . . . . . . . . . . . .3D 102
Lochmore Way LE10: Hinc . . . . . . . . . . .3D 102
Locke Av. LE4: Leic . . . . . . . . . . . . . . . .1K 65
Lockerbie Av. LE4: Leic . . . . . . . . . . . . .2J 65
Lockerbie Wlk. LE4: Leic . . . . . . . . . . . .2K 65
Lock Ga. Cl. LE18: Wig . . . . . . . . . . . . .1G 83
Lockhouse Cl. LE2: Leic . . . . . . . . . . . . .4B 76
LOCKINGTON . . . . . . . . . . . . .4D 8 (2B 158)
Lockington Hall DE74: Lock . . . . . . . . . . .3D 8
Lockington Rd. DE74: Hem . . . . . . . . . . .3B 8
Lock Keeper Cl. LE18: Wig . . . . . . . . . . .1G 83
Lockley Cl. LE6: Ratby . . . . . . . . . . . . . .6B 62
Locks, The LE11: Lou . . . . . . . . . . . . . .4D 18
Lock's Cl. LE15: Gree . . . . . . . . . . . . . .5E 124
Lockside Cl. LE2: G Par . . . . . . . . . . . . .6A 76
Locksley Cl. LE65: Ash Z . . . . . . . . . . . .4J 23
Lockton Cl. LE65: Ash Z . . . . . . . . . . . . .4A 24
LODDINGTON
    Kettering . . . . . . . . . . . . . . . .3B 164
    Leicester . . . . . . . . . . . . . . . .1A 164
Loddington La. LE15: Bel R . . . . . . . . . . .4F 133
Loddington Rd. LE7: T Hil . . . . . . . . . . .3H 131
Loddon Cl. LE13: Mel M . . . . . . . . . . . .6E 116
Lodge, The LE15: O'ham . . . . . . . . . . . .4J 127
                        (not continuous)
Lodge Cl. CV9: Manc . . . . . . . . . . . . . .7A 96
LE4: Thurm . . . . . . . . . . . . . . .7B 60
LE7: Sys . . . . . . . . . . . . . . . . .1E 60
LE8: Kib H . . . . . . . . . . . . . . .1H 89
LE9: Hun . . . . . . . . . . . . . . . . .1B 80
LE10: Bur . . . . . . . . . . . . . . .6K 103
LE12: Bar S . . . . . . . . . . . . . . .4D 32
LE13: Mel M . . . . . . . . . . . . . .5E 116
LE65: Ash Z . . . . . . . . . . . . . . .6J 23
Lodge Farm LE19: Litt . . . . . . . . . . . . . .3F 81
Lodge Farm Rd. LE5: Leic . . . . . . . . . . . .1E 72
Lodge Gdns. LE15: O'ham . . . . . . . . . . .4J 127
Lodge La. LE7: Crop . . . . . . . . . . . . . . .2H 57
Lodge M. DE72: A Tre . . . . . . . . . . . . . .1D 6
LE7: Thurn . . . . . . . . . . . . . . .3G 73
Lodge Rd. LE8: Flec . . . . . . . . . . . . . . .5B 88
Lodgewood Av. LE4: Birs . . . . . . . . . . . .6F 59
Logan Av. LE2: Leic . . . . . . . . . . . . . . .2C 76
Logan Ct. LE16: Mkt H . . . . . . . . . . . . .3D 150
Logan Cres. LE16: Mkt H . . . . . . . . . . . .3C 150
Logan St. LE16: Mkt H . . . . . . . . . . . . .4D 150
Loire Cl. LE65: Ash Z . . . . . . . . . . . . . .4J 23
Lombardy Ri. LE5: Leic . . . . . . . . . . . . .7J 65
Lomond Cl. LE10: Hinc . . . . . . . . . . . . .3E 102
Lomond Cres. LE4: Leic . . . . . . . . . . . . .4C 64
London La. LE12: Wym . . . . . . . . . . . . .2J 21
London Rd. DE72: Shar . . . . . . . . . . . . .1A 8
DE74: Keg . . . . . . . . . . . . . . . .7H 9
LE1: Leic . . . . . . . . . . .6F 5 (3G 71)
LE2: Leic . . . . . . . . . . .6F 5 (3G 71)
LE2: Oad . . . . . . . . . . . . . . . .5F 79
                        (Glen Rd.)
LE2: Oad . . . . . . . . . . . . . . . .3D 78
                        (Leicester Rd.)
LE8: Bur O, G Gle . . . . . . . . . . .6G 79
LE10: Hinc . . . . . . . . . . . . . . .3H 103
LE12: L Wha . . . . . . . . . . . . . . .6H 9
LE15: Upp . . . . . . . . . . . . . . .4C 138
LE67: Coal . . . . . . . . . . . . . . .3D 38

London Rd. LE67: Mark . . . . . . . . . . . . . . . . . .5F 55
London St. LE5: Leic . . . . . . . . . . . . . . . . . . . .1K 71
LONDONTHORPE . . . . . . . . . . . . . . . . . . . . . .1C 161
Longate Rd. LE13: Mel M . . . . . . . . . . . . . . .1F 117
Long Brimley Cl. LE16: L Bow . . . . . . . . . . . .4H 151
LONG CLAWSON . . . . . . . . . . . .2J 111 (2A 160)
Longcliff Cl. LE14: O Dal . . . . . . . . . . . . . . . .7A 110
Longcliffe Gdns. LE11: Nan . . . . . . . . . . . . . .4J 29
Longcliffe Rd. LE5: Leic . . . . . . . . . . . . . . . . .7J 65
  LE12: Shep . . . . . . . . . . . . . . . . . . . . . . . . .7C 16
Longcliff Hill LE14: O Dal . . . . . . . . . . . . . . .7A 110
Longcliff Rd. LE67: Coal . . . . . . . . . . . . . . . .4H 39
Long Cl. LE12: Bar S . . . . . . . . . . . . . . . . . . .3C 32
  LE12: Quo . . . . . . . . . . . . . . . . . . . . . . . . . .4K 31
Long Cft. DE72: A Tre . . . . . . . . . . . . . . . . . . .1C 6
LONG EATON . . . . . . . . . . . . . . . . . . . . . . . .1B 158
Longfellow Rd. LE2: Leic . . . . . . . . . . . . . . . .7G 71
Longfield Way LE13: Mel M . . . . . . . . . . . . .1F 117
LONGFORD . . . . . . . . . . . . . . . . . . . . . . . . . .3A 162
Longford Cl. LE18: Wig . . . . . . . . . . . . . . . . . .1J 83
Long Furlong LE12: Moun . . . . . . . . . . . . . . .4D 44
Long Furrow LE7: East G . . . . . . . . . . . . . . . .5F 47
Long Grey LE8: Flec . . . . . . . . . . . . . . . . . . . .2A 88
Longhade Furlong LE7: Anst . . . . . . . . . . . . .6K 57
Long Hedge La. LE65: Wort . . . . . . . . . . . . . .2A 14
Longhedge La. NG13: Bott . . . . . . . . . . . . . .1F 107
Longhedge La. Ind. Est. NG13: Bott . . . . . . .1F 107
Long Holden DE74: Dis . . . . . . . . . . . . . . . . . .4B 12
Longhurst Cl. LE4: Leic . . . . . . . . . . . . . . . . .1A 66
Longlands, The LE16: L Bow . . . . . . . . . . . . .4H 151
LONGLANE . . . . . . . . . . . . . . . . . . . . . . . . . .1A 158
Long La. DE74: Keg . . . . . . . . . . . . . . . . . . . . .2H 9
  LE1: Leic . . . . . . . . . . . . . . . . .2B 4 (1E 70)
  LE7: Bill . . . . . . . . . . . . . . . . . . . . . . . . . . . .6H 131
  LE14: Bur L . . . . . . . . . . . . . . . . . . . . . . . . .1C 120
  LE14: Sta . . . . . . . . . . . . . . . . . . . . . . . . . . .7D 106
  LE14: Sta . . . . . . . . . . . . . . . . . . . . . . . . . . .1F 109
  LE18: Wig . . . . . . . . . . . . . . . . . . . . . . . . . . .6K 77
  NG13: Bark V, Plun, Red . . . . . . . . . . . . . . .4E 106
LONG LAWFORD . . . . . . . . . . . . . . . . . . . . . .3B 162
Longleat Cl. LE5: Leic . . . . . . . . . . . . . . . . . .6K 65
  LE16: L Bow . . . . . . . . . . . . . . . . . . . . . . . . .4H 151
Long Mdw. LE18: Wig . . . . . . . . . . . . . . . . . . .1A 84
Long Mdw. Dr. LE10: Hinc . . . . . . . . . . . . . . .4C 102
Longmeadow Way LE15: Cott . . . . . . . . . . . .6B 124
Long Mere La. DE74: Dis . . . . . . . . . . . . . . . .6K 11
  LE12: Belt . . . . . . . . . . . . . . . . . . . . . . . . . . .1H 15
Long Row LE15: O'ham . . . . . . . . . . . . . . . . .4H 127
  NG11: King S . . . . . . . . . . . . . . . . . . . . . . . . .4K 9
Long Shoot, The CV11: Nun . . . . . . . . . . . . .4A 102
Longstone Grn. LE5: Leic . . . . . . . . . . . . . . . .7G 67
Long St. LE9: S Stan . . . . . . . . . . . . . . . . . . .7K 101
  LE12: Belt . . . . . . . . . . . . . . . . . . . . . . . . . . .5H 15
  LE18: Wig . . . . . . . . . . . . . . . . . . . . . . . . . . .6J 77
LONG WHATTON . . . . . . . . . . . .5F 13 (2B 158)
Long Whatton Rd. DE74: Dis . . . . . . . . . . . . .4A 12
Longwill Av. LE13: Mel M . . . . . . . . . . . . . . .3G 117
Lonsdale Rd. LE4: Thurm . . . . . . . . . . . . . . . .7A 60
Lonsdale St. LE2: Leic . . . . . . . . . . . . . . . . . .3J 71
Lonsdale Way LE15: O'ham . . . . . . . . . . . . . .4F 127
Lord Byron St. LE2: Leic . . . . . . . . . . . . . . . .7G 71
Lord Cl. LE19: Nar . . . . . . . . . . . . . . . . . . . . . .2F 81
Lord Crewe Cl. LE9: N Ver . . . . . . . . . . . . . . .6H 93
Lords Av. LE4: Beau L . . . . . . . . . . . . . . . . . .6C 58
Lords Cl. LE67: Coal . . . . . . . . . . . . . . . . . . . .5G 39
Lorne Rd. LE2: Leic . . . . . . . . . . . . . . . . . . . .6G 71
Lorraine Rd. LE2: Leic . . . . . . . . . . . . . . . . . .1D 76
Lorrimer Rd. LE2: Leic . . . . . . . . . . . . . . . . . .7E 70
Lorrimer Way LE11: Lou . . . . . . . . . . . . . . . . .5A 18
Loseby La. LE1: Leic . . . . . . . . .4C 4 (2F 71)
Loseby Wlk. LE1: Leic . . . . . . . . . . . . . . . . . . .2F 71
  (off Loseby La.)
Lossiemouth Rd. LE10: Hinc . . . . . . . . . . . . .2C 102
Lothair Rd. LE2: Leic . . . . . . . . . . . . . . . . . . .6E 70
Lothian Pl. DE74: C Don . . . . . . . . . . . . . . . . .5J 7
Loudoun Ct. LE65: Ash Z . . . . . . . . . . . . . . . .5K 23
Loudoun Pl. DE74: C Don . . . . . . . . . . . . . . . .4J 7
Loudoun Way LE65: Ash Z . . . . . . . . . . . . . . .6H 23
LOUGHBOROUGH . . . . . . . . . . .7F 19 (3C 159)
Loughborough Cemetery & Crematorium
  LE11: Lou . . . . . . . . . . . . . . . . . . . . . . . . . . .2G 31
Loughborough Central Station
  Great Central Railway . . . . . . . . . . . . . .7G 19
Loughborough Motorway Trading Est.
  LE12: Shep . . . . . . . . . . . . . . . . . . . . . . . . .1C 28
Loughborough Rd. LE4: Birs . . . . . . . . . . . . . .7G 59
  LE4: Birs, Leic . . . . . . . . . . . . . . . . . . . . . . .1F 65
  LE7: R'ley, Wan . . . . . . . . . . . . . . . . . . . . . .3F 45
  LE12: Bur W . . . . . . . . . . . . . . . . . . . . . . . . .4D 20
  LE12: Cote, Hot . . . . . . . . . . . . . . . . . . . . . .4K 19
  LE12: Hat . . . . . . . . . . . . . . . . . . . . . . . . . . .1J 17
  LE12: P'old . . . . . . . . . . . . . . . . . . . . . . . . . .4K 19
  LE12: Quo . . . . . . . . . . . . . . . . . . . . . . . . . . .7C 32
  (Granite Way)
  LE12: Quo . . . . . . . . . . . . . . . . . . . . . . . . . . .3H 31
  (Quorndon-Mountsorrel By-Pass)
  LE12: Shep . . . . . . . . . . . . . . . . . . . . . . . . .6E 16

Loughborough Rd. LE12: Walt W . . . . . . . . . .6E 20
  LE14: Ash . . . . . . . . . . . . . . . . . . . . . . . . . . .2F 115
  LE67: Cole . . . . . . . . . . . . . . . . . . . . . . . . . .4J 25
  LE67: Thrin . . . . . . . . . . . . . . . . . . . . . . . . . .4D 26
  LE67: Whit . . . . . . . . . . . . . . . . . . . . . . . . . .5E 26
Loughborough Station (Rail) . . . . . . . . . . . .5G 19
Loughborough Technology Pk.
  LE11: Lou . . . . . . . . . . . . . . . . . . . . . . . . . . .2K 29
Loughborough Town Hall Theatre . . . . . . . . .6F 19
Loughborough University . . . . . . . . . . . . . . . .1A 30
Loughland Cl. LE8: Bla . . . . . . . . . . . . . . . . . .1A 82
Louise Av. LE6: Groby . . . . . . . . . . . . . . . . . .4D 62
LOUND . . . . . . . . . . . . . . . . . . . . . . . . . . . . .3D 161
LOUNT . . . . . . . . . . . . . . . . . . . . . . . . . . . . .3A 158
Lount Rd. CV13: Osb . . . . . . . . . . . . . . . . . . .5A 92
Lounts Cres. LE16: G Eas . . . . . . . . . . . . . . .5K 141
Lountside LE65: Ash Z . . . . . . . . . . . . . . . . . .4C 24
Lovelace Cres. LE9: Elm . . . . . . . . . . . . . . . .5E 100
Lovelace Way LE8: Flec . . . . . . . . . . . . . . . . .4C 88
Love La. LE10: Bur . . . . . . . . . . . . . . . . . . . .5K 103
Loves La. LE15: Emp . . . . . . . . . . . . . . . . . .6C 128
  LE17: D Bas . . . . . . . . . . . . . . . . . . . . . . . . .2D 144
Lovett Ct. LE12: Sileby . . . . . . . . . . . . . . . . . .1J 45
Lovetts Cl. LE10: Hinc . . . . . . . . . . . . . . . . .3C 102
Lovey's Cft. DE73: B Hil . . . . . . . . . . . . . . . . .7A 10
Lowcroft Dr. LE2: Oad . . . . . . . . . . . . . . . . . .4E 78
LOWER BENEFIELD . . . . . . . . . . . . . . . . . . .3C 165
Lwr. Bond St. LE10: Hinc . . . . . . . . . . . . . . . .2G 103
Lwr. Brand LE67: Grif . . . . . . . . . . . . . . . . . .5A 14
Lwr. Brown St. LE1: Leic . . . . . . . .5C 4 (3F 71)
Lwr. Cambridge St. LE11: Lou . . . . . . . . . . . .5F 19
Lwr. Church St. LE7: Sys . . . . . . . . . . . . . . . .1D 60
  LE65: Ash Z . . . . . . . . . . . . . . . . . . . . . . . . .5A 24
Lwr. Farm Cl. LE15: Emp . . . . . . . . . . . . . . .6D 128
  (not continuous)
Lwr. Free La. LE1: Leic . . . . . . . . .3D 4 (1F 71)
Lwr. Gladstone St. LE11: Lou . . . . . . . . . . . .5F 19
Lower Grn. LE11: Lou . . . . . . . . . . . . . . . . . . .3B 30
Lwr. Hastings St. LE1: Leic . . . . . . .7E 5 (3G 71)
Lwr. Hill St. LE1: Leic . . . . . . . . . .2D 4 (1F 71)
Lwr. Keyham La. LE5: Leic . . . . . . . . . . . . . .6C 66
  (Humberstone Dr.)
  LE5: Leic . . . . . . . . . . . . . . . . . . . . . . . . . . .5G 67
  (Keyham La. W)
Lwr. Lee St. LE1: Leic . . . . . . . . . .2D 4 (1F 71)
Lwr. Leicester Rd. LE17: Lut . . . . . . . . . . . . .4K 153
Lwr. Moor Rd. LE67: Cole . . . . . . . . . . . . . . .2J 25
Lwr. Packington Rd. LE65: Ash Z . . . . . . . . .6K 23
Lwr. Willow St. LE1: Leic . . . . . . . . . . . . . . . .7G 65
LOWESBY . . . . . . . . . . . . . . . . . . . . . . . . . . .1A 164
Lowesby Cl. LE13: Mel M . . . . . . . . . . . . . . .5H 117
Lowesby La. LE14: T'ord . . . . . . . . . . . . . . . .7H 119
Loweswater Cl. LE12: Bar S . . . . . . . . . . . . . .2D 32
Loweswater Dr. LE11: Lou . . . . . . . . . . . . . . .2A 30
Loweswater Gro. LE65: Ash Z . . . . . . . . . . . .7A 24
LOWICK . . . . . . . . . . . . . . . . . . . . . . . . . . . . .3C 165
Lowick Dr. LE18: Wig . . . . . . . . . . . . . . . . . . .6A 78
Lowland Av. LE3: Leic E . . . . . . . . . . . . . . . . .5E 68
Lowther Cl. LE15: L'ham . . . . . . . . . . . . . . . .5C 122
Lowther Way LE11: Lou . . . . . . . . . . . . . . . . .2F 31
LOW WOODS . . . . . . . . . . . . . . . . . . . . . . . . .7H 15
Low Woods La. LE12: Belt . . . . . . . . . . . . . . .6G 15
Loxley Dr. LE13: Mel M . . . . . . . . . . . . . . . . .6D 116
Loxley Rd. LE3: Glen . . . . . . . . . . . . . . . . . . .5G 63
LUBBESTHORPE . . . . . . . . . . . . . . . . . . . . . .1F 75
Lubbesthorpe Bridle Rd.
  LE3: Brau . . . . . . . . . . . . . . . . . . . . . . . . . . .6J 69
  LE19: End . . . . . . . . . . . . . . . . . . . . . . . . . . .7D 68
Lubbesthorpe Rd. LE3: Brau . . . . . . . . . . . . .1J 75
Lubbesthorpe Way LE3: Brau . . . . . . . . . . . .4H 69
  LE19: Brau . . . . . . . . . . . . . . . . . . . . . . . . . .7H 69
LUBENHAM . . . . . . . . . . . . . . . .7J 149 (3A 164)
Lubenham Hill LE16: Mkt H . . . . . . . . . . . . . .4B 150
Lubenham Rd. LE16: East F . . . . . . . . . . . . . .5A 150
Lucas Rd. LE10: Bur . . . . . . . . . . . . . . . . . . .5G 103
Lucas Way LE9: Earl S . . . . . . . . . . . . . . . . . .3D 100
LUDDINGTON IN THE BROOK . . . . . . . . . . .3D 165
Ludgate Cl. LE4: Birs . . . . . . . . . . . . . . . . . . .5E 58
Ludlam Cl. LE8: Count . . . . . . . . . . . . . . . . . .5C 82
Ludlow Cl. LE2: Oad . . . . . . . . . . . . . . . . . . . .3E 78
  LE11: Lou . . . . . . . . . . . . . . . . . . . . . . . . . . .3A 30
Ludlow Dr. LE13: Mel M . . . . . . . . . . . . . . . . .2F 117
Ludlow Pl. LE12: Shep . . . . . . . . . . . . . . . . . .1C 28
Luffenham Rd. LE15: B'den . . . . . . . . . . . . . .7D 136
  PE9: Ket . . . . . . . . . . . . . . . . . . . . . . . . . . . .7F 137
Lullingstone Cl. LE67: Mark . . . . . . . . . . . . . .4G 55
LULLINGTON . . . . . . . . . . . . . . . . . . . . . . . . .3A 158
Lulworth Cl. LE5: Leic . . . . . . . . . . . . . . . . . .3B 72
  LE18: Wig . . . . . . . . . . . . . . . . . . . . . . . . . . .2K 83
Lundy Cl. LE10: Hinc . . . . . . . . . . . . . . . . . . .2E 102
Lunsford Rd. LE5: Leic . . . . . . . . . . . . . . . . .6K 65
Lupin Cl. LE10: Bur . . . . . . . . . . . . . . . . . . . .5G 103
Luther St. LE3: Leic . . . . . . . . . . . . . . . . . . . .3C 70
LUTTERWORTH . . . . . . . . . . . .5J 153 (3C 163)
Lutterworth Mus. and Historical Society
  . . . . . . . . . . . . . . . . . . . . . . . . . . . . . . . . . .4J 153

Lutterworth Rd. CV23: Will . . . . . . . . . . . . . .7A 152
  LE2: Leic . . . . . . . . . . . . . . . . . . . . . . . . . . . .4C 76
  LE8: Arne . . . . . . . . . . . . . . . . . . . . . . . . . . .4F 147
  LE8: Brun, Arne . . . . . . . . . . . . . . . . . . . . . .4F 147
  LE8: Whet, Bla . . . . . . . . . . . . . . . . . . . . . . .4A 82
  LE9: Cosb . . . . . . . . . . . . . . . . . . . . . . . . . . .2E 144
  LE10: Bur . . . . . . . . . . . . . . . . . . . . . . . . . .6K 103
  LE17: Bitt . . . . . . . . . . . . . . . . . . . . . . . . . . .2H 153
  LE17: Gilm . . . . . . . . . . . . . . . . . . . . . . . . . .7J 145
  LE17: Kim . . . . . . . . . . . . . . . . . . . . . . . . . . .7A 146
  LE17: Lut, D Bas, Cosb . . . . . . . . . . . . . . . .7C 144
  LE17: Lut, Mist, Wal . . . . . . . . . . . . . . . . . .6K 153
  LE17: N Kil . . . . . . . . . . . . . . . . . . . . . . . . . .2F 155
  LE17: Shaw . . . . . . . . . . . . .7E 154 & 2C 156
  LE17: Swin . . . . . . . . . . . . . . . . . . . . . . . . . .1G 157
  LE17: Ull . . . . . . . . . . . . . . . . . . . . . . . . . . . .7F 143
  LE17: Will . . . . . . . . . . . . . . . . . . . . . . . . . . .7A 152
Lutterworth Sports Cen. . . . . . . . . . . . . . . . .4J 153
Lutterworth Swimming Pool . . . . . . . . . . . . .4J 153
LUTTON . . . . . . . . . . . . . . . . . . . . . . . . . . . . .3D 165
Lyall Cl. LE11: Lou . . . . . . . . . . . . . . . . . . . . . .4B 18
  LE10: Bur . . . . . . . . . . . . . . . . . . . . . . . . . .6K 103
Lychgate Cl. LE7: Crop . . . . . . . . . . . . . . . . . .3J 57
  LE10: Bur . . . . . . . . . . . . . . . . . . . . . . . . . .6K 103
Lychgate La. LE10: A Fla, Bur . . . . . . . . . . . .6K 103
Lydall Rd. LE2: Leic . . . . . . . . . . . . . . . . . . . .4E 76
LYDDINGTON . . . . . . . . . . . . .7E 138 (2B 164)
Lyddington Bede House . . . . . . . . . . . . . . . . .7E 138
Lyddington Rd. LE16: C'ott . . . . . . . . . . . . . .2J 141
Lydford Rd. LE4: Leic . . . . . . . . . . . . . . . . . . .4A 66
Lyle Cl. LE4: Leic . . . . . . . . . . . . . . . . . . . . . .1A 66
  LE13: Mel M . . . . . . . . . . . . . . . . . . . . . . . .1F 117
Lyme Rd. LE2: Leic . . . . . . . . . . . . . . . . . . . . .4J 71
Lymington Rd. LE5: Leic . . . . . . . . . . . . . . . .6F 67
Lyn Cl. LE3: Leic . . . . . . . . . . . . . . . . . . . . . . .3K 63
Lyncote Rd. LE3: Leic . . . . . . . . . . . . . . . . . . .7B 70
Lyncroft Leys LE7: Scra . . . . . . . . . . . . . . . . .7G 67
Lyndale Cl. LE4: Thurm . . . . . . . . . . . . . . . . .7A 60
Lyndale Rd. LE3: Brau . . . . . . . . . . . . . . . . . .7K 69
Lyndene Cl. LE9: Earl S . . . . . . . . . . . . . . . .3E 100
Lyndhurst Cl. LE2: Leic . . . . . . . . . . . . . . . . . .5J 71
Lyndhurst Cl. LE10: Bur . . . . . . . . . . . . . . . .5K 103
Lyndhurst Rd. LE2: Oad . . . . . . . . . . . . . . . . .2C 78
LYNDON . . . . . . . . . . . . . . . . . . . . . . . . . . . . .1C 165
Lyndon Dr. LE2: Oad . . . . . . . . . . . . . . . . . . .2B 78
Lyndon Hill Vis. Cen. . . . . . . . . . . . . . . . . . . .1E 134
Lyndon Rd. LE15: Mant . . . . . . . . . . . . . . . . .3B 134
  LE15: N Luf . . . . . . . . . . . . . . . . . . . . . . . . .1A 136
Lyndwood Ct. LE2: Leic . . . . . . . . . . . . . . . . .6K 71
Lyneham Cl. LE10: Hinc . . . . . . . . . . . . . . . .2D 102
Lyngate Av. LE4: Birs . . . . . . . . . . . . . . . . . . .5G 59
Lynholme Rd. LE2: Leic . . . . . . . . . . . . . . . . .2H 77
Lynmouth Cl. LE3: Glen . . . . . . . . . . . . . . . . .7G 63
Lynmouth Dr. LE17: Gilm . . . . . . . . . . . . . . . .7J 145
  LE18: Wig . . . . . . . . . . . . . . . . . . . . . . . . . . .3G 77
Lynmouth Rd. LE5: Leic . . . . . . . . . . . . . . . . .6F 67
Lynton Cl. LE17: Gilm . . . . . . . . . . . . . . . . . .7J 145
Lynton Rd. LE13: Mel M . . . . . . . . . . . . . . . .1D 116
Lynwood Cl. LE9: Des . . . . . . . . . . . . . . . . . . .2H 95
Lyon Cl. LE18: Wig . . . . . . . . . . . . . . . . . . . . .4G 77
Lysander Cl. LE10: Bur . . . . . . . . . . . . . . . . .7H 103
Lytham Rd. LE2: Leic . . . . . . . . . . . . . . . . . . .6G 71
Lytton Rd. LE2: Leic . . . . . . . . . . . . . . . . . . . .5H 71
  (not continuous)

## M

Mablowe Fld. LE18: Wig . . . . . . . . . . . . . . . . .1A 84
Macaulay Rd. LE7: R'ley . . . . . . . . . . . . . . . . .6E 44
  LE17: Lut . . . . . . . . . . . . . . . . . . . . . . . . . . .2J 153
Macaulay St. LE2: Leic . . . . . . . . . . . . . . . . . .7F 71
McCarthy Cl. LE67: Whit . . . . . . . . . . . . . . . . .6E 26
McCarthy Rd. LE12: Shep . . . . . . . . . . . . . . . .6C 16
Macdonald Rd. LE4: Leic . . . . . . . . . . . . . . . .5G 65
McDowell Way LE19: Nar . . . . . . . . . . . . . . . .2F 81
Machin Dr. LE9: B Ast . . . . . . . . . . . . . . . . . .6E 86
Mackaness Cl. LE17: Gilm . . . . . . . . . . . . . . .7J 145
McKenzie Wlk. LE5: Leic . . . . . . . . . . . . . . . .2C 72
Mackenzie Way LE1: Leic . . . . . . . .1F 4 (7G 65)
MACKWORTH . . . . . . . . . . . . . . . . . . . . . . . . .1A 158
Maclean Av. LE11: Lou . . . . . . . . . . . . . . . . . .4A 18
McVicker Cl. LE5: Leic . . . . . . . . . . . . . . . . . .1C 72
Madeline Cl. LE16: G Bow . . . . . . . . . . . . . . .2G 151
Madeline Rd. LE4: Beau L . . . . . . . . . . . . . . .7C 58
Madras Rd. LE1: Leic . . . . . . . . . . .2G 4 (1H 71)
Magazine Wlk. LE1: Leic . . . . . . . .5B 4 (2E 70)
Magee Cl. LE10: Hinc . . . . . . . . . . . . . . . . . . .1F 103
MAGNA PARK . . . . . . . . . . . . . .4C 152 (3C 163)
Magna Rd. LE18: Wig . . . . . . . . . . . . . . . . . . .7G 77
Magna Rd. Ind. Est. LE18: Wig . . . . . . . . . . .7G 77
Magnolia Av. LE11: Lou . . . . . . . . . . . . . . . . .4E 30
Magnolia Cl. LE2: Leic . . . . . . . . . . . . . . . . . .3C 76
  LE3: Leic E . . . . . . . . . . . . . . . . . . . . . . . . . .5C 68
Magnolia Dr. LE17: Lut . . . . . . . . . . . . . . . . .3H 153
Magnus Rd. LE4: Leic . . . . . . . . . . . . . . . . . . .4J 65
Maidenhair Cl. LE11: Lou . . . . . . . . . . . . . . . .5E 30
Maiden St. LE7: Sys . . . . . . . . . . . . . . . . . . . .2B 60

Maidenwell Av.—Maple Av.


**Maidenwell Av.** LE5: Leic, Ham . . . . . 5E **66**
**Maidstone Rd.** LE2: Leic . . . . . 5G **4** (2H **71**)
MAIDWELL . . . . . 3A **164**
**Maidwell Cl.** LE18: Wig . . . . . 6B **78**
**Maino Cres.** LE17: Lut . . . . . 5G **153**
**Main Rd.** CV9: S Mag . . . . . 7A **90**
CV9: Twy . . . . . 2C **90**
CV13: Bils . . . . . 5F **91**
LE14: Ash . . . . . 2J **115**
LE14: N Bro, Up Bro . . . . . 1B **110**
LE14: O Dal . . . . . 7A **110**
LE14: T'ord . . . . . 6G **119**
LE14: Wyc . . . . . 5E **112**
LE15: Barl, O'ham . . . . . 2F **127**
LE15: Glas . . . . . 1H **139**
LE17: C Mag, C Par . . . . . 5C **142**
LE67: Bag . . . . . 1G **93**
NG13: Red . . . . . 1D **106**
**Main St.** CV13: B'one . . . . . 5C **92**
CV13: Cad . . . . . 5B **94**
CV13: Con . . . . . 6G **91**
CV13: Dadl . . . . . 1B **98**
CV13: H Hill . . . . . 6G **97**
CV13: Mkt B . . . . . 2D **94**
CV13: Nail . . . . . 2C **92**
CV13: S Gol . . . . . 3A **98**
DE11: A Vil . . . . . 2A **22**
DE11: Blac . . . . . 3D **22**
DE12: Oak . . . . . 5C **34**
DE12: Snar . . . . . 6G **49**
DE72: W Tre . . . . . 4A **6**
DE73: B Hil . . . . . 7A **10**
DE73: Wils . . . . . 3A **10**
DE74: Hem . . . . . 4B **8**
DE74: Lock . . . . . 4D **8**
LE3: Brau . . . . . 5J **69**
LE3: Glen . . . . . 5F **63**
LE5: Leic . . . . . 6C **66**
(Humberstone Dr.)
LE5: Leic . . . . . 5D **72**
(The Common)
LE6: New L . . . . . 4B **56**
LE6: Ratby . . . . . 6A **62**
LE7: Bark . . . . . 5E **60**
LE7: Bars . . . . . 5C **118**
LE7: Bush, Thurn . . . . . 3H **73**
LE7: Coss . . . . . 4J **45**
LE7: Gad . . . . . 2A **118**
LE7: Hou H . . . . . 3C **130**
LE7: Quen . . . . . 7H **47**
LE7: Rat W . . . . . 3D **46**
LE7: S Cro . . . . . 7A **118**
LE7: Scra . . . . . 6H **67**
LE7: T Hil . . . . . 2H **131**
LE7: Tug . . . . . 2B **132**
LE8: Bur O . . . . . 6D **130**
LE8: Count . . . . . 6F **83**
LE8: Flec . . . . . 4B **88**
LE8: G Gle . . . . . 1K **85**
LE8: Kib H . . . . . 1J **89**
LE8: Peat M . . . . . 2K **147**
LE8: Sad . . . . . 7D **88**
LE8: Smee W . . . . . 5H **89**
LE8: Will W . . . . . 1J **145**
LE9: B Ast . . . . . 3C **86**
LE9: Cosb . . . . . 6H **81**
(not continuous)
LE9: Des . . . . . 1H **95**
LE9: Hun . . . . . 2B **80**
LE9: K Mal . . . . . 6F **95**
LE9: K Mux . . . . . 2B **68**
LE9: N Ver . . . . . 6G **93**
LE9: Peck . . . . . 5J **95**
LE9: Stap . . . . . 1J **99**
LE9: Thurl . . . . . 2C **96**
LE10: A Fla . . . . . 5D **104**
LE12: L Wha . . . . . 5F **13**
LE12: Osg . . . . . 6C **14**
LE12: Stan S . . . . . 1G **19**
LE12: Swith . . . . . 5F **43**
LE12: W Eav . . . . . 2D **42**
LE12: W'orpe . . . . . 4G **31**
LE14: Ash . . . . . 3F **115**
LE14: Bur H . . . . . 6F **121**
LE14: Edm . . . . . 3J **121**
LE14: F Wre . . . . . 5G **115**
LE14: G Dal . . . . . 6C **120**
LE14: Harb . . . . . 2C **108**
LE14: Hob . . . . . 2B **114**
LE14: Hol . . . . . 5K **111**
LE14: O Dal . . . . . 6C **110**
LE14: Roth . . . . . 4C **114**
LE14: Spro . . . . . 2H **113**
LE14: Sta . . . . . 2H **109**
LE14: T Sat . . . . . 4H **119**
LE14: T'ord . . . . . 6G **119**
LE14: W'ham . . . . . 1G **121**
**Main St.** LE15: Alle . . . . . 7F **133**
LE15: Barr . . . . . 4J **123**
LE15: B'den . . . . . 7C **136**
LE15: Bel R . . . . . 5G **133**
LE15: Bisb . . . . . 3F **139**
LE15: Cott . . . . . 7A **124**
LE15: Emp . . . . . 6B **128**
LE15: Gree . . . . . 5E **124**
LE15: Knos . . . . . 2C **126**
LE15: Lyd . . . . . 6D **138**
LE15: Mkt O . . . . . 2H **123**
LE15: Pres . . . . . 7A **134**
LE15: Rid . . . . . 2H **133**
LE15: S Dry . . . . . 7A **138**
LE15: Seat . . . . . 5J **139**
LE15: Ward . . . . . 7K **133**
LE15: Whis . . . . . 2C **122**
LE16: Brin . . . . . 7J **141**
LE16: C'ott . . . . . 2H **141**
LE16: Dray . . . . . 7G **141**
LE16: East F . . . . . 7B **150**
LE16: East L . . . . . 2B **140**
LE16: Fox . . . . . 2G **149**
LE16: G Bow . . . . . 1F **151**
LE16: Lub . . . . . 7H **149**
LE16: Med . . . . . 7C **140**
LE17: Ash P . . . . . 5K **143**
LE17: Brun . . . . . 1D **146**
LE17: C'ach . . . . . 6C **154**
LE17: D Bas . . . . . 1D **144**
LE17: Frol . . . . . 1E **142**
LE17: Gilm . . . . . 6J **145**
LE17: Leire . . . . . 2K **143**
LE17: L'ton . . . . . 2E **148**
LE17: Mows . . . . . 3B **148**
LE17: P Par . . . . . 2A **146**
LE17: Shaw . . . . . 3B **156**
LE17: Shea . . . . . 5J **147**
LE17: Ull . . . . . 7F **143**
LE18: Kilby . . . . . 6B **84**
LE65: Smis . . . . . 1H **23**
LE65: Wort . . . . . 3B **14**
LE67: Bag . . . . . 1F **93**
LE67: Hea . . . . . 3G **51**
LE67: Mark . . . . . 5F **55**
LE67: N Bur . . . . . 6B **50**
LE67: Nor H . . . . . 6D **36**
LE67: Rav . . . . . 4J **37**
LE67: S Bar . . . . . 5A **54**
LE67: Swan . . . . . 5B **26**
LE67: Swep . . . . . 3A **50**
LE67: Thor . . . . . 1J **93**
LE67: Thrin . . . . . 3D **26**
NG13: Red . . . . . 1E **106**
NG32: Bran . . . . . 5J **109**
NG32: Crox . . . . . 6H **107**
NG32: Eat . . . . . 6G **109**
NG33: Buck . . . . . 5G **113**
NG33: Sew . . . . . 7J **113**
PE9: Belm . . . . . 6J **129**
PE9: G Cas . . . . . 2H **137**
**Maitland Av.** LE12: Moun . . . . . 3E **44**
**Maizefield** LE10: Hinc . . . . . 6F **99**
**Makey's Cl.** LE15: E Wes . . . . . 3F **135**
**Malabar Rd.** LE1: Leic . . . . . 2G **4** (1H **71**)
**Malcolm Arc.** LE1: Leic . . . . . 3C **4**
**Malham Cl.** LE4: Leic . . . . . 3C **64**
**Malham Way** LE2: Oad . . . . . 3F **79**
**Mallard Av.** LE6: Groby . . . . . 3C **62**
**Mallard Cl.** DE12: Mea . . . . . 1D **48**
PE9: Ess . . . . . 1K **129**
**Mallard Dr.** LE7: Sys . . . . . 1B **60**
LE10: Hinc . . . . . 4D **102**
**Mallard Rd.** LE12: Bar S . . . . . 3E **32**
LE12: Moun . . . . . 2F **45**
**Mallard Way** LE3: Leic E . . . . . 5C **68**
**Malling Av.** LE9: B Ast . . . . . 3B **86**
**Malling Cl.** LE4: Birs . . . . . 4H **59**
**Mallory Cl.** LE9: N Ver . . . . . 7H **93**
Mallory Pk. Motor Racing Circuit
. . . . . 7F 95 (1B 162)
**Mallory Pl.** LE5: Leic . . . . . 6A **66**
**Mallory St.** LE9: Earl S . . . . . 2B **100**
**Mallow Cl.** LE5: Ham . . . . . 3E **66**
**Malthouse Cl.** CV13: Nail . . . . . 2C **92**
**Maltings, The** LE3: Glen . . . . . 5F **63**
LE5: Ham . . . . . 3F **67**
LE12: Sileby . . . . . 1J **45**
**Maltings Yd.** LE15: Ext . . . . . 2C **128**
**Malt Mill Bank** LE9: Barw . . . . . 4K **99**
**Malton Dr.** LE2: Oad . . . . . 2E **78**
**Malvern Av.** LE12: Shep . . . . . 1E **28**
**Malvern Cres.** LE9: Cosb . . . . . 6H **81**
LE65: Ash Z . . . . . 3J **23**
**Malvern Rd.** LE2: Leic . . . . . 5K **71**
**Malvern Wlk.** *LE15: O'ham . . . . . 4F 127*
*(off Grampian Way)*
**Mammoth St.** LE67: Coal . . . . . 3D **38**
MANCETTER . . . . . 7A 96 (2A 162)
**Mancetter Rd.** CV9: Manc . . . . . 6A **96**
(not continuous)
**Manchester La.** DE11: Harts . . . . . 1F **23**
**Mandarin Cl.** LE10: Hinc . . . . . 5D **102**
**Mandarin Way** LE8: Whet . . . . . 5K **81**
**Mandervell Rd.** LE2: Oad . . . . . 3B **78**
**Mandora La.** LE2: Leic . . . . . 7G **5** (3H **71**)
**Manitoba Rd.** LE1: Leic . . . . . 1E **4** (7G **65**)
**Mann Cl.** LE3: Brau . . . . . 5H **69**
**Manners Dr.** LE13: Mel M . . . . . 1G **117**
**Manners Rd.** LE2: Leic . . . . . 1E **76**
**Mannings Ter.** DE12: Mea . . . . . 1E **48**
**Mnr. Brook Cl.** LE9: S Stan . . . . . 7K **101**
LE67: D Hea . . . . . 7C **38**
**Manor Cl.** LE2: Oad . . . . . 7D **72**
LE10: Bur . . . . . 6F **103**
LE12: L Wha . . . . . 5F **13**
LE13: Mel M . . . . . 2H **117**
LE17: C Mag . . . . . 5B **142**
LE65: Ash Z . . . . . 6A **24**
PE9: Ryh . . . . . 4H **129**
**Manor Ct.** LE8: Bla . . . . . 1C **82**
LE10: Hinc . . . . . 2F **103**
LE12: Wym . . . . . 1K **21**
LE14: W Wol . . . . . 2C **112**
**Manor Cres.** LE9: Stap . . . . . 1H **99**
**Manor Dr.** LE4: Beau L . . . . . 1A **64**
LE11: Lou . . . . . 3F **31**
LE12: Sileby . . . . . 2J **45**
LE65: Wort . . . . . 2B **14**
**Mnr. Farm Cl.** LE9: B Ast . . . . . 4D **86**
**Mnr. Farm Ct.** LE7: T Hil . . . . . 2H **131**
NG11: King S . . . . . 4K **9**
**Mnr. Farm La.** PE9: Ess . . . . . 1K **129**
**Mnr. Farm M.** DE72: A Tre . . . . . 1D **6**
**Mnr. Farm Rd.** DE72: A Tre . . . . . 1D **6**
**Mnr. Farm Wlk.** LE7: T Hil . . . . . 2H **131**
**Mnr. Farm Way** LE3: Glen . . . . . 7G **63**
**Mnr. Farm Yd.** LE7: T Hil . . . . . 2H **131**
**Manor Gdns.** LE3: Glen . . . . . 6G **63**
LE9: Des . . . . . 2G **95**
LE12: Shep . . . . . 6D **16**
**Manor Grn.** PE9: Ket . . . . . 6G **137**
**Manor Ho. Cl.** LE10: A Fla . . . . . 5D **104**
**Manor Ho. Dr.** LE12: Bar S . . . . . 4C **32**
**Manor Ho. Gdns.** LE5: Leic . . . . . 6D **66**
**Manor La.** LE9: Peck . . . . . 6J **95**
LE14: Som . . . . . 6K **121**
LE15: Barl . . . . . 2F **127**
LE15: Glas . . . . . 1J **139**
LE15: L'ham . . . . . 5C **122**
**Manor Pl.** LE10: Hinc . . . . . 2G **103**
**Manor Rd.** CV9: Manc . . . . . 7A **96**
CV13: B'one . . . . . 5B **92**
LE2: Oad . . . . . 7B **72**
LE4: Thurm . . . . . 7K **59**
LE8: Flec . . . . . 4C **88**
LE9: Cosb . . . . . 5H **81**
LE9: Des . . . . . 2G **95**
LE9: Sap . . . . . 3J **105**
LE11: Lou . . . . . 3F **31**
LE15: Stre . . . . . 2K **125**
LE16: G Bow . . . . . 1G **151**
LE16: Med . . . . . 7D **140**
LE17: Bitt . . . . . 2H **153**
LE17: C Mag . . . . . 4B **142**
LE17: Ull . . . . . 7E **142**
LE67: D Hea . . . . . 6B **38**
LE67: Hea . . . . . 3F **51**
NG13: East . . . . . 2H **107**
Manor Road Activity Room . . . . . 1C **78**
**Manor Rd. Extension** LE2: Oad . . . . . 1D **78**
**Manor St.** LE10: Hinc . . . . . 2F **103**
LE18: Wig . . . . . 6H **77**
**Manor Vw.** PE9: Ket . . . . . 5H **137**
**Manor Wlk.** LE16: Mkt H . . . . . 4E **150**
**Manor Way** LE10: Bur . . . . . 6G **103**
**Mansfield Av.** LE12: Quo . . . . . 5A **32**
**Mansfield St.** LE1: Leic . . . . . 2C **4** (1F **71**)
LE12: Quo . . . . . 5A **32**
**Mansion Ho. Gdns.**
LE13: Mel M . . . . . 1F **117**
**Mansion St.** LE10: Hinc . . . . . 2G **103**
**Manston Cl.** LE4: Leic . . . . . 1C **66**
MANTHORPE
Bourne . . . . . 3D 161
Grantham . . . . . 1C 161
**Mantle La.** LE67: Coal . . . . . 2C **38**
**Mantle Rd.** LE3: Leic . . . . . 1D **70**
MANTON . . . . . 2C 134 (1B 164)
**Manton Cl.** LE9: B Ast . . . . . 4F **87**
**Manton Rd.** LE15: E Wes . . . . . 3F **135**
**Maple Av.** LE3: Brau . . . . . 4G **69**
LE8: Bla . . . . . 3B **82**
LE8: Count . . . . . 5F **83**

Maple Cl. LE4: Leic . . . . . . . . . . . . . . . . . .4E **64**
  LE10: Bur . . . . . . . . . . . . . . . . . . . . . . . . .6H **103**
  LE13: Mel M . . . . . . . . . . . . . . . . . . . . . .2E **116**
Maple Ct. LE2: Leic . . . . . . . . . . . . . .5G **4** (2H **71**)
Maple Dr. DE72: A Tre . . . . . . . . . . . . . . . . . .1C **6**
  LE17: Lut . . . . . . . . . . . . . . . . . . . . . . . . .4H **153**
  LE67: Ibs . . . . . . . . . . . . . . . . . . . . . . . . . .3J **51**
Maple Rd. LE4: Thurm . . . . . . . . . . . . . . . . .7K **59**
  LE11: Lou . . . . . . . . . . . . . . . . . . . . . . . . .3F **31**
Maple Rd. Nth. LE11: Lou . . . . . . . . . . . . . .3F **31**
Maple Rd. Sth. LE11: Lou . . . . . . . . . . . . . .4F **31**
Mapleton Rd. LE18: Wig . . . . . . . . . . . . . . .5J **77**
Maple Tree Wlk. LE19: Litt . . . . . . . . . . . . .2G **81**
Maple Way LE9: Des . . . . . . . . . . . . . . . . . .2G **95**
  LE9: Earl S . . . . . . . . . . . . . . . . . . . . . . .4C **100**
Maplewell LE67: Coal . . . . . . . . . . . . . . . . .3H **39**
Maplewell Dr. LE4: Beau L . . . . . . . . . . . . .7A **58**
Maplewell Rd. LE12: W Eav . . . . . . . . . . . .5B **42**
Maplin Rd. LE5: Leic . . . . . . . . . . . . . . . . . .5G **67**
MAPPERLEY
  Ikeston . . . . . . . . . . . . . . . . . . . . . . . . . .1B **158**
  Nottingham . . . . . . . . . . . . . . . . . . . . . .1C **159**
Mapperley Ho. *LE13: Mel M* . . . . . . . . . .4G **117**
                     *(off St Johns Ct.)*
MAPPERLEY PARK . . . . . . . . . . . . . . . . . .1C **159**
Marble St. LE1: Leic . . . . . . . . . . .5C **4** (2F **71**)
Marchant Rd. LE10: Hinc . . . . . . . . . . . . . .3F **103**
Marcian Cl. LE10: Hinc . . . . . . . . . . . . . . .2C **102**
Marcus Cl. LE7: Sys . . . . . . . . . . . . . . . . . .3A **60**
Mardale Way LE11: Lou . . . . . . . . . . . . . . .3B **30**
MAREFIELD . . . . . . . . . . . . . . . . . . . . . . .1A **164**
Marefield Cl. LE7: Thurn . . . . . . . . . . . . . . .1J **73**
Marefield La. LE7: T Hil . . . . . . . . . . . . . . .2H **131**
  LE14: J O'Ga . . . . . . . . . . . . . . . . . . . . .7J **119**
Marfitt St. LE4: Leic . . . . . . . . . . . . . . . . . .4H **65**
Margam Cl. LE3: Leic . . . . . . . . . . . . . . . . .4B **64**
Margaret Anne Rd. LE2: Oad . . . . . . . . . . .4D **78**
Margaret Cl. LE4: Thurm . . . . . . . . . . . . . .5A **60**
Margaret Cres. LE18: Wig . . . . . . . . . . . . . .5H **77**
Margaret Rd. LE5: Leic . . . . . . . . . . . . . . . .2A **72**
                    *(not continuous)*
Margaret St. LE67: Coal . . . . . . . . . . . . . . .3C **38**
MARHOLM . . . . . . . . . . . . . . . . . . . . . . . .1D **165**
Marie Cl. CV9: Manc . . . . . . . . . . . . . . . . .6A **96**
Marigold Cres. LE13: Mel M . . . . . . . . . . . .7E **116**
Marigold Dr. LE10: Bur . . . . . . . . . . . . . . . .6H **103**
Marigold La. LE12: Moun . . . . . . . . . . . . . .2E **44**
Marigold Way LE19: Nar . . . . . . . . . . . . . . .1D **80**
Marina Dr. LE6: Groby . . . . . . . . . . . . . . . .3E **62**
Marina Rd. LE5: Leic . . . . . . . . . . . . . . . . .3K **71**
Marion Cl. LE3: Leic . . . . . . . . . . . . . . . . . .4K **63**
Marions Way LE9: Crof . . . . . . . . . . . . . . . .5B **80**
Marjorie St. LE4: Leic . . . . . . . . . . . . . . . . .5G **65**
MARKEATON . . . . . . . . . . . . . . . . . . . . . .1A **158**
MARKET BOSWORTH . . . . . . . . . .2D **94** (1B **162**)
MARKET DEEPING . . . . . . . . . . . . . . . . . .3D **161**
MARKET END . . . . . . . . . . . . . . . . . . . . . .3A **162**
MARKET HARBOROUGH . . . . . . . .4E **150** (3A **164**)
Market Harborough Station (Rail) . . . . . . . .4G **151**
Market M. CV13: Mkt B . . . . . . . . . . . . . . .2D **94**
MARKET OVERTON . . . . . . . . . .2H **123** (3B **160**)
Market Pl. CV13: Mkt B . . . . . . . . . . . . . . .2D **94**
  DE74: Keg . . . . . . . . . . . . . . . . . . . . . . . . .6H **9**
  LE1: Leic . . . . . . . . . . . . . . . . .4C **4** (2F **71**)
  LE7: Bill . . . . . . . . . . . . . . . . . . . . . . . . .6H **131**
  LE10: Hinc . . . . . . . . . . . . . . . . . . . . . . .3G **103**
  LE11: Lou . . . . . . . . . . . . . . . . . . . . . . . . .6F **19**
  LE12: Moun . . . . . . . . . . . . . . . . . . . . . .1E **44**
  LE12: Shep . . . . . . . . . . . . . . . . . . . . . . .6D **16**
  LE13: Mel M . . . . . . . . . . . . . . . . . . . . . .4F **117**
  LE15: O'ham . . . . . . . . . . . . . . . . . . . . .4J **127**
  LE15: Upp . . . . . . . . . . . . . . . . . . . . . . .2C **138**
  LE67: Whit . . . . . . . . . . . . . . . . . . . . . . .6F **27**
Market Pl. App. LE1: Leic . . . . . . . . .4D **4** (2F **71**)
Market Pl. Sth. LE1: Leic . . . . . . . . .4C **4** (2F **71**)
Market St. DE11: C Gre . . . . . . . . . . . . . . .1A **22**
  DE74: C Don . . . . . . . . . . . . . . . . . . . . . . .5K **7**
  LE1: Leic . . . . . . . . . . . . . . . . .4C **4** (2F **71**)
  LE11: Lou . . . . . . . . . . . . . . . . . . . . . . . . .6E **18**
  LE15: O'ham . . . . . . . . . . . . . . . . . . . . .4J **127**
  LE17: Lut . . . . . . . . . . . . . . . . . . . . . . . .4J **153**
  LE65: Ash Z . . . . . . . . . . . . . . . . . . . . . .5K **23**
  LE67: Coal . . . . . . . . . . . . . . . . . . . . . . .2C **38**
  NG13: Bott . . . . . . . . . . . . . . . . . . . . . .2H **107**
MARKFIELD . . . . . . . . . . . . . . .5G **55** (3B **158**)
Markfield Ct. Retirement Village
  LE67: Mark . . . . . . . . . . . . . . . . . . . . . . .7G **55**
Markfield Ind. Est. LE67: Mark . . . . . . . . . .3E **54**
Markfield La. LE6: New L . . . . . . . . . . . . . .4H **55**
  LE67: Mark . . . . . . . . . . . . . . . . . . . . . . .4H **55**
  LE67: Mark, Thor . . . . . . . . . . . . . . . . . . .1J **93**
Markfield Rd. LE6: Groby . . . . . . . . . . . . . .2B **62**
  LE6: Ratby . . . . . . . . . . . . . . . . . . . . . . .4A **62**
Markland LE2: Leic . . . . . . . . . . . . . . . . . . .4C **76**
Marlborough Cl. LE10: Bur . . . . . . . . . . . . .4A **104**
Marlborough Ct. LE67: Coal . . . . . . . . . . . .3C **38**
Marlborough Dr. LE8: Flec . . . . . . . . . . . . .5C **88**

Marlborough Pl. LE17: Lut . . . . . . . . . . . . . .5J **153**
Marlborough Sq. LE67: Coal . . . . . . . . . . . .3C **38**
Marlborough St. LE1: Leic . . . . . . . .5D **4** (2F **71**)
Marlborough Way LE16: Mkt H . . . . . . . . . .2E **150**
  LE65: Ash Z . . . . . . . . . . . . . . . . . . . . . .5J **23**
Marl Flds. LE7: R'ley . . . . . . . . . . . . . . . . . .3F **45**
Marlow Rd. LE3: Leic . . . . . . . . . . . . . . . . .5D **70**
Marmion Cl. LE8: Flec . . . . . . . . . . . . . . . .5C **88**
Maromme Sq. LE18: Wig . . . . . . . . . . . . . .5K **77**
Marquis Ct. DE12: Moi . . . . . . . . . . . . . . . .6A **22**
Marquis Dr. DE12: Moi . . . . . . . . . . . . . . . .6A **22**
Marquis Rd. LE14: O Dal . . . . . . . . . . . . . .5D **110**
Marquis St. LE1: Leic . . . . . . . . . . .6D **5** (3F **71**)
Marriott Dr. LE8: Leic . . . . . . . . . . . . . . . . .3K **89**
Marriott Rd. LE2: Leic . . . . . . . . . . . . . . . . .3E **76**
Marriot Wlk. LE2: Leic . . . . . . . . . . . . . . . . .2F **77**
Marsden Av. LE7: Quen . . . . . . . . . . . . . . . .7F **47**
Marsden La. LE2: Leic . . . . . . . . . . . . . . . . .2B **76**
Marsden Rd. LE67: Rav . . . . . . . . . . . . . . . .2K **37**
Marshall Av. LE12: Sileby . . . . . . . . . . . . . .7K **33**
Marshall Cl. LE3: Brau . . . . . . . . . . . . . . . .5G **69**
Marshall Ct. LE16: Mkt H . . . . . . . . . . . . . .5F **151**
Marshall Farm Cl. NG13: Bark V . . . . . . . . .3A **106**
Marshall St. LE3: Leic . . . . . . . . . . . . . . . . .7D **64**
Marsham Cl. LE5: Ham . . . . . . . . . . . . . . . .4D **66**
Marsh Av. LE8: Kib H . . . . . . . . . . . . . . . . .2K **89**
Marsh Cl. LE4: Leic . . . . . . . . . . . . . . . . . . .1A **66**
Marsh Ct. NG13: Bott . . . . . . . . . . . . . . . .1H **107**
Marsh Dr. LE8: Kib H . . . . . . . . . . . . . . . . .2J **89**
Marsh Rd. LE12: Moun . . . . . . . . . . . . . . . .3E **44**
MARSTON . . . . . . . . . . . . . . . . . . . . . . . .1B **160**
Marston Cl. DE12: Moi . . . . . . . . . . . . . . . .6C **22**
  LE2: Oad . . . . . . . . . . . . . . . . . . . . . . . . .5C **78**
Marston Cres. LE8: Count . . . . . . . . . . . . . .6E **82**
Marston Dr. LE6: Groby . . . . . . . . . . . . . . . .3D **62**
MARSTON JABBETT . . . . . . . . . . . . . . . . .3A **162**
Marston Rd. LE4: Leic . . . . . . . . . . . . . . . . .4A **66**
  LE9: Crof . . . . . . . . . . . . . . . . . . . . . . . . .4A **80**
MARSTON TRUSSELL . . . . . . . . . . . . . . .3D **163**
Marston Way LE67: Hea . . . . . . . . . . . . . . .3F **51**
Marstown Av. LE18: Wig . . . . . . . . . . . . . . .6F **77**
Marteg Cl. LE13: Mel M . . . . . . . . . . . . . . .6E **116**
Martel Ho. LE8: G Gle . . . . . . . . . . . . . . . . .7K **79**
Martin Av. LE2: Oad . . . . . . . . . . . . . . . . . .3D **78**
  LE9: Leic E . . . . . . . . . . . . . . . . . . . . . . .4D **68**
  LE12: Bar S . . . . . . . . . . . . . . . . . . . . . . .4D **32**
  LE12: Moun . . . . . . . . . . . . . . . . . . . . . .3D **44**
Martin Cl. LE4: Leic . . . . . . . . . . . . . . . . . .6H **65**
  LE9: S Stan . . . . . . . . . . . . . . . . . . . . . .2J **105**
  LE15: O'ham . . . . . . . . . . . . . . . . . . . . .2K **127**
  LE67: Whit . . . . . . . . . . . . . . . . . . . . . . .5D **26**
Martin Ct. LE7: Anst . . . . . . . . . . . . . . . . . .1H **63**
  LE11: Lou . . . . . . . . . . . . . . . . . . . . . . . .2B **30**
Martin Dr. LE7: Sys . . . . . . . . . . . . . . . . . .1A **60**
Martin Ryan Wlk. LE3: Leic . . . . . . .7A **5** (3D **70**)
Martinshaw Cl. LE3: Leic . . . . . . . . . . . . . .3J **63**
Martinshaw La. LE6: Groby . . . . . . . . . . . . .3C **62**
Martin Sq. LE6: Ratby . . . . . . . . . . . . . . . . .6B **62**
Martin St. LE4: Leic . . . . . . . . . . . . . . . . . .6H **65**
Martins Yd. LE16: Mkt H . . . . . . . . . . . . . .4E **150**
Martival LE5: Leic . . . . . . . . . . . . . . . . . . . .6A **66**
Marvin Cl. LE3: Leic . . . . . . . . . . . . . . . . . .7B **64**
Marwell Cl. LE4: Leic . . . . . . . . . . . . . . . . .2F **65**
Marwell Wlk. LE4: Leic . . . . . . . . . . . . . . . .2F **65**
Marwood Rd. LE4: Leic . . . . . . . . . . . . . . . .2D **64**
Mary Ct. LE3: Leic . . . . . . . . . . . . . . . . . . .6B **64**
Marydene Cl. LE5: Leic . . . . . . . . . . . . . . . .4E **72**
Marydene Dr. LE5: Leic . . . . . . . . . . . . . . . .4E **72**
Mary Gee Ho's. LE2: Leic . . . . . . . . . . . . . .7K **71**
Maryland St. LE9: Barw . . . . . . . . . . . . . . . .4J **99**
Mary La. LE14: Besc . . . . . . . . . . . . . . . . . .1E **112**
Marylebone Dr. LE17: Lut . . . . . . . . . . . . . .4K **153**
Mary Rd. LE3: Leic . . . . . . . . . . . . . . . . . . .6B **64**
Mary's Cl. LE12: Wym . . . . . . . . . . . . . . . . .2K **21**
Mary's Ct. LE7: Anst . . . . . . . . . . . . . . . . . .7H **57**
Marywell Cl. LE10: Hinc . . . . . . . . . . . . . . .2C **102**
Masefield Av. LE19: End . . . . . . . . . . . . . . .6E **74**
Masefield Cl. DE12: Mea . . . . . . . . . . . . . . .2D **48**
  LE9: Barw . . . . . . . . . . . . . . . . . . . . . . .2A **100**
Mason Cl. LE10: Hinc . . . . . . . . . . . . . . . . .3E **102**
Mason Row LE5: Ham . . . . . . . . . . . . . . . . .3F **67**
Masons Cl. LE19: Nar . . . . . . . . . . . . . . . . .2F **81**
Matlock Av. LE18: Wig . . . . . . . . . . . . . . . .7G **77**
Matlock St. LE2: Leic . . . . . . . . . . . . . . . . .1J **71**
Matthew Arnold Ct. *LE11: Lou* . . . . . . . . .5B **18**
                   *(off Shelley St.)*
Matthew Ct. LE11: Lou . . . . . . . . . . . . . . . .6H **19**
Matthews Ct. LE65: Ash Z . . . . . . . . . . . . . .5H **23**
Matts Cl. LE2: Leic . . . . . . . . . . . . . . . . . . .3D **76**
Maughan St. LE9: Earl S . . . . . . . . . . . . . . .1E **100**
Maura Cl. LE8: Whet . . . . . . . . . . . . . . . . . .4K **81**
Maurice Dr. LE8: Count . . . . . . . . . . . . . . . .6D **82**
Maurice Rd. LE16: Mkt H . . . . . . . . . . . . . .7D **150**
Mavis Av. LE3: Leic . . . . . . . . . . . . . . . . . . .5C **70**
Mawby Cl. LE8: Whet . . . . . . . . . . . . . . . . .4A **82**
Mawby's La. DE12: A Mag . . . . . . . . . . . . . .5B **48**

MAXEY . . . . . . . . . . . . . . . . . . . . . . . . . .1D **165**
Maxfield Ho. LE2: Leic . . . . . . . . . . . . . . . . .2H **71**
Maxwell Dr. LE11: Lou . . . . . . . . . . . . . . . .4K **17**
Maxwell Way LE17: Lut . . . . . . . . . . . . . . .2J **153**
May Cl. LE3: Leic . . . . . . . . . . . . . . . . . . . .3A **70**
Mayfield LE15: O'ham . . . . . . . . . . . . . . . .2J **127**
Mayfield Dr. LE11: Lou . . . . . . . . . . . . . . . . .1E **30**
  LE18: Wig . . . . . . . . . . . . . . . . . . . . . . . .4K **77**
Mayfield Rd. LE2: Leic . . . . . . . . . . . . . . . . .4J **71**
Mayfield St. LE13: Mel M . . . . . . . . . . . . . .2D **116**
Mayfield Way LE9: Barw . . . . . . . . . . . . . . .3B **100**
Mayflower Cl. LE67: Mark . . . . . . . . . . . . . .5G **55**
Mayflower Ct. LE67: Mark . . . . . . . . . . . . . .5G **55**
Mayflower Rd. LE5: Leic . . . . . . . . . . . . . . .4A **72**
May Mdw. Cl. CV13: B'one . . . . . . . . . . . . .5C **92**
Maynard Cl. LE67: Bag . . . . . . . . . . . . . . . .7G **53**
Maynard Rd. LE2: Leic . . . . . . . . . . . . . . . .1H **71**
                   *(not continuous)*
Maynard Wlk. LE67: Bag . . . . . . . . . . . . . . .7G **53**
Mayns La. LE8: Bur O . . . . . . . . . . . . . . . . .7B **130**
Mayo Cl. LE11: Lou . . . . . . . . . . . . . . . . . . .4D **30**
Mayor's Wlk. LE1: Leic . . . . . . . . . .9F **5** (4G **71**)
Mayre Cl. LE9: B Ast . . . . . . . . . . . . . . . . . .5F **87**
Mays Farm Dr. LE9: S Stan . . . . . . . . . . . . .6J **101**
Maytree Cl. LE9: Leic E . . . . . . . . . . . . . . . .4C **68**
Maytree Dr. LE9: Leic E . . . . . . . . . . . . . . . .4C **68**
May Tree La. LE12: Wood . . . . . . . . . . . . . .7F **31**
Meadhurst Gdns. LE15: Upp . . . . . . . . . . . .2C **138**
Meadhurst Rd. LE3: Leic . . . . . . . . . . . . . . .2A **70**
Meadow, The LE9: B Ast . . . . . . . . . . . . . . .5E **86**
Meadow Av. LE11: Lou . . . . . . . . . . . . . . . . .4F **19**
Meadowbrook Ct. DE12: A Mag . . . . . . . . . .5B **48**
Meadowbrook Rd. LE8: K Bea . . . . . . . . . . .3H **89**
Meadow Cl. CV9: S Mag . . . . . . . . . . . . . . .6C **90**
  LE6: Ratby . . . . . . . . . . . . . . . . . . . . . . .6B **62**
  LE7: East G . . . . . . . . . . . . . . . . . . . . . . .5H **47**
  LE9: S Stan . . . . . . . . . . . . . . . . . . . . . .7J **101**
  LE12: Bar S . . . . . . . . . . . . . . . . . . . . . . .3E **32**
  *LE16: Mkt H* . . . . . . . . . . . . . . . . . . . . .3F **151**
                 *(off Meadow St.)*
  LE67: Bag . . . . . . . . . . . . . . . . . . . . . . . . .1F **93**
Meadow Ct. LE2: Leic . . . . . . . . . . . . . . . . .1C **76**
  LE18: Wig . . . . . . . . . . . . . . . . . . . . . . . .6A **78**
  LE19: Nar . . . . . . . . . . . . . . . . . . . . . . . .7E **74**
Meadow Ct. Rd. LE6: Groby . . . . . . . . . . . . .3D **62**
  LE9: Earl S . . . . . . . . . . . . . . . . . . . . . .3E **100**
Meadowcourt Rd. LE2: Leic . . . . . . . . . . . . .1B **76**
Meadow Cres. DE74: C Don . . . . . . . . . . . . .6K **7**
Meadowcroft Cl. LE3: Glen . . . . . . . . . . . . . .7F **63**
Meadowdale Rd. LE16: L Bow . . . . . . . . . . .3H **151**
Meadow Dr. LE10: Bur . . . . . . . . . . . . . . . .4K **103**
Meadow Farm Marina Cvn. Pk. LE12: Bar S . .5F **33**
Meadowfield LE15: O'ham . . . . . . . . . . . . . .2J **127**
Meadow Gdns. DE12: Mea . . . . . . . . . . . . . .2E **48**
  LE2: Leic . . . . . . . . . . . . . . . . . . . . . . . . .2G **77**
Meadow Hill LE8: G Gle . . . . . . . . . . . . . . . .7J **79**
Meadow La. LE4: Birs . . . . . . . . . . . . . . . . .5H **59**
  LE7: Sys . . . . . . . . . . . . . . . . . . . . . . . . .1K **59**
  LE11: Lou . . . . . . . . . . . . . . . . . . . . . . . . .5F **19**
  LE12: Nor S, Stan S . . . . . . . . . . . . . . . . .2G **19**
  LE12: Osg . . . . . . . . . . . . . . . . . . . . . . . .2C **26**
  LE67: Coal . . . . . . . . . . . . . . . . . . . . . . .3G **39**
  LE67: Mark . . . . . . . . . . . . . . . . . . . . . . .4G **55**
  LE67: S Bar . . . . . . . . . . . . . . . . . . . . . . .4B **54**
  LE67: Thrin . . . . . . . . . . . . . . . . . . . . . . .2C **26**
  PE9: Ryh . . . . . . . . . . . . . . . . . . . . . . . .6G **129**
Meadow La. Ind. Est. LE11: Lou . . . . . . . . . .4G **19**
Meadow Rd. CV13: B'one . . . . . . . . . . . . . .5C **92**
  LE9: Barw . . . . . . . . . . . . . . . . . . . . . . .3B **100**
  LE12: Moun . . . . . . . . . . . . . . . . . . . . . .4D **44**
  LE12: W Eav . . . . . . . . . . . . . . . . . . . . . .3E **42**
MEADOWS . . . . . . . . . . . . . . . . . . . . . . . .1C **159**
Meadows, The LE7: East G . . . . . . . . . . . . . .4G **47**
  LE10: Bur . . . . . . . . . . . . . . . . . . . . . . . .4K **103**
  LE12: Shep . . . . . . . . . . . . . . . . . . . . . . .1C **28**
  LE19: Litt . . . . . . . . . . . . . . . . . . . . . . . .2H **81**
Meadows Edge LE19: End . . . . . . . . . . . . . .6E **74**
MEADOWS ESTATE, THE . . . . . . . . . . . . . .6B **78**
Meadows La. LE14: Hos . . . . . . . . . . . . . . .4A **108**
Meadows Ri. LE14: W'ham . . . . . . . . . . . . .1G **121**
Meadow St. LE16: Mkt H . . . . . . . . . . . . . .3E **150**
Meadowsweet Rd. LE5: Ham . . . . . . . . . . . .4E **66**
Meadowsweet Way LE13: Mel M . . . . . . . . .7D **116**
Meadow Vw. LE2: Oad . . . . . . . . . . . . . . . .3D **78**
  LE67: D Hea . . . . . . . . . . . . . . . . . . . . . .7C **38**
Meadow Wlk. LE67: Ibs . . . . . . . . . . . . . . . .3K **51**
Meadow Way LE6: Groby . . . . . . . . . . . . . . .3D **62**
  LE9: Des . . . . . . . . . . . . . . . . . . . . . . . . .3J **95**
  LE13: Mel M . . . . . . . . . . . . . . . . . . . . . .6G **117**
  LE18: Wig . . . . . . . . . . . . . . . . . . . . . . . .6A **78**
Meads, The LE3: Leic . . . . . . . . . . . . . . . . .2J **69**
Meadvale Rd. LE2: Leic . . . . . . . . . . . . . . . .1H **77**
Meadway LE3: Leic . . . . . . . . . . . . . . . . . . .1A **70**
Meadway, The LE4: Birs . . . . . . . . . . . . . . .5G **59**
  LE7: Sys . . . . . . . . . . . . . . . . . . . . . . . . .3B **60**
  LE10: Bur . . . . . . . . . . . . . . . . . . . . . . . .4J **103**
Meadwell Rd. LE3: Leic . . . . . . . . . . . . . . . .3H **69**

Mease Cl. DE12: Mea . . . . . . . . . . . . . . . .1E 48
MEASHAM . . . . . . . . . . . . . .7E 34 (3A 158)
Measham Leisure Cen. . . . . . . . . . . . . . . .7E 34
Measham Mus. . . . . . . . . . . . . . . . . . . .7E 34
Measham Rd. DE12: A Mag . . . . . . . . . . .3B 48
  DE12: Acre, Oak . . . . . . . . . . . . . . . .6A 34
  DE12: Moi . . . . . . . . . . . . . . . . . . . . .1B 34
                    (not continuous)
  DE12: Snar . . . . . . . . . . . . . . . . . . . .4F 49
  LE65: Pac . . . . . . . . . . . . . . . . . . . . .4H 35
                    (not continuous)
MEDBOURNE . . . . . . . . . . . . .6C 140 (2A 164)
Medbourne Rd. LE16: Dray . . . . . . . . . . .7F 141
  LE16: Hall . . . . . . . . . . . . . . . . . . . .7A 132
  LE16: Slaw . . . . . . . . . . . . . . . . . . . .5A 140
Medhurst Cl. LE8: Whet . . . . . . . . . . . . . .4A 82
Medieval Village of Hamilton . . . . . . . . . . .3G 67
Medina Rd. LE3: Leic . . . . . . . . . . . . . . .6D 64
Medway Cl. LE16: L Bow . . . . . . . . . . . . .4G 151
Medway Dr. LE13: Mel M . . . . . . . . . . . .6E 116
Medway St. LE2: Leic . . . . . . . . . . . . . . .3J 71
Meer, The LE8: Flec . . . . . . . . . . . . . . . .5C 88
Meeting St. LE12: Quo . . . . . . . . . . . . . .6K 31
Megabowl
  Barrow upon Soar . . . . . . . . . . . . . . .4D 32
  Leicester . . . . . . . . . . . . . .3B 4 (1E 70)
Megazone Laser Cen. . . . . . . . . . . . . . . .1D 4
Melba Way LE4: Birs . . . . . . . . . . . . . . . .4H 59
MELBOURNE . . . . . . . . . . . . . . . . . . .2A 158
Melbourne Cl. LE8: K Bea . . . . . . . . . . . .3H 89
Melbourne Dr. LE13: Mel M . . . . . . . . . .4D 116
Melbourne Ho. LE13: Mel M . . . . . . . . . .4G 117
                    (off St Johns Ct.)
Melbourne La. DE73: B Hil . . . . . . . . . . . .6A 10
Melbourne Rd. LE2: Leic . . . . . . . . . . . . .2J 71
  LE65: Stau H . . . . . . . . . . . . . . . . . . .1H 25
  LE67: Ibs . . . . . . . . . . . . . . . . . . . . .5J 51
  LE67: Rav . . . . . . . . . . . . . . . . . . . . .1K 51
Melbourne St. LE2: Leic . . . . . . . . . . . . .1H 71
  LE67: Coal . . . . . . . . . . . . . . . . . . . .3C 38
Melbray Dr. LE13: Mel M . . . . . . . . . . . .1E 116
Melbreak Av. LE11: Lou . . . . . . . . . . . . . .3C 30
Melcombe Wlk. LE4: Leic . . . . . . . . . . . . .3F 65
Melcroft Cl. LE3: Leic . . . . . . . . . . . . . . .2B 70
Melford St. LE5: Leic . . . . . . . . . . . . . . .7B 66
Melland Pl. LE2: Leic . . . . . . . . . . . . . . .3E 76
Mellerstain Wlk. LE5: Leic . . . . . . . . . . . .7A 66
Mellier Ct. LE19: Nar . . . . . . . . . . . . . . .6E 74
Mellor Rd. LE3: Leic . . . . . . . . . . . . . . .2A 70
Melody Av. LE7: Anst . . . . . . . . . . . . . . .7J 57
Melody Dr. LE12: Sileby . . . . . . . . . . . . . .2J 45
Melrose Cl. LE10: Hinc . . . . . . . . . . . . .3E 102
  LE65: Ash Z . . . . . . . . . . . . . . . . . . .6B 24
Melrose Rd. LE67: Thrin . . . . . . . . . . . . .3D 26
Melrose St. LE4: Leic . . . . . . . . . . . . . . .5H 65
Melton Av. LE4: Leic . . . . . . . . . . . . . . .1J 65
Melton Carnegie Mus. . . . . . . . . . . . . . .4G 117
Melton Country Pk. . . . . . . . . . . . . . . . .2G 117
Melton Country Pk. Vis. Cen. . . . . . . . . . .1G 117
Melton Dr. LE9: B Ast . . . . . . . . . . . . . . .2C 86
Melton Indoor Bowls Cen. . . . . . . . . . . . .6D 116
MELTON MOWBRAY . . . . . . . . .4G 117 (3A 160)
Melton Mowbray Station (Rail) . . . . . . . . .5F 117
Melton Rd. LE4: Leic, Thurm . . . . . . . . . . .5H 65
  LE7: Bill . . . . . . . . . . . . . . . . . . . . .4G 131
  LE7: East G, Quen, Rear, Sys . . . . . . . . .1D 60
  LE7: T Hil . . . . . . . . . . . . . . . . . . . .1G 131
  LE12: Bar S . . . . . . . . . . . . . . . . . . . .4D 32
  LE12: Bur W . . . . . . . . . . . . . . . . . . .3G 21
  LE14: Ash H . . . . . . . . . . . . . . . . . . . .2J 115
  LE14: Bur L . . . . . . . . . . . . . . . . . . .1C 120
  LE14: L Cla . . . . . . . . . . . . . . . . . . . .3G 111
  LE14: Scal . . . . . . . . . . . . . . . . . . . .7A 112
  LE14: W Wol . . . . . . . . . . . . . . . . . . .4B 112
  LE14: W'ham . . . . . . . . . . . . . . . . . . .1F 121
  LE15: L'ham . . . . . . . . . . . . . . . . . . .5B 122
  LE15: O'ham . . . . . . . . . . . . . . . . . . .4H 127
  LE15: Whis . . . . . . . . . . . . . . . . . . . .1A 122
  LE16: C Lan, East L . . . . . . . . . . . . . . .1A 140
Melton Spinney Rd. LE13: Mel M . . . . . . . .2J 117
  LE14: Scal . . . . . . . . . . . . . . . . . . . .7D 112
Melton St. LE1: Leic . . . . . . . . . . . . . . . .7G 65
  LE9: Earl S . . . . . . . . . . . . . . . . . . . .2D 100
Melville Cl. LE11: Lou . . . . . . . . . . . . . . .4K 17
Memorial Sq. LE67: Coal . . . . . . . . . . . . .3C 38
Memory La. LE1: Leic . . . . . . . . . . . . . . .7G 65
Mendip Av. LE4: Leic . . . . . . . . . . . . . . .5C 64
Mendip Cl. LE12: Shep . . . . . . . . . . . . . .7E 16
  LE65: Ash Z . . . . . . . . . . . . . . . . . . .6K 23
Mendip Rd. LE15: E Wes . . . . . . . . . . . . .3H 135
  LE15: O'ham . . . . . . . . . . . . . . . . . . .4F 127
Mennecy Cl. LE8: Count . . . . . . . . . . . . .6D 82
Mensa Cl. LE2: Leic . . . . . . . . . . . . . . . .2J 71
Menzies Rd. LE4: Leic . . . . . . . . . . . . . . .4E 64
MERCASTON . . . . . . . . . . . . . . . . . . .1A 158
Mercer's Way LE7: East G . . . . . . . . . . . .5G 47
Merchants Comn. LE7: East G . . . . . . . . . .5G 47

Mercia Dr. LE2: Oad . . . . . . . . . . . . . . .2B 78
Mercury Cl. LE2: Leic . . . . . . . . .5G 4 (2H 71)
Mere, The LE8: G Gle . . . . . . . . . . . . . . .1J 85
Mere Cl. LE5: Leic . . . . . . . . . . . . . . . . .1J 71
  LE12: Moun . . . . . . . . . . . . . . . . . . . .4E 44
Meredith Rd. LE3: Leic . . . . . . . . . . . . . .6B 70
Mere La. LE2: Oad . . . . . . . . . . . . . . . . .6F 79
  LE7: Quen . . . . . . . . . . . . . . . . . . . . .7H 47
Mere Rd. LE2: Gt Stret . . . . . . . . . . . . . .3K 79
  LE5: Leic . . . . . . . . . . . . . . . . . . . . .7J 65
  LE14: W Wol . . . . . . . . . . . . . . . . . . .1C 112
  LE17: Walt . . . . . . . . . . . . . . . . . . . .6C 146
  LE18: Wig . . . . . . . . . . . . . . . . . . . . .5A 78
Meres Wlk. LE18: Wig . . . . . . . . . . . . . . .5B 78
Merevale Av. LE10: Hinc . . . . . . . . . . . . .4F 103
Merevale Cl. LE10: Hinc . . . . . . . . . . . . .4F 103
Mereworth Cl. LE5: Leic . . . . . . . . . . . . .6K 65
Merganster Way LE67: Coal . . . . . . . . . . .4G 39
Meridian Bus. Pk. LE19: Brau . . . . . . . . . .2H 75
Meridian E. LE19: Brau . . . . . . . . . . . . . .6H 69
Meridian Leisure Pk. LE19: Brau . . . . . . . .6J 69
Meridian Nth. LE19: Brau . . . . . . . . . . . . .1H 75
Meridian Sth. LE19: Brau . . . . . . . . . . . . .2H 75
Meridian Way LE19: Brau . . . . . . . . . . . . .6H 69
Meridian W. LE19: Brau . . . . . . . . . . . . . .1H 75
Meriton Rd. LE17: Lut . . . . . . . . . . . . . .5H 153
Merlin Cl. LE3: Leic E . . . . . . . . . . . . . . .5E 68
  LE7: R'ley . . . . . . . . . . . . . . . . . . . . .3F 45
  LE9: B Ast . . . . . . . . . . . . . . . . . . . . .3C 86
Merrick Ct. LE10: Bur . . . . . . . . . . . . . . .6J 103
Merrifield Gdns. LE10: Bur . . . . . . . . . . . .6H 103
Merrin Ct. LE11: Lou . . . . . . . . . . . . . . . .5F 19
Merrydale Ct. LE5: Leic . . . . . . . . . . . . . .6A 66
Merry Hurst Way LE10: Hinc . . . . . . . . . . .4C 102
MERRY LEES . . . . . . . . . . . . . . . . . . .1B 162
Merrylees Rd. LE67: Thor . . . . . . . . . . . . .3K 93
Merton Av. LE3: Leic . . . . . . . . . . . . . . .2C 70
  LE7: Sys . . . . . . . . . . . . . . . . . . . . . .2D 60
Merton Cl. LE9: B Ast . . . . . . . . . . . . . . .3B 86
Merton Way LE8: Kib H . . . . . . . . . . . . . .2H 89
Mervyn Rd. LE5: Leic . . . . . . . . . . . . . . .3K 71
Messenger Cl. LE11: Lou . . . . . . . . . . . . .3C 18
Metcalf Cl. LE9: S Stan . . . . . . . . . . . . . .1J 105
Metcalfe St. LE9: Earl S . . . . . . . . . . . . . .3D 100
Methuen Av. LE4: Thurm . . . . . . . . . . . . .5A 60
Mews Gallery, The . . . . . . . . . . . . . . . . .2F 81
Meynell Cl. LE2: Oad . . . . . . . . . . . . . . .4E 78
  LE13: Mel M . . . . . . . . . . . . . . . . . . .7F 117
Meynell Rd. LE5: Leic . . . . . . . . . . . . . . .7K 65
  LE12: Quo . . . . . . . . . . . . . . . . . . . . .4A 32
Michael Cl. LE7: Quen . . . . . . . . . . . . . .6G 47
Michael Lewis Ho. LE3: Leic . . . . . . . . . . .1B 70
Michael Ramsey Ct. LE2: G Par . . . . . . . . .5C 76
Mickleden Grn. LE67: Whit . . . . . . . . . . . .2G 39
MICKLEOVER . . . . . . . . . . . . . . . . . .1A 158
Mickleton Cl. DE11: C Gre . . . . . . . . . . . .2A 22
Mickleton Dr. LE5: Leic . . . . . . . . . . . . . .4D 72
Middle Av. LE11: Lou . . . . . . . . . . . . . . .4D 18
Middlebrook Cl. LE6: Ratby . . . . . . . . . . .6B 62
Middlebrook Grn. LE16: Mkt H . . . . . . . . . .3F 151
Middledale Rd. LE16: L Bow . . . . . . . . . . .4G 151
MIDDLEFIELD . . . . . . . . . . . . . . . . . .7F 99
Middlefield Cl. LE10: Hinc . . . . . . . . . . . .1G 103
Middlefield Ct. LE10: Hinc . . . . . . . . . . . .1G 103
Middlefield La. LE10: Hinc . . . . . . . . . . . .7G 99
                    (Middlefield Pl.)
  LE10: Hinc . . . . . . . . . . . . . . . . . . . .6F 99
                    (Normandy Way)
Middlefield Pl. LE10: Hinc . . . . . . . . . . . .7G 99
Middlefield Rd. LE7: Coss . . . . . . . . . . . .5K 45
Middle La. LE14: N Bro . . . . . . . . . . . . . .2D 110
Middle Orchard LE12: Sileby . . . . . . . . . . .3J 45
Middle Rd. LE67: Grif . . . . . . . . . . . . . . .2A 26
                    (off The Tentas)
Middlesex Rd. LE2: Leic . . . . . . . . . . . . . .1D 76
Middle St. LE14: Hos . . . . . . . . . . . . . . .6B 108
  LE15: Win . . . . . . . . . . . . . . . . . . . . .5E 134
  NG13: Bark V . . . . . . . . . . . . . . . . . . .3B 106
  NG32: Crox . . . . . . . . . . . . . . . . . . . .5G 107
MIDDLETON . . . . . . . . . . . . . . . . . . .2B 164
Middleton Cl. LE9: S Stan . . . . . . . . . . . .1K 105
  LE18: Wig . . . . . . . . . . . . . . . . . . . . .5B 78
Middleton Pl. LE11: Lou . . . . . . . . . . . . .1E 30
Middleton Rd. LE16: Brin . . . . . . . . . . . . .7J 141
Middletons Cl. LE8: Flec . . . . . . . . . . . . .3B 88
Middleton St. LE2: Leic . . . . . . . . . . . . . .1C 76
Midhurst Av. LE3: Brau . . . . . . . . . . . . . .7K 69
Midland Cotts. LE18: Wig . . . . . . . . . . . . .6G 77
Midland Ct. LE15: O'ham . . . . . . . . . . . . .3H 127
                    (not continuous)
  LE17: Lut . . . . . . . . . . . . . . . . . . . . .2K 153
Midland Rd. LE67: Hug . . . . . . . . . . . . . .7C 38
Midland St. LE1: Leic . . . . . . . . . .3F 4 (1G 71)
MIDWAY . . . . . . . . . . . . . . . . . . . . .2A 158
Midway La. LE17: Walt . . . . . . . . . . . . . .6C 146
Midway Rd. LE5: Leic . . . . . . . . . . . . . . .5K 71
Mildenhall Rd. LE11: Lou . . . . . . . . . . . . .6A 18

Mildmay Cl. LE13: Mel M . . . . . . . . . . . . .1F 117
Milestone Cl. LE8: Kib H . . . . . . . . . . . . .3K 89
Milfoil Cl. LE10: Hinc . . . . . . . . . . . . . . .4C 102
Milford Cl. LE19: Nar . . . . . . . . . . . . . . .1E 80
Milford Rd. LE2: Leic . . . . . . . . . . . . . . .7H 71
Millais Rd. LE10: Hinc . . . . . . . . . . . . . . .7D 98
Mill Bank LE65: Ash Z . . . . . . . . . . . . . . .5K 23
Millbrook Cl. LE4: Leic . . . . . . . . . . . . . .3F 65
Millbrook Dr. LE9: B Ast . . . . . . . . . . . . .5D 86
Millbrook Wlk. LE4: Leic . . . . . . . . . . . . .3F 65
Mill Cl. LE4: Birs . . . . . . . . . . . . . . . . . .7H 59
  LE8: Smee W . . . . . . . . . . . . . . . . . . .5H 89
  LE9: Sap . . . . . . . . . . . . . . . . . . . . .3K 105
  LE9: Stap . . . . . . . . . . . . . . . . . . . . .1H 99
  LE12: Shep . . . . . . . . . . . . . . . . . . . .5E 16
                    (Boundary Way)
  LE12: Shep . . . . . . . . . . . . . . . . . . . .6C 16
                    (Tickow La.)
  LE18: Wig . . . . . . . . . . . . . . . . . . . . .1F 83
Mill Dam LE67: Hug . . . . . . . . . . . . . . . .6D 38
Mill Dr. LE6: Ratby . . . . . . . . . . . . . . . . .7B 62
Millennium Av. DE12: Moi . . . . . . . . . . . .6A 22
Millennium Cl. LE17: N Kil . . . . . . . . . . . .2K 155
Miller Cl. LE4: Leic . . . . . . . . . . . . . . . . .1A 66
Millers Cl. LE3: Glen . . . . . . . . . . . . . . . .6E 62
  LE7: Sys . . . . . . . . . . . . . . . . . . . . . .2C 60
Millersdale Av. LE5: Leic . . . . . . . . . . . . .3F 73
Millers Gdns. LE16: Mkt H . . . . . . . . . . . .5B 150
Millers Grange LE9: B Ast . . . . . . . . . . . .5D 86
Millers Grn. LE10: Bur . . . . . . . . . . . . . .5J 103
Millers Wlk. LE67: Rav . . . . . . . . . . . . . .5J 37
Millers Yd. LE16: Mkt H . . . . . . . . . . . . . .4E 150
Millfield Cl. LE7: Anst . . . . . . . . . . . . . . .1H 63
  LE65: Ash Z . . . . . . . . . . . . . . . . . . .3J 23
Millfield Cres. LE3: Brau . . . . . . . . . . . . .2K 75
Millfield St. DE11: W'lle . . . . . . . . . . . . . .1C 22
Mill Gdns. CV13: H Hill . . . . . . . . . . . . . .6G 90
Mill Gro. LE15: Whis . . . . . . . . . . . . . . . .2B 122
  LE17: Lut . . . . . . . . . . . . . . . . . . . . .5K 153
Mill Hill LE4: Leic . . . . . . . . . . . . . . . . . .4G 65
  LE14: Sta . . . . . . . . . . . . . . . . . . . . .3H 109
  LE16: Lub . . . . . . . . . . . . . . . . . . . . .6H 149
  LE19: End . . . . . . . . . . . . . . . . . . . . .4E 74
Mill Hill Cl. LE8: Whet . . . . . . . . . . . . . . .2A 82
Mill Hill Ind. Est. LE19: End . . . . . . . . . . . .3E 74
                    (Feldspar Cl.)
  LE19: End . . . . . . . . . . . . . . . . . . . . .4E 74
                    (Quarry La.)
Mill Hill La. LE2: Leic . . . . . . . . .7G 5 (3H 71)
  LE67: Mark . . . . . . . . . . . . . . . . . . . .4F 55
Mill Hill Rd. LE8: Arne . . . . . . . . . . . . . . .2H 147
  LE10: Hinc . . . . . . . . . . . . . . . . . . . .2F 103
  LE16: Mkt H . . . . . . . . . . . . . . . . . . .4F 151
Mill Ho. LE13: Mel M . . . . . . . . . . . . . . .4G 117
MILLHOUSE ESTATE . . . . . . . . . . . . . . .3C 26
Milligan Rd. LE2: Leic . . . . . . . . . . . . . . .2E 76
Mill La. CV9: Manc . . . . . . . . . . . . . . . . .7A 96
  CV9: S Mag, S Par . . . . . . . . . . . . . . .5C 90
  CV9: With . . . . . . . . . . . . . . . . . . . . .5A 96
  CV13: Bils . . . . . . . . . . . . . . . . . . . . .6F 91
  DE74: Keg . . . . . . . . . . . . . . . . . . . . .6H 9
  LE2: Leic . . . . . . . . . . . . . . . .6A 5 (3E 70)
  LE4: Thurm . . . . . . . . . . . . . . . . . . . .5K 59
  LE7: Sys . . . . . . . . . . . . . . . . . . . . . .7B 46
  LE8: Bla . . . . . . . . . . . . . . . . . . . . . .1C 82
  LE8: K Bea, Smee W . . . . . . . . . . . . . .4E 88
  LE9: Earl S, Thurl . . . . . . . . . . . . . . . .1F 101
  LE9: N Ver . . . . . . . . . . . . . . . . . . . . .6H 93
  LE10: S'ord . . . . . . . . . . . . . . . . . . . .6H 105
  LE11: Lou . . . . . . . . . . . . . . . . . . . . .6E 18
                    (Market St.)
  LE11: Lou . . . . . . . . . . . . . . . . . . . . .5G 19
                    (Nottingham Rd.)
  LE12: Bar S . . . . . . . . . . . . . . . . . . . .4D 32
  LE12: Belt . . . . . . . . . . . . . . . . . . . . .3H 15
  LE12: L Wha . . . . . . . . . . . . . . . . . . .6G 13
  LE12: Sileby . . . . . . . . . . . . . . . . . . . .2G 45
  LE13: Mel M . . . . . . . . . . . . . . . . . . .5G 117
  LE14: Ash . . . . . . . . . . . . . . . . . . . . .3G 115
  LE14: F Wre . . . . . . . . . . . . . . . . . . . .5H 115
  LE14: L Cla . . . . . . . . . . . . . . . . . . . .2J 111
  LE14: Som . . . . . . . . . . . . . . . . . . . . .6K 121
  LE14: W Wol . . . . . . . . . . . . . . . . . . .2C 112
  LE15: B'den . . . . . . . . . . . . . . . . . . . .7E 136
  LE15: Cott . . . . . . . . . . . . . . . . . . . . .6A 124
  LE15: Emp . . . . . . . . . . . . . . . . . . . . .6D 128
  LE16: C'ott . . . . . . . . . . . . . . . . . . . .2H 141
  LE17: Gilm, P Par . . . . . . . .7J 145 & 3A 146
  LE17: Shea . . . . . . . . . . . . . . . . . . . .5J 147
  LE19: End . . . . . . . . . . . . . . . . . . . . .5F 75
  LE65: Ash Z . . . . . . . . . . . . . . . . . . .5K 23
  LE67: Cole . . . . . . . . . . . . . . . . . . . . .4A 26
  LE67: Hea . . . . . . . . . . . . . . . . . . . . .3G 51
  LE67: Thor . . . . . . . . . . . . . . . . . . . . .2J 93
  NG32: Crox . . . . . . . . . . . . . . . . . . . .6H 107
  PE9: Ket . . . . . . . . . . . . . . . . . . . . . .6H 137
Mill La., The LE3: Glen . . . . . . . . . . . . . .6E 62

Mill La. Ind. Est. LE3: Glen . . . . . . . . . . . . . .5D **62**
Mill-on-the-Soar Falconry & Fishing Cen.
. . . . . . . . . . . . . . . . . . . . . . . . . . . . . . . . . . .2A **86**
Mill Pond LE67: Hug . . . . . . . . . . . . . . . . . .6D **38**
Mill Rd. LE7: Rear . . . . . . . . . . . . . . . . . . . . .3H **47**
    LE7: Thurc . . . . . . . . . . . . . . . . . . . . . . . . .2B **58**
    LE12: W Eav . . . . . . . . . . . . . . . . . . . . . . . .3D **42**
    LE15: Seat, T Wat . . . . . . . . . . . . . . . . . . .7K **139**
        (not continuous)
    LE17: Ull . . . . . . . . . . . . . . . . . . . . . . . . . . .7F **143**
Mills, The LE12: Quo . . . . . . . . . . . . . . . . . .6A **32**
Millstone La. LE1: Leic . . . . . . . . . .5B **4** (2F **71**)
    LE7: Sys . . . . . . . . . . . . . . . . . . . . . . . . . . .7E **46**
Mill St. LE1: Leic . . . . . . . . . . . . . . .6D **5** (3F **71**)
    LE9: Barw . . . . . . . . . . . . . . . . . . . . . . . . . .5J **99**
    LE13: Mel M . . . . . . . . . . . . . . . . . . . . . . . .5F **117**
    LE15: O'ham . . . . . . . . . . . . . . . . . . . . . . . .4J **127**
    LE65: Pac . . . . . . . . . . . . . . . . . . . . . . . . . .2K **35**
    PE9: Ryh . . . . . . . . . . . . . . . . . . . . . . . . . . .4H **129**
Mill St. Ind. Est. LE9: Barw . . . . . . . . . . . .4K **99**
Mills Yd. LE11: Lou . . . . . . . . . . . . . . . . . . . .7F **19**
MILLTHORPE . . . . . . . . . . . . . . . . . . . . . . .1D **161**
Mill Vw. LE9: Hun . . . . . . . . . . . . . . . . . . . .2B **80**
    LE10: Hinc . . . . . . . . . . . . . . . . . . . . . . . . .2H **103**
Millwood Cl. LE4: Leic . . . . . . . . . . . . . . . .1E **64**
Milner Cl. LE12: Sileby . . . . . . . . . . . . . . . .2J **45**
Milnroy Rd. LE5: Leic . . . . . . . . . . . . . . . . .1G **73**
MILTON . . . . . . . . . . . . . . . . . . . . . . . . . . .2A **158**
Milton Cl. DE12: Mea . . . . . . . . . . . . . . . . .2E **48**
    LE10: Hinc . . . . . . . . . . . . . . . . . . . . . . . . .2F **103**
    LE13: Mel M . . . . . . . . . . . . . . . . . . . . . . . .2E **116**
    LE18: Wig . . . . . . . . . . . . . . . . . . . . . . . . . .6A **78**
Milton Ct. LE11: Lou . . . . . . . . . . . . . . . . . .4B **18**
Milton Cres. LE4: Leic . . . . . . . . . . . . . . . .3B **64**
Milton Gdns. LE2: Oad . . . . . . . . . . . . . . . .3C **78**
Milton Ho. LE4: Leic . . . . . . . . . . . . . . . . . .3B **64**
Milton St. LE11: Lou . . . . . . . . . . . . . . . . . .4C **18**
    LE19: Nar . . . . . . . . . . . . . . . . . . . . . . . . . .7E **74**
Milverton Av. LE4: Leic . . . . . . . . . . . . . . .5C **64**
Milverton Cl. LE18: Wig . . . . . . . . . . . . . . .4J **77**
Milverton Dr. LE18: Wig . . . . . . . . . . . . . . .4J **77**
Mimosa Cl. LE11: Lou . . . . . . . . . . . . . . . . .4E **30**
Minehead St. LE3: Leic . . . . . . . . . . . . . . . .2B **70**
Minster Ct. LE1: Leic . . . . . . . . . . . . . . . . . .5C **4**
Minster Cres. LE4: Leic . . . . . . . . . . . . . . . .5D **64**
Minstrel's Wlk. LE7: East G . . . . . . . . . . . . .5F **47**
Minton Rd. DE74: C Don . . . . . . . . . . . . . .4H **7**
Mint Rd. LE2: Leic . . . . . . . . . . . . .7A **5** (3D **70**)
MISTERTON . . . . . . . . . . . . . . . .2B **154** (3C **163**)
Misterton Way LE17: Lut . . . . . . . . . . . . . .5K **153**
Mistral Cl. LE10: Hinc . . . . . . . . . . . . . . . . .3J **103**
Mitchell Dr. LE11: Lou . . . . . . . . . . . . . . . .4K **17**
Mitchell Rd. LE19: End . . . . . . . . . . . . . . . .5E **74**
Moat, The DE74: C Don . . . . . . . . . . . . . . .4K **7**
Moat Cl. LE9: Thurl . . . . . . . . . . . . . . . . . . .2B **96**
Moat Ct. LE5: Leic . . . . . . . . . . . . . . . . . . .6E **66**
Moat Gdns. LE9: Sap . . . . . . . . . . . . . . . . .4J **105**
Moat Rd. LE5: Leic . . . . . . . . . . . . . . . . . . .2K **71**
    LE11: Lou . . . . . . . . . . . . . . . . . . . . . . . . . .3C **30**
Moat St. LE18: Wig . . . . . . . . . . . . . . . . . . .6J **77**
Moat Way LE9: Barw . . . . . . . . . . . . . . . . .4J **99**
Modbury Av. LE4: Leic . . . . . . . . . . . . . . . .2E **64**
Model Farm Cl. LE11: Lou . . . . . . . . . . . . .2C **30**
MOIRA . . . . . . . . . . . . . . . . . .7C **22** (3A **158**)
Moira Dale DE74: C Don . . . . . . . . . . . . . .5K **7**
Moira Furnace Mus. . . . . . . . . . . . . . . . . . .1A **34**
Moira Rd. DE11: W'lle . . . . . . . .3B **22** & 4A **22**
    DE12: Don . . . . . . . . . . . . . . . . . . . . . . . . .3B **34**
    LE65: Ash Z . . . . . . . . . . . . . . . . . . . . . . . .5E **22**
Moira St. LE4: Leic . . . . . . . . . . . . . . . . . . .5H **65**
    LE11: Lou . . . . . . . . . . . . . . . . . . . . . . . . . .7F **19**
Moir Cl. LE12: Sileby . . . . . . . . . . . . . . . . . .1J **45**
Moles La. LE15: Seat . . . . . . . . . . . . . . . . .5K **139**
MOLESWORTH . . . . . . . . . . . . . . . . . . . . .3D **165**
Molesworth Bungs. PE9: Ket . . . . . . . . . . .5H **137**
Molyneux Dr. LE12: Sileby . . . . . . . . . . . . .3K **45**
Monal Cl. LE8: Whet . . . . . . . . . . . . . . . . . .5K **81**
Monarch Cl. LE4: Birs . . . . . . . . . . . . . . . . .5J **59**
Monarch Way LE11: Lou . . . . . . . . . . . . . .4E **18**
Monar Cl. LE4: Leic . . . . . . . . . . . . . . . . . . .2K **65**
Mona St. LE9: Earl S . . . . . . . . . . . . . . . . . .3D **100**
Monckton Cl. LE1: Leic . . . . . . . . .1F **4** (7G **65**)
Money Hill LE65: Ash Z . . . . . . . . . . . . . . .3K **23**
Monica Rd. LE3: Brau . . . . . . . . . . . . . . . . .1K **75**
Monks Cres. LE4: Leic . . . . . . . . . . . . . . . .5C **58**
MONKS KIRBY . . . . . . . . . . . . . . . . . . . . . .3B **162**
Monmouth Dr. LE2: Leic . . . . . . . . . . . . . .6C **76**
Monroe Cl. LE16: Mkt H . . . . . . . . . . . . . .2D **150**
Monsarrat Way LE11: Lou . . . . . . . . . . . . .4B **18**
Monsell Dr. LE2: Leic . . . . . . . . . . . . . . . . .3C **76**
Montague Av. LE7: Sys . . . . . . . . . . . . . . . .3D **60**
Montague Cl. LE9: N Ver . . . . . . . . . . . . . .5H **93**
Montague Dr. LE11: Lou . . . . . . . . . . . . . .3A **30**
Montague Rd. LE2: Leic . . . . . . . . . . . . . . .5H **71**
    LE9: B Ast . . . . . . . . . . . . . . . . . . . . . . . . . .3D **86**
Monteith Pl. DE74: C Don . . . . . . . . . . . . .4K **7**
Montford M. DE74: C Don . . . . . . . . . . . . .4K **7**

Montgomery Cl. LE17: Lut . . . . . . . . . . . . .5G **153**
Montgomery Rd. LE9: Earl S . . . . . . . . . . .2F **101**
        (not continuous)
Montreal Rd. LE1: Leic . . . . . . . . .1F **4** (7G **65**)
Montrose Cl. LE16: Mkt H . . . . . . . . . . . . .6D **150**
Montrose Ct. LE5: Leic . . . . . . . . . . . . . . . .6C **66**
Montrose Rd. LE2: Leic . . . . . . . . . . . . . . . .3C **76**
Montrose Rd. Sth. LE2: Leic . . . . . . . . . . .3C **76**
Montsoreau Way
    LE12: Moun . . . . . . . . . . . . . . . . . . . . . . . .4D **44**
Montvale Gdns. LE4: Leic . . . . . . . . . . . . . .6D **64**
Moon Cl. LE2: Leic . . . . . . . . . . . . .5G **4** (2H **71**)
Moor, The LE67: Cole . . . . . . . . . . . . . . . . .4J **25**
Moorbarns La. LE17: Lut . . . . . . . . . . . . . .7G **153**
Moore Av. DE74: Keg . . . . . . . . . . . . . . . . .5H **9**
Moore Cl. DE12: A Mag . . . . . . . . . . . . . . .5B **48**
Moore Rd. LE9: Barw . . . . . . . . . . . . . . . . .2A **100**
Moores Cl. LE18: Wig . . . . . . . . . . . . . . . . .6E **76**
Moores La. LE19: End . . . . . . . . . . . . . . . . .5F **75**
Moores Rd. LE4: Leic . . . . . . . . . . . . . . . . .4H **65**
Moorfield Pl. LE12: Shep . . . . . . . . . . . . . .6D **16**
Moorfields LE5: Leic . . . . . . . . . . . . . . . . . .6F **67**
Moorgate Av. LE4: Birs . . . . . . . . . . . . . . . .5F **59**
Moorgate St. LE4: Leic . . . . . . . . . . . . . . . .6G **65**
Moorhen Way LE11: Lou . . . . . . . . . . . . . .7D **18**
Moorings, The LE12: Bar S . . . . . . . . . . . . .5E **32**
Moorland Cl. CV13: Mkt B . . . . . . . . . . . . .2D **94**
Moorland Rd. LE7: Sys . . . . . . . . . . . . . . . .2A **60**
Moorlands, The LE67: Cole . . . . . . . . . . . .1H **37**
Moor La. DE72: A Tre . . . . . . . . . . . . . . . . .1D **6**
    DE73: Ton . . . . . . . . . . . . . . . . . . . . . . . . .6D **10**
    LE11: Lou . . . . . . . . . . . . . . . . . . . . . . . . . .6F **19**
        (Aumberry Gap)
    LE11: Lou . . . . . . . . . . . . . . . . . . . . . . . . . .7H **19**
        (Thomas St.)
    LE14: Sta . . . . . . . . . . . . . . . . . . . . . . . . . .1H **109**
    LE15: N Luf . . . . . . . . . . . . . . . . . . . . . . . . .2B **136**
    LE15: Whis . . . . . . . . . . . . . . . . . . . . . . . . .1E **122**
    LE67: Cole . . . . . . . . . . . . . . . . . . . . . . . . .5J **25**
Moor Leys La. LE14: W Wol . . . . . . . . . . . .4A **112**
Moor Rd. LE67: Ell . . . . . . . . . . . . . . . . . . . .2E **52**
Moray Cl. LE10: Hinc . . . . . . . . . . . . . . . . .3D **102**
Morban Rd. LE2: Leic . . . . . . . . . . . . . . . . .2B **76**
MORBORNE . . . . . . . . . . . . . . . . . . . . . . .2D **165**
Morcote Rd. LE3: Leic . . . . . . . . . . . . . . . . .4J **69**
MORCOTT . . . . . . . . . . . . . . . .6J **135** (1C **165**)
Morcott Rd. LE15: B'den, Mor . . . . . . . . . .7A **136**
    LE15: Glas . . . . . . . . . . . . . . . . . . . . . . . . .1J **139**
    LE15: Win . . . . . . . . . . . . . . . . . . . . . . . . . .6E **134**
Moreton Ct. LE67: Coal . . . . . . . . . . . . . . .5D **38**
Moreton Dale LE12: Sileby . . . . . . . . . . . .7K **33**
Morgan Est. CV23: C Dus . . . . . . . . . . . . .5A **156**
Morgans Orchard LE12: Bar S . . . . . . . . . .3D **32**
Morland Av. LE2: Leic . . . . . . . . . . . . . . . . .7A **72**
Morland Dr. LE10: Hinc . . . . . . . . . . . . . . .7E **98**
Morledge St. LE1: Leic . . . . . . . . .3F **4** (1G **71**)
MORLEY . . . . . . . . . . . . . . . . . . . . . . . . . . .1A **158**
Morley Arc. LE1: Leic . . . . . . . . . . . . . . . . .3D **4**
Morley La. LE12: Shep . . . . . . . . . . . . . . . . .2C **28**
Morley Rd. LE5: Leic . . . . . . . . . . . . . . . . . .1J **71**
    LE9: Sap . . . . . . . . . . . . . . . . . . . . . . . . . . .4K **105**
Morley St. LE11: Lou . . . . . . . . . . . . . . . . . .5G **19**
    LE13: Mel M . . . . . . . . . . . . . . . . . . . . . . . .3D **116**
    LE16: Mkt H . . . . . . . . . . . . . . . . . . . . . . . .4D **150**
Mornington St. LE5: Leic . . . . . . . . . . . . . .7K **65**
Morpeth Av. LE4: Leic . . . . . . . . . . . . . . . .1D **64**
Morpeth Cl. LE2: Oad . . . . . . . . . . . . . . . . .4F **79**
Morris Cam Wlk. LE14: Ash . . . . . . . . . . . .2F **115**
Morris Cl. LE3: Brau . . . . . . . . . . . . . . . . . .5H **69**
    LE11: Lou . . . . . . . . . . . . . . . . . . . . . . . . . .6G **19**
Morris Ct. LE17: Brun . . . . . . . . . . . . . . . . .1D **146**
Morrison Ct. LE8: K Bea . . . . . . . . . . . . . . .4J **89**
Morris Rd. LE2: Leic . . . . . . . . . . . . . . . . . .6G **71**
Mortiboys Way LE9: S Stan . . . . . . . . . . . .1J **105**
Mortimer Pl. LE3: Leic . . . . . . . . . . . . . . . .6B **70**
Mortimer Rd. LE13: Mel M . . . . . . . . . . . .3F **117**
    LE19: Nar . . . . . . . . . . . . . . . . . . . . . . . . . .2E **80**
Mortimer Way LE3: Leic . . . . . . . . . . . . . . .6A **70**
    LE11: Lou . . . . . . . . . . . . . . . . . . . . . . . . . .4K **17**
Mortoft Rd. LE4: Leic . . . . . . . . . . . . . . . . .3H **65**
MORTON . . . . . . . . . . . . . . . . . . . . . . . . . .2D **161**
Morton Wlk. LE5: Leic . . . . . . . . . . . . . . . .6K **65**
    LE65: Ash Z . . . . . . . . . . . . . . . . . . . . . . . .7H **23**
Morwoods, The LE2: Oad . . . . . . . . . . . . . .3D **78**
Moscow La. LE12: Shep . . . . . . . . . . . . . . .2C **28**
Mossdale LE67: Whit . . . . . . . . . . . . . . . . .5E **26**
Mossdale Rd. LE3: Brau . . . . . . . . . . . . . . .7J **69**
Mosse Way LE2: Oad . . . . . . . . . . . . . . . . .2E **78**
Mossgate LE4: Leic . . . . . . . . . . . . . . . . . . .7A **64**
Mosswithy LE8: Flec . . . . . . . . . . . . . . . . . .5B **88**
Mostyn Av. LE7: Sys . . . . . . . . . . . . . . . . . .1E **60**
Mostyn St. LE3: Leic . . . . . . . . . . . . . . . . . .2B **70**
Mottisford Rd. LE4: Leic . . . . . . . . . . . . . . .2F **65**
Mottisford Wlk. LE4: Leic . . . . . . . . . . . . .2F **65**
Moulds La. LE16: G Eas . . . . . . . . . . . . . . .5K **141**
Mount, The LE7: Scra . . . . . . . . . . . . . . . . .6H **67**
    LE17: D Bas . . . . . . . . . . . . . . . . . . . . . . . .2C **144**

Mountain Rd. LE4: Leic . . . . . . . . . . . . . . .2C **66**
Mount Av. LE5: Leic . . . . . . . . . . . . . . . . . .1K **71**
    LE9: Barw . . . . . . . . . . . . . . . . . . . . . . . . . .3B **100**
Mountbatten Rd. LE15: O'ham . . . . . . . . .4G **127**
Mountbatten Way LE17: Lut . . . . . . . . . . .5H **153**
Mountcastle Rd. LE3: Leic . . . . . . . . . . . . .5C **70**
Mountfield Rd. LE9: Earl S . . . . . . . . . . . . .2D **100**
Mountfields Dr. LE11: Lou . . . . . . . . . . . . .1C **30**
Mt. Grace Rd. LE11: Lou . . . . . . . . . . . . . .5K **17**
MOUNT PLEASANT . . . . . . . . . . . . . . . . . .3A **158**
Mt. Pleasant DE74: C Don . . . . . . . . . . . . .5K **7**
    DE74: Keg . . . . . . . . . . . . . . . . . . . . . . . . .6G **9**
    LE2: Oad . . . . . . . . . . . . . . . . . . . . . . . . . . .4F **79**
    LE15: Mor . . . . . . . . . . . . . . . . . . . . . . . . . .6J **135**
Mt. Pleasant Rd. LE15: Mor . . . . . . . . . . .6J **135**
Mount Rd. LE2: Oad . . . . . . . . . . . . . . . . . .3D **78**
    LE5: Leic . . . . . . . . . . . . . . . . . . . . . . . . . . .1J **71**
    LE9: Cosb . . . . . . . . . . . . . . . . . . . . . . . . . .6H **81**
    LE10: Hinc . . . . . . . . . . . . . . . . . . . . . . . . .3G **103**
Mount St Bernard Abbey (Monastery) . . . .6K **27**
MOUNTSORREL . . . . . . . . . . . .2E **44** (3C **159**)
Mountsorrel La. LE7: R'ley . . . . . . . . . . . . .4E **44**
    LE12: Sileby . . . . . . . . . . . . . . . . . . . . . . . .1F **45**
Mount Vw. LE8: G Gle . . . . . . . . . . . . . . . .5A **130**
Mount Wlk. LE65: Ash Z . . . . . . . . . . . . . .5A **24**
Mowbray Ct. LE13: Mel M . . . . . . . . . . . . .5E **116**
Mowbray Dr. LE7: Sys . . . . . . . . . . . . . . . .1E **60**
Mowmacre Community & Sports Cen. . . . .1E **64**
MOWMACRE HILL . . . . . . . . . . .1D **64** (1C **163**)
Mowmacre Hill LE4: Leic . . . . . . . . . . . . . .1E **64**
MOWSLEY . . . . . . . . . . . . . . . .2B **148** (3D **163**)
Mowsley Ct. LE17: H Bos . . . . . . . . . . . . . .5C **148**
Mowsley End LE18: Wig . . . . . . . . . . . . . . .6K **77**
Mowsley La. LE17: Walt . . . . . . . . . . . . . . .6C **146**
Mowsley Rd. LE8: Sad . . . . . . . .7D **88** & 1C **148**
    LE17: H Bos . . . . . . . . . . . . . . . . . . . . . . . .6C **148**
Muckle Ga. La. LE12: Sea . . . . .1K **33** & 2J **33**
MUGGINGTON . . . . . . . . . . . . . . . . . . . . .1A **158**
Muirfield Cl. LE3: Leic . . . . . . . . . . . . . . . . .1G **69**
Mulberry Av. LE3: Leic . . . . . . . . . . . . . . . .1G **69**
Mulberry Cl. LE17: Lut . . . . . . . . . . . . . . . .3H **153**
Mulberry Ct. LE16: Dray . . . . . . . . . . . . . . .7G **141**
Mulberry Sq. LE12: Shep . . . . . . . . . . . . . .6D **16**
Mulberry Way DE72: A Tre . . . . . . . . . . . . .2C **6**
Mull Way LE8: Count . . . . . . . . . . . . . . . . .6F **83**
Muncaster Cl. LE9: B Ast . . . . . . . . . . . . . .6E **86**
Mundella St. LE2: Leic . . . . . . . . . . . . . . . .4J **71**
Mundesley Rd. LE5: Ham . . . . . . . . . . . . . .4D **66**
Mundy Cl. LE12: Bur W . . . . . . . . . . . . . . . .3F **21**
Municipal Sq. W. LE1: Leic . . . . . . . . . . . . .4D **4**
Munnings Cl. LE4: Leic . . . . . . . . . . . . . . . .6H **65**
Munnings Dr. LE10: Hinc . . . . . . . . . . . . . .7D **98**
Muntjack Rd. LE8: Whet . . . . . . . . . . . . . . .3K **81**
Murby Way LE3: Brau . . . . . . . . . . . . . . . . .5G **69**
Murdoch Ri. LE11: Lou . . . . . . . . . . . . . . . .4B **18**
Muriel Rd. LE3: Leic . . . . . . . . . . . . . . . . . .2C **70**
Murphy Dr. LE67: Bag . . . . . . . . . . . . . . . . .7F **53**
Murray Cl. LE9: B Ast . . . . . . . . . . . . . . . . .6D **86**
Murrayfield Rd. LE3: Leic . . . . . . . . . . . . . .2G **69**
Murray St. LE2: Leic . . . . . . . . . . . .3G **4** (1H **71**)
Muscovey Rd. LE67: Coal . . . . . . . . . . . . . .4G **39**
Museum Sq. LE1: Leic . . . . . . . . . .6E **5** (3G **71**)
Musgrove Cl. LE3: Leic . . . . . . . . . . . . . . . .2D **70**
Mushroom La. DE11: A Vil . . . . . .2A **22** & 4A **22**
Musk Cl. LE4: Leic . . . . . . . . . . . . . . . . . . . .5K **141**
Musson Dr. LE65: Ash Z . . . . . . . . . . . . . . .6J **23**
Musson Rd. LE3: Leic . . . . . . . . . . . . . . . . .7J **63**
MUSTON . . . . . . . . . . . . . . . . . . . . . . . . . . .1B **160**
Muston Gdns. LE2: Leic . . . . . . . . . . . . . . .1H **77**
Muston La. NG13: East . . . . . . . . . . . . . . . .3J **107**
Myrtle Av. LE4: Birs . . . . . . . . . . . . . . . . . . .4H **59**
Myrtle Cl. LE9: Barw . . . . . . . . . . . . . . . . . .3K **99**
Myrtle Rd. LE2: Leic . . . . . . . . . . . . . . . . . .3J **71**
Mythe La. CV9: With . . . . . . . . . . . . . . . . . .4A **96**

### N

Nagle Gro. LE4: Leic . . . . . . . . . . . . . . . . . .1K **65**
NAILSTONE . . . . . . . . . . . . . . . .2C **92** (1B **162**)
Nailstone Rd. CV13: B Bea . . . . . . . . . . . . .4A **92**
Namur Rd. LE18: Wig . . . . . . . . . . . . . . . . .5E **76**
Nanhill Dr. LE12: W Eav . . . . . . . . . . . . . . .4E **42**
NANPANTAN . . . . . . . . . . . . . . .4K **29** (3C **159**)
Nanpantan Rd. LE11: Lou, Nan . . . . . . . . .6H **29**
    LE12: Nan . . . . . . . . . . . . . . . . . . . . . . . . . .6H **29**
Nansen Rd. LE5: Leic . . . . . . . . . . . . . . . . .3A **72**
NARBOROUGH . . . . . . . . . . . . . .1F **81** (2C **163**)
Narborough Bogs Nature Reserve . . . . . . .7H **75**
Narborough Hall . . . . . . . . . . . . . . . . . . . . .2F **81**
Narborough Rd. LE3: Brau . . . . . . . . . . . . .2K **75**
    LE3: Leic . . . . . . . . . . . . . . . . . . . . . . . . . . .6B **70**
    LE9: Cosb . . . . . . . . . . . . . . . . . . . . . . . . . .4G **81**
    LE9: Hun . . . . . . . . . . . . . . . . . . . . . . . . . . .2B **80**
Narborough Rd. Nth. LE3: Leic . . . . . . . . .2D **70**
Narborough Rd. Sth. LE19: End . . . . . . . . .4J **75**
        (not continuous)

Narborough Station (Rail) . . . . . . . . . . . . . .2G 81
Narborough Wood Bus. Pk. LE19: End . . . . . . .1C 74
Narrow Boat Cl. LE18: Wig . . . . . . . . . . . . . .1G 83
Narrow La. DE12: Don . . . . . . . . . . . . . . . . . .4A 34
  LE2: Leic . . . . . . . . . . . . . . . . . . . . . . . . .2C 76
  LE12: Hat . . . . . . . . . . . . . . . . . . . . . . . . . .1J 17
  LE14: Sta . . . . . . . . . . . . . . . . . . . . . . . .2H 109
Narrows, The LE10: Hinc . . . . . . . . . . . . . . .3H 103
NASEBY . . . . . . . . . . . . . . . . . . . . . . . . . .3D 163
Naseby Cl. LE16: Mkt H . . . . . . . . . . . . . . . .5E 150
  LE18: Wig . . . . . . . . . . . . . . . . . . . . . . . . .6A 78
Naseby Dr. LE11: Lou . . . . . . . . . . . . . . . . . .1J 29
  LE65: Ash Z . . . . . . . . . . . . . . . . . . . . . . . .4B 24
Naseby Rd. LE4: Leic . . . . . . . . . . . . . . . . . .4A 66
Naseby Sq. LE16: Mkt H . . . . . . . . . . . . . . .5E 150
Naseby Way LE8: G Gle . . . . . . . . . . . . . . . .1K 85
NASSINGTON . . . . . . . . . . . . . . . . . . . . . .2D 165
National Diving Cen. . . . . . . . . . . . . . . . . . .2K 105
National Space Science Vis. Cen. . . . . . . . . .4F 65
Navigation Dr. LE2: G Par . . . . . . . . . . . . . . .6A 76
Navigation St. DE12: Mea . . . . . . . . . . . . . . .7E 34
  LE1: Leic . . . . . . . . . . . . . . . . . . . . . . . . . .7F 65
Navigation Way LE11: Lou . . . . . . . . . . . . . . .5E 18
Navins, The LE12: Moun . . . . . . . . . . . . . . . .2E 44
Naylor Av. LE11: Lou . . . . . . . . . . . . . . . . . . .1H 31
Naylor Rd. LE7: Sys . . . . . . . . . . . . . . . . . . .7E 46
Neal Av. LE3: Brau . . . . . . . . . . . . . . . . . . . .5J 69
Neale Ho. LE8: G Gle . . . . . . . . . . . . . . . . . .7K 79
Neales Ct. LE10: Hinc . . . . . . . . . . . . . . . . .2G 103
NEAL'S GREEN . . . . . . . . . . . . . . . . . . . . .3A 162
Necton St. LE7: Sys . . . . . . . . . . . . . . . . . . .2C 60
Nedham St. LE2: Leic . . . . . . . . . . .2G 4 (1H 71)
Needham Av. LE2: G Par . . . . . . . . . . . . . . . .5A 76
Needham Cl. LE2: Oad . . . . . . . . . . . . . . . . .4G 79
  LE13: Mel M . . . . . . . . . . . . . . . . . . . . . .3F 117
Needhams Wlk. LE67: Coal . . . . . . . . . . . . . .3D 38
Needlegate LE1: Leic . . . . . . . . . . . .1B 4 (7E 64)
Needleworks, The LE11: Lou . . . . . . . . . . . . .6F 19
Needwood Way LE19: Nar . . . . . . . . . . . . . . .6D 74
Nelot Way LE5: Leic . . . . . . . . . . . . . . . . . . .2D 72
Nelson Cl. LE12: Shep . . . . . . . . . . . . . . . . . .6F 17
Nelson Dr. LE10: Hinc . . . . . . . . . . . . . . . . .6G 99
Nelson Flds. LE67: Coal . . . . . . . . . . . . . . . .2G 39
Nelson Pl. LE65: Smis . . . . . . . . . . . . . . . . .1H 23
Nelson St. LE1: Leic . . . . . . . . . . . .6F 5 (3G 71)
  LE7: Sys . . . . . . . . . . . . . . . . . . . . . . . . . .2D 60
  LE16: Mkt H . . . . . . . . . . . . . . . . . . . . . .4D 150
Nene Cl. LE13: Mel M . . . . . . . . . . . . . . . . .6E 116
Nene Ct. LE2: Oad . . . . . . . . . . . . . . . . . . . .3E 78
Nene Cres. LE15: O'ham . . . . . . . . . . . . . . .5H 127
Nene Dr. LE2: Oad . . . . . . . . . . . . . . . . . . . .3E 78
Nene Way LE67: Coal . . . . . . . . . . . . . . . . . .5G 39
Neptune Cl. LE2: Leic . . . . . . . . . . . . . . . . . .2J 71
Neston Gdns. LE2: Leic . . . . . . . . . . . . . . . .2F 77
Neston Rd. LE2: Leic . . . . . . . . . . . . . . . . . .2F 77
NETHER BROUGHTON . . . . . . . . .2D 110 (2D 159)
Nether Cl. LE15: Cott . . . . . . . . . . . . . . . . .6B 124
Nethercote LE67: N Bur . . . . . . . . . . . . . . . .6B 50
Nethercroft Dr. LE65: Pac . . . . . . . . . . . . . . .2A 36
Nether End LE7: Gad . . . . . . . . . . . . . . . . .2A 118
  LE14: G Dal . . . . . . . . . . . . . . . . . . . . . .5D 120
Nether Farm Cl. LE17: Gilm . . . . . . . . . . . . .7J 145
NETHERFIELD . . . . . . . . . . . . . . . . . . . . . .1D 159
Netherfield Cl. LE9: B Ast . . . . . . . . . . . . . . .4F 87
Netherfield La. DE74: Hem . . . . . . . . . . . . . . .1C 8
Netherfield Rd. LE7: Anst . . . . . . . . . . . . . . .6H 57
Nether Fld. Way LE3: Brau . . . . . . . . . . . . . .6H 69
Nether Grn. LE16: G Bow . . . . . . . . . . . . . .1H 151
NETHER HALL . . . . . . . . . . . . . . . . . . . . . . .5F 67
Nether Hall La. LE4: Birs . . . . . . . . . . . . . . .7H 59
Netherhall Rd. LE5: Leic . . . . . . . . . . . . . . . .6E 66
Netherley Ct. LE10: Hinc . . . . . . . . . . . . . . .7G 99
Netherley Rd. LE10: Hinc . . . . . . . . . . . . . . .7G 99
NETHERSEAL . . . . . . . . . . . . . . . . . . . . . . .3A 158
Nether St. LE14: Harb . . . . . . . . . . . . . . . . .2C 108
  LE15: Bel R . . . . . . . . . . . . . . . . . . . . . . .5G 133
Nevada Pk. Cvn. Pk. LE13: Mel M . . . . . . . .4D 116
Nevanthon Rd. LE3: Leic . . . . . . . . . . . . . . . .2B 70
Neville Cl. LE12: Shep . . . . . . . . . . . . . . . . . .6D 16
Neville Dr. LE67: Coal . . . . . . . . . . . . . . . . .3G 39
  LE67: Mark . . . . . . . . . . . . . . . . . . . . . . . .5F 55
Neville Rd. LE3: Leic . . . . . . . . . . . . . . . . . .2B 70
Neville Smith Cl. LE9: Sap . . . . . . . . . . . . . .4J 105
Nevill Holt Rd. LE16: Dray . . . . . . . . . . . . . .6F 141
Newall Cl. LE17: Lut . . . . . . . . . . . . . . . . . .4J 153
Newark Cl. LE12: Shep . . . . . . . . . . . . . . . . .7B 16
Newarke, The LE2: Leic . . . . . . . . . .5A 4 (2E 70)
Newarke Cl. LE2: Leic . . . . . . . . . . .6A 5 (3E 70)
Newarke Grn. LE2: Leic . . . . . . . . . .5B 4 (2E 70)
Newarke Houses Mus. . . . . . . . . . . .5B 4 (2E 70)
Newarke Point LE2: Leic . . . . . . . . . .6A 5 (3E 70)
Newarke St. LE1: Leic . . . . . . . . . . .5C 4 (2F 71)
Newark Rd. LE4: Thurm . . . . . . . . . . . . . . . .5A 60
NEW ARLEY . . . . . . . . . . . . . . . . . . . . . . . .3A 162
New Ashby Ct. *LE11: Lou* . . . . . . . . . . . . . .1K 29
  *(off Sharpley Rd.)*

New Ashby Rd. LE11: Lou . . . . . . . . . . . . . . .2G 29
New Av. LE7: Rear . . . . . . . . . . . . . . . . . . . .3J 47
NEWBOLD . . . . . . . . . . . . . . . . . .1G 25 (3B 158)
Newbold Cl. LE12: Sileby . . . . . . . . . . . . . . .7K 33
Newbold Ct. CV13: B'one . . . . . . . . . . . . . . .5C 92
Newbold Dr. DE74: C Don . . . . . . . . . . . . . . .3K 7
Newbold La. LE14: Bur H . . . . . . . . . . . . . .6F 121
  LE65: Wort . . . . . . . . . . . . . . . . . . . . . . . .3A 14
NEWBOLD ON AVON . . . . . . . . . . . . . . . . .3B 162
Newbold Rd. CV13: B'one . . . . . . . . . . . . . . .5C 92
  LE9: Des . . . . . . . . . . . . . . . . . . . . . . . . . .1G 95
  LE9: K Mal . . . . . . . . . . . . . . . . . . . . . . . . .6F 95
NEWBOLD VERDON . . . . . . . . . . .6H 93 (1B 162)
Newbon Cl. LE11: Lou . . . . . . . . . . . . . . . . . .6C 18
New Bond St. LE1: Leic . . . . . . . . . .3C 4 (1F 71)
New Brickyard La. DE74: Keg . . . . . . . . . . . . .7H 9
New Bri. Rd. LE2: G Par . . . . . . . . . . . . . . . .6A 76
New Bri. St. LE2: Leic . . . . . . . . . . .9B 5 (4E 70)
New Bldgs. LE10: Hinc . . . . . . . . . . . . . . . .2G 103
Newbury Av. LE13: Mel M . . . . . . . . . . . . . .2D 116
Newbury Cl. LE18: Wig . . . . . . . . . . . . . . . . .7J 77
Newby Cl. LE8: Whet . . . . . . . . . . . . . . . . . .7K 75
Newby Gdns. LE2: Oad . . . . . . . . . . . . . . . . .4F 79
New Causeway NG13: Bark V . . . . . . . . . . .3A 106
New Cl. LE5: Leic . . . . . . . . . . . . . . . . . . . .3K 71
  LE67: Swan . . . . . . . . . . . . . . . . . . . . . . . .7A 26
Newcombe Rd. LE3: Leic . . . . . . . . . . . . . . . .5B 70
Newcombe St. LE16: Mkt H . . . . . . . . . . . . .5E 150
New Fld. Rd. LE15: Ext . . . . . . . . . . . . . . . .2D 128
Newfields DE12: Moi . . . . . . . . . . . . . . . . . . .7B 22
New Flds. Av. LE3: Leic . . . . . . . . . . . . . . . . .5A 70
New Flds. Sq. LE3: Leic . . . . . . . . . . . . . . . .6B 70
New Forest Cl. LE18: Wig . . . . . . . . . . . . . . .1K 83
NEWFOUNDPOOL . . . . . . . . . . . . . . . . . . . .7C 64
Newgate End LE18: Wig . . . . . . . . . . . . . . . .6J 77
NEWHALL . . . . . . . . . . . . . . . . . . . . . . . . .2A 158
Newham Cl. LE4: Leic . . . . . . . . . . . . . . . . . .1C 66
Newhaven Rd. LE5: Leic . . . . . . . . . . . . . . . .4E 72
New Henry St. LE3: Leic . . . . . . . . . .1A 4 (7E 64)
NEW HUMBERSTONE . . . . . . . . . . . . . . . . . .7B 66
Newington St. LE4: Leic . . . . . . . . . . . . . . . .4H 65
Newington Wlk. LE4: Leic . . . . . . . . . . . . . . .4H 65
New Inn Cl. LE9: B Ast . . . . . . . . . . . . . . . . .5E 86
New King St. LE11: Lou . . . . . . . . . . . . . . . . .7G 19
Newlands Av. LE12: Shep . . . . . . . . . . . . . . .1E 28
Newlands Rd. LE9: Barw . . . . . . . . . . . . . . .3A 100
New La. LE12: Walt W . . . . . . . . . . . . . . . . . .6F 21
Newlyn Pde. LE5: Leic . . . . . . . . . . . . . . . . . .5F 67
Newmans Cl. LE15: N Luf . . . . . . . . . . . . . .1B 136
Newmarket St. LE2: Leic . . . . . . . . . . . . . . . .7H 71
Newmarket Wlk. LE2: Leic . . . . . . . . . . . . . . .7H 71
New Pk. Rd. LE2: Leic . . . . . . . . . . . . . . . . . .7E 70
NEW PARKS . . . . . . . . . . . . . . . . . . . . . . . .6J 63
New Parks Blvd. LE3: Leic . . . . . . . . . . . . . . .2H 69
  *(not continuous)*
New Parks Cres. LE3: Leic . . . . . . . . . . . . . .6A 64
New Parks Leisure Cen. . . . . . . . . . . . . . . . .6K 63
New Pk. St. LE3: Leic . . . . . . . . . . . .5A 4 (2D 70)
New Parks Way LE3: Leic . . . . . . . . . . . . . . .2H 69
New Parliament St. LE1: Leic . . . . . . .2D 4 (1F 71)
New Pingle St. LE3: Leic . . . . . . . . . .1A 4 (7E 64)
Newpool Bank LE2: Oad . . . . . . . . . . . . . . . .4G 79
Newport Av. LE13: Mel M . . . . . . . . . . . . . .3F 117
Newport Pl. LE1: Leic . . . . . . . . . . . .5E 4 (2G 71)
Newport St. LE3: Leic . . . . . . . . . . . . . . . . . .1C 70
Newquay Cl. LE10: Hinc . . . . . . . . . . . . . . . .6H 99
Newquay Dr. LE3: Glen . . . . . . . . . . . . . . . . .5G 63
New Rd. DE12: A Par . . . . . . . . . . . . . . . . . .6A 48
  LE1: Leic . . . . . . . . . . . . . . . . . . .2C 4 (1F 71)
  LE8: K Bea, Kib H . . . . . . . . . . . . . . . . . . .3J 89
  LE9: S Stan . . . . . . . . . . . . . . . . . . . . . . .1J 105
  LE10: Bur . . . . . . . . . . . . . . . . . . . . . . . . .5K 103
  LE14: Bur L . . . . . . . . . . . . . . . . . . . . . . . .2C 120
  LE15: Bel R . . . . . . . . . . . . . . . . . . . . . . .6F 133
  LE15: Gree . . . . . . . . . . . . . . . . . . . . . . . .1G 125
  LE67: Cole . . . . . . . . . . . . . . . . . . . . . . . . .3A 26
  PE9: Ryh . . . . . . . . . . . . . . . . . . . . . . . . . .5G 129
New Romney Cl. LE5: Leic . . . . . . . . . . . . . . .6G 67
New Romney Cres. LE5: Leic . . . . . . . . . . . . .6G 67
New Row DE12: Moi . . . . . . . . . . . . . . . . . . .7C 22
  LE67: Ibs . . . . . . . . . . . . . . . . . . . . . . . . . .5K 51
  PE9: Ryh . . . . . . . . . . . . . . . . . . . . . . . . . .4H 129
  *(not continuous)*
Newry, The LE2: Leic . . . . . . . . . . . . . . . . . .3F 77
New Star Rd. LE4: Leic . . . . . . . . . . . . . . . . .2B 66
Newstead Av. LE3: Leic . . . . . . . . . . . . . . . . .5C 64
  LE7: Bush . . . . . . . . . . . . . . . . . . . . . . . . .3J 73
  LE10: Bur . . . . . . . . . . . . . . . . . . . . . . . . .7G 103
  LE18: Wig . . . . . . . . . . . . . . . . . . . . . . . . .4J 77
Newstead Rd. LE2: Leic . . . . . . . . . . . . . . . .7J 71
Newstead Way LE11: Lou . . . . . . . . . . . . . . .5E 30
New St. CV13: B'one . . . . . . . . . . . . . . . . . . .5C 92
  DE11: C Gre . . . . . . . . . . . . . . . . . . . . . . .1A 22
  DE12: Don . . . . . . . . . . . . . . . . . . . . . . . . .3A 34
  DE12: Mea, Oak . . . . . . . . . . . . . . . . . . . .6D 34

New St. DE12: Oak . . . . . . . . . . . . . . . . . . . .5C 34
  DE74: Keg . . . . . . . . . . . . . . . . . . . . . . . . . .5J 9
  LE1: Leic . . . . . . . . . . . . . . . . . . .4C 4 (2F 71)
  LE2: Oad . . . . . . . . . . . . . . . . . . . . . . . . . .2C 78
  LE7: Quen . . . . . . . . . . . . . . . . . . . . . . . . .7G 47
  LE8: Bla . . . . . . . . . . . . . . . . . . . . . . . . . . .1B 82
  LE8: Count . . . . . . . . . . . . . . . . . . . . . . . . .5F 83
  LE9: Earl S . . . . . . . . . . . . . . . . . . . . . . . .2D 100
  LE9: S Stan . . . . . . . . . . . . . . . . . . . . . . .7J 101
  LE10: Hinc . . . . . . . . . . . . . . . . . . . . . . . .2G 103
  LE11: Lou . . . . . . . . . . . . . . . . . . . . . . . . .7E 18
  LE12: Bar S . . . . . . . . . . . . . . . . . . . . . . . .4D 32
  LE13: Mel M . . . . . . . . . . . . . . . . . . . . . .4F 117
  LE14: Ash . . . . . . . . . . . . . . . . . . . . . . . . .2G 115
  LE14: Scal . . . . . . . . . . . . . . . . . . . . . . . .6C 112
  LE15: O'ham . . . . . . . . . . . . . . . . . . . . . . .4H 127
  LE17: Lut . . . . . . . . . . . . . . . . . . . . . . . . .4J 153
  LE67: Coal . . . . . . . . . . . . . . . . . . . . . . . . .4D 38
NEW SWANNINGTON . . . . . . . . . . .6D 26 (3B 158)
NEWTON
  Kettering . . . . . . . . . . . . . . . . . . . . . . . . .3B 164
  Nottingham . . . . . . . . . . . . . . . . . . . . . . .1D 159
  Rugby . . . . . . . . . . . . . . . . . . . .6A 156 (3C 163)
  Sleaford . . . . . . . . . . . . . . . . . . . . . . . . .1D 161
NEWTON BURGOLAND . . . . . . . . . .7C 50 (1A 162)
Newton Cl. LE11: Lou . . . . . . . . . . . . . . . . . .4B 18
  LE12: Bar S . . . . . . . . . . . . . . . . . . . . . . . .3E 32
Newton Dr. LE4: Birs . . . . . . . . . . . . . . . . . . .5H 59
NEWTON HARCOURT . . . . . . . . . . .3F 85 (2D 163)
Newton La. LE8: G Gle . . . . . . . . . . . . . . . . .2J 85
  LE8: New H . . . . . . . . . . . . . . . . . . . . . . . .2D 84
  LE18: Wig . . . . . . . . . . . . . . . . . . . . . . . . .6K 77
NEWTON REGIS . . . . . . . . . . . . . . . . . . . . .1A 162
Newton Rd. CV13: Ods . . . . . . . . . . . . . . . . .7E 50
  LE10: Hinc . . . . . . . . . . . . . . . . . . . . . . . .4B 102
  LE67: Hea . . . . . . . . . . . . . . . . . . . . . . . . .5F 51
  LE67: N Bur, Swep . . . . . . . . . . . . . . . . . .4B 50
NEWTON SOLNEY . . . . . . . . . . . . . . . . . . .2A 158
NEWTON UNTHANK . . . . . . . . . . . . . . . . . .1B 162
Newton Way LE9: B Ast . . . . . . . . . . . . . . . . .6D 86
New Town Cl. LE8: K Bea . . . . . . . . . . . . . . .3H 89
Newtown Cres. LE15: Upp . . . . . . . . . . . . . .3B 138
NEWTOWN LINFORD . . . . . . . . . . . .5C 56 (3C 159)
Newtown Linford La. LE6: Groby . . . . . . . . . . .7C 56
Newtown Rd. LE15: Upp . . . . . . . . . . . . . . .2A 138
Newtown St. LE1: Leic . . . . . . . . . . . .7D 5 (3F 71)
NEWTOWN UNTHANK . . . . . . . . . . . . . . . . .1K 95
New Wlk. LE1: Leic . . . . . . . . . . . . . .5D 4 (2F 71)
  LE9: Sap . . . . . . . . . . . . . . . . . . . . . . . . . .4J 105
  LE12: Shep . . . . . . . . . . . . . . . . . . . . . . . .6D 16
New Walk Mus. & Art Gallery . . . . . . .6E 5 (3G 71)
New Walks LE11: Lou . . . . . . . . . . . . . . . . . .1G 31
New Way Rd. LE5: Leic . . . . . . . . . . . . . . . . .5K 71
New Wharf LE2: Leic . . . . . . . . . . . . .5A 4 (2E 70)
New Wycliffe Home LE4: Leic . . . . . . . . . . . .3K 65
New Zealand La. LE7: Quen . . . . . . . . . . . . . .6E 46
Nicholas Dr. LE6: Ratby . . . . . . . . . . . . . . . .6B 62
Nichols St. LE1: Leic . . . . . . . . . . . .3F 4 (1G 71)
Nicklaus Rd. LE4: Leic . . . . . . . . . . . . . . . . .2K 65
Nicolson Rd. LE11: Lou . . . . . . . . . . . . . . . . .3A 30
Nidderdale Rd. LE18: Wig . . . . . . . . . . . . . . .6B 78
Nightingale Av. LE12: Hat . . . . . . . . . . . . . . .1K 17
Nightingale Way LE15: O'ham . . . . . . . . . . .3K 127
Nightsbridge Rd. LE2: G Par . . . . . . . . . . . . .7D 76
Nine Acres LE67: Keg . . . . . . . . . . . . . . . . . .6G 9
Nithsdale Av. LE16: Mkt H . . . . . . . . . . . . . .5E 150
Nithsdale Cres. LE16: Mkt H . . . . . . . . . . . .5F 151
Nixon Cl. LE2: Leic . . . . . . . . . . . . . . . . . . . .6G 71
Noble Cl. LE17: Lut . . . . . . . . . . . . . . . . . . .2J 153
Noble St. LE3: Leic . . . . . . . . . . . . . . . . . . . .1D 70
Nock Verges LE9: Earl S . . . . . . . . . . . . . . . .1F 101
  LE9: S Stan . . . . . . . . . . . . . . . . . . . . . . .1J 105
Noel Av. LE15: O'ham . . . . . . . . . . . . . . . . .5G 127
Noel St. LE3: Leic . . . . . . . . . . . . . . . . . . . . .4D 70
NO MAN'S HEATH . . . . . . . . . . . . . . . . . . .1A 162
Nook, The LE7: Anst . . . . . . . . . . . . . . . . . . .7J 57
  LE8: G Gle . . . . . . . . . . . . . . . . . . . . . . . . .1J 85
  LE8: Whet . . . . . . . . . . . . . . . . . . . . . . . . .2K 81
  LE9: Cosb . . . . . . . . . . . . . . . . . . . . . . . . .7H 81
  LE12: Wym . . . . . . . . . . . . . . . . . . . . . . . . .2K 21
  LE14: Spro . . . . . . . . . . . . . . . . . . . . . . . .2H 113
  LE15: Whis . . . . . . . . . . . . . . . . . . . . . . . .2C 122
  LE17: Bitt . . . . . . . . . . . . . . . . . . . . . . . . . .2H 153
  LE17: Wal . . . . . . . . . . . . . . . . . . . . . . . . .2D 154
  LE19: End . . . . . . . . . . . . . . . . . . . . . . . . . .5F 75
  LE67: Mark . . . . . . . . . . . . . . . . . . . . . . . .4F 55
  NG32: Crox . . . . . . . . . . . . . . . . . . . . . . . .6G 107
Nook Cl. LE6: Ratby . . . . . . . . . . . . . . . . . . .5A 62
  LE12: Shep . . . . . . . . . . . . . . . . . . . . . . . .1E 28
Nook La. LE15: Emp . . . . . . . . . . . . . . . . . . .7B 128
Nooks Country Pk., The . . . . . . . . . . . . . . . .5F 85
Nook St. LE3: Leic . . . . . . . . . . . . . . . . . . . .7B 64
Norbury Av. LE4: Leic . . . . . . . . . . . . . . . . . .5J 65
Norbury Cl. LE16: Mkt H . . . . . . . . . . . . . . .3D 150
Norfolk Cl. LE10: Bur . . . . . . . . . . . . . . . . . .7G 103
Norfolk Dr. LE13: Mel M . . . . . . . . . . . . . . .7G 117
Norfolk Lodge LE4: Leic . . . . . . . . . . . . . . . .6H 65

Norfolk Rd.—Odeon Cinema

**Norfolk Rd.** LE9: Des .3H **95**
LE18: Wig .5F **77**
**Norfolk St.** LE3: Leic .2D **70**
**Norfolk Wlk.** LE3: Leic .2D **70**
**Norman Ct.** DE74: Keg .7H **9**
LE2: Oad .4F **79**
**Norman Dagley Cl.** LE9: Earl S .3D **100**
**Normandy Cl.** LE3: Glen .7G **63**
**Normandy Way** LE9: Barw .6H **99**
LE10: Hinc .2C **102**
**Norman Rd.** LE4: Thurm .5K **59**
**Norman St.** LE3: Leic .3D **70**
**NORMANTON**
**Derby** .**1A 158**
**Grantham** .**1B 160**
Normanton Church Mus. .1H 135
**Normanton Dr.** LE11: Lou .4F **19**
LE15: O'ham .3K **127**
**Normanton Gro.** LE9: Thurl .3C **96**
**Normanton La.** LE12: Stan S .1F **19**
LE67: Hea .1F **51**
NG13: Bott .1H **107**
**NORMANTON LE HEATH** .**6D 36 (3A 158)**
**NORMANTON ON SOAR** .**2C 159**
**NORMANTON-ON-THE-WOLDS** .**1D 159**
**Normanton Pk. Rd.** LE15: Emp .7C **128**
LE15: Norm .2H **135**
**Normanton Rd.** LE5: Leic .3J **71**
LE15: E Wes .3G **135**
LE65: Pac .3A **36**
**NORMANTON TURVILLE** .**3A 96**
**Norman Way** LE13: Mel M .4F **117**
**Norris Cl.** LE4: Leic .3A **64**
**NORRIS HILL** .**5D 22 (3A 158)**
**Norris Hill** DE12: Moi .5D **22**
**Northage Cl.** LE12: Quo .6B **32**
**Northampton Rd.** LE16: Mkt H .4E **150**
**Northampton Sq.** LE1: Leic .4E **4** (2G **71**)
**Northampton St.** LE1: Leic .5E **4** (2G **71**)
**North Av.** LE2: Leic .5J **71**
LE67: Coal .5D **38**
**Northbank** LE16: Mkt H .4E **150**
**NORTHBECK** .**1D 161**
**NORTHBOROUGH** .**1D 165**
**North Bri. Pl.** LE3: Leic .1A **4** (7D **64**)
**North Brook Cl.** LE15: Gree .4E **124**
**North Cl.** DE11: Blac .3D **22**
LE10: Bur .5H **103**
**Northcote Rd.** LE2: Leic .7H **71**
**North Cres.** NG13: Bott .2G **107**
**North Deepdale** LE5: Leic .1B **72**
**Northdene Rd.** LE2: Leic .3G **77**
**Northdown Dr.** LE4: Thurm .7A **60**
**North Dr.** LE5: Leic .6C **66**
**NORTH END** .**7C 32 (3C 159)**
**North End** LE16: Hall .6A **132**
**North End Cl.** LE2: Leic .2F **77**
**NORTH EVINGTON** .**1A 72 (1D 163)**
**Northfield** LE67: Bag .6G **53**
**Northfield Av.** LE4: Birs .5H **59**
LE18: Wig .4H **77**
**Northfield Cl.** LE13: Mel M .3F **117**
**Northfield Dr.** LE67: Coal .4G **39**
**Northfield Rd.** LE4: Leic .5A **66**
LE8: Bla .7B **76**
LE10: Hinc .4E **102**
**NORTHFIELDS** .**4K 65**
**Northfields** LE7: Sys .1D **60**
LE65: Ash Z .3K **23**
**Northfold Rd.** LE2: Leic .2J **77**
**Northgate** LE15: O'ham .4H **127**
**Northgates** LE1: Leic .2A **4** (1E **70**)
**Northgate St.** LE3: Leic .1A **4** (7E **64**)
**Nth. Hall Dr.** LE7: Gad .1A **118**
**Northhill Cl.** LE12: Sileby .7K **33**
(not continuous)
**NORTH KILWORTH** .**2K 155 (3D 163)**
**North La.** LE16: Fox .1G **149**
**Northleigh Gro.** LE16: Mkt H .3D **150**
**Northleigh Way** LE9: Earl S .3E **100**
**NORTH LUFFENHAM** .**1A 136 (1C 165)**
**Nth. Luffenham Rd.**
LE15: Mor, N Luf .5J **135** & 3A **136**
LE15: S Luf .3B **136**
**North Mills** LE3: Leic .1A **4** (7D **64**)
**NORTHORPE** .**3D 161**
**North Rd.** LE11: Lou .4F **19**
LE17: S Kil .6H **155**
**North St.** LE2: Oad .2C **78**
LE7: R'ley .6E **44**
LE7: Sys .1C **60**
LE12: Bar S .3D **32**
LE13: Mel M .3F **117**
LE14: Ash .2J **115**
LE17: Swin .3G **157**
LE18: Wig .5K **77**
LE65: Ash Z .5K **23**
**North St.** LE67: Whit .6E **26**
**North St. E.** LE15: Upp .2C **138**
**North St. W.** LE15: Upp .2B **138**
**Northumberland Av.** CV13: Mkt B .3C **94**
LE4: Leic .4J **65**
**Northumberland Rd.** LE18: Wig .5F **77**
**Northumberland St.** LE1: Leic .1A **4** (7E **64**)
**North Vw. Cl.** LE14: Ash .2J **115**
**North Wlk.** DE12: Mea .5F **35**
**North Way** LE7: Hou H .2C **130**
**Northwick Rd.** PE9: Ket .6G **137**
**NORTH WITHAM** .**2C 161**
**Northwood Dr.** LE12: Shep .4E **16**
**NORTON-JUXTA-TWYCROSS** .**1A 162**
**Norton Rd.** LE9: Earl S .3B **100**
**Norton St.** LE1: Leic .6C **5** (3F **71**)
LE15: Upp .2C **138**
**Norwich Cl.** LE12: Shep .1C **28**
**Norwich Rd.** LE4: Leic .3D **64**
**Norwood Cl.** LE10: Hinc .7H **99**
**Norwood Rd.** LE5: Leic .4A **72**
**NOSELEY** .**2A 164**
**Notley Mnr. Dr.** LE9: Barw .2B **100**
**NOTTINGHAM** .**1C 159**
Nottingham East Midlands Airport Aeropark .1B 12
**NOTTINGHAM EAST MIDLANDS INTERNATIONAL AIRPORT** .**1A 12 (2B 158)**
**Nottingham La.** LE14: O Dal .7A **110**
**Nottingham Rd.** DE74: Keg .5H **9**
LE5: Leic .1K **71**
LE11: Lou .6F **19**
LE12: Bur W .4D **20**
LE12: Cote .5G **19**
LE13: Mel M .1D **116**
LE14: Ab K, N Bro .4F **111**
LE14: N Bro .2D **110**
LE65: Ash Z .5A **24**
LE65: Wort .7A **10**
LE67: Cole .3A **26**
NG13: Bott .2F **107**
**Nottingham Rd. Ind. Est.** LE65: Ash Z .4B **24**
**Nottingham St.** LE13: Mel M .4F **117**
**Nowell Cl.** LE2: G Par .7D **76**
**Nuffield Rd.** LE10: Hinc .4B **102**
**Nugent St.** LE3: Leic .1D **70**
**NUNEATON** .**2A 162**
**Nuneaton La.** CV13: H Hill .7G **97**
**Nuneaton Rd.** CV9: Manc .7A **96**
**Nunneley Way** LE16: Mkt H .2F **151**
**Nursery Cl.** LE4: Thurm .7K **59**
LE7: Quen .7G **47**
LE9: Thurl .3C **96**
LE12: Shep .4E **16**
LE15: Emp .6C **128**
**Nursery End** LE11: Lou .3B **30**
**Nursery Gdns.** LE9: Earl S .3C **100**
**Nursery Gro.** LE12: Bar S .3E **32**
**Nursery Hollow** LE2: G Par .5A **76**
**Nursery La.** LE12: Quo .5A **32**
LE14: Ab K, Hol .5J **111**
**Nursery Rd.** LE5: Leic .7F **67**
**Nurses La.** LE14: W'ham .1H **121**
**Nutfield Rd.** LE3: Leic .4C **70**
**Nuthall Gro.** LE2: G Par .4B **76**
**Nutkin Cl.** LE11: Lou .1D **30**
**Nutt's La.** LE10: Hinc .5C **102**

## O

**OADBY** .**2C 78 (1D 163)**
**Oadby Hill Dr.** LE2: Oad .2B **78**
**Oadby Ind. Est.** LE2: Oad .3B **78**
Oadby Leisure Cen. .3B 78
**Oadby Rd.** LE18: Wig .5K **77**
Oadby Swimming Pool .2C 78
**Oak & Ash Bus. Pk.** LE5: Leic .7J **65**
**Oak Av.** LE17: Leire .2J **143**
**Oakberry Rd.** LE17: Lut .2K **153**
**Oakberry Rd. Ind. Est.**
LE17: Lut .2K **153**
**Oak Cl.** DE12: Mea .7E **34**
LE9: Thurl .2C **96**
LE10: Bur .6H **103**
LE11: Lou .5E **30**
LE15: Upp .1B **138**
LE16: Mkt H .3F **151**
LE67: Coal .4G **39**
**Oak Cres.** LE3: Brau .5G **69**
**Oakcroft Av.** LE9: K Mux .2C **68**
**Oakdale Cl.** LE3: Leic .1G **69**
**Oakdale Rd.** LE9: Earl S .3C **100**
**Oakdene Rd.** LE2: Leic .2G **77**
**Oak Dr.** LE7: Sys .3D **60**
LE67: Ibs .4J **51**
**Oakenshaw Cl.** LE4: Leic .1E **64**
**Oakfield** LE15: O'ham .2J **127**
**Oakfield Av.** LE3: Glen .4H **63**
LE4: Birs .6F **59**
LE17: Lut .4H **153**
LE67: Mark .5F **55**
**Oakfield Cl.** LE8: G Gle .7K **79**
**Oakfield Ct.** LE3: Glen .4H **63**
**Oakfield Cres.** LE8: Bla .3C **82**
**Oakfield Rd.** LE2: Leic .4J **71**
**Oakfield Way** CV9: S Mag .5C **90**
**Oak Grn.** LE67: Mark .7G **55**
**OAKHAM** .**4H 127 (1B 164)**
**Oakham Cl.** LE11: Lou .4C **18**
**Oakham Dr.** LE67: Coal .2J **39**
**Oakham Gro.** LE65: Ash Z .4J **23**
**Oakham Rd.** LE7: Hals, T Hil .2J **131**
LE15: B Rut .6C **126**
LE15: Barl, L'ham .6C **122**
LE15: Ext .3A **128**
LE15: Gree .5E **124**
LE15: Knos .2C **126**
LE15: Pres .6A **134**
LE15: Whis .2C **122**
**Oakham Station (Rail)** .**3H 127**
**Oakhill Trad. Est.** LE2: Leic .6F **71**
**Oakhurst Ct.** LE11: Lou .6A **18**
**Oakland Av.** LE4: Leic .1H **65**
**Oakland Rd.** LE2: Leic .6G **71**
**Oaklands Av.** LE11: Lou .1D **30**
**Oaklands Pk.** LE16: L Bow .5F **151**
**Oak La.** LE8: Arne .2H **147**
**Oakleigh Av.** LE2: G Par .7E **76**
**Oakleigh Ct.** LE65: Ash Z .5K **23**
**Oakley Av.** LE12: Shep .6D **16**
**Oakley Cl.** LE12: Shep .5D **16**
**Oakley Dr.** LE11: Lou .2D **30**
LE12: L Wha .7H **13**
**Oakley Est.** LE12: Shep .5D **16**
**Oakley Rd.** LE5: Leic .7K **65**
LE12: Shep .3D **16**
LE15: Cott .4C **124**
**Oakmeadow** LE3: Glen .7F **63**
**Oakmeadow Way** LE6: Groby .4C **62**
**Oakpool Gdns.** LE2: Leic .5D **76**
**Oakridge Cl.** LE5: Ham .3E **66**
**Oak Rd.** LE9: Des .2G **95**
LE13: Mel M .4F **117**
LE19: Litt .3G **81**
**Oaks Ct.** LE19: Nar .1E **80**
**Oaks Dr.** LE8: Bla .2C **82**
LE9: N Ver .6H **93**
**Oakside Cl.** LE5: Leic .3E **72**
**Oakside Cres.** LE5: Leic .2E **72**
**OAKS IN CHARNWOOD** .**6C 28**
**Oaks Ind. Est.** LE9: Earl S .2D **100**
LE11: Lou .4E **18**
LE17: Lut .3K **153**
LE19: Nar .2E **80**
LE67: Coal .3A **38**
**Oak Spinney Pk.** LE3: Leic E .3F **69**
**Oaks Rd.** LE8: G Gle .1K **85**
LE12: Char .5G **27**
LE67: Whit .5G **27**
**Oak St.** LE5: Leic .7J **65**
**Oaks Way** LE2: Oad .7B **72**
LE9: Earl S .2D **100**
**OAKTHORPE** .**5C 34 (3A 158)**
**Oakthorpe Av.** LE3: Leic .3B **70**
Oakthorpe Sports and Leisure Cen. .5D 34
**Oak Tree Cl.** LE5: Ham .4E **66**
**Oaktree Cl.** LE6: Groby .3C **62**
LE8: K Bea .2K **89**
**Oak Tree Rd.** LE67: Hug .5B **38**
**Oak Way** LE14: F Wre .5H **115**
**OAKWOOD** .**1A 158**
**Oakwood Av.** LE18: Wig .4K **77**
**Oakwood Cl.** LE3: Leic E .5D **68**
LE67: Thor .3K **93**
**Oakwood Dr.** LE11: Lou .2K **29**
**Oakwood Rd.** LE4: Leic .5D **64**
**OASBY** .**1D 161**
**Oasis, The** LE3: Glen .6F **63**
**Oban Rd.** LE10: Hinc .4D **102**
**Oban St.** LE3: Leic .1C **70**
**OBTHORPE** .**3D 161**
**Occupation La.** DE11: W'lle .2B **22**
**Occupation Rd.** CV13: Nail .2C **92**
DE11: A Vil .3A **22**
LE9: S Stan .5J **101**
**Ocean Cl.** LE5: Leic .7E **66**
**Ocean Rd.** LE5: Leic .1E **72**
**Ocean Wlk.** LE5: Leic .1E **72**
**OCKBROOK** .**1B 158**
**Odam Cl.** LE3: Leic .5K **69**
**Oddfellows Row** DE12: Mea .7E **34**
**Odeon Arc.** LE1: Leic .4C **4**
Odeon Cinema
Leicester Freemen's Pk. .10C 5 (5F 71)

ODSTONE . LE10: Hinc . . . . . . . . . . . . . . .1A 162
Odstone Dr. LE10: Hinc . . . . . . . . . . . . . . .3C 102
Odstone La. CV13: Nail . . . . . . . . . . . . . . .7J 51
  LE67: N Bur . . . . . . . . . . . . . . . . . .7C 50
Offranville Cl. LE4: Thurm . . . . . . . . . . . .7B 60
Ogwen Cl. LE5: Leic . . . . . . . . . . . . . . . . .1F 73
Okehampton Av. LE5: Leic . . . . . . . . . . . .4B 72
Okehampton Wlk. LE5: Leic . . . . . . . . . . .4B 72
OLD ARLEY . . . . . . . . . . . . . . . . . . . . . .2A 162
Old Ashby Rd. LE11: Lou . . . . . . . . . . . . .1J 29
Old Barn Wlk. LE4: Leic . . . . . . . . . . . . . .3C 64
Old Bridewell LE13: Mel M . . . . . . . . . . . .1G 117
Old Bull Farm Cl. LE12: Sut Bon . . . . . . . .6K 9
OLDBURY . . . . . . . . . . . . . . . . . . . . . . . .2A 162
Old Chapel Wlk. *LE17: C Mag* . . . . . . . .5C 142
  (off Bell St.)
Old Charity Farm LE2: S'ton . . . . . . . . . . .6G 73
Old Church St. LE2: Leic . . . . . . . . . . . . . .2C 76
Old Coach Rd., The LE17: D Bas . . . . . . . .1D 144
OLD DALBY . . . . . . . . . . . . . .7A 110 (2D 159)
Old Dalby La.
  LE14: N Bro, O Dal . . . . . . . .6C 110 & 3C 110
Old Dalby Trad. Est. LE14: O Dal . . . . . . . .7D 110
Old End DE12: A Mag . . . . . . . . . . . . . . . .4B 48
Oldershaw Av. DE74: Keg . . . . . . . . . . . . .6G 9
Old Farm Rd. CV9: Manc . . . . . . . . . . . . .7A 96
Old Fld. Cl. LE8: Count . . . . . . . . . . . . . . .5C 82
Oldfield La. LE7: R'ley . . . . . . . . . . . . . . . .4F 45
Old Forge Cl. LE12: Hat . . . . . . . . . . . . . .1J 17
Old Forge Rd. CV13: F Dray . . . . . . . . . . .2H 97
  LE17: Ash M . . . . . . . . . . . . . . . . . . . .1G 145
Old Gdn. Cl. LE8: Bla . . . . . . . . . . . . . . . .2B 82
Old Ga. Av. DE72: W Tre . . . . . . . . . . . . . .3A 6
Old Ga. Rd. LE7: Thru . . . . . . . . . . . . . . . .4A 114
Old Granary, The LE7: T Hil . . . . . . . . . . .3H 131
Old Gt. North Rd. PE9: G Cas, Stam . . . . .2H 137
Old Grn. LE16: Med . . . . . . . . . . . . . . . . .7C 140
Old Hall Cl. LE4: Thurm . . . . . . . . . . . . . .5A 60
  LE6: Groby . . . . . . . . . . . . . . . . . . . . .4D 62
Old Hall La. LE16: Lub . . . . . . . . . . . . . . .7J 149
Old Holt Rd. LE16: Med . . . . . . . . . . . . . .6D 140
Old Ho. La. LE67: C Oak . . . . . . . . . . . . . .7D 40
Old John Tower . . . . . . . . . . . . . . . . . . . .2D 56
Old La., The NG13: Bark V . . . . . . . . . . . .3A 106
Old Melton Rd. LE7: T Hil . . . . . . . . . . . . .2H 131
Old Mill Cl. LE9: B Ast . . . . . . . . . . . . . . .5D 86
Old Mill La. LE1: Leic . . . . . . . . .1A 4 (7E 64)
Old Mill Rd. LE9: B Ast . . . . . . . . . . . . . . .5D 86
Old Milton St. LE1: Leic . . . . . . . . .1E 4 (7G 65)
Old Nurseries, The LE67: Rav . . . . . . . . . .4K 37
Old Pk. Cl. NG11: Rat S . . . . . . . . . . . . . .2K 9
Old Parks La. LE65: Smis . . . . . . . . . . . . .1J 23
Old Parsonage La. LE12: Hot . . . . . . . . . .1C 20
Old Rectory Cl. LE9: B Ast . . . . . . . . . . . .4C 86
Old Rectory Mus. . . . . . . . . . . . . . . . . . .5F 19
Old Saffron La. LE2: Leic . . . . . . . . . . . . .6E 70
Old School Cl. LE15: N Luf . . . . . . . . . . . .1B 136
  LE17: Walt . . . . . . . . . . . . . . . . . . . . .7B 146
  LE67: Ell . . . . . . . . . . . . . . . . . . . . . . .3D 52
Old School Ho., The LE15: Ext . . . . . . . . . .2C 128
Old School La. LE17: Walt . . . . . . . . . . . . .7B 146
  LE67: Bag . . . . . . . . . . . . . . . . . . . . . .2F 93
Old School M. DE72: A Tre . . . . . . . . . . . .1D 6
  LE15: Upp . . . . . . . . . . . . . . . . . . . . . .3C 138
  LE16: Mkt H . . . . . . . . . . . . . . . . . . . .4E 150
OLD SOMERBY . . . . . . . . . . . . . . . . . . . .1C 161
Old Stableyard, The LE16: East L . . . . . . .2B 140
Old Sta. Cl. LE12: Shep . . . . . . . . . . . . . .1D 28
  LE67: Coal . . . . . . . . . . . . . . . . . . . . .3D 38
Old Sta. Yd. NG13: Bott . . . . . . . . . . . . . .1J 107
Old Tannery Dr. LE12: Sileby . . . . . . . . . . .1J 45
Old Vicarage Gdns. LE14: Ab K . . . . . . . . .6J 111
Old Way LE12: Hat . . . . . . . . . . . . . . . . . .1J 17
OLD WESTON . . . . . . . . . . . . . . . . . . . . .3D 165
Old Woodyard, The LE12: Hat . . . . . . . . . .1J 17
Oliver Ct. LE2: Leic . . . . . . . . . . . . . . . . .6J 71
Oliver Rd. LE4: Leic . . . . . . . . . . . . . . . . .4K 65
  LE11: Lou . . . . . . . . . . . . . . . . . . . . . .1F 31
Oliver St. LE2: Leic . . . . . . . . . . . . . . . . .7E 70
Olphin St. LE4: Leic . . . . . . . . . . . . . . . . .6G 65
Olympic Cl. LE3: Glen . . . . . . . . . . . . . . . .6H 63
One Ash Rdbt. LE12: Quo . . . . . . . . . . . . .4J 31
One Barrow La. LE12: Char . . . . . . . . . . . .5A 28
  LE67: Whit . . . . . . . . . . . . . . . . . . . . .5A 28
Onslow St. LE2: Leic . . . . . . . . . . . . . . . . .3J 71
Ontario Cl. LE1: Leic . . . . . . . . .1E 4 (7G 65)
Opal Ct. LE1: Leic . . . . . . . . . . . .7E 5 (4G 71)
Orange Hill LE17: Lut . . . . . . . . . . . . . . . .5K 153
Orange St. LE15: Upp . . . . . . . . . . . . . . . .2C 138
  LE18: Wig . . . . . . . . . . . . . . . . . . . . . .1F 83
Orchard, The LE2: Leic . . . . . . . . . . . . . . .1K 77
  LE6: Groby . . . . . . . . . . . . . . . . . . . . .3B 62
  LE9: S Stan . . . . . . . . . . . . . . . . . . . .1K 105
  LE12: Sea . . . . . . . . . . . . . . . . . . . . . .3K 33
Orchard Av. DE74: C Don . . . . . . . . . . . . .5J 7
  LE2: G Par . . . . . . . . . . . . . . . . . . . . .5B 76
Orchard Bank LE17: P Par . . . . . . . . . . . .2A 146

Orchard Cl. CV9: With . . . . . . . . . . . . . . . .5B 96
  CV13: B'one . . . . . . . . . . . . . . . . . . . .5C 92
  DE74: Dis . . . . . . . . . . . . . . . . . . . . . .4A 12
  LE2: Oad . . . . . . . . . . . . . . . . . . . . . .4C 78
  LE10: Bur . . . . . . . . . . . . . . . . . . . . . .6K 103
  LE12: Osg . . . . . . . . . . . . . . . . . . . . . .6C 14
  LE12: Shep . . . . . . . . . . . . . . . . . . . . .7D 16
  LE15: Glas . . . . . . . . . . . . . . . . . . . . .1J 139
  LE15: Upp . . . . . . . . . . . . . . . . . . . . . .1C 138
  LE17: Gilm . . . . . . . . . . . . . . . . . . . . .7J 145
  LE67: Rav . . . . . . . . . . . . . . . . . . . . . .2K 37
  NG13: Bark V . . . . . . . . . . . . . . . . . . .3A 106
Orchard Est. LE12: Quo . . . . . . . . . . . . . .5K 31
Orchard Gdns. LE4: Thurm . . . . . . . . . . . .7B 60
Orchard La. LE8: Count . . . . . . . . . . . . . .6F 83
  LE8: G Gle . . . . . . . . . . . . . . . . . . . . .2K 85
Orchard Pk. Mobile Home Pk. LE7: Sys . . .1D 60
Orchard Rd. LE4: Birs . . . . . . . . . . . . . . . .6H 59
  LE8: Will W . . . . . . . . . . . . . . . . . . . . .2J 145
  LE9: B Ast . . . . . . . . . . . . . . . . . . . . . .3C 86
  LE15: L'ham . . . . . . . . . . . . . . . . . . . .5C 122
  LE17: Lut . . . . . . . . . . . . . . . . . . . . . .5H 153
Orchards, The LE5: Leic . . . . . . . . . . . . . .6G 67
  LE67: Thor . . . . . . . . . . . . . . . . . . . . .2K 93
Orchards Dr. LE18: Wig . . . . . . . . . . . . . .6H 77
Orchards Nature Reserve . . . . . . . . . . . . .5B 64
Orchardson Av. LE4: Leic . . . . . . . . . . . . .6G 65
Orchard St. LE1: Leic . . . . . . . . . .1D 4 (7F 65)
  LE8: Flec . . . . . . . . . . . . . . . . . . . . . .4B 88
  LE10: Hinc . . . . . . . . . . . . . . . . . . . . .3H 103
Orchard St. LE11: Lou . . . . . . . . . . . . . . . .6E 18
  LE16: Mkt H . . . . . . . . . . . . . . . . . . . .3E 150
  LE67: Ibs . . . . . . . . . . . . . . . . . . . . . .4K 51
Orchard Vw. LE12: Moun . . . . . . . . . . . . .4E 44
Orchard Wlk. LE17: Ull . . . . . . . . . . . . . . .7F 143
Orchard Way DE12: Mea . . . . . . . . . . . . . .7E 34
  LE7: Sys . . . . . . . . . . . . . . . . . . . . . .2E 60
  LE12: Wym . . . . . . . . . . . . . . . . . . . . .2K 21
Orchid Cl. LE5: Ham . . . . . . . . . . . . . . . . .4F 67
  LE12: Moun . . . . . . . . . . . . . . . . . . . .2F 45
  LE13: Mel M . . . . . . . . . . . . . . . . . . . .7D 116
  LE19: Nar . . . . . . . . . . . . . . . . . . . . . .7E 74
Orchid Pl. LE9: B Ast . . . . . . . . . . . . . . . .6F 87
Oriel Dr. LE7: Sys . . . . . . . . . . . . . . . . . . .2D 60
Orkney Cl. LE10: Hinc . . . . . . . . . . . . . . . .2E 102
Orkney Way LE8: Count . . . . . . . . . . . . . .6F 83
Orlando Rd. LE2: Leic . . . . . . . . . . . . . . . .5H 71
Orly Av. DE74: C Don . . . . . . . . . . . . . . . .6J 7
Orme Cl. LE4: Leic . . . . . . . . . . . . . . . . . .3A 64
Ormen Grn. LE3: Leic . . . . . . . . . . . . . . . .1H 69
Ormond Cl. LE9: Barw . . . . . . . . . . . . . . . .3K 99
Oronsay Rd. LE4: Leic . . . . . . . . . . . . . . .3B 64
Orpine Rd. LE5: Ham . . . . . . . . . . . . . . . .3D 66
Orsett Cl. LE5: Leic . . . . . . . . . . . . . . . . .6C 66
Orson Dr. LE18: Wig . . . . . . . . . . . . . . . . .5H 77
Orson St. LE5: Leic . . . . . . . . . . . . . . . . . .2K 71
ORSTON . . . . . . . . . . . . . . . . . . . . . . . . .1A 160
Orston La. NG13: Bott . . . . . . . . . . . . . . .1F 107
ORTON . . . . . . . . . . . . . . . . . . . . . . . . . .3B 164
Orton Cl. LE7: Rear . . . . . . . . . . . . . . . . . .3H 47
Orton La. CV9: O Hil, Twy . . . . . . . . . . . . .3A 90
ORTON-ON-THE-HILL . . . . . . . . . . . . . . .1A 162
Orton Rd. LE4: Leic . . . . . . . . . . . . . . . . .3E 64
  LE9: Earl S . . . . . . . . . . . . . . . . . . . . .2E 100
Ortons Ind. Est. LE67: Coal . . . . . . . . . . . .3D 38
ORTON WISTOW . . . . . . . . . . . . . . . . . . .2D 165
Orwell Cl. LE11: Lou . . . . . . . . . . . . . . . . .4B 18
Orwell Dr. LE4: Beau L . . . . . . . . . . . . . . .2A 64
OSBASTON . . . . . . . . . . . . . . . .7B 92 (1B 162)
Osbaston Cl. LE10: Hinc . . . . . . . . . . . . . .7J 99
OSBASTON HOLLOW . . . . . . . . . . . . . . . .4A 92
OSBASTON TOLL GATE . . . . . . . . . . . . . .5A 92
Osborne Rd. LE5: Leic . . . . . . . . . . . . . . .2K 71
  LE11: Lou . . . . . . . . . . . . . . . . . . . . . .4A 18
OSBOURNBY . . . . . . . . . . . . . . . . . . . . . .1D 161
Osbourne Ct. LE8: Whet . . . . . . . . . . . . . .1K 81
OSGATHORPE . . . . . . . . . . . . .6E 14 (3B 158)
Osiers, The DE74: Keg . . . . . . . . . . . . . . .6H 9
  LE3: Brau . . . . . . . . . . . . . . . . . . . . . .1K 75
  LE11: Lou . . . . . . . . . . . . . . . . . . . . . .4E 30
  LE12: Moun . . . . . . . . . . . . . . . . . . . .3C 44
Osiers Office Pk., The LE19: Brau . . . . . . .2J 75
OSLESTON . . . . . . . . . . . . . . . . . . . . . . .1A 158
OSMASTON . . . . . . . . . . . . . . . . . . . . . . .1A 158
Osmaston Rd. LE5: Leic . . . . . . . . . . . . . .3J 71
Osprey Cl. LE9: B Ast . . . . . . . . . . . . . . . .3C 86
Osprey Rd. LE4: Beau L . . . . . . . . . . . . . .7A 58
Osterley Cl. LE11: Lou . . . . . . . . . . . . . . . .6A 18
Oswin Rd. LE3: Leic . . . . . . . . . . . . . . . . .2J 69
Ottawa Rd. LE1: Leic . . . . . . . . . .2F 4 (7G 65)
Otter La. LE12: Moun . . . . . . . . . . . . . . . .2F 45
Otter Way LE8: Whet . . . . . . . . . . . . . . . .4K 81
OUNDLE . . . . . . . . . . . . . . . . . . . . . . . . .3D 165
Oundle Cl. LE65: Ash Z . . . . . . . . . . . . . . .3H 23
Outfields Dr. LE7: Crop . . . . . . . . . . . . . . .3K 57
Outlands Dr. LE10: Hinc . . . . . . . . . . . . . .2C 102
Outwood Cl. LE3: Leic . . . . . . . . . . . . . . .2H 69

OUTWOODS . . . . . . . . . . . . . .2J 25 (3B 158)
Outwoods, The LE10: Bur . . . . . . . . . . . . .3J 103
Outwoods Av. LE11: Lou . . . . . . . . . . . . . .2D 30
Outwoods Dr. LE11: Lou . . . . . . . . . . . . . .1D 30
Outwoods La. LE67: Cole . . . . . . . . . . . . .2J 25
Outwoods Rd. LE11: Lou . . . . . . . . . . . . . .3D 30
Oval, The CV13: Nail . . . . . . . . . . . . . . . .2C 92
  LE1: Leic . . . . . . . . . . . . . . . .7F 5 (3G 71)
  LE2: Oad . . . . . . . . . . . . . . . . . . . . . .4B 78
  LE9: S Stan . . . . . . . . . . . . . . . . . . . .1K 105
  LE16: Mkt H . . . . . . . . . . . . . . . . . . . .3E 150
  LE67: Coal . . . . . . . . . . . . . . . . . . . . .5G 39
Oval Cl. LE15: N Luf . . . . . . . . . . . . . . . . .1B 136
Overbrook Grange CV11: Nun . . . . . . . . . .7H 97
OVER BURROWS . . . . . . . . . . . . . . . . . . .1A 158
Overdale Av. LE3: Glen . . . . . . . . . . . . . . .4F 63
Overdale Cl. LE3: Glen . . . . . . . . . . . . . . .4F 63
  LE16: L Bow . . . . . . . . . . . . . . . . . . . .4G 151
Overdale Rd. LE2: Leic . . . . . . . . . . . . . . .2H 77
  LE4: Thurm . . . . . . . . . . . . . . . . . . . . .7B 60
OVER END . . . . . . . . . . . . . . . . . . . . . . . .2D 165
Overfield Av. LE16: Mkt H . . . . . . . . . . . . .2F 151
Overfield Cl. LE6: Ratby . . . . . . . . . . . . . .6B 62
  LE19: Nar . . . . . . . . . . . . . . . . . . . . . .2E 80
Overfield Wlk. LE6: Ratby . . . . . . . . . . . . .5B 62
Overing Cl. LE4: Leic . . . . . . . . . . . . . . . .3G 65
Overpark Av. LE3: Leic . . . . . . . . . . . . . . .3K 69
OVERSEAL . . . . . . . . . . . . . . . . . . . . . . .3A 158
Overseal Rd. LE3: Leic . . . . . . . . . . . . . . .6J 63
Overstrand Rd. LE5: Ham . . . . . . . . . . . . .4D 66
Overton Cl. LE67: Cole . . . . . . . . . . . . . . .4J 25
Overton Rd. LE5: Leic . . . . . . . . . . . . . . . .7K 65
  LE67: Ibs . . . . . . . . . . . . . . . . . . . . . .5K 51
OVER WHITACRE . . . . . . . . . . . . . . . . . .2A 162
Owen Cl. LE3: Brau . . . . . . . . . . . . . . . . . .6H 69
  LE4: Leic . . . . . . . . . . . . . . . . . . . . . .1A 66
Owen Cres. LE13: Mel M . . . . . . . . . . . . .3G 117
Owen Dr. LE13: Mel M . . . . . . . . . . . . . . .2G 117
Owen St. LE67: Coal . . . . . . . . . . . . . . . . .3C 38
OWSTON . . . . . . . . . . . . . . . . . . . . . . . . .1A 164
Owston Dr. LE18: Wig . . . . . . . . . . . . . . . .5H 77
Owston La. LE14: Som . . . . . . . . . . . . . . .7K 121
  LE15: Knos . . . . . . . . . . . . . . . . . . . . .3A 126
Owston Wood Rd. LE15: Knos . . . . . . . . . .3A 126
OWTHORPE . . . . . . . . . . . . . . . . . . . . . . .1D 159
Oxbow Cl. LE13: Mel M . . . . . . . . . . . . . .5D 116
Oxburgh Cl. LE11: Lou . . . . . . . . . . . . . . .5A 18
Oxendon St. LE2: Leic . . . . . . . . . . . . . . .2H 71
Oxendon Wlk. LE2: Leic . . . . . . . . . . . . . .2H 71
Oxford Av. LE2: Leic . . . . . . . . . . . . . . . . .4H 71
Oxford Ct. LE1: Leic . . . . . . . . . .6C 5 (3F 71)
  LE7: Sys . . . . . . . . . . . . . . . . . . . . . .1E 60
Oxford Dr. LE13: Mel M . . . . . . . . . . . . . .7F 117
  LE18: Wig . . . . . . . . . . . . . . . . . . . . . .5F 77
Oxford Rd. LE2: Leic . . . . . . . . . . . . . . . . .5H 71
  LE9: Des . . . . . . . . . . . . . . . . . . . . . . .2G 95
Oxford St. LE1: Leic . . . . . . . . . . .5B 4 (2E 70)
  LE7: Sys . . . . . . . . . . . . . . . . . . . . . .1E 60
  LE9: Barw . . . . . . . . . . . . . . . . . . . . . .3A 100
  LE9: Earl S . . . . . . . . . . . . . . . . . . . . .2E 100
  LE11: Lou . . . . . . . . . . . . . . . . . . . . . .6D 18
  LE12: Shep . . . . . . . . . . . . . . . . . . . . .1D 28
  LE67: Coal . . . . . . . . . . . . . . . . . . . . .3E 38
Oxley Cl. LE12: Shep . . . . . . . . . . . . . . . .7C 16
Oxon Way LE5: Leic . . . . . . . . . . . . . . . . .2C 72
Oxted Ri. LE2: Oad . . . . . . . . . . . . . . . . . .5C 78

**P**

Packer Av. LE3: Leic E . . . . . . . . . . . . . . . .3F 69
Packe St. LE11: Lou . . . . . . . . . . . . . . . . .6E 18
Packhorse Dr. LE19: End . . . . . . . . . . . . . .6H 75
Packhorse Grn. LE2: Leic . . . . . . . . . . . . .5D 76
Pack Horse La. LE11: Lou . . . . . . . . . . . . .7F 19
Packhorse Rd. LE2: Leic . . . . . . . . . . . . . .5D 76
PACKINGTON . . . . . . . . . . . . . .2A 36 (3A 158)
Packington Hill DE74: Keg . . . . . . . . . . . . .5G 9
Packington Nook La.
  LE65: Ash Z . . . . . . . . . . . . . . . . . . . .7J 23
Packman Grn. LE8: Count . . . . . . . . . . . . .6F 83
Packwood Rd. LE4: Leic . . . . . . . . . . . . . .3E 64
Paddock, The LE8: K Bea . . . . . . . . . . . . .3J 89
  LE9: N Ver . . . . . . . . . . . . . . . . . . . . . .6G 93
  LE12: Shep . . . . . . . . . . . . . . . . . . . . .7D 16
  LE17: C Mag . . . . . . . . . . . . . . . . . . . .5C 142
  LE67: Mark . . . . . . . . . . . . . . . . . . . . .4G 55
Paddock Cl. DE74: C Don . . . . . . . . . . . . .5G 7
  LE2: Oad . . . . . . . . . . . . . . . . . . . . . .2B 78
  LE7: R'ley . . . . . . . . . . . . . . . . . . . . . .7E 44
  LE8: Count . . . . . . . . . . . . . . . . . . . . .5E 82
  LE12: Quo . . . . . . . . . . . . . . . . . . . . . .6A 32
  LE13: Mel M . . . . . . . . . . . . . . . . . . . .6G 117
  LE15: Whis . . . . . . . . . . . . . . . . . . . . .2D 122
Paddock Ct. LE12: Stan S . . . . . . . . . . . . .1G 19
  LE16: Mkt H . . . . . . . . . . . . . . . . . . . .3E 150
Paddock La. LE10: Bur . . . . . . . . . . . . . . .6J 103

Paddocks, The—Percy Rd.


**Paddocks, The** LE14: W Wol 1C **112**
LE19: Litt 2G **81**
NG13: Bott 2G **107**
**Paddock St.** LE18: Wig 6K **77**
**Paddock Vw.** LE7: Sys 2B **60**
**Paddock Way** LE10: Hinc 4B **102**
**Padgate Cl.** LE7: Scra 7H **67**
**Padside Rd.** LE5: Ham 2F **67**
**Padstow Rd.** LE4: Leic 3A **66**
**Padwell La.** LE7: Bush 3J **73**
**Page Cl.** LE17: Lut 2J **153**
**Page La.** DE74: Dis 4A **12**
**Paget Av.** LE4: Birs 5H **59**
**Paget Rd.** LE3: Leic 1C **70**
LE16: Lub 7H **149**
LE67: Ibs 2K **51**
**Paget's End** LE14: L Cla 1J **111**
**Paget St.** LE2: Leic 2C **76**
LE8: K Bea 3J **89**
LE11: Lou 6D **18**
**Paigle Rd.** LE2: Leic 2C **76**
PAILTON 3B **162**
**Painter St.** LE1: Leic 6G **65**
**Palace Hill** LE7: Hou H 2E **130**
**Palfreyman La.** LE2: Oad 5F **79**
**Pall Mall** LE13: Mel M 2H **117**
**Palma Gro.** LE11: Lou 5B **18**
**Palmer Av.** LE11: Lou 5D **18**
**Palmer Dr.** LE17: Lut 5J **153**
**Palmer Rd.** LE10: Hinc 1E **102**
**Palmerston Blvd.** LE2: Leic 2J **77**
**Palmerston Cl.** LE8: K Bea 3H **89**
**Palmerston Rd.** LE13: Mel M 1D **116**
**Palmerston Way** LE2: Leic 2J **77**
**Palmer St.** LE4: Leic 3G **65**
**Pamela Pl.** LE4: Leic 2E **64**
**Pankhurst Rd.** LE4: Beau L 7A **58**
**Pantain Rd.** LE11: Lou 3C **30**
**Paper Mill Cl.** LE7: Anst 7H **57**
**Parade, The** LE2: Oad 2C **78**
LE8: Flec 4B **88**
LE12: Shep 1C **28**
**Paradise Cl.** DE12: Moi 7C **22**
**Paradise La.** LE14: O Dal 7A **110**
**Paramore Cl.** LE8: Whet 4A **82**
**Pares Cl.** LE67: Whit 6E **26**
**Parham Cl.** LE3: Leic 5B **64**
**Paris Cl.** LE65: Ash Z 4J **23**
**Park, The** CV13: Mkt B 2D **94**
Park & Ride
Meynells Gorse 3G **69**
**Park Av.** DE74: C Don 5H **7**
LE2: Leic 7E **70**
LE11: Lou 2F **31**
LE12: Shep 1E **28**
LE13: Mel M 4E **116**
LE67: Mark 4F **55**
**Park Cl.** LE9: Cosb 7H **81**
LE9: Earl S 1D **100**
LE12: Shep 6D **16**
LE16: Fox 1G **149**
LE65: Ash Z 7J **23**
**Park Cotts.** LE15: Glas 1H **139**
**Park Ct.** LE11: Lou 1E **30**
**Park Cres.** LE2: Oad 4E **78**
**Parkdale** LE67: Ibs 4J **51**
**Parkdale Rd.** LE4: Thurm 7A **60**
**Park Dr.** LE3: Glen 6G **63**
LE3: Leic E 4G **69**
LE16: Mkt H 3E **150**
**Parker Dr.** LE4: Leic 4D **64**
**Parkers Cl.** DE11: Blac 3D **22**
**Parkers Flds.** LE12: Quo 4A **32**
**Parkfield Cl.** LE6: Ratby 6B **62**
**Parkfield Cres.** DE12: A Mag 4A **48**
**Parkfield Rd.** LE15: O'ham 3G **127**
PE9: Ryh 6H **129**
**Park Hill** LE7: Gad 1A **118**
**Parkhill** LE2: Leic 7D **70**
**Park Hill Av.** LE2: Leic 1D **76**
**Park Hill Dr.** LE2: Leic 1D **76**
**Park Hill La.** LE12: Sea 4K **33**
**Park Ho.** LE15: Emp 6A **128**
LE16: Mkt H 3E **150**
**Park Ho. Cl.** LE4: Birs 1G **65**
**Park Ho. Ct.** LE8: Bla 1B **82**
LE9: Sap 4J **105**
**Parkland Dr.** LE2: Oad 2C **78**
(not continuous)
**Parklands Av.** LE6: Groby 3B **62**
**Parklands Dr.** LE11: Lou 3E **30**
Parklands Leisure Cen. 4B **78**
**Park La.** DE72: W Tre 4A **6**
DE74: C Don 5D **6**
LE2: Leic 5K **71**
LE13: Mel M 4F **117**
LE15: O'ham 4H **127**
**Park La.** LE17: Walt 6C **146**
LE67: Bag 7G **53**
**Park M.** LE16: Mkt H 3E **150**
**Park Ri.** LE3: Leic 2J **69**
LE12: Shep 7D **16**
**Park Rd.** DE12: Moi 2A **34**
LE4: Birs 7F **59**
LE6: Ratby 7B **62**
LE7: Anst 1H **63**
LE8: Bla 1A **82**
LE9: Cosb 7H **81**
LE9: Earl S 2D **100**
LE9: Sap 4J **105**
LE10: Hinc 3H **103**
LE11: Lou 4D **30**
LE12: Sileby 7J **33**
LE13: Mel M 4F **117**
LE18: Wig 1F **83**
LE19: Nar 2F **81**
LE65: Ash Z 4K **23**
LE67: Coal 3D **38**
PE9: Ket 6F **137**
**Parkside** LE6: Groby 2D **62**
**Parkside Cl.** LE4: Beau L 7A **58**
**Parkside Ct.** LE10: Hinc 3H **103**
**Parkstone Cl.** LE18: Wig 1J **83**
**Parkstone Rd.** LE5: Leic 6F **67**
LE7: Sys 7D **46**
LE9: Des 2H **95**
**Park St.** CV13: Mkt B 2D **94**
LE1: Leic 5D **4** (2F **71**)
**Park St.** LE8: Flec 3B **88**
LE11: Lou 7F **19**
**Park Va. Rd.** LE5: Leic 2J **71**
**Park Vw.** CV9: S Mag 6C **90**
DE72: A Tre 1D **6**
LE3: Leic 1J **69**
LE10: S'ord 6G **105**
LE67: Whit 6E **26**
**Park Vw. Cl.** LE9: B Ast 4D **86**
**Parkway, The** LE5: Leic 7D **66**
**Parlour Cl.** LE18: Wig 6J **77**
**Parnell Cl.** LE19: Litt 3G **81**
**Parnham's Cl.** LE14: N Bro 2C **110**
**Parry St.** LE5: Leic 7J **65**
**Parsons Dr.** LE2: G Par 5A **76**
LE12: Sileby 7K **33**
**Parsons La.** LE10: Hinc 3J **103**
LE10: S'ord 7H **105**
**Parsonwood Hill** LE67: Whit 5E **26**
**Partridge Cl.** LE7: Sys 1B **60**
LE12: Moun 2F **45**
LE17: U Bru 4E **146**
**Partridge Rd.** LE4: Thurm 7B **60**
**Partridge Way** LE15: O'ham 2K **127**
**Parva Lodge** LE15: L'ham 6C **122**
**Parvian Rd.** LE2: Leic 4G **77**
**Paske Av.** LE7: Gad 1A **118**
**Pasley Cl.** LE2: Leic 4D **76**
**Pasley Rd.** LE2: Leic 4D **76**
**Pasture La.** LE1: Leic 1B **4** (7E **64**)
LE9: N Ver 6H **93**
LE12: Hat 1J **17**
LE14: Hos 7B **108**
LE14: Sta 4G **109**
LE15: Barl 2F **127**
**Pastures, The** DE72: W Tre 3B **6**
LE2: Oad 4G **79**
LE7: Sys 2A **60**
LE9: B Ast 5D **86**
LE12: Bar S 5E **32**
LE12: Shep 3C **28**
LE15: Cott 6B **124**
LE16: Mkt H 4C **150**
LE19: Nar 7E **74**
**Pastures La.** DE12: Oak 5D **34**
**Patchetts Cl.** NG13: Bott 2J **107**
**Pate Rd.** LE13: Mel M 7C **116**
**Paterson Cl.** LE4: Beau L 7A **58**
**Paterson Dr.** LE12: W Eav 3D **42**
**Paterson Pl.** LE12: Shep 5D **16**
**Paton St.** LE3: Leic 3D **70**
**Patrick St.** LE16: Mkt H 5F **151**
**Patterdale Dr.** LE11: Lou 2A **30**
**Patterdale Rd.** LE4: Thurm 7A **60**
**Paudy La.** LE12: Bar S, Sea 2G **33**
**Paul Dr.** LE4: Leic 2B **66**
**Pauline Av.** LE4: Leic 2H **65**
**Paulyn Way** LE65: Ash Z 6H **23**
**Pavilion Way** LE11: Lou 4E **18**
**Pawley Cl.** LE8: Whet 3A **82**
**Pawley Gdns.** LE2: Leic 4D **76**
**Pawley Grn.** LE2: Leic 4D **76**
**Payne's La.** LE16: Med 7C **140**
**Payne St.** LE4: Leic 3H **65**
**Peacock Dr.** LE8: Whet 4K **81**
**Peacock La.** LE1: Leic 4B **4** (2E **70**)
**Peakdale** LE18: Wig 7B **78**
**Peake Rd.** LE4: Leic 5K **65**
**Peartree Av.** LE12: Shep 7F **17**
**Pear Tree Cl.** LE9: Barw 2A **100**
LE17: Lut 4G **153**
**Peartree Cl.** DE74: C Don 5J **7**
LE3: Glen 7F **63**
LE7: Anst 1H **63**
**Peartree Ct.** LE65: Wort 3B **14**
**Pear Tree Gdns.** LE16: Mkt H 5D **150**
**Pear Tree La.** LE11: Lou 4J **17**
**Peashill Cl.** LE12: Sileby 1A **46**
**Peatling Grange** LE17: Ash M 1G **145**
**Peatling La.** LE8: Count 7F **83**
PEATLING MAGNA 1K **147** (2C **163**)
PEATLING PARVA 2A **146** (3C **163**)
**Peatling Parva Rd.** LE17: Gilm 6K **145**
**Peatling Rd.** LE8: Count 6F **83**
LE17: Ash M 1H **145** & 3K **145**
**Pebble Bank La.** LE13: Mel M 3H **117**
**Pebble Yd.** LE14: G Dal 6C **120**
PECKLETON 6J **95** (1B **162**)
**Peckleton Comn.** LE9: Peck 5K **95**
**Peckleton Grn.** LE9: Barw 2A **100**
**Peckleton La.** LE9: Des 4H **95**
**Peckleton Rd.** LE9: K Mal 6G **95**
**Peckleton Vw.** LE9: Des 3H **95**
**Pedlars Cl.** LE4: Leic 3B **64**
**Pedlars Way** LE7: East G 5F **47**
**Peebles Way** LE4: Leic 3K **65**
**Peel Cl.** LE8: K Bea 3H **89**
**Peel Dr.** LE11: Lou 6G **19**
**Peewit Cl.** LE2: G Par 5A **76**
**Pegasus Bus. Pk.** DE74: N Air 1D **12**
**Pegasus Cl.** LE2: Leic 4G **4** (2H **71**)
**Peggs Cl.** DE12: Mea 7E **34**
LE9: Earl S 2E **100**
**Peggs Grange** LE67: Hug 6D **38**
PEGGS GREEN 3A **26** (3B **158**)
**Peggs La.** LE7: Quen 7H **47**
**Peldar Pl.** LE67: Coal 4H **39**
**Peldon Cl.** LE4: Leic 4D **64**
**Pelham St.** LE1: Leic 6C **5** (3F **71**)
LE2: Oad 2C **78**
**Pelham Way** LE1: Leic 6C **5** (3F **71**)
**Pell Cl.** LE12: Bar S 3E **32**
**Pells Cl.** LE8: Flec 3B **88**
**Pembroke Av.** LE7: Sys 3D **60**
LE18: Wig 6F **77**
**Pembroke St.** LE5: Leic 7J **65**
**Pembroke Wlk.** *LE5: Leic 7J **65***
*(off Pembroke St.)*
**Pembury Cl.** LE8: G Gle 7K **79**
**Pen Cl.** LE2: Leic 4E **76**
**Penclose Rd.** LE8: Flec 3A **88**
**Pendene Rd.** LE2: Leic 6J **71**
**Pendlebury Dr.** LE2: Leic 1G **77**
**Pendragon Way** LE3: Leic E 5E **68**
**Penfold Cl.** LE9: Sap 3J **105**
**Penfold Dr.** LE8: Count 6D **82**
**Penhale Rd.** LE3: Brau 7K **69**
**Penistone St.** LE67: Ibs 3K **51**
**Penkridge Rd.** DE11: C Gre 2A **22**
**Penkridge Wlk.** LE4: Leic 2E **64**
**Penman Way** LE19: End 3J **75**
**Pennant Cl.** LE3: Glen 7H **63**
**Pennant Rd.** LE10: Bur 6G **103**
**Penney Cl.** LE18: Wig 5J **77**
**Pennine Cl.** LE2: Oad 3F **79**
LE12: Shep 1E **28**
**Pennine Dr.** LE15: E Wes 3H **135**
**Pennine Way** LE65: Ash Z 6K **23**
**Penn La.** LE14: Sta 1G **109**
**Penn St.** LE15: O'ham 4J **127**
**Penny La.** LE9: Barw 3K **99**
**Penny Long La.** LE3: Leic E 4D **68**
**Penrith Av.** LE12: Shep 1B **28**
**Penrith Rd.** LE4: Leic 4J **65**
**Penryn Dr.** LE18: Wig 7J **77**
**Pensilva Cl.** LE18: Wig 7J **77**
**Pentland Av.** LE12: Shep 1F **29**
**Pentland Cl.** LE10: Hinc 2E **102**
**Pentland Ct.** LE15: O'ham 4F **127**
**Pentland Rd.** LE65: Ash Z 5B **24**
**Pentridge Cl.** LE18: Wig 1J **83**
**Penzance Av.** LE18: Wig 7J **77**
**Penzance Cl.** LE10: Hinc 6H **99**
**Peppercorn Cl.** LE4: Leic 3C **64**
**Peppercorn Wlk.** LE4: Leic 3D **64**
**Pepper Dr.** LE12: Quo 4K **31**
**Peppers Cl.** LE12: Moun 1D **44**
**Peppers Dr.** DE74: Keg 6F **9**
**Pepper's La.** LE14: Bur L 1C **120**
**Pera Innovation Pk.** LE13: Mel M 3E **116**
**Percival St.** LE5: Leic 7K **65**
**Percy Rd.** LE2: Leic 1E **76**
LE15: Cott 4C **124**

Percy St. LE3: Brau . . . . . . . . . . . . . .7A 70
Peregrine Cl. DE12: Mea . . . . . . . . . . .1E 48
Peregrine Ri. LE4: Beau L . . . . . . . . . .7A 58
Peregrine Rd. LE9: B Ast . . . . . . . . . . .2C 86
Perkins Cl. LE16: Mkt H . . . . . . . . . . .3F 151
Perkyn Rd. LE5: Leic . . . . . . . . . . . . .1E 72
Perran Av. LE67: Whit . . . . . . . . . . . . .2G 39
Perry Cl. LE12: W Eav . . . . . . . . . . . . .2D 42
Perry Gro. LE11: Lou . . . . . . . . . . . . . .2G 31
Perseverance Rd. LE4: Birs . . . . . . . . . .1G 65
Perth Av. LE3: Leic . . . . . . . . . . . . . . .7A 64
(not continuous)
Peterborough Av. LE15: O'ham . . . . . . . . .3J 127
Peterborough Rd.
 LE15: B'den, Mor . . . . . . . . . . . .7K 135
Peterfield Rd. LE67: Whit . . . . . . . . . . .1G 39
Peterleas, The DE12: Don . . . . . . . . . . .3A 34
Peters Av. LE9: N Ver . . . . . . . . . . . . .6H 93
Peters Cl. DE73: Ton . . . . . . . . . . . . . .6D 10
 LE9: S Stan . . . . . . . . . . . . . . . .1H 105
Peters Dr. LE5: Leic . . . . . . . . . . . . . .7D 66
Petersfield LE9: Crof . . . . . . . . . . . . . .5A 80
Petersfield Rd. LE13: Mel M . . . . . . . . .3E 116
Peters Way LE15: Bisb . . . . . . . . . . . . .2G 139
Petunia Cl. LE3: Leic E . . . . . . . . . . . . .5D 68
Petworth Dr. LE3: Leic . . . . . . . . . . . . .1B 70
 LE11: Lou . . . . . . . . . . . . . . . . . .5A 18
 LE16: L Bow . . . . . . . . . . . . . . . . .5H 151
Pevensey Av. LE5: Leic . . . . . . . . . . . . .4F 73
Pevensey Rd. LE11: Lou . . . . . . . . . . . .4C 18
Peverel Ct. LE3: Brau . . . . . . . . . . . . . .6J 69
Peverel Rd. LE3: Leic . . . . . . . . . . . . . .5A 70
Peveril Rd. LE17: Ash M . . . . . . . . . . . .1G 145
Phillip Dr. LE2: G Par . . . . . . . . . . . . . .7E 76
Phillips Cres. LE4: Beau L . . . . . . . . . . .7A 58
Phipps Cl. LE8: Whet . . . . . . . . . . . . . .3A 82
Phoenix Arts Cen. . . . . . . . . . . . . .5C 4 (2F 71)
Phoenix Bus. Pk.
 LE10: Hinc . . . . . . . . . . . . . . . . .3B 102
Phoenix Cl. LE3: Leic . . . . . . . . . . . . . .7B 64
Phoenix Dr. LE12: Sileby . . . . . . . . . . .2K 45
Piccadilly Cinema . . . . . . . . . . . . . . . .7K 65
Piccaver Ri. LE3: Leic . . . . . . . . . . . . . .1H 69
Pickards La. LE14: Wyc . . . . . . . . . . . . .5E 112
Pickering Cl. LE4: Leic . . . . . . . . . . . . . .5K 65
Pickering Dr. LE67: Ell . . . . . . . . . . . . .1C 52
Pickering Rd. LE9: B Ast . . . . . . . . . . . .6D 86
PICKFORD . . . . . . . . . . . . . . . . . . . .3A 162
Picks Cl. LE16: L Bow . . . . . . . . . . . . .4H 151
Pick St. LE12: Shep . . . . . . . . . . . . . . .6D 16
PICKWELL . . . . . . . . . . . . . . . . . . . .3A 160
Pickwell Cl. LE3: Leic . . . . . . . . . . . . . .6J 63
Pickwell La. LE15: Whis . . . . . . . . . . . . .4A 122
(not continuous)
Pickwell Rd. LE14: Som . . . . . . . . . . . .6K 121
PICKWORTH
 Grantham . . . . . . . . . . . . . . . . . .1D 161
 Stamford . . . . . . . . . . . . . . . . . .3C 161
Pickworth Cl. LE15: O'ham . . . . . . . . . .3K 127
Pickworth Rd. PE9: G Cas . . . . . . . . . . .1H 137
Picton Cl. LE5: Ham . . . . . . . . . . . . . . .2E 66
Pied Bull Cl. PE9: Ket . . . . . . . . . . . . . .5H 137
Piers Rd. LE3: Glen . . . . . . . . . . . . . . .5G 63
Pike Cl. LE10: Bur . . . . . . . . . . . . . . . .6G 103
Pilgrim Gdns. LE5: Leic . . . . . . . . . . . . .4C 72
Pilgrims Ga. LE10: Bur . . . . . . . . . . . . .6K 103
Pilkington Rd. LE3: Leic . . . . . . . . . . . . .4J 69
Pillings Rd. LE15: O'ham . . . . . . . . . . . .2H 127
PILSGATE . . . . . . . . . . . . . . . . . . . .1D 165
PILTON
 Peterborough . . . . . . . . . . . . . . .3D 165
 Stamford . . . . . . . . . . . . . . . . . .1C 165
Pilton Cl. LE15: O'ham . . . . . . . . . . . . .4K 127
Pilton Rd. LE15: N Luf . . . . . . . . . . . . . .2A 136
Pimpernel Cl. LE19: Nar . . . . . . . . . . . . .7D 74
Pincet La. LE17: N Kil . . . . . . . . . . . . . .2K 155
Pindar Rd. LE3: Leic . . . . . . . . . . . . . . .6A 64
Pine Cl. CV13: S Gol . . . . . . . . . . . . . . .3B 98
 LE11: Lou . . . . . . . . . . . . . . . . . .4E 30
 LE17: Lut . . . . . . . . . . . . . . . . . .4G 153
 LE65: Ash Z . . . . . . . . . . . . . . . . .4B 24
Pine Ct. DE12: Moi . . . . . . . . . . . . . . . .5D 22
Pine Dr. LE7: Sys . . . . . . . . . . . . . . . . .3D 60
Pinehurst Cl. LE3: Leic . . . . . . . . . . . . .1G 69
Pinel Cl. LE9: B Ast . . . . . . . . . . . . . . .6E 86
Pine Rd. LE3: Glen . . . . . . . . . . . . . . . .6G 63
Pines, The LE7: Bush . . . . . . . . . . . . . .3K 73
 LE67: Whit . . . . . . . . . . . . . . . . . .1G 39
Pine Tree Av. LE5: Leic . . . . . . . . . . . . .7C 66
 LE6: Groby . . . . . . . . . . . . . . . . . .4D 62
Pine Tree Cl. LE2: Oad . . . . . . . . . . . . .4D 78
 LE9: N Ver . . . . . . . . . . . . . . . . . .6J 93
Pine Tree Gdn. LE2: Oad . . . . . . . . . . . .4D 78
Pine Tree Gro. LE9: Leic E . . . . . . . . . . .5C 68
Pine Tree Wlk. LE5: Leic . . . . . . . . . . . .6C 66
Pine Vw. LE3: Leic E . . . . . . . . . . . . . . .3F 69
Pinewood Av. LE4: Thurm . . . . . . . . . . .1A 66

Pinewood Cl. LE4: Beau L . . . . . . . . . . .1A 64
 LE8: Count . . . . . . . . . . . . . . . . . .5E 82
Pinewood Ct. LE67: Mark . . . . . . . . . . . .7G 55
Pinewood Dr. LE67: Mark . . . . . . . . . . . .7G 55
Pinfold LE3: Brau . . . . . . . . . . . . . . . . .1K 75
Pinfold, The LE6: Ratby . . . . . . . . . . . . .6A 62
 LE8: Mark . . . . . . . . . . . . . . . . . .5G 55
 LE67: N Bur . . . . . . . . . . . . . . . . .7B 50
Pinfold Cl. LE10: Hinc . . . . . . . . . . . . . .4C 102
 LE15: N Luf . . . . . . . . . . . . . . . . .1A 136
 LE15: S Luf . . . . . . . . . . . . . . . . .4C 136
 NG13: Bott . . . . . . . . . . . . . . . . . .1G 107
Pinfold Ct. LE14: T Sat . . . . . . . . . . . . .3H 119
Pinfold Gdns. LE11: Lou . . . . . . . . . . . . .6G 19
Pinfold Footpath LE9: Earl S . . . . . . . . .1F 101
Pinfold Ga. LE11: Lou . . . . . . . . . . . . . .6F 19
Pinfold Jetty LE11: Lou . . . . . . . . . . . . .6F 19
Pinfold La. LE14: Harb . . . . . . . . . . . . . .2E 108
 LE15: Mkt O . . . . . . . . . . . . . . . . .2J 123
(Main St.)
 LE15: Mkt O . . . . . . . . . . . . . . . . .1H 123
(Thistleton Rd.)
 LE15: N Luf . . . . . . . . . . . . . . . . .1A 136
 LE15: S Luf . . . . . . . . . . . . . . . . .3C 136
 NG13: Bott . . . . . . . . . . . . . . . . . .1G 107
Pinfold Pl. LE14: Harb . . . . . . . . . . . . . .2E 108
Pinfold Rd. LE4: Thurm . . . . . . . . . . . . .7K 59
Pingle, The CV13: B'one . . . . . . . . . . . .5C 92
 LE12: Quo . . . . . . . . . . . . . . . . . .6J 31
Pingle La. LE9: Pott M . . . . . . . . . . . . . .4K 101
 LE15: Mor . . . . . . . . . . . . . . . . . .6K 135
Pingle St. LE3: Leic . . . . . . . . . . . .1A 4 (7E 64)
PINLEY . . . . . . . . . . . . . . . . . . . . . . .3A 162
Pintail Cl. LE8: Whet . . . . . . . . . . . . . . .5K 81
Pintail Ct. DE12: Mea . . . . . . . . . . . . . .1D 48
(off Widgeon Dr.)
Piper Cl. LE3: Leic . . . . . . . . . . . . . . . .7A 64
 LE11: Lou . . . . . . . . . . . . . . . . . .2D 30
 LE12: L Wha . . . . . . . . . . . . . . . . .7G 13
 LE12: Shep . . . . . . . . . . . . . . . . . .4E 16
Piper Dr. LE12: L Wha . . . . . . . . . . . . . .6G 13
Piper La. LE67: Rav . . . . . . . . . . . . . . . .3K 37
Piper Way LE3: Leic . . . . . . . . . . . . . . .7A 64
PIPEWELL . . . . . . . . . . . . . . . . . . . .3B 164
Pipewell Wlk. LE4: Leic . . . . . . . . . . . . .3E 64
Pipistrelle Dr. CV13: Mkt B . . . . . . . . . .2A 94
Pipistrelle Way LE2: Oad . . . . . . . . . . . .4G 79
Pipit Cl. DE12: Mea . . . . . . . . . . . . . . . .1E 48
Pisca La. LE67: Hea . . . . . . . . . . . . . . . .3G 51
Pitchens Cl. LE4: Beau L . . . . . . . . . . . .1K 63
Pitchers La. LE16: G Eas . . . . . . . . . . . .5K 141
Pit Hill LE8: Smee W . . . . . . . . . . . . . . .5H 89
Pithiviers Cl. LE65: Ash Z . . . . . . . . . . . .6J 23
Pit La. PE9: Ket . . . . . . . . . . . . . . . . . .4H 137
Pits Av. LE3: Brau . . . . . . . . . . . . . . . . .1J 75
Pitsford Dr. LE11: Lou . . . . . . . . . . . . . .1J 29
Pitt La. LE67: Cole . . . . . . . . . . . . . . . . .5J 25
Pitton Cl. LE18: Wig . . . . . . . . . . . . . . . .1J 83
Plain Ga. LE7: R'ley . . . . . . . . . . . . . . . .4C 44
Plantagenet Way LE65: Ash Z . . . . . . . . .4B 24
Plantation, The LE8: Count . . . . . . . . . . .5E 82
Plantation Av. LE2: Leic . . . . . . . . . . . . .2C 76
Platts La. LE17: Coss . . . . . . . . . . . . . . .5J 45
Player Cl. LE4: Leic . . . . . . . . . . . . . . . .1K 65
Pleasant Cl. LE3: Leic E . . . . . . . . . . . . .5D 68
 LE11: Lou . . . . . . . . . . . . . . . . . . .6E 18
Pleasant Pl. DE74: Keg . . . . . . . . . . . . . .6H 9
Pleasant Ter. LE15: Upp . . . . . . . . . . . . .2C 138
Plough Cl. LE3: Leic E . . . . . . . . . . . . . .6D 68
 LE9: B Ast . . . . . . . . . . . . . . . . . .6E 86
Ploughmans Dr. LE12: Shep . . . . . . . . . .5E 16
Ploughmans' Lea LE7: East G . . . . . . . . .5F 47
Plover Cl. LE15: O'ham . . . . . . . . . . . . .2K 127
Plover Cres. LE4: Beau L . . . . . . . . . . . .7B 58
Plover Rd. PE9: Ess . . . . . . . . . . . . . . .1J 129
Plowman Cl. LE3: Glen . . . . . . . . . . . . . .5G 63
Plummer La. DE74: Keg . . . . . . . . . . . . . .6G 9
PLUMTREE . . . . . . . . . . . . . . . . . . . .1D 159
Plumtree Cl. LE11: Lou . . . . . . . . . . . . . .4D 18
Plumtree Cotts. DE12: Don . . . . . . . . . . .3A 34
PLUMTREE PARK . . . . . . . . . . . . . . . .1D 159
Plumtree Way LE7: Sys . . . . . . . . . . . . . .3D 60
PLUNGAR . . . . . . . . . . . . . . . .6C 106 (1A 160)
Plungar La. NG13: Bark V . . . . . . . . . . . .3A 106
Pluto Cl. LE2: Leic . . . . . . . . . . . . . . . . .2H 71
Plymouth Dr. LE5: Leic . . . . . . . . . . . . . .4B 72
Plymstock Cl. LE3: Leic . . . . . . . . . . . . . .1B 70
Poachers Cl. LE3: Glen . . . . . . . . . . . . . .6F 63
Poachers Pl. LE2: Oad . . . . . . . . . . . . . .4F 79
Pochin Cl. LE13: Mel M . . . . . . . . . . . . .5E 116
Pochin Dr. LE16: Mkt H . . . . . . . . . . . . .2E 150
Pochin's Bri. Rd. LE18: Wig . . . . . . . . . . .1G 83
Pochins Cl. LE18: Wig . . . . . . . . . . . . . . .7J 77
Pochin St. LE9: Crof . . . . . . . . . . . . . . . .5A 80
Pochin Way LE12: Sileby . . . . . . . . . . . . .7K 33
Pocket End LE11: Lou . . . . . . . . . . . . . .3B 30

Pocklingtons Wlk. LE1: Leic . . . . . . . .4C 4 (2F 71)
Point, The LE16: L Bow . . . . . . . . . . . . .3H 151
POINTON . . . . . . . . . . . . . . . . . . . . . .1D 161
Polaris Cl. LE2: Leic . . . . . . . . . . . . . . . .2H 71
Polden Cl. LE12: Shep . . . . . . . . . . . . . .1E 28
POLEBROOK . . . . . . . . . . . . . . . . . . .3D 165
Polebrook Cl. LE3: Leic . . . . . . . . . . . . . .3J 63
POLESWORTH . . . . . . . . . . . . . . . . . .1A 162
Polka Wlk. LE14: W'ham . . . . . . . . . . . . .1G 121
Pollard Cl. LE13: Mel M . . . . . . . . . . . . .2H 117
Pollard Ct. LE2: Leic . . . . . . . . . . . . . . . .5K 71
Pollard Rd. LE3: Leic . . . . . . . . . . . . . . .4J 69
Pollards Cl. LE15: B'den . . . . . . . . . . . . .7D 136
Pollard Way LE67: Rav . . . . . . . . . . . . . .2A 38
Polly Bott's La. LE67: Ulv . . . . . . . . . . . .1H 55
Pomeroy Dr. LE2: Oad . . . . . . . . . . . . . .3B 78
Pond End DE74: C Don . . . . . . . . . . . . . .2K 7
Pond La. LE15: Gree . . . . . . . . . . . . . . .5F 125
Pond St. LE12: Sea . . . . . . . . . . . . . . . .4K 33
Pontylue Way LE7: Sys . . . . . . . . . . . . . .3A 60
Pool Rd. LE3: Leic . . . . . . . . . . . . . . . . .1B 70
Pool St. DE11: C Gre . . . . . . . . . . . . . . .1B 22
Pope Cres. LE15: End . . . . . . . . . . . . . . .5E 74
Pope St. LE2: Leic . . . . . . . . . . . . . . . . .7G 71
Poplar Av. DE12: Moi . . . . . . . . . . . . . . .2A 34
 LE4: Birs . . . . . . . . . . . . . . . . . . . .5G 59
 LE8: Count . . . . . . . . . . . . . . . . . .6E 82
 LE17: Lut . . . . . . . . . . . . . . . . . . .4H 153
 LE67: Mark . . . . . . . . . . . . . . . . . .5F 55
Poplar Cl. LE15: Upp . . . . . . . . . . . . . . .1C 138
Poplar Dr. DE12: Mea . . . . . . . . . . . . . . .6E 34
Poplar Hill LE12: Walt W . . . . . . . . . . . . .6G 21
Poplar Rd. LE11: Lou . . . . . . . . . . . . . . .3F 31
 LE19: Litt . . . . . . . . . . . . . . . . . . . .3F 81
Poplars, The LE3: Brau . . . . . . . . . . . . . .1A 76
 LE6: Ratby . . . . . . . . . . . . . . . . . .5A 62
 LE7: Bill . . . . . . . . . . . . . . . . . . . .6J 131
 LE9: Earl S . . . . . . . . . . . . . . . . . .1F 101
Poplars Cl. LE6: Groby . . . . . . . . . . . . . .3C 62
Poplars Ct. LE16: Mkt H . . . . . . . . . . . . .3D 150
Poplars Farm Ct. LE8: Count . . . . . . . . . .5E 82
Poplar Ter. CV13: Con . . . . . . . . . . . . . .5H 91
Poppins, The LE4: Beau L . . . . . . . . . . . .7B 58
Popple Cl. LE9: B Ast . . . . . . . . . . . . . . .5E 86
Poppy Cl. LE2: Leic . . . . . . . . . . . . . . . .4F 77
 LE6: Groby . . . . . . . . . . . . . . . . . .3E 62
 LE11: Lou . . . . . . . . . . . . . . . . . . .5E 30
 LE67: Coal . . . . . . . . . . . . . . . . . .5G 39
Porlock Cl. LE12: Shep . . . . . . . . . . . . . .1E 28
 LE17: Gilm . . . . . . . . . . . . . . . . . .7J 145
Porlock St. LE3: Leic . . . . . . . . . . . . . . .2B 70
Portcullis Rd. LE5: Leic . . . . . . . . . . . . . .5G 67
Portgate LE18: Wig . . . . . . . . . . . . . . . .7A 78
Portishead Rd. LE5: Leic . . . . . . . . . . . . .6A 66
Portland Bldg. LE2: Leic . . . . . . . . . . . . .6A 5
Portland Dr. LE10: Hinc . . . . . . . . . . . . . .7H 99
Portland Gdns. LE9: Cosb . . . . . . . . . . . .5H 81
Portland Rd. LE2: Leic . . . . . . . . . . . . . . .6J 71
 LE9: K Mux . . . . . . . . . . . . . . . . . .3C 68
Portland St. LE9: Cosb . . . . . . . . . . . . . .5H 81
Portland Towers LE2: Leic . . . . . . . . . . . .7A 72
Portland Wlk. LE2: Oad . . . . . . . . . . . . . .5E 78
Portloc Dr. LE18: Wig . . . . . . . . . . . . . . .1K 83
Portman St. LE4: Leic . . . . . . . . . . . . . . .4H 65
Portmore Cl. LE4: Leic . . . . . . . . . . . . . .4C 64
Portsdown Rd. LE2: Leic . . . . . . . . . . . . .2K 77
Portslade Ho. LE3: Glen . . . . . . . . . . . . .1G 69
Portsmouth Rd. LE4: Leic . . . . . . . . . . . .5G 65
Portwey, The LE5: Leic . . . . . . . . . . . . . .6A 66
Posey La. DE72: A Tre . . . . . . . . . . . . . .1C 6
Post Office La. CV9: With . . . . . . . . . . . .6B 96
 LE8: New H . . . . . . . . . . . . . . . . . .3F 85
 LE14: T'ord . . . . . . . . . . . . . . . . . .6H 119
 NG13: Plun . . . . . . . . . . . . . . . . . .5C 106
 NG13: Red . . . . . . . . . . . . . . . . . .2E 106
Post Rd. LE4: Thurm . . . . . . . . . . . . . . .4A 60
Pott Acre LE7: R'ley . . . . . . . . . . . . . . . .3F 45
POTTER HILL . . . . . . . . . . . . . . . . . . .2A 160
Potters Marston La.
 LE9: Thurl . . . . . . . . . . . . . . . . . . .2K 101
Potter St. LE1: Leic . . . . . . . . . .2E 4 (1G 71)
Potterton Rd. LE4: Leic . . . . . . . . . . . . . .2D 64
Pougher Cl. LE9: Sap . . . . . . . . . . . . . . .4K 105
Poulteney Dr. LE12: Quo . . . . . . . . . . . . .5K 31
Poultney La. LE17: Kim . . . . . . . . . . . . . .7A 146
Powers Rd. LE9: Barw . . . . . . . . . . . . . .5J 99
Powys Av. LE2: Leic . . . . . . . . . . . . . . . .6A 72
Powys Gdns. LE2: Leic . . . . . . . . . . . . . .6A 72
Poynings Av. LE3: Leic . . . . . . . . . . . . . .1A 70
Praetor Ho. LE10: Hinc . . . . . . . . . . . . . .2G 103
Prebendal Ho. LE15: Emp . . . . . . . . . . . .7C 128
Prebend St. LE2: Leic . . . . . . . . . . .6F 5 (3G 71)
Precinct, The LE17: C'ach . . . . . . . . . . . .6C 154
Prentice Cl. DE12: Moi . . . . . . . . . . . . . .7C 22
Presents La. LE12: Belt . . . . . . . . . . . . . .4H 15
Prestbury Rd. LE11: Lou . . . . . . . . . . . . .6K 17
PRESTON . . . . . . . . . . . . . . . . . .7A 134 (1B 164)

| | | |
|---|---|---|
| Preston Cl. LE6: Ratby . . . . . . . . . . . . . . . .6C **62** | Putney Rd. W. LE2: Leic . . . . . . . . . . . . . . .5F **71** | Quorndon Ri. LE6: Groby . . . . . . . . . . . . . .4C **62** |
| LE12: Sileby . . . . . . . . . . . . . . . . . . . . .2J **45** | Pyeharps Rd. LE10: Bur . . . . . . . . . . . . . .6H **103** | Quorndon Ter. LE12: Quo . . . . . . . . . . . . .5K **31** |
| LE67: S Bar . . . . . . . . . . . . . . . . . . . . .4A **54** | Pyke, The LE7: R'ley . . . . . . . . . . . . . . . . .3F **45** | Quorndon Water Ct. LE12: Quo . . . . . . . . .5K **31** |
| Preston Ct. LE15: Pres . . . . . . . . . . . . . . .7A **134** | Pymm Ley Cl. LE6: Groby . . . . . . . . . . . . . .3D **62** | Quorn Pk. LE12: Bar S . . . . . . . . . . . . . . .2H **33** |
| Preston Dr. LE9: N Ver . . . . . . . . . . . . . . .5H **93** | Pymm Ley Gdns. LE6: Groby . . . . . . . . . . .3D **62** | Quorn Rd. LE5: Leic . . . . . . . . . . . . . . . . . .7K **65** |
| Preston Ri. LE5: Leic . . . . . . . . . . . . . . . . .5E **66** | Pymm Ley La. LE6: Groby . . . . . . . . . . . . .4D **62** | |
| Preston Rd. LE10: Hinc . . . . . . . . . . . . . . .1E **102** | Pytchley Cl. LE4: Leic . . . . . . . . . . . . . . . .1E **64** | |
| LE15: Win . . . . . . . . . . . . . . . . . . . . .6C **134** | LE15: Cott . . . . . . . . . . . . . . . . . . .2D **124** | |
| Preston's La. LE67: Cole . . . . . . . . . . . . . .5J **25** | *(not continuous)* | **R** |
| Prestop Dr. LE65: Ash Z . . . . . . . . . . . . . .4H **23** | Pytchley Dr. LE11: Lou . . . . . . . . . . . . . . .3D **30** | |
| PRESTWOLD . . . . . . . . . . . . .2C **20** (2C **159**) | | Racecourse La. LE14: Bur L . . . . . . . . . . .2D **120** |
| Prestwold La. LE12: Bur W, P'old . . . . . . . .1C **20** | | Radar Rd. LE3: Leic . . . . . . . . . . . . . . . . .2H **69** |
| Prestwold Rd. LE5: Leic . . . . . . . . . . . . . .6J **65** | **Q** | RADBOURNE . . . . . . . . . . . . . . . . . . . .1A **158** |
| Pretoria Cl. LE4: Beau L . . . . . . . . . . . . . .6C **58** | | RADCLIFFE ON TRENT . . . . . . . . . . . . . .1D **159** |
| Pretoria Rd. LE9: K Mux . . . . . . . . . . . . . .2B **68** | Quadrant, The LE4: Leic . . . . . . . . . . . . . .4F **65** | Radcot Lawns LE2: Leic . . . . . . . . . . . . . .5D **76** |
| LE67: Ell, Ibs . . . . . . . . . . . . . . . . . . . .3A **52** | LE15: Upp . . . . . . . . . . . . . . . . . . . . .2C **138** | RADFORD |
| Prevost Gdns. LE12: Quo . . . . . . . . . . . . .4A **32** | Quainton Rd. LE2: Leic . . . . . . . . . . . .9A **5** (4D **70**) | Coventry . . . . . . . . . . . . . . . . . . . . .3A **162** |
| Price Way LE4: Thurm . . . . . . . . . . . . . . . .6C **60** | Quaker Cl. CV13: F Dray . . . . . . . . . . . . . .2H **97** | Nottingham . . . . . . . . . . . . . . . . . . . .1C **159** |
| Pride Pl. LE16: Mkt H . . . . . . . . . . . . . . . .5D **150** | Quaker Rd. LE12: Sileby . . . . . . . . . . . . . .3J **45** | Radford Dr. LE3: Brau . . . . . . . . . . . . . . .4G **69** |
| Priesthills Rd. LE10: Hinc . . . . . . . . . . . . .3G **103** | Quantock Ri. LE12: Shep . . . . . . . . . . . . . .1E **28** | Radford Ho. LE3: Brau . . . . . . . . . . . . . . .4G **69** |
| Priestley Rd. LE3: Leic . . . . . . . . . . . . . . .2A **70** | QUARNDON . . . . . . . . . . . . . . . . . . . . .1A **158** | Radford Mdw. DE74: C Don . . . . . . . . . . . .5H **7** |
| Priestman Rd. LE3: Brau . . . . . . . . . . . . . .6G **69** | QUARNDON COMMON . . . . . . . . . . . . . .1A **158** | Radiant Rd. LE5: Leic . . . . . . . . . . . . . . . .7E **66** |
| Priest Mdw. LE8: Flec . . . . . . . . . . . . . . . .3B **88** | Quarry La. CV9: Manc . . . . . . . . . . . . . . . .7A **96** | Radley Cl. LE65: Ash Z . . . . . . . . . . . . . . .3J **23** |
| Priestwells LE15: Gree . . . . . . . . . . . . . . .5E **124** | DE12: Snar . . . . . . . . . . . . . . . . . . . .6H **49** | Radmoor Rd. LE11: Lou . . . . . . . . . . . . . .7D **18** |
| PRIMETHORPE . . . . . . . . . . . .3C **86** (2C **163**) | LE19: End . . . . . . . . . . . . . . . . . . . . .4E **74** | Radmore Rd. LE10: Hinc . . . . . . . . . . . . . .7G **99** |
| Primethorpe Wlk. LE9: B Ast . . . . . . . . . . .3C **86** | Quarrymans Ct. LE67: Mark . . . . . . . . . . . .4F **55** | Radnor Ct. LE19: Nar . . . . . . . . . . . . . . . .6D **74** |
| Primrose Cl. LE6: Groby . . . . . . . . . . . . . .3E **62** | Quartz Cl. LE19: End . . . . . . . . . . . . . . . .3F **75** | Radnor Dr. LE12: Shep . . . . . . . . . . . . . . .5D **16** |
| LE19: Nar . . . . . . . . . . . . . . . . . . . . .1E **80** | Quebec Rd. LE1: Leic . . . . . . . . . .2F **4** (1G **71**) | Radnor Rd. LE18: Wig . . . . . . . . . . . . . . . .5G **77** |
| Primrose Dr. LE10: Bur . . . . . . . . . . . . . . .6H **103** | Queen Elizabeths Wlk. LE3: Leic . . . . . . . .1D **70** | Radstone Wlk. LE5: Leic . . . . . . . . . . . . . .1B **72** |
| Primrose Hill LE2: Oad . . . . . . . . . . . . . . .2B **78** | Queen Elizabeth Theatre, The . . . . . . . . .3J **127** | Raeburn Rd. LE2: Leic . . . . . . . . . . . . . . .6H **71** |
| Primrose Way LE7: Quen . . . . . . . . . . . . . .6G **47** | Queen's Cl. LE14: Scal . . . . . . . . . . . . . . .6C **112** | RAGDALE . . . . . . . . . . . . . . . . . . . . . .3D **159** |
| LE9: K Mux . . . . . . . . . . . . . . . . . . . .1D **68** | Queens Dr. LE3: Leic E . . . . . . . . . . . . . . .4E **68** | Ragdale Rd. LE4: Leic . . . . . . . . . . . . . . .5K **65** |
| Prince Albert Dr. LE3: Glen . . . . . . . . . . . .7G **63** | LE18: Wig . . . . . . . . . . . . . . . . . . . . .6H **77** | LE14: Hob . . . . . . . . . . . . . . . . . . . . .1B **114** |
| Prince Charles St. LE14: Ash . . . . . . . . . . .2G **115** | LE19: End . . . . . . . . . . . . . . . . . . . . .6H **75** | Railway St. LE18: Wig . . . . . . . . . . . . . . .1F **83** |
| Prince Dr. LE2: Oad . . . . . . . . . . . . . . . . .3E **78** | Queensferry Pde. LE2: Leic . . . . . . . . . . . .5C **76** | Railway Ter. DE12: Mea . . . . . . . . . . . . . .1E **48** |
| Princes Cl. LE7: Anst . . . . . . . . . . . . . . . .7J **57** | Queensgate Dr. LE4: Birs . . . . . . . . . . . . .5E **58** | LE11: Lou . . . . . . . . . . . . . . . . . . . . .5G **19** |
| Princes Rd. LE14: O Dal . . . . . . . . . . . . . .5D **110** | Queensmead Cl. LE6: Groby . . . . . . . . . . .4C **62** | Raine Way LE2: Oad . . . . . . . . . . . . . . . . .5F **79** |
| Princess Anne Sq. LE14: Ash . . . . . . . . . . .2G **115** | Queens Pk. Ct. LE10: Hinc . . . . . . . . . . . .3H **103** | Rainsborough Gdns. LE16: Mkt H . . . . . . . .6D **150** |
| Princess Av. LE2: Oad . . . . . . . . . . . . . . .4E **78** | Queen's Pk. Flats LE10: Hinc . . . . . . . . . .3H **103** | Rainsford Cres. LE4: Leic . . . . . . . . . . . . .3E **64** |
| LE15: O'ham . . . . . . . . . . . . . . . . . . .4G **127** | *(off Queen's Rd.)* | Raleigh Cl. LE10: Hinc . . . . . . . . . . . . . . .6G **99** |
| Princess Dr. LE9: K Mux . . . . . . . . . . . . . .2B **68** | Queens Pk. Ter. LE10: Hinc . . . . . . . . . . . .3H **103** | Ralph Cl. LE11: Lou . . . . . . . . . . . . . . . . .3B **30** |
| LE13: Mel M . . . . . . . . . . . . . . . . . . .7F **117** | Queens Pk. Way LE2: Leic . . . . . . . . . . . . .6D **76** | Ralphs Cl. LE17: D Bas . . . . . . . . . . . . . .1D **144** |
| Princess Rd. LE10: Hinc . . . . . . . . . . . . . .3H **103** | *(not continuous)* | Ralph Toon Ct. LE14: Ash . . . . . . . . . . . . .2G **115** |
| Princess Rd. Backways LE1: Leic . . . .6D **5** (3F **71**) | Queens Rd. DE74: Keg . . . . . . . . . . . . . . .5H **9** | *(off Regency Rd.)* |
| Princess Rd. E. LE1: Leic . . . . . . . . . .7E **5** (3G **71**) | LE2: Leic . . . . . . . . . . . . . . . .10G **5** (5H **71**) | Ramsbury Rd. LE2: Leic . . . . . . . . . . . . . .3H **77** |
| Princess Rd. W. LE1: Leic . . . . . . . . . .6D **5** (3F **71**) | LE8: Bla . . . . . . . . . . . . . . . . . . . . . .2A **82** | Ramscliff Av. DE12: Don . . . . . . . . . . . . . .4B **34** |
| Princess St. LE11: Lou . . . . . . . . . . . . . . .7F **19** | LE10: Hinc . . . . . . . . . . . . . . . . . . . .3H **103** | Ramsdean Av. LE18: Wig . . . . . . . . . . . . .5J **77** |
| LE19: Nar . . . . . . . . . . . . . . . . . . . . .1G **81** | LE11: Lou . . . . . . . . . . . . . . . . . . . . .5G **19** | Ramsden Rd. CV9: Manc . . . . . . . . . . . . . .6A **96** |
| Prince St. LE67: Coal . . . . . . . . . . . . . . . .4D **38** | LE15: O'ham . . . . . . . . . . . . . . . . . . .3J **127** | Ramsey Cl. LE10: Hinc . . . . . . . . . . . . . . .2E **102** |
| Prince William Rd. LE11: Lou . . . . . . . . . . .4E **18** | LE15: Upp . . . . . . . . . . . . . . . . . . . .2B **138** | LE17: Lut . . . . . . . . . . . . . . . . . . . . .4K **153** |
| Prince William Way LE11: Lou . . . . . . . . . .4E **18** | Queen's Royal Lancers Regimental Mus., The | Ramsey Gdns. LE5: Leic . . . . . . . . . . . . . .5G **67** |
| Printers Yd. LE15: Upp . . . . . . . . . . . . . . .2C **138** | . . . . . . . . . . . . . . . . . . . . . . . . . . . .1B **160** | Ramsey Way LE5: Leic . . . . . . . . . . . . . . .5G **67** |
| *(off Market Pl., not continuous)* | Queen's St. DE12: Mea . . . . . . . . . . . . . . .7E **34** | Ramson Cl. LE5: Ham . . . . . . . . . . . . . . . .4E **66** |
| Priorfields LE65: Ash Z . . . . . . . . . . . . . . .6A **24** | Queen St. LE1: Leic . . . . . . . . . . .3E **4** (2G **71**) | Rancliffe Cres. LE3: Leic . . . . . . . . . . . . . .3A **70** |
| *(not continuous)* | LE2: Oad . . . . . . . . . . . . . . . . . . . . .2D **78** | Randall Cl. LE7: Bars . . . . . . . . . . . . . . . .5C **118** |
| Prior Pk. LE65: Ash Z . . . . . . . . . . . . . . . .6A **24** | LE7: Bark T . . . . . . . . . . . . . . . . . . . .6E **60** | Randles Cl. LE7: Bush . . . . . . . . . . . . . . .3J **73** |
| *(off Up. Packington Rd.)* | LE9: Barw . . . . . . . . . . . . . . . . . . . .4A **100** | Range, The LE15: L'ham . . . . . . . . . . . . . .5B **122** |
| Prior Pk. Rd. LE65: Ash Z . . . . . . . . . . . . .5K **23** | LE11: Lou . . . . . . . . . . . . . . . . . . . . .7G **19** | Range Rd. LE65: Ash Z . . . . . . . . . . . . . . .5A **24** |
| Priory Cl. LE7: Sys . . . . . . . . . . . . . . . . . .2B **60** | LE12: Shep . . . . . . . . . . . . . . . . . . . .6E **16** | Ranksborough Dr. LE15: L'ham . . . . . . . . .5B **122** |
| LE67: Thrin . . . . . . . . . . . . . . . . . . . .3C **26** | LE15: Upp . . . . . . . . . . . . . . . . . . . .2C **138** | LE10: Hinc . . . . . . . . . . . . . . . . . . . .3E **102** |
| Priory Cres. LE3: Leic . . . . . . . . . . . . . . . .2J **69** | LE16: L Bow . . . . . . . . . . . . . . . . . . .5G **151** | Rannoch Cl. LE4: Leic . . . . . . . . . . . . . . .3C **64** |
| Priory La. LE67: Ulv . . . . . . . . . . . . . . . . .2F **55** | LE67: Coal . . . . . . . . . . . . . . . . . . . .4D **38** | Ranton Way LE3: Leic . . . . . . . . . . . . . . .6C **64** |
| Priory Rd. CV13: Mkt B . . . . . . . . . . . . . .3B **94** | LE67: Mark . . . . . . . . . . . . . . . . . . . .6G **55** | Ranworth Wlk. LE4: Leic . . . . . . . . . . . . . .2E **64** |
| LE11: Lou . . . . . . . . . . . . . . . . . . . . .3C **30** | NG13: Bott . . . . . . . . . . . . . . . . . . . .2H **107** | RATBY . . . . . . . . . . . . . . . . . . .6A **62** (1C **163**) |
| LE15: Mant . . . . . . . . . . . . . . . . . . . .2C **134** | Queensway DE74: C Don . . . . . . . . . . . . . .4H **7** | Ratby Cl. LE3: Leic E . . . . . . . . . . . . . . . .2E **68** |
| Priory Wlk. CV9: Manc . . . . . . . . . . . . . . .7A **96** | LE3: Leic . . . . . . . . . . . . . . . . . . . . .3A **100** | LE9: K Mux . . . . . . . . . . . . . . . . . . . .7C **62** |
| LE3: Leic E . . . . . . . . . . . . . . . . . . . .4E **68** | LE13: Mel M . . . . . . . . . . . . . . . . . . .7F **117** | LE67: Mark . . . . . . . . . . . . . . . . . . . .6G **55** |
| LE10: Hinc . . . . . . . . . . . . . . . . . . . .2H **103** | LE14: O Dal . . . . . . . . . . . . . . . . . . .5E **110** | Ratby Mdw. La. LE19: End . . . . . . . . . . . .5J **75** |
| Priory Water Nature Reserve . . . . . . . . . .3H **115** | Queensway Ho. DE12: Mea . . . . . . . . . . . .7E **34** | Ratby Rd. LE6: Groby . . . . . . . . . . . . . . . .4C **62** |
| Private Rd. LE9: S Stan . . . . . . . . . . . . . . .7J **101** | Queen Victoria Ct. LE10: Hinc . . . . . . . . . .2G **103** | Ratcliff Cl. LE65: Ash Z . . . . . . . . . . . . . . .5J **23** |
| LE67: Hug . . . . . . . . . . . . . . . . . . . . .5B **38** | Quelch Cl. LE67: Hug . . . . . . . . . . . . . . . .6D **38** | Ratcliffe Cl. LE2: Leic . . . . . . . . . . . . . . . .7J **71** |
| *(not continuous)* | Quemby Cl. LE4: Leic . . . . . . . . . . . . . . . .4G **65** | Ratcliffe La. LE2: Leic . . . . . . . . . . . . . . . .7K **71** |
| Proctors Pk. Rd. LE12: Bar S . . . . . . . . . . .4C **32** | Quenby Cres. LE7: Sys . . . . . . . . . . . . . . .2E **60** | RATCLIFFE CULEY . . . . . . . . . . . . . . . . .2A **162** |
| Proctor's Pleasure Pk. LE12: Bar S . . . . . . .4C **32** | Quenby St. LE5: Leic . . . . . . . . . . . . . . . .7K **65** | Ratcliffe Dr. LE9: Hun . . . . . . . . . . . . . . . .2B **80** |
| Progress Way LE4: Leic . . . . . . . . . . . . . .3C **66** | QUENIBOROUGH . . . . . . . . . .7G **47** (3D **159**) | Ratcliffe La. CV9: S Mag . . . . . . . . . . . . . .7B **90** |
| Prospect Hill LE5: Leic . . . . . . . . . . . . . . .1J **71** | Queniborough Ind. Dr. LE7: Quen . . . . . . . .7J **47** | DE74: Lock . . . . . . . . . . . . . . . . . . . .1F **9** |
| Prospect Rd. LE5: Leic . . . . . . . . . . . . . . .1K **71** | Queniborough Ind. Est. LE7: Quen . . . . . . .7F **47** | RATCLIFFE ON SOAR . . . . . . . .2K **9** (2B **158**) |
| LE8: K Bea . . . . . . . . . . . . . . . . . . . .3H **89** | Queniborough Rd. LE4: Leic . . . . . . . . . . .5J **65** | RATCLIFFE ON THE WREAKE . . . .3D **46** (3D **159**) |
| Prospect Way LE9: Earl S . . . . . . . . . . . . .2D **100** | LE7: Bark, Sys . . . . . . . . . . . . . . . . . .5F **61** | Ratcliffe Rd. LE2: Leic . . . . . . . . . . . . . . . .7J **71** |
| Pryor Rd. LE12: Sileby . . . . . . . . . . . . . . .7K **33** | LE7: Quen . . . . . . . . . . . . . . . . . . . .7G **47** | LE7: Coss, Rat W . . . . . . . . . . . . . . . .1K **45** |
| Pudding Bag La. LE12: Shep . . . . . . . . . . .3B **28** | Quickthorns LE2: Oad . . . . . . . . . . . . . . .1D **78** | LE7: Thru . . . . . . . . . . . . . . . . . . . . .7B **114** |
| Pudding Bay La. LE15: Ext . . . . . . . . . . . .2C **128** | Quiney Way LE2: Oad . . . . . . . . . . . . . . . .2E **78** | LE10: Bur . . . . . . . . . . . . . . . . . . . . .5J **103** |
| Pughe's Cl. LE10: Bur . . . . . . . . . . . . . . . .6K **103** | Quinton Ri. LE2: Oad . . . . . . . . . . . . . . . .4C **78** | LE11: Lou . . . . . . . . . . . . . . . . . . . . .5F **19** |
| Pulford Dr. LE7: Scra, Thurn . . . . . . . . . . .1H **73** | QUORN . . . . . . . . . . . . . . . . .5A **32** (3C **159**) | LE12: Sileby . . . . . . . . . . . . . . . . . . .1K **45** |
| Pullman Rd. LE18: Wig . . . . . . . . . . . . . . .5H **77** | Quorn & Woodhouse Station | Ratcliffe St. LE4: Leic . . . . . . . . . . . . . . . .4H **65** |
| Pullman Trad. Est. LE15: Upp . . . . . . . . . .3D **138** | Great Central Railway . . . . . . . . . . . . .6H **31** | Ratts La. LE15: B Rut . . . . . . . . . . . . . . . .6C **126** |
| Pulteney Av. LE11: Lou . . . . . . . . . . . . . . .3F **31** | Quorn Av. LE2: Oad . . . . . . . . . . . . . . . . .4E **78** | Raven Cl. DE12: Mea . . . . . . . . . . . . . . . .1D **48** |
| Pulteney Rd. LE11: Lou . . . . . . . . . . . . . . .3F **31** | LE13: Mel M . . . . . . . . . . . . . . . . . . .4E **116** | Ravenhurst Rd. LE3: Brau . . . . . . . . . . . . .6K **69** |
| Pump La. LE14: Ash . . . . . . . . . . . . . . . . .3G **115** | LE14: Ab K . . . . . . . . . . . . . . . . . . . .7H **111** | Raven Rd. LE3: Leic . . . . . . . . . . . . . . . . .4J **69** |
| Purbeck Av. LE12: Shep . . . . . . . . . . . . . .7F **17** | Quorn Cl. LE11: Lou . . . . . . . . . . . . . . . . .1G **31** | Ravensbridge Dr. LE4: Leic . . . . . . . . . . . .6D **64** |
| Purbeck Cl. LE18: Wig . . . . . . . . . . . . . . .1K **83** | Quorn Ct. LE12: Quo . . . . . . . . . . . . . . . .6K **31** | Ravenslea LE67: Rav . . . . . . . . . . . . . . . .4J **37** |
| Purcell Rd. LE4: Leic . . . . . . . . . . . . . . . .6G **65** | Quorn Cres. LE15: Cott . . . . . . . . . . . . . .3D **124** | Ravensthorpe Dr. LE11: Lou . . . . . . . . . . .7K **17** |
| Purdy Ct. LE15: O'ham . . . . . . . . . . . . . . .4H **127** | LE67: Coal . . . . . . . . . . . . . . . . . . . .4H **39** | Ravensthorpe Rd. LE18: Wig . . . . . . . . . . .5G **77** |
| Purley Ri. LE12: Shep . . . . . . . . . . . . . . . .1E **28** | QUORNDON . . . . . . . . . . . . . .5A **32** (3C **159**) | RAVENSTONE . . . . . . . . . . . . . .4J **37** (3B **158**) |
| Purley Rd. LE4: Leic . . . . . . . . . . . . . . . . .5J **65** | Quorndon Mountsorrel By-Pass | Ravenstone Ct. LE67: Rav . . . . . . . . . . . . .4J **37** |
| Putney Rd. LE2: Leic . . . . . . . . . . . . . . . .5F **71** | LE7: R'ley . . . . . . . . . . . . . . . . . . . . .4G **45** | Ravenstone Rd. LE67: Coal . . . . . . . . . . . .2A **38** |
| Putney Rd. E. LE2: Leic . . . . . . . . . . . . . .6G **71** | LE12: Bar S, Moun, Quo . . . . . . . . . . . .4J **31** | LE67: Hea . . . . . . . . . . . . . . . . . . . . .2G **51** |
| | | LE67: Ibs . . . . . . . . . . . . . . . . . . . . .2J **51** |

Ravenwood DE11: Swad . . . . . . . . . . . . . . . . . . .1A 22
Rawdon Cl. DE74: C Don . . . . . . . . . . . . . . . . . . .4J 7
Rawdon Rd. DE12: Moi . . . . . . . . . . . . . . . . . . .5A 22
Raw Dykes Rd. LE2: Leic . . . . . . . .10B 5 (5E 70)
Rawlings Ct. LE2: Oad . . . . . . . . . . . . . . . . . . .4G 79
Rawlings Pas. LE2: Oad . . . . . . . . . . . . . . . . . . .2C 78
Rawlins Cl. LE12: W Eav . . . . . . . . . . . . . . . . . . .3E 42
Rawlins Community College Swimming Pool
. . . . . . . . . . . . . . . . . . . . . . . . . . . . . . . . . .5A 32
Rawlinson Wlk. LE4: Leic . . . . . . . . . . . . . . . . .3C 64
Rawson St. LE1: Leic . . . . . . . . . . .6D 5 (3G 71)
LE19: End . . . . . . . . . . . . . . . . . . . . . . . . . .5F 75
Rawsthorne Wlk. LE4: Leic . . . . . . . . . . . . . . .6G 65
Rayleigh Grn. LE5: Leic . . . . . . . . . . . . . . . . . .5G 67
Rayleigh Way LE5: Leic . . . . . . . . . . . . . . . . . .5G 67
Raymond Av. LE11: Lou . . . . . . . . . . . . . . . . . . .4B 18
Raymond Rd. LE3: Leic . . . . . . . . . . . . . . . . . . .4C 70
Rayner Rd. LE4: Leic . . . . . . . . . . . . . . . . . . . . .2B 66
Raynes Wlk. LE13: Mel M . . . . . . . . . . . . . . . .3G 117
Raynham Dr. LE11: Lou . . . . . . . . . . . . . . . . . . .5A 18
Rayns Way LE7: Sys . . . . . . . . . . . . . . . . . . . . .3A 60
REARSBY . . . . . . . . . . . . . . . . . .3J 47 (3D 159)
Rearsby La. LE7: Gad . . . . . . . . . . . . . . . . . . .1A 118
Rearsby Rd. LE4: Leic . . . . . . . . . . . . . . . . . . . .5J 65
LE7: Quen . . . . . . . . . . . . . . . . . . . . . . . . . .6G 47
LE7: Thru . . . . . . . . . . . . . . . . . . . . . . . . . .7B 114
Rectory Cl. DE73: B Hil . . . . . . . . . . . . . . . . . . .7A 10
LE17: Swin . . . . . . . . . . . . . . . . . . . . . . . .3H 157
LE18: Wig . . . . . . . . . . . . . . . . . . . . . . . . . .7K 77
Rectory Ct. NG13: Bott . . . . . . . . . . . . . . . . . .1H 107
Rectory Dr. LE14: Up Bro . . . . . . . . . . . . . . . .1A 110
Rectory End LE8: Bur O . . . . . . . . . . . . . . . . .5D 130
Rectory Farm M. DE72: W Tre . . . . . . . . . . . . .4A 6
Rectory Gdns. DE72: A Tre . . . . . . . . . . . . . . . .1C 6
LE2: Leic . . . . . . . . . . . . . . . . . . . . . . . . . .5D 72
Rectory La. CV13: Cad . . . . . . . . . . . . . . . . . . .6C 94
CV13: Mkt B . . . . . . . . . . . . . . . . . . . . . . .2D 94
CV13: Nail . . . . . . . . . . . . . . . . . . . . . . . . .2C 92
DE12: A Mag . . . . . . . . . . . . . . . . . . . . . . .4A 48
LE7: Thurc . . . . . . . . . . . . . . . . . . . . . . . . .3B 58
LE8: K Bea . . . . . . . . . . . . . . . . . . . . . . . . .2J 89
LE14: Bur H . . . . . . . . . . . . . . . . . . . . . . .6F 121
LE15: E Wes . . . . . . . . . . . . . . . . . . . . . . .3G 135
LE16: L Bow . . . . . . . . . . . . . . . . . . . . . . .5G 151
LE16: Med . . . . . . . . . . . . . . . . . . . . . . . . .6D 140
NG13: Bott . . . . . . . . . . . . . . . . . . . . . . . .1H 107
Rectory M. DE72: A Tre . . . . . . . . . . . . . . . . . . .1C 6
Rectory Pl. LE11: Lou . . . . . . . . . . . . . . . . . . . .6F 19
LE12: Wym . . . . . . . . . . . . . . . . . . . . . . . . .2K 21
Rectory Rd. LE7: Wan . . . . . . . . . . . . . . . . . . .3H 59
LE11: Lou . . . . . . . . . . . . . . . . . . . . . . . . . .5F 19
LE67: Mark . . . . . . . . . . . . . . . . . . . . . . . . .4G 55
Redbrook Cres. LE13: Mel M . . . . . . . . . . . . .6D 116
Red Burrow La. LE65: Pac . . . . . . . . . . . . . . . .4A 36
LE67: Nor H . . . . . . . . . . . . . . . . . . . . . . . .4A 36
Redcar Rd. LE4: Leic . . . . . . . . . . . . . . . . . . . .5H 65
Red Hall Dr. LE9: Barw . . . . . . . . . . . . . . . . . .3A 100
Red Hall Rd. LE9: Barw . . . . . . . . . . . . . . . . . .3B 100
Red Hill LE4: Birs . . . . . . . . . . . . . . . . . . . . . . .1F 65
Red Hill Av. LE19: Nar . . . . . . . . . . . . . . . . . . . .1E 80
Red Hill Circ. LE4: Leic . . . . . . . . . . . . . . . . . . .2G 65
Red Hill Cl. LE4: Thurm . . . . . . . . . . . . . . . . . .5A 60
Red Hill La. LE4: Thurm . . . . . . . . . . . . . . . . . .5A 60
(not continuous)
LE67: Swan, Thrin, Whit . . . . . . . . . . . . . . .6B 26
Red Hill Way LE4: Leic . . . . . . . . . . . . . . . . . . .1D 64
Red Ho. Cl. LE2: Leic . . . . . . . . . . . . . . . . . . . .4C 76
Red Ho. Gdns. LE2: Leic . . . . . . . . . . . . . . . . .4C 76
Red Ho. Ri. LE2: Leic . . . . . . . . . . . . . . . . . . . .4C 76
Red Ho. Rd. LE2: Leic . . . . . . . . . . . . . . . . . . .4C 76
Redland Cl. LE15: B'den . . . . . . . . . . . . . . . . .7D 136
Redland Rd. LE15: O'ham . . . . . . . . . . . . . . . .4F 127
Redlands Est. LE67: Ibs . . . . . . . . . . . . . . . . . .2A 52
Redlich Cl. LE16: L Bow . . . . . . . . . . . . . . . . .4H 151
Red Lion La. LE9: N Ver . . . . . . . . . . . . . . . . . .6J 93
Red Lion St. LE14: Sta . . . . . . . . . . . . . . . . . .2H 109
Red Lodge Rd. LE7: T Hil . . . . . . . . . . . . . . . .1J 131
Redmarle Rd. LE3: Leic . . . . . . . . . . . . . . . . . .4A 70
REDMILE . . . . . . . . . . . . . . . . .1E 106 (1A 160)
Redmile La. NG13: Bark V . . . . . . . . . . . . . . .2B 106
Redmile's La. PE9: Ket . . . . . . . . . . . . . . . . . .6H 137
Redmires Cl. LE11: Lou . . . . . . . . . . . . . . . . . . .7K 17
Redmoor Cl. CV13: Mkt B . . . . . . . . . . . . . . . .3B 94
Redpath Cl. LE4: Leic . . . . . . . . . . . . . . . . . . . .7H 65
Redruth Av. LE18: Wig . . . . . . . . . . . . . . . . . . .7J 77
Redruth Ct. LE18: Wig . . . . . . . . . . . . . . . . . . .1J 83
(off Launceston Rd.)
Redruth Rd. LE4: Beau L . . . . . . . . . . . . . . . . .6C 58
Redwing Cl. LE15: O'ham . . . . . . . . . . . . . . . .3K 127
Redwing Wlk. LE5: Leic . . . . . . . . . . . . . . . . . .7J 65
Redwood Av. LE13: Mel M . . . . . . . . . . . . . . . .2F 117
Redwood Rd. LE11: Lou . . . . . . . . . . . . . . . . . .4E 30
Redwood Wlk. LE5: Leic . . . . . . . . . . . . . . . . . .7J 65
Reed Pool Cl. LE8: Count . . . . . . . . . . . . . . . . .5F 83
Rees Cl. LE15: Upp . . . . . . . . . . . . . . . . . . . . .1B 138
Rees Gro. LE4: Leic . . . . . . . . . . . . . . . . . . . . .1K 65
Reeth Cl. LE4: Leic . . . . . . . . . . . . . . . . . . . . . .3C 64

Reeves Cl. LE8: Whet . . . . . . . . . . . . . . . . . . . .4K 81
Reeves La. LE15: Win . . . . . . . . . . . . . . . . . . .5E 134
Reeves Rd. LE10: Bur . . . . . . . . . . . . . . . . . . . .5J 103
Reeve's Yd. LE15: Upp . . . . . . . . . . . . . . . . . .2C 138
Reform Rd. LE67: Ibs . . . . . . . . . . . . . . . . . . . .5K 51
Regal Cinema
Melton Mowbray . . . . . . . . . . . . . . . . . . . .4F 117
Regal Ct. LE19: End . . . . . . . . . . . . . . . . . . . . .6H 75
Regan Rd. DE12: Moi . . . . . . . . . . . . . . . . . . . .7C 22
Regency Cl. LE2: G Par . . . . . . . . . . . . . . . . . . .7D 76
Regency Ct. LE3: Leic . . . . . . . . . . . . . . . . . . . .2C 70
LE10: Bur . . . . . . . . . . . . . . . . . . . . . . . . .4K 103
Regency Rd. LE14: Ash . . . . . . . . . . . . . . . . . .2G 115
Regent Cl. LE18: Wig . . . . . . . . . . . . . . . . . . . .6H 77
Regent Ct. DE11: C Gre . . . . . . . . . . . . . . . . . .1A 22
LE10: Hinc . . . . . . . . . . . . . . . . . . . . . . . .3G 103
LE11: Lou . . . . . . . . . . . . . . . . . . . . . . . . . .5E 18
LE14: Lut . . . . . . . . . . . . . . . . . . . . . . . . . .5J 153
Regent Pde. LE10: Hinc . . . . . . . . . . . . . . . . .3G 103
(off Regent St.)
Regent Pl. LE13: Mel M . . . . . . . . . . . . . . . . . .5G 117
Regent Pl. Retail Pk. LE11: Lou . . . . . . . . . . . .6E 18
Regent Rd. LE1: Leic . . . . . . . . . . . .6D 5 (3F 71)
LE8: Count . . . . . . . . . . . . . . . . . . . . . . . . .5F 83
LE14: Hob . . . . . . . . . . . . . . . . . . . . . . . . .2B 114
Regent St. DE11: C Gre . . . . . . . . . . . . . . . . . .1A 22
LE1: Leic . . . . . . . . . . . . . . . . . . .6F 5 (3G 71)
LE2: Oad . . . . . . . . . . . . . . . . . . . . . . . . . .2C 78
LE7: Thru . . . . . . . . . . . . . . . . . . . . . . . . .7B 114
LE9: Barw . . . . . . . . . . . . . . . . . . . . . . . . .3A 100
LE10: Hinc . . . . . . . . . . . . . . . . . . . . . . . .3G 103
LE11: Lou . . . . . . . . . . . . . . . . . . . . . . . . . .6E 18
LE13: Mel M . . . . . . . . . . . . . . . . . . . . . . .5G 117
LE17: Lut . . . . . . . . . . . . . . . . . . . . . . . . . .5J 153
LE19: Nar . . . . . . . . . . . . . . . . . . . . . . . . . .1G 81
Regent St. Ind. Est. LE19: Nar . . . . . . . . . . . . .2H 81
Regents Wlk. LE3: Leic E . . . . . . . . . . . . . . . . .4E 68
Regs Way LE67: Bar . . . . . . . . . . . . . . . . . . . . .7H 39
REMPSTONE . . . . . . . . . . . . . . . . . . . . . . . .2C 159
Rempstone Rd. LE12: Belt . . . . . . . . . . . . . . . . .4J 15
LE12: Hot . . . . . . . . . . . . . . . . . . . . . . . . . .1C 20
LE12: Wym . . . . . . . . . . . . . . . . . . . . . . . . .1J 21
LE67: Cole, Grif . . . . . . . . . . . . . . . . . . . . .4G 25
Rendell Rd. LE4: Leic . . . . . . . . . . . . . . . . . . . .5G 65
Rendell St. LE11: Lou . . . . . . . . . . . . . . . . . . . .5F 19
(not continuous)
Renfrew Rd. LE5: Leic . . . . . . . . . . . . . . . . . . . .6G 67
Renishaw Dr. LE5: Leic . . . . . . . . . . . . . . . . . . .5A 72
Rennes Cl. LE65: Ash Z . . . . . . . . . . . . . . . . . . .5J 23
Renning End LE12: Moun . . . . . . . . . . . . . . . . .4E 44
Repington Row LE2: Leic . . . . . . . . . . . . . . . . .3F 77
REPTON . . . . . . . . . . . . . . . . . . . . . . . . . . . .2A 158
Repton Cl. LE65: Ash Z . . . . . . . . . . . . . . . . . . .3J 23
LE18: Wig . . . . . . . . . . . . . . . . . . . . . . . . . .4H 77
Repton Rd. DE12: Mea . . . . . . . . . . . . . . . . . . .7B 34
Repton St. LE3: Leic . . . . . . . . . . . . . . . . . . . . .7D 64
Reservoir Hill DE11: A Vil . . . . . . . . . . . . . . . . .4A 22
DE12: Moi . . . . . . . . . . . . . . . . . . . . . . . . .4A 22
Reservoir Rd. LE7: Crop . . . . . . . . . . . . . . . . . .2H 57
LE67: Thor . . . . . . . . . . . . . . . . . . . . . . . . .3K 93
Resolution Rd. LE65: Ash Z . . . . . . . . . . . . . . .4B 24
Retreat, The LE5: Leic . . . . . . . . . . . . . . . . . . . .2B 72
LE12: Bar S . . . . . . . . . . . . . . . . . . . . . . . . .3D 32
Revell Cl. LE12: Quo . . . . . . . . . . . . . . . . . . . . .5B 32
Reynolds Chase LE18: Wig . . . . . . . . . . . . . . . .5K 77
Reynolds Cl. LE10: Hinc . . . . . . . . . . . . . . . . . .7D 98
Reynolds Pl. LE3: Leic . . . . . . . . . . . . . . . . . . .5A 70
Rhodes Cl. LE16: Mkt H . . . . . . . . . . . . . . . . . .5C 150
Ribble Av. LE2: Oad . . . . . . . . . . . . . . . . . . . . .2F 79
Ribble Dr. LE12: Bar S . . . . . . . . . . . . . . . . . . .5D 32
Ribblesdale Av. LE10: Hinc . . . . . . . . . . . . . . . .7H 99
Ribble Wlk. LE15: O'ham . . . . . . . . . . . . . . . . .5G 127
Ribble Way LE13: Mel M . . . . . . . . . . . . . . . . .6E 116
Richard III Rd. LE3: Leic . . . . . . . . . .3A 4 (1D 70)
Richard Cl. LE3: Brau . . . . . . . . . . . . . . . . . . . .4G 69
Richardson Cl. LE9: S Stan . . . . . . . . . . . . . . .2J 105
Richardsons Cl. LE9: B Ast . . . . . . . . . . . . . . . .5E 86
Richmond Av. LE2: Leic . . . . . . . . . . . . . . . . . . .7E 70
Richmond Cl. LE2: Leic . . . . . . . . . . . . . . . . . . .7E 70
LE8: Flec . . . . . . . . . . . . . . . . . . . . . . . . . .4B 88
LE9: Cosb . . . . . . . . . . . . . . . . . . . . . . . . . .7G 81
LE9: Des . . . . . . . . . . . . . . . . . . . . . . . . . .3H 95
Richmond Dr. LE2: G Par . . . . . . . . . . . . . . . . . .7E 76
LE13: Mel M . . . . . . . . . . . . . . . . . . . . . . .7G 117
Richmond Rd. LE2: Leic . . . . . . . . . . . . . . . . . .7E 70
LE10: Hinc . . . . . . . . . . . . . . . . . . . . . . . . .7F 99
LE67: D Hea . . . . . . . . . . . . . . . . . . . . . . . .1B 52
Richmond Way LE2: Oad . . . . . . . . . . . . . . . . . .5E 78
Richmore Rd. LE5: Ham . . . . . . . . . . . . . . . . . .3F 67
Riddington Rd. LE3: Brau . . . . . . . . . . . . . . . . .1K 75
LE19: Litt . . . . . . . . . . . . . . . . . . . . . . . . . . .3G 81
Riddon Dr. LE10: Hinc . . . . . . . . . . . . . . . . . . .3E 102
Ridgemere Cl. LE7: Sys . . . . . . . . . . . . . . . . . . .1F 61
Ridgemere La. LE7: Sys . . . . . . . . . . . . . . . . . .2G 61
Ridge Vw. LE16: Mkt H . . . . . . . . . . . . . . . . . .2E 150
Ridgeway LE2: Oad . . . . . . . . . . . . . . . . . . . . . .5D 78
LE19: Litt . . . . . . . . . . . . . . . . . . . . . . . . . . .3G 81

Ridgeway, The LE3: Leic . . . . . . . . . . . . . . . . . .7A 64
LE7: R'ley . . . . . . . . . . . . . . . . . . . . . . . . . .7B 44
LE10: Bur . . . . . . . . . . . . . . . . . . . . . . . . .5G 103
LE16: Mkt H . . . . . . . . . . . . . . . . . . . . . . .2F 151
Ridgeway Dr. LE4: Thurm . . . . . . . . . . . . . . . . .7B 60
Ridgeway W. LE16: Mkt H . . . . . . . . . . . . . . . .2E 150
Ridgway Rd. LE2: Leic . . . . . . . . . . . . . . . . . . . .7K 71
LE65: Ash Z . . . . . . . . . . . . . . . . . . . . . . . .6H 23
Riding, The LE4: Beau L . . . . . . . . . . . . . . . . . .7B 58
Ridings, The LE7: Quen . . . . . . . . . . . . . . . . . .7G 47
LE7: R'ley . . . . . . . . . . . . . . . . . . . . . . . . . .5A 44
Ridley Cl. LE7: Crop . . . . . . . . . . . . . . . . . . . . .3K 57
LE8: Bla . . . . . . . . . . . . . . . . . . . . . . . . . . .3A 82
Ridley St. LE3: Leic . . . . . . . . . . . . . . . . . . . . .3D 70
RIDLINGTON . . . . . . . . . . . . . . . .2H 133 (1B 164)
Ridlington Rd. LE15: Pres . . . . . . . . . . . . . . . . .7A 134
Rigsty, The LE12: Quo . . . . . . . . . . . . . . . . . . . .5J 31
Riley Cl. LE9: S Stan . . . . . . . . . . . . . . . . . . . .2J 105
LE16: Mkt H . . . . . . . . . . . . . . . . . . . . . . .5B 150
Rills, The LE10: Hinc . . . . . . . . . . . . . . . . . . . .1H 103
Ringers Cl. LE2: Oad . . . . . . . . . . . . . . . . . . . . .7C 72
Ringers Spinney LE2: Oad . . . . . . . . . . . . . . . .7C 72
Ring Fence LE12: Shep . . . . . . . . . . . . . . . . . . .1D 28
RINGING HILL . . . . . . . . . . . . . . . .2H 27 (3B 158)
Ring Rd. LE2: Leic . . . . . . . . . . . . . . . . . . . . . . .2K 77
(not continuous)
Ringway, The LE7: Quen . . . . . . . . . . . . . . . . . .6G 47
Ringwood Cl. LE9: Des . . . . . . . . . . . . . . . . . . .2H 95
LE18: Wig . . . . . . . . . . . . . . . . . . . . . . . . . .7J 77
Ringwood Rd. LE5: Leic . . . . . . . . . . . . . . . . . .5G 67
LE12: Shep . . . . . . . . . . . . . . . . . . . . . . . . .5D 16
Ripley Cl. LE16: L Bow . . . . . . . . . . . . . . . . . . .4H 151
Ripon Dr. LE8: Bla . . . . . . . . . . . . . . . . . . . . . . .3B 82
Ripon St. LE2: Leic . . . . . . . . . . . . . . . . . . . . . .4J 71
RIPPINGALE . . . . . . . . . . . . . . . . . . . . . . . . .2D 161
Rise, The LE7: Hou H . . . . . . . . . . . . . . . . . . . .2C 130
LE7: R'ley . . . . . . . . . . . . . . . . . . . . . . . . . .6G 45
LE19: Nar . . . . . . . . . . . . . . . . . . . . . . . . . .6E 74
Riseholme Cl. LE3: Brau . . . . . . . . . . . . . . . . . .1K 75
RISLEY . . . . . . . . . . . . . . . . . . . . . . . . . . . . . .1B 158
Riston Cl. LE2: Oad . . . . . . . . . . . . . . . . . . . . . .5D 78
Ritchie Pk. LE16: Mkt H . . . . . . . . . . . . . . . . . .7E 150
Riversdale Cl. LE4: Birs . . . . . . . . . . . . . . . . . . .7H 59
Riversdale Rd. CV9: Ath . . . . . . . . . . . . . . . . . . .5A 96
River Sence Way LE67: Hug . . . . . . . . . . . . . . . .6D 38
Riverside CV9: With . . . . . . . . . . . . . . . . . . . . . .6B 96
LE16: Mkt H . . . . . . . . . . . . . . . . . . . . . . .4G 151
Riverside Cl. CV9: S Mag . . . . . . . . . . . . . . . . . .5C 90
LE8: G Gle . . . . . . . . . . . . . . . . . . . . . . . . .7K 79
NG13: Bott . . . . . . . . . . . . . . . . . . . . . . . .1G 107
Riverside Ct. DE12: Mea . . . . . . . . . . . . . . . . . .1C 48
LE4: Birs . . . . . . . . . . . . . . . . . . . . . . . . . .7H 59
LE19: Litt . . . . . . . . . . . . . . . . . . . . . . . . . . .2G 81
Riverside Dr. LE2: Leic . . . . . . . . . . . . . . . . . . .2C 76
Riverside Ind. Est. LE16: Mkt H . . . . . . . . . . . .3G 151
Riverside M. LE7: Wan . . . . . . . . . . . . . . . . . . . .3J 59
Riverside Rd. LE13: Mel M . . . . . . . . . . . . . . . .4C 116
LE17: Lut . . . . . . . . . . . . . . . . . . . . . . . . . .5K 153
Riverside Wlk. LE14: Ash . . . . . . . . . . . . . . . . .3G 115
LE16: Mkt H . . . . . . . . . . . . . . . . . . . . . . .4F 151
NG13: Bott . . . . . . . . . . . . . . . . . . . . . . . .1G 107
Riverside Way LE4: Leic . . . . . . . . . . . . . . . . . . .5F 65
LE19: Litt . . . . . . . . . . . . . . . . . . . . . . . . . . .2G 81
Rivers St. LE3: Leic . . . . . . . . . . . . . . . . . . . . . .1D 70
River Vw. LE12: Bar S . . . . . . . . . . . . . . . . . . . .5E 32
Rivet's Mdw. Cl. LE3: Brau . . . . . . . . . . . . . . . .6H 69
Rivington Dr. LE11: Lou . . . . . . . . . . . . . . . . . . .1K 29
Robert Hall Rd. LE8: Arne . . . . . . . . . . . . . . . . .2H 147
Robert Hall St. LE4: Leic . . . . . . . . . . . . . . . . . .3F 65
Robert Hardy Wharf LE11: Lou . . . . . . . . . . . . .6H 19
Robertsbridge Av. LE4: Leic . . . . . . . . . . . . . . .3E 64
Robertsbridge Wlk. LE4: Leic . . . . . . . . . . . . . .3E 64
Roberts Cl. DE74: Keg . . . . . . . . . . . . . . . . . . . .7H 9
Roberts Dr. NG13: Bott . . . . . . . . . . . . . . . . . .1F 107
Robertson Cl. LE9: S Stan . . . . . . . . . . . . . . . .1J 105
Roberts Rd. LE4: Leic . . . . . . . . . . . . . . . . . . . .5G 65
Robin Cl. LE2: Leic . . . . . . . . . . . . . . . . . . . . . .1E 76
LE15: O'ham . . . . . . . . . . . . . . . . . . . . . . .2K 127
Robin Cres. LE13: Mel M . . . . . . . . . . . . . . . . .7E 116
Robin Hood Pl. DE11: C Gre . . . . . . . . . . . . . . .1A 22
Robinia Cl. LE17: Lut . . . . . . . . . . . . . . . . . . . .5G 153
Robin M. LE11: Lou . . . . . . . . . . . . . . . . . . . . . .7E 18
Robin Rd. LE67: Coal . . . . . . . . . . . . . . . . . . . . .4F 39
Robins Fld. LE67: Ratby . . . . . . . . . . . . . . . . . . .6B 62
Robinson Rd. LE5: Leic . . . . . . . . . . . . . . . . . . .7B 66
LE67: Whit . . . . . . . . . . . . . . . . . . . . . . . . .6D 26
Robinson Way LE10: Bur . . . . . . . . . . . . . . . . .7J 103
LE67: Mark . . . . . . . . . . . . . . . . . . . . . . . . .5H 55
Roborough Grn. LE5: Leic . . . . . . . . . . . . . . . . .1G 73
Robotham Cl. LE9: Hun . . . . . . . . . . . . . . . . . . .2C 80
LE19: Nar . . . . . . . . . . . . . . . . . . . . . . . . . .2F 81
Roby Lea DE74: C Don . . . . . . . . . . . . . . . . . . . .4H 7
Rochdale Cres. LE67: Coal . . . . . . . . . . . . . . . .3K 39
Roche Cl. LE2: Leic . . . . . . . . . . . . . . . . . . . . . .4C 76
Rochester Cl. LE8: Kib H . . . . . . . . . . . . . . . . .1H 89
LE12: Moun . . . . . . . . . . . . . . . . . . . . . . . .4C 44
Rochester Gdns. LE16: Mkt H . . . . . . . . . . . . .6D 150

Rock, The NG32: Bran . . . . . . . . . . . . . .6K **109**
Rockbridge Rd. LE2: Oad . . . . . . . . . .4F **79**
Rockery Cl. LE5: Leic . . . . . . . . . . . . . .7C **66**
Rockhill Dr. LE12: Moun . . . . . . . . . . .4D **44**
ROCKINGHAM . . . . . . . . . . . . . . . . . .2B **164**
Rockingham Cl. LE5: Leic . . . . . . . . . .1D **72**
 LE8: Bla . . . . . . . . . . . . . . . . . . . . .3B **82**
 LE12: Shep . . . . . . . . . . . . . . . . . .1C **28**
 LE65: Ash Z . . . . . . . . . . . . . . . . . .6A **24**
Rockingham Dr. LE13: Mel M . . . . . . .3D **116**
Rockingham Ind. Est. LE16: Mkt H . . .3H **151**
Rockingham Rd. LE11: Lou . . . . . . . . .4C **18**
 LE12: Moun . . . . . . . . . . . . . . . . . .4C **44**
 LE16: C'ott . . . . . . . . . . . . . . . . . .4H **141**
 LE16: L Bow, Mkt H . . . . . . . . . . . .4F **151**
Rockland Ri. LE67: Whit . . . . . . . . . . .5F **27**
Rockleigh Gdns. LE65: Ash Z . . . . . . .5J **23**
Rockley Rd. LE4: Leic . . . . . . . . . . . . .5C **64**
Roecliffe Cl. LE67: Mark . . . . . . . . . .5G **55**
Roecliffe Rd. LE7: Crop . . . . . . . . . . .7E **42**
 LE12: W Eav . . . . . . . . . . . . . . . . .7E **42**
Roedean Cl. LE65: Ash Z . . . . . . . . . .4J **23**
Roehampton Dr. LE18: Wig . . . . . . . .3H **77**
Roesia Cl. LE12: Belt . . . . . . . . . . . . .4H **15**
Rogerstone Rd. LE5: Leic . . . . . . . . .3F **73**
Rogue's La. LE10: Hinc . . . . . . . . . . .5D **98**
 LE15: Cott . . . . . . . . . . . . . . . . . .6B **124**
ROLLESTON . . . . . . . . . . . . . . . . . . .1A **164**
Rolleston Cl. LE16: L Bow . . . . . . . . .4G **151**
Rolleston Rd. LE7: Bill . . . . . . . . . . . .7J **131**
 LE18: Wig . . . . . . . . . . . . . . . . . . .5H **77**
Rolleston St. LE5: Leic . . . . . . . . . . . .1K **71**
Roman Cl. LE9: Des . . . . . . . . . . . . . .2J **95**
 LE9: Earl S . . . . . . . . . . . . . . . . . .1F **101**
 LE17: C Mag . . . . . . . . . . . . . . . . .5C **142**
Roman Hill LE18: Wig . . . . . . . . . . . .1A **84**
Roman Rd. LE4: Birs . . . . . . . . . . . . .1G **65**
Romans, The LE12: Moun . . . . . . . . .3D **44**
Romans Cres. LE67: Coal . . . . . . . . . .3K **39**
Roman St. LE3: Leic . . . . . . . . . . . . . .3D **70**
Roman Way LE7: Sys . . . . . . . . . . . . .3A **60**
 LE16: Mkt H . . . . . . . . . . . . . . . . .4E **150**
Romney Cl. LE10: Hinc . . . . . . . . . . .7D **98**
Romulus Ct. LE19: Brau . . . . . . . . . . .7H **69**
Romway Av. LE5: Leic . . . . . . . . . . . .5A **72**
Romway Cl. LE12: Shep . . . . . . . . . . .7E **16**
Romway Rd. LE5: Leic . . . . . . . . . . . .5A **72**
Rona Gdns. LE5: Leic . . . . . . . . . . . .7G **67**
Ronald Ct. LE2: Leic . . . . . . . . . . . . . .6J **71**
Ronald Toon Rd. LE9: Earl S . . . . . . .2F **101**
Ronald W. Ct. LE11: Lou . . . . . . . . . .2B **30**
Roods, The LE7: R'ley . . . . . . . . . . . .6E **44**
Rookery, The LE6: Groby . . . . . . . . . .3D **62**
 LE12: Bar S . . . . . . . . . . . . . . . . . .3C **32**
 LE15: L'ham . . . . . . . . . . . . . . . . .5D **122**
 LE67: Hea . . . . . . . . . . . . . . . . . . .3F **51**
Rookery Cl. CV13: F Dray . . . . . . . . .1H **97**
 LE8: K Bea . . . . . . . . . . . . . . . . . .3K **89**
Rookery La. LE4: Thurm . . . . . . . . . .7K **59**
 LE6: Groby . . . . . . . . . . . . . . . . . .3C **62**
 LE14: W'ham . . . . . . . . . . . . . . . .1G **121**
 LE15: Stre . . . . . . . . . . . . . . . . . .2K **125**
Rookwell Dr. LE16: L Bow . . . . . . . . .6F **151**
Ropewalk DE74: Keg . . . . . . . . . . . . .6G **9**
ROPSLEY . . . . . . . . . . . . . . . . . . . . .1C **161**
Rosamund Av. LE3: Brau . . . . . . . . . .7A **70**
Rose Acre Cl. LE7: Scra . . . . . . . . . . .7H **67**
Rosebank Rd. LE8: Count . . . . . . . . . .6F **83**
Rosebank Vw. DE12: Mea . . . . . . . . .7D **34**
Rosebarn Way LE5: Leic . . . . . . . . . .5F **67**
Roseberry Av. LE8: K Bea . . . . . . . . .3H **89**
Rosebery Av. LE14: Ash . . . . . . . . . . .2J **115**
Rosebery Rd. LE7: Anst . . . . . . . . . . .7J **57**
Rosebery St. LE5: Leic . . . . . . . . . . . .1K **71**
 LE11: Lou . . . . . . . . . . . . . . . . . . .6D **18**
Rosebury Av. LE13: Mel M . . . . . . . .4G **117**
Rose Cl. LE15: N Luf . . . . . . . . . . . . .1B **136**
Rose Cres. LE3: Leic E . . . . . . . . . . . .5D **68**
Rosecroft Gdns. DE11: Swad . . . . . . .1A **22**
Rose Dale LE17: N Kil . . . . . . . . . . . .2K **155**
Rosedale LE67: Whit . . . . . . . . . . . . . .4E **26**
Rosedale Av. LE4: Leic . . . . . . . . . . . .4K **65**
Rosedale Rd. LE18: Wig . . . . . . . . . . .6B **78**
Rosedene Av. LE4: Thurm . . . . . . . . .7K **59**
Rose Farm Bus. Pk. LE8: Count . . . . .3F **83**
Rose Farm Cl. LE3: Leic . . . . . . . . . . .3K **69**
Rosehill LE11: Lou . . . . . . . . . . . . . . .6A **18**
Rosemary Cres. LE67: Whit . . . . . . . .7G **27**
Rosemary Way LE10: Hinc . . . . . . . . .4E **102**
Rosemead Dr. LE2: Oad . . . . . . . . . . .3C **78**
Rosemoor Cl. LE16: L Bow . . . . . . . .4H **151**
Rosendene Cl. LE9: K Mux . . . . . . . . .3D **68**
Roseneath Av. LE4: Leic . . . . . . . . . .4A **66**
Rose St. LE4: Leic . . . . . . . . . . . . . . . .4F **65**
Rosetree Av. LE4: Birs . . . . . . . . . . . .5G **59**

Roseway CV13: S Gol . . . . . . . . . . . . .3A **98**
 LE4: Leic . . . . . . . . . . . . . . . . . . .3K **65**
Rosewood Cl. LE10: Bur . . . . . . . . . . .5J **103**
Rosewood Way LE11: Lou . . . . . . . . .5D **30**
Roslyn St. LE2: Leic . . . . . . . . . . . . . .3J **71**
Rosminian Way LE7: Coss . . . . . . . . .2B **46**
Rossall Dr. LE65: Ash Z . . . . . . . . . . .4J **23**
Ross Cl. LE13: Mel M . . . . . . . . . . . .2H **117**
Rossendale Rd. LE9: Earl S . . . . . . . .2C **100**
Rossett Dr. LE4: Leic . . . . . . . . . . . . .4D **64**
Rossetti Rd. LE19: End . . . . . . . . . . . .5E **74**
Rosshill Cres. LE5: Leic . . . . . . . . . . .7G **67**
Rosslyn Av. LE12: Moun . . . . . . . . . . .4C **44**
Rosslyn Rd. LE67: Whit . . . . . . . . . . . .7F **27**
Ross's La. LE18: Wig . . . . . . . . . . . . .6K **77**
Ross Wlk. LE4: Leic . . . . . . . . . . . . . .6G **65**
 (not continuous)
Roston Dr. LE10: Hinc . . . . . . . . . . . .2C **102**
ROTHERBY . . . . . . . . . . . .3D **114** (3D **159**)
Rotherby Av. LE4: Leic . . . . . . . . . . . .5K **65**
Rotherby La. LE14: F Wre . . . . . . . . .2E **114**
Rotherby Rd. LE7: Gad . . . . . . . . . . . .1A **118**
Rotherby Top LE14: Roth . . . . . . . . . .3E **114**
Rotherwood Dr. LE65: Ash Z . . . . . . .4K **23**
ROTHLEY . . . . . . . . . . . . .6E **44** (3C **159**)
ROTHLEY PLAIN . . . . . . . . . . . . . . . .4B **44**
Rothley Rd. LE12: Moun . . . . . . . . . . .2E **44**
Rothley Station
 Great Central Railway . . . . . . . . .7B **44**
Rothley St. LE4: Leic . . . . . . . . . . . . .5G **65**
ROTHWELL . . . . . . . . . . . . . . . . . . . .3B **164**
Rouen Way LE65: Ash Z . . . . . . . . . . .5J **23**
Roughton St. LE4: Leic . . . . . . . . . . . .4G **65**
Roundhay Rd. LE3: Leic . . . . . . . . . . .5C **70**
Roundhill LE9: K Mux . . . . . . . . . . . . .2C **68**
Roundhill Cl. LE7: Sys . . . . . . . . . . . .3B **60**
 LE16: L Bow . . . . . . . . . . . . . . . . .5H **151**
Roundhill Rd. LE5: Leic . . . . . . . . . . .4K **71**
Roundhills, The LE9: Elm . . . . . . . . . .5E **100**
Roundhill Way LE11: Lou . . . . . . . . . .7K **17**
Roundway, The LE4: Leic . . . . . . . . . .1B **66**
Routh Av. DE74: C Don . . . . . . . . . . . .6K **7**
Row, The LE14: Roth . . . . . . . . . . . . .4D **114**
Rowan Av. LE12: Hat . . . . . . . . . . . . .7K **13**
 LE16: Mkt H . . . . . . . . . . . . . . . . .6E **150**
 LE67: Coal . . . . . . . . . . . . . . . . . .4H **39**
Rowanberry Av. LE3: Leic . . . . . . . . . .1G **69**
Rowan Cl. DE12: Mea . . . . . . . . . . . .6E **34**
 DE12: Moi . . . . . . . . . . . . . . . . . .5D **22**
Rowan Dr. LE17: Lut . . . . . . . . . . . . .4H **153**
 LE67: Ibs . . . . . . . . . . . . . . . . . . . .4J **51**
Rowans, The LE8: Count . . . . . . . . . . .5E **82**
Rowan St. LE3: Leic . . . . . . . . . . . . . .1C **70**
Rowan Way LE9: Des . . . . . . . . . . . . .2H **95**
 (off St Martin's Dr.)
Rowbank Way LE11: Lou . . . . . . . . . .7K **17**
Rowe Leyes Furlong LE7: R'ley . . . . .3F **45**
Rowena Ct. LE12: Moun . . . . . . . . . . .4E **44**
Rowena Dr. LE65: Ash Z . . . . . . . . . .4K **23**
Rowlands, The LE67: Cole . . . . . . . . . .6J **25**
Rowlandson Cl. LE4: Leic . . . . . . . . . .4D **58**
Rowlands Way LE2: G Par . . . . . . . . .6B **76**
Rowlatts Hill Rd. LE5: Leic . . . . . . . . .1B **72**
Rowley Cl. LE8: Flec . . . . . . . . . . . . . .5C **88**
ROWLEY FIELDS . . . . . . . . . . . . . . . .5B **70**
Rowley Fields Av. LE3: Leic . . . . . . . .6B **70**
Rowlinson Ct. LE3: Leic . . . . . . . . . . .5A **64**
Rowsley Av. LE5: Leic . . . . . . . . . . . . .3K **71**
Rowsley St. LE5: Leic . . . . . . . . . . . . .4J **71**
Royal Arc. LE1: Leic . . . . . . . . . . . . . .3C **4**
Royal Ct. LE10: Hinc . . . . . . . . . . . . .4G **103**
 LE19: Nar . . . . . . . . . . . . . . . . . . .1G **81**
Royal E. St. LE1: Leic . . . . . . .1D **4** (7F **65**)
Royal Kent St. LE1: Leic . . . . . .1B **4** (7E **64**)
Royal Leicestershire Mus., The . . .5B **4** (2E **70**)
Royal Oak Cl. LE67: Ibs . . . . . . . . . . .5J **51**
Royal Rd. LE4: Leic . . . . . . . . . . . . . .4H **65**
Royal Way LE11: Lou . . . . . . . . . . . . .4E **18**
Royce Cl. LE3: Brau . . . . . . . . . . . . . .5G **69**
Roy Cl. LE19: Nar . . . . . . . . . . . . . . . .1G **81**
Roydale Cl. LE11: Lou . . . . . . . . . . . .4C **18**
Roydene Cres. LE4: Leic . . . . . . . . . . .4C **64**
Royland Rd. LE11: Lou . . . . . . . . . . . .7F **19**
Royston Cl. LE2: Leic . . . . . . . . . . . . .6D **76**
Rubicon Cl. LE12: Moun . . . . . . . . . . .3F **45**
Ruby St. LE3: Leic . . . . . . . . . . . . . . . .1C **70**
Rudbeck Av. LE13: Mel M . . . . . . . . .4D **116**
RUDDINGTON . . . . . . . . . . . . . . . . . .1C **159**
Ruddington Wlk. LE4: Leic . . . . . . . . .2E **64**
Ruddle Way LE15: L'ham . . . . . . . . . .5C **122**
Ruding Rd. LE3: Leic . . . . . . . . . . . . . .3D **70**
Ruding St. LE3: Leic . . . . . . . . .3A **4** (1E **70**)
 (not continuous)
Rudyard Cl. LE11: Lou . . . . . . . . . . . .1K **29**
Rufford Cl. LE10: Bur . . . . . . . . . . . . .7G **103**
 LE11: Lou . . . . . . . . . . . . . . . . . . .5K **17**
Rufford St. LE5: Leic . . . . . . . . . . . . . .1A **72**

RUGBY . . . . . . . . . . . . . . . . . . . . . . . .3C **163**
Rugby Cl. LE16: Mkt H . . . . . . . . . . . .5D **150**
 LE65: Ash Z . . . . . . . . . . . . . . . . .3J **23**
Rugby Rd. LE10: Bur, Hinc . . . . . . . . .3F **103**
 LE17: C'ach, Lut . . . . . . . . . . . . . .7B **154**
 LE17: Lut . . . . . . . . . . . . . . . . . . .5J **153**
 LE17: S Kil . . . . . . . . . . . . . . . . . .7F **155**
 LE17: S Kil, Swin . . . . . . . . . . . . . .2J **157**
 LE17: Swin . . . . . . . . . . . . . . . . . .4F **157**
Rugby St. LE3: Leic . . . . . . . . . . . . . .7D **64**
Rumsey Cl. LE12: Quo . . . . . . . . . . . .5J **31**
 LE67: Thrin . . . . . . . . . . . . . . . . . .3C **26**
Rumsey Dr. LE8: Whet . . . . . . . . . . . .1A **82**
Runcorn Cl. LE2: Leic . . . . . . . . . . . . .5C **76**
Runcorn Rd. LE2: Leic . . . . . . . . . . . .5D **76**
Runnymede Gdns. LE3: Glen . . . . . . .7H **63**
Rupert Brooke Rd. LE11: Lou . . . . . . .6B **18**
Rupert Cres. LE7: Quen . . . . . . . . . . .6G **47**
Rupert Law Cl. LE12: Quo . . . . . . . . .4K **31**
Rupert Rd. LE16: Mkt H . . . . . . . . . . .6E **150**
Rupert St. LE1: Leic . . . . . . . . .5C **4** (2F **71**)
Ruperts Way LE8: G Gle . . . . . . . . . . .1K **85**
Rushby Rd. LE67: Ell . . . . . . . . . . . . .2E **52**
Rush Cl. LE9: N Ver . . . . . . . . . . . . . .7H **93**
Rushden Ho. LE3: Glen . . . . . . . . . . . .1G **69**
Rushes, The LE11: Lou . . . . . . . . . . . .6E **18**
 LE67: Mark . . . . . . . . . . . . . . . . . .4G **55**
Rushes La. LE16: Lub . . . . . . . . . . . . .7H **149**
Rushes Shop. Cen., The LE11: Lou . . .6E **18**
Rushey Cl. CV13: B'one . . . . . . . . . . .6C **92**
 LE4: Leic . . . . . . . . . . . . . . . . . . .2J **65**
Rushey La. LE7: R'ley . . . . . . . . . . . .2B **44**
RUSHEY MEAD . . . . . . . . . . . . . . . . .1A **66**
Rushford Cl. LE4: Leic . . . . . . . . . . . .5K **65**
Rushford Dr. LE4: Leic . . . . . . . . . . . .5K **65**
Rushmere Wlk. LE3: Leic E . . . . . . . .5E **68**
RUSHTON . . . . . . . . . . . . . . . . . . . . .3B **164**
Rushton Dr. LE2: Leic . . . . . . . . . . . . .4B **76**
Ruskin Av. LE7: Sys . . . . . . . . . . . . . .3E **60**
Ruskington Dr. LE18: Wig . . . . . . . . . .3K **77**
Russ Cl. LE12: Quo . . . . . . . . . . . . . . .4K **31**
Russell Ct. LE2: Leic . . . . . . . . . . . . . .2C **76**
Russell Sq. LE1: Leic . . . . . . . . . . . . .7G **65**
Russell St. LE11: Lou . . . . . . . . . . . . .6G **19**
Russett Cl. LE9: Barw . . . . . . . . . . . . .3F **95**
 LE16: Mkt H . . . . . . . . . . . . . . . . .2F **151**
Russett Way LE4: Birs . . . . . . . . . . . .4J **59**
Rutherford Rd. LE4: Beau L . . . . . . . .1A **64**
Rutland Av. LE2: Leic . . . . . . . . . . . . .6E **70**
 LE10: Hinc . . . . . . . . . . . . . . . . . .4F **103**
 LE18: Wig . . . . . . . . . . . . . . . . . . .5H **77**
Rutland Cen. LE1: Leic . . . . . . .3E **4** (1G **71**)
Rutland Cl. LE3: Leic E . . . . . . . . . . . .4E **68**
 LE15: Upp . . . . . . . . . . . . . . . . . .1B **138**
Rutland Dr. LE4: Thurm . . . . . . . . . . .6A **60**
Rutland Ho. LE13: Mel M . . . . . . . . . .4G **117**
 (off Rutland St.)
Rutland La. NG13: Bott . . . . . . . . . . . .2H **107**
Rutland Sailing Club . . . . . . . . . . . . .2F **135**
Rutland Sq. NG13: Bark V . . . . . . . . .3B **106**
Rutland St. LE1: Leic . . . . . . . .4D **4** (2F **71**)
 (not continuous)
 LE11: Lou . . . . . . . . . . . . . . . . . . .7G **19**
 LE13: Mel M . . . . . . . . . . . . . . . . .4G **117**
Rutland Wlk. LE16: Mkt H . . . . . . . . .2F **151**
Rutland Water Butterfly Farm . . . . . . .7A **128**
Rutland Way PE9: Ryh . . . . . . . . . . . .6G **129**
Rydal Av. LE11: Lou . . . . . . . . . . . . . .2B **30**
Rydal Cl. LE10: Hinc . . . . . . . . . . . . .4C **102**
Rydal Gdns. LE65: Ash Z . . . . . . . . . .7A **24**
Rydal St. LE2: Leic . . . . . . . . .7A **5** (3E **70**)
Ryde Av. LE2: Leic . . . . . . . . . . . . . . .1K **77**
Ryder Rd. LE3: Leic . . . . . . . . . . . . . .1G **69**
Ryderway LE17: Lut . . . . . . . . . . . . . .5H **153**
Rye Cl. LE2: Leic . . . . . . . . . . . . . . . .4E **76**
Ryecroft Rd. DE74: Hem . . . . . . . . . . .1B **8**
Ryefield LE15: O'ham . . . . . . . . . . . . .2J **127**
Ryegate Cres. LE4: Birs . . . . . . . . . . .5F **59**
Rye Hill Av. LE17: Lut . . . . . . . . . . . . .5K **153**
Ryelands Cl. LE16: L Bow . . . . . . . . .3H **151**
RYHALL . . . . . . . . . . . . . . .5H **129** (3D **161**)
Ryhall Rd. PE9: G Cas . . . . . . . . . . . .2J **137**
RYLANDS . . . . . . . . . . . . . . . . . . . . .1C **159**
RYTON . . . . . . . . . . . . . . . . . . . . . . . .3A **162**

**S**

Sacheverell Way LE6: Groby . . . . . . . .5B **62**
Sacheverel Rd. LE3: Leic . . . . . . . . . .1H **69**
Sackville Gdns. LE2: Leic . . . . . . . . . .7J **71**
SADDINGTON . . . . . . . . . . . .7D **88** (2D **163**)
Saddington Rd. LE8: Flec . . . . . . . . . .4B **88**
 LE8: Smee W . . . . . . . . . . . . . . . . .5F **89**
 LE17: Mows . . . . . . . . . . . . . . . . .2B **148**
 LE17: Shea . . . . . . . . . . . . . . . . . .5K **147**
Saddle Cl. LE13: Mel M . . . . . . . . . . .2D **116**

Saddler Rd.—Sandringham Way


Saddler Rd. LE5: Ham 3E 66
Saddlers Cl. LE3: Glen 6F 63
LE7: East G 5F 47
LE10: Bur 5J 103
LE11: Lou 4D 18
Sadlers Wells LE12: Belt 4H 15
Saffron Cl. LE9: Barw 2B 100
Saffron Ct. LE2: Leic 3F 77
LE9: Barw 4K 99
Saffron Hill Rd. LE2: Leic 7E 70
Saffron La. LE2: Leic 5E 70
Saffron Lane Sports Cen. 6F 71
Saffron Rd. LE18: Wig 5E 76
Saffron Way LE2: Leic 2E 76
Sage Cross St. LE13: Mel M 4F 117
Sage Rd. LE2: Leic 7A 5 (3D 70)
Sahara Cl. LE4: Leic 3H 65
St Aidan's Av. LE7: Sys 2B 60
St Albans Cl. LE15: O'ham 4J 127
St Albans Rd. LE2: Leic 7G 5 (3H 71)
St Andrews Cl. LE12: Bur W 3G 21
LE15: Whis 2C 122
LE16: G Eas 5K 141
LE67: Thrin 3D 26
St Andrews Dr. LE2: Leic 6B 72
St Andrew's Ri. DE74: Keg 7G 9
St Andrew's Rd. LE2: Leic 1E 76
St Annes Cl. LE7: Sys 3E 60
LE15: O'ham 4H 127
St Anne's Dr. LE2: Leic 2D 76
St Anne's La. DE74: C Don 5K 7
St Augustine Rd. LE3: Leic 4A 4 (2D 70)
St Austell Rd. LE5: Leic 7G 67
St Barnabas Rd. LE5: Leic 1A 72
St Bartholomews Way
LE14: Mel M, Welb 1B 116
St Bernard's Av. LE4: Leic 3H 65
St Bernard's Cl. LE12: Shep 7C 16
St Bernard's Rd. LE67: Whit 7F 27
St Bernard St. LE4: Leic 4H 65
St Botolph Rd. LE12: Shep 7D 16
Saintbury Rd. LE3: Glen 5H 63
St Catharines Ter. LE7: Hou H 2C 130
St Catharines Way LE7: Hou H 3C 130
St Catherines Av. CV13: Mkt B 2C 94
St Catherine's Cl. LE10: Bur 4J 103
St Christophers Pk. Homes
LE67: Ell 3E 52
St Christopher's Rd. LE67: Ell 3E 52
St Clares Ct. LE67: Coal 4E 38
St Columba Way LE7: Sys 1B 60
St Crispins Way LE4: Thurm 4A 60
St Cuthbert's Av. LE8: G Gle 1K 85
St Davids Cl. LE3: Leic E 4D 68
St David's Ct. LE67: Coal 3J 39
St David's Cres. LE2: Leic 6A 72
LE67: Coal 2J 39
St David's Rd. LE3: Leic 1G 69
St Denys' Cres. LE67: Ibs 4J 51
St Denys Rd. LE5: Leic 3D 72
St Dunstan Rd. LE3: Leic 1C 70
St Edward's Rd. DE74: C Don 6K 7
St Faiths Rd. LE67: Coal 5C 38
St Francis Cl. LE10: Hinc 7F 99
St George's Av. LE10: Hinc 2F 103
St Georges Cl. LE9: N Ver 5G 93
St George's Hill LE67: Swan 4A 26
St George's Retail Pk.
LE1: Leic 3G 4 (1H 71)
St George St. LE1: Leic 4F 4 (2G 71)
St George's Way LE1: Leic 4F 4 (2G 71)
St Giles Cl. CV13: B'one 5C 92
St Gregorys Dr. LE12: Sileby 1K 45
ST HELENA 1A 162
St Helens Cl. LE4: Leic 5C 64
LE10: S'ord 6H 105
St Helens Dr. LE4: Leic 5D 64
St Hilda's Cl. LE7: Sys 3E 60
St Ives LE67: Coal 4H 39
St Ives Rd. LE4: Leic 4A 66
LE18: Wig 7J 77
St James Cl. CV9: Twy 3C 90
LE2: Oad 5E 78
LE9: Hun 2B 80
LE12: Shep 1D 28
St James Ct. *LE2: Leic 4J 71*
*(off St James Rd.)*
LE4: Birs 6H 59
St James Rd. LE2: Leic 4J 71
LE12: Shep 7D 16
St James's Cl. LE10: Bur 6G 103
St James St. LE1: Leic 2E 4 (1G 71)
St James Ter. LE2: Leic 4J 71
St John Bus. Pk. LE17: Lut 5K 153
St Johns LE10: Hinc 2H 103
LE19: End 6H 75
St John's Av. LE7: Sys 2E 60
St John's Cl. LE17: Lut 5H 153
LE67: Hea 3F 51
LE67: Hug 6D 38
PE9: Ryh 5H 129
St Johns Ct. LE13: Mel M 4G 117
St Johns Dr. LE13: Mel M 2F 117
St Johns Rd. LE2: Leic 5J 71
LE14: Ash H 4A 116
St John St. LE1: Leic 1C 4 (7F 65)
St Johns Wlk. LE1: Leic 5E 4
St Leonards Cl. LE12: Bur W 3G 21
St Leonard's Ct. LE2: Leic 10G 5 (5H 71)
St Leonard's Rd. LE2: Leic 5H 71
St Luke's Cl. LE7: Thurn 3H 73
St Margaret Rd. CV13: S Gol 3B 98
St Margarets Dr. LE17: Leire 3J 143
St Margarets Pastures Sports Cen. 1A 4 (7E 64)
St Margaret's St. LE1: Leic 1C 4 (7F 65)
St Margaret's Way LE1: Leic 1B 4 (7E 64)
LE4: Leic 6E 64
St Mark's St. LE1: Leic 1E 4 (7G 65)
St Martins LE1: Leic 4C 4 (2F 71)
LE9: Stap 1H 99
LE10: Bur 5G 103
St Martin's Dr. LE9: Des 2G 95
St Martins E. LE1: Leic 4C 4 (2F 71)
St Martins Sq. LE1: Leic 4C 4
St Martins Sq. Shop. Cen. LE1: Leic 4C 4 (2F 71)
St Martins Wlk. LE1: Leic 4C 4
(Cank St.)
LE1: Leic 4B 4 (2E 70)
(Guildhall La.)
St Mary's Av. LE3: Brau 4G 69
LE5: Leic 6E 66
LE9: Barw 5J 99
LE67: D Hea 6B 38
St Mary's Bus. Pk. LE16: Mkt H 3F 151
St Marys Cl. CV13: Con 6G 91
LE9: B Ast 4C 86
LE11: Lou 6D 18
LE12: Bur W 3G 21
LE12: Osg 6E 14
*LE13: Mel M 4F 117*
*(off St Mary's Way)*
LE15: E Wes 3G 135
NG13: Bott 1H 107
St Mary's Ct. LE3: Brau 4G 69
LE5: Leic 6E 66
LE9: Barw 4K 99
*LE16: Mkt H 3G 151*
*(off Middlebrook Grn.)*
LE67: D Hea 6B 38
St Mary's La. LE67: Rav 5K 37
*NG13: Bott 2H 107*
*(off Church St.)*
St Mary's Pl. LE16: Mkt H 4F 151
St Mary's Rd. LE2: Leic 5H 71
LE10: Hinc 3G 103
LE12: Sileby 7J 33
LE15: Mant 2B 134
LE16: Mkt H 4E 150
LE17: Lut 4H 153
St Mary's Way LE13: Mel M 4F 117
ST MATTHEW'S 1F 4 (7G 65)
St Matthew's Av. LE65: Wort 2B 14
St Matthews Bus. Cen. LE1: Leic 1E 4
St Matthew's Way LE1: Leic 1E 4 (7G 65)
St Maxine Ct. LE2: Leic 6J 71
St Mellion Cl. LE4: Beau L 6B 58
St Michael's Av. LE4: Leic 3H 65
St Michael's Cl. LE65: Ash Z 6A 24
LE67: Mark 4F 55
St Michaels Ct. LE4: Thurm 6K 59
LE9: S Stan 1J 105
St Michael's Dr. DE12: A Mag 5B 48
St Michaels' Dr. LE67: Rav 4J 37
St Nicholas Circ. LE1: Leic 4A 4 (2E 70)
St Nicholas Cl. LE16: L Bow 5F 151
St Nicholas Ct. LE15: Cott 6A 124
St Nicholas Pl. LE1: Leic 4B 4 (2E 70)
St Nicholas Wlk. *LE1: Leic 3A 4*
*(off St Nicholas Circ.)*
St Nicholas Way LE16: L Bow 5F 151
St Olaves Cl. LE11: Lou 5K 17
St Oswalds Rd. LE3: Leic 7K 63
St Pauls Cl. LE2: Oad 2F 79
St Pauls Ct. LE7: Sys 1D 60
St Paul's Dr. LE7: Sys 3C 60
St Paul's Gdns. LE10: Hinc 2H 103
St Pauls Rd. LE3: Leic 1C 70
St Peter's Av. CV9: With 6B 96
LE12: Hat 1J 17
St Peter's Cl. CV9: With 6B 96
CV13: Mkt B 2B 94
LE3: Glen 6F 63
LE15: O'ham 4J 127
LE17: Leire 2K 143
St Peter's Ct. CV13: Mkt B 2D 94
LE7: Sys 1D 60
St Peter's Dr. LE8: Whet 1K 81
LE67: Thor 3K 93
St Peter's La. LE1: Leic 3B 4 (1E 70)
St Peters Path LE2: Oad 3C 78
St Peters Pl. CV13: S'one 3H 91
St Peters Rd. CV9: Manc 6A 96
LE2: Leic 3H 71
LE8: Arne 2H 147
St Peter's St. LE7: Sys 2C 60
St Peters Ter. LE7: T Hil 2H 131
St Peters Wlk. LE13: Mel M 3E 116
St Philips Rd. LE12: Bur W 3G 21
St Phillip's Rd. LE5: Leic 4K 71
St Saviour's Hill LE5: Leic 1J 71
St Saviours Rd. LE5: Leic 1J 71
LE67: Coal 4C 38
St Saviour's Wlk. LE5: Leic 2B 72
St Stephens Rd. LE2: Leic 3J 71
St Swithin's Rd. LE5: Leic 2F 73
St Thomas Rd. LE18: Wig 7E 76
St Thomas's Rd. LE8: G Gle 5A 130
St Tibba Way PE9: Ryh 6G 129
St Vincents Cl. LE67: Coal 5C 38
St Wilfrid's Cl. LE8: K Bea 2J 89
St Winefride Rd. LE12: Shep 7D 16
St Winifreds Ct. NG11: King S 4K 9
St Wolstan's Cl. LE18: Wig 5K 77
Salcombe Cl. LE18: Wig 7J 77
Salcombe Dr. LE3: Glen 6G 63
Salem Rd. LE10: Bur 6J 103
Salisbury Av. LE1: Leic 7G 5 (3H 71)
LE9: Crof 5A 80
LE13: Mel M 3G 117
Salisbury Cl. LE8: Bla 3B 82
LE9: Des 3H 95
Salisbury Rd. LE1: Leic 8G 5 (4H 71)
LE10: Bur 4K 103
Salisbury Rd. Backways LE1: Leic 7G 5
Salisbury St. LE11: Lou 6G 19
Salkeld Rd. LE2: Leic 6C 76
Salmon M. LE12: Shep 6D 16
Saltash Cl. LE18: Wig 7J 77
SALTBY 2B 160
Saltby Rd. LE14: Spro 1G 113
NG32: Crox 6H 107
Saltcoats Av. LE4: Leic 2J 65
Salter Cl. DE74: C Don 4H 7
Saltersagte Dr. LE4: Birs 5G 59
Saltersford Rd. LE5: Leic 7B 66
Saltersgate Dr. LE4: Birs 5G 59
Salter's Hill Dr. LE14: T Sat 3H 119
Salts Cl. LE19: End 6F 75
Samphire Cl. LE5: Ham 4F 67
Samson Rd. LE3: Leic 7B 64
LE67: Coal 1D 38
Samuel Ct. LE15: Upp 1B 138
Samuel St. LE1: Leic 3G 4 (1H 71)
Sandacre St. LE1: Leic 2C 4 (1F 71)
Sandalwood Rd. LE11: Lou 2C 30
Sanderson Cl. LE8: Whet 3A 82
Sanders Rd. LE12: Quo 5K 31
Sandfield Cl. LE4: Leic 1A 66
Sandford Cl. LE5: Leic 1C 72
LE10: Hinc 2J 103
Sandford Ct. LE5: Leic 1C 72
Sandford Rd. LE7: Sys 2C 60
Sand Furrows PE9: Ket 6G 137
Sandgate Av. LE4: Birs 5F 59
Sandham Bri. Rd. LE7: Crop 2K 57
Sandhill Dr. LE19: End 7H 75
Sandhills, The LE12: Quo 5J 31
Sandhills Av. LE5: Ham 3C 66
Sandhills Cl. DE12: Mea 1E 48
LE12: Belt 4H 15
Sandhole La. LE12: Shep 3K 27
Sandhurst Cl. LE3: Leic 1B 70
Sandhurst Gdns. LE3: Leic 1B 70
Sandhurst Rd. LE3: Leic 7B 64
Sandhurst St. LE2: Oad 2C 78
SANDIACRE 1B 158
Sandiacre Dr. LE4: Thurm 5B 60
Sandown Ct. LE3: Glen 5G 63
Sandown Rd. LE2: Leic 6K 71
LE3: Glen 5G 63
LE18: Wig 4K 77
Sandpiper Cl. LE5: Leic 7J 65
Sand Pit La. LE14: L Cla 2H 111
Sandringham Av. LE4: Leic 3H 65
LE9: Earl S 3C 100
Sandringham Cl. LE15: O'ham 5G 127
Sandringham Dr. LE11: Lou 5B 18
Sandringham Ri. LE12: Shep 1B 28
Sandringham Rd. LE2: G Par 7E 76
LE67: Coal 4F 39
Sandringham Way LE16: L Bow 5H 151


A-Z Leicestershire Atlas 211

Sands, The. LE14: L Cla . . . . . . . . . . . .2J **111**
Sandtop Cl. DE11: Blac . . . . . . . . . . . .3D **22**
Sandtop La. DE11: Blac . . . . . . . . . . . .3D **22**
Sandy Cres. LE10: Hinc . . . . . . . . . . . .2F **103**
Sandy La. LE13: Mel M . . . . . . . . . . . .6F **117**
   LE14: Mel M . . . . . . . . . . . .1A **120**
   LE14: Scal . . . . . . . . . . . .6C **112**
Sandy Ri. LE18: Wig . . . . . . . . . . . .4B **78**
Sandy Wlk. LE10: Hinc . . . . . . . . . . . .1E **102**
Sankey Dr. DE11: A Vil . . . . . . . . . . . .2A **22**
Sanvey Cl. LE2: Leic . . . . . . . . . . . .2C **76**
Sanvey Ga. LE1: Leic . . . . . . . . . . .2A **4** (1E **70**)
Sanvey La. LE2: Leic . . . . . . . . . . . .2B **76**
SAPCOTE . . . . . . . . . . . .4J **105** (2B **162**)
Sapcote Ct. LE13: Mel M . . . . . . . . . . . .6G **117**
Sapcote Dr. LE13: Mel M . . . . . . . . . . . .6H **117**
Sapcote Ind. Est. LE10: Bur . . . . . . . . . . . .4K **103**
Sapcote Rd. LE9: S Stan . . . . . . . . . . . .1K **105**
   LE10: Bur . . . . . . . . . . . .4K **103**
SAPPERTON . . . . . . . . . . . .1D **161**
Sarson Cl. LE4: Ash . . . . . . . . . . . .3H **115**
Sarson St. LE12: Quo . . . . . . . . . . . .5K **31**
Sarvodaya Samaj . . . . . . . . . . . .6G **5**
Saunderson Rd. LE4: Leic . . . . . . . . . . . .2D **64**
Savernake Rd. LE4: Leic . . . . . . . . . . . .5C **64**
Saville Cl. LE10: Hinc . . . . . . . . . . . .7H **99**
Saville Dr. LE12: Sileby . . . . . . . . . . . .2J **45**
Saville Rd. LE8: Bla . . . . . . . . . . . .3C **82**
Saville St. LE5: Leic . . . . . . . . . . . .1A **72**
Sawbridge Cl. LE67: Ell . . . . . . . . . . . .2E **52**
Sawbrook LE8: Flec . . . . . . . . . . . .4C **88**
Sawday St. LE2: Leic . . . . . . . . . . .9B **5** (4E **70**)
Sawgate Rd. LE14: Bur L . . . . . . . . . . . .1D **120**
SAWLEY . . . . . . . . . . . .1B **158**
Sawley St. LE5: Leic . . . . . . . . . . . .4K **71**
SAXBY . . . . . . . . . . . .2B **160**
Saxby Rd. LE13: Mel M . . . . . . . . . . . .4G **117**
   LE14: Bren . . . . . . . . . . . .4G **117**
Saxby St. LE2: Leic . . . . . . . . . . .6G **5** (3H **71**)
SAXELBY . . . . . . . . . . . .2D **159**
Saxelby Rd. LE14: Ash . . . . . . . . . . . .1F **115**
Saxilby Rd. LE14: Ab K . . . . . . . . . . . .7F **111**
Saxon Cl. DE73: B Hil . . . . . . . . . . . .7B **10**
   LE16: Mkt H . . . . . . . . . . . .3F **151**
SAXONDALE . . . . . . . . . . . .1D **159**
Saxon Dale LE2: G Par . . . . . . . . . . . .6C **76**
Saxondale Rd. LE18: Wig . . . . . . . . . . . .1A **84**
Saxons Ri. LE6: Ratby . . . . . . . . . . . .5A **62**
Saxon St. LE3: Leic . . . . . . . . . . . .3D **70**
Saxon Way LE65: Ash Z . . . . . . . . . . . .4J **23**
Saxthorpe Rd. LE5: Ham . . . . . . . . . . . .4D **66**
Scalborough Cl. LE8: Count . . . . . . . . . . . .5C **82**
SCALFORD . . . . . . . . . . . .6C **112** (2A **160**)
Scalford Rd. LE13: Mel M . . . . . . . . . . . .1F **117**
Scallywags Adventureland . . . . . . . . . . . .1F **101**
Scalpay Cl. LE4: Leic . . . . . . . . . . . .3B **64**
Scarborough Rd. LE4: Leic . . . . . . . . . . . .4H **65**
SCARRINGTON . . . . . . . . . . . .1A **160**
Schofield Rd. LE11: Lou . . . . . . . . . . . .7A **18**
   LE15: O'ham . . . . . . . . . . . .2J **127**
Scholars Wlk. LE2: Leic . . . . . . . . . . . .5J **71**
School Cl. DE11: A Vil . . . . . . . . . . . .2A **22**
   LE9: Crof . . . . . . . . . . . .6A **80**
   LE10: Bur . . . . . . . . . . . .5K **103**
School Cres. LE9: B Ast . . . . . . . . . . . .3C **86**
Schoolgate LE2: Leic . . . . . . . . . . . .3F **77**
School Hill LE12: Walt W . . . . . . . . . . . .6G **21**
   LE14: Spro . . . . . . . . . . . .2H **113**
School Ho. Cl. LE7: Anst . . . . . . . . . . . .1H **63**
School La. DE74: C Don . . . . . . . . . . . .4J **7**
   LE4: Birs . . . . . . . . . . . .7G **59**
   LE5: Leic . . . . . . . . . . . .5D **72**
   LE7: Bark . . . . . . . . . . . .5F **61**
   LE7: Hou H . . . . . . . . . . . .3C **130**
   LE7: Quen . . . . . . . . . . . .7H **47**
   LE7: S Cro . . . . . . . . . . . .7A **118**
   LE8: Peat M . . . . . . . . . . . .1K **147**
   LE9: Hun . . . . . . . . . . . .2B **80**
   LE10: S'ord . . . . . . . . . . . .7H **105**
   LE12: Belt . . . . . . . . . . . .4H **15**
   LE12: Quo . . . . . . . . . . . .6A **32**
   LE12: Wood . . . . . . . . . . . .2F **43**
   LE14: Harb . . . . . . . . . . . .2C **108**
   LE14: L Bow . . . . . . . . . . . .2H **111**
   LE14: Scal . . . . . . . . . . . .7C **112**
   LE14: Sta . . . . . . . . . . . .3H **109**
   LE15: B'den . . . . . . . . . . . .7D **136**
   LE15: Emp . . . . . . . . . . . .6D **128**
   LE15: Mor . . . . . . . . . . . .6J **135**
   LE15: Upp . . . . . . . . . . . .2C **138**
   LE16: Lub . . . . . . . . . . . .7J **149**
   LE16: Mkt H . . . . . . . . . . . .4E **150**
   LE17: H Bos . . . . . . . . . . . .6C **148**
   LE17: Swin . . . . . . . . . . . .3G **157**
   LE19: Nar . . . . . . . . . . . .2G **81**
   LE67: Cole . . . . . . . . . . . .2A **26**
   LE67: N Bur . . . . . . . . . . . .6C **50**

School La. LE67: New . . . . . . . . . . . .1J **25**
   LE67: Nor H . . . . . . . . . . . .6D **36**
   LE67: Whit . . . . . . . . . . . .5D **26**
   NG32: Crox . . . . . . . . . . . .6G **107**
   NG33: Buck, Sew . . . . . . . . . . . .5H **113**
School Rd. LE8: K Bea . . . . . . . . . . . .3J **89**
   LE15: O'ham . . . . . . . . . . . .3J **127**
School St. DE12: Moi . . . . . . . . . . . .2B **34**
   DE12: Oak . . . . . . . . . . . .5C **34**
   LE7: R'ley . . . . . . . . . . . .6F **45**
   LE7: Sys . . . . . . . . . . . .1D **60**
   LE8: Flec . . . . . . . . . . . .4B **88**
   LE11: Lou . . . . . . . . . . . .6F **19**
School Vw. NG13: Bott . . . . . . . . . . . .2G **107**
School Wlk. LE8: K Bea . . . . . . . . . . . .3J **89**
Scotland La. LE7: Hou H . . . . . . . . . . . .2C **130**
   LE8: Bur O . . . . . . . . . . . .5D **130**
Scotland Rd. LE16: L Bow . . . . . . . . . . . .6F **151**
Scotlands Dr. LE67: Coal . . . . . . . . . . . .4D **38**
Scotlands Ind. Est. LE67: Coal . . . . . . . . . . . .4E **38**
Scotlands Rd. LE67: Coal . . . . . . . . . . . .4D **38**
Scotland Way LE8: Count . . . . . . . . . . . .6F **83**
Scotswood Cres. LE2: Leic . . . . . . . . . . . .5C **76**
Scott Cl. LE15: Upp . . . . . . . . . . . .3C **138**
   LE16: Mkt H . . . . . . . . . . . .2E **150**
   LE65: Ash Z . . . . . . . . . . . .4J **23**
Scott Ct. LE2: Leic . . . . . . . . . . . .7G **71**
SCOTTLETHORPE . . . . . . . . . . . .2D **161**
Scott St. LE2: Leic . . . . . . . . . . . .7G **71**
SCRAPTOFT . . . . . . . . . . . .6H **67** (1D **163**)
Scraptoft La. LE5: Leic . . . . . . . . . . . .7C **66**
   LE7: Bee . . . . . . . . . . . .3K **67**
   LE7: Scra . . . . . . . . . . . .6G **67**
Scraptoft M. LE5: Leic . . . . . . . . . . . .7C **66**
Scraptoft Ri. LE7: Scra . . . . . . . . . . . .6H **67**
Scraptoft Wlk. LE5: Leic . . . . . . . . . . . .6F **67**
SCREDINGTON . . . . . . . . . . . .1D **161**
SCREVETON . . . . . . . . . . . .1A **160**
Scrivener Cl. LE7: Bush . . . . . . . . . . . .2J **73**
Scudamore Rd. LE3: Leic . . . . . . . . . . . .2F **69**
Sculthorpe Cl. LE15: O'ham . . . . . . . . . . . .4K **127**
Seacole Cl. LE3: Brau . . . . . . . . . . . .5H **69**
Seaford Rd. LE2: Leic . . . . . . . . . . . .3D **76**
Seaforth Dr. LE10: Hinc . . . . . . . . . . . .2D **102**
SEAGRAVE . . . . . . . . . . . .3K **33** (3D **159**)
Seagrave Cl. LE67: Coal . . . . . . . . . . . .3J **39**
Seagrave Dr. LE2: Oad . . . . . . . . . . . .2B **78**
Seagrave Rd. LE7: Thru . . . . . . . . . . . .6A **114**
   LE12: Sileby . . . . . . . . . . . .7J **33** & 4J **33**
Seals Cl. LE12: Bur W . . . . . . . . . . . .3G **21**
Seals Rd. DE12: Don . . . . . . . . . . . .3A **34**
SEATON . . . . . . . . . . . .5K **139** (2C **165**)
Seaton Cl. LE10: Bur . . . . . . . . . . . .4A **104**
Seaton Dr. LE15: Upp . . . . . . . . . . . .2D **138**
Seaton Ri. LE5: Leic . . . . . . . . . . . .5G **67**
Seaton Rd. LE3: Brau . . . . . . . . . . . .6G **69**
   LE15: B'den . . . . . . . . . . . .7B **136**
   LE15: Glas . . . . . . . . . . . .1J **139**
   LE15: Seat, Upp . . . . . . . . . . . .2D **138**
   LE18: Wig . . . . . . . . . . . .7J **77**
SECKINGTON . . . . . . . . . . . .1A **162**
Seddons Cl. LE4: Leic . . . . . . . . . . . .2D **64**
SEDGEBROOK . . . . . . . . . . . .1B **160**
Sedgebrook Cl. LE5: Leic . . . . . . . . . . . .3G **73**
Sedgebrook Rd. LE5: Leic . . . . . . . . . . . .3F **73**
Sedgefield Dr. LE7: Sys . . . . . . . . . . . .2A **60**
   LE7: Thurn . . . . . . . . . . . .1H **73**
Segrave Rd. LE3: Leic . . . . . . . . . . . .5B **70**
Seine La. LE19: End . . . . . . . . . . . .4D **74**
Selbourne Ct. LE11: Lou . . . . . . . . . . . .6G **19**
Selbourne St. LE11: Lou . . . . . . . . . . . .6G **19**
Selbury Dr. LE2: Oad . . . . . . . . . . . .3B **78**
Selby Av. LE5: Leic . . . . . . . . . . . .5F **67**
Selby Cl. LE16: Mkt H . . . . . . . . . . . .7E **150**
Selina Cl. DE74: C Don . . . . . . . . . . . .4J **7**
Selkirk Rd. LE4: Leic . . . . . . . . . . . .2K **65**
Selvester Dr. LE12: Quo . . . . . . . . . . . .6B **32**
Senator Cl. LE7: Sys . . . . . . . . . . . .3B **60**
Sence Cres. LE8: G Gle . . . . . . . . . . . .1J **85**
Seton Cl. LE11: Lou . . . . . . . . . . . .4A **18**
Severn Av. LE10: Hinc . . . . . . . . . . . .3D **102**
Severn Cl. LE9: Cosb . . . . . . . . . . . .6H **81**
   LE15: O'ham . . . . . . . . . . . .5G **127**
Severn Cres. LE15: E Wes . . . . . . . . . . . .3J **135**
Severn Hill LE13: Mel M . . . . . . . . . . . .6E **116**
Severn Rd. LE2: Oad . . . . . . . . . . . .3E **78**
Severn St. LE2: Leic . . . . . . . . . . .6G **5** (3H **71**)
Seward St. LE11: Lou . . . . . . . . . . . .7E **18**
SEWSTERN . . . . . . . . . . . .7J **113** (2B **160**)
Sextant Rd. LE5: Leic . . . . . . . . . . . .7E **66**
Seymour Cl. LE11: Lou . . . . . . . . . . . .5K **17**
Seymour Rd. LE2: Leic . . . . . . . . . . . .6H **71**
   LE12: Bur W . . . . . . . . . . . .3F **21**
Seymour St. LE2: Leic . . . . . . . . . . .6G **5** (3H **71**)
Seymour Way LE3: Leic E . . . . . . . . . . . .5D **68**
Shackerdale Rd. LE2: Leic . . . . . . . . . . . .4G **77**
   LE18: Wig . . . . . . . . . . . .4G **77**

SHACKERSTONE . . . . . . . . . . . .3H **91** (1A **162**)
Shackerstone Railwayana Mus., The
   . . . . . . . . . . . .4J **91**
Shackerstone Rd. CV13: Con . . . . . . . . . . . .5G **91**
Shackerstone Station
   Battlefield Line . . . . . . . . . . . .3J **91**
Shackland Dr. DE12: Mea . . . . . . . . . . . .7F **35**
Shackleton Dr. LE10: Bur . . . . . . . . . . . .7H **103**
Shackleton St. LE1: Leic . . . . . . . . . . .1E **4** (7G **65**)
Shackleton Way LE17: Lut . . . . . . . . . . . .5C **152**
Shades Cl. LE9: Crof . . . . . . . . . . . .5A **80**
Shadows La. CV13: Con . . . . . . . . . . . .6G **91**
Shadrack Cl. LE9: S Stan . . . . . . . . . . . .2J **105**
Shady La. LE5: Leic . . . . . . . . . . . .6D **72**
Shaeffer Cl. LE4: Leic . . . . . . . . . . . .4B **64**
Shaftesbury Av. LE4: Leic . . . . . . . . . . . .4H **65**
Shaftesbury Rd. LE3: Leic . . . . . . . . . . . .3C **70**
Shakespeare Cl. LE3: Brau . . . . . . . . . . . .6J **69**
Shakespeare Dr. DE74: Dis . . . . . . . . . . . .3A **12**
   LE3: Brau . . . . . . . . . . . .6K **69**
   LE10: Hinc . . . . . . . . . . . .2F **103**
Shakespeare St. LE2: Leic . . . . . . . . . . . .7F **71**
   LE11: Lou . . . . . . . . . . . .6F **19**
SHANGTON . . . . . . . . . . . .2A **164**
Shanklin Av. LE2: Leic . . . . . . . . . . . .1K **77**
Shanklin Dr. LE2: Leic . . . . . . . . . . . .1K **77**
Shanklin Gdns. LE2: Leic . . . . . . . . . . . .1K **77**
   LE3: Leic E . . . . . . . . . . . .5F **69**
Shanklin Wlk. LE2: Leic . . . . . . . . . . . .2K **77**
Shannon Way LE15: O'ham . . . . . . . . . . . .5G **127**
Shanti Margh LE4: Leic . . . . . . . . . . . .4J **65**
SHARDLOW . . . . . . . . . . . .1B **158**
Shardlow Rd. DE72: A Tre . . . . . . . . . . . .1D **6**
   LE18: Wig . . . . . . . . . . . .5J **77**
Sharmon Cres. LE3: Leic . . . . . . . . . . . .1H **69**
Sharnbrook Gdns.
   LE10: S'ord . . . . . . . . . . . .7H **105**
SHARNFORD . . . . . . . . . . . .7H **105** (2B **162**)
Sharnford Rd. LE9: Sap . . . . . . . . . . . .4K **105**
   LE10: A Fla . . . . . . . . . . . .5D **104**
Sharpe's Plain PE9: Ket . . . . . . . . . . . .6G **137**
Sharpes Row NG33: Sew . . . . . . . . . . . .7K **113**
Sharpe Way LE19: Nar . . . . . . . . . . . .2F **81**
Sharpland LE2: Leic . . . . . . . . . . . .3C **76**
Sharpless Rd. LE10: Bur . . . . . . . . . . . .4H **103**
Sharpley Av. LE67: Coal . . . . . . . . . . . .2G **39**
Sharpley Dr. LE4: Beau L . . . . . . . . . . . .7A **58**
Sharpley Hill LE6: New L . . . . . . . . . . . .3B **56**
Sharpley Rd. LE11: Lou . . . . . . . . . . . .1K **29**
Sharp's Cl. LE67: Thor . . . . . . . . . . . .2K **93**
Sharrads Way LE15: L'ham . . . . . . . . . . . .5D **122**
Shaw Cl. LE8: Whet . . . . . . . . . . . .3K **81**
SHAWELL . . . . . . . . . . . .2C **156** (3C **163**)
Shawell Rd. LE17: C'ach . . . . . . . . . . . .5D **154**
   LE17: Swin . . . . . . . . . . . .4E **156**
Shaw La. LE67: Bar . . . . . . . . . . . .1K **53**
Shaw Wood Cl. LE6: Groby . . . . . . . . . . . .3C **62**
Shearer Cl. LE4: Leic . . . . . . . . . . . .2A **66**
Shearers Ct. LE11: Lou . . . . . . . . . . . .5G **19**
   (off Mill La.)
SHEARSBY . . . . . . . . . . . .5J **147** (2D **163**)
Shearsby Cl. LE18: Wig . . . . . . . . . . . .6K **77**
Shearsby Rd. LE8: Sad . . . . . . . . . . . .7A **88**
Sheene Rd. LE4: Beau L . . . . . . . . . . . .2A **64**
Sheepcote LE7: R'ley . . . . . . . . . . . .5E **44**
Sheepdyke LE15: Cott . . . . . . . . . . . .6A **124**
Sheepwash La. LE7: Anst . . . . . . . . . . . .7J **57**
Sheepy Cl. LE10: Hinc . . . . . . . . . . . .2J **103**
SHEEPY MAGNA . . . . . . . . . . . .6C **90** (1A **162**)
SHEEPY PARVA . . . . . . . . . . . .5D **90** (1A **162**)
Sheepy Rd. CV9: Pin, S Mag . . . . . . . . . . . .7A **90**
   CV9: Twy . . . . . . . . . . . .4B **90**
Sheffield St. LE3: Leic . . . . . . . . . . . .4D **70**
Shelbourne St. LE5: Leic . . . . . . . . . . . .1J **71**
Sheldon Cl. LE11: Lou . . . . . . . . . . . .4K **17**
Sheldon St. LE5: Leic . . . . . . . . . . .2G **4** (1H **71**)
Shelduck Cl. LE8: Whet . . . . . . . . . . . .5K **81**
SHELFORD . . . . . . . . . . . .1D **159**
   . . . . . . . . . . . .3B **162**
Shelford Wlk. LE4: Leic . . . . . . . . . . . .3E **64**
   LE16: L Bow . . . . . . . . . . . .5J **151**
SHELLBROOK . . . . . . . . . . . .5G **23**
Shellbrook Cl. LE65: Ash Z . . . . . . . . . . . .5G **23**
Shelley Av. LE13: Mel M . . . . . . . . . . . .1E **116**
Shelley Cl. DE12: Mea . . . . . . . . . . . .2E **48**
Shelley Dr. LE17: Lut . . . . . . . . . . . .3J **153**
Shelley Gdns. LE10: Hinc . . . . . . . . . . . .7H **99**
Shelley Rd. LE19: End . . . . . . . . . . . .6E **74**
Shelley St. LE2: Leic . . . . . . . . . . . .7G **71**
   LE11: Lou . . . . . . . . . . . .5B **18**
SHELTHORPE . . . . . . . . . . . .2F **31** (3C **159**)
Shelthorpe Av. LE11: Lou . . . . . . . . . . . .2F **31**
Shelthorpe Ho. LE11: Lou . . . . . . . . . . . .3F **31**
Shelthorpe Rd. LE11: Lou . . . . . . . . . . . .2F **31**
SHELTON LOCK . . . . . . . . . . . .1A **158**
Shenley Rd. LE18: Wig . . . . . . . . . . . .4A **78**
SHENTON . . . . . . . . . . . .1A **162**

Shenton Cl. CV13: S Gol . . . . . . . . . . . . . .3B 98
  LE4: Thurm . . . . . . . . . . . . . . . . . . . .7C 60
  LE8: Whet . . . . . . . . . . . . . . . . . . . . . .2K 81
  LE18: Wig . . . . . . . . . . . . . . . . . . . . . .5J 77
Shenton La. CV13: Dadl . . . . . . . . . . . . . . .1A 98
  CV13: Mkt B . . . . . . . . . . . . . . . . . . . .4C 94
Shenton Rd. LE9: Barw . . . . . . . . . . . . . .3A 100
Shenton Station Info. Point . . . . . . . . . . . . .1B 162
Shepherd Cl. LE5: Ham . . . . . . . . . . . . . . .3E 66
  LE9: Leic E . . . . . . . . . . . . . . . . . . . . .4C 68
Shepherds Cl. LE11: Lou . . . . . . . . . . . . . .2B 30
  LE12: Shep . . . . . . . . . . . . . . . . . . . . .5E 16
Shepherds Cft. LE13: Mel M . . . . . . . . . . .2E 116
Shepherds La. LE15: Gree . . . . . . . . . . . . .4F 125
Shepherd's Wlk. LE7: East G . . . . . . . . . . . .5F 47
  PE9: Belm . . . . . . . . . . . . . . . . . . . . .6J 129
Shepherd's Way LE15: Upp . . . . . . . . . . . .1A 138
Shepherd Wlk. DE74: Keg . . . . . . . . . . . . . .7G 9
Sheppards Orchard LE12: Wym . . . . . . . . . .1K 21
SHEPSHED . . . . . . . . . . . . . .7D 16 (3B 158)
Shepshed Dynamo FC . . . . . . . . . . . . . . . .6E 16
Shepshed Rd. LE12: Hat . . . . . . . . . . . . . . .2G 17
Sherborne Av. LE18: Wig . . . . . . . . . . . . . .1J 83
Sherborne Rd. LE10: Bur . . . . . . . . . . . . .4A 104
Sherbourne Dr. LE65: Ash Z . . . . . . . . . . . .4J 23
Sherford Cl. LE18: Wig . . . . . . . . . . . . . . .6J 77
Sheridan Cl. LE19: End . . . . . . . . . . . . . . .6E 74
Sheridan St. LE2: Leic . . . . . . . . . . . . . . . .7F 71
Sheringham Rd. LE4: Leic . . . . . . . . . . . . .4D 64
Sherloyd Cl. LE4: Leic . . . . . . . . . . . . . . . .2B 66
Sherrard Cl. LE15: Whis . . . . . . . . . . . . . .1B 122
Sherrard Dr. LE12: Sileby . . . . . . . . . . . . . .3J 45
Sherrard Rd. LE5: Leic . . . . . . . . . . . . . . . .1J 71
  LE16: Mkt H . . . . . . . . . . . . . . . . . . .2E 150
Sherrard St. LE13: Mel M . . . . . . . . . . . . .4F 117
Sherrard Way LE3: Brau . . . . . . . . . . . . . . .6H 69
Sherrier Way LE17: Lut . . . . . . . . . . . . . . .2J 153
SHERWOOD . . . . . . . . . . . . . . . . . . . . .1C 159
Sherwood Cl. LE67: Ell . . . . . . . . . . . . . . . .1D 52
Sherwood Dr. LE13: Mel M . . . . . . . . . . . .3D 116
Sherwood Rd. CV13: S Gol . . . . . . . . . . . .3A 98
Sherwood St. LE5: Leic . . . . . . . . . . . . . . .1A 72
Shetland Rd. LE4: Leic . . . . . . . . . . . . . . .4J 65
Shetland Way LE8: Count . . . . . . . . . . . . . .5F 83
Shield Cres. LE2: Leic . . . . . . . . . . . . . . . .6C 76
Shields Cres. DE74: C Don . . . . . . . . . . . . .5H 7
SHILTON . . . . . . . . . . . . . . . . . . . . . . . .3B 162
Shilton Rd. LE9: Barw . . . . . . . . . . . . . . .4A 100
  LE9: K Mal . . . . . . . . . . . . . . . . . . . . .6G 95
Shipley Rd. LE5: Leic . . . . . . . . . . . . . . . . .3K 71
Shipman Rd. LE3: Brau . . . . . . . . . . . . . . .2K 75
Shipston Hill LE2: Oad . . . . . . . . . . . . . . .4C 78
Shipton Cl. LE18: Wig . . . . . . . . . . . . . . . .6B 78
Shipton Rd. LE5: Ham . . . . . . . . . . . . . . . .3E 66
Shire Cl. LE3: Leic . . . . . . . . . . . . . . . . . .2J 69
Shires Cen., The LE1: Leic . . . . . . .3C 4 (1F 71)
Shires La. LE1: Leic . . . . . . . . . . .3B 4 (1E 70)
Shires Orchard NG32: Crox . . . . . . . . . . . .6H 107
Shires Wlk. LE1: Leic . . . . . . . . . .3C 4 (1F 71)
Shirley Av. LE2: Leic . . . . . . . . . . . . . . . . .7K 71
Shirley Cl. DE74: C Don . . . . . . . . . . . . . . .4J 7
Shirley Dr. LE7: Sys . . . . . . . . . . . . . . . . .7D 46
Shirley Pk. LE72: A Tre . . . . . . . . . . . . . . . .1D 6
Shirley Rd. LE2: Leic . . . . . . . . . . . . . . . . .7K 71
Shirley St. LE4: Leic . . . . . . . . . . . . . . . . .4G 65
Shirreffs Cl. LE12: Bar S . . . . . . . . . . . . . .3E 32
SHOBY . . . . . . . . . . . . . . . . . . . . . . . . .2D 159
Shoemakers, The LE7: Anst . . . . . . . . . . . .7H 57
Shoesmith Cl. LE9: Barw . . . . . . . . . . . . . .4K 99
Shooting Cl. La. LE12: Bar S . . . . . . . . . . . .4D 32
Short Cl. LE8: Flec . . . . . . . . . . . . . . . . . .4C 88
SHORT HEATH . . . . . . . . . . . . . . . . . . . .3A 158
Shortheath Rd. DE12: Moi . . . . . . . . . . . . .1A 34
Short Hill DE73: Wils . . . . . . . . . . . . . . . . .3A 10
Short La. DE74: C Don . . . . . . . . . . . . . . . .4H 7
Shortridge La. LE19: End . . . . . . . . . . . . . .5F 75
Short St. LE1: Leic . . . . . . . . . . . .2C 4 (1F 71)
Shottens Cl. LE4: Leic . . . . . . . . . . . . . . . .4B 64
Shottery Av. LE3: Brau . . . . . . . . . . . . . . .6K 69
Shoulbard LE8: Flec . . . . . . . . . . . . . . . . .3A 88
Shrewsbury Av. LE2: Leic . . . . . . . . . . . . . .2G 77
  LE16: L Bow . . . . . . . . . . . . . . . . . . .5H 151
Shrewsbury Cl. LE9: Barw . . . . . . . . . . . . .3K 99
Shrewsbury Wlk. LE67: Thrin . . . . . . . . . . . .3D 26
Shropshire Cl. LE16: Mkt H . . . . . . . . . . . .3E 150
Shropshire Pl. LE16: Mkt H . . . . . . . . . . . .3E 150
Shropshire Rd. LE2: Leic . . . . . . . . . . . . . .1D 76
Shrubbery, The DE11: W'lle . . . . . . . . . . . .1C 22
SHUTTINGTON . . . . . . . . . . . . . . . . . . . .1A 162
Shuttleworth La. LE9: Cosb . . . . . . . . . . . .1G 87
SIBBERTOFT . . . . . . . . . . . . . . . . . . . . .3D 163
SIBSON
  Nuneaton . . . . . . . . . . . . . . . . . . . . .1A 162
  Peterborough . . . . . . . . . . . . . . . . . .2D 165
Sibson Dr. DE74: Keg . . . . . . . . . . . . . . . . .6F 9
Sibson Rd. CV9: S Par . . . . . . . . . . . . . . .6D 90
  LE4: Birs . . . . . . . . . . . . . . . . . . . . . .6G 59

Sibton La. LE2: Oad . . . . . . . . . . . . . . . . .4C 78
Sickleholm Dr. LE5: Leic . . . . . . . . . . . . . .5A 72
Siddons Wlk. LE1: Leic . . . . . . . . . . . . . . . .3D 4
Side Ley DE74: Keg . . . . . . . . . . . . . . . . . .5G 9
Sidings, The LE4: Leic . . . . . . . . . . . . . . . .2F 65
Sidmouth Av. LE5: Leic . . . . . . . . . . . . . . .4C 72
Sidney Rd. LE2: Leic . . . . . . . . . . . . . . . . .1K 77
Sidwell St. LE5: Leic . . . . . . . . . . . . . . . . .2A 72
Signal Rd. LE14: O Dal . . . . . . . . . . . . . .6C 110
Silbury Rd. LE4: Leic . . . . . . . . . . . . . . . . .5C 64
SILEBY . . . . . . . . . . . . . . . . . . .1J 45 (3D 159)
Sileby Mill Boatyard . . . . . . . . . . . . . . . . . .2G 45
Sileby Rd. LE12: Bar S . . . . . . . . . . . . . . .4D 32
  LE12: Moun . . . . . . . . . . . . . . . . . . . .1E 44
Sileby Rd. Ind. Est. LE12: Bar S . . . . . . . . .5F 33
Sileby Station (Rail) . . . . . . . . . . . . . . . . . .1J 45
SILK WILLOUGHBY . . . . . . . . . . . . . . . . .1D 161
Silsden Ri. LE4: Leic . . . . . . . . . . . . . . . . .5D 76
Silver Arc. LE1: Leic . . . . . . . . . . . . . . . . . .3C 4
Silver Birches LE12: Quo . . . . . . . . . . . . . .5K 31
Silver Birch Way LE7: East G . . . . . . . . . . .4G 47
Silverbirch Way LE11: Lou . . . . . . . . . . . . .5E 30
Silverdale Dr. LE4: Thurm . . . . . . . . . . . . . .7B 60
Silverstone Dr. LE4: Leic . . . . . . . . . . . . . .1K 65
Silver St. DE12: Oak . . . . . . . . . . . . . . . . .6C 34
  LE1: Leic . . . . . . . . . . . . . .3C 4 (1F 71)
  LE67: Whit . . . . . . . . . . . . . . . . . . . . .7E 26
Silverton Rd. LE2: Oad . . . . . . . . . . . . . . .2E 78
  LE11: Lou . . . . . . . . . . . . . . . . . . . . .3D 30
Silver Wlk. LE1: Leic . . . . . . . . . . . . . . . . . .3C 4
                    (off Silver St.)
Silverwood Cl. LE5: Leic . . . . . . . . . . . . . .2E 72
Silverwood Rd. NG13: Bott . . . . . . . . . . . .2G 107
Simborough Way LE16: L Bow . . . . . . . . . .4H 151
Simmins Cl. LE2: Leic . . . . . . . . . . . . . . . .4D 76
Simmins Cres. LE2: Leic . . . . . . . . . . . . . .4D 76
Simons Cl. LE18: Wig . . . . . . . . . . . . . . . .1A 84
Simons Dr. LE12: Sileby . . . . . . . . . . . . . . .1J 45
Simon's Orchard LE17: Ash P . . . . . . . . . .6K 143
                (not continuous)
Simpson Cl. LE7: Sys . . . . . . . . . . . . . . . . .3A 60
  LE8: Whet . . . . . . . . . . . . . . . . . . . . .3A 82
SINFIN . . . . . . . . . . . . . . . . . . . . . . . . . .1A 158
SINOPE . . . . . . . . . . . . . . . . . . . . . . . . .1H 37
Sir Robert Martin Ct. LE11: Lou . . . . . . . . .5B 18
Siskin Dr. DE12: Mea . . . . . . . . . . . . . . . .1D 48
Siskin Hill LE2: Oad . . . . . . . . . . . . . . . . .4C 78
Siskin Rd. LE15: Upp . . . . . . . . . . . . . . . .1B 138
Sisley Way LE10: Hinc . . . . . . . . . . . . . . . .7D 98
Sitch Cl. LE9: B Ast . . . . . . . . . . . . . . . . . .5E 86
Sitwell Wlk. LE5: Leic . . . . . . . . . . . . . . . .5B 72
Six Acre Cl. LE6: Ratby . . . . . . . . . . . . . . .6B 62
Six Acres LE9: B Ast . . . . . . . . . . . . . . . . .4C 86
SIX HILLS . . . . . . . . . . . . . . . . . . . . . . . .2D 159
Six Hills Rd. LE12: Walt W . . . . . . . . . . . . .6G 21
Skampton Grn. LE5: Leic . . . . . . . . . . . . . .2D 72
Skampton Rd. LE5: Leic . . . . . . . . . . . . . .2D 72
SKEFFINGTON . . . . . . . . . . . . . . . . . . . .1A 164
Skeffington Glebe Rd. LE7: T Hil . . . . . . . .4H 131
Skelton Dr. LE2: Leic . . . . . . . . . . . . . . . . .2G 77
SKETCHLEY . . . . . . . . . . . . . .6H 103 (2B 162)
Sketchley Cl. LE5: Leic . . . . . . . . . . . . . . . .1F 73
Sketchley Hall Gdns. LE10: Bur . . . . . . . . .6F 103
SKETCHLEY HILL . . . . . . . . . . . . . . . . . . .5H 103
Sketchley La. LE10: Bur . . . . . . . . . . . . . .6E 102
Sketchley La. Ind. Est. LE10: Bur . . . . . . . .6E 102
Sketchley Mnr. La. LE10: Bur . . . . . . . . . . .6G 103
Sketchley Mdws. LE10: Bur . . . . . . . . . . . .6F 103
Sketchley Mdws. Bus. Pk.
  LE10: Bur . . . . . . . . . . . . . . . . . . . . .6F 103
Sketchley Old Village LE10: Bur . . . . . . . . .6F 103
Sketchley Rd. LE10: Bur . . . . . . . . . . . . . .6H 103
Skevington Av. LE11: Lou . . . . . . . . . . . . . .6C 18
SKILLINGTON . . . . . . . . . . . . . . . . . . . . .2B 160
Skinner's La. LE67: Whit . . . . . . . . . . . . . . .6F 27
Skippon Cl. LE16: Mkt H . . . . . . . . . . . . . .5D 150
Skipworth St. LE2: Leic . . . . . . . . . . . . . . .3J 71
Skye Way LE8: Count . . . . . . . . . . . . . . . .6F 83
Skylark Av. LE12: Moun . . . . . . . . . . . . . . .3F 45
Skylark Cl. DE12: Mea . . . . . . . . . . . . . . .1D 48
Slade Greens, The LE2: Leic . . . . . . . . . . .4C 76
Slade La. DE73: Wils . . . . . . . . . . . . . . . . .3B 10
Slade Pl. LE2: Leic . . . . . . . . . . . . . . . . . .4C 76
Slash La. LE12: Bar S, Sileby . . . . . . . . . . .6F 33
Slate Brook Cl. LE6: Groby . . . . . . . . . . . . .3D 62
Slate Cl. LE3: Glen . . . . . . . . . . . . . . . . . .6F 63
Slater St. LE1: Leic . . . . . . . . . . . .1B 4 (7E 64)
  LE3: Leic . . . . . . . . . . . . . .1A 4 (7E 64)
Slate St. LE2: Leic . . . . . . . . . . . .5F 4 (2G 71)
SLAWSTON . . . . . . . . . . . . . . . . . . . . . .2A 164
Slawston Rd. LE16: Med . . . . . . . . . . . . . .5A 140
Slaybarns Way LE67: Ibs . . . . . . . . . . . . . .3K 51
Sloane Cl. LE19: End . . . . . . . . . . . . . . . . .5E 74
                (not continuous)
Smart Cl. LE3: Brau . . . . . . . . . . . . . . . . . .5H 69
Smedley Cl. LE65: Ash Z . . . . . . . . . . . . . .6H 23
Smedmore Rd. LE5: Leic . . . . . . . . . . . . . .6K 65

Smeeton Ct. LE8: K Bea . . . . . . . . . . . . . . .3J 89
Smeeton Rd. LE8: K Bea . . . . . . . . . . . . . .4J 89
SMEETON WESTERBY . . . . . . . . . .5H 89 (2D 163)
SMISBY . . . . . . . . . . . . . . . . . . .1H 23 (3A 158)
Smisby Rd. LE65: Ash Z . . . . . . . . . . . . . . .1J 23
Smith Av. LE4: Thurm . . . . . . . . . . . . . . . . .7B 60
Smith Ct. LE67: Whit . . . . . . . . . . . . . . . . .6D 26
Smith Cres. LE67: Coal . . . . . . . . . . . . . . . .3J 39
Smith Dorrien Rd. LE5: Leic . . . . . . . . . . . .7A 66
Smith Way LE19: End . . . . . . . . . . . . . . . . .4J 75
Smithy Cl. CV13: B'one . . . . . . . . . . . . . . .5C 92
Smithy Farm Dr. LE7: S Stan . . . . . . . . . . .1H 105
Smithy La. LE9: Sap . . . . . . . . . . . . . . . . .2B 104
  LE10: Bur . . . . . . . . . . . . . . . . . . . . .2B 104
  LE12: L Wha . . . . . . . . . . . . . . . . . . . .7E 12
  LE65: Ash Z . . . . . . . . . . . . . . . . . . . .4C 24
Smithy Way LE12: Shep . . . . . . . . . . . . . . .6E 16
SMOCKINGTON . . . . . . . . . . . . . . . . . . . .3B 162
Smore Slade Hills LE2: Oad . . . . . . . . . . . .4G 79
Smyth Cl. LE16: Mkt H . . . . . . . . . . . . . . .2E 150
SNARESTONE . . . . . . . . . . . . . . .6G 49 (1A 162)
Snarestone Rd. DE12: A Mag . . . . . . . . . . .5B 48
  LE67: N Bur . . . . . . . . . . . . . . . . . . . .5K 49
Snarrow's Dr. LE67: Thrin . . . . . . . . . . . . . .7E 14
Snell's Nook La. LE11: Nan . . . . . . . . . . . . .2J 29
Snelston Cl. LE15: O'ham . . . . . . . . . . . . .3K 127
SNIBSTON . . . . . . . . . . . . . . . . .5B 38 (3B 158)
Snibston Cl. LE67: Coal . . . . . . . . . . . . . . .2B 38
Snibston Dr. LE67: Coal . . . . . . . . . . . . . . .2A 38
Snipe Cl. LE67: Coal . . . . . . . . . . . . . . . . .3C 38
  LE67: Hug . . . . . . . . . . . . . . . . . . . . .5B 38
Snowdens End LE18: Wig . . . . . . . . . . . . . .7A 78
Snowdon Av. LE15: O'ham . . . . . . . . . . . .4G 127
Snowdon Cl. LE12: Shep . . . . . . . . . . . . . .1E 28
Snowdrop Cl. LE19: Nar . . . . . . . . . . . . . . .1D 80
Snow Hill LE4: Leic . . . . . . . . . . . . . . . . . .5C 64
  LE13: Mel M . . . . . . . . . . . . . . . . . . .4F 117
Soarbank Way LE11: Lou . . . . . . . . . . . . . .3C 18
Soar Cl. LE13: Mel M . . . . . . . . . . . . . . . .6E 116
Soar La. LE3: Leic . . . . . . . . . . . .2A 4 (1D 70)
  LE12: Sut Bon . . . . . . . . . . . . . . . . . .1J 13
Soar Mill La. LE9: B Ast . . . . . . . . . . . . . . .2B 86
Soar Rd. LE4: Thurm . . . . . . . . . . . . . . . . .4A 60
  LE12: Quo . . . . . . . . . . . . . . . . . . . . .5B 32
Soar Valley Leisure Cen. . . . . . . . . . . . . . . .2E 44
Soar Valley Way LE2: Leic . . . . . . . . . . . . .4K 75
  LE3: Leic . . . . . . . . . . . . . . . . . . . . .4K 75
  LE19: End . . . . . . . . . . . . . . . . . . . . .4K 75
Soar Way LE10: Hinc . . . . . . . . . . . . . . . .3D 102
Solway Cl. LE13: Mel M . . . . . . . . . . . . . .6E 116
SOMERBY . . . . . . . . . . . . . . . . .6K 121 (3A 160)
Somerby Dr. LE2: Oad . . . . . . . . . . . . . . . .3E 78
Somerby Rd. LE7: Thurn . . . . . . . . . . . . . . .1H 73
  LE14: Bur H . . . . . . . . . . . . . . . . . . .6F 121
  LE15: Knos . . . . . . . . . . . . . . . . . . . .1A 126
Somerfield Wlk. LE4: Leic . . . . . . . . . . . . . .4B 64
Somerfield Way LE3: Leic E . . . . . . . . . . . .5D 68
Somerscales Wlk. LE4: Leic . . . . . . . . . . . .7H 65
Somerset Av. LE4: Leic . . . . . . . . . . . . . . . .4D 64
Somerset Cl. LE12: Bur W . . . . . . . . . . . . . .3F 21
  LE13: Mel M . . . . . . . . . . . . . . . . . . .1A 120
Somerset Dr. LE3: Glen . . . . . . . . . . . . . . .7F 63
Somerset Rd. LE15: Cott . . . . . . . . . . . . . .4C 124
Somers Rd. LE5: Leic . . . . . . . . . . . . . . . . .1E 72
Somerville Rd. LE3: Leic . . . . . . . . . . . . . . .6B 70
Sonning Way LE2: G Par . . . . . . . . . . . . . .6C 76
Sopers Rd. LE9: Crof . . . . . . . . . . . . . . . . .6A 80
Sorrel Cl. LE12: Moun . . . . . . . . . . . . . . . .2E 44
Sorrell Rd. LE5: Ham . . . . . . . . . . . . . . . . .4E 66
Sorrel Way LE19: Nar . . . . . . . . . . . . . . . . .7D 74
Sth. Albion St. LE1: Leic . . . . . . . . .5E 4 (2G 71)
Southampton St. LE1: Leic . . . . . . . .3E 4 (1G 71)
South Av. LE3: Leic E . . . . . . . . . . . . . . . . .4F 69
  LE17: Ull . . . . . . . . . . . . . . . . . . . . . .7F 143
  LE18: Wig . . . . . . . . . . . . . . . . . . . . .6J 77
South Charnwood Swimming Pool . . . . . . . .7E 46
Sth. Church Ga. LE1: Leic . . . . . . . .1B 4 (7F 64)
South Cl. DE11: Blac . . . . . . . . . . . . . . . . .3D 22
  LE8: Arne . . . . . . . . . . . . . . . . . . . . .2H 147
  LE14: Scal . . . . . . . . . . . . . . . . . . . .6C 112
South Cres. NG13: Bott . . . . . . . . . . . . . .2G 107
SOUTH CROXTON . . . . . . . . . . . .7A 118 (3D 159)
Sth. Croxton Rd. LE7: Quen . . . . . . . . . . . . .7J 47
  LE7: S Cro . . . . . . . . . . . . . . . . . . . .5A 118
                (not continuous)
South Derbyshire Ski Cen. . . . . . . . . . . . . . .1A 22
Southdown Dr. LE4: Thurm . . . . . . . . . . . . .1A 66
Southdown Rd. LE5: Leic . . . . . . . . . . . . . .1K 71
  LE11: Lou . . . . . . . . . . . . . . . . . . . . .4E 30
Southdown Wlk. LE15: Cott . . . . . . . . . . . .4C 124
              (off Tiverton Rd.)
South Dr. LE5: Leic . . . . . . . . . . . . . . . . . .6C 66
  LE9: S Stan . . . . . . . . . . . . . . . . . . . .2K 105
SOUTH END . . . . . . . . . . . . . . . . . . . . . . .2F 45
Southernhay Av. LE2: Leic . . . . . . . . . . . . . .7J 71
Southernhay Cl. LE2: Leic . . . . . . . . . . . . . .6J 71
Southernhay Rd. LE2: Leic . . . . . . . . . . . . .7J 71

Southey Cl. LE4: Leic . . . . . . . . . . . . . . . .6H 65
 LE19: End . . . . . . . . . . . . . . . . . . . . . .6E 74
Southfield Av. LE7: Sys . . . . . . . . . . . . . .2D 60
Southfield Cl. LE2: G Par . . . . . . . . . . . . .5A 76
 LE7: Scra . . . . . . . . . . . . . . . . . . . . . .7H 67
Southfield Rd. LE10: Hinc . . . . . . . . . . . .4G 103
 LE11: Lou . . . . . . . . . . . . . . . . . . . . . .7F 19
SOUTH FIELDS . . . . . . . . . . . . . . . . . . .4E 70
South Flds. LE1: Leic . . . . . . . . .7E 5 (3G 71)
Southfields Av. LE2: Oad . . . . . . . . . . . . .2B 78
Southfields Dr. LE2: Leic . . . . . . . . . . . . .3E 76
 (not continuous)
Southfields Drive Sports Cen. . . . . . . . . . .3F 77
Southfields Wlk. LE2: Leic . . . . . . . . . . . .3F 77
Southfield Way CV13: Mkt B . . . . . . . . . .3C 94
Southgate Ho. LE1: Leic . . . . . . . . . . . . . .5B 4
 (off Millstone La.)
Southgates LE1: Leic . . . . . . . . .4B 4 (2E 70)
Southgates Underpass LE1: Leic . . . .4B 4 (2E 70)
SOUTH KILWORTH . . . . . . . . .6G 155 (3D 163)
Sth. Kilworth Rd. LE17: N Kil . . . . . . . .4J 155
 LE17: Wal . . . . . . . . . . . . . . . . . . . . .2E 154
 NN6: Welf . . . . . . . . . . . . . . . . . . . . .7J 155
Sth. Kingsmead Rd. LE2: Leic . . . . . . . . .2J 77
SOUTH KNIGHTON . . . . . . . . . . . . . . . . .1K 77
Sth. Knighton Rd. LE2: Leic . . . . . . . . . .1K 77
Southland Rd. LE2: Leic . . . . . . . . . . . . .2K 77
South La. LE67: Bar . . . . . . . . . . . . . . . . .1J 53
Sth. Leicester Ind. Est. LE67: Ell . . . . . . .1E 52
Southleigh Gro. LE16: Mkt H . . . . . . . . . .3D 150
SOUTH LUFFENHAM . . . . . .4C 136 (1C 165)
Southmeads Cl. LE2: Leic . . . . . . . . . . . .1C 78
Southmeads Rd. LE2: Leic, Oad . . . . . . . .1B 78
SOUTHORPE . . . . . . . . . . . . . . . . . . . .1D 165
South Pde. LE13: Mel M . . . . . . . . . . . . .4F 117
 (off King St.)
South Rd. LE67: Ibs . . . . . . . . . . . . . . . .5K 51
Southside Rd. LE3: Brau . . . . . . . . . . . . .2K 75
South St. DE11: W'lle . . . . . . . . . . . . . . .1C 22
 LE2: Oad . . . . . . . . . . . . . . . . . . . . . .2C 78
 LE11: Lou . . . . . . . . . . . . . . . . . . . . . .7F 19
 LE12: Bar S . . . . . . . . . . . . . . . . . . . .4D 32
 LE14: Ash H . . . . . . . . . . . . . . . . . . .2K 115
 LE14: Scal . . . . . . . . . . . . . . . . . . . .6C 112
 LE15: O'ham . . . . . . . . . . . . . . . . . . .4H 127
 LE65: Ash Z . . . . . . . . . . . . . . . . . . . .5K 23
 LE67: Ell . . . . . . . . . . . . . . . . . . . . . .1D 52
 (not continuous)
South Vw. LE14: Ash . . . . . . . . . . . . . . .3F 115
 LE14: Bur H . . . . . . . . . . . . . . . . . . . .6F 121
 LE15: Upp . . . . . . . . . . . . . . . . . . . . .2C 138
 LE17: Frol . . . . . . . . . . . . . . . . . . . . .1E 142
South Vw. Cl. LE15: Mant . . . . . . . . . . .3C 134
Southview Ct. LE9: K Mux . . . . . . . . . . . .3D 68
Southview Dr. LE5: Leic . . . . . . . . . . . . .5B 72
South Wlk. LE6: Ratby . . . . . . . . . . . . . .5A 62
South Way LE8: K Bea . . . . . . . . . . . . . .2K 89
Southway LE8: Bla . . . . . . . . . . . . . . . . .3B 82
SOUTHWICK . . . . . . . . . . . . . . . . . . . .2D 165
SOUTH WIGSTON . . . . . . . .7F 77 (2C 163)
South Wigston Station (Rail) . . . . . . . . . . .6F 77
SOUTH WITHAM . . . . . . . . . . . . . . . . . .3C 161
Southworth Rd. DE73: B Hil . . . . . . . . . . .7A 10
Sovereign Ct. LE11: Lou . . . . . . . . . . . . .7F 19
Sovereign Pk. LE16: Mkt H . . . . . . . . . . .6F 151
Sovereign Pk. Ind. Est. LE16: Mkt H . . . . .6F 151
Sowters La. LE12: Bur W . . . . . . . . . . . . .3G 21
Spa Cl. LE10: Hinc . . . . . . . . . . . . . . . .2H 103
Spa Dr. LE9: Sap . . . . . . . . . . . . . . . . .3J 105
Spa La. LE10: Hinc . . . . . . . . . . . . . . . .2H 103
 LE18: Wig . . . . . . . . . . . . . . . . . . . . .6K 77
Spalding St. LE5: Leic . . . . . . . . . . . . . .1A 72
SPANBY . . . . . . . . . . . . . . . . . . . . . . .1D 161
Sparkenhoe LE9: Crof . . . . . . . . . . . . . .6A 80
 LE9: N Ver . . . . . . . . . . . . . . . . . . . . .6H 93
Sparkenhoe Est. LE67: Hea . . . . . . . . . . .3J 51
Sparkenhoe St. LE2: Leic . . . . . .5G 4 (2H 71)
Sparrow Hill LE11: Lou . . . . . . . . . . . . . .6F 19
Sparsis Gdns. LE19: End . . . . . . . . . . . . .7H 75
Speeds Pingle LE11: Lou . . . . . . . . . . . . .6E 18
Speedwell Cl. LE19: Nar . . . . . . . . . . . . .7D 74
 LE67: Coal . . . . . . . . . . . . . . . . . . . . .3E 38
Speedwell Dr. LE5: Ham . . . . . . . . . . . . .3D 66
 LE9: B Ast . . . . . . . . . . . . . . . . . . . . .6E 86
Speedwell Rd. LE12: Moun . . . . . . . . . . .2F 45
Speers Rd. LE3: Leic . . . . . . . . . . . . . . .6J 63
Spencefield Dr. LE5: Leic . . . . . . . . . . . .4D 72
Spencefield La. LE5: Leic . . . . . . . . . . . .4D 72
Spencer Av. LE4: Thurm . . . . . . . . . . . . .6A 60
Spencer Rd. LE17: Lut . . . . . . . . . . . . . .4J 153
Spencers Rd. PE9: Ket . . . . . . . . . . . . . .6G 137
Spencer St. LE2: Oad . . . . . . . . . . . . . . .2C 78
 LE10: Hinc . . . . . . . . . . . . . . . . . . . . .2G 103
 LE16: Mkt H . . . . . . . . . . . . . . . . . . .4D 150
Spencer Vw. LE67: Ell . . . . . . . . . . . . . .2E 52
Spence St. LE5: Leic . . . . . . . . . . . . . . .7K 65
Spence Street Swimming Pool . . . . . . . . .7K 65

Spendlow Gdns. LE2: Leic . . . . . . . . . . . .4E 76
Spendlow Grn. LE2: Leic . . . . . . . . . . . . .4E 76
Sperry Ct. LE67: Ibs . . . . . . . . . . . . . . . .4K 51
Spiers Cl. LE19: Nar . . . . . . . . . . . . . . . .2F 81
Spindle Rd. LE11: Lou . . . . . . . . . . . . . .5E 30
Spindles, The LE10: Bur . . . . . . . . . . . . .6J 103
Spinner Cl. LE9: B Ast . . . . . . . . . . . . . .4F 87
Spinners Way LE12: Shep . . . . . . . . . . . .7D 16
Spinney, The CV9: Manc . . . . . . . . . . . . .6A 96
 DE74: C Don . . . . . . . . . . . . . . . . . . . .4J 7
 LE2: Oad . . . . . . . . . . . . . . . . . . . . . .4J 79
 LE7: Thurn . . . . . . . . . . . . . . . . . . . . .3G 73
 LE15: Cott . . . . . . . . . . . . . . . . . . . . .7A 124
 LE67: Hug . . . . . . . . . . . . . . . . . . . . .6C 38
Spinney Av. LE8: Count . . . . . . . . . . . . . .5F 83
Spinney Cl. LE2: G Par . . . . . . . . . . . . . .5A 76
 LE3: Brau . . . . . . . . . . . . . . . . . . . . . .5G 69
 LE6: Groby . . . . . . . . . . . . . . . . . . . . .4C 62
 LE7: Sys . . . . . . . . . . . . . . . . . . . . . .2A 60
 LE13: Mel M . . . . . . . . . . . . . . . . . . .2H 117
 LE16: Mkt H . . . . . . . . . . . . . . . . . . .4C 150
 LE17: Gilm . . . . . . . . . . . . . . . . . . . . .7J 145
 LE65: Ash Z . . . . . . . . . . . . . . . . . . . .6K 23
 (off Stuart Way)
 PE9: Ryh . . . . . . . . . . . . . . . . . . . . . .5G 129
Spinney Ct. LE9: Crof . . . . . . . . . . . . . . .5A 80
Spinney Dr. CV13: B'one . . . . . . . . . . . . .6C 92
 LE8: Kib H . . . . . . . . . . . . . . . . . . . . .2J 89
 LE12: Quo . . . . . . . . . . . . . . . . . . . . .6K 31
Spinney Halt LE8: Whet . . . . . . . . . . . . . .2J 81
Spinney Hill CV13: Mkt B . . . . . . . . . . . .2B 94
Spinney Hill Dr. LE11: Lou . . . . . . . . . . . .1B 30
Spinney Hill Rd. LE5: Leic . . . . . . . . . . . .7J 65
SPINNEY HILLS . . . . . . . . . . . .1K 71 (1D 163)
Spinney La. LE15: Stre . . . . . . . . . . . . . .2K 125
 PE9: Ryh . . . . . . . . . . . . . . . . . . . . . .5G 129
Spinney Mdw. LE7: Bill . . . . . . . . . . . . . .7J 131
Spinney Nook LE7: Tug . . . . . . . . . . . . . .2C 132
Spinney Ri. LE4: Birs . . . . . . . . . . . . . . . .6F 59
Spinney Rd. LE10: Bur . . . . . . . . . . . . . .5F 103
 PE9: Ket . . . . . . . . . . . . . . . . . . . . . .6G 137
Spinney Side LE6: Groby . . . . . . . . . . . . .4C 62
Spinney Vw. LE8: G Gle . . . . . . . . . . . . .5A 130
Spire Vw. NG13: Bott . . . . . . . . . . . . . . .1H 107
Spital, The DE74: C Don . . . . . . . . . . . . . .4J 7
Spital Hill DE74: C Don . . . . . . . . . . . . . .4J 7
SPONDON . . . . . . . . . . . . . . . . . . . . . .1B 158
SPON END . . . . . . . . . . . . . . . . . . . . . .3A 162
Sponne Ri. LE2: Leic . . . . . . . . . . . . . . . .4E 76
Sports Fld. La. LE9: Hun . . . . . . . . . . . . .1B 80
Sports Rd. LE3: Glen . . . . . . . . . . . . . . .6G 63
Spring Bk. Way LE15: Upp . . . . . . . . . . .2B 138
Springbank LE16: Med . . . . . . . . . . . . . .6C 140
Springbrook Dr. LE7: Scra . . . . . . . . . . . .1H 73
Spring Cl. LE2: Leic . . . . . . . . . . . . . . . .3D 76
 LE6: Ratby . . . . . . . . . . . . . . . . . . . . .6B 62
 LE12: Shep . . . . . . . . . . . . . . . . . . . .1E 28
 LE15: Mkt O . . . . . . . . . . . . . . . . . . .2H 123
 (not continuous)
 LE17: Lut . . . . . . . . . . . . . . . . . . . . .5J 153
Spring Cott. Rd.
 DE12: Over . . . . . . . . . . . . . . . . . . . . .5A 22
Springdale Rd. LE4: Thurm . . . . . . . . . . .7A 60
Springfield DE74: Keg . . . . . . . . . . . . . . .6F 9
 LE67: Thurn . . . . . . . . . . . . . . . . . . . .3E 26
Springfield Av. CV13: Mkt B . . . . . . . . . .2B 94
Springfield Cl. LE3: Glen . . . . . . . . . . . . .7F 63
 LE9: R'ley . . . . . . . . . . . . . . . . . . . . . .5E 44
 LE8: K Bea . . . . . . . . . . . . . . . . . . . . .4K 89
 LE9: B Ast . . . . . . . . . . . . . . . . . . . . .5D 86
 LE11: Lou . . . . . . . . . . . . . . . . . . . . . .3C 30
 LE12: Bur W . . . . . . . . . . . . . . . . . . . .3F 21
 LE67: Ibs . . . . . . . . . . . . . . . . . . . . . .4K 51
Springfield Ct. LE16: Mkt H . . . . . . . . . . .5F 151
Springfield Cres. LE8: K Bea . . . . . . . . . .4J 89
Springfield La. LE8: Smee W . . . . . . . . . .5J 89
Springfield Pk. LE10: Hinc . . . . . . . . . . .1D 102
Springfield Rd. LE2: Leic . . . . . . . . . . . . .5J 71
 LE10: Hinc . . . . . . . . . . . . . . . . . . . . .4G 103
 LE12: Shep . . . . . . . . . . . . . . . . . . . .7C 16
 LE12: Sileby . . . . . . . . . . . . . . . . . . . .7K 33
Springfield St. LE13: Mel M . . . . . . . . . .2E 116
 LE16: Mkt H . . . . . . . . . . . . . . . . . . .5F 151
Springfield Way LE15: O'ham . . . . . . . . .2J 127
Spring Gdns. LE9: Earl S . . . . . . . . . . . .1E 100
 LE9: Sap . . . . . . . . . . . . . . . . . . . . . .3K 105
 LE19: Litt . . . . . . . . . . . . . . . . . . . . . .3G 81
Springhill Gdns. LE16: Mkt H . . . . . . . . .5C 150
Spring La. LE12: L Wha . . . . . . . . . . . . . .7H 13
 LE12: Shep . . . . . . . . . . . . . . . . . . . .1D 28
 LE14: Wart . . . . . . . . . . . . . . . . . . . . .6F 111
 LE14: W'ham . . . . . . . . . . . . . . . . . . .1G 121
 LE15: Glas . . . . . . . . . . . . . . . . . . . . .1J 139
 LE18: Wig . . . . . . . . . . . . . . . . . . . . . .5K 77
 LE65: Pac . . . . . . . . . . . . . . . . . . . . . .2A 36
 LE67: Coal, Swan . . . . . . . . . . . . . . . .7B 26
Spring Rd. LE67: Ibs . . . . . . . . . . . . . . . .3A 52

Springs, The LE9: B Ast . . . . . . . . . . . . .4C 86
 LE17: Swin . . . . . . . . . . . . . . . . . . . . .3H 157
Spring Ter. LE16: Med . . . . . . . . . . . . . . .7D 140
Springway Cl. LE5: Leic . . . . . . . . . . . . . .2G 73
Springwell Cl. LE8: Count . . . . . . . . . . . .5E 82
Springwell Dr. LE8: Count . . . . . . . . . . . .5D 82
Springwell La. LE8: Whet . . . . . . . . . . . . .4K 81
SPROXTON . . . . . . . . . . . .2H 113 (2B 160)
Sproxton Rd. NG33: Buck . . . . . . . . . . . .5G 113
Spruce Av. LE11: Lou . . . . . . . . . . . . . . .4D 30
Spruce Way LE17: Lut . . . . . . . . . . . . . . .3H 153
Square, The DE12: Oak . . . . . . . . . . . . . .5C 34
 LE3: Glen . . . . . . . . . . . . . . . . . . . . . .5F 63
 LE7: Thurn . . . . . . . . . . . . . . . . . . . . .3H 73
 LE8: Count . . . . . . . . . . . . . . . . . . . . .5F 83
 LE8: New H . . . . . . . . . . . . . . . . . . . . .3F 85
 LE9: Earl S . . . . . . . . . . . . . . . . . . . .2D 100
 LE9: Sap . . . . . . . . . . . . . . . . . . . . . .4J 105
 LE12: L Wha . . . . . . . . . . . . . . . . . . . .5F 13
 LE3: S Luf . . . . . . . . . . . . . . . . . . . . .3B 136
 LE16: Mkt H . . . . . . . . . . . . . . . . . . .4E 150
 LE17: Frol . . . . . . . . . . . . . . . . . . . . .2F 143
 LE17: Shea . . . . . . . . . . . . . . . . . . . .5J 147
 LE19: Litt . . . . . . . . . . . . . . . . . . . . . .3G 81
 LE67: Bag . . . . . . . . . . . . . . . . . . . . .1F 93
 NG13: Bott . . . . . . . . . . . . . . . . . . . .1G 107
 PE9: Ryh . . . . . . . . . . . . . . . . . . . . . .5H 129
Square Ct. LE4: Birs . . . . . . . . . . . . . . . .6H 59
Squires Cl. LE15: L'ham . . . . . . . . . . . . .5C 122
Squires Grn. LE10: Bur . . . . . . . . . . . . . .5J 103
Squire's Ride LE7: East G . . . . . . . . . . . .4F 47
Squirrel La. LE19: Nar . . . . . . . . . . . . . . .2E 80
Squirrel's Cnr. LE7: East G . . . . . . . . . . .4G 47
Squirrel Way LE11: Lou . . . . . . . . . . . . . .1D 30
Stable Cl. LE19: Litt . . . . . . . . . . . . . . . .2G 81
Stableford Cl. LE12: Shep . . . . . . . . . . . .6D 16
Stablegate Way LE16: L Bow . . . . . . . . . .4G 151
Stables, The LE10: Bur . . . . . . . . . . . . . .6G 103
Stables Ct. LE15: O'ham . . . . . . . . . . . . .4H 127
Stackley Rd. LE8: G Gle . . . . . . . . . . . . . .7K 79
Stadium Cl. LE67: Coal . . . . . . . . . . . . . .4C 38
Stadium Pl. LE4: Leic . . . . . . . . . . . . . . .4E 64
Stadium Ri. LE4: Leic . . . . . . . . . . . . . . .4D 64
Stadon Rd. LE7: Anst . . . . . . . . . . . . . . .7H 57
Stafford Av. LE13: Mel M . . . . . . . . . . . . .3G 117
Stafford Dr. LE18: Wig . . . . . . . . . . . . . . .6F 77
Stafford Leys LE3: Leic E . . . . . . . . . . . . .4D 68
Staffords Acre DE74: Keg . . . . . . . . . . . . .6G 9
Stafford St. LE4: Leic . . . . . . . . . . . . . . .3J 65
 LE9: Barw . . . . . . . . . . . . . . . . . . . . . .4K 99
STAINBY . . . . . . . . . . . . . . . . . . . . . . .2C 161
Stainby Rd. NG33: Buck . . . . . . . . . . . . .5H 113
Staindale LE18: Wig . . . . . . . . . . . . . . . .6B 78
STAINFIELD . . . . . . . . . . . . . . . . . . . . .2D 161
Stainmore Av. LE19: Nar . . . . . . . . . . . . .6E 74
Stainsdale Grn. LE67: Whit . . . . . . . . . . .2G 39
Staley Av. LE65: Ash Z . . . . . . . . . . . . . .7H 23
STAMFORD . . . . . . . . . . . . . . . . . . . . .1D 165
Stamford Cl. LE3: Glen . . . . . . . . . . . . . .6F 63
 LE6: Ratby . . . . . . . . . . . . . . . . . . . . .5A 62
 LE16: Mkt H . . . . . . . . . . . . . . . . . . .5E 150
Stamford Dr. LE6: Groby . . . . . . . . . . . . .4D 62
 LE7: Crop . . . . . . . . . . . . . . . . . . . . . .3K 57
 LE67: Coal . . . . . . . . . . . . . . . . . . . . .2J 39
Stamford End LE15: Ext . . . . . . . . . . . . .2D 128
Stamford Hall LE2: Leic . . . . . . . . . . . . . .7B 72
Stamford Rd. LE9: K Mux . . . . . . . . . . . .3C 68
 LE15: Emp . . . . . . . . . . . . . . . . . . . . .7C 128
 LE15: Ext . . . . . . . . . . . . . . . . . . . . .2D 128
 LE15: Mor, S Luf . . . . . . . . . . . . . . . . .7K 135
 LE15: O'ham . . . . . . . . . . . . . . . . . . .4J 127
 NG33: Sew . . . . . . . . . . . . . . . . . . . .7K 113
 PE9: Ess . . . . . . . . . . . . . . . . . . . . . .3J 129
 PE9: Ket . . . . . . . . . . . . . . . .7K 135 & 4J 137
Stamford St. LE1: Leic . . . . . . . . .5D 4 (2F 71)
 LE3: Glen . . . . . . . . . . . . . . . . . . . . . .5F 63
 LE6: Ratby . . . . . . . . . . . . . . . . . . . . .5A 62
Stanage Rd. LE12: Sileby . . . . . . . . . . . .7K 33
Stanbrig LE18: Wig . . . . . . . . . . . . . . . . .1A 84
Stancliff Rd. LE4: Leic . . . . . . . . . . . . . . .1B 66
Standard Hill LE67: Hug . . . . . . . . . . . . . .5B 38
Stanfell Rd. LE2: Leic . . . . . . . . . . . . . . .7G 71
Stanford Hall . . . . . . . . . . . . . . . . . . . . .4K 157
Stanford Hill LE11: Lou . . . . . . . . . . . . . .4F 19
Stanford La. LE12: Cote . . . . . . . . . . . . . .2H 19
STANFORD ON AVON . . . . . . . . . . . . . .3C 163
STANFORD ON SOAR . . . . . . .1G 19 (2C 159)
Stanford Rd. LE12: Nor S . . . . . . . . . . . . .1C 18
 LE17: Swin . . . . . . . . . . . . . . . . . . . . .4H 157
 NN6: Swin . . . . . . . . . . . . . . . . . . . . .4H 157
Stanhope Rd. DE11: Swad . . . . . . . . . . . .1A 22
 LE18: Wig . . . . . . . . . . . . . . . . . . . . . .7A 78
Stanhope St. LE5: Leic . . . . . . . . . . . . . .2K 71
Stanier Dr. LE4: Leic . . . . . . . . . . . . . . . .2B 66
Stanier Rd. LE9: B Ast . . . . . . . . . . . . . . .4E 86
Stanilands LE15: Whis . . . . . . . . . . . . . .2B 122

STANION . . . . . . . . . . . . . . . . . . . .3C 165
Stanleigh Gdns. DE12: Don . . . . . . . . . .4A 34
STANLEY . . . . . . . . . . . . . . . . . . . . .1B 158
Stanley Burroughs Almshouse LE9: Sap . .4J 105
STANLEY COMMON . . . . . . . . . . . . . .1B 158
Stanley Dr. LE5: Leic . . . . . . . . . . . . . . .6C 66
Stanley Rd. CV13: Mkt B . . . . . . . . . . . .3C 94
LE2: Leic . . . . . . . . . . . . . . . . . . . . . .4J 71
LE10: Hinc . . . . . . . . . . . . . . . . . . . . .1F 103
Stanley St. LE9: Barw . . . . . . . . . . . . . .4K 99
LE11: Lou . . . . . . . . . . . . . . . . . . . . . .1F 31
LE13: Mel M . . . . . . . . . . . . . . . . . . .4G 117
STANTON . . . . . . . . . . . . . . . . . . . . . .3A 158
STANTON BY BRIDGE . . . . . . . . . . . . .2A 158
STANTON BY DALE . . . . . . . . . . . . . .1B 158
Stanton La. LE9: Crof, Pott M . . . . . . . . .3A 80
LE9: Sap, S Stan . . . . . . . . . . . . . . . .3G 105
LE67: Eli, S Bar . . . . . . . . . . . . . . . . . .4H 53
LE67: S Bar . . . . . . . . . . . . . . . . . . . . .2B 54
LE67: Thor . . . . . . . . . . . . . . . . . . . . .1J 93
STANTON-ON-THE-WOLDS . . . . . . . . .1D 159
Stanton Rd. LE9: Elm . . . . . . . . . . . . . .6F 101
LE9: Sap . . . . . . . . . . . . . . . . . . . . . .4J 105
LE14: Ash H . . . . . . . . . . . . . . . . . . . .4A 116
Stanton Row LE2: Leic . . . . . . . . . . . . . .2F 77
STANTON UNDER BARDON . . . . . . .4B 54 (3B 158)
Stanway Cl. LE16: L Bow . . . . . . . . . . .4G 151
Stanyon Cl. LE8: Count . . . . . . . . . . . . .5E 82
STAPENHILL . . . . . . . . . . . . . . . . . . . .2A 158
STAPLEFORD
  Melton Mowbray . . . . . . . . . . . . . . . .3B 160
  Salisbury . . . . . . . . . . . . . . . . . . . . .1B 158
Stapleford Rd. LE4: Leic . . . . . . . . . . . .2D 64
LE15: Whis . . . . . . . . . . . . . . . . . . . .1B 122
Staplehurst Av. LE3: Brau . . . . . . . . . . .7J 69
STAPLETON . . . . . . . . . . . . . . . .1J 99 (2B 162)
Stapleton La. CV13: Dadl . . . . . . . . . . . .2C 98
CV13: S Che . . . . . . . . . . . . . . . . . . . .7C 94
LE9: Barw . . . . . . . . . . . . . . . . . . . . .1J 99
LE9: K Mal . . . . . . . . . . . . . . . . . . . . .6F 95
Star Cotts. LE9: S Stan . . . . . . . . . . . .6J 101
Starkie Av. DE74: C Don . . . . . . . . . . . . .5H 7
Starmer Cl. LE9: Cosb . . . . . . . . . . . . . .6J 81
Statham St. LE9: N Ver . . . . . . . . . . . . .5H 93
STATHERN . . . . . . . . . . . . . . .2H 109 (1A 160)
Stathern La. LE14: Harb . . . . . . . . . . . .3D 108
Stathern Rd. LE14: Harb . . . . . . . . . . . .2D 108
Station App. LE15: O'ham . . . . . . . . . . .3H 127
Station App. Ind. Est. LE15: O'ham . . . . .3H 127
(not continuous)
Station Av. LE11: Lou . . . . . . . . . . . . . . .5D 18
Station Cl. LE9: K Mux . . . . . . . . . . . . . .3C 68
Station Dr. DE12: Moi . . . . . . . . . . . . . . .7B 22
LE9: K Mux . . . . . . . . . . . . . . . . . . . . .3C 68
Station Hill LE14: J O'Ga . . . . . . . . . . . .7J 119
LE67: Swan . . . . . . . . . . . . . . . . . . . .7A 26
Station Hollow LE8: K Bea . . . . . . . . . . .3J 89
Station La. LE7: Scra . . . . . . . . . . . . . . .1H 73
LE14: Ash, K Bel . . . . . . . . . . . . . . . .3F 115
LE14: O Dal . . . . . . . . . . . . . . . . . . . .7B 110
LE17: Leire . . . . . . . . . . . . . . . . . . . .2J 143
Station M. LE65: Ash Z . . . . . . . . . . . . . .6K 23
Station Rd. CV13: H Hill . . . . . . . . . . . . .5G 97
CV13: Mkt B . . . . . . . . . . . . . . . . . . . .2A 94
CV13: S Gol . . . . . . . . . . . . . . . . . . . .3A 98
CV13: S'one . . . . . . . . . . . . . . . . . . . .3H 91
CV23: Lilb . . . . . . . . . . . . . . . . . . . . .7F 157
DE73: Mel . . . . . . . . . . . . . . . . . . . . . .7A 6
DE74: C Don . . . . . . . . . . . . . . . . . . . .4K 7
DE74: Hem . . . . . . . . . . . . . . . . . . . . .2A 8
DE74: Keg . . . . . . . . . . . . . . . . . . . . . .5H 9
LE3: Glen . . . . . . . . . . . . . . . . . . . . . .5F 63
LE4: Birs . . . . . . . . . . . . . . . . . . . . . .1F 65
LE6: Ratby . . . . . . . . . . . . . . . . . . . . .6A 62
LE7: Crop, R'ley . . . . . . . . . . . . . . . . .3J 57
LE7: Rear . . . . . . . . . . . . . . . . . . . . .1J 47
(not continuous)
LE7: Sys . . . . . . . . . . . . . . . . . . . . . .2C 60
LE7: Thurn . . . . . . . . . . . . . . . . . . . .2H 73
LE8: Count . . . . . . . . . . . . . . . . . . . . .6D 82
LE8: G Gle, Wist . . . . . . . . . . . . . . . . .5H 85
LE9: B Ast . . . . . . . . . . . . . . . . . . . . .4D 86
(not continuous)
LE9: Crof . . . . . . . . . . . . . . . . . . . . . .5A 80
LE9: Des . . . . . . . . . . . . . . . . . . . . . .2J 95
LE9: Earl S . . . . . . . . . . . . . . . . . . . .4D 100
LE9: Elm . . . . . . . . . . . . . . . . . . . . . .5D 100
LE9: K Mux . . . . . . . . . . . . . . . . . . . .2B 68
LE9: S Stan . . . . . . . . . . . . . . . . . . . .7G 101
LE10: Hinc . . . . . . . . . . . . . . . . . . . . .3G 103
LE12: Quo . . . . . . . . . . . . . . . . . . . . .5A 32
LE12: Sut Bon . . . . . . . . . . . . . . . . . . . .5J 9
LE14: G Dal . . . . . . . . . . . . . . . . . . . .6B 120
LE14: Up Bro . . . . . . . . . . . . . . . . . . .1A 110
LE15: Mor . . . . . . . . . . . . . . . . . . . . .6K 135
LE15: N Luf, S Luf . . . . . . . . . . . . . . .1B 136
LE15: O'ham . . . . . . . . . . . . . . . . . . .4H 127

Station Rd. LE15: Upp . . . . . . . . . . . . . .2C 138
LE15: Whis . . . . . . . . . . . . . . . . . . . .2D 122
LE15: Win . . . . . . . . . . . . . . . . . . . . .5C 134
LE16: G Bow . . . . . . . . . . . . . . . . . . .2G 151
LE17: Cat . . . . . . . . . . . . . . . . . . . . .7F 157
LE17: D Bas . . . . . . . . . . . . . . . . . . . .1E 144
LE17: H Bos . . . . . . . . . . . . . . . . . . . .7A 148
LE17: Lut . . . . . . . . . . . . . . . . . . . . .5K 153
LE17: N Kil . . . . . . . . . . . . . . . . . . . .2K 155
LE17: Ull . . . . . . . . . . . . . . . . . . . . . .7F 143
LE18: Wig . . . . . . . . . . . . . . . . . . . . .6H 77
LE19: Litt, Nar . . . . . . . . . . . . . . . . . .2G 81
LE65: Ash Z . . . . . . . . . . . . . . . . . . . .6K 23
LE67: Bag . . . . . . . . . . . . . . . . . . . . .5F 53
LE67: Hug . . . . . . . . . . . . . . . . . . . . .7C 38
LE67: Ibs . . . . . . . . . . . . . . . . . . . . . .4H 51
NG11: King S . . . . . . . . . . . . . . . . . . . .4K 9
NG13: Bott . . . . . . . . . . . . . . . . . . . .1H 107
PE9: Ess . . . . . . . . . . . . . . . . . . . . . .1K 129
PE9: Ket . . . . . . . . . . . . . . . . . . . . . .6H 137
Station Rd. Ind. Est. CV13: Mkt B . . . . . .2A 94
Station St. LE1: Leic . . . . . . . . . .5F 4 (2G 71)
LE8: K Bea . . . . . . . . . . . . . . . . . . . . .3J 89
LE8: Whet . . . . . . . . . . . . . . . . . . . . .1J 81
LE11: Lou . . . . . . . . . . . . . . . . . . . . .6D 18
LE18: Wig . . . . . . . . . . . . . . . . . . . . .6G 77
Station Ter. LE67: Bag . . . . . . . . . . . . . .6G 53
LE67: Hea . . . . . . . . . . . . . . . . . . . . .4G 51
Station Yd. LE10: Hinc . . . . . . . . . . . . .4G 103
Staunton Cl. DE74: C Don . . . . . . . . . . . .4J 7
STAUNTON IN THE VALE . . . . . . . . . .1B 160
Staveley Cl. LE12: Sileby . . . . . . . . . . . .2K 45
LE18: Wig . . . . . . . . . . . . . . . . . . . . .6A 78
Staveley Ct. LE11: Lou . . . . . . . . . . . . . .5F 19
Staveley Rd. LE5: Leic . . . . . . . . . . . . . .4K 71
Staythorpe Rd. LE4: Leic . . . . . . . . . . . .1C 66
Stebbings Rd. LE2: Leic . . . . . . . . . . . . .3D 76
Steele Cl. LE5: Leic . . . . . . . . . . . . . . . .2C 72
Steeple Cl. LE18: Wig . . . . . . . . . . . . . .4A 78
STEEPLE GIDDING . . . . . . . . . . . . . . .3D 165
Steeple Row LE11: Lou . . . . . . . . . . . . . .6F 19
Steins La. LE5: Leic . . . . . . . . . . . . . . . .6D 66
Stelle Way LE3: Glen . . . . . . . . . . . . . . .3H 63
Stemborough La. LE17: Leire . . . . . . . . .2K 143
Stenor Cl. LE8: Flec . . . . . . . . . . . . . . . .3A 88
STENSON . . . . . . . . . . . . . . . . . . . . . .2A 158
STENSON FIELDS . . . . . . . . . . . . . . . .1A 158
Stenson Rd. LE3: Leic . . . . . . . . . . . . . .5A 64
LE67: Coal . . . . . . . . . . . . . . . . . . . . .2D 38
STENWITH . . . . . . . . . . . . . . . . . . . . .1B 160
Stephenson Cl. LE6: Groby . . . . . . . . . . .3C 62
LE9: B Ast . . . . . . . . . . . . . . . . . . . . .6E 86
Stephenson Ct. LE3: Glen . . . . . . . . . . . .4G 63
LE67: Coal . . . . . . . . . . . . . . . . . . . . .2A 38
Stephenson Dr. LE3: Leic . . . . . . . . . . . .7B 64
Stephenson Ind. Est. LE67: Coal . . . . . . .2B 38
Stephenson Rd. LE10: Hinc . . . . . . . . . .4B 102
Stephenson Way LE6: Groby . . . . . . . . . .3C 62
LE67: Coal . . . . . . . . . . . . . . . . . . . . .1A 38
Stevens Cl. LE9: S Stan . . . . . . . . . . . .1K 105
LE17: Ull . . . . . . . . . . . . . . . . . . . . . .7F 143
Stevens Gdns. LE9: Cosb . . . . . . . . . . . .5H 81
Stevens St. LE16: Mkt H . . . . . . . . . . . .4D 150
Stevenstone Cl. LE2: Oad . . . . . . . . . . . .3F 79
Stewards Ct. LE9: Des . . . . . . . . . . . . . .2H 95
Stewart Av. LE19: End . . . . . . . . . . . . . .7E 74
Stewart Dr. LE11: Lou . . . . . . . . . . . . . .4A 18
Steyning Cres. LE3: Glen . . . . . . . . . . . .5H 63
STIBBINGTON . . . . . . . . . . . . . . . . . .2D 165
Stiles, The LE7: Sys . . . . . . . . . . . . . . .1D 60
Stiles Cl. LE9: B Ast . . . . . . . . . . . . . . .5D 86
Stimpson Rd. LE67: Coal . . . . . . . . . . . .3E 38
Stinford Leys LE16: L Bow . . . . . . . . . . .4H 151
Stinson Way LE67: Whit . . . . . . . . . . . . .6D 26
Stirling Av. LE10: Hinc . . . . . . . . . . . . .2D 102
LE11: Lou . . . . . . . . . . . . . . . . . . . . . .5B 18
Stirling Cl. LE12: Moun . . . . . . . . . . . . .4C 44
LE12: Quo . . . . . . . . . . . . . . . . . . . . .4K 31
Stirling Dr. LE7: Thurn . . . . . . . . . . . . .1H 73
Stirling Rd. LE13: Mel M . . . . . . . . . . . .4D 116
STIVICHALL . . . . . . . . . . . . . . . . . . . .3A 162
STOCKERSTON . . . . . . . . . . . . . . . . .2B 164
Stockerston Cres. LE15: Upp . . . . . . . . .3A 138
Stockerston La. LE16: G Eas . . . . . . . . .4K 141
Stockerston Rd. LE15: Upp . . . . . . . . . .3A 138
Stockerton Rd. LE15: Alle . . . . . . . . . . .7G 133
Stockingers Ct. LE11: Lou . . . . . . . . . . . .5G 19
(off Mill La.)
STOCKINGFORD . . . . . . . . . . . . . . . . .2A 162
Stocking Leys LE10: Bur . . . . . . . . . . . .4K 103
Stockland Rd. LE2: Leic . . . . . . . . . . . . .4E 76
Stocks Hill LE15: Mant . . . . . . . . . . . . .2C 134
PE9: Ket . . . . . . . . . . . . . . . . . . . . . .6H 137
Stocks Rd. LE7: Scra . . . . . . . . . . . . . . .6H 67
Stockton Ho. LE3: Glen . . . . . . . . . . . . .1H 69
Stockton Rd. LE4: Leic . . . . . . . . . . . . . .5A 66

Stockwell, The LE12: Wym . . . . . . . . . . .2K 21
Stockwell Cl. LE16: L Bow . . . . . . . . . . .4H 151
Stockwell Head LE10: Hinc . . . . . . . . . .2G 103
Stockwell Rd. LE2: Leic . . . . . . . . . . . . .1K 77
STOKE . . . . . . . . . . . . . . . . . . . . . . . .3A 162
STOKE ALBANY . . . . . . . . . . . . . . . . .3B 164
STOKE BARDOLPH . . . . . . . . . . . . . . .1D 159
STOKE DOYLE . . . . . . . . . . . . . . . . . .3D 165
STOKE DRY . . . . . . . . . . . . . . .7A 138 (2B 164)
STOKE GOLDING . . . . . . . . . . . .3A 98 (2A 162)
Stoke La. CV13: Dadl . . . . . . . . . . . . . . .2B 98
CV13: H Hill, S Gol . . . . . . . . . . . . . . . .5H 97
LE10: Wyk . . . . . . . . . . . . . . . . . . . . .6C 98
Stoke Rd. CV13: S Gol . . . . . . . . . . . . . .3C 98
LE10: Hinc . . . . . . . . . . . . . . . . . . . . .5D 98
LE15: Lyd . . . . . . . . . . . . . . . . . . . . .7D 138
STOKE ROCHFORD . . . . . . . . . . . . . . .2C 161
Stokesby Ri. LE2: Leic . . . . . . . . . . . . . .7C 76
Stokes Cl. LE8: Bla . . . . . . . . . . . . . . . .1A 82
Stokes Dr. LE3: Leic . . . . . . . . . . . . . . . .6B 64
Stokes Paddock LE14: L Cla . . . . . . . . . .2G 111
Stonebow Cl. LE11: Lou . . . . . . . . . . . . .4K 17
Stonebow Wlk. LE11: Lou . . . . . . . . . . . .4J 17
Stonebridge St. LE5: Leic . . . . . . . . . . . .1K 71
Stonechat Wlk. LE5: Leic . . . . . . . . . . . .1J 71
Stone Cl. LE4: Beau L . . . . . . . . . . . . . .7A 58
Stonecroft LE8: Count . . . . . . . . . . . . . .6C 82
Stonecrop Rd. LE5: Ham . . . . . . . . . . . .4E 66
Stonehaven Cl. LE67: Coal . . . . . . . . . . .3J 39
Stonehaven Rd. LE4: Leic . . . . . . . . . . . .2K 65
Stonehill DE74: C Don . . . . . . . . . . . . . .6K 7
Stonehill Av. LE4: Birs . . . . . . . . . . . . . .4G 59
Stonehill Ct. LE8: G Gle . . . . . . . . . . . .5A 130
Stonehill Dr. LE8: G Gle . . . . . . . . . . . .5A 130
Stonehills DE74: Keg . . . . . . . . . . . . . . .6G 9
Stonehurst Family Farm & Motor Mus. . . .1D 44
Stonehurst Rd. LE3: Brau . . . . . . . . . . . .7K 69
Stoneleigh Mnr. LE2: Leic . . . . . . . . . . . .5K 71
Stoneleigh Way LE3: Leic . . . . . . . . . . . .6B 64
Stoneley Rd. CV13: S Gol . . . . . . . . . . . .4A 98
Stone Row LE67: Coal . . . . . . . . . . . . . .2D 38
STONESBY . . . . . . . . . . . . . . . . . . . . .2B 160
Stonesby Av. LE2: Leic . . . . . . . . . . . . . .3E 76
Stonesby Rd. LE14: Spro . . . . . . . . . . . .2G 113
LE14: W Wol . . . . . . . . . . . . . . . . . . .2D 112
Stonesby Wlk. LE2: Leic . . . . . . . . . . . . .3F 77
Stone Style Gdns. LE14: Scal . . . . . . . . .6C 112
Stoneycroft Rd. LE9: Earl S . . . . . . . . . .3C 100
STONEYGATE
  Hinckley . . . . . . . . . . . . . . . . . . . . .1H 103
  Leicester . . . . . . . . . . . . . . .6K 71 (1D 163)
Stoneygate Av. LE2: Leic . . . . . . . . . . . .6J 71
Stoneygate Ct. LE2: Leic . . . . . . . . . . . .5J 71
Stoneygate Dr. LE10: Hinc . . . . . . . . . . .7H 99
Stoneygate Rd. LE2: Leic . . . . . . . . . . . .5J 71
Stoney Hollow LE17: Lut . . . . . . . . . . . .5J 153
Stoney La. DE12: A Mag . . . . . . . . . . . . .4B 48
LE67: Cole . . . . . . . . . . . . . . . . . . . . .4J 25
LE67: S Bar . . . . . . . . . . . . . . . . . . . .4D 54
STONEY STANTON . . . . . . . . . . .1K 105 (2B 162)
Stoneywell Rd. LE4: Beau L . . . . . . . . . . .1K 63
Stonton Rd. LE16: C Lan . . . . . . . . . . . .1A 140
STONTON WYVILLE . . . . . . . . . . . . . .2A 164
Stoop La. LE12: Quo . . . . . . . . . . . . . . .5A 32
Stordon La. LE67: Grif, Thrin . . . . . . . . . .7A 14
Storer Cl. LE12: Sileby . . . . . . . . . . . . . .1K 45
Storer Hall LE11: Lou . . . . . . . . . . . . . . .6D 18
Storer Rd. LE11: Lou . . . . . . . . . . . . . . .6D 18
Stores La. LE8: Flec . . . . . . . . . . . . . . . .4B 88
Storey St. LE3: Leic . . . . . . . . . . . . . . . .7D 64
Storkit La. LE12: Wym . . . . . . . . . . . . . .1J 21
Stornaway Rd. LE5: Leic . . . . . . . . . . . . .7F 67
STOUGHTON . . . . . . . . . . . . . .6G 73 (1D 163)
Stoughton Av. LE2: Leic . . . . . . . . . . . . .6K 71
Stoughton Cl. LE2: Oad . . . . . . . . . . . . .2D 78
Stoughton Dr. LE5: Leic . . . . . . . . . . . . .5B 72
Stoughton Dr. Nth. LE5: Leic . . . . . . . . . .4K 71
Stoughton Dr. Sth. LE2: Leic . . . . . . . . . .6B 72
Stoughton La. LE2: Leic . . . . . . . . . . . . .5D 72
Stoughton Rd. LE2: Leic . . . . . . . . . . . . .6K 71
(Stoneygate)
LE2: Leic . . . . . . . . . . . . . . . . . . . . . .4G 73
(Thurnby)
Stoughton St. LE2: Leic . . . . . . . . . . . . .2H 71
Stoughton St. Sth. LE2: Leic . . . . .5G 4 (2H 71)
Stour Cl. LE2: Oad . . . . . . . . . . . . . . . . .2F 79
STOW . . . . . . . . . . . . . . . . . . . . . . . .1D 161
Stowe Cl. LE3: Leic . . . . . . . . . . . . . . . .5A 64
LE65: Ash Z . . . . . . . . . . . . . . . . . . . .4J 23
Stow Hill LE14: Spro . . . . . . . . . . . . . . .2H 113
Strachan Cl. LE12: Moun . . . . . . . . . . . . .3F 45
STRAGGLETHORPE . . . . . . . . . . . . . .1D 159
Strancliffe La. LE12: Bar S . . . . . . . . . . .2C 32
Strand, The LE2: Leic . . . . . . . . . . . . . . .6G 71
Strasbourg Dr. LE4: Leic . . . . . . . . . . . . .3B 64
Stratford Rd. LE3: Brau . . . . . . . . . . . . .6K 69

| | | |
|---|---|---|
| Strathaven Rd. LE4: Leic . . . .2K **65** | Sutherland St. LE2: Leic . . . . . . .3J **71** | Swithland Cl. LE11: Lou . . . . . . . .5A **18** |
| Strathern Rd. LE3: Leic . . . . .4K **63** | Suthern Cl. LE15: O'ham . . . . . . .2J **127** | LE67: Mark . . . . . . . . . . .5G **55** |
| Strathmore Av. LE4: Leic . . . .4K **65** | Suthers Rd. DE74: Keg . . . . . . . .6F **9** | Swithland Ct. LE3: Brau . . . . . . .1K **75** |
| Strathmore Cl. LE67: Coal . . . .4J **39** | SUTTON | LE12: W Eav . . . . . . . . . .4E **42** |
| Strathmore Rd. LE10: Hinc . . .4D **102** | Nottingham . . . . . . . . . .1A **160** | Swithland La. LE7: R'ley . . . . . . .3B **44** |
| Stratton Cl. LE16: Mkt H . . . .6D **150** | Peterborough . . . . . . . . .2D **165** | Swithland Rd. LE12: Swith . . . . .1J **57** |
| Strawberry Gdns. LE19: End . . .4D **74** | Sutton Av. LE4: Leic . . . . . . . . .5J **65** | LE12: W Eav . . . . . . . . . .7E **42** |
| Strawberry La. DE11: Blac . . . .3D **22** | SUTTON BASSETT . . . . . . . . .2A **164** | LE67: Coal . . . . . . . . . . .4J **39** |
| Streamside Cl. LE9: B Ast . . . .5D **86** | SUTTON BONINGTON . . . . . . .2C **159** | Sword Cl. LE3: Glen . . . . . . . . .7G **63** |
| Street, The LE15: S Luf . . . . .4C **136** | SUTTON CHENEY . . . . . . . . .1B **162** | Sword Dr. LE10: Hinc . . . . . . . .7E **98** |
| STRELLEY . . . . . . . . . . . . . . . .1C **159** | Sutton Cl. LE2: Oad . . . . . . . . .5D **78** | Sybil Rd. LE3: Leic . . . . . . . . . .6B **70** |
| Strensall Rd. LE2: Leic . . . . .5D **76** | LE10: Hinc . . . . . . . . . .7J **99** | Sycamore Cl. LE2: Leic . . . . . . .6B **72** |
| STRETTON | LE12: Quo . . . . . . . . . . .6K **31** | LE2: Oad . . . . . . . . . . . .5J **79** |
| Burton upon Trent . . . . . . .2A **158** | Sutton Ct. LE9: B Ast . . . . . . . .2C **86** | LE7: Sys . . . . . . . . . . . . .3D **60** |
| Oakham . . . . . . . .2K **125** (3C **161**) | LE16: Mkt H . . . . . . . . .6E **150** | LE9: N Ver . . . . . . . . . . .6G **93** |
| Stretton Cl. LE10: Bur . . . . . .5G **103** | SUTTON IN THE ELMS . . .2C **86** (2C **163**) | LE10: Bur . . . . . . . . . . .6H **103** |
| Stretton Ct. LE8: G Gle . . . . . .1K **85** | Sutton La. CV13: Cad . . . . . . . .6C **94** | LE13: Mel M . . . . . . . . . .2E **116** |
| Stretton Dr. LE67: Coal . . . . . .3J **39** | CV13: Dadl . . . . . . . . . .1B **98** | LE65: Ash Z . . . . . . . . . .4J **51** |
| STRETTON EN LE FIELD . . . . .3A **158** | CV13: Mkt B . . . . . . . . .4D **94** | Sycamore Dr. DE12: Moi . . . . . .5D **22** |
| Stretton Hall Dr. LE2: Oad . . .5H **79** | Sutton Lodge LE15: O'ham . . . .4K **127** | LE6: Groby . . . . . . . . . . .3D **62** |
| Stretton La. LE7: Hou H . . . . .3B **130** | Sutton Pl. LE4: Leic . . . . . . . . .4J **65** | LE17: Lut . . . . . . . . . . . .4G **153** |
| Stretton Rd. LE3: Leic . . . . . .2C **70** | Sutton Rd. DE74: Keg . . . . . . . .7G **9** | LE65: Ash Z . . . . . . . . . .4B **24** |
| LE8: G Gle . . . . . . . . . . .7K **79** | LE2: Leic . . . . . . . . . . .7G **71** | Sycamore Gro. LE6: Groby . . . . .3D **62** |
| LE15: Gree, Stre . . . . . .5G **125** | LE16: G Bow . . . . . . . . .1H **151** | Sycamore La. LE14: W'ham . . . .1G **121** |
| STRETTON UNDER FOSSE . . . . .3B **162** | (Dingley Rd.) | Sycamore Rd. DE74: C Don . . . .3K **7** |
| Stretton Vw. DE12: Oak . . . . . .6B **34** | LE16: G Bow . . . . . . . . .2J **151** | LE4: Birs . . . . . . . . . . . .4G **59** |
| Strollers Way LE7: East G . . . .5F **47** | (Harborough Rd.) | LE15: N Luf . . . . . . . . . .1B **136** |
| Stroma Way LE8: Count . . . . .1F **83** | SWADLINCOTE . . . . . . . . .1A **22** (3A **158**) | LE67: Coal . . . . . . . . . . .4G **39** |
| Stroud Ct. NG13: Bott . . . . . .1H **107** | Swadlincote Rd. DE11: W'lle . . .1B **22** | Sycamores, The LE17: S Kil . . . .6H **155** |
| Stroud Rd. LE5: Leic . . . . . . .7K **65** | Swains Grn. LE10: Bur . . . . . . . .5J **103** | Sycamore St. LE8: Bla . . . . . . . .1B **82** |
| Stroud's Cl. LE14: Hos . . . . . .5B **108** | Swainson Rd. LE4: Leic . . . . . . .6A **66** | Sycamore Way CV13: Mkt B . . . .3D **94** |
| STROXTON . . . . . . . . . . . . . . .1C **161** | Swain St. LE1: Leic . . . . . .4F **4** (2G **71**) | LE11: Lou . . . . . . . . . . .4E **30** |
| Strudwick Way LE8: Whet . . . .7A **76** | Swale Cl. LE2: Oad . . . . . . . . .2F **79** | LE19: Litt . . . . . . . . . . .3F **81** |
| Strutt Rd. LE10: Bur . . . . . . .6K **103** | LE13: Mel M . . . . . . . . .6E **116** | Sykefield Av. LE3: Leic . . . . . . .3C **70** |
| Stuart Ct. LE2: Leic . . . . . . . .6J **71** | Swallow Cl. LE3: Leic E . . . . . . .6C **68** | Sykes La. LE15: Emp . . . . . . . . .7A **128** |
| LE8: K Bea . . . . . . . . . .3J **89** | LE12: Moun . . . . . . . . . .2F **45** | Sylvan Av. LE5: Leic . . . . . . . . .1K **71** |
| Stuart Cres. LE16: Gar . . . . . .3J **149** | Swallow Ct. LE10: Hinc . . . . . . .4C **102** | Sylvan St. LE3: Leic . . . . . . . . .1C **70** |
| Stuart Rd. LE2: G Par . . . . . . .5C **76** | Swallow Dale LE67: Thrin . . . . . .4D **26** | Sylvan Way LE3: Leic E . . . . . . .3F **69** |
| LE16: Mkt H . . . . . . . . .6D **150** | Swallowdale Dr. LE4: Beau L . . . .7B **58** | Symington Way LE16: Mkt H . . . .4E **150** |
| Stuart St. LE3: Leic . . . . . . . .4D **70** | Swallowdale Rd. LE13: Mel M . . .7E **116** | SYSONBY . . . . . . . . . . . . . . . .4C **116** |
| LE8: K Bea . . . . . . . . . .3J **89** | Swallow Dr. LE7: Sys . . . . . . . .1A **60** | Sysonby Grange La. | 
| Stuart Way LE65: Ash Z . . . . .6K **23** | Swallows Dale LE7: East G . . . . .4G **47** | LE13: Mel M . . . . . . . . .5C **116** |
| Stubbs Rd. LE4: Leic . . . . . . .6H **65** | Swallows Dr. LE14: Sta . . . . . . .2G **109** | Sysonby St. LE13: Mel M . . . . . .3D **116** |
| Studbrook Cl. DE74: C Don . . .5H **7** | Swallow Wlk. LE7: Hat . . . . . . . .1J **17** | SYSTON |
| Stud Farm Cl. DE73: B Hil . . . .7A **10** | Swan Cl. LE2: G Par . . . . . . . . .6A **76** | Grantham . . . . . . . . . . .1C **161** |
| Sturdee Cl. LE2: Leic . . . . . . .4D **76** | LE12: Bar S . . . . . . . . . .3E **32** | Leicester . . . . . . . . .1D **60** (3D **159**) |
| Sturdee Grn. LE2: Leic . . . . . .4C **76** | LE12: Moun . . . . . . . . . .2F **45** | Syston By-Pass LE4: Thurm . . . .4A **60** |
| Sturdee Rd. LE2: Leic . . . . . .4C **76** | LE13: Mel M . . . . . . . . .7E **116** | LE7: Coss, Rat W . . . . . .7A **46** |
| (not continuous) | Swanington Incline LE67: Swan . . .6B **26** | Syston Northern By-Pass |
| Sturrock Cl. LE7: Thurn . . . . . .1H **73** | Swann Cl. LE15: N Luf . . . . . . . .1B **136** | LE7: Quen, Rat W . . . . .6C **46** |
| Styon Rd. LE3: Leic . . . . . . . .5J **63** | SWANNINGTON . . . . . . .6B **26** (3B **158**) | Syston RFC . . . . . . . . . . . . . . .1G **61** |
| SUDBOROUGH . . . . . . . . . . . . .3C **165** | Swannington Rd. LE3: Leic . . . . .7C **64** | Syston Rd. LE7: Coss . . . . . . . .5H **45** |
| Sudeley Av. LE4: Leic . . . . . . .4E **64** | LE9: B Ast . . . . . . . . . . .4E **86** | LE7: Quen . . . . . . . . . . .6F **47** |
| Suffolk Cl. LE13: Mel M . . . . .7G **117** | LE67: Coal . . . . . . . . . .3K **37** | LE7: S Cro . . . . . . . . . .7A **118** |
| LE18: Wig . . . . . . . . . . .5G **77** | Swannymote Rd. LE12: Shep . . .5G **27** | Syston Station (Rail) . . . . . . . .2C **60** |
| Suffolk St. LE5: Leic . . . . . . . .2A **72** | LE67: Whit . . . . . . . . . .5G **27** | Syston St. E. LE1: Leic . . . . . . .7H **65** |
| Suffolk Way LE9: Des . . . . . . .3H **95** | Swanscombe Rd. LE2: Leic . . . . .6D **70** | Syston St. W. LE1: Leic . . . . . . .6G **65** |
| Sulgrave Rd. LE5: Leic . . . . . .7K **65** | Swan St. LE3: Leic . . . . . .2A **4** (1E **70**) | Sywell Av. LE11: Lou . . . . . . . . .7A **18** |
| Sullington Rd. LE12: Shep . . . .1D **28** | LE11: Lou . . . . . . . . . . .6F **19** | Sywell Dr. LE18: Wig . . . . . . . . .6A **78** |
| Sullivans Way LE11: Lou . . . . .3D **18** | LE12: Sea . . . . . . . . . . .3K **33** | |
| Sulney Cl. LE14: Up Bro . . . . .1A **110** | LE12: Sileby . . . . . . . . .1J **45** | |
| Sulthorpe Rd. PE9: Ket . . . . . .6F **137** | Swan Way LE7: Sys . . . . . . . . . .1A **60** | |
| Summerfield LE15: O'ham . . . .2J **127** | LE67: Coal . . . . . . . . . .4F **39** | **T** |
| Summerlea Rd. LE5: Leic . . . . .1E **72** | SWARBY . . . . . . . . . . . . . . . .1D **161** | |
| Summerpool Rd. LE11: Lou . . .3D **18** | SWARKESTONE . . . . . . . . . . .2A **158** | Tabberer Cl. LE15: O'ham . . . . .2J **127** |
| Summers Cl. LE9: K Mal . . . . .6G **95** | Swarkestone Rd. DE72: Swark . . .4A **6** | Tadcaster Av. LE2: Leic . . . . . . .5D **76** |
| Summers Way LE16: Mkt H . . .5D **150** | SWATON . . . . . . . . . . . . . . . .1D **161** | Tadcaster Grn. LE2: Leic . . . . . .5D **76** |
| Sunbury Grn. LE5: Leic . . . . . .7G **67** | SWAYFIELD . . . . . . . . . . . . . .2C **161** | Tailby Av. LE5: Leic . . . . . . . . . .6A **66** |
| Sunbury Ri. LE8: Count . . . . . .5C **82** | Swedish Cl. LE16: Fox . . . . . . . .1H **149** | Tailors Link LE7: East G . . . . . . .5F **47** |
| Sundew Rd. LE5: Ham . . . . . . .4E **66** | Sweetbriar Rd. LE3: Leic . . . . . .4C **70** | Talbot La. LE1: Leic . . . . . .4A **4** (2E **70**) |
| Sundial Rd. LE5: Ham . . . . . . .3E **66** | Sweethill DE12: Moi . . . . . . . . .6C **22** | LE67: Swan, Whit . . . . . .4B **26** |
| Sunningdale Ind. Pk. LE3: Leic . .3G **69** | SWEPSTONE . . . . . . . . . .3B **50** (3A **158**) | Talbot Pl. DE12: Don . . . . . . . . .4A **34** |
| Sunningdale Rd. LE3: Leic . . . .3F **69** | Swepstone Rd. DE12: Mea . . . . .7G **35** | Talbot St. LE4: Leic . . . . . . . . . .3G **65** |
| LE67: Coal . . . . . . . . . .4F **39** | LE67: Hea, Swep . . . . . . .3C **50** | LE67: Whit . . . . . . . . . .4D **26** |
| Sunnycroft Rd. LE3: Leic . . . . .2A **70** | LE67: Swep . . . . . . . . . .5K **49** | Talbott Cl. LE9: B Ast . . . . . . . .6E **86** |
| Sunnydale Cres. LE10: Hinc . . .4D **102** | Swift Cl. LE7: Sys . . . . . . . . . . .1B **60** | Talbot Yd. LE16: Mkt H . . . . . . .4E **150** |
| Sunnydale Rd. LE10: Hinc . . . .4C **102** | LE13: Mel M . . . . . . . . .7E **116** | TALLINGTON . . . . . . . . . . . . . .1D **165** |
| Sunnyfield LE15: O'ham . . . . .2J **127** | Swifts Cl. LE12: Wym . . . . . . . .2K **21** | Tamar Rd. LE2: Oad . . . . . . . . .3F **79** |
| Sunnyfield Cl. LE5: Leic . . . . .2E **72** | LE67: Ibs . . . . . . . . . . .3K **51** | LE4: Leic . . . . . . . . . . .4A **66** |
| SUNNY HILL . . . . . . . . . . . . . .1A **158** | Swiftway LE17: Lut . . . . . . . . . .3J **153** | LE13: Mel M . . . . . . . . .6D **116** |
| Sunnyhill LE10: Bur . . . . . . . .4J **103** | Swinburne Rd. LE10: Hinc . . . . .2F **103** | Tamerton Rd. LE2: Leic . . . . . . .3E **76** |
| Sunnyhill Rd. LE11: Lou . . . . .2D **30** | Swindale Cl. LE2: Leic . . . . .7B **5** (3E **70**) | Tame Way LE10: Hinc . . . . . . . .3D **102** |
| Sunnyhill Sth. LE10: Bur . . . . .5J **103** | Swinfen Cl. LE67: Ell . . . . . . . . .2C **52** | Tamworth Cl. LE12: Shep . . . . . .1B **28** |
| Sunnyside LE2: Oad . . . . . . . .4E **78** | Swinfield Rd. LE12: Quo . . . . . . .5A **32** | Tamworth Rd. DE12: A Mag, Mea . .4A **48** |
| LE10: Hinc . . . . . . . . . .7H **99** | SWINFORD . . . . . . . . .4H **157** (3C **163**) | DE72: Swar . . . . . . . . . .1B **8** |
| LE67: Ibs . . . . . . . . . . .5J **51** | Swinford Av. LE2: Leic . . . . . . . .6D **76** | DE74: C Don . . . . . . . . .1A **8** |
| Sunnyside Cl. LE8: Whet . . . . .7K **75** | Swinford Ct. LE2: Leic . . . . . . . .6D **76** | (not continuous) |
| Sunnyside Ind. Est. LE10: Hinc . .6G **99** | Swinford Rd. LE17: C'ach, Lut . . .6K **153** | LE65: Ash Z . . . . . . . . . .7J **23** |
| Sunnyside Pk. LE10: Hinc . . . .6G **99** | LE17: Shaw . . . . . . . . . .2C **156** | Tandy Av. DE12: Moi . . . . . . . . .6D **22** |
| Sun Way LE3: Brau . . . . . . . . .4H **69** | LE17: Wal . . . . . . . . . . .2D **154** | Tanners La. LE12: Hat . . . . . . . .1J **17** |
| Surrey Cl. LE10: Bur . . . . . . . .7H **103** | Swingbridge Rd. LE11: Lou . . . . .4D **18** | Tannery, The LE15: B'den . . . . . .7D **136** |
| Surrey St. LE4: Leic . . . . . . . .5H **65** | Swingbridge St. LE16: Fox . . . . . .2G **149** | Tanni Grey Ho. LE11: Lou . . . . . .6E **18** |
| Susan Av. LE5: Leic . . . . . . . .4D **72** | SWINSTEAD . . . . . . . . . . . . . .2D **161** | (off Union St.) |
| Sussex Av. LE13: Mel M . . . . .7F **117** | Swinstead Rd. LE5: Leic . . . . . . .3F **73** | Tansey Cres. LE9: S Stan . . . . . .1H **105** |
| Sussex Rd. LE18: Wig . . . . . . .7J **77** | Swinton Cl. LE5: Ham . . . . . . . .3F **67** | Tansley Av. LE18: Wig . . . . . . . .7G **77** |
| Sussex St. LE5: Leic . . . . .2G **4** (1H **71**) | SWITHLAND . . . . . . . . . .5G **43** (3C **159**) | TANSOR . . . . . . . . . . . . . . . .2D **165** |
| Sutherington Way LE7: Anst . . .6J **57** | Swithland Av. LE4: Leic . . . . . . .5E **64** | Tan Yd. LE67: Swan . . . . . . . . .6B **26** |
| | | Tanyard Cl. DE74: C Don . . . . . .4K **7** |

Tara St. LE67: Bar . . . . . . . . . . . . . . . . . . .1H **53**
Tarbat Rd. LE5: Leic . . . . . . . . . . . . . . . .7F **67**
Tarragon Rd. LE2: Leic . . . . . . .7A **5** (3D **70**)
Tatlow Ho. LE3: Glen . . . . . . . . . . . . . . . .1H **69**
Tatlow Rd. LE3: Glen . . . . . . . . . . . . . . . .1G **69**
Tatmarsh LE11: Lou . . . . . . . . . . . . . . . . .5F **17**
Tatton Cl. LE3: Leic . . . . . . . . . . . . . . . . .5A **64**
Taunton Cl. LE18: Wig . . . . . . . . . . . . . . .7J **77**
Taunton Rd. LE3: Leic . . . . . . . . . . . . . . .2B **70**
Taurus Cl. LE2: Leic . . . . . . . . . . . . . . . . .2H **71**
Taverner Dr. LE6: Ratby . . . . . . . . . . . . . .7B **62**
Taverners Rd. LE4: Beau L . . . . . . . . . . . .6C **58**
Tavistock Cl. LE67: Hug . . . . . . . . . . . . . .6C **38**
Tavistock Dr. LE5: Leic . . . . . . . . . . . . . .4B **72**
Tay Cl. LE15: O'ham . . . . . . . . . . . . . . . .6G **127**
Tayleur Cl. LE67: Coal . . . . . . . . . . . . . . .4E **38**
Taylor Cl. DE12: Moi . . . . . . . . . . . . . . . .7C **22**
  LE7: Sys . . . . . . . . . . . . . . . . . . . . . . .2C **60**
  LE9: S Stan . . . . . . . . . . . . . . . . . . . .1J **105**
Taylor Rd. LE1: Leic . . . . . . . .1F **4** (7G **65**)
Taylor's Bri. Rd. LE18: Wig . . . . . . . . . . .7G **77**
Teal Bus. Pk. LE10: Hinc . . . . . . . . . . . . .4B **102**
Tealby Cl. LE17: Gilm . . . . . . . . . . . . . . .7J **145**
Teal Cl. LE3: Leic E . . . . . . . . . . . . . . . . .5C **68**
  LE67: Coal . . . . . . . . . . . . . . . . . . . . .4F **39**
Teal Dr. LE10: Hinc . . . . . . . . . . . . . . . . .5D **102**
Teal Way LE7: Sys . . . . . . . . . . . . . . . . .1A **60**
Teasel Cl. LE19: Nar . . . . . . . . . . . . . . . .1E **80**
Teasel Dr. LE13: Mel M . . . . . . . . . . . . . .7D **116**
Tebbs Cl. LE8: Count . . . . . . . . . . . . . . . .5C **82**
Tedder Cl. LE17: Lut . . . . . . . . . . . . . . . .5G **153**
Tedworth Grn. LE4: Leic . . . . . . . . . . . . .1D **64**
Tees Cl. LE15: O'ham . . . . . . . . . . . . . . .5H **127**
TEIGH . . . . . . . . . . . . . . . . . . . . . . . . .3B **160**
Teigh La. LE15: Whis . . . . . . . . . . . . . . .1E **122**
Teigh Rd. LE15: A'll . . . . . . . . . . . . . . . .4G **123**
  LE15: Mkt O . . . . . . . . . . . . . . . . . . . .2F **123**
Teignbank Cl. LE10: Hinc . . . . . . . . . . . . .1G **103**
Teign Bank Rd. LE10: Hinc . . . . . . . . . . .7F **99**
Teignmouth Cl. LE5: Leic . . . . . . . . . . . .4B **72**
Teignmouth Wlk. LE5: Leic . . . . . . . . . . .4B **72**
Telford Way LE5: Leic . . . . . . . . . . . . . . .2G **73**
  LE67: Coal . . . . . . . . . . . . . . . . . . . . .1A **38**
Tellis Pl. DE12: Mea . . . . . . . . . . . . . . . .7F **35**
Tempest Rd. LE4: Birs . . . . . . . . . . . . . . .1F **65**
Templars Way LE67: Whit . . . . . . . . . . . .6F **27**
Templar Way LE7: R'ley . . . . . . . . . . . . . .6D **44**
Temple Cl. LE12: Shep . . . . . . . . . . . . . .2E **28**
Temple Hill LE67: Whit . . . . . . . . . . . . . .5F **27**
Temple Rd. LE5: Leic . . . . . . . . . . . . . . .2A **72**
Tendring Dr. LE18: Wig . . . . . . . . . . . . . .5B **78**
Tennis Av. LE13: Mel M . . . . . . . . . . . . .6F **117**
Tennis Ct. Dr. LE5: Leic . . . . . . . . . . . . .7C **66**
Tennyson Cl. DE12: Mea . . . . . . . . . . . . .1D **48**
Tennyson Rd. LE10: Hinc . . . . . . . . . . . .2E **102**
  LE11: Lou . . . . . . . . . . . . . . . . . . . . . .6B **18**
  LE17: Lut . . . . . . . . . . . . . . . . . . . . . .3J **153**
Tennyson St. LE2: Leic . . . . . . . . . . . . . .4J **71**
  LE19: Nar . . . . . . . . . . . . . . . . . . . . . .7E **74**
Tennyson Way LE13: Mel M . . . . . . . . . . .1E **116**
Tentas, The LE67: Grif . . . . . . . . . . . . . .1A **26**
Tentercroft Av. LE7: Sys . . . . . . . . . . . . .1E **60**
Terrace Cotts. LE9: Crof . . . . . . . . . . . . .5A **80**
Terrace Rd. LE67: Ell . . . . . . . . . . . . . . .4F **53**
Tetbury Dr. LE12: Shep . . . . . . . . . . . . . .1B **28**
Tetuan Rd. LE3: Leic . . . . . . . . . . . . . . .1B **70**
Tewkesbury St. LE3: Leic . . . . . . . . . . . .1D **70**
Thackeray St. LE2: Leic . . . . . . . . . . . . . .7F **71**
Thames Dr. LE13: Mel M . . . . . . . . . . . .6E **116**
Thames St. LE1: Leic . . . . . . . .1D **4** (7F **65**)
Thatcher Cl. LE4: Leic . . . . . . . . . . . . . . .2B **64**
Thatchers Cnr. LE7: East G . . . . . . . . . . .5F **47**
Thatchmeadow Dr. LE16: L Bow . . . . . . . .4H **151**
Theatre Mall *LE1: Leic* . . . . . . . . . . . . . .*3D* **4**
  *(off Haymarket Cen.)*
THEDDINGWORTH . . . . . . . . . . . . . . .3D **163**
Theddingworth Rd. LE16: Lub . . . . . . . . .7G **149**
  LE17: H Bos . . . . . . . . . . . . . . . . . . . .6D **148**
  LE17: Mows . . . . . . . . . . . . . . . . . . . .3B **148**
THETFORD . . . . . . . . . . . . . . . . . . . .3D **161**
Thimble Hall Rd. LE7: Low . . . . . . . . . . .7F **119**
  LE14: T'ord . . . . . . . . . . . . . . . . . . . .7F **119**
Thirlemere Rd. LE12: Bar S . . . . . . . . . . .2D **32**
Thirlmere LE67: Coal . . . . . . . . . . . . . . .3J **39**
Thirlmere Ct. LE12: Bar S . . . . . . . . . . . .3D **32**
Thirlmere Dr. LE11: Lou . . . . . . . . . . . . .2B **30**
Thirlmere Gdns. LE65: Ash Z . . . . . . . . . .7A **24**
Thirlmere Rd. LE10: Hinc . . . . . . . . . . . .3D **102**
  LE18: Wig . . . . . . . . . . . . . . . . . . . . . .5B **78**
Thirlmere St. LE2: Leic . . . . . . . .8B **5** (4E **70**)
Thistle Cl. LE7: Crop . . . . . . . . . . . . . . .3K **57**
  LE19: Nar . . . . . . . . . . . . . . . . . . . . . .1E **80**
THISTLETON . . . . . . . . . . . . . . . . . . .3C **161**
Thistleton La. LE15: Mkt O . . . . . . . . . . .1H **123**
Thistley Cl. LE3: Brau . . . . . . . . . . . . . . .5G **69**
Thomas Cl. LE3: Brau . . . . . . . . . . . . . . .7A **70**
  LE7: Hou H . . . . . . . . . . . . . . . . . . . .2C **130**

Thomas Dalby Wlk. *LE15: O'ham* . . . . . . . .4H **127**
  *(off South St., not continuous)*
Thomas Rd. DE74: Keg . . . . . . . . . . . . . .7G **9**
  LE67: Whit . . . . . . . . . . . . . . . . . . . . .6D **26**
Thomasson Rd. LE5: Leic . . . . . . . . . . . .1D **72**
Thomas St. LE11: Lou . . . . . . . . . . . . . . .7H **19**
  LE67: Ibs . . . . . . . . . . . . . . . . . . . . . .5K **51**
Thompson Av. LE12: Belt . . . . . . . . . . . .4H **15**
Thompson Cl. LE12: Quo . . . . . . . . . . . .5K **31**
Thompsons La. LE15: Seat . . . . . . . . . . .5K **139**
Thompson Wlk. LE14: N Bro . . . . . . . . . .3C **110**
Thomson Cl. LE4: Leic . . . . . . . . . . . . . .7K **59**
Thomson Ct. LE67: Mark . . . . . . . . . . . .5H **55**
Thoresby St. LE5: Leic . . . . . . . . . . . . . .1A **72**
THORNBOROUGH . . . . . . . . . . . . . . .1C **38**
Thornborough Cl. LE16: L Bow . . . . . . . . .5G **151**
  LE19: Nar . . . . . . . . . . . . . . . . . . . . . .2D **80**
Thornborough Rd. LE67: Coal . . . . . . . . . .2C **38**
Thornby Gdns. LE18: Wig . . . . . . . . . . . .6A **78**
Thorndale LE67: Ibs . . . . . . . . . . . . . . . .4J **51**
Thorndale Rd. LE4: Thurm . . . . . . . . . . . .6B **60**
Thorneycroft Cl. LE9: B Ast . . . . . . . . . . .6F **87**
Thornfield Av. CV13: S Gol . . . . . . . . . . .3B **98**
Thornfield Way LE10: Hinc . . . . . . . . . . .3H **103**
Thornham Gro. LE67: Ibs . . . . . . . . . . . .3K **51**
THORNHAUGH . . . . . . . . . . . . . . . . .1D **165**
Thornhills LE19: Nar . . . . . . . . . . . . . . . .6E **74**
Thornhills Gro. LE19: Nar . . . . . . . . . . . .6E **74**
Thornholme Cl. LE4: Leic . . . . . . . . . . . .2C **64**
THORNTON . . . . . . . . . . . . . .2K **93** (1B **162**)
Thornton Cl. LE3: Leic . . . . . . . . . . . . . .4H **69**
  LE9: B Ast . . . . . . . . . . . . . . . . . . . . .6E **86**
  LE67: Coal . . . . . . . . . . . . . . . . . . . . .3J **39**
Thornton Cres. LE16: C Lan . . . . . . . . . . .1B **140**
Thornton Dr. LE19: Nar . . . . . . . . . . . . . .1G **81**
Thornton La. LE67: Bag . . . . . . . . . . . . . .2G **93**
  LE67: Mark . . . . . . . . . . . . . . . . . . . .7E **54**
  LE67: S Bar . . . . . . . . . . . . . . . . . . . .6A **54**
Thornton Wlk. LE1: Leic . . . . . . . . . . . . .4B **4**
Thorntop Cl. DE11: Blac . . . . . . . . . . . . .3D **22**
Thorntree Cl. LE3: Leic . . . . . . . . . . . . . .4K **63**
  LE67: Rav . . . . . . . . . . . . . . . . . . . . .2K **37**
Thornville Cl. LE4: Leic . . . . . . . . . . . . . .5A **66**
Thorny Cl. LE11: Lou . . . . . . . . . . . . . . .4B **18**
Thornycroft Rd. LE10: Hinc . . . . . . . . . . .3H **103**
THOROTON . . . . . . . . . . . . . . . . . . . .1A **160**
THORPE ACRE . . . . . . . . . . . .5A **18** (2C **159**)
Thorpe Acre Rd. LE11: Lou . . . . . . . . . . .6B **18**
THORPE ARNOLD . . . . . . . . .2K **117** (2A **160**)
THORPE ASTLEY . . . . . . . . . . . . . . . .5H **69**
THORPE BY WATER . . . . . . . . . . . . . .2B **164**
THORPE CONSTANTINE . . . . . . . . . . .1A **162**
Thorpe Downs Rd. DE11: C Gre . . . . . . . .2A **22**
Thorpe Dr. LE18: Wig . . . . . . . . . . . . . . .4K **77**
Thorpe End LE13: Mel M . . . . . . . . . . . .4G **117**
Thorpe Fld. Dr. LE4: Thurm . . . . . . . . . . .5B **60**
Thorpe Gdns. LE15: Whis . . . . . . . . . . . .2B **122**
Thorpe Hill LE11: Lou . . . . . . . . . . . . . . .7A **18**
Thorpe La. LE7: Bark . . . . . . . . . . . . . . .6E **60**
THORPE LANGTON . . . . . . . . .3E **140** (2A **164**)
Thorpe Langton Rd.
  LE16: C Lan, East L . . . . . . . . . . . . . . .2A **140**
THORPE LATIMER . . . . . . . . . . . . . . . .1D **161**
THORPE MALSOR . . . . . . . . . . . . . . .3B **164**
Thorpe Rd. LE12: Shep . . . . . . . . . . . . . .7C **16**
  LE13: Mel M . . . . . . . . . . . . . . . . . . .4G **117**
THORPE SATCHVILLE . . . . . . .3H **119** (3A **160**)
Thorpe Satchville Rd.
  LE14: G Dal, T Sat . . . . . .1H **119** & 7B **120**
  LE14: T'ord . . . . . . . . . . . . . . . . . . . .6H **119**
Thorpe Side LE14: Scal, T Arn . . . . . . . . .6C **112**
Thorpes La. NG32: Crox . . . . . . . . . . . . .6H **107**
Thorpe's Ter. LE15: Upp . . . . . . . . . . . . .2B **138**
Thorpe St. LE3: Leic . . . . . . . . .5A **4** (2D **70**)
THORPE WATERVILLE . . . . . . . . . . . . .3D **165**
Thorpe Way LE19: End . . . . . . . . . . . . . .4H **75**
Thorpewell LE5: Leic . . . . . . . . . . . . . . .1B **72**
Thorpewell Wlk. LE5: Leic . . . . . . . . . . . .1B **72**
THRAPSTON . . . . . . . . . . . . . . . . . . .3C **165**
Thraves Ter. LE14: Harb . . . . . . . . . . . . .2C **108**
Threadcutters Way LE12: Shep . . . . . . . . .7D **16**
Threadgold Cl. LE4: Beau L . . . . . . . . . . .7B **58**
THREEKINGHAM . . . . . . . . . . . . . . . .1D **161**
Three Pots Rd. LE10: Bur . . . . . . . . . . . .7H **103**
Three Turns La. LE7: S Cro . . . . . . . . . . .5A **118**
Thresher's Ter. LE7: East G . . . . . . . . . . .5F **47**
THRINGSTONE . . . . . . . . . . . .4D **26** (3B **158**)
THRUMPTON . . . . . . . . . . . . . . . . . .1C **159**
Thrush Cl. LE13: Mel M . . . . . . . . . . . . .4H **116**
THRUSSINGTON . . . . . . . . . .7B **114** (3D **159**)
Thrussington Rd. LE7: Rat W, Thru . . . . . .2F **47**
  LE14: Hob . . . . . . . . . . . . . . . . . . . . .3A **114**
THULSTON . . . . . . . . . . . . . . . . . . . .1B **158**
THURCASTON . . . . . . . . . . . .2B **58** (3C **159**)
Thurcaston La. LE7: R'ley, Thurc . . . . . . . .1B **58**
Thurcaston Rd. LE4: Leic . . . . . . . . . . . .6D **58**
  *(Greengate La.)*

Thurcaston Rd. LE4: Leic . . . . . . . . . . . .2F **59**
  *(Red Hill Way)*
Thurcroft Cl. LE2: G Par . . . . . . . . . . . . .5D **76**
THURLASTON . . . . . . . . . . . . .2C **96** (2C **163**)
Thurlaston La. LE9: Crof . . . . . . . . . . . . .2A **80**
  LE9: Earl S . . . . . . . . . . . . . . . . . . . .1G **101**
Thurlaston Rd. LE9: Hun . . . . . . . . . . . . .5B **74**
THURLBY . . . . . . . . . . . . . . . . . . . . .3D **161**
Thurlby Rd. LE5: Leic . . . . . . . . . . . . . . .7K **65**
Thurlington Rd. LE3: Leic . . . . . . . . . . . .4A **70**
Thurlow Cl. LE2: Oad . . . . . . . . . . . . . . .4F **79**
Thurlow Rd. LE2: Leic . . . . . . . . . . . . . .6G **71**
THURMASTON . . . . . . . . . . . .7A **60** (1D **163**)
Thurmaston Blvd. LE4: Leic . . . . . . . . . . .2A **66**
  *(not continuous)*
Thurmaston Footpath LE4: Leic . . . . . . . . .2A **66**
Thurmaston La. LE4: Leic . . . . . . . . . . . .2B **66**
  LE5: Leic . . . . . . . . . . . . . . . . . . . . . .6C **66**
THURNBY . . . . . . . . . . . . . . .3H **73** (1D **163**)
Thurnby Hill LE7: Thurn . . . . . . . . . . . . .2G **73**
Thurnby La. LE5: S'ton . . . . . . . . . . . . . .6G **73**
THURNBY LODGE . . . . . . . . . . . . . . .1G **73**
Thurn Ct. LE5: Leic . . . . . . . . . . . . . . . .7F **67**
Thurncourt Cl. LE5: Leic . . . . . . . . . . . . .7E **66**
Thurncourt Gdns. LE5: Leic . . . . . . . . . . .1H **73**
Thurncourt Rd. LE5: Leic . . . . . . . . . . . .7E **66**
THURNING . . . . . . . . . . . . . . . . . . . .3D **165**
Thurnview Rd. LE5: Leic . . . . . . . . . . . . .4E **72**
Thyme Cl. LE2: Leic . . . . . . . . . . . . . . . .7A **5**
Tiber Way LE19: Brau . . . . . . . . . . . . . . .7H **69**
Tichborne Ct. LE2: Leic . . . . . . .6G **5** (3H **71**)
Tichborne St. LE2: Leic . . . . . . .6G **5** (3H **71**)
TICKENCOTE . . . . . . . . . . . .2G **137** (1C **165**)
TICKNALL . . . . . . . . . . . . . . . . . . . . .2A **158**
Tickow La. LE12: Shep . . . . . . . . . . . . . .2A **28**
Tiffany Ct. LE2: Leic . . . . . . . . . . . . . . . .5K **71**
Tigers Cl. LE18: Wig . . . . . . . . . . . . . . .6E **76**
Tigers Rd. LE18: Wig . . . . . . . . . . . . . . .6E **76**
Tigers Way LE1: Leic . . . . . . . .8D **5** (4F **71**)
Tilbury Cres. LE4: Leic . . . . . . . . . . . . . .1C **66**
TILE HILL . . . . . . . . . . . . . . . . . . . . .3A **162**
Tilford Cres. LE2: Leic . . . . . . . . . . . . . .6D **76**
Tillett Rd. LE3: Brau . . . . . . . . . . . . . . . .5H **69**
Tilley Cl. LE3: Brau . . . . . . . . . . . . . . . .6H **69**
Tillingham Rd. LE5: Leic . . . . . . . . . . . . .6B **66**
Tilling Rd. LE4: Leic . . . . . . . . . . . . . . . .3C **64**
Tilling Wlk. LE4: Leic . . . . . . . . . . . . . . .2C **64**
Tilton Dr. LE2: Oad . . . . . . . . . . . . . . . .5C **78**
Tilton La. LE7: Bill . . . . . . . . . . . . . . . . .3F **131**
TILTON ON THE HILL . . . . . . .2H **131** (1A **164**)
Tilton Rd. LE7: Bill . . . . . . . . . . . . . . . . .5K **131**
  LE10: Bur . . . . . . . . . . . . . . . . . . . . .5H **103**
  LE14: T'ord . . . . . . . . . . . . . . . . . . . .6G **119**
Timbergate Rd. PE9: Ket . . . . . . . . . . . . .6F **137**
Timber Hill NG33: Sew . . . . . . . . . . . . . .7K **113**
Timber St. LE18: Wig . . . . . . . . . . . . . . .7F **77**
Timberwood Dr. LE6: Groby . . . . . . . . . . .4C **62**
Timson Cl. LE16: Mkt H . . . . . . . . . . . . .2D **150**
Tindall Sq. LE15: Cott . . . . . . . . . . . . . . .4B **124**
Tinkers Dell LE7: East G . . . . . . . . . . . . .4F **47**
TINWELL . . . . . . . . . . . . . . . . . . . . .1D **165**
Tipnall Rd. DE74: S'thpe . . . . . . . . . . . . .5J **7**
Tippings La. LE15: B'den . . . . . . . . . . . . .7D **136**
Tiptree Cl. LE4: Leic . . . . . . . . . . . . . . . .4D **64**
TITCHMARSH . . . . . . . . . . . . . . . . . .3D **165**
TITHBY . . . . . . . . . . . . . . . . . . . . . . .1D **159**
Tithe Barn Row LE15: Gree . . . . . . . . . . .4F **125**
  *(not continuous)*
Tithe Cl. CV13: S Gol . . . . . . . . . . . . . . .4A **98**
  LE67: Thrin . . . . . . . . . . . . . . . . . . . .3C **26**
Tithe St. LE5: Leic . . . . . . . . . . . . . . . . .7A **66**
Tithings, The LE8: K Bea . . . . . . . . . . . . .2J **89**
Tiverton Av. LE4: Leic . . . . . . . . . . . . . . .4J **65**
  LE67: Whit . . . . . . . . . . . . . . . . . . . . .2G **39**
Tiverton Cl. LE2: Oad . . . . . . . . . . . . . . .3E **78**
  LE19: Nar . . . . . . . . . . . . . . . . . . . . . .1D **80**
Tiverton M. LE4: Leic . . . . . . . . . . . . . . .4J **65**
Tiverton Rd. LE11: Lou . . . . . . . . . . . . . .4D **30**
  LE15: Cott . . . . . . . . . . . . . . . . . . . . .4C **124**
TIXOVER . . . . . . . . . . . . . . . . . . . . . .1C **165**
Tod's Ter. LE15: Upp . . . . . . . . . . . . . . .2C **138**
TOFT . . . . . . . . . . . . . . . . . . . . . . . .3D **161**
Toft, The LE67: Bar S . . . . . . . . . . . . . . .4H **15**
Tofts, The LE18: Wig . . . . . . . . . . . . . . .7K **77**
Toft's Hill LE14: Sta . . . . . . . . . . . . . . . .2H **109**
  NG32: Knip . . . . . . . . . . . . . . . . . . . .2H **109**
Tokye's Cl. LE15: Bel R . . . . . . . . . . . . . .5G **133**
Tolcarne Rd. LE5: Leic . . . . . . . . . . . . . .6E **66**
Tolchard Cl. LE5: Leic . . . . . . . . . . . . . . .2C **72**
Tolethorpe Cl. LE15: O'ham . . . . . . . . . . .4K **127**
TOLL BAR . . . . . . . . . . . . . . . . . . . . .3J **137**
Toll Bar LE15: Cott . . . . . . . . . . . . . . . . .6B **124**
Tollbar PE9: G Gas . . . . . . . . . . . . . . . . .3J **137**
Toll Bar Av. NG13: Bott . . . . . . . . . . . . . .1G **107**
Tollemache Av. LE4: Leic . . . . . . . . . . . .4E **64**
Toller Rd. LE2: Leic . . . . . . . . . . . . . . . .6J **71**
  LE12: Quo . . . . . . . . . . . . . . . . . . . . .6J **31**

TOLLERTON . . . . . . . . . . . . . . . . .1D 159
Tollgate, The CV13: Osb . . . . . . . . . .5A 92
Tollwell Rd. LE4: Beau L . . . . . . . . . .1C 64
Tolton Rd. LE4: Leic . . . . . . . . . . . . .2D 64
Tom Eatough Ct. LE9: Earl S . . . . . . .2F 101
Tomlin Rd. LE4: Leic . . . . . . . . . . . . .5A 66
Tomlinson Ct. LE2: Oad . . . . . . . . . . .2C 78
Tom Paine Cl. LE3: Brau . . . . . . . . . .5H 69
TONGE . . . . . . . . . . . . . .6D 10 (2B 158)
Tonge La. DE73: B Hil . . . . . . . . . . . .6B 10
Tongue Hall Ct. DE73: Ton . . . . . . . . .6D 10
Toon Cl. LE12: Shep . . . . . . . . . . . . .2C 28
Toothill Rd. LE11: Lou . . . . . . . . . . . .5F 19
Topcliffe Wlk. LE4: Leic . . . . . . . . . . .3E 64
Top Cl. LE3: Brau . . . . . . . . . . . . . . .6H 69
Top End LE14: G Dal . . . . . . . . . . . . .6C 120
Top Grn. LE14: Up Bro . . . . . . . . . . . .1A 110
Tophall Dr. LE8: Count . . . . . . . . . . . .6E 82
Top La. LE15: Bisb . . . . . . . . . . . . . .2F 139
Top Rd. LE14: Welb . . . . . . . . . . . . . .1B 116
  LE15: Rid . . . . . . . . . . . . . . . . . . .2H 133
  LE67: Grif . . . . . . . . . . . . . . . . . . .2A 26
  NG32: Crox . . . . . . . . . . . . . . . . . .6H 107
Top St. DE12: A Mag . . . . . . . . . . . . .6A 48
  LE15: Ext . . . . . . . . . . . . . . . . . . .2D 128
  LE15: Win . . . . . . . . . . . . . . . . . . .6E 134
Top Yd. Farm LE16: G Bow . . . . . . . . .1F 151
Torch Cl. LE16: Hall . . . . . . . . . . . . . .6B 132
Torch Way LE16: Mkt H . . . . . . . . . . .7F 151
Torcross Cl. LE3: Glen . . . . . . . . . . . .6J 63
Toronto Cl. LE1: Leic . . . . . . . .1F 4 (7G 65)
Torrance Dr. LE13: Mel M . . . . . . . . . .1F 117
Torridon Cl. LE4: Leic . . . . . . . . . . . . .3D 64
Torridon Way LE10: Hinc . . . . . . . . . . .2E 102
Torrington Av. LE67: Whit . . . . . . . . . .2G 39
Torrington Cl. LE18: Wig . . . . . . . . . . .1K 83
Totland Rd. LE3: Leic . . . . . . . . . . . . .6C 64
Totnes Cl. LE67: Hug . . . . . . . . . . . . .6C 38
TOTON . . . . . . . . . . . . . . . . . . . . . .1B 158
Toulouse Pl. LE65: Ash Z . . . . . . . . . .5J 23
Tourist Info. Cen.
  Ashby-de-la-Zouch . . . . . . . . . . .5K 23
  Hinckley . . . . . . . . . . . . . . . . . . .3G 103
  Leicester . . . . . . . . . . . . . .4D 4 (2F 71)
  Loughborough . . . . . . . . . . . . . . .7E 18
  Market Harborough . . . . . . . . . . .4E 150
  Melton Mowbray . . . . . . . . . . . . .4G 117
  Wigston . . . . . . . . . . . . . . . . . . .5K 77
Tournament Rd. LE3: Glen . . . . . . . . . .7H 63
Tournament Way LE65: Ash Z . . . . . . . .3J 23
Tovey Cres. LE2: Leic . . . . . . . . . . . . .4D 76
Tower Ct. LE16: Lub . . . . . . . . . . . . . .7J 149
Tower Gdns. LE65: Ash Z . . . . . . . . . .5J 23
Tower Rd. LE9: Earl S . . . . . . . . . . . . .2E 100
Towers, The LE11: Lou . . . . . . . . . . . .1C 30
Towers Cl. LE9: K Mux . . . . . . . . . . . .3C 68
Towers Dr. LE9: K Mux . . . . . . . . . . . .3C 68
Tower St. LE1: Leic . . . . . . . . .7D 5 (3F 71)
Towle Rd. LE3: Leic . . . . . . . . . . . . . .6J 63
Towles Flds. LE12: Bur W . . . . . . . . . .4F 21
Towles Mill LE11: Lou . . . . . . . . . . . . .5G 19
  (off Queen's Rd.)
Towles Pastures DE74: C Don . . . . . . . .5J 7
Town End LE14: Som . . . . . . . . . . . . .7K 121
  NG13: Bark V . . . . . . . . . . . . . . . .3B 106
Town End Cl. LE2: Leic . . . . . . . . . . . .7J 71
  LE14: Ash . . . . . . . . . . . . . . . . . .3F 115
Townend Rd. LE9: Barw . . . . . . . . . . .3K 99
TOWNGATE . . . . . . . . . . . . . . . . . . .3D 161
TOWN GREEN . . . . . . . . . . . . . . . . .7E 44
Town Grn. St. LE7: R'ley . . . . . . . . . . .7E 44
Town Hall Pas. LE11: Lou . . . . . . . . . .7F 19
Town Hall Sq. LE1: Leic . . . . . . . . . . . .4D 4
  (off Every St.)
Townsend Cl. LE4: Leic . . . . . . . . . . . .1K 65
  LE9: B Ast . . . . . . . . . . . . . . . . . .5F 87
Townsend Ct. LE2: Leic . . . . . . . . . . . .2C 76
Townsend La. LE67: D Hea . . . . . . . . .7B 38
Townsend Rd. LE9: S Stan . . . . . . . . .2J 105
  LE19: End . . . . . . . . . . . . . . . . . .5F 75
Town Sq. Shop. Cen. LE7: Sys . . . . . . .1D 60
Town St. LE8: Bur O . . . . . . . . . . . . . .6D 130
Towpath Cl. LE11: Lou . . . . . . . . . . . .5G 19
Towpath Link LE18: Wig . . . . . . . . . . .1G 83
Trackside Cl. LE11: Lou . . . . . . . . . . . .6B 18
Trading Est. LE2: Leic . . . . . . . .3G 4 (1H 71)
Trafalgar Cl. LE7: Sys . . . . . . . . . . . . .2C 60
Trafalgar Way LE2: G Par . . . . . . . . . . .7D 76
Trafford Rd. LE5: Leic . . . . . . . . . . . . .7B 66
  LE10: Hinc . . . . . . . . . . . . . . . . . .1J 103
Tranter Pl. LE4: Leic . . . . . . . . . . . . . .4K 65
Treasure Cl. LE3: Glen . . . . . . . . . . . .7G 63
Treaty Rd. LE3: Glen . . . . . . . . . . . . .7H 63
Tredington Rd. LE3: Glen . . . . . . . . . .5H 63
Treetops Cl. LE5: Leic . . . . . . . . . . . . .7C 66
Trefoil Cl. LE5: Ham . . . . . . . . . . . . . .4E 66
  LE9: B Ast . . . . . . . . . . . . . . . . . .6F 87

Trefoil Cl. LE13: Mel M . . . . . . . . . . . .7E 116
Trelissick Cl. LE11: Lou . . . . . . . . . . . .5K 17
Tremaine Dr. LE18: Wig . . . . . . . . . . . .7J 77
Trenant Rd. LE2: Leic . . . . . . . . . . . . .4E 76
Trent Av. LE4: Beau L . . . . . . . . . . . . .6D 58
Trent Bank LE13: Mel M . . . . . . . . . . .6D 116
Trent Bri. LE67: Coal . . . . . . . . . . . . . .5G 39
Trent Cl. LE2: Oad . . . . . . . . . . . . . . .3F 79
  LE9: B Ast . . . . . . . . . . . . . . . . . .4E 86
Trent La. DE72: W Tre . . . . . . . . . . . . .4A 6
  DE74: C Don . . . . . . . . . . . . . . . . .3J 7
Trent La. Ind. Est. DE74: C Don . . . . . .3K 7
TRENTLOCK . . . . . . . . . . . . . . . . . . .1B 158
Trent Rd. LE10: Hinc . . . . . . . . . . . . . .3D 102
  LE15: O'ham . . . . . . . . . . . . . . . . .6G 127
Trescoe Ri. LE3: Leic . . . . . . . . . . . . .2J 69
Tressall Rd. LE67: Whit . . . . . . . . . . . .1G 39
Tressell Way LE3: Brau . . . . . . . . . . . .5H 69
Trevanth Rd. LE4: Leic . . . . . . . . . . . .3B 66
Trevino Dr. LE4: Leic . . . . . . . . . . . . . .1A 66
Trevor Rd. LE10: Hinc . . . . . . . . . . . . .2J 103
Trevose Gdns. LE5: Leic . . . . . . . . . . .7F 67
Tribune Ho. LE10: Hinc . . . . . . . . . . . .2G 103
  (off Factory Rd.)
Trigo Cl. LE4: Beau L . . . . . . . . . . . . .2A 64
Trillium Cl. LE5: Ham . . . . . . . . . . . . . .3E 66
Trinity Cl. LE7: Sys . . . . . . . . . . . . . . .2D 60
  LE65: Ash Z . . . . . . . . . . . . . . . . .5J 23
Trinity Ct. LE10: Hinc . . . . . . . . . . . . . .3F 103
  LE65: Ash Z . . . . . . . . . . . . . . . . .5K 23
Trinity Cres. LE12: Wym . . . . . . . . . . . .2J 21
Trinity Ho. LE2: Leic . . . . . . . . . . . . . .5A 4
Trinity La. LE1: Leic . . . . . . . . .6D 5 (3F 71)
  LE10: Hinc . . . . . . . . . . . . . . . . . .3F 103
Trinity Rd. LE8: Whet . . . . . . . . . . . . . .1K 81
  LE19: End . . . . . . . . . . . . . . . . . .6J 75
Trinity St. LE11: Lou . . . . . . . . . . . . . .7G 19
Trinity Vicarage Rd. LE10: Hinc . . . . . . .3F 103
Tripontium Bus. Cen. CV23: N'ton . . . . .3A 156
Tristram Cl. LE3: Leic E . . . . . . . . . . . .5E 68
Triumph Rd. LE3: Glen . . . . . . . . . . . .7G 63
Trojan Way LE7: Sys . . . . . . . . . . . . . .3A 60
Troon Ind. Est. LE4: Leic . . . . . . . . . . .2C 66
  (not continuous)
Troon Way LE4: Leic . . . . . . . . . . . . . .1K 65
  LE10: Bur . . . . . . . . . . . . . . . . . . .6G 103
Troon Way Bus. Cen. LE4: Leic . . . . . . .2B 66
Tropical Birdland . . . . . . . . . . . . . . . . .1G 95
Trout Ponds Farm Camp Site
  CV9: S Mag . . . . . . . . . . . . . . . . .5B 90
TROWELL . . . . . . . . . . . . . . . . . . . . .1B 158
True Lovers Wlk. LE11: Lou . . . . . . . . . .6D 18
Trueway Dr. LE12: Shep . . . . . . . . . . . .7E 16
Trueway Dr. Sth. LE12: Shep . . . . . . . .1E 28
Trueway Rd. LE5: Leic . . . . . . . . . . . . .5A 72
Truro Cl. LE10: Hinc . . . . . . . . . . . . . . .6H 99
Truro Dr. LE18: Wig . . . . . . . . . . . . . . .7K 77
TRUSLEY . . . . . . . . . . . . . . . . . . . . .1A 158
Tuckers Cl. LE11: Lou . . . . . . . . . . . . .1G 31
Tuckers Holt La. LE67: N Bur . . . . . . . .7D 50
Tuckers Rd. LE11: Lou . . . . . . . . . . . . .1G 31
Tuckett Rd. LE12: W Eav . . . . . . . . . . .2D 42
Tuckey Cl. LE9: Sap . . . . . . . . . . . . . .3K 105
Tudor Cl. CV13: Mkt B . . . . . . . . . . . . .3C 94
  LE3: Leic . . . . . . . . . . . . . . . . . . .2D 70
  LE65: Ash Z . . . . . . . . . . . . . . . . .6K 23
Tudor Dr. LE2: Oad . . . . . . . . . . . . . . .2D 78
  LE9: Cosb . . . . . . . . . . . . . . . . . .7H 81
Tudor Gro. LE6: Groby . . . . . . . . . . . . .5C 62
Tudor Hill LE13: Mel M . . . . . . . . . . . . .1A 120
Tudor Rd. LE3: Leic . . . . . . . . .4A 4 (7D 64)
  LE10: Hinc . . . . . . . . . . . . . . . . . .1F 103
Tudor Wlk. LE3: Leic . . . . . . . . . . . . . .2D 70
Tuffleys Way LE3: Brau . . . . . . . . . . . .6G 69
TUGBY . . . . . . . . . . . . . . . .2C 132 (1A 164)
Tugwell La. LE16: Hall . . . . . . . . . . . . .6A 132
Tunstall Cres. LE4: Leic . . . . . . . . . . . .6A 66
TUR LANGTON . . . . . . . . . . . . . . . . .2A 164
Turnbull Cl. LE7: Bill . . . . . . . . . . . . . .6H 131
Turnbull Dr. LE3: Brau . . . . . . . . . . . . .7K 69
Turnbury Way LE5: Leic . . . . . . . . . . . .5A 72
Turner Av. LE11: Lou . . . . . . . . . . . . . .1E 30
Turner Cl. LE12: Quo . . . . . . . . . . . . . .4K 31
Turner Dr. LE10: Hinc . . . . . . . . . . . . .7D 98
Turner Ri. LE2: Oad . . . . . . . . . . . . . . .4D 78
Turner Rd. LE5: Leic . . . . . . . . . . . . . .7B 66
Turner St. LE1: Leic . . . . . . . . .7D 5 (3F 71)
Turner Wlk. LE5: Leic . . . . . . . . . . . . . .1C 72
Turnpike Cl. LE16: Mkt H . . . . . . . . . . .6A 150
  LE17: Lut . . . . . . . . . . . . . . . . . . .2K 153
Turnpike Rd. PE9: Ryh . . . . . . . . . . . . .4G 129
Turnpike Way LE67: Mark . . . . . . . . . . .5G 55
Turnstone Wlk. LE5: Leic . . . . . . . . . . .7J 65
Turn St. LE7: Sys . . . . . . . . . . . . . . . .1C 60
Turolough Rd. LE67: Whit . . . . . . . . . . .4E 26
TURVEY . . . . . . . . . . . . . . . . . . . . . .7H 13
Turvey La. LE12: L Wha . . . . . . . . . . . .6H 13

Turville Cl. LE10: Bur . . . . . . . . . . . . . .6J 103
  LE18: Wig . . . . . . . . . . . . . . . . . . .1A 84
Turville Rd. LE3: Leic . . . . . . . . . . . . . .4B 70
  LE17: Gilm . . . . . . . . . . . . . . . . . .6J 145
Tuskar Rd. LE5: Leic . . . . . . . . . . . . . .7F 67
Tutbury Cl. LE65: Ash Z . . . . . . . . . . . .6A 24
Tuxford Rd. LE4: Leic . . . . . . . . . . . . .3C 66
Tweed Dr. LE13: Mel M . . . . . . . . . . . .6E 116
Tweedside Cl. LE10: Hinc . . . . . . . . . . .7J 99
Tweentown LE67: D Hea . . . . . . . . . . .7C 38
Twells Rd. LE14: W Wol . . . . . . . . . . . .2D 112
TWENTY . . . . . . . . . . . . . . . . . . . . . .2D 161
Twickenham Rd. LE2: Leic . . . . . . . . . .6C 76
Twinlakes Pk. . . . . . . . . . . . . . . . . . . .1K 117
Twitchbed La. LE15: Upp . . . . . . . . . . .1C 138
Twitchell La. CV9: S Mag . . . . . . . . . . .6C 90
Twitten, The LE2: G Par . . . . . . . . . . . .7D 76
TWYCROSS . . . . . . . . . . . . . .2C 90 (1A 162)
Twycross Rd. CV9: S Mag . . . . . . . . . . .5C 90
  CV13: Bils . . . . . . . . . . . . . . . . . . .6F 91
  LE10: Bur . . . . . . . . . . . . . . . . . . .5J 103
Twycross St. LE2: Leic . . . . . . . . . . . . .2J 71
Twycross Zoo . . . . . . . . . . . . . . . . . . .1A 162
TWYFORD
  Derby . . . . . . . . . . . . . . . . . . . . . .2A 158
  Melton Mowbray . . . . . . . .6G 119 (3A 160)
Twyford Cl. LE67: Coal . . . . . . . . . . . . .3J 39
Twyford Ct. LE9: Barw . . . . . . . . . . . . .3A 100
Twyford Rd. LE7: S Cro . . . . . . . . . . . .6C 118
  LE14: Bur H . . . . . . . . . . . . . . . . .7K 119
  LE14: Mare . . . . . . . . . . . . . . . . . .7J 119
  LE14: T Sat . . . . . . . . . . . . . . . . .5H 119
TWYWELL . . . . . . . . . . . . . . . . . . . . .3C 165
Tyburn Cl. LE3: Leic . . . . . . . . . . . . . . .3K 63
Tycross Rd. DE12: Snar . . . . . . . . . . . .7G 49
Tyers Cl. LE9: Thurl . . . . . . . . . . . . . . .2C 96
Tyes End LE4: Leic . . . . . . . . . . . . . . .3A 64
Tyler Av. LE11: Lou . . . . . . . . . . . . . . .5D 18
Tyler Cl. LE15: E Wes . . . . . . . . . . . . .3G 135
Tyler Ct. LE12: Shep . . . . . . . . . . . . . .4E 16
Tyler Rd. LE6: Ratby . . . . . . . . . . . . . .6B 62
Tyler's Rd. LE12: Belt . . . . . . . . . . . . . .4H 15
Tymecrosse Gdns.
  LE16: Mkt H . . . . . . . . . . . . . . . . .2D 150
Tyndale St. LE3: Leic . . . . . . . . . . . . . .3D 70
Tyndale Cl. LE2: Oad . . . . . . . . . . . . . .3F 79
Tynedale Rd. LE11: Lou . . . . . . . . . . . .3A 30
Tyringham Rd. LE18: Wig . . . . . . . . . . .6A 78
Tyrrell St. LE3: Leic . . . . . . . . . . . . . . .1D 70
Tysoe Hill LE3: Glen . . . . . . . . . . . . . .5H 63
Tythorn Dr. LE18: Wig . . . . . . . . . . . . .3G 77

## U

UFFINGTON . . . . . . . . . . . . . . . . . . . .1D 165
UFFORD . . . . . . . . . . . . . . . . . . . . . .1D 165
Uldale Gro. DE11: C Gre . . . . . . . . . . . .2A 22
ULLESTHORPE . . . . . . . . . . .7F 143 (3C 163)
Ullesthorpe Rd. LE17: Ash P . . . . . . . . .7H 143
  LE17: Bitt . . . . . . . . . . . . . . . . . . .1E 152
  LE17: Frol . . . . . . . . . . . . . . . . . . .2F 143
  LE17: Gilm . . . . . . . . . . . . . . . . . .7E 144
Ullswater Cres. LE65: Ash Z . . . . . . . . .7A 24
Ullswater Av. LE12: Bar S . . . . . . . . . . .2D 32
Ullswater Cl. LE9: Earl S . . . . . . . . . . .3E 100
Ullswater Dr. LE2: Oad . . . . . . . . . . . . .3E 78
Ullswater Rd. LE13: Mel M . . . . . . . . . .5D 116
Ullswater St. LE2: Leic . . . . . . . .7A 5 (3E 70)
Ullswater Wlk. LE2: Oad . . . . . . . . . . . .3E 78
Ulverscroft Dr. LE6: Groby . . . . . . . . . . .4D 62
Ulverscroft La. LE6: New L . . . . . . . . . .7J 41
  LE67: Ulv . . . . . . . . . . . . . . . . . . .7J 41
Ulverscroft Priory (remains of) . . . . . . . .6J 41
Ulverscroft Rd. LE4: Leic . . . . . . . . . . .6H 65
  LE11: Lou . . . . . . . . . . . . . . . . . . .3C 30
Ulverscroft Way LE67: Mark . . . . . . . . .4G 55
Una Av. LE3: Brau . . . . . . . . . . . . . . . .7A 70
Underwood Ct. LE3: Glen . . . . . . . . . . .6F 63
Underwood Cres. LE9: Sap . . . . . . . . . .3K 105
Underwood Dr. LE9: S Stan . . . . . . . . .2H 105
Unicorn Mobile Home Pk.
  LE4: Thurm . . . . . . . . . . . . . . . . . .5K 59
Unicorn St. LE4: Thurm . . . . . . . . . . . .5K 59
Union Pas. LE65: Ash Z . . . . . . . . . . . .5K 23
Union St. LE11: Lou . . . . . . . . . . . . . . .6E 18
Union Wharf LE16: Mkt H . . . . . . . . . . .3D 150
Union Wharf Narrowboats . . . . . . . . . . .3D 150
Unit Ind. Est. LE10: Hinc . . . . . . . . . . . .5D 102
Unitt Rd. LE12: Quo . . . . . . . . . . . . . . .7B 32
Unity Rd. LE3: Glen . . . . . . . . . . . . . . .6G 63
University Cl. LE7: Sys . . . . . . . . . . . . .2D 60
University of Leicester . . . . . . . . . . . . . .7C 5
University Rd. LE1: Leic . . . . . . .10E 5 (5G 71)
  LE11: Lou . . . . . . . . . . . . . . . . . . .1A 30
  (not continuous)
Upex Cl. LE8: Whet . . . . . . . . . . . . . . .5K 81
Upland Cl. LE67: Mark . . . . . . . . . . . . .4F 55

Upland Dr. LE67: Mark . . . . . . . . . . . . . . . .4F **55**
Uplands, The LE13: Mel M . . . . . . . . . . . .5E **116**
Uplands Farm LE12: L Wha . . . . . . . . . . .5E **12**
Uplands Pl. LE12: L Wha . . . . . . . . . . . . .5E **12**
Uplands Rd. DE12: Mea . . . . . . . . . . . . . .1E **48**
   LE2: Leic . . . . . . . . . . . . . . . . . . . . . . .3F **77**
   LE2: Oad . . . . . . . . . . . . . . . . . . . . . . .2D **78**
Uplands Wlk. LE2: Leic . . . . . . . . . . . . . .3F **77**
UPPER BENEFIELD . . . . . . . . . . . . . . . .3C **165**
Upper Bond St. LE10: Hinc . . . . . . . . . . .2G **103**
UPPER BROUGHTON . . . . . . . . .1A **110** (2D **159**)
Up. Brown St. LE1: Leic . . . . . . . . .5C **4** (2F **71**)
UPPER BRUNTINGTHORPE . . . . . . . . .4E **146**
Up. Charnwood St. LE2: Leic . . . . . . . . .1H **71**
Up. Church St. LE7: Sys . . . . . . . . . . . . .1D **60**
   LE65: Ash Z . . . . . . . . . . . . . . . . . . . .5A **24**
UPPER EASTERN GREEN . . . . . . . . . . .3A **162**
Up. George St. LE1: Leic . . . . . . .1E **4** (7G **65**)
Upper Grn. LE11: Lou . . . . . . . . . . . . . . .3B **30**
Upper Grn. La. LE16: G Bow . . . . . . . . .1G **151**
Up. Green Pl. LE16: G Bow . . . . . . . . . .1G **151**
Up. Hall Cl. LE5: Leic . . . . . . . . . . . . . . .6E **66**
Up. Hall Grn. LE5: Leic . . . . . . . . . . . . . .6E **66**
UPPER HAMBLETON . . . . . . . . . . . . . . .1C **165**
Up. King St. LE1: Leic . . . . . . . . . .7D **5** (3F **71**)
UPPER MIDWAY . . . . . . . . . . . . . . . . . .2A **158**
Up. Nelson St. LE1: Leic . . . . . . . .6F **5** (3G **71**)
Up. New Wlk. LE1: Leic . . . . . . . . .7G **5** (3H **71**)
Up. Packington Rd.
   LE65: Ash Z . . . . . . . . . . . . . . . . . . . .7A **24**
Up. Temple Wlk. LE4: Leic . . . . . . . . . . .3A **64**
Up. Tichborne St. LE2: Leic . . . . . .6G **5** (3H **71**)
Upperton Ri. LE3: Leic . . . . . . . . . . . . . .3C **70**
Upperton Rd. LE2: Leic . . . . . . . . . . . . .4D **70**
   LE3: Leic . . . . . . . . . . . . . . . .8A **5** (3C **70**)
UPPINGHAM . . . . . . . . . . . . . . . .2C **138** (2B **164**)
Uppingham Cl. LE5: Leic . . . . . . . . . . . . .2E **72**
Uppingham Dr. LE9: B Ast . . . . . . . . . . .2B **86**
   LE65: Ash Z . . . . . . . . . . . . . . . . . . . .4J **23**
Uppingham Rd. LE5: Leic . . . . . . . . . . . .7K **65**
   LE7: Bill . . . . . . . . . . . . . . . . . . . . . . .6J **131**
                    (not continuous)
   LE7: Bush, Hou H . . . . . .2F **73** & 2A **130**
   LE7: Keyt, Tug . . . . . . . . . . . . . . . . .1B **132**
   LE15: Bisb . . . . . . . . . . . . . . . . . . . .1F **139**
   LE15: O'ham . . . . . . . . . . . . . . . . . .5J **127**
   LE15: Pres . . . . . . . . . . . . . . . . . . . .7A **134**
   LE16: C'ott . . . . . . . . . . . . . . . . . . . .1H **141**
   LE16: Med . . . . . . . . . . . . . . . . . . . .6D **140**
Uppingham School Theatre . . . . . . . . . .2B **138**
UPTON
   Nuneaton . . . . . . . . . . . . . . . . . . . .2A **162**
   Peterborough . . . . . . . . . . . . . . . . . .1D **165**
Upton Cl. DE74: C Don . . . . . . . . . . . . . .4K **7**
Upton Dr. LE18: Wig . . . . . . . . . . . . . . . .6B **78**
Utah Cl. LE3: Glen . . . . . . . . . . . . . . . . . .7G **63**
Uttoxeter Cl. LE4: Leic . . . . . . . . . . . . . .1K **65**
Uxbridge Rd. LE4: Leic . . . . . . . . . . . . . .2J **65**

## V

Vale, The LE15: O'ham . . . . . . . . . . . . . .5J **127**
Valebrook Rd. LE14: Sta . . . . . . . . . . . . .2G **109**
Vale Cl. LE5: Leic . . . . . . . . . . . . . . . . . .7E **66**
   LE11: Lou . . . . . . . . . . . . . . . . . . . . .4F **31**
Vale End LE7: Thurn . . . . . . . . . . . . . . . .2H **73**
Valence Rd. LE3: Leic . . . . . . . . . . . . . . .4B **70**
Valentine Dr. LE2: Oad . . . . . . . . . . . . . .2B **78**
Valentine Rd. LE5: Leic . . . . . . . . . . . . . .2F **73**
Valerie Rd. DE72: A Tre . . . . . . . . . . . . . .1B **6**
Valiant Cl. LE3: Glen . . . . . . . . . . . . . . . .7H **63**
Valjean Cres. LE9: Leic E . . . . . . . . . . . .4C **68**
VALLEY, THE . . . . . . . . . . . . . . . . . . . . .2J **115**
Valley Dr. LE3: Brau . . . . . . . . . . . . . . . .5G **69**
                     (not continuous)
Valley La. LE17: Bitt . . . . . . . . . . . . . . . .2H **153**
Valley Rd. LE5: Ham . . . . . . . . . . . . . . . .2D **66**
   LE11: Lou . . . . . . . . . . . . . . . . . . . . .2B **30**
   LE13: Mel M . . . . . . . . . . . . . . . . . .7E **116**
   LE67: Ibs . . . . . . . . . . . . . . . . . . . . . .4J **51**
   LE67: Mark . . . . . . . . . . . . . . . . . . . .5G **55**
Valley Vw. LE67: New . . . . . . . . . . . . . . .1G **55**
Valley Way LE16: L Bow . . . . . . . . . . . . .3H **151**
   LE67: Whit . . . . . . . . . . . . . . . . . . . .6D **26**
Valliant Cl. LE10: Bur . . . . . . . . . . . . . . .7H **103**
Val Wilson Ct. LE11: Lou . . . . . . . . . . . . .1K **29**
Vancouver Rd. LE1: Leic . . . . . . .1F **4** (7G **65**)
Vandyke Rd. LE2: Oad . . . . . . . . . . . . . .4D **78**
Vanguard Rd. DE74: N Air . . . . . . . . . . . .1J **11**
Vann Wlk. LE4: Leic . . . . . . . . . . . . . . . .4G **65**
Vaughan Av. NG13: Bott . . . . . . . . . . . . .1J **107**
Vaughan Cl. LE16: Mkt H . . . . . . . . . . .7E **150**
Vaughan Rd. LE2: Leic . . . . . . . . . . . . . .1E **76**
Vaughan St. LE3: Leic . . . . . . . . . . . . . .1D **70**
   LE67: Coal . . . . . . . . . . . . . . . . . . . .4C **38**
Vaughan Way LE1: Leic . . . . . . . . .3B **4** (1E **70**)

Ventnor Rd. LE2: Leic . . . . . . . . . . . . . . .1K **77**
Ventnor Rd. Sth. LE2: Leic . . . . . . . . . . .2K **77**
Ventnor St. LE5: Leic . . . . . . . . . . . . . . .2K **71**
Venture Cl. LE10: Hinc . . . . . . . . . . . . . .3B **102**
Venture Theatre, The . . . . . . . . . . . . . . .5K **23**
Vercor Cl. LE67: Coal . . . . . . . . . . . . . . .3K **39**
Verdale Av. LE4: Leic . . . . . . . . . . . . . . .1B **66**
Verdon Cres. LE67: Coal . . . . . . . . . . . . .3H **39**
Vernon Rd. LE2: Leic . . . . . . . . . . . . . . .1E **76**
Vernon St. LE3: Leic . . . . . . . . . . . . . . . .1D **70**
Vero's La. CV13: Nail . . . . . . . . . . . . . . .2C **92**
Vestry Ho. LE1: Leic . . . . . . . . . . .3E **4** (1G **71**)
Vestry St. LE1: Leic . . . . . . . . . . . .3E **4** (1G **71**)
Vetch Cl. LE19: Nar . . . . . . . . . . . . . . . .1D **80**
Viadevana DE12: Moi . . . . . . . . . . . . . . .1A **34**
Vicarage Cl. DE11: Blac . . . . . . . . . . . . .2E **22**
   LE7: Bill . . . . . . . . . . . . . . . . . . . . . . .7J **131**
   LE7: Sys . . . . . . . . . . . . . . . . . . . . . .1D **60**
   LE9: K Mux . . . . . . . . . . . . . . . . . . . .1C **68**
   LE67: New . . . . . . . . . . . . . . . . . . . .1G **25**
Vicarage Ct. LE9: Earl S . . . . . . . . . . . . .2E **100**
Vicarage Dr. LE16: Fox . . . . . . . . . . . . . .1H **149**
Vicarage La. LE4: Leic . . . . . . . . . . . . . .3G **65**
   LE5: Leic . . . . . . . . . . . . . . . . . . . . .6D **66**
   LE7: Bark . . . . . . . . . . . . . . . . . . . . .5F **61**
   LE8: Whet . . . . . . . . . . . . . . . . . . . .1K **81**
   LE12: Belt . . . . . . . . . . . . . . . . . . . . .4H **15**
   LE65: Pac . . . . . . . . . . . . . . . . . . . . .2K **35**
   NG32: Eat . . . . . . . . . . . . . . . . . . . .6G **109**
Vicarage Rd. LE15: O'ham . . . . . . . . . . .3J **127**
Vicarage St. LE9: Earl S . . . . . . . . . . . . .2E **100**
   LE67: Whit . . . . . . . . . . . . . . . . . . . .6F **27**
Vicars Cl. LE15: Ext . . . . . . . . . . . . . . . .2D **128**
Vicary La. LE12: Wood . . . . . . . . . . . . . .1F **43**
Victoria Av. LE2: Leic . . . . . . . . . .6G **5** (3H **71**)
   LE16: Mkt H . . . . . . . . . . . . . . . . . .3D **150**
Victoria Cl. LE67: Whit . . . . . . . . . . . . . .6D **26**
Victoria Ct. LE2: Leic . . . . . . . . . . . . . . .5J **71**
   LE2: Oad . . . . . . . . . . . . . . . . . . . . .1B **78**
Victoria Dr. LE6: Groby . . . . . . . . . . . . . .4D **62**
Victoria Gdns. LE2: Leic . . . . . . . . . . . . .4J **71**
Victoria Hall LE1: Leic . . . . . . . . . . . . . .4B **4**
Victoria M. LE1: Leic . . . . . . . . . .6F **5** (3G **71**)
Victorian Lawn Tennis Club . . . . . . . . . . .5K **71**
Victoria Pde. LE1: Leic . . . . . . . . . . . . . .3D **4**
Victoria Pk. Rd. LE2: Leic . . . . . .10G **5** (5G **71**)
Victoria Pas. LE1: Leic . . . . . . . . .6F **5** (3G **71**)
Victoria Pl. LE11: Lou . . . . . . . . . . . . . . .7F **19**
Victoria Rd. CV9: Manc . . . . . . . . . . . . .7A **96**
   LE8: Whet . . . . . . . . . . . . . . . . . . . .1K **81**
   LE10: Bur . . . . . . . . . . . . . . . . . . . .6J **103**
   LE12: W Eav . . . . . . . . . . . . . . . . . .4D **42**
   LE67: Coal . . . . . . . . . . . . . . . . . . . .3D **38**
   LE67: Ibs . . . . . . . . . . . . . . . . . . . . . .2K **51**
Victoria Rd. E. LE5: Leic . . . . . . . . . . . . .6A **66**
Victoria Rd. Nth. LE4: Leic . . . . . . . . . . .3G **65**
Victoria St. DE74: C Don . . . . . . . . . . . . .3K **7**
   LE4: Thurm . . . . . . . . . . . . . . . . . . .5A **60**
   LE7: Sys . . . . . . . . . . . . . . . . . . . . . .2D **60**
   LE8: Flec . . . . . . . . . . . . . . . . . . . . .4B **88**
   LE10: Hinc . . . . . . . . . . . . . . . . . . . .2G **103**
   LE11: Lou . . . . . . . . . . . . . . . . . . . . .7F **19**
   LE12: Quo . . . . . . . . . . . . . . . . . . . .5B **32**
   LE13: Mel M . . . . . . . . . . . . . . . . . .6F **117**
   LE18: Wig . . . . . . . . . . . . . . . . . . . .5K **77**
   LE19: Nar . . . . . . . . . . . . . . . . . . . . .1G **81**
Victoria Ter. LE2: Leic . . . . . . . . . . . . . . .4H **71**
Victor Rd. LE3: Glen . . . . . . . . . . . . . . . .6H **63**
Victors Cl. LE2: Leic . . . . . . . . . . . . . . . .4C **76**
Viking Rd. LE18: Wig . . . . . . . . . . . . . . .4G **77**
Vilia Cl. LE10: Bur . . . . . . . . . . . . . . . . .7J **103**
Villas, The LE8: K Bea . . . . . . . . . . . . . .2J **89**
Villers Ct. LE8: Bla . . . . . . . . . . . . . . . . .1B **82**
Villiers Hall LE2: Oad . . . . . . . . . . . . . . .7B **72**
Vincent Cl. LE3: Leic . . . . . . . . . . . . . . .1B **70**
Vine Cl. NG13: Bott . . . . . . . . . . . . . . . .3G **107**
Vinehouse Cl. LE7: Thurc . . . . . . . . . . . .2B **58**
Vineries, The LE8: Count . . . . . . . . . . . .6D **82**
Vinetree Ter. LE12: Hot . . . . . . . . . . . . . .1C **20**
Violet Cl. DE12: Don . . . . . . . . . . . . . . . .3A **34**
Viscount Rd. DE74: N Air . . . . . . . . . . . .2K **11**
Vitruvius Way LE19: Brau . . . . . . . . . . . .7G **69**
Vostock Cl. LE2: Leic . . . . . . . . . .4G **4** (2H **71**)
Vue Cinema
   Leicester . . . . . . . . . . . . . . . . . . . . .6J **69**
Vulcan Bus. Cen. LE5: Leic . . . . . . . . . . .7J **65**
Vulcan Ct. LE67: Coal . . . . . . . . . . . . . .2D **38**
Vulcan Rd. LE5: Leic . . . . . . . . . . . . . . .1H **71**
Vulcan Way LE17: Lut . . . . . . . . . . . . . .3B **152**
   LE67: Coal . . . . . . . . . . . . . . . . . . . .2D **38**
Vyner Cl. LE3: Brau . . . . . . . . . . . . . . . .5G **69**

## W

Waddesdon Wlk. LE4: Leic . . . . . . . . . . .6K **65**
WADENHOE . . . . . . . . . . . . . . . . . . . . . .3D **165**

Wade's Ter. LE15: Upp . . . . . . . . . . . . . .2C **138**
Wade St. LE4: Leic . . . . . . . . . . . . . . . . .3F **65**
Wadkins Way LE7: Bush . . . . . . . . . . . . .2J **73**
Wagtail Cl. LE8: Flec . . . . . . . . . . . . . . . .5C **88**
Wain Dr. LE11: Lou . . . . . . . . . . . . . . . . .3A **18**
Waingrove Wlk. LE4: Leic . . . . . . . . . . . .2F **65**
Wainwright Av. LE5: Ham . . . . . . . . . . . .3E **66**
Wainwright Footpath LE5: Ham . . . . . . . .3E **66**
                  (off Sandhills Av.)
Wainwright Rd. LE67: Hug . . . . . . . . . . . .6D **38**
Wakefield Ct. DE74: C Don . . . . . . . . . . .4A **8**
Wakefield Dr. LE67: Whit . . . . . . . . . . . .6E **26**
Wakefield Pl. LE4: Leic . . . . . . . . . . . . . .4K **65**
Wakeley Cl. LE19: Nar . . . . . . . . . . . . . .2E **80**
Wakeley Ct. LE5: Leic . . . . . . . . . . . . . . .1K **71**
Wakeling Cl. LE8: Whet . . . . . . . . . . . . . .4K **81**
WAKERLEY . . . . . . . . . . . . . . . . . . . . . . .2C **165**
Wakerley Cl. LE5: Leic . . . . . . . . . . . . . .1K **71**
Wakerley Rd. LE5: Leic . . . . . . . . . . . . . .4B **72**
   LE15: B'den . . . . . . . . . . . . . . . . . .7D **136**
Wakes Cl. LE17: D Bas . . . . . . . . . . . . .1D **144**
Wakes Rd. LE18: Wig . . . . . . . . . . . . . . .5K **77**
WALCOT . . . . . . . . . . . . . . . . . . . . . . . . .1D **161**
WALCOTE . . . . . . . . . . . . . . . . . .2D **154** (3C **163**)
Walcote Cl. LE10: Hinc . . . . . . . . . . . . . .3C **102**
Walcote Rd. LE4: Leic . . . . . . . . . . . . . . .4A **66**
   LE17: S Kil . . . . . . . . . . . . . . . . . . . .4F **155**
Walcot Rd. LE16: Mkt H . . . . . . . . . . . . .4E **150**
Waldale Dr. LE2: Leic . . . . . . . . . . . . . . .5J **71**
Waldron Ct. LE11: Lou . . . . . . . . . . . . . .4E **18**
Waldron Dr. LE2: Oad . . . . . . . . . . . . . . .3E **78**
Wales Orchard LE17: Leire . . . . . . . . . . .2J **143**
Walford Cl. NG13: Bott . . . . . . . . . . . . .2G **107**
Walker Cl. LE9: B Ast . . . . . . . . . . . . . . .6E **86**
Walker Mnr. Ct. LE17: Lut . . . . . . . . . . . .4K **153**
Walker Rd. LE4: Birs . . . . . . . . . . . . . . . .7F **59**
   LE4: Thurm . . . . . . . . . . . . . . . . . . .7B **60**
   LE67: Bar . . . . . . . . . . . . . . . . . . . . .1J **53**
Walkers Cl. NG13: Bott . . . . . . . . . . . . .2K **107**
Walkers La. LE7: R'ley . . . . . . . . . . . . . .7E **44**
Walkers Stadium, The . . . . . . . .10A **5** (5E **70**)
Walkers Way LE7: Sys . . . . . . . . . . . . . .1D **60**
Wallace Ct. LE2: Leic . . . . . . . . . . . . . . .6K **71**
Wallace Dr. LE6: Groby . . . . . . . . . . . . .1A **62**
   LE12: Sileby . . . . . . . . . . . . . . . . . .3J **45**
Wallace Rd. LE11: Lou . . . . . . . . . . . . . .1E **30**
Wallingford Rd. LE4: Leic . . . . . . . . . . . .4F **65**
Wallis Cl. LE7: Thurc . . . . . . . . . . . . . . .2B **58**
Walney Cl. LE10: Hinc . . . . . . . . . . . . . .2E **102**
Walnut Av. LE4: Birs . . . . . . . . . . . . . . . .6F **59**
Walnut Cl. DE72: A Tre . . . . . . . . . . . . . .1D **6**
   LE2: Oad . . . . . . . . . . . . . . . . . . . . .3C **78**
   LE9: B Ast . . . . . . . . . . . . . . . . . . . .4D **86**
   LE14: Stap . . . . . . . . . . . . . . . . . . .3H **109**
   LE15: Bisb . . . . . . . . . . . . . . . . . . . .3F **139**
   LE15: Emp . . . . . . . . . . . . . . . . . . . .6C **128**
   LE15: Stre . . . . . . . . . . . . . . . . . . . .2K **125**
   LE67: Mark . . . . . . . . . . . . . . . . . . . .5F **55**
Walnut Gro. LE2: G Par . . . . . . . . . . . . . .4B **76**
Walnut Leys LE9: Cosb . . . . . . . . . . . . . .7H **81**
Walnut Paddock LE14: Harb . . . . . . . . . .2D **108**
Walnut Rd. LE11: Lou . . . . . . . . . . . . . . .3E **30**
   NG13: Bott . . . . . . . . . . . . . . . . . . .2G **107**
Walnut St. LE2: Leic . . . . . . . . . . .8A **5** (4E **70**)
Walnut Way LE8: Bla . . . . . . . . . . . . . . . .3B **82**
   LE8: Count . . . . . . . . . . . . . . . . . . .5E **82**
Walpole Ct. LE3: Leic . . . . . . . . . . . . . . .2K **69**
Walsgrave Av. LE5: Leic . . . . . . . . . . . . .3F **73**
WALSGRAVE ON SOWE . . . . . . . . . . . .3A **162**
Walshe Rd. LE5: Leic . . . . . . . . . . . . . . .1D **72**
Walsingham Cres. LE3: Leic E . . . . . . . . .4F **69**
Waltham Av. LE3: Leic . . . . . . . . . . . . . .5A **70**
Waltham Ho. LE15: O'ham . . . . . . . . . . .5H **127**
                   (not continuous)
Waltham La. LE14: Harb . . . . . . . . . . . . .3D **108**
   LE14: L Cla . . . . . . . . . . . . . . . . . . .2J **111**
   NG32: Eat . . . . . . . . . . . . . . . . . . . .7G **109**
WALTHAM ON THE WOLDS . . . .1C **112** (2B **160**)
Waltham Ri. LE13: Mel M . . . . . . . . . . . .6H **117**
Waltham Rd. LE14: Ston . . . . . . . . . . . . .2E **112**
   LE14: T Arn . . . . . . . . . . . . . . . . . . .2J **117**
   NG32: Bran . . . . . . . . . . . . . . . . . . .6J **109**
WALTON . . . . . . . . . . . . . . . . . . .6C **146** (3C **163**)
Walton Cl. LE9: K Mux . . . . . . . . . . . . . .3D **68**
   LE15: Whis . . . . . . . . . . . . . . . . . . .2B **122**
Walton Ct. DE74: Keg . . . . . . . . . . . . . . .5G **9**
Walton Hill DE74: C Don . . . . . . . . . . . . .4J **7**
   DE74: I Wal . . . . . . . . . . . . . . . . . . .2F **11**
Walton La. LE12: Bar S . . . . . . . . . . . . . .6B **20**
   LE17: H Bos . . . . . . . . . . . . . . . . . .4A **148**
WALTON ON THE WOLDS . . . . . . .6G **21** (3C **159**)
Walton Rd. LE17: Kim . . . . . . . . . . . . . . .7A **146**
Walton St. LE3: Leic . . . . . . . . . . . . . . . .4C **70**
Walton Way LE12: Moun . . . . . . . . . . . . .3D **44**
Wand St. LE4: Leic . . . . . . . . . . . . . . . . .5G **65**
WANLIP . . . . . . . . . . . . . . . . . . . .3J **59** (3D **159**)
Wanlip Av. LE4: Birs . . . . . . . . . . . . . . . .6G **59**

Wanlip La. LE4: Birs . . . . . . . . . . . . . .6H 59
Wanlip Rd. LE7: Sys . . . . . . . . . . . . . .2K 59
Wanlip St. LE1: Leic . . . . . . . . . . . . . .7G 65
Wansbeck Gdns. LE5: Leic . . . . . . . . .6E 66
WANSFORD . . . . . . . . . . . . . . . . . . .2D 165
Wanstead Rd. LE3: Leic . . . . . . . . . . . .2E 68
Wanstead Rd. Ind. Pk. LE3: Leic . . . . .2E 68
Ward Cl. LE2: Leic . . . . . . . . . . . . . . . .1C 76
Wardens Wlk. LE3: Leic E . . . . . . . . . . .4F 69
WARDLEY . . . . . . . . . . . . . . . .7K 133 (1B 164)
Wards Closes LE18: Wig . . . . . . . . . . .1A 84
Wards Cres. LE12: Sileby . . . . . . . . . . .1K 45
Wards End LE11: Lou . . . . . . . . . . . . . .7E 18
Wareham Rd. LE8: Bla . . . . . . . . . . . . .3B 82
Waring Cl. LE3: Glen . . . . . . . . . . . . . .5J 63
Warke Flatt DE74: C Don . . . . . . . . . . .2K 7
War Memorial App. LE1: Leic . . . .8F 5 (4G 71)
WARMINGTON . . . . . . . . . . . . . . . . .2D 165
Warmsley Av. LE18: Wig . . . . . . . . . . .4J 77
Warn Cres. LE15: O'ham . . . . . . . . . . .4F 127
Warner Cl. LE8: Whet . . . . . . . . . . . . .4A 82
   LE67: Mark . . . . . . . . . . . . . . . . . .4F 55
Warner Pl. LE11: Lou . . . . . . . . . . . . . .6G 19
Warner's La. LE11: Lou . . . . . . . . . . . .6F 19
Warner St. LE12: Bar S . . . . . . . . . . . .4D 32
Warren, The LE7: East G . . . . . . . . . . .5E 46
   (not continuous)
Warren Av. LE4: Leic . . . . . . . . . . . . . .1C 66
Warren Cl. LE3: Leic E . . . . . . . . . . . . .5D 68
   LE5: Leic . . . . . . . . . . . . . . . . . . .6C 66
   LE67: Mark . . . . . . . . . . . . . . . . . .5G 55
Warren Dr. LE4: Leic . . . . . . . . . . . . . .1C 66
Warren Hill LE6: New L . . . . . . . . . . . .1C 56
Warren Hills Rd. LE67: Coal . . . . . . . . .1J 39
Warren La. DE74: Lock . . . . . . . . . . . . .2E 8
   LE3: Leic E . . . . . . . . . . . . . . . . . .6C 68
   LE67: Whit . . . . . . . . . . . . . . . . . .4F 27
Warren Pk. Way LE19: End . . . . . . . . .4E 74
Warren Rd. LE19: End . . . . . . . . . . . . .7H 75
Warren St. LE3: Leic . . . . . . . . . . . . . .1D 70
Warren Vw. LE4: Leic . . . . . . . . . . . . . .1C 66
Warrington Dr. LE6: Groby . . . . . . . . . .4C 62
Warrington St. LE3: Leic . . . . . . .2A 4 (1E 70)
WARTNABY . . . . . . . . . . . . . .6F 111 (2A 160)
Wartnaby Rd. LE14: Ab K . . . . . . . . . .7G 111
Wartnaby St. LE16: Mkt H . . . . . . . . . .4C 150
WARTON . . . . . . . . . . . . . . . . . . . . . .1A 162
Warwick Av. LE12: Quo . . . . . . . . . . . .5J 31
Warwick Cl. CV13: Mkt B . . . . . . . . . . .2D 94
   LE9: Des . . . . . . . . . . . . . . . . . . . .3G 95
   LE16: Mkt H . . . . . . . . . . . . . . . . .2F 151
   LE67: Bag . . . . . . . . . . . . . . . . . . .7H 53
   LE67: Thor . . . . . . . . . . . . . . . . . .3K 93
Warwick Ct. LE11: Lou . . . . . . . . . . . . .5B 18
Warwick Flats NG13: Bott . . . . . . . . . .2G 107
Warwick Gdns. LE10: Hinc . . . . . . . . . .7H 99
Warwick La. CV13: Mkt B . . . . . . . . . . .2C 94
Warwick Rd. LE8: K Bea, Kib H . . . . . . .3F 89
   LE8: Whet . . . . . . . . . . . . . . . . . . .3H 81
   LE9: B Ast . . . . . . . . . . . . . . . . . . .2B 86
   LE13: Mel M . . . . . . . . . . . . . . . . .6F 117
   LE18: Wig . . . . . . . . . . . . . . . . . . .5H 77
   LE19: Litt . . . . . . . . . . . . . . . . . . .3G 81
Warwick St. LE3: Leic . . . . . . . . . . . . .1D 70
Warwick Way LE11: Lou . . . . . . . . . . . .5B 18
   LE65: Ash Z . . . . . . . . . . . . . . . . . .6A 24
Washbrook La. LE2: Oad . . . . . . . . . . .4B 78
Washington Cl. LE9: Barw . . . . . . . . . .4K 99
Wash La. LE67: Rav . . . . . . . . . . . . . . .4K 37
Wash Pit La. CV13: B'one . . . . . . . . . . .5C 92
   LE17: N Kil . . . . . . . . . . . . . . . . . .2K 155
Washpit La. LE16: Lub . . . . . . . . . . . . .7H 149
Washstones La. LE14: F Wre . . . . . . . .5F 115
Watchcrete Av. LE7: Quen . . . . . . . . . .7J 99
Watchorn Ct. LE15: O'ham . . . . . . . . . .3H 127
Waterfall Way LE9: Barw . . . . . . . . . . .5J 99
   LE16: Med . . . . . . . . . . . . . . . . . . .7C 140
Waterfield Cl. LE5: Leic . . . . . . . . . . . .2D 72
Waterfield Pl. LE16: Mkt H . . . . . . . . . .2E 150
Waterfield Rd. LE7: Crop . . . . . . . . . . .3K 57
Waterfield Way LE10: Bur . . . . . . . . . . .6E 102
Waterfront, The LE3: Leic . . . . . .4A 4 (2E 70)
Watergate LE7: East G . . . . . . . . . . . . .5G 47
Watergate Ct. LE3: Brau . . . . . . . . . . . .2K 75
Watergate La. LE3: Brau . . . . . . . . . . . .1H 75
Water La. LE12: Sea . . . . . . . . . . . . . . .3K 33
   LE14: F Wre . . . . . . . . . . . . . . . . .5G 115
   LE14: L Cla . . . . . . . . . . . . . . . . . .1K 111
   LE14: Sta . . . . . . . . . . . . . . . . . . .3H 109
   LE15: A'll . . . . . . . . . . . . . . . . . . .7H 123
Water Lea LE15: A'll . . . . . . . . . . . . . . .6H 123
Waterloo Cres. LE8: Count . . . . . . . . . .6D 82
   LE18: Wig . . . . . . . . . . . . . . . . . . .5A 78
Waterloo Rd. LE10: Hinc . . . . . . . . . . .3F 103
Waterloo Spinney La. LE12: Wood . . . . . .7F 31

Waterloo Way LE1: Leic . . . . . . .7E 5 (3G 71)
Watermead Country Pk. . . . . . . . . . . .6J 59
Watermead La. LE11: Lou . . . . . . . . . . .3B 30
Water Mdw. Way LE67: Ibs . . . . . . . . . .5K 51
Watermead Way LE4: Leic . . . . . . . . . .2G 65
WATER NEWTON . . . . . . . . . . . . . . . .2D 165
Watersedge Way LE7: Sys . . . . . . . . . .2A 60
Waters End LE9: Barw . . . . . . . . . . . . .5K 99
Waterside PE9: Ryh . . . . . . . . . . . . . . .5H 129
Waterside Cen. . . . . . . . . . . . . . . . . . .5F 65
Waterside Cl. LE11: Lou . . . . . . . . . . . .5F 19
   LE13: Mel M . . . . . . . . . . . . . . . . .1G 117
Waterside Ct. LE10: Hinc . . . . . . . . . . .4C 102
Waterside Dr. LE12: Moun . . . . . . . . . .1D 44
Waterside Rd. LE5: Ham . . . . . . . . . . .3C 66
Waterville Cl. LE3: Leic . . . . . . . . . . . .1G 69
Waterworks Rd. LE67: Coal . . . . . . . . .5G 39
Waterworks Way LE17: H Bos . . . . . . .6C 148
Watery Ga. La. LE9: Thurl . . . . . . . . . .2K 101
Watkin Rd. LE2: Leic . . . . . .8A 5 & 10A 5 (4D 70)
Watling Cl. LE10: Bur . . . . . . . . . . . . . .7F 103
Watling Cres. CV23: C Dus . . . . . . . . .6B 156
Watling Dr. LE10: Bur . . . . . . . . . . . . . .7F 103
Watling St. CV9: Manc, With . . . . . . . . .6A 96
   CV10: Cald, H'hill . . . . . . . .7B 96 & 3F 97
   CV11: Nun . . . . . . . . . . . . .7F 97 & 4A 102
   CV23: Shaw . . . . . . . . . . . . . . . . . .3A 156
   LE1: Leic . . . . . . . . . . . . . . .1C 4 (7F 65)
   LE10: Bur, Hinc . . . . . . . . . . . . . . .5B 102
   LE12: Moun . . . . . . . . . . . . . . . . . .2E 44
   LE17: Shaw . . . . . . . . . . . . . . . . . .3A 156
Watson Av. LE16: Mkt H . . . . . . . . . . .7C 150
Watson Rd. LE4: Leic . . . . . . . . . . . . . .4J 65
Watson's La. LE14: Harb . . . . . . . . . . .2D 108
Watt La. LE8: Peat M . . . . . . . . . . . . . .1K 147
Watts Cl. LE4: Leic . . . . . . . . . . . . . . . .3A 64
Waudby Cl. LE19: Litt . . . . . . . . . . . . . .3G 81
Waugh's Dr. LE12: Moun . . . . . . . . . . .4D 44
Waveney Cl. LE10: Hinc . . . . . . . . . . . .3D 102
Waveney Ri. LE2: Oad . . . . . . . . . . . . .2F 79
Waverley Cl. LE11: Lou . . . . . . . . . . . . .5K 17
Waverley Ct. LE13: Mel M . . . . . . . . . .6G 117
Waverley Rd. LE8: Bla . . . . . . . . . . . . .3C 82
   LE18: Wig . . . . . . . . . . . . . . . . . . .6F 77
Wavertree LE2: Leic . . . . . . . . . . . . . . .7J 71
Wavertree Cl. LE9: Cosb . . . . . . . . . . . .5H 81
Wavertree Dr. LE4: Leic . . . . . . . . . . . .3H 65
Wayfarer Dr. LE7: East G . . . . . . . . . . .4G 47
Wayne Way, The LE4: Birs . . . . . . . . . .6G 59
   LE5: Leic . . . . . . . . . . . . . . . . . . . .1B 72
   (not continuous)
Wayside Dr. LE2: Oad . . . . . . . . . . . . .2E 78
   LE4: Thurm . . . . . . . . . . . . . . . . . .7K 59
Weare Cl. LE7: Bill . . . . . . . . . . . . . . . .7J 131
Weares Cl. LE15: Mor . . . . . . . . . . . . .6K 135
Weaver Cl. LE11: Lou . . . . . . . . . . . . . .2G 31
Weaver Grn. LE13: Mel M . . . . . . . . . .3E 116
Weaver Rd. LE5: Leic . . . . . . . . . . . . . .7F 67
   LE9: Earl S . . . . . . . . . . . . . . . . . . .2F 101
Weavers Av. LE12: Shep . . . . . . . . . . .7D 16
Weavers Cl. LE12: Quo . . . . . . . . . . . . .6A 32
Weavers Ct. LE19: Nar . . . . . . . . . . . . .1F 81
Weaver's Wynd LE7: East G . . . . . . . . .5F 47
Webb Cl. LE3: Leic E . . . . . . . . . . . . . .5F 69
Webbs Way LE13: Mel M . . . . . . . . . . .1J 105
Webster Rd. LE3: Leic . . . . . . . . . . . . .3J 69
Websters Cl. LE12: Shep . . . . . . . . . . .2C 28
WEDDINGTON . . . . . . . . . . . . . . . . . .2A 162
WEEKLEY . . . . . . . . . . . . . . . . . . . . . .3B 164
Weir Cl. LE18: Wig . . . . . . . . . . . . . . . .1H 83
Weir La. LE7: Hou H . . . . . . . . . . . . . .2D 130
Weir Rd. LE8: K Bea . . . . . . . . . . . . . . .3J 89
   LE8: Sad . . . . . . . . . . . . . . . . . . . .7D 88
Welbeck Av. LE4: Leic . . . . . . . . . . . . .4E 64
   LE10: Bur . . . . . . . . . . . . . . . . . . .7G 103
Welbeck Cl. LE8: Bla . . . . . . . . . . . . . .3C 82
Welbury Rd. LE5: Ham . . . . . . . . . . . . .2E 66
WELBY
   Grantham . . . . . . . . . . . . . . . . . .1C 161
   Melton Mowbray . . . . . . . . . . . .1A 116
Welby La. LE13: Mel M . . . . . . . . . . . . .1B 116
   LE14: Ab K . . . . . . . . . . . . . . . . . .7H 111
   LE14: Welb . . . . . . . . . . . . . . . . . .1A 116
Welby Rd. LE14: Ash H . . . . . . . . . . . .4A 116
Welcombe Av. LE3: Brau . . . . . . . . . . .6K 69
WELDON . . . . . . . . . . . . . . . . . . . . . .3C 165
Weldon Av. LE12: Sileby . . . . . . . . . . . .7K 33
Weldon Rd. LE11: Lou . . . . . . . . . . . . .3C 18
   LE18: Wig . . . . . . . . . . . . . . . . . . .5K 77
WELFORD . . . . . . . . . . . . . . . . . . . . . .3D 163
Welford Ct. LE2: Leic . . . . . . . . . . . . . .1H 77
Welford Pl. LE1: Leic . . . . . . . . .5C 4 (2F 71)
Welford Rd. LE1: Leic . . . . . . . .5C 4 (2F 71)
   LE2: Leic . . . . . . . . . . . . . .10D 5 (4F 71)
   LE8: Arne . . . . . . . . . . . . . . . . . . .1H 147
   LE8: Bla . . . . . . . . . . . . . . . . . . . .1B 82
   LE8: Fost . . . . . . . . . . . . . . . . . . . .5A 84

Welford Rd. LE17: H Bos . . . . . . . . . . .7C 148
Welford Rd. LE17: Knap, Shea . . . . . . .1H 147
   LE17: S Kil . . . . . . . . . . . . . . . . . .6H 155
   LE17: Shea . . . . . . . . . . . . . . . . . .5J 147
   LE18: Wig . . . . . . . . . . . . . . . . . . .7K 77
WELHAM . . . . . . . . . . . . . . . . . . . . . .2A 164
Welham Rd. LE16: G Bow . . . . . . . . . .1G 151
   LE16: T Lan . . . . . . . . . . . . . . . . . .2D 140
Welham Wlk. LE4: Leic . . . . . . . . . . . . .2B 66
Welland Av. LE16: Gar . . . . . . . . . . . . .4G 149
Welland Cl. LE16: C'ott . . . . . . . . . . . . .2J 141
   LE67: Coal . . . . . . . . . . . . . . . . . .3H 39
   (Charnborough Rd.)
   LE67: Coal . . . . . . . . . . . . . . . . . .4G 39
   (Nene Way)
Welland Ct. LE16: Mkt H . . . . . . . . . . .5F 151
   (Northampton Rd.)
   LE16: Mkt H . . . . . . . . . . . . . . . . .3G 151
   (Riverside)
Welland Ind. Est. LE16: L Bow . . . . . . .3H 151
Welland Pk. Rd. LE16: Mkt H . . . . . . . .5D 150
Welland Ri. LE13: Mel M . . . . . . . . . . .6F 117
Welland Rd. LE12: Bar S . . . . . . . . . . .5D 32
   LE15: E Wes . . . . . . . . . . . . . . . . .3J 135
Welland St. LE2: Leic . . . . . . . . . . . . . .3H 71
Welland Va. Rd. LE5: Leic . . . . . . . . . .3E 72
Welland Way LE15: O'ham . . . . . . . . . .6G 127
Wellbrook Av. LE12: Sileby . . . . . . . . . .1K 45
Well Ct. LE15: Emp . . . . . . . . . . . . . . .6B 128
   (not continuous)
Well Cross LE15: E Wes . . . . . . . . . . . .3G 135
Wellesbourne Dr. LE3: Glen . . . . . . . . .5H 63
Welles St. LE3: Leic . . . . . . . . . .4A 4 (1E 70)
Wellfield Cl. LE7: Tug . . . . . . . . . . . . . .2C 132
Well Field La. LE14: F Wre . . . . . . . . . .5G 115
Wellgate Av. LE4: Birs . . . . . . . . . . . . .5F 59
Wellhouse Cl. LE18: Wig . . . . . . . . . . . .1J 83
Wellingar Cl. LE3: Brau . . . . . . . . . . . . .5G 69
Wellinger Way LE3: Leic . . . . . . . . . . . .3J 69
Wellington Cl. LE10: Bur . . . . . . . . . . .7H 103
Wellington Parkway LE17: Lut . . . . . . .3C 152
Wellington St. LE1: Leic . . . . . . .5D 4 (2F 71)
   LE7: Sys . . . . . . . . . . . . . . . . . . . .2C 60
   LE11: Lou . . . . . . . . . . . . . . . . . . .7G 19
Wellington Way LE13: Mel M . . . . . . . .2D 116
Well La. DE11: Blac . . . . . . . . . . . . . . .2D 22
   LE10: Hinc . . . . . . . . . . . . . . . . . .2G 103
   LE14: Ab K . . . . . . . . . . . . . . . . . .7H 111
   LE14: Up Bro . . . . . . . . . . . . . . . .1A 110
   LE17: D Bas . . . . . . . . . . . . . . . . .1D 144
Wells Av. LE18: Kilby . . . . . . . . . . . . . .6B 84
WELLSBOROUGH . . . . . . . . . . . . . . . .1A 162
Wellsborough Rd. CV9: S Par . . . . . . . .5D 90
   CV13: Mkt B . . . . . . . . . . . . . . . . .2A 94
Wells Cl. LE17: H Bos . . . . . . . . . . . . .6C 148
Wellsic La. LE7: R'ley . . . . . . . . . . . . . .6E 44
Well Spring Cl. CV9: Ath . . . . . . . . . . . .5A 96
Well Spring Hill LE18: Wig . . . . . . . . . . .1A 84
Wells Rd. LE65: Ash Z . . . . . . . . . . . . .7H 23
Well St. LE15: L'ham . . . . . . . . . . . . . .5C 122
Wellyard Cl. LE12: Shep . . . . . . . . . . . .7E 16
Welton Cl. LE8: K Bea . . . . . . . . . . . . . .3H 89
Welwyn Rd. LE10: Hinc . . . . . . . . . . . .2J 103
Wembley Rd. LE3: Leic . . . . . . . . . . . . .2F 69
Wembury Gdns. LE4: Leic . . . . . . . . . .2E 64
Wendover Dr. LE10: Hinc . . . . . . . . . . .6H 99
Wendy's Cl. LE5: Leic . . . . . . . . . . . . . .7F 67
Wenlock Way LE4: Leic . . . . . . . . . . . . .3C 66
Wensleydale Av. LE9: Barw . . . . . . . . . .5K 99
Wensleydale Cl. LE9: Barw . . . . . . . . . .5K 99
Wensleydale Rd. LE18: Wig . . . . . . . . .7B 78
Wensley Ri. LE2: Leic . . . . . . . . . . . . . .6C 76
Wensum Cl. LE10: Hinc . . . . . . . . . . . .3E 102
   LE15: O'ham . . . . . . . . . . . . . . . . .3K 127
Wentbridge Rd. LE4: Leic . . . . . . . . . . .3K 65
Wenton Cl. LE15: Cott . . . . . . . . . . . . .7A 124
Went Rd. LE4: Birs . . . . . . . . . . . . . . . .7G 59
Wentworth Cl. LE8: K Bea . . . . . . . . . . .4K 89
   LE10: Hinc . . . . . . . . . . . . . . . . . .7H 99
Wentworth Grn. LE9: K Mux . . . . . . . . .3B 68
Wentworth Rd. LE3: Leic . . . . . . . . . . .1C 70
   LE8: Flec . . . . . . . . . . . . . . . . . . . .4C 88
   LE67: Coal . . . . . . . . . . . . . . . . . .4C 38
Werpoint Bus. Cen. LE9: Earl S . . . . . .2E 100
   (off High St.)
Wesley Cl. LE6: Ratby . . . . . . . . . . . . . .6A 62
   LE9: Sap . . . . . . . . . . . . . . . . . . . .4K 105
   LE11: Lou . . . . . . . . . . . . . . . . . . .4K 17
   LE12: Hat . . . . . . . . . . . . . . . . . . .1J 17
Wesley Hillman Ct. DE12: Mea . . . . . . .7E 34
   (off Pegg's Cl.)
Wesley St. LE4: Leic . . . . . . . . . . . . . . .3F 65
Wesley Wlk. LE10: Bur . . . . . . . . . . . . .6K 103
Wesley Way LE67: Mark . . . . . . . . . . . .5H 55
Wessex Dr. LE3: Leic . . . . . . . . . . . . . .2J 69
West Av. LE2: Leic . . . . . . . . . . . . . . . .5H 71
   LE13: Mel M . . . . . . . . . . . . . . . . .3D 116

West Av.—Wilkes Av.


West Av. LE18: Wig .4H 77
W. Bank M. DE74: Keg .6G 9
Westbourne St. LE4: Leic .6G 65
Westbridge LE2: Leic .4A 4 (2E 70)
Westbridge Cl. LE3: Leic .5A 4 (2E 70)
Westbridge Ind. Pk. LE3: Leic .4A 4 (2E 70)
Westbridge Pl. LE2: Leic .5A 4 (2E 70)
WEST BRIDGFORD .1C 159
Westbury Rd. LE2: Leic .6G 71
WESTBY .2C 161
West Cl. LE10: Bur .4G 103
Westcotes Bowling Club .3C 70
Westcotes Dr. LE3: Leic .3C 70
West Ct. LE1: Leic .7F 5 (3G 71)
W. Cross La. LE12: Moun .5C 44
Westdale Av. LE2: G Par .6A 76
WEST DEEPING .1D 165
Westdown Dr. LE4: Thurm .1A 66
West Dr. LE5: Leic .6C 66
WEST END
Leicester .3C 70
Loughborough .6C 14
West End CV13: B'one .5C 92
LE12: L Wha .5D 12
LE14: L Cla .3G 111
LE14: W'ham .1G 121
LE15: Ext .2C 128
LE17: Bitt .2H 153
West End Cl. NG13: Bott .1G 107
Westerby Cl. LE18: Wig .4K 77
Westerby Ct. LE17: Lut .5H 153
Westerby La. LE8: Smee W .5H 89
Westerdale Rd. LE18: Wig .6B 78
Western Av. LE8: Flec .5B 88
LE16: Mkt H .6D 150
LE67: Coal .2A 38
Western Blvd. LE2: Leic .5A 4 (2E 70)
Western Cl. LE65: Ash Z .7K 23
Western Cotts. LE17: N Kil .2J 155
Western Dr. LE8: Bla .2B 82
LE17: C Par .6C 142
Westernhay Rd. LE2: Leic .6J 71
WESTERN PARK .2A 70
Western Pk. LE65: Ash Z .7J 23
Western Pk. Rd. LE3: Leic .2A 70
Western Rd. LE3: Leic .4D 70
LE14: Ash .3G 115
LE14: O Dal .6C 110
W. Farm Dr. LE15: B'den .7C 136
Westfield Av. LE8: Count .5D 82
LE15: O'ham .4G 127
LE18: Wig .4H 77
Westfield Cl. LE7: Rear .4H 47
LE16: Mkt H .4C 150
Westfield Ct. LE10: Hinc .4F 103
Westfield Dr. LE11: Lou .7C 18
Westfield La. LE7: R'ley .7B 44
Westfield Rd. LE3: Leic .2A 70
LE10: Hinc .4E 102
Westfields CV13: B'one .5C 92
Westfields Av. LE65: Ash Z .5H 23
Westfields Ter. LE65: Ash Z .4H 23
Westgate Av. LE4: Birs .5E 58
Westgate La. LE16: Lub .7H 149
Westgate Rd. LE2: Leic .2H 77
Westgate St. LE15: O'ham .4H 127
WEST HALLAM .1B 158
Westhaven Ct. CV13: Mkt B .2C 94
Westhill Rd. LE3: Leic .1A 70
W. Holme St. LE3: Leic .2D 70
Westhorpe Cl. LE15: Win .5E 134
West Hyde LE10: Hinc .4C 102
WEST KNIGHTON .2G 77
Westland Cl. LE16: Lub .7H 149
Westland Rd. LE15: Cott .6B 124
West La. LE7: Bill .6H 131
LE15: Rid .2H 133
LE67: Ell .3H 53
WEST LANGTON .2A 140
W. Langton Rd. LE16: W Lan .2A 140
WEST LEAKE .2C 159
Westleigh Av. LE3: Leic .4C 70
Westleigh Bus. Pk. LE8: Bla .7B 76
Westleigh Rd. LE2: G Par .7E 76
LE3: Leic .4C 70
Westley Grange LE18: Wig .5G 77
Westmeadow La. LE12: L Wha .6C 12
Westmeath Av. LE5: Leic .1D 72
Westminster Cl. LE13: Mel M .1D 116
Westminster Dr. LE2: G Par .7D 76
LE10: Bur .7J 103
(not continuous)
Westminster Ind. Est. DE12: Mea .1D 48
Westminster Rd. LE2: Leic .6A 72
Westminster Way LE65: Ash Z .3J 23
Westmorland Av. LE4: Leic .4J 65
LE11: Lou .2B 30
Westmorland Av. LE18: Wig .6F 77
Westoby Cl. LE12: Shep .6E 16
WESTON BY WELLAND .2A 164
Weston Cl. LE2: Oad .4G 79
LE7: Rear .3H 47
LE10: Hinc .2D 102
Weston Ct. DE72: W Tre .4A 6
Weston Dr. CV13: Mkt B .3C 94
WESTON IN ARDEN .3A 162
WESTON-ON-TRENT .3B 6 (2B 158)
Weston Rd. DE72: A Tre, W Tre .3B 6
LE15: E Wes .3F 135
Westons La. LE15: L'ham .5C 122
WESTON UNDERWOOD .1A 158
W. Orchard LE12: Sileby .3J 45
Westover Rd. LE3: Brau .5H 69
Westray Dr. LE10: Hinc .2E 102
West Rd. LE15: O'ham .4H 127
West Side LE14: Ash H .4A 116
West St. LE1: Leic .7D 5 (3F 71)
LE3: Glen .5G 63
LE7: Sys .1C 60
LE8: Bla .1A 82
LE9: Earl S .1E 100
LE19: End .6F 75
West St. Open LE3: Leic .6A 5 (3D 70)
West Vw. LE14: Som .7K 121
PE9: G Cas .2H 137
(not continuous)
West Vw. Av. LE2: G Par .5B 76
West Wlk. LE1: Leic .7F 5 (3G 71)
(not continuous)
LE67: Ibs .4K 51
WEST WILLOUGHBY .1C 161
Wetherby Cl. LE7: Quen .6G 47
Wetherby Rd. LE4: Leic .2K 65
Wexford Cl. LE2: Oad .4F 79
Weymouth Cl. LE18: Wig .1K 83
Weymouth St. LE4: Leic .6H 65
Whaddon Chase LE15: Cott .4C 124
Whaddon Dr. LE11: Lou .2G 31
Whall Cl. LE12: Quo .6A 32
Wharf St. LE4: Thurm .5K 59
Wharf St. Nth. LE1: Leic .1E 4 (7G 65)
Wharf St. Sth. LE1: Leic .1E 4 (1G 71)
Wharf Way LE2: G Par .6B 76
Wharf Yd. LE10: Hinc .4D 102
Wharncliffe Rd. LE11: Lou .7G 19
Whatoff Lodge & Country Walk .6G 31
WHATTON .1A 160
Whatton Est. LE12: L Wha .4J 13
Whatton House & Gardens .4J 13
Whatton Oaks LE7: R'ley .4E 44
Whatton Rd. DE74: Keg .7G 9
LE12: Hat .7J 13
Wheat Cl. LE12: Moun .1D 44
Wheatfield Cl. LE3: Glen .7G 63
Wheatfield Way LE10: Hinc .7F 99
Wheatland Cl. LE2: Oad .3F 79
Wheatland Dr. LE11: Lou .2G 31
Wheatland Rd. LE4: Leic .1D 64
Wheatlands Cl. PE9: Ket .5G 137
Wheatlands Dr. LE8: Count .5D 82
Wheatley Av. LE15: Upp .1C 138
Wheatley Cl. LE12: Bar S .4E 32
Wheatley Rd. LE4: Leic .2D 64
Wheatleys Rd. LE4: Thurm .6K 59
Wheatsheaf La. LE15: Gree .5F 125
Wheat St. LE1: Leic .2E 4 (1G 71)
Wheeldale LE18: Wig .6B 78
Wheeldale Cl. LE4: Leic .3D 64
Wheeler Cl. LE17: Lut .5J 153
Wheel La. LE15: B'den .7D 136
Wheel Tappers Way LE11: Lou .6D 18
Wheelwright Cl. LE17: N Kil .2K 155
Wheelwright Pl. CV9: S Mag .7B 90
WHETSTONE .1K 81 (2C 163)
Whetstone Ct. LE8: Whet .2K 81
Whetstone Dr. LE67: Coal .3E 38
Whetstone Gorse La. LE8: Whet .7A 82
Whetstone Way LE8: Whet .2J 81
Whiles La. LE4: Birs .6H 59
Whinchat Ct. *DE12: Mea* .*1D 48*
*(off Widgeon Dr.)*
Whinchat Rd. LE5: Leic .1J 71
(not continuous)
Whinham Av. LE9: B Ast .3B 86
WHISSENDINE .2C 122 (3B 160)
Whissendine Rd. LE15: A'll .6F 123
Whistle Way LE19: Nar .1D 80
Whiston Cl. LE5: Leic .1F 73
Whitby Cl. LE9: B Ast .2C 86
LE11: Lou .5K 17
Whitcroft Cl. LE67: Mark .5G 55
Whitcrofts La. LE67: Ulv .5E 40
Whiteacres LE8: Whet .4J 81
White Barn Dr. LE9: Cosb .6H 81
Whitebeam Cl. LE19: Nar .1E 80
Whitebeam Rd. LE2: Oad .1C 78
White Cl. LE9: B Ast .4E 86
Whitefield Rd. LE4: Leic .3F 65
Whitegate LE11: Lou .5G 19
Whitegates Fld. LE18: Wig .7A 78
Whitehall Rd. LE5: Leic .3D 72
White Hart Cl. LE7: Bill .6H 131
Whitehead Cres. LE18: Wig .5H 77
White Heart M. LE7: Bill .6H 131
Whitehill Rd. LE67: Ell .2D 52
Whitehorse Ct. LE12: Wym .2K 21
White Horse La. LE4: Birs .7H 59
Whitehouse Av. LE11: Lou .1G 31
White Ho. Cl. LE6: Groby .3C 62
LE17: Leire .2J 143
LE67: Bag .1F 93
Whitehouse Way DE12: Mea .6E 34
White Lake Cl. LE13: Mel M .6D 116
White Leys Ct. *LE67: Coal* .*3C 38*
*(off Melbourne St.)*
White Lion Gdns. *LE15: O'ham* .*4H 127*
*(off St Annes Cl., not continuous)*
Whitemoors Cl. CV13: S Gol .3B 98
Whitemoors Rd. CV13: S Gol .3B 98
Whiteoaks Rd. LE2: Oad .5E 78
Whitesand Cl. LE3: Glen .5H 63
White St. LE8: K Bea .3H 89
LE12: Quo .5K 31
Whitethorns Cl. LE17: Swin .4G 157
Whitley Cl. LE3: Leic .6B 64
Whitlock Way LE14: Ash .2G 115
Whitman Cl. LE3: Leic .1H 69
Whitteney Dr. Nth. LE2: Leic .4C 76
Whitteney Dr. Sth. LE2: Leic .4D 76
Whittier Rd. LE2: Leic .1F 77
WHITTINGTON .2A 162
Whittington Dr. LE6: Ratby .5A 62
Whittington Rd. LE3: Leic .3K 63
Whittle Cl. LE8: Whet .3K 81
WHITTLEFORD .2A 162
Whittle Rd. LE10: Hinc .3B 102
LE17: Lut .5H 153
WHITWELL .1C 165
Whitwell Rd. LE15: Emp .7A 128
Whitwell Row LE2: Leic .3E 76
WHITWICK .6F 27 (3B 158)
Whitwick Bus. Pk. LE67: Coal .2E 38
Whitwick Moor LE67: Thrin .4D 26
Whitwick Rd. LE67: C Oak, Ulv, Mark .6E 40
LE67: Coal .3D 38
LE67: Coal, C Oak .3A 40
Whitwick Way LE3: Leic .6C 64
Whitworth Av. LE10: Hinc .4C 102
Whitworth Cl. DE12: Moi .7A 22
WHOBERLEY .3A 162
WIBTOFT .7A 142 (3B 162)
Wicken Ri. LE18: Wig .4A 78
Wickham Rd. LE2: Oad .4D 78
Wicklow Av. LE13: Mel M .6G 117
Wicklow Cl. LE12: Shep .1E 28
Wicklow Dr. LE5: Leic .1C 72
Wiclif Way LE17: Lut .3J 153
Wide La. LE12: Hat .1J 17
Wide St. LE12: Hat .2J 17
Widford Cl. LE5: Leic .6C 66
WIDMERPOOL .2D 159
Widon, The LE11: Lou .3C 30
Wigeon Dr. DE12: Mea .1D 48
Wightman Cl. LE9: S Stan .7J 101
LE12: Shep .7D 16
Wightman Rd. LE9: Barw .3B 100
Wigley Rd. LE5: Leic .6E 66
WIGSTHORPE .3D 165
WIGSTON .5K 77 (2D 163)
WIGSTON FIELDS .3H 77
Wigston Framework Knitters Mus. .6J 77
WIGSTON HARCOURT .1A 84
Wigston La. LE2: Leic .2C 76
WIGSTON MAGNA .6A 78
Wigston Rd. LE2: Oad .4B 78
LE8: Bla .1B 82
Wigston's House Mus. .4B 4 (2E 70)
Wigston St. LE1: Leic .4E 4 (2G 71)
LE8: Count .5F 83
Wigston Swimming Pool .7H 77
WILBARSTON .3B 164
Wilberforce Rd. LE3: Leic .4D 70
Wilcox Dr. LE13: Mel M .6H 117
Wildgoose Cl. LE67: Ibs .3K 51
Wild Rose Wlk. LE7: East G .4G 47
Wileman's Cl. LE9: Earl S .4D 100
Wilf Bown Cl. LE9: Earl S .1G 101
WILFORD .1C 159
Wilfred Gdns. LE65: Ash Z .6J 23
Wilfred Pl. LE65: Ash Z .6J 23
Wilkes Av. DE12: Mea .1E 48


A-Z Leicestershire Atlas 221

Wilkes Gdns. LE15: Upp . . . . . . . . . . . . . . . .2C **138**
Wilkes Way LE7: Sys . . . . . . . . . . . . . . . . . . .3B **60**
Wilkinson La. LE9: Elm . . . . . . . . . . . . . . . .4D **100**
Willars Way LE67: Rav . . . . . . . . . . . . . . . . .4K **37**
WILLENHALL . . . . . . . . . . . . . . . . . . . . . . . . .3A **162**
Willesley Cl. LE65: Ash Z . . . . . . . . . . . . . . .7H **23**
Willesley Gdns. LE65: Ash Z . . . . . . . . . . . .7H **23**
Willesley Rd. LE65: Ash Z, W'ley . . . . . . . . .2F **35**
Willesley Wood Side LE65: Ash Z, W'ley . . .6D **22**
(not continuous)
Willet Cl. LE12: Sileby . . . . . . . . . . . . . . . . . .1J **45**
WILLEY . . . . . . . . . . . . . . . . . . . . . . . . . . . . .3B **162**
William Cl. LE7: Quen . . . . . . . . . . . . . . . . . .6G **47**
William Iliffe Flats LE10: Hinc . . . . . . . . . .4D **102**
William Iliffe St. LE10: Hinc . . . . . . . . . . . .4E **102**
William Lyon Ct. LE11: Lou . . . . . . . . . . . . . .5F **19**
William Peardon Ct. LE18: Wig . . . . . . . . . .5J **77**
Williams Cl. LE19: Litt . . . . . . . . . . . . . . . . .3G **81**
William St. LE1: Leic . . . . . . . . . .3F **4** (1H **71**)
   LE11: Lou . . . . . . . . . . . . . . . . . . . . . . . . .7D **18**
   LE19: Nar . . . . . . . . . . . . . . . . . . . . . . . . .2F **81**
WILLINGTON . . . . . . . . . . . . . . . . . . . . . . . .2A **158**
Willn Cl. LE67: Coal . . . . . . . . . . . . . . . . . . .4H **39**
Willoughby Cl. LE13: Mel M . . . . . . . . . . . .5G **117**
Willoughby Ct. LE15: Upp . . . . . . . . . . . . . .2B **138**
Willoughby Dr. LE15: Emp . . . . . . . . . . . . . .6C **128**
Willoughby Gdns. LE15: O'ham . . . . . . . . . .4H **127**
   LE3: Leic E . . . . . . . . . . . . . . . . . . . . . . . .4E **68**
WILLOUGHBY ON THE WOLDS . . . . . . . . .2D **159**
Willoughby Rd. LE8: Count, Will W . . . . . . .6C **82**
   LE3: Mor . . . . . . . . . . . . . . . . . . . . . . . . . .6J **135**
   LE17: Ash M . . . . . . . . . . . . . . . . . . . . . . .1E **144**
   LE17: Ash M, Will W . . . . . . . . . . . . . . . .1G **145**
WILLOUGHBY WATERLEYS . . . . . . .2K **145** (2C **163**)
Willowbank Rd. LE10: Hinc . . . . . . . . . . . . .4F **103**
Willow Brook Cl. LE3: Glen . . . . . . . . . . . . .4G **63**
Willowbrook Cl. LE7: Quen . . . . . . . . . . . . .6G **47**
   LE9: B Ast . . . . . . . . . . . . . . . . . . . . . . . . .3D **86**
   LE10: S'ord . . . . . . . . . . . . . . . . . . . . . . . .7H **105**
   LE65: Ash Z . . . . . . . . . . . . . . . . . . . . . . .3K **23**
Willowbrook Pk. LE11: Lou . . . . . . . . . . . . .4C **18**
Willow Brook Rd. LE5: Leic . . . . . . . . . . . . .7J **65**
Willowbrook Vw. LE5: Leic . . . . . . . . . . . . .1G **73**
Willow Cl. DE12: Mea . . . . . . . . . . . . . . . . .6E **34**
   DE12: Moi . . . . . . . . . . . . . . . . . . . . . . . . .5D **22**
   DE72: A Tre . . . . . . . . . . . . . . . . . . . . . . . .1D **6**
   LE9: N Ver . . . . . . . . . . . . . . . . . . . . . . . .7H **93**
   LE10: Bur . . . . . . . . . . . . . . . . . . . . . . . . .6H **103**
   LE15: Upp . . . . . . . . . . . . . . . . . . . . . . . .1C **138**
   LE15: Whis . . . . . . . . . . . . . . . . . . . . . . . .1B **122**
   LE19: Litt . . . . . . . . . . . . . . . . . . . . . . . . .3G **81**
Willow Ct. LE2: Leic . . . . . . . . . . .5G **4** (2H **71**)
   LE3: Brau . . . . . . . . . . . . . . . . . . . . . . . . .1K **75**
Willow Cres. LE15: O'ham . . . . . . . . . . . . . .3K **127**
   LE16: Mkt H . . . . . . . . . . . . . . . . . . . . . . .5C **150**
Willowcroft LE12: Quo . . . . . . . . . . . . . . . .6J **31**
   LE15: Whis . . . . . . . . . . . . . . . . . . . . . . . .2B **122**
Willowdale LE10: Hinc . . . . . . . . . . . . . . . .4D **102**
Willowdene Way LE9: Barw . . . . . . . . . . . .4A **100**
Willow Dr. LE6: Groby . . . . . . . . . . . . . . . . .5C **62**
   LE8: Count . . . . . . . . . . . . . . . . . . . . . . . .5E **82**
   LE13: Mel M . . . . . . . . . . . . . . . . . . . . . . .3G **117**
Willow Farm Bus. Pk. DE74: C Don . . . . . .2K **7**
Willow Grn. LE67: Coal . . . . . . . . . . . . . . . .2J **39**
Willow Gro. LE12: Moun . . . . . . . . . . . . . . .3C **44**
Willow Herb Cl. LE2: Oad . . . . . . . . . . . . . .4G **79**
Willow Pk. Dr. LE18: Wig . . . . . . . . . . . . . .5J **77**
Willow Pl. LE18: Wig . . . . . . . . . . . . . . . . . .6K **77**
Willow Rd. DE74: C Don . . . . . . . . . . . . . . .3K **7**
   LE8: Bla . . . . . . . . . . . . . . . . . . . . . . . . . .2B **82**
   LE11: Lou . . . . . . . . . . . . . . . . . . . . . . . . .3E **30**
   LE12: Bar S . . . . . . . . . . . . . . . . . . . . . . . .2D **32**
Willows, The LE12: Bur W . . . . . . . . . . . . .4F **21**
Willow St. LE1: Leic . . . . . . . . . . . . . . . . . . .7G **65**
   LE9: Des . . . . . . . . . . . . . . . . . . . . . . . . . .2G **95**
Willow Tree Cl. LE9: Barw . . . . . . . . . . . . .2A **100**
Willowtree Cl. LE5: Ham . . . . . . . . . . . . . . .4E **66**
Willow Tree Cres. LE17: Lut . . . . . . . . . . . .4G **153**
Willow Wlk. LE7: Sys . . . . . . . . . . . . . . . . . .2B **60**
Willow Way LE67: Ibs . . . . . . . . . . . . . . . . .4J **51**
Willsmer Cl. LE9: B Ast . . . . . . . . . . . . . . . .5E **86**
Willson Cl. LE16: L Bow . . . . . . . . . . . . . . .4G **151**
Wilmington Ct. LE2: Leic . . . . . . . . . . . . . .7A **72**
   LE11: Lou . . . . . . . . . . . . . . . . . . . . . . . . .1G **31**
Wilmington Rd. LE3: Leic . . . . . . . . . . . . . .4C **70**
Wilmore Cres. LE4: Leic . . . . . . . . . . . . . . .4H **69**
Wilmot Av. DE72: W Tre . . . . . . . . . . . . . . . .3A **6**
Wilmot Rd. DE11: Swad . . . . . . . . . . . . . . .1A **22**
Wilne Ct. LE2: Leic . . . . . . . . . . . . . . . . . . .3J **71**
Wilnicott Rd. LE3: Brau . . . . . . . . . . . . . . .6K **69**
WILSFORD . . . . . . . . . . . . . . . . . . . . . . . . . .1D **161**
Wilsford Cl. LE18: Wig . . . . . . . . . . . . . . . .1J **83**
Wilshere Cl. LE9: K Mux . . . . . . . . . . . . . . .2B **68**
WILSON . . . . . . . . . . . . . . . . . . . .3A **10** (2B **158**)
Wilson Cl. LE3: Brau . . . . . . . . . . . . . . . . . .5H **69**
Wilson Ri. DE73: Wils . . . . . . . . . . . . . . . . .3A **10**

Wilson Rd. LE18: Wig . . . . . . . . . . . . . . . . .7E **76**
Wilson St. LE2: Leic . . . . . . . . . . . . . . . . . .1J **71**
WILSTHORPE . . . . . . . . . . . . . . . . . . . . . . . .3D **161**
Wilstone Cl. LE11: Lou . . . . . . . . . . . . . . . .7A **18**
Wilton Av. LE11: Lou . . . . . . . . . . . . . . . . . .1G **31**
Wilton Cl. LE2: Oad . . . . . . . . . . . . . . . . . . .3E **78**
Wilton Ct. LE13: Mel M . . . . . . . . . . . . . . .4E **116**
Wilton Pl. LE13: Mel M . . . . . . . . . . . . . . .4F **117**
Wilton Rd. LE13: Mel M . . . . . . . . . . . . . . .4E **116**
Wilton St. LE1: Leic . . . . . . . . . . . .1D **4** (7F **65**)
Wiltshire Ho. LE4: Leic . . . . . . . . . . . . . . . .4D **64**
Wiltshire Rd. LE4: Leic . . . . . . . . . . . . . . . .4D **64**
   LE18: Wig . . . . . . . . . . . . . . . . . . . . . . . . .5H **77**
Wimbish Thorpe Cl. NG13: Bott . . . . . . . . .1G **107**
Wimbledon St. LE1: Leic . . . . . . .3E **4** (1G **71**)
Wimborne Cl. LE18: Wig . . . . . . . . . . . . . . .7J **77**
Wimborne Rd. LE2: Leic . . . . . . . . . . . . . . .2K **77**
Winchendon Cl. LE5: Leic . . . . . . . . . . . . . .7A **66**
Winchester Av. LE3: Leic . . . . . . . . . . . . . . .4B **70**
   LE8: Bla . . . . . . . . . . . . . . . . . . . . . . . . . .1A **82**
Winchester Av. Ind. Pk. LE8: Bla . . . . . . . .1A **82**
Winchester Ct. LE67: Ibs . . . . . . . . . . . . . .3K **51**
Winchester Dr. LE10: Bur . . . . . . . . . . . . . .4K **103**
   LE13: Mel M . . . . . . . . . . . . . . . . . . . . . .1D **116**
Winchester Rd. LE8: Bla, Count . . . . . . . . .2C **82**
Winchester Way LE65: Ash Z . . . . . . . . . . .4J **23**
Winckley Cl. LE7: Hou H . . . . . . . . . . . . . . .2C **130**
Windermere Av. LE65: Ash Z . . . . . . . . . . .6A **24**
Windermere Cl. LE9: Earl S . . . . . . . . . . . . .2E **100**
Windermere Dr. LE9: Crof . . . . . . . . . . . . . .5B **80**
Windermere Rd. LE12: Bar S . . . . . . . . . . .3D **32**
   LE15: E Wes . . . . . . . . . . . . . . . . . . . . . . .3F **135**
   LE18: Wig . . . . . . . . . . . . . . . . . . . . . . . . .5B **78**
Windermere St. LE2: Leic . . . . . . . .8A **5** (4E **70**)
Winders Ct. LE2: Leic . . . . . . . . . . . . . . . . .3D **76**
Winders Way LE2: Leic . . . . . . . . . . . . . . . .3D **76**
Windleden Rd. LE11: Lou . . . . . . . . . . . . . .7K **17**
Windley Rd. LE2: Leic . . . . . . . . . . . . . . . . .2F **77**
Windmill Av. LE4: Birs . . . . . . . . . . . . . . . . .5H **59**
Windmill Bank LE18: Wig . . . . . . . . . . . . . .7A **78**
Windmill Cl. DE74: C Don . . . . . . . . . . . . . .6K **7**
   LE4: Thurm . . . . . . . . . . . . . . . . . . . . . . . .5B **60**
   LE6: Ratby . . . . . . . . . . . . . . . . . . . . . . . . .6B **62**
   LE12: Moun . . . . . . . . . . . . . . . . . . . . . . .1D **44**
   LE65: Ash Z . . . . . . . . . . . . . . . . . . . . . . .6A **24**
   LE67: Rav . . . . . . . . . . . . . . . . . . . . . . . . .5J **37**
Windmill End LE7: R'ley . . . . . . . . . . . . . . . .5E **44**
Windmill Gdns. LE8: Kib H . . . . . . . . . . . . .1J **89**
Windmill Ri. LE6: Groby . . . . . . . . . . . . . . .3C **62**
   LE12: W Eav . . . . . . . . . . . . . . . . . . . . . . .3D **42**
Windmill Rd. LE11: Lou . . . . . . . . . . . . . . .7H **19**
Windmill Rd. Ind. Est. LE11: Lou . . . . . . . .7H **19**
Windmill Vw. LE67: Swan . . . . . . . . . . . . . .5A **26**
Windmill Way DE74: Keg . . . . . . . . . . . . . .6F **9**
   LE15: Lyd . . . . . . . . . . . . . . . . . . . . . . . . .7E **138**
Windrush Dr. LE2: Oad . . . . . . . . . . . . . . . .2F **79**
   LE10: Hinc . . . . . . . . . . . . . . . . . . . . . . . .3D **102**
Windsor Av. LE2: G Par . . . . . . . . . . . . . . . .7E **76**
   LE4: Leic . . . . . . . . . . . . . . . . . . . . . . . . .4H **65**
   LE6: Groby . . . . . . . . . . . . . . . . . . . . . . . .4D **62**
Windsor Cl. LE2: Oad . . . . . . . . . . . . . . . . .5E **78**
   LE12: Moun . . . . . . . . . . . . . . . . . . . . . . .4D **44**
   LE12: Quo . . . . . . . . . . . . . . . . . . . . . . . . .5B **32**
   LE67: Coal . . . . . . . . . . . . . . . . . . . . . . . .3H **39**
Windsor Ct. LE10: Bur . . . . . . . . . . . . . . . .6K **103**
   LE16: Mkt H . . . . . . . . . . . . . . . . . . . . . . .3D **150**
Windsor Dr. LE12: Shep . . . . . . . . . . . . . . .1C **28**
   LE15: O'ham . . . . . . . . . . . . . . . . . . . . . .5G **127**
Windsor Rd. LE11: Lou . . . . . . . . . . . . . . . .5B **18**
   LE14: W Wol . . . . . . . . . . . . . . . . . . . . . . .1D **112**
   LE65: Ash Z . . . . . . . . . . . . . . . . . . . . . . .6K **23**
Windsor St. LE10: Bur . . . . . . . . . . . . . . . .6J **103**
   LE13: Mel M . . . . . . . . . . . . . . . . . . . . . .4F **117**
Winforde Cres. LE3: Leic . . . . . . . . . . . . . . .3H **69**
WING . . . . . . . . . . . . . . . . . . . . .5E **134** (1B **164**)
Wingfield St. LE4: Leic . . . . . . . . . . . . . . . .4H **65**
Wing Hall LE15: Win . . . . . . . . . . . . . . . . . .6E **134**
Wing Maze . . . . . . . . . . . . . . . . . . . . . . . . . .6E **134**
Wing Rd. LE15: Glas . . . . . . . . . . . . . . . . . .1J **139**
   LE15: Mant . . . . . . . . . . . . . . . . . . . . . . . .3B **134**
   LE15: Mor . . . . . . . . . . . . . . . . . . . . . . . . .4H **135**
Winifred St. LE2: Leic . . . . . . . . . .7B **5** (3E **70**)
WINSHILL . . . . . . . . . . . . . . . . . . . . . . . . . . .2A **158**
Winslow Dr. LE18: Wig . . . . . . . . . . . . . . . .4A **78**
Winslow Grn. LE5: Leic . . . . . . . . . . . . . . . .6E **66**
Winstanley Dr. LE3: Leic . . . . . . . . . . . . . .3K **69**
Winster Cres. LE13: Mel M . . . . . . . . . . . .6D **116**
Winster Dr. LE4: Thurm . . . . . . . . . . . . . . .5A **60**
Winston Av. LE9: Crof . . . . . . . . . . . . . . . . .5B **80**
Winston Cl. PE9: Ket . . . . . . . . . . . . . . . . . .6G **137**
Winterbeck Cl. NG13: Bott . . . . . . . . . . . . .1G **107**
Winterbeck Ind. Est. NG13: Bott . . . . . . . .1F **107**
Winterburn Gdns. LE8: Whet . . . . . . . . . . .2K **81**
Winterburn Way LE11: Lou . . . . . . . . . . . . .7K **17**
Winterfield Cl. LE3: Glen . . . . . . . . . . . . . . .7F **63**
Wintergreen Cl. LE5: Ham . . . . . . . . . . . . . .3E **66**
Wintersdale Rd. LE5: Leic . . . . . . . . . . . . . .1E **72**

Wintersdale Wlk. LE5: Leic . . . . . . . . . . . . .1F **73**
Winterton Cl. LE4: Thurm . . . . . . . . . . . . . .5B **60**
Winton Av. LE3: Leic . . . . . . . . . . . . . . . . . .5C **70**
Winton Wlk. LE3: Leic . . . . . . . . . . . . . . . . .5C **70**
WINWICK . . . . . . . . . . . . . . . . . . . . . . . . . . .3D **165**
Wireless Hill Ind. Est. LE15: S Luf . . . . . . . .3E **136**
(not continuous)
Wisp, The LE15: B Rut . . . . . . . . . . . . . . . . .7A **126**
WISTOW . . . . . . . . . . . . . . . . . . . . . . . . . . . .5F **85**
Wistow Cl. LE18: Kilby . . . . . . . . . . . . . . . . .6C **84**
Wistow La. LE8: Kib H . . . . . . . . . . . . . . . . .1E **88**
Wistow Rd. LE8: New H . . . . . . . . . . . . . . . .2F **85**
   LE8: Wist . . . . . . . . . . . . . . . . . . . . . . . . .5G **85**
   LE18: Kilby . . . . . . . . . . . . . . . . . . . . . . . .6C **84**
   LE18: Wig . . . . . . . . . . . . . . . . . . . . . . . . .7K **77**
Wistow Rural Cen. . . . . . . . . . . . . . . . . . . . .5F **85**
Witchley Cl. LE15: O'ham . . . . . . . . . . . . . .4K **127**
Witham Av. LE15: O'ham . . . . . . . . . . . . . .5G **127**
Witham Cl. LE13: Mel M . . . . . . . . . . . . . . .6E **116**
WITHAM ON THE HILL . . . . . . . . . . . . . . . .3D **161**
Withcote Av. LE5: Leic . . . . . . . . . . . . . . . . .1D **72**
Withens Cl. LE3: Leic . . . . . . . . . . . . . . . . . .7A **64**
Witherdell LE4: Leic . . . . . . . . . . . . . . . . . . .3A **64**
WITHERLEY . . . . . . . . . . . . . . . . .6B **96** (2A **162**)
Witherley Rd. CV9: Ath . . . . . . . . . . . . . . . .6A **96**
Withers Cl. LE15: O'ham . . . . . . . . . . . . . . .2J **127**
Withers Way LE3: Brau . . . . . . . . . . . . . . . .5H **69**
Withington Cl. LE3: Brau . . . . . . . . . . . . . . .5H **69**
WITHYBROOK . . . . . . . . . . . . . . . . . . . . . . . .3B **162**
WITTERING . . . . . . . . . . . . . . . . . . . . . . . . . .1D **165**
Woburn Cl. LE2: Leic . . . . . . . . . . . . . . . . . .4C **76**
   LE10: Hinc . . . . . . . . . . . . . . . . . . . . . . . .7H **99**
   LE11: Lou . . . . . . . . . . . . . . . . . . . . . . . . .6A **18**
   LE16: L Bow . . . . . . . . . . . . . . . . . . . . . . .4G **151**
   LE18: Wig . . . . . . . . . . . . . . . . . . . . . . . . .6A **78**
Wodehouse Rd. LE3: Leic . . . . . . . . . . . . . .3A **70**
Wokingham Av. LE2: Leic . . . . . . . . . . . . . .6D **76**
Wolds, The LE7: East G . . . . . . . . . . . . . . . .4G **47**
WOLLATON . . . . . . . . . . . . . . . . . . . . . . . . . .1C **159**
Wollaton Av. LE11: Lou . . . . . . . . . . . . . . . .6A **18**
Wollaton Cl. LE3: Glen . . . . . . . . . . . . . . . .6F **63**
Wolsey Cl. LE3: Leic E . . . . . . . . . . . . . . . . .5D **68**
   LE6: Groby . . . . . . . . . . . . . . . . . . . . . . . .4C **62**
   LE8: Flec . . . . . . . . . . . . . . . . . . . . . . . . . .3B **88**
Wolsey Dr. LE6: Ratby . . . . . . . . . . . . . . . . .5A **62**
Wolsey La. LE8: Flec . . . . . . . . . . . . . . . . . .3B **88**
(off Wolsey Cl.)
   LE8: Flec . . . . . . . . . . . . . . . . . . . . . . . . . .3B **88**
(Stores La.)
Wolsey Rd. LE67: Coal . . . . . . . . . . . . . . . .2C **38**
Wolsey St. LE4: Leic . . . . . . . . . . . . . . . . . .6E **64**
Wolsey Way LE7: Sys . . . . . . . . . . . . . . . . . .2B **60**
   LE11: Lou . . . . . . . . . . . . . . . . . . . . . . . . .6G **19**
Wolverton Rd. LE3: Leic . . . . . . . . . . . . . . .5C **70**
WOLVEY . . . . . . . . . . . . . . . . . . . . . . . . . . . .3B **162**
WOLVEY HEATH . . . . . . . . . . . . . . . . . . . . . .3B **162**
Wolvey Rd. LE10: Bur . . . . . . . . . . . . . . . . .7H **103**
Woodbank LE2: G Par . . . . . . . . . . . . . . . . .6B **76**
   LE10: Bur . . . . . . . . . . . . . . . . . . . . . . . . .4K **103**
Woodbank Rd. LE2: Leic . . . . . . . . . . . . . . .2J **77**
   LE6: Groby . . . . . . . . . . . . . . . . . . . . . . . .3B **62**
Woodbine Av. LE2: Leic . . . . . . . . .7G **5** (3H **71**)
Woodbine Cres. LE17: Lut . . . . . . . . . . . . . .5J **153**
Woodborough Rd. LE5: Leic . . . . . . . . . . . .3C **72**
Woodboy St. LE1: Leic . . . . . . . . . .1E **4** (7G **65**)
Woodbreach Dr. LE16: L Bow . . . . . . . . . . .4H **151**
Woodbridge Rd. LE4: Leic . . . . . . . . . . . . . .3H **65**
Woodbrook Rd. LE11: Lou . . . . . . . . . . . . . .2C **30**
Woodbury Ri. LE8: G Gle . . . . . . . . . . . . . . .5A **130**
Woodby La. LE17: Bitt . . . . . . . . . . . . . . . . .2E **152**
Wood Cl. LE12: Shep . . . . . . . . . . . . . . . . . .7F **17**
Woodcock Cl. LE17: Gilm . . . . . . . . . . . . . .7J **145**
Woodcock Dr. LE13: Mel M . . . . . . . . . . . .7E **116**
Woodcock Way LE65: Ash Z . . . . . . . . . . . .4A **24**
Woodcote LE65: Ash Z . . . . . . . . . . . . . . . .3K **23**
Woodcote Rd. LE3: Brau . . . . . . . . . . . . . . .1J **75**
Woodcroft, The DE74: Dis . . . . . . . . . . . . . .4A **12**
Woodcroft Av. LE2: Leic . . . . . . . . . . . . . . .2G **77**
WOOD END . . . . . . . . . . . . . . . . . . . . . . . . . .3A **162**
Wood End LE3: Leic . . . . . . . . . . . . . . . . . . .7A **64**
Woodfield Cl. LE19: Nar . . . . . . . . . . . . . . . .1F **81**
Woodfield Cotts. DE12: Mea . . . . . . . . . . . .7F **35**
Woodfield Rd. LE2: Oad . . . . . . . . . . . . . . .1D **78**
   LE7: R'ley . . . . . . . . . . . . . . . . . . . . . . . . .6E **44**
   LE10: Bur . . . . . . . . . . . . . . . . . . . . . . . . .5F **103**
WOODFORD . . . . . . . . . . . . . . . . . . . . . . . . .3C **165**
Woodford Cl. LE18: Wig . . . . . . . . . . . . . . .1J **83**
Woodford La. CV10: H'hill . . . . . . . . . . . . . .7D **96**
Woodford Rd. LE2: Leic . . . . . . . . .9A **5** (4D **70**)
Woodgate LE3: Leic . . . . . . . . . . . . . . . . . . .7D **64**
   LE7: R'ley . . . . . . . . . . . . . . . . . . . . . . . . .6E **44**
   LE11: Lou . . . . . . . . . . . . . . . . . . . . . . . . .7F **19**
   LE16: Fox . . . . . . . . . . . . . . . . . . . . . . . . .2H **149**
Woodgate Cl. LE16: L Bow . . . . . . . . . . . . .5H **151**
Woodgate Dr. LE4: Birs . . . . . . . . . . . . . . . .5F **59**
   LE11: Lou . . . . . . . . . . . . . . . . . . . . . . . . .1D **30**
Woodgate Hill LE14: G Dal . . . . . . . . . . . . .6D **120**

Woodgate Rd. LE10: Bur ...3K 103
Woodgon Rd. LE7: Anst ...7H 57
Woodgreen Rd. LE4: Leic ...5K 65
Woodgreen Wlk. LE4: Leic ...5K 65
Woodhall Cl. LE3: Leic ...2H 69
Woodhead Cl. LE15: Mkt O ...2H 123
Wood Hill LE5: Leic ...1J 71
  LE14: O Dal ...7A 110
WOODHOUSE ...7G 31 (3C 159)
Woodhouse Cl. LE67: Mark ...4G 55
WOODHOUSE EAVES ...3E 42 (3C 159)
Woodhouse La. LE11: Nan ...4K 29
  LE12: Nan ...4K 29
Woodhouse Rd. LE12: Quo, Wood ...7G 31
  LE14: Ash ...2F 115
  LE19: Nar ...1E 80
  LE67: Coal ...4H 39
Woodhouse St. DE11: W'lle ...1B 22
Woodland Av. LE2: Leic ...6J 71
  LE10: Bur ...5K 103
  LE13: Mel M ...6G 117
  LE17: C Mag ...5C 142
  LE19: Nar ...7F 75
Woodland Cl. LE67: Mark ...5G 55
Woodland Dr. LE3: Brau ...5H 69
Woodland Rd. LE5: Leic ...7K 65
  LE10: Hinc ...2J 103
  LE15: Cott ...4C 124
Woodlands, The LE8: Count ...5D 82
  LE16: Mkt H ...3C 150
  LE18: Wig ...4B 78
Woodlands Cl. LE2: Oad ...4J 79
  LE12: Wym ...2K 21
Woodlands Ct. LE2: Oad ...4G 79
Woodlands Dr. LE6: Groby ...2B 62
  LE11: Lou ...2E 30
  LE12: Shep ...5E 16
Woodlands La. LE9: K Mux ...1C 68
Woodlands Way DE12: Moi ...5D 22
Woodland Vw. LE15: O'ham ...3J 127
Wood La. CV10: H Hill ...6F 97
  CV13: Cad ...6B 94
  CV13: H Hill ...6F 97
  LE7: Tug ...1C 132
  LE12: Quo ...6B 32
  LE14: Sta ...1H 109
  LE15: B Rut ...7B 126
  LE15: Ward ...7K 133
  NG13: Bark V ...3B 106
Woodlea Av. LE17: Lut ...3G 153
Woodley Rd. LE6: Ratby ...6A 62
Woodman's Chase LE7: East G ...5F 47
Woodmans Way LE12: Shep ...5E 16
Woodmarket LE17: Lut ...5H 153
WOODNEWTON ...2D 165
Woodnewton Dr. LE5: Leic ...3F 73
WOODNOOK ...1C 161
Woodpecker Dr. LE3: Leic E ...5C 68
Wood Rd. CV13: Nail ...1E 92
  LE67: Ell ...7D 52
Woods Cl. LE2: Oad ...2E 78
  LE67: Hug ...6C 38
Woodshawe Ri. LE3: Leic ...4J 69
WOODSIDE ...1A 158
Woodside LE12: Bar S ...3C 32
  LE65: Bar S ...6H 23
Woodside Cl. LE4: Leic ...5K 65
  LE19: Nar ...1D 80
Woodside Rd. LE2: Oad ...5F 79
Woodstock Cl. LE4: Leic ...2E 64
  LE10: Bur ...5K 103
Woodstock Rd. LE4: Leic ...2E 64
Wood St. LE1: Leic ...1D 4 (7F 65)
  LE9: Earl S ...2D 100
  LE10: Hinc ...2G 103
  LE65: Ash Z ...5A 24
Wood St. Cl. LE10: Hinc ...2G 103
WOODTHORPE ...4G 31 (3C 159)
Woodthorpe Av. LE11: Lou ...2F 31
Woodthorpe Rd. LE11: Lou ...2F 31
WOODVILLE ...3A 158
Woodville Gdns. LE18: Wig ...3J 77
Woodville Rd. LE3: Leic ...2B 70
Woodward Av. LE12: Quo ...5J 31
Woodway LE8: Whet ...1K 81
Woodway La. LE17: C Par ...7B 142
Woodway Rd. LE17: Lut ...5G 153
Woodwell Head La. LE14: Edm ...3K 121

Woodyard La. LE8: Whet ...1K 81
Wooldale Cl. LE7: Anst ...6J 57
Woolrooms, The LE67: Cole ...3K 25
WOOLSTHORPE
  Colsterworth ...2C 161
  Grantham ...1B 160
Woolsthorpe Wlk. LE5: Leic ...6A 66
Wootton Cl. LE8: Whet ...3K 81
Wootton Ri. LE2: Leic ...3D 76
Worcester Av. LE4: Birs ...4H 59
Worcester Cl. LE9: Barw ...3K 99
Worcester Dr. LE13: Mel M ...7G 117
  LE16: Mkt H ...2E 150
  LE18: Wig ...6F 77
Worcester Rd. LE2: Leic ...1D 76
Wordsworth Cl. LE67: Cole ...4J 25
Wordsworth Cres. LE19: Nar ...7E 74
Wordsworth Rd. LE2: Leic ...7G 71
  LE11: Lou ...6B 18
Wordsworth Way DE12: Mea ...2D 48
Workhouse La. LE10: Bur ...6K 103
  (not continuous)
Workspace 17 LE67: Coal ...5C 38
Worrall Cl. LE3: Leic ...3H 69
Worrall Rd. LE3: Leic ...3H 69
Worsh Cl. LE8: Whet ...4K 81
Worsley Way LE8: Whet ...3A 82
WORTHINGTON ...2B 14 (2B 158)
Worthington La. LE73: B Hil ...7B 10
  LE65: Wort ...2A 14
  LE67: New ...1G 25 & 3A 14
Worthington St. LE2: Leic ...2J 71
Wortley Cl. LE12: Shep ...4E 16
  LE67: Coal ...3E 38
Wortley Ct. LE11: Lou ...6F 19
WOTHORPE ...1D 165
Woulds Ct. DE12: Moi ...5D 22
  (off Ashfield Dr.)
Wranglands, The LE8: Flec ...4C 68
Wreake Cl. LE7: Sys ...1D 60
Wreake Cres. LE14: Ash ...3F 115
Wreake Dr. LE7: Rear ...1J 47
Wreake Rd. LE4: Thurm ...4A 60
Wreake Wlk. LE15: O'ham ...5G 127
  (off Welland Way)
Wreford Cres. LE5: Leic ...7G 67
Wrekin Cl. LE65: Ash Z ...7A 24
Wren Cl. DE12: A Mag ...5A 48
  LE2: Leic ...1E 76
  LE7: Sys ...1A 60
  LE11: Lou ...7D 18
  LE13: Mel M ...7E 116
  LE15: O'ham ...2J 127
Wrendyke Cl. LE15: Mor ...6J 135
Wright Cl. LE8: Whet ...5K 81
Wright La. LE2: Oad ...4F 79
Wrights Acre LE12: Sileby ...7H 33
Wrights Cl. LE12: Quo ...6K 31
Wrights La. LE14: W'ham ...1H 121
Wroxall Way LE3: Leic ...6C 64
Wyatt Cl. LE3: Leic ...3G 69
Wyatt Rd. LE67: Coal ...2E 38
Wych Elm Cl. LE8: G Gle ...7K 79
Wych Elm Rd. LE2: Oad ...1C 78
Wychwood Rd. LE8: Whet ...4A 82
Wycliffe Av. LE12: Bar S ...3D 32
  LE13: Mel M ...3F 117
Wycliffe Ind. Est. LE17: Lut ...3K 153
Wycliffe St. LE1: Leic ...4C 4 (2F 71)
Wycliffe Ter. LE17: Lut ...4K 153
WYCOMB ...5E 112
Wycombe Gro. LE13: Mel M ...5H 117
Wycombe Rd. LE5: Leic ...6B 66
Wycomb La. LE14: Wyc ...4E 112
Wye Cl. LE10: Hinc ...3D 102
Wye Dean Dr. LE18: Wig ...6K 77
WYFORDBY ...3A 160
Wyfordby Cl. LE13: Mel M ...6H 117
Wyggeston Av. NG13: Bott ...1H 107
Wyggeston Hospital LE3: Leic ...2C 70
Wyggeston Rd. LE67: Coal ...4D 38
  NG13: Bott ...1H 107
Wyggeston Ter. NG13: Bott ...2H 107
Wykeham Cl. LE8: Bla ...3B 82
WYKEN ...3A 162
WYKIN ...7C 98 (2B 162)
Wykin La. CV13: S Gol ...4A 98
Wykin Rd. LE10: Hinc, Wyk ...7C 98

Wylam Cl. LE3: Leic ...6A 64
Wymar Cl. LE4: Leic ...3C 64
WYMESWOLD ...1K 21 (2D 159)
Wymeswold Bowls Club ...2J 21
Wymeswold Ind. Est. LE12: Bur W ...1G 21
Wymeswold La. LE12: Bur W ...2G 21
Wymeswold Rd. LE12: Hot ...1D 20
WYMONDHAM ...1H 121 (3B 160)
Wymondham Drift LE14: W'ham ...1J 121
Wymondham Towermill ...3B 160
Wymondham Way LE13: Mel M ...1F 117
Wyndale Dr. LE7: Sys ...7D 46
Wyndale Rd. LE2: Leic ...1H 77
Wyndham Av. LE13: Mel M ...6F 117
Wyndham Cl. LE2: Oad ...1E 78
Wyndham Rd. LE11: Lou ...4K 17
Wynfield Rd. LE3: Leic ...2B 70
Wyngate Dr. LE3: Leic ...3B 70
Wynthorpe Ri. LE3: Leic ...3A 70
Wynton Cl. LE8: Bla ...3C 82
WYSALL ...2D 159
Wysall La. LE12: Wym ...1K 21
Wytchley Rd. PE9: Ket ...6F 137
Wythburn Cl. LE11: Lou ...2B 30
Wyvelle Cres. DE74: Keg ...5G 9
Wyvern Av. LE4: Leic ...3K 65
Wyvern Cl. LE9: B Ast ...5E 86
  LE10: Bur ...7H 103
Wyvernhoe Dr. LE12: Quo ...6J 31
Wyvern Ter. LE13: Mel M ...4G 117
WYVILLE ...2B 160
Wyville Row LE3: Leic ...6A 70

## Y

Yardley Dr. LE2: Leic ...3H 77
Yarmouth St. LE1: Leic ...1D 4
Yarrow Cl. LE5: Ham ...5E 66
YARWELL ...2D 165
Yarwell Dr. LE18: Wig ...6A 78
Yates Av. DE72: A Tre ...1C 6
Yates Cl. DE12: Moi ...6C 22
Yaxley Cl. LE7: Thurn ...1H 73
Yeats Cl. LE3: Brau ...6H 69
Yelverton Av. LE5: Leic ...4E 72
Ye Olde Pork Pie Shoppe ...4F 117
Yeoman La. LE1: Leic ...3E 4 (1G 71)
Yeomanry Ct. LE16: Mkt H ...4E 150
Yeoman's Dale LE7: East G ...4F 47
Yeomans Keep LE17: Bitt ...2H 153
Yeoman St. LE1: Leic ...3E 4 (1G 71)
Yew Cl. LE3: Leic E ...6D 68
Yews, The LE2: Oad ...2D 78
  LE14: G Dal ...5D 120
Yew Tree Cl. LE8: Will W ...1K 145
  LE9: Barw ...2B 100
  LE17: Lut ...4G 153
Yew Tree Cres. LE13: Mel M ...2F 117
Yew Tree Dr. LE3: Leic ...1G 69
York Cl. CV13: Mkt B ...3C 94
  DE12: Mea ...7E 34
  LE2: G Par ...7E 76
  LE12: Moun ...4D 44
York Pl. LE1: Leic ...5E 4 (2G 71)
  LE67: Coal ...3K 39
York Rd. DE11: C Gre ...1A 22
  LE1: Leic ...5C 4 (2F 71)
  LE10: Hinc ...7F 99
  LE11: Lou ...6E 18
Yorkshire Rd. LE4: Leic ...5J 65
York St. LE1: Leic ...5D 4 (2F 71)
  LE16: Mkt H ...4F 151
Y Theatre, The ...5E 4 (2G 71)
Yukon Way LE1: Leic ...1F 4 (7G 65)

## Z

Zealand Cl. LE10: Hinc ...7J 99
Zetland Cl. LE67: Coal ...4C 38
Zetland Sq. LE15: Cott ...2D 124
  (not continuous)
Zetland Wlk. LE4: Leic ...1E 64
Zion Hill LE67: Cole ...3A 26
ZOUCH ...2C 159
Zouch Rd. LE12: Hat ...7K 13

# HOSPITALS and HOSPICES
## covered by this atlas.

N.B. Where Hospitals and Hospices are not named on the map, the reference
given is for the road in which they are situated.

ASHBY & DISTRICT HOSPITAL —5A **24**
Leicester Road
ASHBY-DE-LA-ZOUCH
LE65 1DG
Tel: 01530 566900

COALVILLE COMMUNITY HOSPITAL —3G **39**
Broom Leys Road
COALVILLE
LE67 4DE
Tel: 01530 467400

DOVE COTTAGE DAY HOSPICE —7A **106**
Canal Lane
Stathern
MELTON MOWBRAY
LE14 4EX
Tel: 01949 860303

FEILDING PALMER HOSPITAL —4K **153**
Gilmorton Road
LUTTERWORTH
LE17 4DZ
Tel: 01455 552 150

GLENFIELD HOSPITAL —4K **63**
Groby Road
LEICESTER
LE3 9QP
Tel: 0116 287 1471

GORSE HILL HOSPITAL —2K **63**
Anstey Lane
Anstey
LEICESTER
LE7 7GX
Tel: 0116 225 5400

HINCKLEY & DISTRICT HOSPITAL —3G **103**
Mount Road
HINCKLEY
LE10 1AG
Tel: 01455 441 800

HINCKLEY AND BOSWORTH COMMUNITY HOSPITAL —5G **99**
Ashby Road
HINCKLEY
LE10 3DA
Tel: 01455 441800

LEICESTER BUPA HOSPITAL —6C **72**
Gartree Road
Oadby
LEICESTER
LE2 2FF
Tel: 0116 272 0888

LEICESTER FRITH HOSPITAL (WITHIN GLENFIELD HOSP.) —4K **63**
Groby Road
LEICESTER
LE3 9QF
Tel: 0116 2255200

LEICESTER GENERAL HOSPITAL —3C **72**
Gwendolen Road
LEICESTER
LE5 4PW
Tel: 0116 249 0490

LEICESTER NUFFIELD HOSPITAL —6D **66**
Scraptoft Lane
LEICESTER
LE5 1HY
Tel: 0116 276 9401

LEICESTER ROYAL INFIRMARY —3F **71** (7C **5**)
Infirmary Square
LEICESTER
LE1 5WW
Tel: 0116 254 1414

LOROS HOSPICE —4A **64**
Groby Road
LEICESTER
LE3 9QE
Tel: 0116 2313771

LOUGHBOROUGH HOSPITAL —6C **18**
Hospital Way
Epinal Way
LOUGHBOROUGH
LE11 5JY
Tel: 01509 611 600

MARKET HARBOROUGH & DISTRICT HOSPITAL —4D **150**
58 Coventry Road
MARKET HARBOROUGH
LE16 9DD
Tel: 01858 410 500

MELTON WAR MEMORIAL HOSPITAL —5F **117**
Ankle Hill
MELTON MOWBRAY
LE13 0QL
Tel: 01664 854 900

RAINBOWS CHILDRENS HOSPICE —5E **30**
Lark Rise
LOUGHBOROUGH
LE11 2HS
Tel: 01509 638000

RUTLAND MEMORIAL HOSPITAL —4G **127**
Cold Overton Road
OAKHAM
LE15 6NT
Tel: 01572 722 552

ST LUKE'S HOSPITAL —2D **150**
33 Leicester Road
MARKET HARBOROUGH
LE16 7BN
Tel: 01858 410 300

ST MARY'S HOSPITAL —4G **117**
Thorpe Road
MELTON MOWBRAY
LE13 1SJ
Tel: 01664 855533

SKETCHLEY HALL (PRIORY) —6F **103**
Manor Way
Sketchley
HINCKLEY
LE10 3HT
Tel: 01455 890023